Oracle Press™

Oracle DBA 101

Oracle Press™

Oracle DBA 101

Marlene Theriault, Rachel Carmichael,
and James Viscusi

Osborne/**McGraw-Hill**

Berkeley New York St. Louis San Francisco
Auckland Bogotá Hamburg London Madrid
Mexico City Milan Montreal New Delhi Panama City
Paris São Paulo Singapore Sydney
Tokyo Toronto

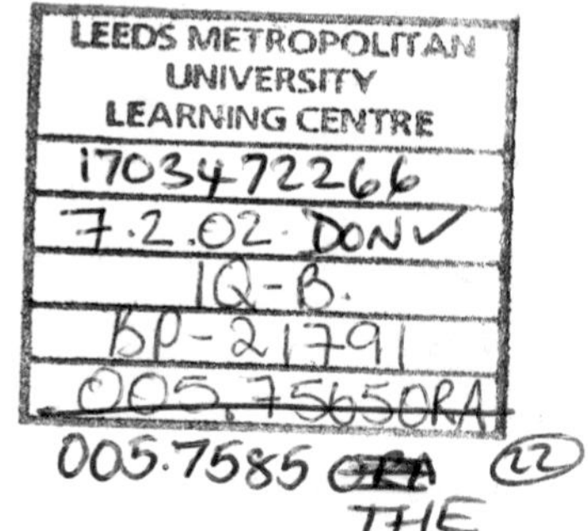

Osborne/**McGraw-Hill**
2600 Tenth Street
Berkeley, California 94710
U.S.A.

For information on translations or book distributors outside the U.S.A., or to arrange bulk purchase discounts for sales promotions, premiums, or fund-raisers, please contact Osborne/**McGraw-Hill** at the above address.

Oracle DBA 101

34567890 CUS CUS 019876543210

ISBN 0-07-212120-3

Publisher
Brandon A. Nordin

Associate Publisher and Editor-in-Chief
Scott Rogers

Acquisitions Editor
Jeremy Judson

Project Editor
Madhu Prasher

Editorial Assistant
Monika Faltiss

Technical Editor
Ian Fickling

Copy Editor
Judith Brown

Proofreader
C2 Editorial Services

Indexer
Valerie Robbins

Computer Designers
Jim Kussow
Richard Schwartz

Illustrator
Gary Corrigan

Series Design
Jani Beckwith

This book was composed with Corel VENTURA ™ Publisher.

About the Authors

Marlene Theriault has been an Oracle DBA for over 17 years and has worked with Oracle products since version 2.0 of the Oracle RDBMS. She has been published in magazines and conference proceedings throughout the world. Ms. Theriault received the "Best User Presentation" award at EOUG 1999, "Outstanding Speaker" at ECO'98, and the "Distinguished Speaker" award for presentations at both ECO'95 and ECO'96. She coauthored *Oracle Security* with William Heney (O'Reilly and Associates, 1998); The *Oracle8i DBA Handbook* with Kevin Loney (Oracle Press, 2000); and *Oracle DBA 101* with Rachel Carmichael and James Viscusi (Oracle Press, 2000). She is chair of the MAOP DBA SIG and authors an "Ask The DBA" column for the MAOP newsletter. Ms. Theriault is an avid recreational walker (Volksmarching) and has done at least one 6-mile walk in each of the 50 United States. Marlene can be reached at mtheriault@mindspring.com.

Rachel Carmichael has been an Oracle DBA for over nine years. She chairs the DBA Special Interest Group for the New York Oracle Users Group, is both Chauncey and OCP certified, and has presented at various international and national conferences, including the ECO all-day DBA seminar for the past three years. She coauthored the Oracle Press book, *Oracle SQL and PL/SQL Annotated Archives*, 1998, with Kevin Loney, and this Oracle Press book, *Oracle DBA 101*, 2000, with Marlene Theriault and James Viscusi.

James Viscusi has been working with relational database products for over 10 years and specifically with Oracle for the last six years. He currently works with Oracle Corporation in the Support Division Center of Expertise, in particular working with customers experiencing performance problems. He has presented at several conferences worldwide including Oracle Open World, IOUG-A, and UKOUG. Mr. Viscusi is also a husband and father of two children and volunteers as an Emergency Medical Technician when he can find the time.

In memory of my father, Paul Robert Siegel, M.D. (1907–1998),
who spent his life helping and healing others

And to my mother, Lillian Mona Siegel, age 90,
who just keeps on truckin' along!

—Marlene Theriault

To Peter, always. And dragonflies.

—Rachel Carmichael

To Sara and James, who were patient
when Daddy had to be "busy"

and

To Sandi, who understood why and covered for me
when I needed it most.

—James Viscusi

Contents at a Glance

PART III

Oracle Tools and Performance

PART IV

Database Protection

PART V

Appendixes

Contents

PART II

The World of Views

PART III
Oracle Tools and Performance

PART IV
Database Protection

PART V
Appendixes

Acknowledgments

Acknowledgments from Marlene Theriault

Perhaps this was the easiest book for me to be involved with writing because it is a book that I have wanted to write for a very long time. Or perhaps this book was easy to write because Rachel and I have been writing and presenting together for so long that we now have a very compatible writing style. In any event, this book has been a joy to be involved in from start to finish. The effort put forth by everyone involved has been stellar.

My thanks, as always, go first and foremost to Rachel Carmichael, who has been my beloved friend and writing partner for many years. We have often talked about our ability to enhance each other's work, and this effort has been no different. Whether she writes the music and I write the words, or vice versa, the work seems to become a greater whole than the sum of its parts. Words cannot express what her friendship has meant to me over the years.

I am very grateful that Jim Viscusi has been a special friend to me for so long. His caring and concern have made my problems seem much lighter. His contribution to this book has been significant, and I thank him wholeheartedly for being willing to take precious time away from his family to be involved with this task. First efforts are always the hardest, and he's done a super job.

I've never met Ian Fickling but have grown to know him through his technical review of both this book and the *Oracle8i DBA Handbook*. To take on two books at once and do a fantastic, professional job with each has been a Herculean task that

Ian performed beautifully. Thank you so much, Ian, for juggling the technical review of two books along with raising a family and maintaining a full-time job. Well done!

Tony Ziemba has been a huge contributing factor to where I am today—wherever *that* is! He has supported and encouraged me every step of the way, making opportunities materialize for me that I could never have manufactured myself. I can't really thank him enough for the help he's always provided to me.

A special thanks to the group of folks comprising Oracle User Resources, Inc.: Mary Bonish, Warren Capps, Michael La Magna, Dale Lowery, and Tony Ziemba. Without the ECO conference, there would be no book! To Michael La Magna, I'd like to give a separate acknowledgment for, without his willingness to let Rachel and me "run amok" each year, *DBA 101* in any form would probably never have been created.

Kevin Loney deserves more thanks than I can properly give here for both inviting me to be involved with the *Oracle8i DBA Handbook* and for being patient and tolerant when I was late with chapter deliveries because I was juggling two books at once. His friendship and willingness to share his knowledge are things I truly treasure.

Thanks to everyone at Osborne/McGraw-Hill. You have all worked very hard to make this book a reality: Scott Rogers, Jeremy Judson, Madhu Prasher, Monika Faltiss, Judith Brown, and the rest of the staff involved.

I'd like to personally thank Carl Dudley for his contribution of Recovery Manager information and his willingness to share knowledge, and Bert Spencer for his continued contribution to the European Oracle User community, and, more importantly, for their friendship. Barbara McBrien deserves special thanks for her review of the early chapters and her suggestions for making them better, as does Dan Peacock for his contribution: the different types of DBAs. Eyal Aronoff continues to be both one of my personal top Oracle gurus and, more importantly, a very special friend.

Friends play a vital part in helping to bring a book to completion, and I must thank Sue Hornbuckle, Cathy Lockwood, and Roz Croog for always being there to help and support me.

As always, I must thank my significant other, Nelson Cahill, for his quiet acceptance when I announce that I'm getting involved in yet another book effort. Without him to keep the household running smoothly and helping to keep me sane and grounded, I could not do any of this. And, finally, thank you to my family, especially my son, Marc Goodman, and my friends and associates at the Johns Hopkins University Applied Physics Laboratory who helped me through the early part of this book's development.

Acknowledgments from Rachel Carmichael

In September 1990, never having seen an Oracle database, I became the Oracle DBA. (We need a DBA. "Poof!" You're the DBA.) The memory of those first frantic months, desperately trying to learn enough, to understand the workings of the database, will never leave me and, in part, is the reason for this book. In March 1991, I attended the first East Coast Oracle user's conference, where I met Marlene Theriault. She's been stuck with me ever since. In 1996, at IOUW in San Francisco, Kevin Loney introduced Marlene and me to James Viscusi, and Jim has been stuck with us ever since.

I would like to thank the wonderful people of Oracle Users Resource, who have put on the ECO conference each year since 1991. You have given Marlene and me a home. Most especially I want to thank Tony Ziemba, who has urged me every year to present and who eventually had to hire me so he could *tell* me to present, and Mike LaMagna, who runs the DBA seminar. Mike finally just gave in to the inevitable and now allows Marlene and me to take over the seminar each year. It was at these seminars that we began the DBA 101 course, the basis of this book.

The people at Osborne/McGraw-Hill have been marvelous and supportive through this effort. Scott Rogers, Jeremy Judson, Madhu Prasher, Monika Faltiss, and Judith Brown—thank you! My special thanks to my "kid brother" Ian Fickling, our technical editor. Ian has improved this book with his insights, corrections, and suggestions. I expect to see his name on the cover of an Oracle Press book very soon.

I spend a good deal of time hanging out on the DBA e-mail listserv at www.lazydba.com. The people on this list have taught me that as little as I think I know, I have a great deal to give. And no matter how much I have learned, there is always something new. My deepest thanks to Henry O'Keeffe, listowner and dear friend, for giving me a forum to help others.

I want to thank Kevin Loney, who got me started on this writing merry-go-round by inviting me to coauthor the *Oracle SQL & PL/SQL Annotated Archives* with him. One of these days I may forgive him for that! His belief in my abilities and his willingness to correct my misunderstandings have made me a much better DBA.

Jim Viscusi has been a friend for a number of years. He has always been available to help me solve problems, both personal and professional, spending time he doesn't have to spare to answer my questions. He has been there with advice, friendship, and support at all turns. His contributions to this book have been invaluable, and I am indebted to him for so much.

As for my friend Ross Mohan, I am bound and determined to get his name on a book with mine, even though it did not turn out to be this one. His graciousness is much appreciated but nothing less than I have come to expect of him. He keeps me laughing and gives me perspective, and I thank him for his friendship.

My friendship with Marlene Theriault began in the middle of a sentence with talks about Oracle and has expanded to fill every area of my life. She has been there for me at every moment, encouraging me, supporting me, and urging me to grow and develop. I am not sure there are words adequate enough to express what she means to me. I love her dearly and am grateful every day for her friendship.

I owe a good deal to my family and friends, who put up with my distraction and lack of time while we were writing this. Mom and Dad, I could not have survived these months without your help. I love you.

Finally, and always, my love and thanks go to Peter. I will live with the lessons he taught me forever.

Acknowledgments from James Viscusi

This book is about helping people start something new. In your case it is being an Oracle DBA. In my case it was the process of writing and contributing to a book. My first steps on this road would not have been nearly as successful without a willingness to try something new and without support from many sources, only some of which I can thank here.

I first met Marlene Theriault at Oracle Open World in 1996, and the more I have gotten to know her, the more impressed I have become. Marlene's success in life is extraordinary by any standards, but I admire it even more knowing some of the paths she has had to travel along the way. She handled the job of leading this project with grace and style and always had an encouraging word along the way—even when she was busy juggling her own commitments—making my part in the process that much more rewarding. Great job, Marlene!

Meeting Rachel Carmichael and Marlene on the same night is like winning the lottery twice in the same day! Over the years, Rachel has always been a good friend to turn to, professionally and personally. She has always had one of the best qualities in a friend—the ability to know when to give advice and when to just listen. I'm grateful for her friendship and our many conversations over the years—none of which were casual!

Kevin Loney's name shows up all through these acknowledgments and with good reason. I cannot thank Kevin enough for his encouragement while we worked together and for asking me to present with him at Open World. In that act, Kevin's actions embodied the spirit of this book. His willingness to take on a "partner" and his support and encouragement of my beginning efforts set me on the path to be a better DBA and led inevitably to my contributions here.

I'm deeply indebted to many people at Oracle who took the time to share their experiences and in many cases their friendship. One who deserves special recognition is Anjo Kolk, performance guru and the person who exposed me to some of the philosophies behind tuning databases. Thanks as well to Andy Tremanye for many days and nights of conversation and debate on how to build practical experience into a set of diagnostic questions. Also to Rob Grant, who worked to find the answers on how I should approach this effort without telling me I was crazy to try. Many thanks to my current workmates who were willing to share and collaborate when the topic of performance came up: Steve Andrew, Karl Daday, Ray Dutcher, Susan Kim, Vijay Lunawat, Roderick Manalac, Erhan Odok, Sameer Patkar, Stefan Pommerenk, Hector Pujol, Kevin Reardon, and Lawerence To.

Thanks to everyone at Osborne/McGraw-Hill who waded through what might be the longest stream of e-mail in the history of the Internet just to arrive at the title for this book! Thanks for believing in this idea and then working hard to turn it into a reality.

A special nod to Bruce Costa for long years of friendship and advice and a swift kick in the tail when required. My completing any contributions at all is in part due to a long night of conversation and advice that could be best boiled down to, "Sit down, shut up, and write!"

In the end, it was my family who was the most consistent source of support. Thanks to my parents, who were always supportive and willing to pitch in whenever things got really hectic. Most importantly, special thanks to my wife Sandi, who helped in so many ways. Whether it was reading drafts, listening to me rant, or just knowing when to bring me a cup of coffee and shut the door, she was there through this entire process. I'm grateful for her support in more ways than I can ever fully express.

Getting Started

new•bie *n*
/n[y]oo'bee/ (Originally from British public-school and military slang variant of "new boy") An inexperienced user of a system.

Beginnings are scary. Whether it's starting in a new school, beginning a new job, or learning a new skill, despite the exciting prospect, there's always an element of fear, a feeling of being overwhelmed, of "How will I ever manage to learn it all?" We call this feeling the "New Kid on the Block" syndrome, and it applies to every new venture we begin. We are all, always, newbies about something.

In 1991, Rachel Carmichael was a brand-new Oracle DBA, without having ever seen or worked with Oracle before. And although Marlene Theriault had been working with Oracle for a while, the new release, version 6, was an almost complete rewrite of the database, making her a newbie all over again. Fortunately for them both, in March of that year, a small group of people, incorporated as Oracle User Resources, held their first-ever East Coast Oracle (ECO) conference in Washington, D.C. The conference was titled "A Wizard's Gathering."

Standing in the hotel registration line, Marlene found herself in conversation with the woman next to her. That woman was Rachel. Neither one of them can remember how that conversation started or what it was about, but there is one thing that both of them are very sure of. That conversation started in the middle of a sentence! And they haven't stopped talking since.

Over the next few years, with very few other resources available, they used snail mail and phone calls to help one another learn each new release of Oracle—all the time wishing that someone else could help them learn the new things so they didn't constantly feel overwhelmed.

As their knowledge grew, they began to give back to the Oracle community, presenting at conferences and trying to help the newer newbies. At the IOUW conference in 1996, Kevin Loney, a friend and, later, coauthor with both Marlene and Rachel, introduced them to Jim Viscusi. The three kept in touch via e-mail, answering each other's questions, expanding each other's knowledge. And Marlene and Rachel always went "home," to ECO, to present and help each year.

In 1997, the two of them put together a workshop called "DBA 101: A Refresher Course." The workshop was turned into a paper and was presented at several conferences. The response was tremendous. And they realized that the best way to help as many people as possible was to turn this presentation into a book. Fortunately, Osborne/McGraw-Hill agreed with them, and now you hold the results in your hands. Jim, with his detailed knowledge of performance tuning and Oracle database administration, was a natural choice to be the third member of this book's writing team.

As you may have noticed by now, this is not a "normal" book introduction. So far, it does not have one word about "Here's what this book contains" or "Here's what this book is (or isn't)." You see, we wanted you to get a brief introduction to who we are and how this book came into being. We felt it was important for you to get a sense of who we are and how we write. You'll be getting more glimpses of "us" as you read.

Okay, here's a little bit "about this book." The style you see here is the style we've used throughout the book. Our goal was to write a book that Marlene's 90-year-old mother can read and (mostly) understand. This book is not your typical Oracle textbook, but does contain many advanced concepts in what we hope is an easy-to-understand form.

So, keep in mind that everyone is a newbie at times, there is no such thing as a dumb question, and please do sit back and enjoy the ride as we help you learn just what is involved in becoming an Oracle DBA.

PART I

Getting Down to Basics

CHAPTER 1

About Being an Oracle DBA

We've heard it said that "Nobody knows exactly what an Oracle database administrator *really* does, but every company is very sure they need at least one or, probably, two or more of them." Even as late as a couple of years ago, if you asked a group of Oracle database administrators (DBAs), "How many of you grew up saying, 'When I grow up, I want to be an Oracle DBA'?" there would be no hands raised. More recently, the same question will produce several hands waving in the air. High school students are becoming more aware of the industry need for trained Oracle professionals and are entering college with the intent of becoming Oracle DBAs. More and more people interested in changing careers are looking toward Oracle technology as a great (and potentially lucrative) field in which to work.

In this chapter, we will examine not only what a database is but also what an Oracle DBA is and does. We'll show you the possible tasks that you could spend your days doing and the steps you might take to help you realize your goal of becoming an Oracle DBA.

How You "Talk" to a Database

In order to communicate with an Oracle database, you must be able to "speak" the language that an Oracle database understands. Originally, that language was called User Friendly Interface (UFI). UFI was a very early and limited language, and you could not do much more than basic database actions. You could perform the following basic tasks:

- Insert, which allowed you to put information into your database
- Update, which allowed you to modify existing information
- Select, which allowed you to look at the information stored in the database
- Delete, which allowed you to remove information from the database
- Perform mathematical operations
- Perform some limited date manipulations

As the language evolved, it was renamed Structured Query Language or SQL (pronounced "see-quel"). Over the years, SQL has become the standard that you use to speak to a database. We realize that a basic understanding of SQL is necessary to help you understand the scripts and other code that we will be presenting in this book. We have taken great care to explain each script and piece of code thoroughly. However, teaching you SQL is outside the scope of this book, and if you find that you are having trouble understanding the scripts and code and how they work, we recommend you look for a basic book on SQL to study.

What Is an Oracle DBA, and What Does One Do?

So, what *is* an Oracle DBA? To answer this question, we'll have to look at what an Oracle database is. Or, better yet, let's talk first about what a general database is. Take just a minute to look around you. How many databases do you see? Well, if you are sitting in a room that has any books or magazines lying around, you can count each of them as a database of sorts. Loosely stated, a *database* is a collection of information. A dictionary is a collection or database of words, while a cookbook is a database of recipes. If you have a telephone book, you have a database of names and their associated telephone numbers and addresses.

Now, let's take this one step further and think about what electronic databases you have in your home. If you have a speed dialer on your phone, you have a database of numbers that you frequently call. Likewise, a caller identification box would be a database of people who call you frequently. If you have cable television, usually one or more channels show the television program schedule. Wow, there's yet another database to count. My gosh, you're surrounded by them! If you are a person who owns and uses a personal digital assistant (PDA), such as a Palm Pilot, you carry a multipurpose database around with you.

A Banking Example

If you have an account at a bank and use their automatic teller machine (ATM), you are interacting with a database that holds your account information. You might have a checking account, a savings account, a money market account, some kind of loan account—to buy a car or a house—a Christmas fund, and even an individual retirement account (IRA), all at the same bank. The database that stores all the information about all of your accounts might even be an Oracle database.

What happens when you can't get to your specific bank branch and you need money? You can usually use a "fast cash" machine at a grocery store or go to an ATM at another bank branch, and not necessarily another branch of your specific bank. The machine that you use can tap into several different systems to interact with many different banks and enable you to get money from your personal account remotely. Pretty amazing!

The mechanism that lets you get money from your account is actually one or more computer programs made up of lists of commands or instructions that tell a computer what to do. Once you have inserted your card in the ATM and entered your personal identification number (PIN) for the account, a group of computer programs (called an application) present information and ask you questions to perform the following actions:

- Determine what action you want to take—in this case, withdraw cash
- Find out how much cash you want
- Compare how much money you are requesting with how much you have available
- Determine whether you have enough money to remove some and still have whatever minimum amount is required by your bank to keep the account solvent
- Dispense the requested amount to you if you have enough money available

The programs that have been run to perform all of these tasks are written to interact with a database. The programs ask for information, or *query*, the database during some of the steps listed here. When you insert your card into the machine and are prompted for your PIN, the program checks the information on the magnetic strip on the back of the card to determine that the PIN you have entered matches the value stored on the strip. After the program has obtained the inputs from you for what action you want to perform and how much money you want, the database is queried to find out your account balance. The program takes the following actions:

- Verifies whether the card has been reported as stolen
- Does the math to verify that you have sufficient funds for the transaction
- Checks to make sure the transaction will not exceed your daily withdrawal limit
- Updates your account to show a withdrawal has occurred
- Modifies the balance to reflect the withdrawn amount plus any service charges your bank imposes on ATM withdrawals
- Modifies your old balance to reflect your new balance
- Dispenses the money to you

How does the program know it has located the correct account? What information is stored in the database? Where exactly is it stored? What mechanisms are used to ensure that your account information is really yours? We'll look at the answers to these questions in the next section.

Storing the Information

The pieces of information that the bank's database would need to store for your account might be

- Your name
- Your address
- Your telephone number
- A way to uniquely identify your account (account number)
- A way to verify you are who you say you are (mother's maiden name, perhaps)
- The amount of money you have available

You can probably think of other pieces of information that might also be required. Taking a look at the composition of the information, we see that your name actually might have up to five parts:

- A salutation, such as Mr., Mrs., Ms.
- First name
- Middle name or middle initial
- Last name
- A suffix, such as Junior, or a number (the first, second, third, etc.)

Your address could have the following parts:

- Street number
- Street name
- Apartment number
- City
- State
- Zip code

In other words, each area of information could be broken down into smaller pieces. A database is used to organize and store the pieces of information.

So, What's an Oracle Database?

Oracle Corporation has produced a set of very complex software programs that enable people to build and populate databases with all kinds of information. Since the information is defined based on the relational model, the databases are referred to as relational database management systems (RDBMS). In Chapter 2, we will begin to tell you how the Oracle software is used to handle and organize the information.

As Oracle's products have matured, the databases have become bigger and more complex. Controlling the configuration and performance has become almost an art form that requires both skill and knowledge on the part of the people who administer the databases. The status and tasks required of an Oracle DBA have changed and matured as well.

Now we've established what a database is and have a brief definition of what an Oracle database is. Let's take a few minutes to examine whether you have what it takes to be an Oracle DBA.

This "test" assumes you have been out in the work world for some period of time. If you have not worked for a living yet, try to think about a comparable situation that you have been through. After you've had a chance to mull over your answers to the following questions, we'll look at the possible evolution of a DBA from junior DBA through expert.

Do You Have What It Takes to Be a DBA?

This bit of humor was circulating around electronic mail a while ago. We don't know who wrote it, but it's a fun twist on an old joke:

CIOs leap tall buildings in a single bound
Are faster than a speeding bullet (rats, missed him again)
Are more powerful than a locomotive
Talk to God

Sr. Managers leap short buildings with a running start
Are faster than a BB gun
Are more powerful than a streetcar
Ask God questions

Midlevel DBAs can clear a single-story house most of the time
Can outrun the arrows that users shoot at them, with a head start
Get run over by bicycles
Beg God not to notice them

Junior DBAs trip over the stoop
Wonder why there are holes in their body
Say "Look at the choo-choo"
Make God mad by asking, "What happens if I turn off the server?"

Senior DBAs run through buildings
Eat the bullets
Throw the locomotive at the users
Are Oracle Gods (or Goddesses)!

Below are some questions to ask yourself to determine whether you have the proper personality and mind-set to enjoy being a DBA. We've included some of our perspectives on the interpretation of the questions. Remember that this is all for fun (with just a little bit of reality thrown in), so relax and enjoy it. Please realize, too, that if some of these questions seem too negative, there is really a positive side to each one. We'll try to show you the positive in each of these questions.

Do You Have What It Takes to Be a DBA?

Are you able to function at top efficiency with little or no sleep—possibly for days at a time?

It was suggested that the above question might be better stated as "four days at a time." The truth is that DBAs are often called upon to work nonstop to recover a database that has crashed, regardless of how long that might take. Somehow, your users tend to view their ability to interact with a database as having precedence over your personal schedule. Generally, companies will expect you to do whatever is necessary to "get the job done," and if that includes working around the clock to solve a problem, you'll probably work around the clock. The other side of the coin is that, if you are a really thorough DBA who takes pride in your work, you will probably *want* to work around the clock, even if your boss says to you, "Hey, take a break and come back in the morning." Rachel's manager had to literally force her to go home one night (day? Eternity!) after a database crash. Yes, she successfully recovered the database.

The status of being known as "the person to rely on" in an emergency is both a blessing and a curse. Although you may end up working some long hours, you will usually earn management's loyalty and respect and much higher salary than your fellow employees, and you have the satisfaction of knowing that you truly are needed in your company.

Do you like getting phone calls in the middle of the night that *aren't* wrong numbers?

If something goes wrong with your database, it won't matter to your users whether it is day or night. They will want the database back up and available as soon as possible. If you are running a database that must be available 24 hours a day, you will probably be expected to respond whenever you are called. We've all spent some number of nights blearily answering the phone and then getting up to fix the problem.

On the other side, you can often work from home if the need arises, and your management will usually give you compensation time for the extra hours you have worked.

Do you enjoy being the "invisible" person in your organization, that is, until something goes wrong?

It's sad but true. As long as everything is running smoothly and at an optimal performance level, no one notices you. That situation can quickly change if something breaks. Suddenly, you are the most important, most visible person in your organization, that is, until the problem gets fixed.

Over time, the role of the DBA has changed some, and most of us are no longer quite as "invisible" as we once were. If you are doing a really good job of keeping your databases tuned and sized correctly, you may be called upon to participate more fully in the decision-making processes for design and implementation. By keeping your databases tuned and protected, you will have ensured that you have the time to participate in other areas of the database arena.

You might also want to learn to "toot your own horn" occasionally and be sure to let your management know that you interceded to avert a problem *before* it became a real show stopper. It's perfectly all right to keep your boss up to speed on your activities by saying something like, "I just noticed we were switching redo log files too often, so I added log files and increased the size of all of them before it became a problem for our users."

Do you enjoy life under a microscope?

As stated above, when something breaks, you are suddenly under severe scrutiny. Marlene can remember having a downed production system two weeks after her database "went live" that took several hours to recover. When it came time to recover the database, she looked up to find 12 people hovering around her doorway just watching her typing. Fortunately, the database was recovered with no lost data, and she was "hero for a day."

Do you enjoy long lines of people outside your door?

No, this doesn't refer to the previous question.

There will usually be a steady stream of DBAs and developers stopping by your office to get answers to questions, allocation of disk space, help with problems, or just general moral support. You really need to like people and believe that anyone stopping by your door is a user who needs assistance. You also should be able to pick up where you left off with what you were doing, even if it is several hours later! "Now, where was I?" is a phrase that you may often mutter.

Do you enjoy spending hours on the telephone—listening to awful music (compliments of Oracle Support)—wondering if you will ever talk to a human being?

Truly, Oracle Support Services has improved radically over the years. Even their music has improved (honest!). Calls to support are a way of life for DBAs. That's a cold, hard fact. Regardless of the version of software you are running or the platform you are running on, you will have to call support fairly frequently, and you really need to have both patience and a sense of humor to survive. You also have to realize that the first person you talk to may be only the messenger and not the one to help you with your problem. That situation seems to be improving too.

The good news is that Oracle Support Services can usually help you find the answers you need to get your job done more efficiently. There is wonderful information available on Oracle's support home page and through their Metalink website.

Do you love solving puzzles that make no sense?

Well, the last time we said, "But that makes absolutely no sense," we had found a bug... er... undocumented feature... in a product. Solving problems and troubleshooting go hand in hand with being a DBA. We are often called upon to work through very fascinating (to us) problems or questions.

We've found that if you enjoy doing crossword puzzles or word problems or love to watch and puzzle through mysteries, you will make a wonderful DBA. The mind-set that enjoys puzzle solving will also enjoy DBA tasks.

Is your favorite weekend meal Twinkies and Coca-Cola, and do you view pizza as a seven-day-a-week healthy meal plan?

In most companies, the only time upgrades, maintenance, or changes can be made to a system are over weekends, late at night, or very early in the morning. If you work for a company that has databases running seven days a week 24 hours a day ("24 x 7 shops"), the times that you can get your very necessary work done are even more limited. Unfortunately, the jobs usually require you to be there to make sure everything goes smoothly. The good news is that most companies now have vending machines that are restocked on a fairly frequent basis—or we would have starved to death years ago. Hey, lots of pizza places deliver late at night. Every good DBA we know has a wide collection of take-out menus from places that deliver.

As with working odd hours when something goes wrong with your database, doing maintenance on off-hours will usually earn you compensation time to use when something important comes up for you to do outside of work. Things tend to balance out, either with higher pay raises or time off when you need it. Most companies recognize that you are making extraordinary efforts on their behalf and reward you for the extra effort.

Do you love being on a perpetual *steep* learning curve?

In industry, most professionals have a predictable learning curve. After graduation from college, the learning curve will be very steep. Over time, the curve tapers off and levels off in most careers. Later, the curve may actually start sliding downhill, and many people end up trudging along in a nonproductive and boring job. Not so with an Oracle DBA!

Just as you begin to feel that you have truly grasped the workings of your current release (or even before that happy point in time), Oracle comes out with a new, much more complex version, and you get to start all over again. It's great. You need never be bored. You can also never learn it all, so there is always something to do or study. How wonderful to know that you will continue to learn and grow over your entire career!

Do you enjoy the challenge of moving between different computer platforms?
More and more companies are finding they need different computer platforms for different types of work. It's not unusual to find Oracle installed on several different flavors of Unix (each with its own little quirks) and several Windows NT boxes or other platforms—all in the same shop.

Do you believe you'll have enough time to teach yourself <fill in the blank> (possible choices: TCL, 8i, PL/SQL, Built-in Packages, Java, etc.)?
In other words, are you the eternal optimist, who believes that you will have time on your hands to read or study? Do you love the thought that you will always have choices in what direction you want to learn and grow? Although there are times when you will be too busy to even think about stopping to learn something new, there will also be times when you will be able to just sit and read and learn.

You may be encouraged to try out different software and evaluate various tools to help make your job easier. If you are the typical Oracle DBA, you will end up having a whole list of things you want to learn about or work with. As we said earlier, there is just no way to know it all. The software changes too rapidly to ever completely catch up with all of the latest, greatest features. Ah, but isn't the chase exciting? And the more you learn and grow, the more in demand your skills and you will be. There is something to be said for never having to fear unemployment.

In most work environments, DBAs are often forced to learn things on the fly. They are generally people who love to "tinker" and find ways to solve problems on their own. Many DBAs have been known to take the approach, "I wonder what would happen if..." and then go about finding out what happens. (Usually we don't crash the database when doing this!)

Reading the documentation is done in small "sips," since there is rarely enough time to read complete chapters at one sitting. It is quite common to grab a manual, search for the topic of interest, read enough to figure out what's wrong in the situation you are currently troubleshooting, fix the problem, and set the manual aside. This approach can lead to a very real problem: you end up with incomplete knowledge and information. Later in this chapter, we'll look at training courses you can take to help provide you with a more rounded, thorough background.

If you answered yes to some of the questions presented here, you will love being a DBA.

Types of DBAs

You can look at the database administrator's changing roles and tasks within organizations in several different ways. Today's DBA may end up specializing in one area of administration or performing a subset of tasks within all of the following areas:

- The systems or operational DBA, who monitors all of the instances and servers and makes structural changes to the databases themselves, such as adding users, tablespaces, and so on
- The architectural DBA, who works closely with an application development team to provide an optimal database solution
- The application DBA, who does more coding in PL/SQL or Java (for Oracle8i), HTML, WebDB, and other database programming methods to provide either end-user solutions or foundations for other applications development
- The data DBA, who specializes in data integrity and cleansing issues, primarily within a data warehouse or data mart environment

A data modeler understands the requirements, the process flow, and all entities within a business and creates a data model to reflect these things. It is often the responsibility of the data DBA to convert the data model into a physical database.

Because the beginning DBA will usually start out performing basic database tasks, we will emphasize the systems DBA's tasks here.

We have attempted to present as thorough a list of tasks as possible. Tasks that may be unique to your company's environment may not appear here. There may also be tasks presented here that are viewed as inappropriate for a DBA to perform in your organization. The tasks are not presented here in order of priority or with complete detail. Throughout the book, we will try to ensure that the tasks listed here are covered in enough detail to enable you to perform them effectively.

The Tasks

Your top priorities as a database administrator are to ensure optimal performance of the databases and monitor the resources available for the various database systems to assure reliability, accessibility, and recoverability. The general health and well-being of the databases are of prime concern.

The normal scope of your functions can include (but is not limited to) the following set of tasks. Don't worry if you do not understand some of the tasks mentioned below; they are explained in later sections. The purpose here is for you to become familiar with the various terms and tasks that a DBA may perform.

Software Installations/Upgrades

In the software installation and upgrade area, you will need to

- Stay abreast of the most current releases of Oracle software and compatibility issues with the appropriate operating systems as well as intra-Oracle software compatibility.
- Determine whether a new release is stable enough to consider placing it on the development system for testing and integration with your application.
- Create an environment area for new release installation.
- Verify (on a high-level basis) the proper functioning of the new software release.
- Plan and coordinate the testing of the new release for each database and each application area.
- Plan, coordinate, and execute the implementation of the upgrade on the development system for all applications once the software has been tested and certified against all the applications on all of the databases in development.
- Plan, coordinate, and execute the implementation of the upgrade on the production system once the software has been verified for all applications.
- Log Technical Action Reports (TARs), as necessary, against a new or upgraded version of the RDBMS, and arrange for, apply, and verify patches when they are needed and available.

You might also have to monitor and advise management on licensing issues.

Database Actions

By "database actions," we mean those tasks you perform that directly change the composition and configuration of your database. You might need to

- Determine the space (disk storage) requirements for a proposed database, working with the developers and system administrator.
- Allocate the space for and build the database per Oracle's Optimal Flexible Architecture standards within the available hardware configuration.
- Determine and implement the backup/recovery plan for each database, both while in development and as the application moves to production, and coordinate that plan against database availability requirements.

- Monitor and coordinate updates of the database recoverability plan with the site's disaster recovery plan.
- Monitor the database performance while the application is in development on an ongoing, database-by-database basis, to identify potential performance problems before getting to a production status.
- Provide an ongoing tuning process for a database once an application goes into production, for example, adjust shared pool size, database block buffers, log buffers, and so on, as needed.
- Monitor table and tablespace growth and fragmentation on a periodic basis to ensure that space allocation does not become a critical issue.
- Maintain an ongoing configuration map for each database on both development and production, including any links to other databases.
- Test the backup/recovery plan for each database on a regular basis, coordinating the test with the site's disaster recovery plan testing.

System Issues

- We use the term "system issues" to specify the actions that you take at the operating system level that directly or indirectly affect your database. These actions affect the environment in which your database exists.Verify on a daily basis that nightly (or periodic) backups have run successfully; examine all appropriate logs (alert logs, startup logs, shutdown logs, tuning information, etc.); verify that all databases that should be up and running are available and accessible.
- Perform housecleaning tasks as required, such as purging old files from the Oracle software areas, ensuring that archive logs have enough disk space (if applicable), and so on.
- Perform ongoing database performance tuning, and work with the system administrator on operating system-specific performance issues related to the Oracle databases, such as system patches that may be required or system parameters that may need adjustment.
- Monitor the space used by each database and space availability on a systemwide basis, and generate future capacity plans for management's use.
- Coordinate upgrades of system software products to resolve any Oracle/operating system issues/conflicts.
- Research, test, and recommend for purchase tools related to Oracle database administration, or propose tools for development in-house.

Education Issues

By "education issues" we mean those actions that ensure that you, as the DBA, are not the only person who knows what is available in the latest releases of the database.

- Disseminate Oracle information to the developers and users when appropriate.
- Train backup DBAs, operation center staff, and other appropriate staff.
- Attend training classes and user group conferences to stay on top of the latest information and newest products interacting with Oracle.
- Subscribe to and read trade journals such as *Oracle Magazine* and *Oracle Technical Journal*.
- Subscribe to and participate in Internet listservs and usenet groups to collect information from your peers.

Developer Issues

- Most DBAs live in a world where they either directly or indirectly interact with the developers who are writing applications that use their databases. By "developer issues" we mean those actions that help the development team accomplish their goals. Know enough about the Oracle tools' normal functional behavior to be able to determine whether a problem is tools based or application based.
- Be able to log Technical Action Reports (TARs), apply patches, and coordinate with developers to verify that a patch has corrected a problem without causing other problems.
- Assist developers with database design issues and problem resolution, including knowledge on how to run and understand the output from both TKPROF and the Explain Plan utilities to tune the SQL queries.

Security Issues

Unless the database is accessible, it's not going to be particularly useful. At the same time, not all users should be allowed to see all the data in the database. By "security issues" we mean developing and maintaining processes and procedures that control the access to your database.

- Set and maintain user and DBA passwords for all databases, and document same.

- Create user and developer accounts, and distribute appropriate privileges as needed to approved people by authority of approved people, and document same.
- When appropriate, use Oracle's audit facilities to monitor table/user activities.
- Develop, document, and maintain change control procedures to prevent unauthorized changes to database objects.

Database Standards

By "database standards" we mean a set of policies that make the maintenance of the database simpler by defining naming conventions, general practices, and repetitive procedures.

- Define, document, and maintain database standards for the organization to ensure consistency in database creation, schema definitions, and tablespace, table, constraint, trigger, package, procedure, and index naming conventions.
- Create naming conventions for SQL*Net files (LISTENER.ORA, TNSNAMES.ORA, etc.) for ease of installation, configuration, and maintainability.
- Where appropriate, write and distribute procedures (both step-by-step narratives and actual code) for tasks that must be performed frequently.
- Define standards for database documentation.
- Create a "Database Administrator's Handbook" of documentation on all customized code and procedures, and keep the documentation as current as possible.

A Logical Progression

A truth must be pointed out before we examine the growth path of a DBA. Just as with any other occupation, some people will easily grow into expert DBAs and some never will. There is a slogan being used by a newspaper in the Washington, D.C., area to the effect that "If you don't get it, you don't GET it"© (© The Washington Post). This is also true in the area of Oracle database administration. We have seen bright, gifted computer people who just never "got" how to be an effective DBA. They never made it past the tasks listed in the first section below, "In the Beginning...".

The progression presented here is based on our observations of the way many DBAs have developed in companies in which we have worked. As a most junior-level DBA, you will tend to spend a great deal of time learning the basics of doing your job. As you become adept at the basic skills, you will begin to have enough time to progress into more advanced concerns. When you have reached a level of having several years as a working DBA, you will probably have progressed to a point where others around you will do the lower-level functions so that you can devote more time to the advanced topics. We believe the progression represents a set of mind-sets, and as a person becomes more senior, he or she reaches new levels of awareness about the functionality of an Oracle database and the care that it requires.

In the Beginning...

As a new DBA you will spend most of your time learning to perform and performing the most "necessary" tasks. These tasks can include building and maintaining one or more databases. You will need to learn how to create users and create and grant roles to those users. When you have a problem and there is no senior DBA around to ask, you will need to call Oracle Support Services. You will need to learn how to log Technical Action Reports (TARs). Performing installations of Oracle software, relinking the software, and applying patches to the software are all tasks that you will learn. A big part of your education will be learning how to read and understand what the Oracle documentation is *really* saying (not an easy feat), learning how to find things out for yourself within the database, and sharpening your SQL skills.

Over Time...

As you become more experienced, you will spend time developing and testing an effective backup/recovery plan. You will begin to see areas that you can automate and will start to write scripts to perform your daily tasks through batch jobs so that you will be free to spend more time monitoring database growth and performance. You will tend to spend more time performing developer and user support functions. As you gain knowledge about your database, you will spend more time learning to tune the database—developing a daily routine to check the health of your databases. Although you might be permitted to attend conferences and Oracle user group meetings as a junior DBA, you will begin to gain much more from conferences as your base of knowledge and reference grows. As new versions of Oracle are released, you will want to attend Oracle classes on the latest version so that you can begin to evaluate the impact of the new features on your systems. You will start to develop more effective problem-solving and troubleshooting approaches.

As Your Experience Grows...

Once you become a more senior DBA, you will tend to stay abreast of current releases and learn the tricks involved in determining what version is stable enough to use. You will plan, coordinate, and migrate databases to new releases. You will have developed a toolkit of scripts to help you monitor your databases effectively.

You will be able to advise your upper-level management on licensing issues. One of your most important tasks will be to create an effective site disaster recovery plan and ensure that your backup and recovery strategies work well. You will usually maintain configuration maps and documentation on your databases. You will be expected to disseminate information, train backup DBAs and operations staff, and coach and mentor others. You may become involved with database design. Because of your advanced knowledge, you may be called upon to define and maintain database standards; write and distribute procedures. You will monitor space use and space availability and generate capacity plans for management. You will research, test, and recommend tools for database administration and development. You may be expected to call to management's attention areas of potential trouble (for example, Year 2000 issues).

Education and Jobs

Sometimes you have a chance to decide "what you want to be when you grow up" and can therefore plan a concentrated course of study (otherwise known as getting that undergraduate degree) in your field of choice. Sometimes you decide later that what you are doing is not what you love and you need to make a change. And sometimes your boss decides for you: "We need a DBA, you're the only one available, you're the DBA."

No matter how you make the decision to become a database administrator, one thing is certain. You are going to need some form of training or schooling. Why do we differentiate between schooling and training? Schooling tends to be a series of classes, taken one after another, one leading into another, given in a formal setting, transferring a general body of both theoretical and practical knowledge. Training usually is a single class, concentrating on one specific aspect of the subject matter, teaching you the "how to do this" and not necessarily the "why you are doing this."

Getting Education and Training

As recently as ten years ago, the only actions you could take to become an Oracle DBA were these:

- Experiment with your database and hope you did not corrupt it beyond recoverability
- Read the Oracle documentation (a very daunting task, indeed)
- Go to Oracle-supplied education classes
- Attend Oracle user group meetings and beat the information out of your fellow DBAs (which tended to make you a very unpopular attendee)

As Oracle products have become more mature and popular, we have seen a shortage of Oracle DBAs in industry. Because of the high demand for trained DBAs, more and more companies have been created to supply Oracle-based training. Oracle Corporation has expanded its training offerings. Even colleges and universities are now offering courses.

College Courses

More and more colleges are offering degrees not only in computer science or information technology but also in database administration. These classes are usually generic, teaching you the principles behind database administration. You will need a grounding in data modeling—the practice of taking the real-world information flow and turning it into entities and relationships that can then be translated into the physical world, the database structures, and objects. You will learn how to write and tune SQL, the Structured Query Language that is used to access most databases, Oracle included.

Some schools offer degree programs in Oracle database administration specifically. How do you go about finding these schools? The best place to start is with your local colleges and universities. Get a catalog (you just found another database!) and start looking through it. Call college bookstores and ask which books are a part of the Computer curriculum.

If your local schools don't offer the classes you need, the Internet is the next place to go. Do a search on "database administration." Look for the schools that offer classes, in Oracle in particular, but in general database principles as well.

But what if you already have a degree and want to change what you do? Going back to college for a four-year degree isn't always an option. That's when you have to be a bit more creative. Take classes from Oracle Corporation, or take the certification classes (we'll discuss those in more detail in a little while). Join your local Oracle users group. You will find people and companies there who offer training courses designed to teach you the specifics of administering a database.

Ask your company for training. Many companies will pay for classes that make you more valuable to them. It's often easier and less expensive for a company to train an employee who knows their business in the new technology than to hire someone proficient in the technology who doesn't know their business. So don't be afraid to ask your current employer about opportunities to be trained as an Oracle DBA. Your manager may not be able to take immediate action in helping you get training, but if you don't speak up, how will anyone know that you want to become a DBA?

Search the Internet (try a search on "Oracle education") for companies that offer training classes on a variety of specific Oracle topics. Use several search engines, as you can often get hits from one engine that don't appear on a second engine's search results list.

Train Yourself

When all else fails, start training yourself. Oracle often offers free trial software. Download it, install it, and start playing. Read the Oracle documentation (yes, all of it!). Build yourself a test database and play. Look for and read the many and varied technical books available at your local bookstore or online bookstores. Join a newsgroup or list server (listserv). There are several excellent ones out there, populated by all levels of DBAs who are willing to answer questions from the novice. A word of caution though: many of the listservs are very active and you might receive as many as 50 to 100 emails per day from them. This can be an overwhelming amount of electronic mail and can easily flood some email storage allowances. However, the volume of educational information you can receive may be worth the amount of email traffic generated from some of these groups.

Connect to the Oracle website and join the Metalink support service (available to you if you or your company has purchased Oracle support). Metalink gives you access both to the public Oracle papers and bulletins and the technical forums where you can post questions or read about problems and questions that other DBAs have had. These forums are monitored by Oracle technical support staff, and they are quick to investigate and post responses. In addition, you will find that most DBAs who read these forums will post answers to others' questions.

Performing a Job Search

An article in *Oracle Magazine*'s May/June 1999 issue was titled, "If You Are Breathing, You're Hired." This may be the very minimum job requirement for a DBA! The need for trained Oracle professionals has increased so dramatically in the last several years that it would seem like almost anyone can get hired to fill an Oracle position. But is this true? Where do you begin to look for the position that is right for you? What qualifications should you emphasize on a resume to help you get an entry-level position?

First, look in your local newspaper listings (oops, another database!). Be creative in your search; database jobs can and will be listed under "Computers," "Database," "Oracle," and "Programmers." Join the local users group, and start networking. Talk to people who are presenting or who are running the meetings. Introduce yourself to other DBAs and talk to them. These are the people who will hear about jobs or know recruiters who are looking for DBAs. Look through the internal job listings at your current company. Many companies would rather promote or train someone from within.

Again, search the Internet. Just as you can find Oracle courses on the web to train yourself, you will see companies that specialize in job placements. Look on the websites of the companies that make third-party products to help DBAs monitor and maintain their databases. Often these companies will have an email address to which you can send your resume.

That said, what should you put on your resume to make a company want to hire you? The reality is, entry-level jobs are hard to find. Most companies want someone who already has experience as an Oracle DBA. Highlight the projects you have done in school. Include jobs and projects that are not directly related to database work, but that do reflect your strengths in planning and implementing projects.

About the Oracle Certified Professional Program

"Are you certifiable?" reads an advertisement from Oracle Education about their Oracle Certified Professional program. What's this certification about? What does it cover? Is it worthwhile?

For many years when someone applied for a job as an Oracle DBA, an employer had only the applicant's resume and the interviewer's skills to use to evaluate a prospective employee. This combination was not always enough to ensure that the person who was hired could perform the expected tasks effectively. To solve this problem, a group of Oracle professionals created and arranged for Sylvan Learning Centers to proxy an Oracle database administrator certification program. The idea behind the program was to help the industry easily recognize a trained DBA from an untrained one. Although this program was not maintained, another program has been created to help fulfill this purpose. In the next section, we'll tell you about this new program.

Oracle Certified Professional (OCP) Test

In 1997 at the Oracle Open World Conference in Los Angeles, Oracle Education unveiled a new version 7.3 certification program. As new versions of the database are released, Oracle Education releases matching versions of the tests to allow you to maintain and upgrade your certification. In addition to offering an Oracle 7.3 Database Administrator certification, Oracle Education offers certification in the following areas:

- Oracle8 Database Administrator certification in Oracle8 and Oracle8i
- Oracle Database Operator certification in a subset of the database administration functions
- Application Developer certification in Developer 2000

The initial set of tests for a DBA, dubbed the "Oracle Certified Professional" exam, consists of four parts:

- Test 1: Introduction to Oracle: SQL and PL/SQL
- Test 2: Database Administration

- Test 3: Backup and Recovery Workshop
- Test 4: Performance Tuning Workshop

Although the tests can be taken in any order, Test 1 is really the base test upon which all the other tests are built. The tests cover the following information:

I. Introduction to Oracle: SQL and PL/SQL

- Tests knowledge of SQL and PL/SQL language constructs, syntax, and usage
- Data Definition Language (DDL), Data Manipulation Language (DML), and Data Control Language (DCL)
- Basic data modeling and database design
- Basic Oracle Procedure Builder usage

II. Database Administration (Oracle RDBMS version 7.3 administration issues)

- Database architecture
- Startup and shutdown
- Database creation
- Managing database internals and externals, such as redo log files, rollback segments, control files, tablespaces, tables, indexes
- Database auditing
- National Language Support (NLS) features
- Oracle utilities, such as SQL*Loader

III. Backup and Recovery Workshop

- Knowledge of backup and recovery motives and models
- Backup and recovery architecture
- Methods for recovery and procedures for archive logging
- Considerations for supporting high-availability databases (24 x 7)
- Use of the new (in version 7.3) standby database features
- Troubleshooting

IV. Performance Tuning Workshop (all aspects of version 7.3 tuning)

- Diagnosis of tuning problems

- Database optimal configuration (Optimal Flexible Architecture standards)
- Ability to tune the shared pool, buffer cache, rollback segments, redo logs, sorts
- Detecting and tuning lock contention
- Oracle block usage
- Differences in tuning On-line Transaction Processing (OLTP) environments as opposed to Decision Support Systems (DSS) and mixed environments
- Load optimization

When you sign up to take one of the tests, you will refer to the test by its name instead of the numbers listed here, since the test numbers are rarely used. You must pass all four tests in order to receive the OCP-DBA designation, but you can take the tests in any order you choose. Unfortunately, it is not unusual for a person not to pass one or more of the tests on the first attempt. If you do not pass a test, you will have to wait at least one month before you can attempt the test again. Several books are available that you can use to study for the tests, and there are several third-party training courses you can take. Oracle Corporation also offers practice examinations on their education website that you can use to gauge how well prepared you are to take the exam.

Once you feel ready to attempt an exam, Sylvan Prometric, which can be reached at 1-800-755-EXAM (3926), proctors the tests. Other telephone numbers you can try are 612-896-7000 or 612-820-5707 if you can't get through on the 800 number. When you call, you will need to supply the following:

- Your name, organization, and mailing address
- The name of the test you want to take
- A method of payment—your order taker can supply details on the various payment options

You'll receive a confirmation of your appointment, and on the day of the test, you will need to produce two forms of identification, with a photo ID being one of them. You will be requested to arrive at least 15 minutes early so you can register and fill in the appropriate paperwork. Once you have taken the exam, the software will immediately tell you whether you have passed or not. Each test has a potential of 800 points, and the points are broken into several topic areas. The test administrator should print a detailed report of your test results. Whether you pass or not, be sure to get and keep this report.

Once you have passed all four parts of the exam, you will automatically receive your certification package. However, it may take anywhere from four to six weeks for your certification to arrive. Once you have passed the examinations, you are entitled to use the OCP-DBA designation and logo on your business cards, letterhead, advertisements, and resume.

OCP-DBA certification is an ongoing activity. With each new release of the Oracle RDBMS, a new set of examinations will be made available, and you will have six months in which to become certified in the new version. Once you have passed the version 7.3 examination, an Oracle8 New Features examination is currently available to bring you up to the next level of certification. You may, however, decide to take the complete set of Oracle8 examinations instead and skip the version 7.3 tests entirely.

Oracle Database Layout

When you were little and learning to tell time, did you find it difficult? There was the physical clock that you looked at, but it was hard to relate that to the intangible time.

How about learning to use a calendar? You could look at a calendar to see what day a particular date was going to be. You could keep track of how far off your birthday, the first day of summer vacation, or the first day of the new school year was.

The clock and the calendar are both physical representations of a logical entity—time. As the clock measures the passage of time in seconds, minutes, and hours, the calendar measures the passage of time in days, weeks, months, and years. Of course, modern watches combine both functions to provide the day, date, and time.

Within an Oracle system, you have both physical and logical entities. In this chapter, we are going to talk about the various objects and entities that make up an Oracle system. Some people find these concepts a little hard to understand, so hang on to your hat because this is liable to be a bumpy ride!

Logical vs. Physical Objects

Let's pretend for a moment that you are a file clerk in a large company. Your company sells hardware supplies to the general public. Almost daily, deliveries of various forms of hardware are received from your suppliers. Your job is to take all the invoices describing the items that your company has received and all the bills that have been paid and file them together in a large black filing cabinet.

Gee, what would you do if your boss needed to know how many skingwattles were delivered from the XYZ Company last March? You'd have to go through the various folders in the cabinet until you located the folder for the XYZ Company. Removing the folder from the cabinet, you'd have to locate all of the bills for the month of March and then add up each purchase of skingwattles listed in the invoices. Sounds like a pretty tedious job, doesn't it?

"Wouldn't it be wonderful," you might ponder after working for many hours to compile your report, "if all the invoices and bills were together in one easy-to-access electronic location that everyone could get to?" Companies have spent millions of dollars because they agree with you that storing all of their business information in a central electronic repository makes wonderful sense. But how do you store the data, and what do you use to see the information?

Oracle Corporation has for many years supplied computer software to accomplish both the task of storing information and the means to view it. In the case of information storage, Oracle supplies tools that enable you to build one or more databases. To view information, Oracle provides several tools that developers can use to build software *applications*—groups of computer programs that help you to view and interact with the information stored in your database. Oracle also provides applications for several different forms of information tracking that you can buy "off the shelf." For this book, we will concentrate on the database side of the Oracle product set. As a DBA, this is the software you will interact with most of the time, and this is the software you will "take care of."

To help you understand the differences between the logical and physical entities that we are going to be talking about in this chapter, we introduce these concepts by looking at three different "worlds":

- The human world
- The computer hardware world
- The database world

An object can be physical in one world but logical in another. Confusing? Let's look at some examples of the different worlds to see how this nomenclature works. In Table 2-1, we have listed the three worlds and some of the objects in those worlds. You can see that in our human world, we have what we consider to be solid objects and perceptions or concepts. You can touch and hold a pencil or a piece of paper because it has three dimensions and a solid composition. You can see a dream with your mind's eye and can hold on to it with your mind but not with your hands.

In the computer world, you can touch a computer, its disks, and all of its physical components. If you use a monitor screen, you can see the directories and files on the disks, but you can't hold them in your hands.

In the database world, you can hold the CD_ROM disc that you receive from Oracle. Now, here's where the tricky part comes in. Files appear as "logical" in our computer world, but in the database world, they are thought of as "physical." This is one case where an object has crossed over from the logical to the physical when it went from one world to another. We know, it's kind of a hokey concept and hard to really pin down, but consider that through a database's software, you can really touch the objects that we refer to as physical. So, in the database world, files on a disk are considered as physical, and there are objects inside the database that we think of as logical, such as tables, views, and indexes.

To begin our exploration of the composition of an Oracle database, let's look at the so-called physical pieces. Because we are talking about computers, even some of what we refer to and view as physical objects can't be picked up and carried around individually. Just keep in mind that these different worlds exist, and let's go from there.

Type of World	Physical Example	Logical Example
Human world	Filing cabinet, paper, pencils	Thoughts, dreams
Computer world	Disk, CPU	File on disk, computer program
Database world	Datafile, redo log file, control file	Table, view, index, tablespace

TABLE 2-1. *The Three Worlds Example*

Physical Objects

Although we are not here to teach you about basic computer hardware, we need to look briefly at the general composition of a computer to understand how and where Oracle fits into the picture. A computer is composed of a multitude of different pieces. If you were to take a computer apart—and please don't try this at home without a net—you would find an assortment of

- Computer chips
- Resistors
- At least one central processing unit (CPU)
- An internal disk on which you can store computer programs or data
- Possible external disks connected to the computer for more storage
- Memory modules
- Many other components

Okay, so there are lots of electronic components that make up a computer. The disks—both internal and external—are used to store information in a measure known as a *byte*. The bytes are grouped together in operating system *blocks* of (usually) 512 bytes. So, you could say that 512 bytes make up a block of operating system space. Oracle also measures its storage in bytes and blocks, but you get to pick the size of an Oracle block from several choices when you create the database. The default number of bytes in an Oracle block is 2048, which is a very small block size by today's standards. We'll look more closely at Oracle block sizing in Chapter 3.

There is also operating system software associated with your computer. In the next section, we'll look at the structure of some software components.

About Operating Systems

Operating systems vary depending on the type of hardware you are using. Oracle Corporation offers versions of the Oracle software for a variety of operating systems and computers.

The operating system (OS) is a layer between the computer hardware and computer software. The OS understands how to speak to a disk drive when the software issues a command such as "write to this file." There are many different operating systems, and some computer hardware is designed to work properly with only certain kinds of operating systems. Oracle software may not be available for some of the operating systems or for various versions of the same operating system. The general areas in which information is stored are called *directories,* and the information is stored in *files* within a directory. In Figure 2-1, you can see the top-level directory structure for a Windows NT installation of Oracle RDBMS v8.0.5.0.0.

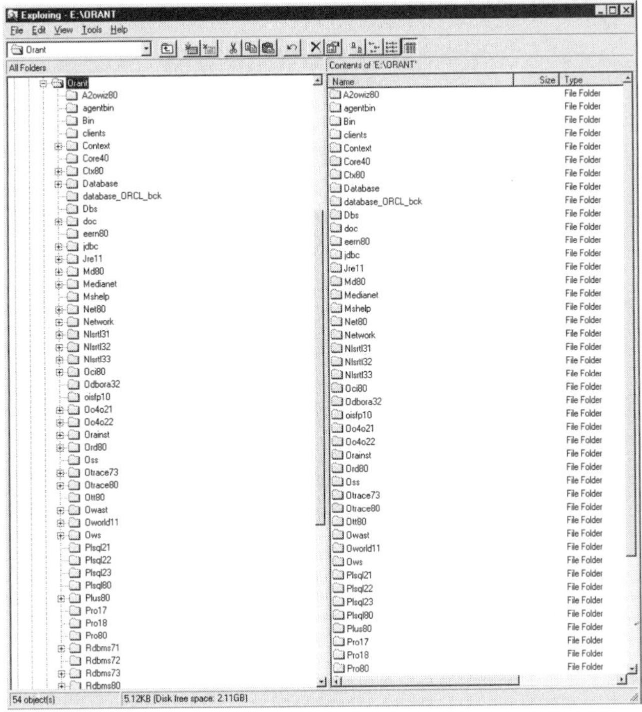

FIGURE 2-1. *Windows NT Oracle v8.0.5.0.0 directory structure*

About Version Numbers

Note the version number 8.0.5.0.0. Over time, you will become very familiar with and fluent in keeping track of and talking about the various versions that Oracle has released or that you are working with. In fact, that's one of the first things most DBAs will ask each other. A possible conversation between two DBAs might sound like the following:

DBA1: "I just had the worst experience."

DBA2: "What happened?"

DBA1: "Well, I was migrating a database, and the Migration Assistant failed."

DBA2: "What version were you migrating from and to?"

DBA1: "Oh, 7.3.3.6 to 8.1.5."

DBA2: "Bummer!"

In actuality, the complete version number is always five digits long, separated by decimal points, but DBAs generally talk in the shortest significant numbers available and tend to leave off any trailing zeros when zeros are present. After all, why make any more work for ourselves than necessary, right?

Well, back to directory structures and Figure 2-1. On a Windows NT system, the directory indicators, or *icons*, look like the folders you might use to file papers in a filing cabinet. The files within a directory are displayed on the right side of the screen. Each file has an icon that shows you its function.

If you are using a Unix operating system, the directory structure will be displayed with file names. Figure 2-2 displays a directory listing for a Unix system.

The listing gives similar information but without the icons. By comparison, the listing from an Alpha OpenVMS system is shown in Figure 2-3.

Again, you can see that the listing is without icons. However, the directory contents are displayed very differently, even though they contain many similar names, such as the rdbms and network directories. What you will also notice from comparing the three listings is that although the basic structure for a directory is different, the contents seem to be very similar. In reality, for Oracle software, there are many files with the same names across all of the different operating systems. A file called pupbld.sql on a Windows NT system will be identical to a file with the same name on a Unix system. That's one of the great things about Oracle software. There are consistencies across the different operating systems that you, as a DBA, can rely on.

```
$ ls -l $ORACLE_HOME
total 74
drwxr-xr-x   2 oracle   dba         1536 Nov  8 17:43 bin
drwxr-xr-x   3 oracle   dba          512 Oct 19  1998 book22
drwxr-xr-x   2 oracle   dba          512 Apr 15 06:26 dbs
drwxr-xr-x   3 oracle   dba          512 Oct 19  1998 guicommon2
drwxr-xr-x   4 oracle   dba         1536 Oct 19  1998 lib
drwxr-xr-x  14 oracle   dba          512 Oct 19  1998 network
drwxr-xr-x   3 oracle   dba          512 Oct 19  1998 nlsrtl3
drwxr-xr-x   9 oracle   dba          512 Oct 19  1998 obackup
drwxr-xr-x   4 oracle   dba          512 Oct 19  1998 ocommon
drwxr-xr-x   3 oracle   dba          512 Oct 19  1998 oracore3
drwxr-xr-x   7 oracle   dba         5120 Oct 20  1998 orainst
drwxr-xr-x   8 oracle   dba          512 Oct 19  1998 otrace
drwxr-xr-x   3 oracle   dba          512 Feb 17 20:09 patchset
drwxr-xr-x   6 oracle   dba          512 Oct 20  1998 plsql
drwxr-xr-x   9 oracle   dba          512 Nov  5 10:51 precomp
drwxr-xr-x  11 oracle   dba          512 Oct 19  1998 rdbms
drwxr-xr-x   4 oracle   dba          512 Oct 19  1998 slax
drwxr-xr-x   8 oracle   dba          512 Oct 19  1998 sqlplus
drwxr-xr-x   7 oracle   dba          512 Oct 19  1998 svrmgr
-rw-r--r--   1 oracle   dba        11865 Oct 20  1998 unix.prd
```

FIGURE 2-2. *Unix Oracle directory structure*

Windows NT, Compaq OpenVMS, and Unix all have a text interface, which means you can "talk" to the operating system through text commands. In Windows NT, you use a DOS window, while for Compaq OpenVMS and Unix, you use a command line. Windows NT and Unix also have a graphical interface (Explorer, X11 File Manager). However, because most people use the Windows NT graphical interface and the Unix command line, we are displaying them here in these formats.

How Oracle Fits In

Where does Oracle fit into all of this? Well, for one thing, Oracle takes advantage of the various components of any operating system to help perform its processing. Oracle uses the computer's disks to store many different types of files and many different types of information. These files are viewed as physical objects because you can copy them from one disk to another or even copy them onto portable disks and carry them to another computer with the same operating system.

```
Directory MYDISK01:[ORACLE.V7336]

AGENT.DIR;1         AROPT.DIR;1         CRT.DIR;1          DDBEXT.DIR;1
FORMS45.DIR;1       GRAPHICS25.DIR;1    GUICORE23.DIR;1    INSTALL.DIR;1
NETCONFIG.DIR;1     NETWORK.DIR;1       OCOMMON.DIR;1      OTRACE.DIR;1
PARREXT.DIR;1       PATCHSET.DIR;1      PQOPT.DIR;1        PROCBUILDER.DIR;1
PROGINT.DIR;1       RDBMS.DIR;1         REPORTS25.DIR;1    SQLFORMS.DIR;1
SQLPLUS.DIR;1       SQLREPORT.DIR;1     SVRMGR.DIR;1       UTIL.DIR;1

Total of 24 files.
```

FIGURE 2-3. *Alpha OpenVMS Oracle directory structure*

Oracle Software

Among the files that make up an Oracle system is the Oracle Corporation-supplied software that you will use to build and manage your databases. This software is made up of different files that serve various functions.

When you install the Oracle software, you will be given the option of letting Oracle create a small demonstration database for you. If this is the first time you are installing this version of the Oracle software, you will want to let Oracle create a database so you will have an area in which you can explore and learn the new features and just generally "play." The best way for you to learn to be an Oracle DBA is to practice and experiment with a database that you can safely mess up or even destroy.

Oracle's "Physical" Composition

In Chapter 3, we'll look more closely at installing the Oracle-supplied software. For now, you just need to remember that the Oracle software will "live" on a computer disk on your system in files within directories.

When you create an Oracle database, there are two types of files that Oracle uses to store information. It stores the information about the database structure (the *metadata*) in one set of files and your company's actual data in another form of files. There are four types of physical files associated with an Oracle database: control files, redo log files, datafiles, and informational log files, such as the alert and trace log files. In addition, parameter files—used to initialize Oracle's memory area—are necessary to start the database but are not actually part of it. A sixth type of file—backup files that are copies of the datafiles—may also exist for the database but, again, are not an actual part of it.

- **Datafiles** contain the actual data that you think of when you hear the word *database*.
- **Parameter files** contain the initialization parameters that you can modify to tell Oracle how to create the memory area it will use to manage the database.
- **Control files** map the physical files of a database to the logical tablespaces and online redo log files in the database dictionary as well as maintain information Oracle needs to ensure that your database is consistent.
- **Redo log files** contain enough information to allow Oracle to reconstruct or back out transactions should the database be shut down before the changes have been written to the disk files.
- **Alert and trace log files** contain information about the health of the database and provide warnings when problems occur.
- **Backup files** contain copies of the database files that can be used to recover both structural and datafiles.

The database metadata is stored within the Oracle data dictionary. Information is stored in the data dictionary about the logical entities that make up the database, such as tables, views, synonyms, triggers, and procedures, and the locations of the physical objects, such as the datafiles, control files, redo log files, and log files. In the following sections, we'll talk about the various types of files in more detail.

Datafiles

If you let Oracle create a small demonstration database for you when you install the Oracle-supplied software and you look at the directory structure, you will find several files associated with your new database. Figure 2-4 shows a list of file names for a new database called ORC1. Yes, each database you create will have a name and a *system identification name* or SID. This system identification name is usually, but not always, the same as the database name. A database is used to store and

```
Crtl1Orc1.ctl
Crtl2Orc1.ctl
Dat1Orc1.dbf
Idx1Orc1.dbf
Rbs1Orc1.dbf
Sys1Orc1.dbf
Tmp1Orc1.dbf
Tool1Orc1.dbf
Usr1Orc1.dbf
ConOrc1.ora
InitOrc1.ora
Log1Orc1.rdo
Log2Orc1.rdo
```

FIGURE 2-4. *Directory structure for a new, demonstration database*

manipulate data in a logical way. When a database is up, several Oracle processes are running in the background. We'll talk more about these processes in Chapter 3. These processes make up the instance and allow the data to be accessed. Oracle uses a SID to differentiate between instances and to ensure the correct processes, and in turn the correct data, are being manipulated. When you are using the Oracle Parallel Server option, the SIDs of the instances must be different from one another, although one may be the same as the database name. Oracle needs to be able to differentiate among requests from the different instances and the machines they reside on, and it uses the instance name to keep track of this.

There can be many datafiles within a database, and Oracle uses each datafile to store information. Oracle writes to the datafiles using a binary format, so you can't really read or modify the contents of a datafile yourself. Datafiles are the physical areas of database storage. Most DBAs use a standard convention for naming their database files so they can easily tell the type of file and its specific use. In the list in Figure 2-4, you can see that several different file *extensions*, or ending names, are used:

- .CTL for control files
- .ORA for parameter files
- .RDO for redo log files
- .DBF for datafiles

Looking again at Figure 2-4, you can see that the database name is used in each file name to show that the file is an element of the ORC1 database. The beginning of each name shows the function or object with which the file is associated. A number is used after the beginning of the name to uniquely identify a file.

- **CON** Configuration parameter file
- **CRTL** Control file
- **DAT** Datafile in which company information might be stored
- **IDX** Datafile in which index information might be stored
- **INIT** Initialization parameter file
- **LOG** Redo log file
- **RBS** Rollback segment datafile
- **SYS** System datafile
- **TMP** Temporary segment datafile
- **TOOL** Datafile in which application tool information might be stored
- **USR** Datafile in which user information might be stored

If you saw the file name TmpMydb3.dbf in a directory, you would immediately be able to guess that the file was the third datafile used for temporary segment information for the Mydb database. Please realize that the convention we are showing here is just one of many that you could use. There are no set rules for naming your tablespaces, tables, indexes, and other objects. We recommend, however, that you use a consistent naming approach when working with the various Oracle files. You will then be able to easily identify the associations between the objects and their intended use. Consistent naming conventions will help make your life much easier!

At the very lowest physical level, an Oracle database is composed of database blocks. The database blocks are used to store all of the database data. As a DBA, you will determine the Oracle database block size when you create a database. The size is set using the parameter **db_block_size**. You'll put this parameter either in the init.ora or config.ora file. Once you create a database with a specific block size, the size cannot be changed unless the database is rebuilt. Because the block size is "cast in concrete," you will need to be careful when you select a database block size so that you will enhance and help optimize the performance of the application that will use the database. On modern, memory-rich systems, database block sizes of 4, 8, 16, or even 32 kilobytes are within reason. So, how do you decide what size to make your database blocks? In Chapter 3, we'll look more closely at how to size your database blocks to best match the performance requirements for your database.

In an Oracle database, an *extent* is a contiguous allocation of database blocks. An extent is dedicated to a specific table, cluster, index, temporary segment, or rollback segment. An extent is created whenever a segment is created or a current segment is not large enough to hold information that is being inserted. A *segment* is a collection of extents that make up a single table, index, temporary segment, or rollback segment.

Parameter Files

In the previous section, you saw that there are two different files with a file extension of .ORA. In the explanations, you saw that the .ORA extension is used to indicate a parameter file—either an initialization parameter file or a configuration parameter file. These files are used to tell Oracle that you want to change the value that Oracle would normally use as its default for a specific parameter when the database is started. These parameters are used to influence how Oracle will perform its various tasks.

The Initialization Parameter File

When you create a database, Oracle creates a sample, default init.ora file. If you do not modify any values in the Oracle-supplied file, Oracle will use all default settings when it starts your database. Why do you care what values are used? Well, you care because the parameters influence how quickly users can obtain information from your database—otherwise known as database performance. Let's face it. If you have to sit in front of a computer screen waiting for information to be returned from a database and you sit for more than about 45 seconds, you will feel like you've been waiting for several minutes! It's human nature to believe that more time has gone by than really has when you're waiting for a response. As a DBA, you want the information to be retrieved from your database as quickly as possible, especially if it's the president of the company waiting for the data. So, you will end up being vitally interested in how quickly your database is returning information.

There are many other parameters in the init.ora file that you can modify for purposes other than performance tuning. We'll talk more about the other parameters as we get into the software installation information in Chapter 3. Just as a piece of inside information, even though the actual initialization file that will be created for a database named orc1 will be named initorc1.ora, in DBA-speak, the initialization file is referred to as the init.ora file. The same applies to the config.ora file discussed next. Oh, and the file is really talked about as the "init dot ora" file or "config dot ora" file. Go figure!

The Configuration Parameter File

The configuration file, which is generally named config.ora, is used for instance-specific information. This file is a text file that is called or activated by the init.ora file. The INIT.ORA file will contain a parameter called **ifile**. The **ifile** parameter will be set equal to the location of the config.ora file. The value will look something like the following for a Windows NT location:

```
ifile=c:\orant\database\config.ora
```

You may not even have or need a configuration file on your system for your database, and that's okay. You may have multiple configuration files in your init.ora, each one setting the parameters for various database options. A configuration file will contain values for parameters that generally do not change in your database.

Oracle provides an extra-cost option that enables you to have more than one instance attach to a single database. This option is called the Oracle Parallel Server (OPS) option. If you have this option and are performing parallel server operations, you will use a configuration file to hold the configuration for each specific instance that attaches to your database. We'll talk more about the nomenclature of *instance* versus *database* in Chapter 3. For now, just keep in mind that the information you usually store in a configuration file consists of the following:

- Location of the control files
- Name of the database
- Oracle block size for the database
- Location of the dump files for users and for the instance

Since there is more than one instance connecting to a single database, the elements listed in the configuration file can be very different for each instance. Of course, if there is only one instance connected to a database, all of this information can be stored in the init.ora file, and no config.ora file is really necessary.

Log Files

If you were going to keep track of the food you eat daily, you might buy a small notebook to carry around with you. You could label the notebook with something like "Daily Food Diary." Each time you ate something (if you were really serious about this venture), you might record any or all of the following information:

- The kind of food you ate
- Quantity
- Amount of calories, fat, carbohydrate, or protein the food contained

- When you ate—day, date, and time
- What mood you were in when you ate
- Why you chose that particular time to eat

All of this information would give you a pretty good view of what was going on with your daily eating patterns. You might review your food diary every evening, and once a week you might note how you felt about your eating patterns. We could refer to your food diary as a "Daily Food Log" since you are logging your eating activities.

Oracle creates two different forms of logs: informational logs and internal activity logs. Each log type keeps track of a different form of database activity. Here are lists of the different types of logs that are created and a notation of what type of information each log contains. We'll look more closely at each of the different logs in Chapter 3.

The informational logs that are generally created by an Oracle database at various times include

- **Database startup log** Created each time a database is started
- **Database shutdown log** Created each time a database is closed and shut down
- **Alert log** Created when the database is first created to log various database events and updated with all subsequent database events
- **Trace files** Created when a database or process system error occurs
- **SQL*Net Listener log** Created or written to each time a listener event occurs

The log files that are created and used by Oracle for its own internal activity tracking include

- **Redo log files** Used to track corporate data changes
- **Control files** Used to track the location of database files on the system
- **Archive log files** (if archive logging is enabled) Used for database recovery

All of these logs will be discussed more thoroughly in Chapter 3.

Backup Files

Think for a moment about car or household insurance that you purchase to ensure that if something happens to your possessions, you will be able to replace them. Making copies—called *backups*—of the Oracle files and their contents helps you ensure that you will be able to replace your company's data if an accident or hardware failure occurs. Your data could be lost in several different ways. Any one of the following kinds of events could occur:

- Hardware failure
- Software failure
- Natural disaster, such as a flood or fire
- Human error

In each of these cases, if you do not have a copy of your database with the most current data available, your company could lose large amounts of both time and money replacing the lost information.

Oracle provides many useful options to help you protect your data. In most cases, the options you choose to back up your database will generate files that will be stored on your computer disks. The command procedures you will use to create the backups will also be stored on physical disks.

In Chapter 13, we'll tell you more about your backup options and how they work.

Logical Database Objects

In the preceding sections, you have been introduced to the physical files associated with an Oracle database. It's now time to learn about the logical files. As we mentioned in the earlier section, "Oracle's 'Physical' Composition," the information about the contents of the logical files is all stored in the data dictionary. In the following sections, you will see how the contents of the data dictionary correspond to the contents in the database physical files.

Tablespaces

One of the most difficult concepts to understand about an Oracle database is a *tablespace*. It's also one of the most difficult to explain! Think for a minute about your last trip to a library. The library was filled with books, magazines, videocassettes, music CDs, newspapers, possibly artwork, and reference materials. In other words, the library contained a wide assortment of different kinds of information. Well, a tablespace is the logical representation of stored information. There is a direct correlation between a tablespace and the datafiles that store the data. When you create a tablespace, you tell Oracle the location for the initial datafile with which the tablespace will be associated. You also tell Oracle the size of the datafile. There are many parameters that you can use to describe how your new tablespace will "look."

Managing tablespaces involves many considerations and issues. In Chapter 5, we'll look at tablespace composition and management in depth.

Tables

Whether you realize it or not, you have already been looking at potential Oracle database table structures both in this chapter and in Chapter 1. Sneaky, aren't we! So, what is a database *table*? Is it like my kitchen table at home—the one where I keep piling all those magazines I get? Well, sort of. In a way, a database table is more like a storage cabinet with drawers. Each drawer can be of a different size or the same size, and you can put something in each drawer or the drawer can be left empty for a period of time (or forever). A table is a location where you put pieces of information of various sizes.

Creating a Table

Remember back in Chapter 1 when we were talking about the information that a bank needs in order to keep track of your transactions? We listed the following information about your name:

- A salutation, such as Mister (Mr), Mistress (Mrs), Miss (Ms)
- First name
- Middle name or middle initial
- Last name
- A suffix, such as Junior (Jr) or a number (the first, second, third, etc.)

Technically, for our table, each drawer is called a *column*. Each complete customer name is called a *row*, and the cabinet is called a table. Once you have decided on the components you need for your table to be able to store the customer names, you must decide what size each column needs to be. Let's assign some tentative sizes (we'll count each alphabetical letter as one character) to each column in the proposed customer names table, as shown in Table 2-2.

This particular table only has alphabetical letters. Can you have numbers in your column sizes? What about calendar dates? Of course! You can have many different *data types*, and there are wonderful SQL language books that can tell you all about the different types.

For now, the only data types we'll talk about are the character ones so that we can develop our table. Most documentation will tell you that there are three different ways to define a character data type: CHAR, VARCHAR, and VARCHAR2. In reality, as of Oracle8, only two of these types are actually used: CHAR and VARCHAR2. Even if you tell Oracle that you want to use, or *declare*, a column as VARCHAR, Oracle will automatically convert your declaration to VARCHAR2. So, what's the difference between CHAR and VARCHAR2?

If you have a column that you say will be 15 characters long and the value that you want to store in the column is only 5 characters long, what will happen? If the column is declared as CHAR, Oracle will insert blank characters onto the end of the value so that there are actually 15 characters stored. If the column is declared as VARCHAR2, Oracle will only store the 5 actual characters, with no blanks "padded on to the end." If you have a million rows in your table, the amount of storage space required could be drastically different depending on how the columns are defined. There are times that you will want the complete column length held for data, and you will want to use CHAR. Most of the time, you will probably use VARCHAR2.

Column	**Size**
Salutation	5 characters
First Name	15 characters
Middle Name	15 characters
Last Name	25 characters
Suffix	10 characters

TABLE 2-2. *Sizing a Table's Columns*

Naming Tables and Columns

The next step you will take to create the customer names table is to decide what names you will give each column. There aren't a lot of hard-and-fast rules for naming tables and columns, but it's nice to have meaningful names so you can recognize the purpose that each name represents. You could choose a name for your table such as CUSTOMER_NAMES or CUST_NAMES. If you decide to really cut back the number of letters used, you might choose CST_NMS, but, as you can see, the more letters you drop, the less meaningful the name becomes. For this table, let's go with CUST_NAMES.

Now, let's think about the column names and their data types. How about:

```
Salut          varchar2(5)
First_Name     varchar2(15)
Middle_Name    varchar2(15)
Last_Name      varchar2(25)
Suffix         varchar2(10)
```

That looks pretty good. The names are short enough to be easily typed and used but long enough to be meaningful.

Table Creation Code

You have the table name, the column names, their data types and sizes. You have enough information and are now ready to actually create your first, small, simple table. The command you will use is as follows:

```
create table CUST_NAMES
(Salut         varchar2(5),
First_Name     varchar2(15),
Middle_Name    varchar2(15),
Last_Name      varchar2(25),
Suffix         varchar2(10))
```

To let Oracle know that you've completed your command and want the program to perform the requested task, you use either a semicolon (;) or a slash (/). Let's go ahead and run the table creation script in an Oracle v8.0.4 database and see what happens.

```
create table CUST_NAMES
 (Salut  varchar2(5),
  First_Name varchar2(15),
  Middle_Name varchar2(15),
```

```
  Last_Name varchar2(25),
  Suffix  varchar2(10))
/

Table created.

describe CUST_NAMES;

Name                                               Null?    Type
-------------------------------------------------- -------- ------------
SALUT                                                       VARCHAR2(5)
FIRST_NAME                                                  VARCHAR2(15)
MIDDLE_NAME                                                 VARCHAR2(15)
LAST_NAME                                                   VARCHAR2(25)
SUFFIX                                                      VARCHAR2(10)
```

Once the table is created, you can store information in it by writing

```
insert into CUST_NAMES
(Salut, First_Name, Middle_Name, Last_Name, Suffix)
values ('MS','MARLENE','LYNN','THERIAULT',NULL);
```

There are three interesting things to look at in the last statement:

- All of the column names are listed in the insert statement.
- There is no owner listed in the table name because the owner of the schema is doing the insert. If another person were doing the insert, an owner would need to be designated in the insert statement in the form owner.table_name.
- All of the name values are capitalized to make comparisons easier in future queries.
- The word "NULL" is used to show that there is no value for the Suffix column.

This is a very simple table without any rules enforced. We'll talk more about owner references in the "To Role or Not to Role" section later in the chapter.

Enforcing Business Rules

What are some of the rules you might want to enforce on a table and why? You might want one or more of the following rules enforced to ensure the consistency of the data being entered:

- Every customer's name must include at least a first name and a last name
- The only values that can be used in the Salut column are DR, MS, MR, MRS
- The only values that can be used in the Suffix column are JR, SR, I, II, III

To impose the rules, you can use an Oracle feature called a *constraint*. There are two different categories of constraints available: table constraints and column constraints. If you want to ensure that the information is consistent across the entire table, you use a table constraint. For example, if you need a way to uniquely identify each row in a table, you can use a constraint that says, "Each row must have a column with a unique number in it for identification purposes." You create a *primary key constraint* to enforce that rule across the entire table. If you want to ensure that the contents of a column only contain specific information (such as our Salut or Suffix columns), you use a constraint that checks the value being added to the column to ensure that only the permitted values are accepted. You use a column-level *check constraint*.

Within the categories of table and column constraints, different types of constraints are available to ensure that your business rules are enforced. Here is a list of some of the available constraints:

- **Primary key constraint** Table constraint used to ensure unique rows across a table
- **Foreign key constraint** Table constraint used to ensure consistency across tables
- **Unique column constraint** Column constraint used to ensure unique values in a column
- **Null constraint** Column constraint used to allow or disallow the absence of a value in a specific column
- **Check constraint** Column constraint used to ensure that only specific values will be allowed for storage in a column

In earlier versions of Oracle, you would have to write application code to enforce these business rules. With the addition of constraints in later versions of Oracle, you can now use the database to enforce these rules both efficiently and effectively.

More Complex Tables

So far, all you've seen is a very simple table and some rules that you can apply, called constraints, to help you enforce your company's business rules. However, there are many different kinds of tables that you could use in Oracle8 and 8i to help you manage and administer your data.

Here is a list of some new table types introduced in Oracle8 and enhanced in 8i:

- **Partitioned tables** Used to spread a large table over a set of smaller tables for ease of maintainability and more efficient data retrieval
- **Advanced Queue tables** Used to integrate a message queuing system within the database
- **Index-Organized tables** (also called Index-Only) Used to store index columns as a table to aid in faster data retrieval
- **Nested tables** Used to store multiple columns of data within one column of a table
- **Object tables** Used to enable the creation of object types that more closely represent their composition in the real world

More information about these table types can be found in the *Oracle8i DBA Handbook*, by Kevin Loney and Marlene Theriault (Osborne/McGraw-Hill, 2000).

Indexes

Just as you have many more databases around you than you realized, you have many indexes as well. You probably use indexes already as a way to quickly find information you need. Think about a cookbook. The recipes are often grouped by type of meal (breakfast, lunch, dinner, etc.). Suppose you wanted to find recipes using chicken. Well, you could read the whole book, checking each and every recipe's ingredient list for the word *chicken*. Of course, if your family will be home in an hour and you need to find a recipe to make for dinner, this isn't going to be useful, unless this is a very short cookbook! To quickly go to the recipes that have chicken in them, of course, you turn to the back of the book, where you can look up the word *chicken* and find a list of recipes and pages. Much faster, and you might even have time to relax before dinner.

Let's look at some other indexes. The catalog at the local library is actually several indexes. The catalog lists books by author (first index), subject (second index), and title (third index). And a book may appear several times within the same index, perhaps because it has several authors or because it can be listed under many subjects (this book, for example, could be listed in the author index three times). Even the shelves holding the books are a kind of index. If you are in the fiction section, the racks of shelves will have ranges of letters of the alphabet attached to them. This way, if you know the author you are looking for, you can move quickly to the section where his books can be found. You may have to look through several shelves to find the book you want, but it's still faster than looking through every book in the library.

So how do we translate this concept to a database? Let's look again at the hardware company we discussed earlier in this chapter. The company has converted that filing cabinet system to a computerized one and now has a database that stores its invoice information. One of the tables in the database has information about the invoices the company sends out. The invoice table has to have the following pieces of information:

- Customer name
- Customer account
- Customer address
- A shipping address if it is different from the customer's address
- Date of the invoice
- List of products
- Quantity sold
- Price per individual product
- Total charges

Without indexes, you have to look at every row in your table. The action of examining every row in a table is known as a *full table scan*. If your boss wants you to tell him the total skingwattles sold to the XYZ Company between March and April, you will have to look at each and every invoice row in the invoice table, decide if it is for the XYZ Company, and then look at the date and product on the invoice before deciding whether or not to count this invoice. Hmm… looks like you haven't come very far in getting the system to be easier and more friendly to interact with yet. As long as you don't have many invoices, looking at every one of them is not a problem. But if your company is doing well, you are going to have lots and lots of invoices, and it may take more time than your boss is willing to wait to come up with the information.

Now let's add an index to the invoice table. We could add one on customer, and then you would only have to look at the invoices sent to the XYZ Company. But what if your boss wants to see the total of skingwattles sold, and doesn't care which customer you sold them to? In that case, the index on customer is not going to help. Just as the library has many indexes, and a single book can appear in more than one of them, so a database can have many indexes on a single table. And the indexes don't have to be on only one column in the table. So you can have an index on customer, and another one on product, and a third on date, or you can have each of those indexes plus an index that is made up of both customer and product information, or customer, product, and date information. In other words, you can mix and match columns in a table to have multiple indexes to perform different jobs.

However, keep in mind that you don't want a bunch of indexes on a table just to have indexes. You really do want to have good business reasons to have an index. While indexes can help you find information faster, having too many of them can slow you down when it comes to adding data to your database. Every time you add a new row to a table, you have to add a row to each and every one of the indexes for that table. So the more indexes you have, the slower your database may respond when you add data.

Database Triggers

In order to shoot a gun, you must pull the trigger. The effect of pulling the trigger is as follows:

1. The trigger causes a hammer to strike the firing pin.
2. The firing pin strikes the percussion cap, which causes a minor explosion.
3. The minor explosion causes a major explosion that propels the bullet out of the chamber through the barrel.

What does shooting a gun have to do with an Oracle database? In the same way that pulling a trigger of a gun causes specific actions to occur, "firing" a database trigger causes Oracle to take specific actions in the database. For example, let's say that every time the Salary column of the PAYROLL table is modified, you want to capture the name of the person making the change and the day on which the change occurs. You want to save this information to the PAYROLL_AUDIT table. Oracle provides various forms of *triggers* that you can use to capture information or load other tables with data as needed.

There are four different types of triggers:

- Data Manipulation Language (DML) triggers on tables
- "Instead of" triggers on views
- System triggers on databases that fire for each event for every user in the entire database
- Schema triggers on schemas that fire for each event for a specific schema

Triggers can be written to fire on DML statements such as insert, update, or delete. They can be written to fire on Data Definition Language (DDL) statements such as create, alter, or drop. They can also be written to fire when a specific database action occurs, such as database shutdown or startup. Triggers can be created to take action before or after a behavior occurs. In our PAYROLL_AUDIT example, you want to capture the information after the payroll record is modified, so you would use an "after update" trigger.

You can have triggers that will fire when data is inserted, updated, or deleted from a table, and you can have the trigger fire either before or after the action has occurred. Triggers can be created to fire for every row that is affected as well as only once per statement. You can also have an "instead of" trigger that can be used to modify data through a view. Coupled with the "instead of" trigger, you can use the parameter **for each row** to tell Oracle that you want the action applied to each row in the table that is affected by the trigger.

Views

When you use a camera to take a picture, you use a viewfinder to isolate only the area you want to capture on film. If you look out over a horizon, you will see the full scope of the scenery. When you look through the camera's viewfinder, you see only a narrow portion of the whole scene.

An Oracle view works much the same way as a viewfinder on a camera. It is a mask laid over a table or tables to change the picture the user sees when accessing the data. A view can be created by selecting columns from a larger table, or a view can be written to restrict the number of rows or type of data returned from a select. You can define a view that joins several tables together, with complicated selection criteria, so that you can optimize the access path to the data.

Why use views? If a complicated query is run often, it is simpler to access a view with a simple select statement than it is to constantly rewrite the statement. Should the query change, you only have to change the view definition, rather than change the SQL in every program that has this query. You can control access to data with the where clause in a view, limiting your user's access to certain columns or rows.

Oracle also decides whether or not to parse a SQL statement by first checking to see if the statement already exists in the SQL area of the system global area (SGA). The statement must match *exactly*, down to capitalization and spacing. By using views to store complicated queries that are run often, the statement does not have to be reparsed, saving time and increasing database performance. We'll talk more about the SQL area and the SGA in Chapter 3.

Snapshots

If you think of photography, a *snapshot* is a picture of the world, frozen at the time the picture was taken. Oracle snapshots are similar. An Oracle snapshot is a picture of a table or set of tables that is captured at a point in time. Snapshots are copies of data in one database that have been copied to another database. You can create either of the following kinds of snapshots:

- **Simple snapshots** Created by selecting information from a single table or a simple set of tables that are joined together
- **Complex snapshots** Created by selecting information from multiple tables with subqueries or "group by" clauses

Let's say you have created a snapshot of your CUST_NAMES table called CUST_NAMES_SNAP in another database. This is a very simple snapshot that has been created from a very simple table. You create the snapshot on Monday morning. Throughout the day on Monday, people come into the bank and open accounts, so several names are added to your CUST_NAMES table. By the end of the day, the CUST_NAMES_SNAP snapshot no longer matches the CUST_NAMES table. Whatever will you do? The table and the snapshot are now out of sync! You will now somehow need to make the table and snapshot match again. The act of resynchronization is called a *snapshot refresh.*

Oracle makes a distinction between simple and complex snapshots in order to distinguish how the snapshots can be refreshed. A simple snapshot can be refreshed with changes to the data only. This is called a *fast refresh.* The data in a complex snapshot has to be completely copied to the remote database. This is called a *full refresh.* You can either manually refresh your snapshots, or you can schedule to have them refreshed via the job queues.

Why use snapshots? If some of your users want to do reporting on the data and don't need an up-to-the minute picture of the database, you can move the reporting functions to another database and keep your main database for online activity. This allows you to tune each database for better performance based on the workload each database has.

Another great way to use snapshots is if you have an application in one database that relies on having the latest information from another database, but stored in a little different format. For example, let's say you have personnel location information in Database A and need pieces of that information in Database B. In Database A you have all of each employee's data, while in Database B you only need the employee's name, room number, and phone number. An employee's location could change from one day to the next, so you need the information refreshed on a daily basis to keep the locations current. Snapshots are a perfect way to accomplish this task.

Rollback Segments

Think about a bank and how it handles a transfer of money from one account to another. The money is first taken from one account and then added to another account—a single transaction in which both parts must be completed or else both must be wiped out. If for some reason the money can't be added to the second account after it is removed from the first account, what happens? The money can't just disappear. The books have to balance. The bank program (or database program) has to hold the previous balance of the account somewhere so that it can "roll back" the removal of the money if it has to and replace the account balance with the original amount. In an Oracle database, the information about the previous balance will be held in a rollback segment so that Oracle can keep track of the *before image*, or appearance of the data, in case the transaction is not completed.

How does a rollback segment work? As your program begins to change data in the database, Oracle is changing the physical blocks that contain that information. Before writing the changed information into the data block buffers in the SGA, or to disk, Oracle first assigns your transaction to a rollback segment and makes a copy of the original information in the rollback segment. So if you change your mind and cancel the transaction, the original information is there and can be written back to the disk. If you have a very large transaction, Oracle will expand the rollback segment by adding extents, just as it expands a table when you add information to it. We'll talk more about the data block buffers and the SGA in Chapter 3.

As you can see in Figure 2-5, Oracle views a rollback segment like a circle and expands the circle by adding extents if your transaction needs more space. Oracle will only "wrap" back to the beginning of a rollback segment and reuse the extents in it if the first extent in the rollback segment no longer has a transaction in it.

Using rollback segments also enables Oracle to allow other users of the database to access the table you are changing. Oracle builds a consistent view of the data from the rollback segment, so someone accessing a table while you are in the middle of an update will see a picture of the data in the table before you began your changes. Even if you commit the changes to the database, Oracle will attempt to continue providing a consistent picture to the other user by continuing to read from the rollback segment.

Rollback segments take up physical space in the database, usually in a tablespace that has been reserved exclusively for them. Why reserve a separate tablespace just for rollback segments? Well, the rollback segments are accessed by many transactions and can grow quickly if a lot of data is being changed, so they can take up a lot of the free blocks in a tablespace, leaving little room for the tables. And they can also shrink back to their original size, either automatically by setting a parameter called **optimal** when you create them, or by the DBA manually issuing a **shrink** command. This extension and shrinkage can cause fragmentation in the tablespace and, if other data is stored there, could cause the database to be unable to allocate space when it needs to.

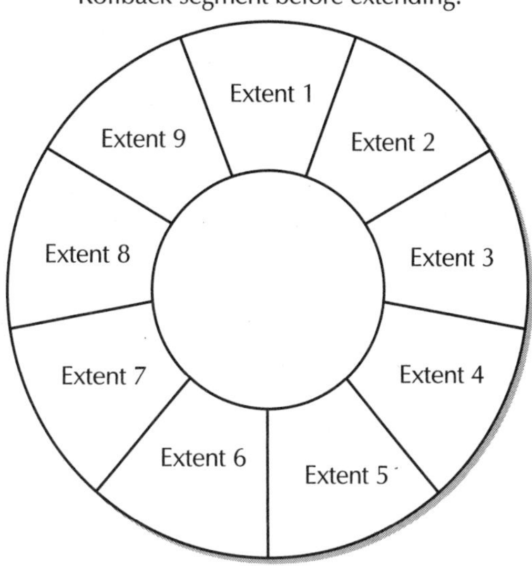

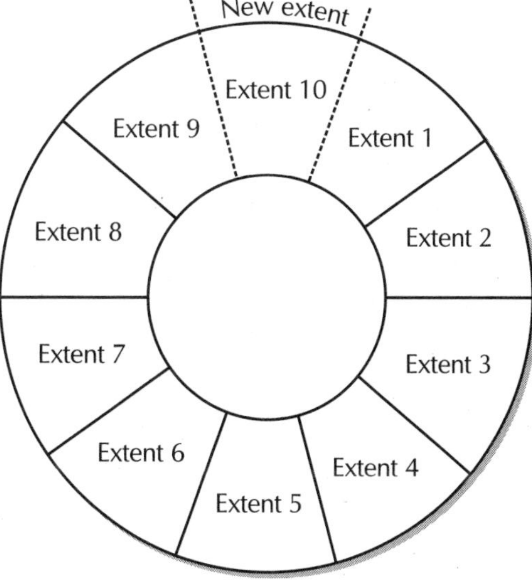

FIGURE 2-5. *Rollback segment before and after extending*

Temporary Segments

Have you ever alphabetized a stack of cards? If the stack was small enough, you could hold all the cards in your hands while putting them in order. But if the stack was large, you wouldn't be able to hold them all at once. In order to make it easier on yourself, you might first separate the cards into two piles, one for the letters A–L and the other for M–Z. Then you would take the piles and break them down even further, A–G, H–L, M–R, and S–Z. You would keep breaking the piles into smaller piles, until you had few enough cards in a pile to hold in your hands while ordering them. Each of the piles you made was temporary, used only for holding the cards until you could get to that pile and put it in order or break it down further. Once you had finished sorting the cards, the piles disappeared.

For certain database actions, Oracle needs to build a temporary staging area to contain the data from the intermediary steps of the processing. Creating an index, selecting data using "union" or "group by" or "order by" clauses, or doing a join on columns that do not have an index will cause Oracle to sort the data and use this staging area. As part of your init.ora parameter file, you can set aside a section of memory in the process global area (PGA) called the **sort_area_size**, for sorting. The PGA is allocated for each user process connecting to the database. If Oracle can fit everything it needs to sort into this memory area, it will not use a temporary segment.

If, however, the data being manipulated is larger than the **sort_area_size**, Oracle will write chunks of the data to disk, allocating temporary segments. Temporary segments are allocated in the tablespace defined as the temporary tablespace for the user running the query. Each database user can have a different temporary tablespace assigned to him or her.

Once Oracle is done with the operation that needed the temporary segments, they are released back to the free space of the tablespace. To help speed performance, Oracle allows you to designate the contents of a tablespace as TEMPORARY. If you do this, the temporary segments are not immediately released, but stay available for reuse by another operation. Tablespaces defined as TEMPORARY cannot contain anything other than temporary segments. You can't create a "temporary" table or other object in a tablespace that has been marked as TEMPORARY, even though you are sure the table you are creating will only exist for a little while. Once a tablespace has been marked as TEMPORARY, Oracle will not allow you to create anything other than temporary segments there.

Roles

Do you remember playing make-believe when you were young? You'd go outside with your friends, and suddenly the neighborhood was the Old West, and you and your best friend were cowboys. You took on the role of "cowboy," and with that role came the ability to ride a horse, rope a cow, and shoot a six-gun. You had gunfights and shoot-outs and generally had a great time. Or maybe you daydreamed yourself into your favorite television show. There you were, the dashing young doctor saving lives, or the heroic police officer fighting crime, or the graceful ballerina dancing across the stage. Each character you became had defined abilities and actions they could perform.

As you grew, the roles you played changed. You became a student. Perhaps you participated in after-school activities or became an athlete. In order to get spending cash, you took an after-school or summer job and worked as a baby-sitter or in the local fast-food restaurant or as a lifeguard. You were then playing many roles at once, but each one you played was played individually—one at a time.

These roles can also be made up of other roles. The lifeguard might also teach swimming, so "swimming teacher" becomes a subrole of lifeguard. What never changes about these roles is that with each role comes a set of abilities, privileges, and actions that you can perform, just by stepping into the role. So a role can be defined as a set of actions and rights granted to the person adopting that role.

Now, let's go back to the hardware company and your job as a file clerk. If you've come to the conclusion that file clerk is a role, you're right. A person filling the file clerk role needs access to the invoices that the company receives from its suppliers. A person filling the role of accounting clerk needs access to the invoices from suppliers and to the invoices the company has sent to its customers. This means the accounting clerk role is actually made up of the file clerk role and some additional rights and actions.

In Figure 2-6 we see that the manager role has the ability to function as both the file clerk role and the accounting clerk role. In addition, some actions can't be done by either role, but only by the manager role.

How do we translate the actions and privileges we do and have in our roles in life to a database? Well, the file clerk action of looking up invoices could be moved to a computer, with all the invoice information stored in a database. When you automate the work that people do, or just move some of the paperwork to a computer, you are defining roles in a database.

With version 6, Oracle introduced the concept of database roles. Roles were designed to make it easier to administer user system and object privileges. You can grant and revoke privileges to the application objects (tables, views, packages, procedures, etc.) without directly granting them to each user who needs them. So, how and why would you want to use roles, and what are their advantages and drawbacks? In the next section, we'll try to answer these questions for you.

To Role or Not to Role

Why use roles rather than grant privileges directly? Let's look at an example. If you have an application with 100 objects, and you have 100 users, you need to make

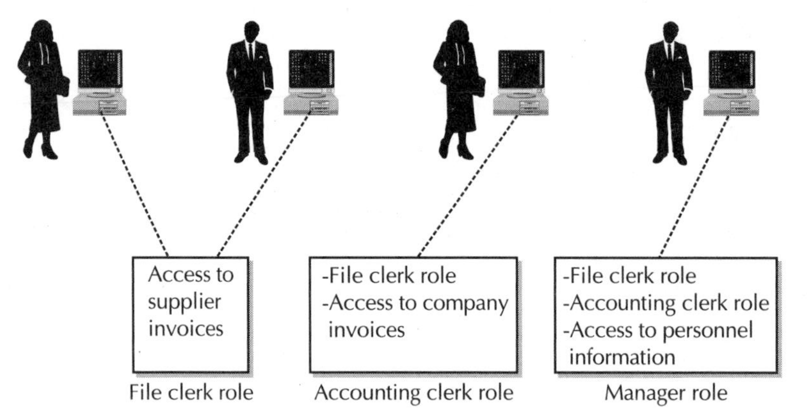

FIGURE 2-6. *Assignment of roles*

10,000 grants (100 grants each for 100 users). If one user leaves, you have to revoke 100 grants to maintain security. And if you add a new object, you need to grant access to it to 100 users. Magnify this by multiple tables and multiple users, and you end up spending all your time just granting access to objects. Now complicate this even further by assuming that your users fall into different categories, and each category of user should have access to only some of the objects. How do you ensure that users get access to only those objects that they should?

To help control this problem, Oracle introduced roles. Rather than grant privileges to users directly, you grant privileges to a role and then grant the role to users. Now, when you add a new object, you only have to grant access to the role, and all users who are granted that role automatically inherit that access. And when a user leaves, you don't have to revoke access at all.

Sounds perfect, doesn't it? Before you rush out and create roles for everything and grant them to all your users, you should be aware of a few drawbacks to using roles. First, roles cannot own objects. Why is this important? Well, if you do a "**select distinct Object_Type from DBA_OBJECTS**," one of the object types that is returned is SYNONYM. So roles can't own synonyms. Why is that important?

A synonym is an alias for an object. When you reference an object in your program, unless you own the object or there is a synonym defined for it, you need to reference the object using the syntax "object_owner.object_name" (marlene.CUST_NAMES instead of CUST_NAMES). This can become a problem as you move programs and procedures from one database to another and the owner of the object changes. You would have to remember to change your code everywhere you reference the object and remember who the owner is in that particular database. If you create a synonym for the object, you only need to refer to the object by its synonym in your program. You can create a synonym of the same name in different databases, and they can refer to different objects, or different object owners, or both. So your program does not have to change.

Now back to why it's important that a role can't own a synonym. This means that the only way you can allow a role to access an object is by either hard-coding the owner of the object into every object access or creating public synonyms. A public synonym is a synonym that is available to everyone, not just you. And the problem with public synonyms is that if you have two applications in your database, and each one has a table named HOLIDAYS that contains different data for each application, you can't create the same public synonym name for the two tables.

Second, you can't create stored procedures, functions, or packages using the access privileges you get from a role. So all your developers will have to have access granted directly. Because of this restriction, it's generally a good idea in production to have a single userid that owns all the objects and the procedures that access the objects.

Advantages of Roles

Managed properly, roles can make your life a good deal easier. Let's go back to the hardware supplies company example we used earlier. Your management has decided to keep all information in one database, so you have data about the invoices, your inventory, and even personnel information in the database. As a file clerk, you need access to the invoices, and you may, or may not, need information on the remaining items in stock. But you do *not* need personnel information. In fact, it's illegal for you to have it. So how does your company allow you access to the data you need and keep you from the data you aren't supposed to see?

You can define separate roles, one for a file clerk (CLERK) and one for personnel (PAYROLL) and assign access to the invoices and inventory data to CLERK and access to the employee information to PAYROLL. Then the DBA assigns you the role CLERK, and you can see the information you need to do your job. If there is only one file clerk in the company, you don't need a role. But as we discussed before, what if there are many people working as file clerks? And what if there are many additions to the objects that a file clerk needs to work with? Tracking all the changes and making sure each object is assigned to the proper person and that each person is assigned all the objects they need becomes a full-time job! And what if you change jobs within the company and now need access to the personnel information? The DBA would have to ensure that he or she revokes all the privileges you had to the file clerk data and then add all the privileges you will need for the personnel data. It's easy to miss either revoking one or adding one. But if the privileges have been grouped into roles, the grants and revokes become single statements.

Packages, Procedures, and Functions

Once you have your data in your tables in your database, you need a way to get the data back out to your users. You could give them each a list of all the SQL statements they would need to use in order to retrieve the data. However, that is awkward and someone would inevitably either mistype the statements or need to manipulate the information in a way that can't be done using SQL alone.

Oracle has provided a procedural language extension to SQL, called PL/SQL, that you can use to mix SQL statements with programming constructs such as loops. This allows you to write programs that can be stored within the database. These programs are stored in the database already compiled and parsed and will execute faster than if they are called from outside the database.

There are several forms of stored programs, all of which are written in PL/SQL and stored within the database. Each type of program can take input and return output. Functions always return a single value to the caller, while procedures can return none, one, or more values. With version 7.0, Oracle added a new form of stored program—a package. Packages are made up of combinations of procedures and functions and allow you to group related functions, procedures, and cursors as a single program unit.

Sequences

Going back to when you were young, think about when you went to a movie theater. You purchased a ticket, and when you entered the theater, the attendant ripped the ticket in half and gave you one half and kept the other. Each ticket had a number on it, and each ticket was unique. In this way, the theater could keep track of exactly how many tickets were sold and ensure that they did not sell more tickets than they had seats in which people could sit.

People have bank accounts with an account number, books have an International Standard Book Number (ISBN), Oracle has TAR (Technical Action Request) numbers. Each of these numbers is used to identify the object they are assigned to, because there is no other way to uniquely identify these things.

In the hardware company, you need a way to uniquely identify your customers, your suppliers, your invoices, and your employees. You need to ensure that information about one customer and her bills is not connected to information about any other customer. What steps would you need to take to assign a unique number to each customer, supplier, invoice, or employee? You could keep a table somewhere that contained a number. Each time you needed a new, unique number, you could have your program do the following steps:

1. Lock the row in your unique number table so that no one else could read or change the number until you were done looking at and using it.
2. Select the current number to assign to your customer.

3. Add one to the number in the table to make it unique and different from the number you just selected.

4. Unlock the record so someone else who needed a unique number could use the table.

The problem with this method is that it's time consuming, resource intensive, and if the person who requested the number goes to lunch in the middle of the work, everyone waits while the number table is locked. This is not an efficient solution.

Oracle provides sequences as a way around this problem. Sequences are unique number generators, providing sequential numbers that can be used to uniquely identify rows in a table. They are not linked to a table, so you can define one sequence to generate all the numbers in your database, or you can have multiple sequence generators to serve different purposes.

If you don't need every number in the sequence (for customer numbers that just have to be unique), you can tell Oracle to *cache* (or save) numbers from the sequence into memory. This means that while you may lose numbers when the database shuts down, you can retrieve a sequence number more quickly. For numbers that must be sequential (invoice numbers), you can define the sequence to read from disk for each number. Information about sequences is stored in a single data dictionary table in the SYSTEM tablespace, so it is always available. Once a number has been generated from the sequence, it will never be generated again unless the sequence has been created to cycle back to the beginning.

Privileges

Now that you have all the information stored in your database, and you have defined the various roles that people will play in your application, you need to grant access to the objects and privileges to do certain things within the database. Oracle distinguishes between privileges to manipulate data and privileges to perform actions. Privileges to manipulate data are called *object privileges,* and privileges to perform actions are called *system privileges.*

Object privileges include the following rights:

- Look at rows and columns in your tables and views (select)
- Add new rows (insert)
- Update existing rows (update)
- Delete information (delete)
- Execute stored programs (execute)

System privileges allow you to perform actions that affect the overall state of the database. System privileges enable you or your users to change the structure of the database. A few simple privileges are as follows:

- Create a table, index, view, snapshot
- Drop a table, index, view, snapshot
- Create a session in the database in order to connect to the database to perform work

We'll look more closely at system privileges in a minute. For now, let's consider why you need privileges on objects in your database.

Why not make everything accessible to everyone and allow any user to modify system structures? Not all data should be available to every user. If you store personnel information in your database as well as business data, you want to ensure that only those people authorized to look at personnel information have access to it. You don't want an employee to be able to look at another employee's salary or medical information, nor do you want someone to be able to update his or her own payroll, vacation, or sick leave accrual records.

Another form of information that you might not want everyone to have access to is your company-private information. At the April 1999 International Oracle User Group (IOUG-A Live) conference, a DBA described how a contractor who had been hired to work on his database copied company-private information and then left the company and used the copied information to win a contract at a lower bid. Although this is totally unprofessional, it might be difficult to prove the information was removed and used against the company.

Let's first talk about object privileges. These are rights you give to other users to access your objects. You can grant different privileges to different users, letting some only select data and others change it. You can also grant access to other users **with grant option** to allow them to grant access for you. This allows you to keep ownership of all objects within a single schema, create a role for administration of access (DATASEC), grant access to all objects with grant option to DATASEC, and grant the DATASEC role to your data center operations staff. By granting a privilege with grant option to someone else, it allows you to keep access to the owner schema restricted and yet allows others to grant access to the application objects.

For example, if Rachel grants Marlene select privilege on the CUST_NAMES table **with grant option**, Marlene can grant select on the CUST_NAMES table to Ross. Now Marlene and Ross can both see what's in the CUST_NAMES table. But what happens if Rachel changes her mind and decides that Marlene should no longer be able to see this table? Rachel can *revoke* select from Marlene. Gee, what happens to Ross's ability to select from the table? Well, Ross loses his ability to select from the table as soon as Marlene loses her privileges. You will need to remember the ramifications of revoking privileges from someone who has had grant option on an object because of this ripple effect.

Now let's talk about system privileges. These privileges allow you to connect to the database, to affect database objects such as rollback segments and tablespaces, and to create user objects such as tables, views, indexes, and stored procedures. Like object privileges, you can pass on the ability to grant these privileges to another user or role, with the **with admin option**.

If you grant a privilege to someone else **with admin option** and then revoke the privilege from that person, anyone who has been granted privileges through that option would still retain his or her privileges. That sounds kind of confusing, so let's look at an example. Marlene grants **create table with admin option** to Rachel. Rachel then grants **create table** to Ross. Marlene decides that it was not a good idea to grant Rachel this privilege, so she revokes the privilege from Rachel. Guess what. Ross will still have the **create table** privilege!

You will need to take your time and use care as you decide who should have the ability to create objects and who should be able to perform work or grant privileges in your databases.

CHAPTER 3

Oracle Installation, Configuration, and Build

n an ideal world, you would begin employment as an Oracle DBA in a company with a fresh system and a clean slate. There would be no Oracle software installed, no databases built, no decisions already made about how your world would look or run. Of course, there is no ideal world; so, when you start a new job as a DBA, you usually inherit a system that may or may not be set up in the most effective way to promote optimal performance or ensure ease of manageability.

In this chapter, we will start from the very beginning and show you how a database can be installed and configured to make your life easier and the database work better. We'll look at the steps you can take from the time you receive your new CD-ROM software disc from Oracle to make your installation go more smoothly. As you explore this chapter, you will find information that will help you to recognize areas of your database that may need reconfiguration or reorganization to improve performance or manageability. You'll find scripts and tips to help you learn to be more effective as a DBA.

About Software Installation

Before we dive into the steps you should take when you receive your Oracle software CD-ROM disc, let's talk for a minute about the differences between an installation, an upgrade, and a migration. You will hear these words all used interchangeably, but they really have very different actions and meanings associated with them.

When you take the disc that you receive from Oracle and put it in your CD-ROM drive and, through the Oracle installation routines, move the files into directories on your system, you are performing an installation. During the installation session, you usually have the option of letting Oracle install a basic demonstration database. We'll talk a little later about why you should accept this offer. During the installation, Oracle also offers other configuration and installation options that we'll talk about later as well.

Upgrade vs. Migration

The words *upgrade* and *migration* have two different connotations. We'll look first at what is meant by the terms *software upgrade* versus *software migration*. After exploring these terms, we'll examine the differences between a database upgrade and database migration.

Software Upgrade vs. Migration

In earlier versions of Oracle, it was not uncommon for a DBA to receive a disc (or in those days, a nine-track tape or TK50 tape) and just install the new software on top of the old software. When you overwrite the old Oracle software with the new files, you are performing a *software upgrade*. By placing the software files in the same directory structure in which the old software resided, you will be overwriting and deleting any files that have the same name as the original files. Any files that have different names will be left behind. Therefore, you will be left with a complete set of files from the new version and some old files from previous versions. That can get very messy and confusing, especially if you have a problem down the road and need to look at files in a specific directory.

The second approach that you can use and that we heartily recommend—called a *software migration* or fresh installation—is to create a separate directory structure for the new software version. You will have two (or more) copies of Oracle software on your system at one time in completely separate directories. Unless space is a critical issue, we recommend that you always keep separate versions of the software on your system for the following reasons:

- If you overwrite your current version, you will be running your applications in an untested environment.
- Overwriting the old version with a new one may leave behind a mix of old and new files.
- You will not have a chance to verify the new database features delivered with your new software.
- Your developers will not be able to pretest their applications with the new software or incorporate new features that may improve their applications.
- You may have customized some of the files in one of the directories that will be overwritten by the new installation.
- If anything goes wrong, you will have to back out the installation and restore your old environment. Having to stop users from working while you upgrade the software and, again, while you back out the upgrade can be both time consuming and frustrating for them and for you.

If you perform a software migration or fresh installation, you will be able to accomplish the following:

- Verify the new software.
- Be sure the version of software you are working with is untainted by previous software.
- Determine what is different between the old version and the new one.
- Test all the new features thoroughly before you put the new version into production.

- Allow developers to test new features and adapt them to their applications.
- Make the change without disturbing your users.
- Allow for easy migration—when you have finished testing, your migration can be as simple as changing the path for ORACLE_HOME.

In today's fast-paced, "got to get it done *now*" environment, fresh installations are the approach that makes the most sense.

Going One Step Further

In today's computing environment, it's not unusual to find that companies are using more than one computer with a full complement of disks to provide a development environment that is separate from their production system. If you have separate environments, you will be able to "field" the new version of Oracle software to your development system, test it, enhance the applications, and then carry the new version to production. This approach gives you the best of both worlds. You'll have a protected place in which to work with the new version while maintaining your old environment.

Database Upgrade vs. Migration

Another use of the word *upgrade* applies to upgrading a database. If you have a database at version 7.3.2.3.2 and you want it to be a 7.3.3.6 database, you have two choices, as follows:

1. You can shut down your current database under the old version, start it up under the new version, and immediately run some configuration scripts to convert the database to the new version. This approach is called a *database upgrade.*
2. You can create a new database under the new version, make a copy of your old database, and put that copy into your new database. This approach is called a *database migration.*

Just as keeping software versions separate makes a lot of sense, keeping database versions separate can also provide you with the same kinds of benefits. You'll be able to test the performance of your new version while the old database is still available to your users. If there are changes in the way features work between versions, or if new features are available, you will be able to modify your application to handle the change or take advantage of the new feature. Oracle also fixes bugs between releases. We've had occasions when programmers took advantage of one of the quirks of a bug, and when the upgrade was done, suddenly the application stopped working. Separate database versions would have allowed us to catch this and correct the application before end users were hurt by the change.

A Suggested Configuration

In many shops, the approach that has proven to be the most sound and productive is to have two different machines (also referred to as platforms or boxes)—one for development and preproduction, or quality assurance (QA), and one for production. The development box will have at least two copies of the database that reflect the production database. One database will be used for the developers to create and debug their enhancements to the current application, while the second database will be kept as a mirror of the production database. The second database will be used for preproduction and quality assurance testing to ensure that any new features scheduled for release into production will work correctly and not cause unexpected problems in the production environment. Figure 3-1 shows this configuration.

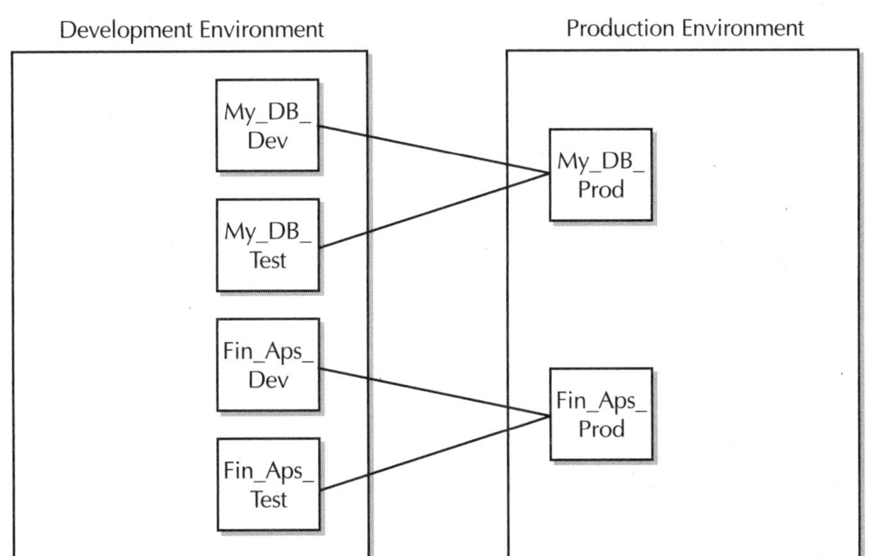

My_DB_Dev - Development database for My_DB application
My_DB_Test - exact copy of current production database for test
Fin_Aps_Dev - Development database for Fin_Aps application
Fin_Aps_Test - exact copy of current production database for test

FIGURE 3-1. *Two systems with associated databases*

In Figure 3-1, we show more than one database on each system. One database is used for tracking the company's property, and another database is used for personnel information. On the production box, there are two databases—one for each application. On the development box, there are four databases—one for each application's development and one for each application's preproduction work. If at all possible, we recommend that you use this approach.

Keep in mind that the production database may be too large to move to a development box in a cost-effective manner. In one shop, the DBA creates a copy of the production database on development. He then loads the data and uses a set of routines generated in-house to pare down the database to a manageable, usable size while still retaining enough test data for the developers to be able to work effectively. You may need to use the same approach in your area.

In many shops, the disk space allocated for development is not large enough to make a full copy of the production database before resizing. In a case like that, you'll need to be a bit more creative in providing a development environment. One approach is to do a full database export with no data and use this to create scripts that can be modified to resize the tables and indexes. Then create the smaller test database, tablespaces, and tables; use SQL*Plus or PL/SQL to extract a subset of the data and generate files that can be used as input to SQL*Loader (Oracle's data load utility program); and load these files into development. This is a time-consuming process, but it may be the only means you will have to generate a useful development database.

Software Installation Steps

Although specific information about installing the Oracle-supplied software is beyond the scope of this book, we will briefly cover the steps that you normally follow when you receive the Oracle software CD-ROM disc and any hard-copy documentation. Unfortunately, Oracle has, of late, been shipping less and less hard-copy documentation with their software releases.

Initial Actions to Take

Although making copies of software for distribution to unlicensed people is illegal, making copies of the software for your own protection and use is okay. Therefore, if you have a CD-ROM copier, the very first thing you should do is make at least three copies of the CD-ROM disc—one for your documentation room, one as your private disc, and one to keep for group access. Once you have made your copies, you should insert the CD-ROM and look for any files with *readme* or *installation* in their names. This may be all of the installation documentation that you are going to receive, and these files can contain very important information that you need to know *before* you begin to install the Oracle software. If your company has purchased a support contract from Oracle, call Oracle Support Services to ask about any known problems with the version you received and any associated patches for that version.

If you have not received a platform-specific version of the installation manual, you should ask Oracle to send you a copy. Each platform has its own peculiarities when it comes to software installations, and a hard-copy installation guide should be available for your specific machine.

When you call support, verify that the operating system you are using is the version—with all associated operating system patches installed—that is required for the specific version of the Oracle server software you have received. Do not assume anything! It's very easy to believe you are on version 4.0.d of an operating system and find out later that you are actually on version 4.0.b. You may find that you need operating system patch number XXXXXXX in order to run Oracle's version X.X on your Unix, OpenVMS, or Windows NT system. And, yes, this just recently happened to one of us. Marlene was asked to help a group installing Oracle version 8.0.5 on a Compaq Unix box. The link kept failing, with two undefined symbols. After several hours, it was finally determined that the operating system level that was installed was not the correct version required for this Oracle installation. Everyone assumed the system administrator had upgraded the operating system. She had upgraded all of the other machines to the correct operating system version but not the machine on which the installation was being performed. Making sure you have the right operating system and operating system patches can save you a lot of time in the long run.

Once you have verified that the operating system versions and patches are correct, read through the installation instructions to verify that your system memory and disk resources are adequate for the Oracle version you are going to use. Be sure to read through all of the instructions so you have the appropriate answers for each question for which you will be prompted. Decide before you begin the installation process whether you will want the Oracle installation to create a default database. In later versions of the software installation, you will have to decide whether you want Oracle to link the appropriate software; install, configure, and start up your Listener and Intelligent Agent; and install and configure a Names Server.

About the Demonstration Database

We recommend letting Oracle create a small default database during your software installation for the following reasons:

- If the database creation succeeds, you will have verified your installation as well as proven that a database can be built.
- You can "poke around" in the default database to see what roles, role composition, and default users (along with their privileges) are being created by Oracle.

- In some versions, Oracle creates default users with easily guessed passwords and DBA privileges! It's important to know which they are so you can change these passwords or privileges.
- You will have a model of the naming conventions and files that Oracle feels are important, although the sizing of these files may be unrealistic for your development or production needs.
- You will have a small test database that you can use as a "sandbox" to perform practice scenarios for disaster recovery and sanity checks if things fail to work correctly in another database.

Some Installation Decisions

Based on the version of Oracle you are installing, you may be asked whether you would like the installation to perform any of the following tasks:

- Link the application software, which is the Oracle-supplied code
- Configure the SQL*Net Listener, which is used to support client connections to the database
- Configure the Intelligent Agent, which is used to communicate between the database and the Oracle Enterprise Manager (the Oracle-supplied, remote database administration tool)
- Configure the Oracle Names Server, which is used to provide SQL*Net connection locations to clients

If these options are presented to you, we recommend that you allow Oracle to link the application software and configure the Listener and Intelligent Agent so that you will be able to see how Oracle performed these tasks. Configuring these tools can be a very confusing task, so letting Oracle perform the work for you can be a great starting point to ensure that you will be able to add your site-specific databases successfully by following the default examples. If you already have a version of Oracle on your system with SQL*Net running and you are going to use the same directory structure to install the new version of Oracle, we recommend that you make a copy of your current TNSNAMES.ORA, SQLNET.ORA, and LISTENER.ORA files (used by the SQL*Net Listener). By making a copy of these files, you ensure that you will retain the correctly configured files for your system. If the same directory structure is used, these files will be overwritten with sample files and your current configuration will be lost. Installing and configuring the Oracle Names Server is another option about which you may be asked to make a decision. The Names Server is a mechanism that you can use to enable SQL*Net clients to look up the correct IP address of the machine and database to which they want to connect. With a Names Server, you won't need to maintain a TNSNAMES.ORA file on each client machine, and centralized connection information will be easy to obtain.

During the installation, you are prompted about whether you want the Oracle installation to create a demonstration database (discussed in the previous section) or whether you want to perform a customized database build or customized installation (only install a selected subset of software instead of installing the complete default configuration).

We suggest that you script everything you do, as you do it, so you will be able to re-create your actions later. We can almost guarantee that you will repeat these actions, either because you are creating yet another database or because there was a problem, as simple as a typo, the first time. Scripting lets you see what you did and either repeat it or correct it. Besides which, who wants to keep typing in the same commands over and over and over again? We sure don't!

In addition to scripting, you should keep a spool file of the results of running your scripts. Often, error messages scroll so fast on the screen that you miss them. With a spooled log file, you can review what went wrong and fix it.

Finding the Versions on Your System

When you call Oracle Support Services for information or help in solving a problem, you will often be asked to tell the support person the exact versions of various software installed on your platform. But where are you going to look to find out the specific product version numbers for the installation? Don't panic! We are here to help you. All you need to do is look at the following files, depending on the operating system you are using:

- On Windows NT, look in $ORACLE_HOME\orainst\nt.rgs.
- On OpenVMS, look in $ora_root:[util]products.txt.
- On Unix, look in $ORACLE_HOME/orainst/unix.rgs.

The versions of the Oracle products will be stored in these files. To find out the products and versions installed on your operating system, ask your system administrator.

After Installation

After the software has been installed and proven to work correctly (by creating a default database, etc.), you want to create your own *real* database. Before you create your first database, you need to make decisions about the following:

- How many copies of the control file you will want and where they will be located

- How many redo log files you will want and if you want to have Oracle mirror them
- The database block size for your database

As you learned in Chapter 2, the control files are used to map the physical files to the logical database objects. If you have only one control file on your system and something damages it, you may have major problems recovering your database. The control files take up very little space, and Oracle recommends that you have at least two control files as a precaution. We recommend that you create and keep three copies of the control file on your system—in different directories on different disks—to ensure recoverability.

Redo log files contain enough information to allow Oracle to reconstruct or back out transactions. If you are creating a database with which a few developers will be working and very little load will be placed on the system, you will probably only need a few redo log files for your database. You must have at least two redo log files in order for Oracle to operate correctly. We recommend that you have at least three to five. We'll talk more about redo log files and how to monitor them in Chapter 4.

The default block size that Oracle uses to create a database is 2K (2048 bytes), and that's generally just too small to be practical in anything other than a very small test database! If you are working on a Windows NT system, you will probably want to make your database block size 4K, or 4096 bytes. On Unix and Compaq OpenVMS systems, you can size your database block size as large as 16K or even 32K. For a database just beginning to be developed, we recommend that you begin with a 4K or 8K block size. We'll talk more about database block sizes a bit later in this chapter.

Once Your Database Is Created

Once you have created your database, you will need to perform several tasks. Smart DBAs write a script to perform these tasks automatically. Writing a script gives you a chance to review what tasks you want to do and the order in which you want to do them; and, as we mentioned before, most DBAs create databases over and over again. Why retype when you don't have to? Another benefit of scripting is that the output can be captured in an output file. Having the output captured is very useful—especially if you are running a database creation script and want to verify that all of the tablespaces were created successfully.

Before we look at the tasks you must complete after building your database, let's take a few minutes to look at the users SYS and SYSTEM.

About SYS and SYSTEM

When a new database is created, Oracle populates the database with some default users. The following two users will always be created:

- **SYS** The most powerful user in the database, owns all of the internal objects that make up the database

- **SYSTEM** The original account from which you do most of your object creation

There are two ways you can access the SYS and SYSTEM accounts: through SQL*Plus or through the Server Manager (svrmgr) utility. Each operating system has a different way of accessing the svrmgr utility, and the utility can also be accessed as a command line program, using svrmgrl. There are several permutations of this command, for example, **svrmgr23**, **svrmgr30**, **svrmgrm**, etc.

The default password for SYSTEM is "manager," while SYS has a default password of "change_on_install." These default passwords are widely known, and you should change them as soon as you finish creating the database, or you will leave a security hole. We know of an application manager who insisted that his database was totally secure. When called in to help fix a problem, we were able to log on to this "secure" system using the password "manager" for SYSTEM.

Okay, so what's the difference between these two accounts and how do you know when to log on as one or the other? Up until version 8i, the only way you can create, start up, or shut down a database is through the Server Manager utility, using a special login that has four different forms, as follows:

- Connect internal as sysdba
- Connect / as sysdba
- Connect internal as sysoper
- Connect / as sysoper

When you log in to the database using the svrmgr and connect as "/" or "internal," you are really connecting to the SYS account with the highest privileges available. You can do great harm to a database using this account, so approach it with caution. When you need to create tablespaces, rollback segments, redo logs, and other objects, you can log on to the database either through SQL*Plus or svrmgr as SYS or SYSTEM, or another account with these specific DBA privileges. We feel that the safest approach is to create these objects from SQL*Plus as an account with the specific privileges to do these operations and do only the tasks that absolutely must be done through the svrmgr, SYS, or SYSTEM account.

The "CAT" Scripts

Some scripts can only be run from svrmgr as SYS connected as "internal." The "cat" scripts are an example of the scripts that must usually be run as SYS from svrmgr. You will find these scripts in the following directories:

- On Windows NT, look in $ORACLE_HOME\rdbms<version_number>\admin

- On OpenVMS, look in $ora_root:[rdbms]
- On Unix, look in $ORACLE_HOME/rdbms/admin

Take the time to look at these scripts and review them so you know what they are doing. They are used to establish the data dictionary for the database and create and load many internal tables, views, and procedures.

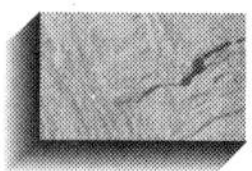

NOTE
*In Oracle 8i, these scripts can be run from SQL*Plus connected as the user "internal".*

When you have completed creating your database, you need to run the "cat" scripts (catalog.sql, catproc.sql, catexp.sql, etc.). Be sure always to run catalog.sql first, catproc.sql second, and then any of the other "cat" scripts in whatever order you want. You will find, if you look at these scripts, that they each call other scripts. If you have already run catalog.sql and catproc.sql, you do not have to run them again to run any of the other "cat" scripts.

Your next step is to create one small rollback segment in the SYSTEM tablespace. You cannot create any other objects or segments in the database until you have created this rollback segment and brought it online. Once you have created the SYSTEM rollback segment, you can create the other tablespaces, rollback segments, and so on, that you want in your database.

In the next section, we will look at how to determine what your base tablespace configuration should look like.

On the Number of Tablespaces and Their Layout

At the 1991 International Oracle User Week conference, Cary Millsap presented a paper on a standardized approach to the naming of Oracle directories, placement of files on a system, and the amount and type of tablespaces that a basic database should have. The approach was developed to improve Oracle performance in earlier versions of the RDBMS and to enable consistency in database file location. Cary called his approach the Optimal Flexible Architecture (OFA).

Over time, Cary's concepts have proven to be an invaluable approach to configuring a database for optimal performance. Although his approach to directory structure and file-naming conventions is excellent, we'll concentrate more on his recommendations for database architecture. While performing research as he developed his concepts, Cary found that a database with at least seven initial, basic tablespaces located on different disks—preferably on different controllers—will yield better performance. Table 3-1 shows the recommended minimum tablespaces that should be created for a database and a proposed naming convention for each of them.

Now, let's take a look at these tablespaces and see what type of segments should be stored in each.

The SYSTEM Tablespace

At first glance, it would seem that the SYSTEM tablespace is self-explanatory—a tablespace to be used to store the objects that belong to the user SYSTEM. However, the SYSTEM tablespace should be used to store only those objects that belong to the user SYS. Once you have created the first five tablespaces listed in Table 3-1, we suggest you alter the SYSTEM user to use the TOOLS tablespace as its default tablespace and the TEMP tablespace as the temporary tablespace. We also suggest you alter the SYS user to point to the TEMP tablespace as its temporary tablespace for sort operations. The commands you will use are as follows:

```
alter user SYSTEM default tablespace TOOLS temporary tablespace TEMP;
alter user SYS temporary tablespace TEMP;
```

Why would you want to do this? To ensure that the only user who will be using the SYSTEM tablespace is SYS and that the SYSTEM tablespace will not be used to store temporary segments during sorting operations. Since, by default, Oracle creates users with their default tablespace as SYSTEM and their temporary

Tablespace Name	File Name
SYSTEM	SYSTEM01.DBF
RBS	RBS01.DBF
TEMP or TEMPORARY	TEMP01.DBF
TOOLS	TOOLS01.DBF
USERS	USER01.DBF
DATA	DATA01.DBF
INDEX	INDEX01.DBF

TABLE 3-1. *Seven Basic Tablespaces*

tablespace as SYSTEM, as you create each new user in your database, ensure that you assign the user a specific default tablespace and temporary tablespace. If you do not ensure that SYS is the only user assigned to the SYSTEM tablespace, that tablespace will

- Tend to get very fragmented
- Have potentially severe contention against it and affect performance

Because you cannot alter the SYSTEM tablespace offline, there is no way to rebuild this tablespace without rebuilding the entire database, and this can be very time consuming. If you are scripting everything as we've suggested, you will already have your create_user script, so it's easy to build the script to prompt you for a username, default tablespace name, and temporary tablespace name to ensure that these values are set properly.

Okay, so the only user in the SYSTEM tablespace is SYS.

The Rollback Tablespace

The rollback tablespace is conventionally called RBS. You can create more than one rollback segment tablespace, each with a unique name, placed on different disks to improve performance. The rollback tablespace is used specifically to store rollback segments. If you have enough disks and controllers and find that you have high rollback segment contention, you might even want to have two or more sets of rollback segment tablespaces with the rollback segments spread evenly over them. In Chapter 4, we'll talk more about rollback segments and how to monitor them.

The TEMP or TEMPORARY Tablespace

The next tablespace on the list is TEMP or TEMPORARY. As the name implies, this tablespace is assigned to each user as the temporary tablespace that is used each time a sort operation is performed. What causes a sort operation? Any time a SQL statement includes a clause with "order by," "group by," or "union," for example, a sort is performed. When you create an index, a sort is also performed.

We want these sorts to be performed in a separate tablespace used specifically to store temporary segments so that other tablespaces are not fragmented. We find that it is a really good policy to store *only* temporary segments in a TEMP tablespace. Do not put any other objects in there, even if they are viewed as temporary objects. You can also have more than one temporary tablespace, but each one should have a unique name that will help indicate with which application it is associated. If you have a payroll application in your database in which there is a great deal of sort activity, you might create an additional temporary tablespace named TEMP_PAYROLL and assign it as the temporary tablespace for the

PAYROLL_USER schema. We'll talk more about temporary segments and tablespaces defined as "temporary" in Chapter 5.

The TOOLS Tablespace

The fourth tablespace on our list is the TOOLS tablespace. As we mentioned earlier, it is a good policy to alter the SYSTEM user's default tablespace to point to the TOOLS tablespace. If you are licensed to use the Oracle Developer, Oracle Discoverer, Oracle Web Applications software, or another Oracle product, you should install the base tables for these products either in their own schema area tablespaces or in the TOOLS tablespace. You can also use this tablespace for third-party products that require a tablespace in which to house their objects.

The USERS Tablespace

Our fifth tablespace is USERS. You can use this tablespace to provide an area where a user can create and store small objects such as test tables or the prototype of a new application under development. If the application seems to be turning into a "real" application, you want to move it from the USERS tablespace to an area of its own—a set of DATA and INDEX tablespaces. In a production database, users should not be creating objects, so you may not need this tablespace when you create a database that will be used for production.

In Oracle8i, true temporary tables can be created, so the USERS tablespace might be a good place to create them on production, although a more fitting name would be TEMP_TABLES for such a tablespace.

The DATA and INDEX Tablespaces

If your database were going to be used for one very small application, you would assign your schema developer to the DATA tablespace and request that the developer use the INDEX tablespace to store indexes for the application. If you are going to house many applications or one large application in the database, you might want to create several tablespaces for data and indexes. The developer will have to name the specific index tablespace to be used in the index creation script because, by default, Oracle will place all objects created by a user in his or her default tablespace. In general, it is a good idea for developers to specify the tablespace for each table or index they create, even if they want it in their default tablespace. The DBA may decide to change the default tablespace of a user at any time, and the object may not end up where it was intended to go.

How the Default Tablespace Assignment Works

To better understand how the designation of a default tablespace works, we'll look at the following example. Let's say you are the PAYROLL application developer and you are working in the PAYROLL schema. The schema was created with the following statement:

```
create user PAYROLL
identified by payme
default tablespace PAYROLL_DATA
temporary tablespace TEMP_PAYROLL
quota unlimited on PAYROLL_DATA
quota unlimited on PAYROLL_INDEX
/
```

You could grant the schema the Oracle-defined CONNECT role using the statement

```
grant connect to PAYROLL
/
```

Next, you could create a basic table for the PAYROLL application using a statement like this:

```
create table PAY_SALARY (
       Empname            VARCHAR2(20),
       Empnum             NUMBER,
       Job_Title          VARCHAR2(10),
       Salary             NUMBER(9,2))
/
```

Now, you'll need to create a basic unique index for the PAYROLL application. The statement you'll use to create this index might look like the following:

```
create unique index PAY_SALARY_IDX
on PAY_SALARY (Empname, Empnum)
tablespace PAYROLL_INDEX
/
```

Notice that the table creation statement does not have a tablespace explicitly named, while the index does. By default, since the PAYROLL user was created pointing to the default tablespace PAYROLL_DATA, any objects that the PAYROLL user creates with no tablespace clause will be created in that tablespace. Notice also the granting of an amount of quota on each of the tablespaces to which the user will have access. Even though the user has been granted the ability to create tables through the CONNECT role, without quota being granted on a tablespace, the user could not create objects—he or she would not be allowed to use any physical space in the tablespace. In "About the Demo Tables" later in the chapter, we'll talk more about the CONNECT and RESOURCE Oracle-supplied roles.

Quota is granted either as a specific amount of physical space (for example, 10M) or as "unlimited." If you grant a specific amount of space, the user will be able to create and extend objects until the total amount of space used by these objects reaches that specific limit. If you grant quota as unlimited, the objects belonging to that user can grow to use up all available space in the tablespace.

Sizing Your Tablespaces

You deal with sizing issues every day, but you don't think about them very much. When you go into a grocery store, you make one sizing decision after another—what size can of corn to buy or how much meat is enough to feed you and your dinner guests. Will the economy size package of ice cream be too big to be used in a reasonable amount of time? By now, you can make these decisions pretty automatically because you've been shopping for a while. But how do you know, if you've never sized a tablespace, how big, or small, to make it? When you start out as a DBA, you will be called upon to size not only tablespaces but also the objects that will go into them.

There are several ways to determine the size that you can make your database tablespaces. Let's look at some possible scenarios to see the different approaches you can use in determining the sizes your tablespaces need to be.

A Development Database Moving into Production

If an existing database is moving from development into production, you can look at the volume of existing space currently being used. Once you have the current usage, you can meet with the developers and try to estimate how large each object in the database is projected to grow within the next year or two. You will have to consider how much disk space is available to you for establishing your new database. One goal you could have is to try to ensure that each tablespace will be large enough for each object to grow within it without running out of space for at least six months to a year. Sizing of production tablespaces becomes much more critical if you are supporting a database that will be available 24 hours a day, 7 days a week, 365 days a year (referred to as a 24 x 7 x 365 shop). As more electronic commerce sites come into being, there will be more and more demand for these types of shops.

A Copy of an Existing Database

If you are building a new database that will be a copy of an existing database, your job in sizing the tablespaces becomes much easier. You can perform the following steps:

1. Copy the scripts that were used to create the original database into the new database's directory structure.

2. Modify the creation scripts to contain the new database's tablespace names and directory locations.
3. Consider any changes to the new database that will increase its tablespace size requirements.
4. Build the new database.

Wow, that was easy! Once you've established an initial database on your system and scripted everything about the database build, things can get to be almost that simple.

Vendor-Supplied Products

If you are using an Oracle-supplied product, Oracle will generally tell you just how much space you need to build the database to support that product. We recommend adding extra space to Oracle's suggested values; they sometimes underestimate the amount of space you really need. Most third-party vendors will provide guidelines for their products' space requirements. Reading the documentation for any product that will be going into your database will help you determine the space requirements more accurately.

The Tablespace Default Storage Clause

Once you've decided on the size of each of your tablespaces, you'll need to look at a sizing clause that's available when you create each tablespace. This clause is very confusing at first, so we'll go slowly and see if we can make it easier to understand. This clause, called the tablespace default storage clause, is like a safety net beneath a trapeze artist. It is used when someone creates a segment—such as a table, index, cluster, temporary segment, or rollback segment—in a tablespace and doesn't tell Oracle what size to make the segment. For example, let's say you issue the following table creation statement with no storage clause:

```
create table MY_TAB
(My_Name   VARCHAR2(40))
/
```

Since no sizing is listed anywhere in the statement, Oracle will look at the tablespace default storage clause on the tablespace that is declared as your default tablespace to see what sizing parameters to use.

Storage Parameters

The storage parameters available for a segment are as follows:

- **initial extent** How big the segment's first extent will be

- **next extent** How big the segment's next extent will be
- **pctincrease** A factor by which each successive extent will geometrically grow
- **maxextents** Maximum number of extents the segment can have
- **minextents** Minimum number of extents the segment can have

After the segment has been created, the initial and minextents values cannot be changed without dropping and rebuilding the segment.

But what happens if you do not provide Oracle with a tablespace default storage clause? Well, Oracle has a predetermined (very small) storage clause that it will use if you do not provide one when you create the tablespace. You are always better off providing a default storage clause for each tablespace that you create.

If you are not sure what values have been assigned to the default parameters for a tablespace, you can see the sizes in the DBA_TABLESPACES and USER_TABLESPACES views. Remember, these parameters are only used when a segment is created with no storage clause.

How Extents Work

When a segment is created, it will acquire at least one or more extents based on the value you put in for minextents. Let's say you've specified minextents equal to one. The initial extent will be used to store data until it no longer has any free space available. Will the extent be completely filled up? Well, that depends on the size established in the pctfree clause. This clause tells Oracle the percentage of each block in each extent to reserve for updates of existing rows. In other words, if you are inserting data into a row of a table but you don't know all the values for the row, the pctfree clause will tell Oracle how much space to save so you can come back later and expand the row without having to move it to a new block.

There is also a **pctused** clause, which informs Oracle that no new inserts can be placed into the block unless the block is less than the value of **pctused** full. For example, suppose **pctfree** is 10% and **pctused** is 40% (the defaults). Inserts will be placed into the block until the block becomes 90 percent full, which is 100 percent of the **pctfree** value. Since you have the minimum amount of space free (as determined by the **pctfree** value), a new insert cannot be placed into the block, so a new block will be allocated and the row will be placed there. Updates to existing rows within the block will use the 10 percent of free space. If, or when, space in the block is freed via data being removed, inserts will not take place into the block until the block becomes less than 40 percent full—the **pctused** value. Once the block becomes less than 40 percent full, inserts will be written into the block until it becomes 90 percent full again.

When additional data is added to the segment, the segment will extend by obtaining a second extent of the size specified by the **next** parameter. There is no guarantee that the second extent will be stored physically next to (or contiguous to) the first extent.

You can use the **pctincrease** parameter to minimize the number of extents to which a table will grow. If you set the **pctincrease** value to zero, each extent will be exactly the same size as the last extent in the table. If you set the **pctincrease** parameter to a value greater than zero, you might be letting yourself in for some trouble. You see, a non-zero value for this parameter can be dangerous because it causes the size of each successive extent to increase geometrically by the **pctincrease** factor that you have specified. For example, say you create a data table with an initial extent of 20 database blocks. You have declared the next extent to be 20 database blocks. You have also declared that the **pctincrease** will be 50%. Table 3-2 maps out the size that the fifth extent will be.

Gee, did that table get big fast. And the table will continue to grow even bigger at a much faster rate as the extents grow. In just ten extents, the table's size will be increased by 7700 percent! Keep in mind that the 185 database blocks mentioned in Table 3-2 could represent a large number of bytes. If the database block size is set to 8K (8192 bytes), the actual bytes needed for this extent would be 8192 * 185 or 1,515,520 bytes or 1.5MB of space. Imagine what the size of the next extent will be after 20 more extents!

Look again at Table 3-2. Notice that each extent after the initial one is based on the value that is given in the **next** extent parameter and not the size of the current extent. If you change the **pctincrease** parameter value, be sure to reevaluate what the **next** value should now be. For example, if you change the value of **pctincrease** to zero after the fifth extent, the sixth extent would be 20 database blocks and not 290 database blocks. Figure 3-2 graphs the growth of a table with **pctincrease** set to a number greater than zero or one. Figure 3-3 graphs the growth of a table with **pctincrease** set to a value of zero or one.

Extent	Extent Size	Total Blocks	The Math
Initial extent	20	20	Initial
Next extent	20	40	Next
Third extent	30	70	Next*1.5
Fourth extent	45	115	Next*1.5*1.5
Fifth extent	70	185	Next*1.5*1.5*1.5

TABLE 3-2. *Effects of pctincrease*

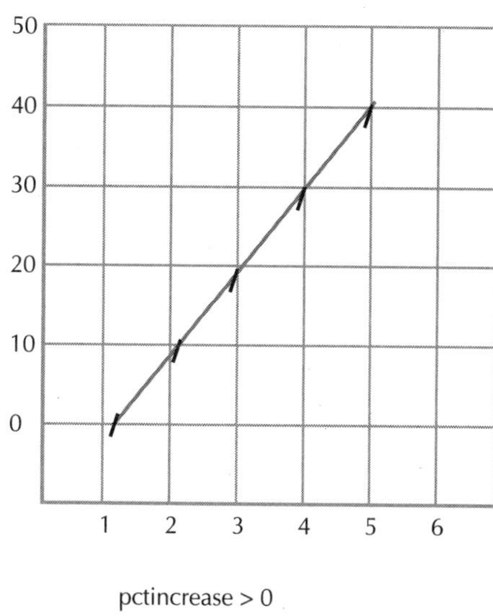

FIGURE 3-2. *Growth of a table with pctincrease greater than zero*

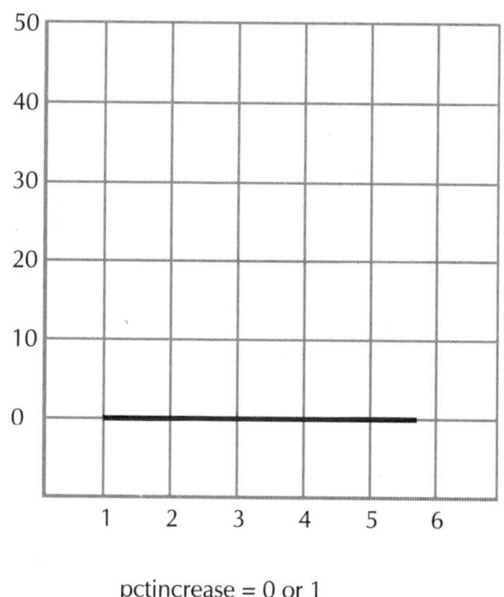

FIGURE 3-3. *Growth of a table with pctincrease set to zero or one*

Instance vs. Database

What constitutes an instance, and what makes up a database? Although the terms are often used interchangeably, *instance* and *database* in the Oracle world have very specific meanings. Since nomenclature is often important, let's take a quick look at the meanings of each of these words.

At a minimum, an Oracle instance is made up of the following background processes:

- **SMON** System monitor
- **PMON** Process monitor
- **DBWR** Database writer
- **LGWR** Log writer

It may also include other processes, such as:

- **RECO** Recovery manager for distributed databases
- **ARCH** Archive log writer
- **CKPT** Checkpoint writer
- **SNP#** Job queue processes
- **Other processes** Any other detached processes used to support parallel servers or multithreaded servers

Although the system global area (SGA), which is a reserved shared memory area, is not a process, it is included with the detached processes as part of the instance. So the detached processes, coupled with the SGA, make up the instance. In the next section, we'll look more closely at the SGA and its composition.

As we explained in Chapter 2, the database is the set of physical files in which all of the objects (tables, indexes, views, synonyms, procedures, programs, etc.) and all of the metadata (data dictionary information) are stored. There is often a mix of logical and physical references when we talk about a database. The logical entities are the tablespaces, tables, indexes, views, and other objects, while the physical entities are the actual datafiles that reside at the operating system level and the blocks allocated within those datafiles. Table 3-3 shows the relationship between the logical constructs and the physical objects that make up an Oracle database.

Logical Construct	Physical Implementation
Instance	Database
Tablespace	Datafiles
Tables/indexes/rollback and temporary segments	Segments
Extents	Blocks

TABLE 3-3. *Relationships of Logical to Physical Database Constructs*

Composition of the SGA

Let's take a moment to think about your office or work area at your place of business. You probably have a desk in which to store things like office supplies. You may have your personal computer sitting on your desk or on a table next to or attached to your desk. Regardless of your profession, you have books in either a bookshelf or cupboard so that you can easily use them for references. In other words, you have a specific area in which you do your work and store your documents or reference materials. Oracle is the same way except that Oracle uses a part of the computer's memory as its work place.

Now, what happens if someone comes in and rummages through your desk to look for something or takes books from your shelf without telling you? Chances are, your area will be disrupted and you will not be able to find the information you need when you need it. So, what do you do? Well, if you are in an office with a door, you install a lock, and whenever you are away from your office, you lock the door so no one else can get in and disturb your possessions. Oracle locks an area of the computer's memory and performs its work there. This area is called the system global area or SGA.

From a different perspective, Oracle uses the SGA to enable processes to share information and resources. When you run a SQL script, the first time the script is presented, Oracle performs several tasks to process the code before it is run. If you run the same piece of code over again and Oracle still has the information available in the SGA, Oracle can use the information that is already stored about the code to reduce the amount of processing time. If many users run the same code, Oracle's reuse of the stored information can substantially reduce the amount of processing time for each execution of the code.

Defining the SGA

So, what is the SGA really, and why do you care what's in it? Remember that the SGA plus the processes described earlier make up an Oracle instance. Oracle uses the SGA to manage interaction between all the user processes and the database itself. By compartmentalizing the SGA, multiple users can share data within memory, avoiding the need to physically access data from disks repeatedly—a time-consuming process.

The SGA may enable the sharing of data blocks, rollback segment blocks, SQL statements, and multithreaded server information. If you get the SGA tuned well for your application, you will be able to eliminate the database's memory usage as a potential performance problem. We'll talk more about performance in Chapter 12.

Controlling the Size of the SGA

You control the size of the SGA by the values that you use for the following parameters in the init.ora parameter file:

- db_block_buffers
- log_buffer
- shared_pool_size

We'll look at each of these parameters individually. First, can you name all of the seven dwarves from the Snow White story? Stop! Don't read any further until you have tried to name all seven of the little fellows. We know this seems as if we are drifting away from the topic, but do bear with us for a moment. There's Dopey, Doc, Sleepy, Sneezy, Happy, Bashful, and Grumpy. Did you get them all right on the first try, or did you peek? If you named even a few of them, how did you manage to do that? What mechanism enabled you to remember the names? You looked into your memory and sorted through all the data stored there until you found the place where your brain had stored the values for the names. If you could not remember the names and we had not told you what they were, you would have to go back to a book to look them up. In the same way, Oracle uses the SGA as its memory and the disks as its book to look things up. It's a lot faster to look into your memory for information than to stop and hunt for the correct book and correct page to find the information you want, isn't it? We could say that you now have the dwarves' names *cached* in your memory because the values are currently stored there. So a cache is just a place in memory in which something is or can be stored.

The Database Buffer Cache

The **db_block_buffers** parameter is probably the most significant parameter in determining the size of the SGA and the impact on performance. One database block equals one buffer. The **db_block_buffers** parameter is the number of database blocks cached in memory in the SGA. The amount of memory used is a multiple of **db_block_buffers** and **db_block_size** for the cache. If you want to figure out how much memory is going to be used in your SGA for your database buffer cache, you can do the following calculation:

```
Database buffer cache = db_block_buffers * db_block_size
```

Since you specify the number of blocks and not the number of bytes to allocate when you specify the value for **db_block_buffers**, the actual amount of memory used is a multiple of **db_block_buffers** times the database block size (**db_block_size**). For instance, if your database block size is 2K, or 2048 bytes, per block and you specify 10,000 buffers, with each buffer equal to one database block, the amount of memory used is 20,480,000 bytes.

```
Database buffer cache = 10000 * 2048
Database buffer cache = 20480000
```

There are advantages and disadvantages to having a high value for **db_block_buffers**. The higher the number of buffers you have, the more likely a block will be in memory when a user needs it. By having more information in memory, you reduce the number of times Oracle has to go back to disk to get information—referred to as the *physical I/O*. However, if the number of buffers is too high, you will use more memory than you really need to, and Oracle will have to look through more blocks to find the one you want, which can actually decrease performance.

Log Buffers

The next parameter, **log_buffer**, is the number of bytes allocated to the redo log buffer in the SGA. The redo log buffer stores a record of all changes made to the database. The redo log buffer is flushed to the online redo log files, which are used if the database needs recovery. More log buffers reduce the number of times data is flushed to the redo logs. The default value for this parameter is set to four times the database block size.

Shared Pool Size

The last parameter, **shared_pool_size**, determines the amount of memory Oracle allocates to shared SQL areas, library cache, dictionary cache, and to the packages and procedures that you *pin* (ask Oracle to keep resident) in memory. Pinning packages and procedures that are used frequently increases your database performance because they are not flushed out of memory when Oracle needs space for a new SQL statement.

In addition to these shared structures, Oracle keeps information about each user process that is attached to the database in the SGA.

How to See the Size of the SGA Using a V$ View

You can query the V$ view V$SGA to see the size of the SGA, as shown in the following listing:

```
REM   SGA Size
REM
select *
  from V$SGA;
```

Sample output from V$SGA is shown below. The output shows the size of the different areas within the SGA.

```
NAME                        VALUE
-------------------- ------------
Fixed Size                  38904
Variable Size            10313056
Database Buffers         10240000
Redo Buffers                16384
```

As shown in the V$SGA query output, the database has 10,240,000 bytes dedicated to its database block buffer cache (the "Database Buffers" line). The redo log buffer cache (the "Redo Buffers" line) is 16,384 bytes in size. The shared SQL area is the chief component of the "Variable Size" of the SGA, which accounts for 10,313,056 bytes in the example. We'll talk more about V$SGA and the V$ views in Chapters 9, 10, and 11.

How to See the Size of the SGA Using Server Manager

The SGA sizing information is also available within Server Manager. In the following example, the **svrmgrl** command is used to access the line mode interface of Server Manager. The **show sga** command retrieves data from V$SGA and adds a "Total" line to show the total memory area required by the SGA.

```
svrmgrl
SVRMGR> connect internal
SVRMGR>  show sga
Total System Global Area       20608344 bytes
Fixed Size                        38904 bytes
Variable Size                  10313056 bytes
Database Buffers               10240000 bytes
Redo Buffers                      16384 bytes
```

In general, increasing the size of the SGA will improve the performance of your database environment. The size of the SGA is usually 2 percent of the size of the total allocated datafile space for the database. However, you should ensure that the SGA is not so large that it causes swapping and paging to occur at the operating system level. (Swapping and paging are mechanisms that the operating system and Oracle use to move information in and out of the computer's memory. Each time a chunk of information is moved into or out of a computer's memory, there is a set amount of "cost" for the operation in time lost from doing the actual work of processing. Therefore, each time a paging or swapping operation occurs, system and database performance can be affected.)

Those Things You Do

There are many tasks that you, as the DBA, will perform on a daily basis. In this section, we'll examine some scripts that Oracle has supplied to help you see into the inner workings of the Oracle RDBMS or that help you gain information about your database. In Chapters 6 through 11, we'll look at the composition of the DBA_ and V$ views. For right now, we'll look at specific scripts that you may need to run to help you establish the environment for your new database.

CATDBSYN.SQL

An Oracle database uses memory-resident structures known as x$ tables to store information dynamically while the database is open. Oracle provides v$ performance tables that the DBA can view to help in performance tuning. The metadata is stored in the Oracle data dictionary and has the following three levels of information available:

- **USER_** Any objects that the user personally owns
- **ALL_** Any objects to which the user has access
- **DBA_** All objects in the database (reserved for users granted DBA privileges)

In an Oracle version 7.3 or earlier database, after you create the database, run the "cat" scripts, and create the tablespaces and rollback segments, you need to log on to the SYSTEM account and run the script catdbsyn.sql. This script creates the data dictionary views so that you can easily see the database metadata. Users who will be performing DBA tasks and have DBA privileges granted to them also need to run this script from their account.

In Oracle version 8.0.2 and higher, the approach used by Oracle is slightly different. Anyone assigned the DBA role will automatically be able to "see" the data dictionary views.

PUPBLD.SQL

If you've ever logged on to a newly created database, you may have gotten a message stating that the "product user profile does not exist" with a notation to run pupbld.sql. What's going on here? Why did you get this message?

From the early days of Oracle databases, you, as the DBA, have had the ability to block a user's access to the database by any method other than through an application. You could prevent users from logging directly into SQL*Plus and could block their ability to "Host" out; that is, get to the operating system level without disconnecting from the database by issuing a command in the form

```
SQL> host
```

After issuing this command from a Windows NT system, Oracle will open a DOS window and place your cursor in that window. You would be able to issue system commands and do whatever your account has privileges to do at the operating system level. This can be a huge security risk, and most companies try to avoid allowing users to reach the operating system level from an application or from SQL*Plus.

In earlier versions of SQL, you could even block products such as SQL*Forms and SQL*ReportWriter from being run either interactively or from an application. When a user attempted to connect to the database using SQL*Plus or one of the early products, Oracle would check a table called PRODUCT_USER_PROFILE to determine whether the user was allowed to perform the action requested. If Oracle went to check the table and it did not exist, a warning would be issued that the table did not exist. Oracle would assume that because there was no PRODUCT_USER_PROFILE table, there was no requirement to block SQL access. The user would be permitted to log on to the database from the SQL*Plus level. Of course, each user received the error message each time he or she logged on to the database, and you would receive irate calls from the users.

If you were lucky, you either remembered to run pupbld.sql, or you were the first person to log on to the database and the error message was enough to "spur you to action" and run the script. Once the table was created in the database and the appropriate views were created, you no longer got the error message because Oracle now had a table that it could check to verify whether the user should be permitted to access the database through SQL*Plus or any other designated Oracle product.

Over the years, what you can block and what you can't block has changed. However, the need to run pupbld.sql in your newly created database has remained until version 8.0.5, when Oracle started to automatically run this script when it creates a default database.

If you manually create your database, you will still need to run pupbld.sql. You can use this utility to block access to SQL, PL/SQL, and SQL*Plus commands by any of the following:

- One specific user
- An entire group of users
- All users in the database

You can keep one or more users from being able to reach the operating system level from an application or from the SQL*Plus command line. This utility is a way to enhance your database security, but it should be used with caution since you might inadvertently block someone's access when that access is required for the person to perform his or her job.

HELPINS.SQL

Up until Oracle version 8.0.5, if you wanted to provide online information about SQL and SQL*Plus commands, you could run the script helpins.sql to build the information area. You could then type **help <*subject*>** at the SQL*Plus command line and receive information immediately. You can still do this with versions of Oracle earlier than 8.0.5. We have found this feature very helpful and appropriate to use in a development environment. We do not recommend that you install the help utility in a production database for the following reasons:

- No one should be doing development there.
- No one should have access to the SQL*Plus command line.
- A certain amount of storage resource is used with the utility.

If you type **help** in an Oracle version 8.0.5 database on a Windows NT platform, you will receive the following message:

```
SQL>help
SQL*Plus Help Files are included in Oracle Documentation.
You have to read SQL*Plus Help Files from Oracle Documentation.
```

In truth, the help files are still supplied in 8.0.5 and higher versions; you just have to look for them. The routines are located in the \sqlplus\admin\help folder on a Windows NT system or in the /<disk>/sqlplus/admin/help directory on a Unix machine. You can check in your directory structure in approximately the same location for them on an OpenVMS system. You should see a group of files with the word *help* somewhere in the name. On Windows NT, the files are as follows:

```
Helpindx.sql
Helptbl.sql
Plshelp.ctl
Plushelp.ctl
Readme.doc
Sqlhelp.ctl
```

The Readme.doc describes the steps you must take to install the help information.

In versions of Oracle earlier than 8.0.5, you will find the helpins routines in the sqlplus directory. You run the file as SYSTEM to install the information. The routine uses SQL*Loader to load the help information into the database. Once the information is loaded, anyone logged on to the database through SQL*Plus can type **help** and a subject, for example, **help set**, and the documentation will be provided.

About the Demo Tables

When you create a database, several scripts are run—either by Oracle or by you. If you accept Oracle's offer to build a default database (and even if you don't), we recommend that you take some time immediately after creating the database to examine the DBA_USERS area to determine which default users are created there. You can do this by logging on as SYSTEM/MANAGER and typing

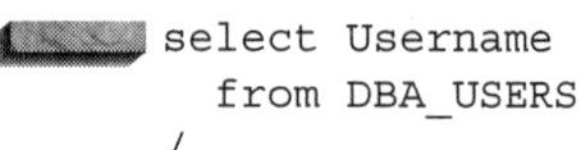

```
select Username
  from DBA_USERS
/
```

The results from a default database created in version 8.0.5 on a Windows NT system are

```
USERNAME
------------------------------
SYS
SYSTEM
ORDSYS
DEMO
DBSNMP
SCOTT
MDSYS

 7 rows selected.
```

The results from an 8.1.5 (8i) default database are as follows:

```
select Username
from DBA_USERS
/

USERNAME
------------------------------
SYS
SYSTEM
OUTLN
DBSNMP
MTSSYS
AURORA$ORB$UNAUTHENTICATED
SCOTT
DEMO
ORDSYS
ORDPLUGINS
MDSYS
CTXSYS
ORACLE

 13 rows selected.
```

After you have determined the usernames, you will want to find out which privileges have been granted to each user in your database. Most of the users listed above have been granted CONNECT and usually RESOURCE privileges. The MDSYS user was not granted any Oracle-supplied roles but, instead, has been granted 90 system privileges and owns 21 procedures. The problems with the default users created here are threefold:

1. The RESOURCE role supplied by Oracle explicitly grants UNLIMITED TABLESPACE privilege to the user granted this role. This privilege means that a user can override any assigned quotas and place objects anywhere in the database that he or she desires—even the SYSTEM tablespace.
2. The default password—which may be unchangeable—is very easily guessed. For example, the DEMO password is "demo," and the MDSYS password (with 90 system privileges available in version 8.0.5) is "mdsys." The only passwords that differ from their associated usernames are SYS ("change_on_install"), SYSTEM ("manager"), and SCOTT ("tiger"). All of these passwords are well documented and well known.
3. As you can see, the default users that are created from version to version will change, and if you perform an upgrade of your database, the default users that you deleted may reappear.

You will need to determine whether the default users that have been created in your new database are necessary—in both your development and your production databases—and whether their passwords can be changed. SYS, SYSTEM, and SCOTT can all be safely modified, and we strongly urge you to do so as soon as possible after your database has been created.

The DBSNMP User

The DBSNMP user is used by the Intelligent Agent to perform tasks within your database from a remote console. If you are not going to use the Oracle Enterprise Manager (See Chapter 11) for remote database administration tasks or event or job scheduling, you can drop the DBSNMP user from your database. If, however, you plan to perform remote database monitoring or administration, you can take the following steps to modify both the username and the password that this account will use. The DBSNMP account is created automatically when you create or upgrade your database. The account is created by running a script called catsnmp.sql. This script first creates the role SNMPAGENT and then creates the DBSNMP user with the following script:

```
drop user DBSNMP cascade;
grant CONNECT, RESOURCE, SNMPAGENT, create public synonym to DBSNMP
identified by DBSNMP;

create synonym DBSNMP.DBA_TABLESPACES for SYS.DBA_TABLESPACES;
create synonym DBSNMP.DBA_DATA_FILES for SYS.DBA_DATA_FILES;
create synonym DBSNMP.DBA_FREE_SPACE for SYS.DBA_FREE_SPACE;
create synonym DBSNMP.DBA_SEGMENTS for SYS.DBA_SEGMENTS;
```

You can modify this script and change the references to DBSNMP to a username and password of your choice. If you change the username, you will also need to change the references in the "create synonym" statements to the username that you have chosen. Finally, you will need to add the following two commands to the snmp_rw.ora file in the network/admin directory:

```
SNMP.CONNECT.<service_name>.NAME = <The new username>
SNMP.CONNECT.<service_name>.PASSWORD = <The new password>
```

So the entries for a new username "intagnt" with a new password of "myagnt" in the mydb database would look like the following:

```
SNMP.CONNECT.MYDB.NAME = intagnt
SNMP.CONNECT.MYDB.PASSWORD = myagnt
```

Steps in Copying and Renaming a Database

Why would you want to copy a database from one place to another? Why would you ever want to rename a database? In this section, we're going to look at the reasons for copying and/or renaming a database as well as the procedures you can use to accomplish these tasks.

To answer the "why" questions, think about the steps you need to take if your application programmers are about to release a major enhancement to an application. Before they are really ready to release their new version, you want to make sure it is thoroughly tested against a database that is as close to the production database as possible. You could test it against the production database, if you were sure that the changes would not change the production data or impact production performance. However, testing in production is just not a good idea because unexpected things do happen and new code is often problematic in ways that are completely unexpected. If you test the new code in a production environment and "blow the system out of the water," how long will it take you to repair the damage? How long can your production system remain unavailable without having a financial impact on your company?

So, what approach do you want to use? The safest way to ensure that you can move a new feature to your production system is to make a copy of the production database by creating another database with a different name and allow (or require) your programmers to test their changes. If you have two different computers, you could just copy the database without renaming it; but in general, we've found that it is a good idea to rename the database to avoid confusion about which database is really being used. Speaking from past experience, we have found that it's just too easy to get mixed up about which machine you are on and which database you are accessing. We have found that it's much easier to append a letter *t* to the end of a current database name so that we know it is our test database. For example, a Human Resources database named HRP in production could be named HRT in the test environment and HRD in the development environment.

Choices in Renaming a Database

There are two ways to copy and rename a database: either by a full database export and re-import to a new database or by using the command **alter database backup controlfile to trace**. Each approach has advantages and disadvantages. The full database export and re-import approach can take considerable time, depending on the size of your database. The **alter database backup controlfile to trace** command can be done in a significantly shorter period of time. However, although the **alter**

database approach will allow you to move your datafiles, you will not be able to resize them.

The Database Export/Re-Import Approach

A full export allows you the opportunity to do the following tasks:

- Resize the datafiles and locate them on different disks on a different machine
- Re-create the tables with new storage parameters and in different tablespaces
- Rename the database itself

Using the full database export approach, you will perform the following steps:

1. Export the entire database (full=y).
2. Create a new init.ora file with the new database name.
3. Create an initial database containing at least SYSTEM, rollback, and temporary tablespaces.
4. Oracle's import utility will automatically create datafiles if they don't exist, so if you want to change the size or location of datafiles, pre-create them now, before the import, in the new locations and/or sizes.
5. Oracle's import utility will also automatically create tables, in the same tablespace and the same size as they originally were. If you want to resize tables or change their tablespace, pre-create them now.
6. Import the export with ignore=y. (Note that the SYS user does not get exported or imported.)
7. Rerun catalog, catproc, and any other Oracle-provided scripts you want.

Depending on the size of your database and the amount of data you have, this procedure could take several days! When you use the export/import method, you want to create all of the tablespaces in your new, renamed database before you perform the import.

Let's see what happens if you are importing the database on the same machine and you do not create the tablespaces with the datafiles in different locations and with different file names. When you go to import, Oracle will try to re-create the tablespaces with their datafiles in the same location and with the same names as the current production versions. The import will encounter errors and fail. If you create the tablespaces with the datafiles in their new directories, when Oracle attempts to do the import, it will see that the tablespaces already exist and will ignore the **create**

tablespace statements in the export file. The only time you will not want or need to create the tablespaces and datafiles is when you have a second system that is an exact replica of the first system—with all of the disks labeled with the same names. If the disks exist with the same names as the original database's system, Oracle will create the datafiles pointing to the new disks on the new system with no problems.

The Alter Database Approach

The alternate method of moving and renaming a database uses the **alter database backup controlfile to trace** command to make a readable, editable copy of the commands needed to create a new control file and open the database. You can use this file, along with a copy of the init.ora, redo log files, and datafiles, to create a new copy of your database. This command can be run from either Server Manager or SQL*Plus by a user with DBA privileges.

When you run the **alter database backup controlfile to trace** command, the command creates a trace file in your udump directory. You tell Oracle where the udump directory is located by placing an entry in your init.ora parameter file. The trace file is created with the standard Oracle trace file name; on Unix, this is ora_*<sid>*_*<Unix process id>*.trc. If your Unix process ID is 372 and your database SID is mydb, the trace file will have the name ora_mydb_372.trc. You should rename this file to a more meaningful file name as soon as you have created it so that the file does not get lost among the other trace files that Oracle may generate. Figure 3-4 shows a sample file generated by the **alter database** command on a Compaq OpenVMS system.

Once you have generated the trace file, you can edit it and make the change to rename the datafiles to their new locations and to rename the database. You will want to delete the entire text above the line that reads as follows:

```
# The following commands will create a new control file and use it
```

Although the text above this line is interesting and contains some valuable information about your database, the entire text above this line is not executable code and will cause errors to be generated if you try to run it. The lines with pound signs (#) are comment lines and can be left in the script since they provide information about what the script is doing without interfering with the script's processing.

In addition to editing the control file, you will need to make either a cold or hot backup of the original database. The edit of the trace file must include changing the **create controlfile** command from **reuse database *<sid>*** to **set database *<new_sid>***.

The steps involved in copying and renaming an existing database are simple:

1. Generate the trace file to create the new control file using the **alter database backup controlfile to trace** command.

```
Dump file ora_dump:MYNODE_MYDB_FG_SRV_008.trc
 4-MAY-1999 11:14:25.60:
Parallel server mode inactive
------------------------------------------------------------
Proc: 0x20200e9e ORA_MYDBB0887 User: [650,20000] ORACLE       Term:
Image: $1$DKD105:[ORACLE.V7336.RDBMS]SRV.EXE
  CPU Time Used (10ms): 11
  $CREPRC flags: 260,  Current Privs: f71dedad
  Event Flags 0-31/32-63/Mask: e0009001/80000000/dfffffff
  Job Subprocesses/Current Mode/PHD Flags: 0/0/1015a20
  ASTs Active/Avail./Enabled/Limit: 0/998/15/1000
  Buffered IO Count Avail./Limit: 149/150
  Buffered IO Byte Count Avail./Limit: 148272/148272
  Direct IO Count Avail./Limit/Operations: 150/150/67
  Enqueue Count Avail./Limit: 294/300
  Open File Count Avail./Limit/ShFilLm: 992/1000/0
  Page File Count Avail./Limit/Location: 191040/200000/100663296
  Active Page Table Count: 0,  Page Faults: 756
  Pages in Working Set - Global/Process-Private:  6208/3776
  FreePTEs (unsigned longwords 0:1): 4261201264:3
  Subprocess Count/Limit: 0/50
  Timer Queue Count Avail/Limit: 99/100
Working Set Max. Size/Max. Extent/Quota: 11392/786432/11392
  Working Set Current Extent/Size/Peak: 786432/10496/9984
------------------------------------------------------------
vsnsql=b vsnxtr=3
Oracle7 Server Release 7.3.3.6.0 - Production Release<LF>With the
distributed, „
cpu ALPH 80000000 vms V7.1-2   clustered with 1 nodes
scsnd: MYNODE   , ndname: MYNODE, sys$node MYNODE::
cpuid 80 rev 0522000000000000000000016 archflg 3C000
hwmdl: 1314 hwnm: AlphaServer 4X00 5/600 8MB cpus: FFFFFFFF cpush:
active: 2,„
locktbl size 7617 max 270805 resource hash size 16384
Instance name: MYDB<LF>
Redo thread mounted by this instance: 1<LF>
Oracle process number: 8<LF>
pid: 20200e9e, image: MYDISK1:[ORACLE.RDBMS]SRV.EXE
<LF>
4-MAY-1999 11:14:25.60:
*** SESSION ID:(7.90) 1999.05.04.11.14.25.060
# The following commands will create a new control file and use it
# to open the database.
# No data other than log history will be lost. Additional logs may
```

FIGURE 3-4. *Sample control file creation script*

```
# be required for media recovery of offline data files. Use this
# only if the current version of all online logs are available.
STARTUP NOMOUNT
CREATE CONTROLFILE REUSE DATABASE "MYDB" NORESETLOGS NOARCHIVELOG
    MAXLOGFILES 32
    MAXLOGMEMBERS 5
    MAXDATAFILES 100
    MAXINSTANCES 16
    MAXLOGHISTORY 1600
LOGFILE
  GROUP 1 (
    'MYDISK3:[ORACLE.MYDB]REDO01.LOG',
    'MYDISK1:[ORACLE.MYDB]REDO01.LOG'
  ) SIZE 10M,
  GROUP 2 (
    'MYDISK3:[ORACLE.MYDB]REDO02.LOG',
    'MYDISK4:[ORACLE.MYDB]REDO02.LOG'
  ) SIZE 10M,
  GROUP 3 (
    'MYDISK3:[ORACLE.MYDB]REDO03.LOG',
    'MYDISK4:[ORACLE.MYDB]REDO03.LOG'
  ) SIZE 10M
DATAFILE
  'MYDISK3:[ORACLE.MYDB]ORA_SYSTEM.DBF',
  'MYDISK7:[ORACLE.MYDB]TEMP01.DBF',
  'MYDISK3:[ORACLE.MYDB]RBS01.DBF',
  'MYDISK4:[ORACLE.MYDB]TOOLS01.DBF',
  'MYDISK4:[ORACLE.MYDB]USERS01.DBF',
  'MYDISK4:[ORACLE.MYDB]MY_TS01.DBF'
;
# Recovery is required if any of the datafiles are restored backups,
# or if the last shutdown was not normal or immediate.
RECOVER DATABASE
# Database can now be opened normally.
ALTER DATABASE OPEN;
```

FIGURE 3-4 *Sample control file creation script* (continued)

2. Edit the trace file and init.ora files to change the database name.
3. Back up the original database, either by shutting it down and doing a full files level backup, or by altering the tablespaces into backup mode and doing a hot backup.

4. Change the environment variables to point to the new instance.
5. If you want to rename or move the datafiles or log files as well, edit their locations in the trace file and copy the backed up datafiles to the new locations. Additionally, change any files that include the full file specification, such as backup scripts.
6. Run the trace file in Server Manager, connected as internal.
7. Run the **alter database rename global_name to <*newdb*>;** command.
8. Rename the init.ora and config.ora files to reflect the new database name.
9. Edit the configuration files that are instance name specific, such as oratab, listener.ora, and tnsnames.ora.

You only need to do step 7, above, if your database is part of a global network. The global name, also referred to as a service name, is defined as the database name and a domain name, and is used in database links in remote databases to access your database. Changing the global name of the new database does not change it at any remote site that references it, and it is up to the remote database administrator to change the references to your database.

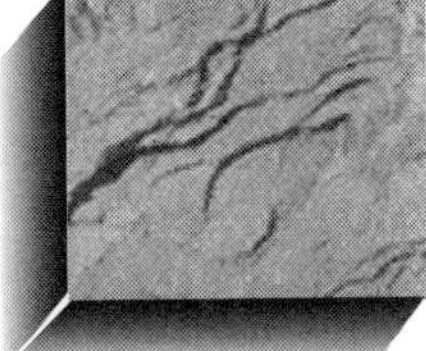

CHAPTER 4

What We Do Daily

hink about the routines in your life. Every weekday, you get up at the same time, brush your teeth, take a shower, make and eat breakfast. On your way to work you stop off and get a newspaper and a cup of coffee. You take the same train or bus into work. If you are still in school, you have a schedule of classes you attend. Once a week you go grocery shopping or do laundry. Once a month you might get a haircut. Every year you visit your doctor and dentist and have your car inspected. Okay, so maybe your life isn't quite that orderly, but human beings tend to be creatures of habit, so chances are that if you have a steady job, you tend to follow some kind of a schedule or routine.

We believe that, just as you have routines in your daily life, you should have routines in your work as a DBA. Following procedures and processes helps to make your job easier by letting you know about potential problems and trends so that you can take action before things go wrong. Becoming a proactive DBA is a wonderful goal to have. Not only will you increase your chances of having a smooth-running database, but you will decrease the number of weekends you have to spend at work. You will help ensure that mole hills do not grow into overwhelming mountains.

Throughout this chapter, we will include some scripts to help you implement new "routines" in your life. To run each of the scripts described in this chapter, you will need to be logged on to the database as a privileged user. You can use the SYS or SYSTEM account with the Oracle-supplied DBA role or create a user with the DBA role or the equivalent privileges. We recommend that you create a specific account for monitoring your database.

General Monitoring

Why monitor your database on a regular basis instead of just setting up processes to notify you of errors? Looking at your database daily can give you a feel for many of the following elements:

- What is normal
- Growth patterns of space usage
- Timing of log switches
- Number of users connecting

Once you have a feel for the normal functioning of your database, anything unusual will catch your eye immediately, and you can fix the problem before it actually becomes one. It's much better to say to your management, "I noticed we were running low on space for the application master table so I added a datafile," than to have an entire department's work grind to a halt because there is no room for a table to grow.

That said, let's take a look at what kinds of things you should be monitoring.

Alert Logs

When your database is created, Oracle also creates a log, known as the *alert log*, in which it writes information about

- Each time the database is started.
- Any recovery that was performed on database startup.
- Each time the database is shut down.
- Each time a log switch occurs (referred to as a *thread switch*).
- What parameters (from the init.ora file) were used within the database at startup and are not default parameters.
- Any DDL commands that change the structure of the database, such as "alter tablespace PAYROLL_TS add datafile..."
- Space allocation errors that have occurred (ORA-1650 through ORA-1659).
- Errors that occur and the location and name of the error file (called *trace files* because they have the extension .trc). Oracle creates these files to more fully document the error and provide Oracle Support with information to help them help you resolve the cause of the error.

As you can see, the alert log, which is given the following names in different systems, contains a good deal of important information and, oddly enough, is never reduced in size automatically.

- alert_<SID>.log on a Unix system
- <SID>alert.log on a Windows NT system
- <node>_<SID>_alert.log on an OpenVMS system

In other words, the alert log is created when the database is created, and information is appended to the file each time one of the actions listed above occurs. As you can imagine, this file can grow very large, especially if your database has been around for a long time. If you have an alert log that's been around for, say, a year, and you need to look at an entry from last week, you may have a huge amount of data to wade through just to get to the information in which you are interested. So, what can you do?

Here is an interesting fact for you: Oracle will create a new alert log, with the default name, if it can't find one when it wants to write an entry to the log. That means you can rename the file daily and back up the old ones and remove them from your disk on a regular basis. This does two things: keeps your current alert log relatively small so that you don't run out of disk space and lets you keep old alert logs to review for trends. We have a batch job that runs nightly and renames each of our database alert log files by adding the current date as the extension. The routine then emails the log to our email account so we can quickly scan the file to see if anything looks like a problem area—for example, a 600 error occurring or too frequent thread switches. An Oracle error that ends with a number in the 600 range is referred to as "an ORA-600 error." Although not always a signal for database disaster, these errors can be a very serious form of internal database error and should be given strict attention. Unless you are familiar with the specific ORA-600 error that you have received, you will want to call support to verify what, if any, actions you should take to correct the error.

Some DBAs have created routines that check for errors and email notification only if an error is found. If you work in an environment where any errors or downtime is unacceptable, you might want to develop or purchase software that will constantly monitor for errors and page you if one occurs. Generally speaking, it takes only a few minutes daily to scan through a day's worth of alerts from your database. Some of us have routines that email the alert logs from our production databases to our own email accounts. If you send the alert log to yourself daily, you can check it for entries that will enable you to do the following:

- Quickly see any problems.
- Manually check the files to ensure that your redo logs are not switching too frequently.
- Verify that the log writer is not being overwhelmed, which would indicate that there are not enough and/or large enough redo logs on your system.

If you set the init.ora parameter **log_checkpoint_to_alert** to TRUE, Oracle will add more information to the alert log about your log switches. While this will increase the size of your alert log, it will also give you more information about what is going on in your database. Below is a sample section of an alert log from a database with **log_checkpoint_to_alert** set to TRUE.

```
Fri May  7 22:39:10 1999
Beginning database checkpoint by background
Fri May  7 22:39:11 1999
Thread 1 advanced to log sequence 14249
  Current log# 4 seq# 14249 mem# 0: /ORADATA7/TEST/TEST_redo4.rdo
```

```
Fri May  7 22:39:22 1999
Completed database checkpoint by background
Fri May  7 22:42:50 1999
Beginning database checkpoint by background
Fri May  7 22:42:50 1999
Thread 1 advanced to log sequence 14250
  Current log# 1 seq# 14250 mem# 0: /ORADATA6/TEST/TEST_redo1.rdo
Fri May  7 22:43:04 1999
Completed database checkpoint by background
Fri May  7 22:45:27 1999
ORA-1653: unable to extend table/cluster TEST.MSG_IN by 1458 in tablespace USERS
```

Oops. It looks like the TEST database had a space problem at 10:45 p.m. on Friday, May 7, 1999. Assuming that there were no users on the test system that late at night, you might conclude that a batch job was running and loading the MSG_IN table. Unfortunately, the tablespace for that table did not have enough contiguous space to allocate an extent. An error was written to the alert log, and the process trying to load the table failed. As a proactive DBA, you will see the error first thing in the morning, since you check your email as soon as you come in to work. You will know, probably well before whoever submitted the job that failed, that a tablespace needs more space. You will be able to add the necessary space and send out a follow-up email to everyone involved with that data load (and your boss—just to keep her informed), letting them know the problem has been addressed and resolved. See? You now look like an efficient, on-top-of-problems DBA. Good job!

LISTENER.LOG

The SQL*Net listener (called Net8 in all versions of Oracle8) generates a log when it is started and writes to the log—either with a great deal of information or minimally, depending on what level of logging has been enabled. With minimal messaging enabled on a Net8 listener, the information that is provided

- Shows when the listener was started
- Lists the ports being listened on
- Shows the machine on which the listener is running
- Contains a notation for every connection made through this listener

A sample entry looks like this:

```
TNSLSNR80 for 32-bit Windows: Version 8.0.5.0.0 - Production on 25-SEP-98 14:24:30
(c) Copyright 1997 Oracle Corporation. All rights reserved.
System parameter file is C:\orant\NET80\admin\listener.ora
Log messages written to C:\orant\NET80\log\listener.log
Listening on: (ADDRESS=(PROTOCOL=ipc)(PIPENAME=\\.\pipe\oracle.worldipc))
```

```
Listening on: (ADDRESS=(PROTOCOL=ipc)(PIPENAME=\\.\pipe\ORCLipc))
Listening on: (ADDRESS=(PROTOCOL=ipc)(PIPENAME=\\.\pipe\EXTPROC0ipc))
Listening on: (ADDRESS=(PROTOCOL=nmp)(PIPENAME=\\MYOWN-PC\pipe\ORAPIPE))
Listening on: (ADDRESS=(PROTOCOL=tcp)(DEV=136)(HOST=128.299.5.45)(PORT=1521))
Listening on: (ADDRESS=(PROTOCOL=tcp)(DEV=124)(HOST=128.299.5.45)(PORT=1526))
Listening on: (ADDRESS=(PROTOCOL=tcp)(DEV=144)(HOST=110.0.0.1)(PORT=1521))
TIMESTAMP * CONNECT DATA [* PROTOCOL INFO] * EVENT [* SID] * RETURN CODE
```

If you enable logging at a more intensive level, more information will be written to the log but more overhead traffic will be incurred. We recommend you periodically check your listener.log for errors. If you seem to be encountering SQL*Net problems, turn on more trace information at that time. Note that earlier versions of SQL*Net will give different log information. The only way to remove a listener log file that has become too large is to stop the listener process, delete the log file, and restart the listener process. Unlike the alert log, if you rename the listener log file, Oracle will continue to write to the renamed file. When you stop the listener process, you do not lose any existing connections to the database, but no new connections can be made until you restart the process. For that reason, we normally start at least two listener processes for each instance and put both ports into all the TNSNAMES.ORA files on our clients. When SQL*Net attempts to connect to a listener from the client, it tries the first port listed in the TNSNAMES.ORA file. If there is no listener active on that port, it will attempt to connect to the next port in the TNSNAMES entry. So you can take your listeners down one at a time, delete or rename the log files, and then restart them, and not interfere with your users' connections.

The only overhead to having multiple listeners is in the management of the listeners and the additional server process that will be created for each new listener. Multiple listeners allow you to spread network traffic over multiple NICs (Network Interface Cards), which will allow you to load-balance connections to your database server.

Redo Log Status

Why check on the status of your redo logs? Well, you may want to change the size of your redo logs because you are switching too frequently. If you want to retain the names of your redo logs, you'll need to drop them before re-creating them at the new size. You need to know the status of the redo log you want to drop before you drop it. Dropping the current redo log is not good practice, unless you are testing recovery scenarios!

Information about the online redo logs is kept in two of the V$ views, V$LOG and V$LOGFILE. The views can be joined on the column Group# to get information from both. Redo logs can be part of a redo log group, which allows you to mirror your redo logs using an Oracle software feature and provides yet another layer of protection against the loss of a redo log. If you lose an online redo log, you will have to perform recovery on your database.

The script below selects information about the redo logs in a test database. A SYSTEM-like account is used to run this script.

```
col Member format a40
col Logstat format a10 heading 'Use Status'
select Member,
       a.Group#,
       b.Status,
       a.Status Logstat
  from V$LOGFILE a, V$LOG b
 where a.Group#=b.Group#
/
```

Looking at the output of this script, you can tell certain things about this database. For instance, you can gain the following facts from looking at the report below:

- The DBA for this database has decided not to take advantage of Oracle's log mirroring, because there is only one redo log (member) per group#.
- There are four redo logs, and all are part of the database.
- The USE STATUS column, which is the Status column from V$LOGFILE, is blank if the redo log is in use by the database.
- The redo logs are placed on two different disks, and the DBA has attempted to improve performance by alternating the placement of the redo logs on these disks. Since Oracle will read the prior log to archive it, you can have disk head contention if the two logs are on the same disk. By placing them on different disks, one disk can be read while the other is being written to. If possible, you should always put your redo logs on disks that have nothing else on them (or at least files that are accessed very infrequently).
- The current and in-use redo log is redo2 (Status column is CURRENT).
- The redo log that was last used is redo1 (Status is ACTIVE).
- It is possible that the file redo1 is either being archived or is still needed for instance recovery if the database should crash. A status of INACTIVE means the redo log is not needed for instance recovery.

Other values for the Status column of V$LOG can be found in the Oracle documentation.

```
MEMBER                             GROUP# STATUS           USE STATUS
------------------------------ -------------- ---------------- ----------
/ORADATA6/TEST/TEST_redo1.rdo               1 ACTIVE
/ORADATA7/TEST/TEST_redo2.rdo               2 CURRENT
/ORADATA6/TEST/TEST_redo3.rdo               3 INACTIVE
/ORADATA7/TEST/TEST_redo4.rdo               4 INACTIVE
```

Fragmentation

Why do you want to check on the level of fragmentation in your tablespaces? Think of your tablespace as a puzzle that you are trying to piece together. As you find spots for more and more puzzle pieces, the empty spaces become more and more difficult to fill with just any piece. You have to have precisely the right size space for the next piece you want to use, or you can't make it fit.

Finding space in your tablespace to add another extent works in a similar way. You may have a large amount of free space left in a tablespace, but none of it is in a large enough chunk to fill the request for the extent. While the extents in an object do not have to be contiguous (one right after another on disk), the blocks within an extent must be. So you need to monitor your tablespaces to make sure you have large enough chunks of free blocks to fill the requests you get.

The PL/SQL script below will display the extents available within your tablespace and the size of each extent. To run the script, you first have to create a table to hold the intermediate results, using the **create table** script. You will use an account with SYSTEM-like privileges to run the fragmentation script.

```
create table FREESP (
Fname  VARCHAR2(513),
Tspace VARCHAR2(30),
First  NUMBER(10),
Blocks NUMBER(10),
Last   NUMBER(10))
/
```

Rather than create this table each time the PL/SQL script is run (and further fragment the tablespace), FREESP is created once and the **truncate** command is used to empty it before each use in the fragment.sql script.

```
set feedback off term off verify off pagesize 60 newpage 0 linesize 66
truncate table FREESP;
declare
  Fileid    NUMBER(9);
  Filename  VARCHAR2(513);
  Tsname    VARCHAR2(30);
  Cursor Tablespaces is
```

```
    select File_Name, File_ID, Tablespace_Name
      from DBA_DATA_FILES
     where Tablespace_Name = upper('&1');
begin
open Tablespaces;
loop
  fetch Tablespaces into Filename, Fileid, Tsname;
  exit when Tablespaces%NOTFOUND;
declare
  First   NUMBER(10);
  Blocks  NUMBER(10);
  Last    NUMBER(10);
  Tfirst  NUMBER(10);
  Tblocks NUMBER(10);
  Tlast   NUMBER(10);
  Cursor Free is
    select Block_ID a, Blocks b, Block_ID+Blocks c
      from DBA_FREE_SPACE
     where File_ID = Fileid
     order by Block_ID;
begin
  open Free;
  fetch Free into First, Blocks, Last;
  if Free%NOTFOUND
   then
       goto close_free;
  end if;
  loop
    fetch Free into Tfirst, Tblocks, Tlast;
    exit when Free%NOTFOUND;
    if Tfirst = Last
      then
        Blocks := Blocks + Tblocks;
        Last := Tlast;
      else
        insert into FREESP
          values (Filename, Tsname, First, Blocks, Last-1);
        commit;
        First := Tfirst;
        Blocks := Tblocks;
        Last := Tlast;
    end if;
  end loop;
      insert into FREESP
         values (Filename, Tsname, First, Blocks, Last-1);
  commit;
```

```
<<close_free>>
  close Free;
end;
end loop;
commit;
close Tablespaces;
end;
/
set term off echo off
col Db_Name new_value Instance
select 'INSTANCE NAME' Description, value Db_Name
  from V$PARAMETER
 where UPPER(Name) = 'DB_NAME'
/
ttitle center Instance ' TABLESPACE FRAGMENTATION REPORT'
col Tspace heading 'TABLESPACE|NAME' format a10 trunc
col Fname heading 'FILE' format A30 trunc
col First heading 'START|BLOCK' format 999,999
col Blocks heading 'SIZE(BLKS)' format 99,999,999
break on report on Tspace skip 1 on Fname skip 1
compute sum of Blocks on Fname
compute sum of Blocks on report

spool fragmentation.rpt
select Tspace, Fname, First, Blocks
  from FREESP
 order by Tspace,Fname,First;

spool off
```

The script runs for a single tablespace and expects the tablespace name as input. Before we explain the script in detail, let's take a look at the output of the script.

```
               test TABLESPACE FRAGMENTATION REPORT

TABLESPACE                                       START
NAME       FILE                                  BLOCK  SIZE(BLKS)
---------- ------------------------------ -------- -----------
USR1       /home01/oracle/user_1_test            3,215           3
                                                 4,065          40
                                                 5,586          75
                                                 8,475         145
                                                10,080         110
                                                10,545         100
                                                21,832       3,215
                                                50,563          85
```

```
                                 61,054        111
                                 85,045      1,420
                                 95,996          7
                                108,526         70
                                121,503        121
                                125,689        275
                                127,250        450
                                131,418         58
                                151,903        895
                                159,394         50
                                171,876        325
                                270,022        665
                                292,477         18
                                328,862         50
                                328,922         85
                                334,617        110
                                344,614        285
                                359,493        670
                                360,328        675
                                365,297        125
                                366,197        325
                                366,567        435
                                369,117         33
                                371,945         13
                                372,033        220
                                372,833        155
                                375,651        150
                                423,382        195
                                425,657        100
                                431,110         72
                                434,692      1,905
                                481,830         40
******************************           ----------
sum                                         13,881

/home01/oracle/user_2_test        4,812        125
                                 10,849         50
                                 10,924         40
                                 26,151        102
                                 28,888        360
                                 29,758        455
                                 31,909        355
                                 51,235        105
                                135,832        145
                                136,197        325
                                166,270         18
```

```
                                              186,381         590
                                              202,906       2,503

                    test TABLESPACE FRAGMENTATION REPORT

TABLESPACE                                       START
NAME       FILE                                  BLOCK  SIZE(BLKS)
---------- ---------------------------------- -------- -----------
USR1       /home01/oracle/user_2_test          258,757       2,910
                                               346,192          50
                                               401,162       1,705
                                               442,167          40
                                               468,537       1,090
                                               476,277       1,205
                                               478,717          50
                                               481,342         110
                                               481,477       1,450
                                               483,367         235
                                               487,142         915
                                               502,107         345
           ******************************               -----------
           sum                                              15,278


**********                                                -----------
sum                                                           29,159
```

Yikes! This tablespace is badly fragmented. There are 65 extents making up the 29,159 free blocks—an average of less than 500 bytes per extent! If all you did was add up the number of blocks available in the DBA_FREE_SPACE view for this tablespace, it would look like you had tons of space left. Too many inexperienced DBAs fall into the trap of checking total space available and thinking they have enough space, when in reality, the space is so fragmented that there really is not enough contiguous space to allocate another extent. When you look closely at the space in the tablespace in the report above, most of the extents are less than 500 blocks. Unless this tablespace is either read-only or contains tables that are updated infrequently, you're going to have problems allocating space in here.

Oracle does not merge contiguous free extents unless there is no other alternative; so your tablespace becomes more and more fragmented as Oracle first allocates space from the largest free extent it encounters in the tablespace before reusing and coalescing the smaller free extents that are created as objects are dropped. Figure 4-1 illustrates available extents within a tablespace before and after a request for an extent has been allocated.

(a)

USED	Free 5 blocks	Free 20 Blocks	USED	Free 15 Blocks	USED	Free 20 Blocks

(b)

USED	Allocated 25 Blocks	USED	Free 15 Blocks	USED	Free 20 Blocks

FIGURE 4-1. *Contiguous extents coalesced:*
(a) Fragmentation with two contiguous extents before a 25-block extent request
(b) Fragmentation after the extents are coalesced and allocated

Now let's take a more detailed look at the script and what it's doing.

The DBA_FREE_SPACE data dictionary view contains information about every free extent in the datafiles that make up the database. Oracle does not go through the view to see if any of the extents are contiguous. So you can have information about two extents that are right next to each other (as they are in Figure 4-1a), but you will see them as two separate rows in this view. This is not too efficient, and not too useful, since it's not a true picture of the free space available in your datafiles! The fragment.sql script reads the DBA_FREE_SPACE data dictionary view, looks for extents that are contiguous, adds up the number of blocks in the contiguous extents (or just reports the number if the extents are not contiguous), stores the results in a temporary table, and reports, by datafile, on the fragmentation in your tablespace. By saving prior days' versions of this report, you can see how your tablespace is being used and fragmented and how frequently fragmentation is occurring.

In order to run the fragment.sql script for the first time, you have to create a table called FREESP, which is used to store information about the datafiles and extents. To create the FREESP table, execute the following script with SYSTEM-like privileges:

```
create table FREESP (
Fname  VARCHAR2(513),
Tspace VARCHAR2(30),
```

```
First  NUMBER(10),
Blocks NUMBER(10),
Last   NUMBER(10))
/
```

The first section of the fragment.sql script will read through the DBA_DATA_FILES view for the datafiles associated with the requested tablespace. The **cursor** statement is used in PL/SQL to define a SQL statement that will return more than one row, so you can write a loop to read the rows one-by-one. The DBA_FREE_SPACE view stores information about free space in each datafile, not each tablespace. So for each datafile it finds in the tablespace, the script runs an inner loop through DBA_FREE_SPACE to get the extent information.

```
set feedback off term off verify off pagesize 60 newpage 0 linesize 66
truncate table FREESP;
declare
  Fileid     NUMBER(9);
  Filename   VARCHAR2(513);
  Tsname     VARCHAR2(30);
  Cursor Tablespaces is
     select File_Name, File_ID, Tablespace_Name
       from DBA_DATA_FILES
      where Tablespace_Name = upper('&1');
begin
open Tablespaces;
loop
  fetch Tablespaces into Filename, Fileid, Tsname;
  exit when Tablespaces%NOTFOUND;
```

For every datafile it finds, the script opens a cursor and reads through DBA_FREE_SPACE, summing up the contiguous extents as it goes. The Block_ID is the starting block identifier for that extent in that particular file. Separate extents are contiguous if the Block_ID value plus the number of blocks equals the next Block_ID found. As an example, if there are two extents in DBA_FREE_SPACE for a datafile, and the Block_ID of the first extent is 10 and it has 5 blocks, then if the Block_ID of the second extent is 15 (10 + 5), the two extents are contiguous (block numbers 10, 11, 12, 13, and 14 in the first extent and blocks 15 through the number of blocks in the second extent), and Oracle will coalesce them if it needs to, to get enough space for a requested extent. So we want to report on them as if they were a single extent. If the extents are contiguous, the script continues to add up the number of blocks in each contiguous extent and reads the next Block_ID. Once we find an extent that does not immediately follow the prior one, the holding information is inserted into the FREESP table and the holding variables are reset. Once all the extents for a datafile have been processed, the inner cursor is closed and the next datafile information is retrieved.

Once all datafiles have been processed, the outer cursor is closed and the data in the intermediate table FREESP is reported.

```
declare
  First   NUMBER(10);
  Blocks  NUMBER(10);
  Last    NUMBER(10);
  Tfirst  NUMBER(10);
  Tblocks NUMBER(10);
  Tlast   NUMBER(10);
  Cursor Free is
    select Block_ID a, Blocks b, Block_ID+Blocks c
      from DBA_FREE_SPACE
     where File_ID = Fileid
     order by Block_ID;
begin
  open Free;
  fetch Free into First, Blocks, Last;
  if Free%NOTFOUND
   then
       goto close_free;
  end if;
  loop
    fetch Free into Tfirst, Tblocks, Tlast;
    exit when Free%NOTFOUND;
    if Tfirst = Last
      then
        Blocks := Blocks + Tblocks;
        Last := Tlast;
      else
        insert into FREESP
          values (Filename, Tsname, First, Blocks, Last-1);
        commit;
        First := Tfirst;
        Blocks := Tblocks;
        Last := Tlast;
    end if;
  end loop;
      insert into FREESP
         values (Filename, Tsname, First, Blocks, Last-1);
  commit;
<<close_free>>
  close Free;
end;
end loop;
commit;
close Tablespaces;
end;
/
```

Once all the datafiles have been checked, the information gathered in the FREESP table is displayed via SQL*Plus reporting commands. Using the **value** parameter, the instance name is captured for display in all page headers. The **break** and **compute** commands are used to create subtotal, total, and grand total values.

```
set term off echo off
col Db_Name new_value Instance
select 'INSTANCE NAME' Description, value Db_Name
  from V$PARAMETER
 where UPPER(Name) = 'DB_NAME'
/
ttitle center Instance ' TABLESPACE FRAGMENTATION REPORT'
col Tspace heading 'TABLESPACE|NAME' format a10 trunc
col Fname heading 'FILE' format A30 trunc
col First heading 'START|BLOCK' format 999,999
col Blocks heading 'SIZE(BLKS)' format 99,999,999
break on report on Tspace skip 1 on Fname skip 1
compute sum of Blocks on Fname
compute sum of Blocks on report

spool fragmentation.rpt
select Tspace, Fname, First, Blocks
  from FREESP
 order by Tspace,Fname,First;

spool off
```

The output in the following listing shows that the tablespace USR1 in the TEST database is extremely fragmented. Although 29,159 total blocks are available in the USR1 tablespace, the largest single extent that can be allocated is 3,215 blocks, with most of the extents much smaller. This tablespace may appear to have a good deal of space left, based on the total blocks available, but closer examination indicates possible problems. Monitoring the changes in this report over several days or weeks will show when additional datafiles will be needed.

```
                  test TABLESPACE FRAGMENTATION REPORT

TABLESPACE                                          START
NAME        FILE                                    BLOCK  SIZE(BLKS)
---------- ------------------------------ -------- -----------
USR1        /home01/oracle/user_1_test              3,215           3
                                                    4,065          40
                                                    5,586          75
                                                    8,475         145
                                                   10,080         110
                                                   10,545         100
                                                   21,832       3,215
```

```
                                  50,563          85
                                  61,054         111
                                  85,045       1,420
                                  95,996           7
                                 108,526          70
                                 121,503         121
                                 125,689         275
                                 127,250         450
                                 131,418          58
                                 151,903         895
                                 159,394          50
                                 171,876         325
                                 270,022         665
                                 292,477          18
                                 328,862          50
                                 328,922          85
                                 334,617         110
                                 344,614         285
                                 359,493         670
                                 360,328         675
                                 365,297         125
                                 366,197         325
                                 366,567         435
                                 369,117          33
                                 371,945          13
                                 372,033         220
                                 372,833         155
                                 375,651         150
                                 423,382         195
                                 425,657         100
                                 431,110          72
                                 434,692       1,905
                                 481,830          40
*****************************            -----------
sum                                           13,881

/home01/oracle/user_2_test         4,812         125
                                  10,849          50
                                  10,924          40
                                  26,151         102
                                  28,888         360
                                  29,758         455
                                  31,909         355
                                  51,235         105
                                 135,832         145
                                 136,197         325
                                 166,270          18
                                 186,381         590
                                 202,906       2,503
```

```
                 test TABLESPACE FRAGMENTATION REPORT

TABLESPACE                                          START
NAME        FILE                                    BLOCK  SIZE(BLKS)
----------  ----------------------------  --------  -----------
USR1        /home01/oracle/user_2_test     258,757        2,910
                                           346,192           50
                                           401,162        1,705
                                           442,167           40
                                           468,537        1,090
                                           476,277        1,205
                                           478,717           50
                                           481,342          110
                                           481,477        1,450
                                           483,367          235
                                           487,142          915
                                           502,107          345
            ******************************             -----------
            sum                                           15,278


**********                                              -----------
sum                                                       29,159
```

Rollback Segments

Have you ever had to write a poem? You start with an idea and, maybe, a first line or theme. You might write several lines and then decide the poem is just awful, and you start over again. You get halfway through and decide that most of what you've written is wonderful, but a line here or there needs to be changed. Finally, you get to the end of the poem and realize that a line you took out should have been left in. Now, you have to scramble to try to remember exactly what that line said (which, by now, you are convinced will make the poem spectacular and must be recaptured). If you carefully wrote each line and started out fresh—recopying everything you wanted to keep—each time you began to rewrite the poem, you would have a copy of exactly what the poem looked like through each phase of the writing. You could easily go back and see what that one, wonderful line said. Once you completed each version of the poem and made a clean copy of it (committed it), you could hand off that clean copy to someone else to read while you continued to revise the poem. Oracle uses rollback segments, just like you use that clean copy, to keep track of exactly how data looked before it was modified—called *before images*.

Why store the before image of data? Oracle promises that "readers won't block writers, and writers won't block readers." What does this mean? Suppose you start to look at the payroll table and are reporting on salaries. Now someone else comes along and changes some of the salaries. Without the rollback segment, your report would show inconsistent data—some from before the change and some from after the change. Oracle ensures that you won't see a mix of unmodified and modified data by using the rollback segments to give you a consistent picture of the data, even if someone is making changes to it.

When a user begins to do work, such as generate a report or modify rows of a table, a rollback segment is assigned to the user's process. In Chapter 3, we talked about how rollback segments are allocated and how they are extended. But what happens if a rollback segment runs out of space? If a large transaction requires more space than the rollback segment has already allocated, the rollback segment will extend into the free space remaining in the tablespace, just as a table extends when you add more data to it. If the rollback segment requires more space than is available in the tablespace, then the transaction causing the rollback segment to extend will fail. If the transaction fails, you can probably expect a call from an irate user! So, what can you do about ensuring that there is enough space in the rollback segment tablespace to support the volume of data transactions that are occurring? Why, you can monitor the number of times the rollback segments have to extend to support the load.

If the extents within the rollback segment are too small, then the transaction will "wrap" from one extent to another within the rollback segment. Each time a rollback segment wraps, Oracle has to take the time to perform internal space management tasks. These tasks take time and performance resources away from processing time. So, ideally, you want to size a transaction's rollback segment entry to fit entirely within one extent of the rollback segment, thus minimizing the performance and internal space management issues associated with wraps. You can monitor the number of times the rollback segment entries wrap from one extent to another within the rollback segment. We'll show you how in the section "Monitoring Rollback Segment Extent Size" a bit later in this chapter.

Monitoring Rollback Segment Size

Rollback segments are assigned to processes in a circular manner, and all transactions, regardless of their size, compete for the same available rollback segments. Unless you specifically use the **set transaction use rollback segment** command as the first statement after every **commit** to allocate a specific rollback segment to your next transaction, you have no control over which rollback segment will be used during your transaction processing. The **set transaction use rollback segment** statement, if you are going to use it, must be the first statement in the transaction, and the **commit** or **rollback** statement is the last statement of the transaction.

If you use the **set transaction use rollback segment** command to support a large transaction, you should create a rollback segment that is specially sized for the transaction. If you do not use the **set transaction use rollback segment** command, a rollback segment will be assigned to your transaction in a round-robin fashion. Since most rollback segment assignments for transactions are random, you should use a standard size for all of your rollback segments (except for those that specifically support large transactions). There is no guarantee that the large rollback segment you have placed online to be used just for your large transaction will not be allocated to other processes before your process is started. Although many transactions can and do share rollback segments, you cannot ever be 100 percent sure that yours will be the only transaction in your large rollback segment unless there are no other users on the system while your process is running.

As we said, a single rollback segment can store the data from multiple transactions. Any of the entries within the rollback segment can force the rollback segment to extend. Therefore, if you have a lot of small transactions in a rollback segment, you are just as likely to have extension occur as you would with a single large transaction.

The Rollback Segment Optimal Parameter

Now, let's say that a rollback segment has been extending and now reaches a point where it has used up all of the available space in the rollback segment tablespace. What will happen next? The transaction that is attempting to extend will fail. As other rollback segments attempt to extend, since there is no available space left to extend into, more transactions will fail. What are your options at this point? Well, there is really only one thing you can do: add a datafile to the rollback segment tablespace to make more space available.

However, before things ever get that critical, there is something you can do to help ensure that you will not run out of space in the rollback segment tablespace. To control the extension of rollback segments, you can rebuild the rollback segments (one at a time, if necessary) and set an optimal size for each of the rollback segments. You can use the optimal parameter of the **storage** clause to set an optimal value when you are performing a **create rollback segment** or **alter rollback segment** command. You can find the value of the rollback segment's optimal parameter setting, along with other rollback segment statistics, in the V$ROLLSTAT view, which records cumulative statistics about all rollback segment usage since the database was last started.

If you have set an optimal size for your rollback segments, then rollback segments that have extended beyond their optimal size can shrink. The optimal size should be set to minimize the number of extensions and shrinks required for the rollback segment to support the size and volume of transactions.

Looking at the Optimal Value, Shrinks, and Extends

The following script queries V$ROLLSTAT along with V$ROLLNAME. The V$ROLLNAME view shows the names of the online rollback segments, while in V$ROLLSTAT, the rollback segments are identified only by their USN (Undo Segment Number) value. The query in the following listing will show the optimal size, number of shrinks, average size per shrink, and number of extensions per rollback segment.

```
REM  Rollback Segment Extensions
REM
column Name format A20
select Name, OptSize, Shrinks, AveShrink, Extends
  from V$ROLLSTAT, V$ROLLNAME
 where V$ROLLSTAT.USN=V$ROLLNAME.USN;
```

Sample output for the V$ROLLSTAT query is shown in the following listing:

```
NAME                    OPTSIZE    SHRINKS  AVESHRINK    EXTENDS
-------------------- ---------- ---------- ----------  ----------
SYSTEM                                   0          0           0
R01                    10485760          4   41943040          32
R02                    10485760          2   44564480          17
```

Let's take a look at the report and see what we have. There are three active rollback segments in the database. The SYSTEM rollback segment is used for data dictionary transactions. Users' transactions are assigned to either the R01 or R02 rollback segment. Each of the user rollback segments has an optimal size of 10MB (10,485,760 bytes). Each user rollback segment has extended beyond its optimal value and has been forced to shrink back to its optimal size two or more times.

The rollback segments have shrunk by an average of almost 40MB each time they have shrunk. If you think carefully about the report output, you will realize that the R01 and R02 rollback segments are not properly sized for the transactions they are supporting. They are frequently extending (49 times since the last database startup) and extend, on average, to five times their optimal size. If a rollback segment has to constantly extend beyond its optimal setting and then shrink back to its optimal setting, Oracle is performing a great deal of unnecessary space management work. To reduce the number of rollback segment extensions, you should modify the rollback segments' optimal settings, increasing them to at least 40MB. After modifying the rollback segments' storage settings, you can periodically reexecute the script to determine the impact of the changes. You might also want to consider adding more rollback segments to the database to help accommodate the transaction load.

When a rollback segment extends beyond its optimal setting the first time, the rollback segment will not shrink. The second time the rollback segment extends beyond its optimal setting, the rollback segment will shrink—provided the second transaction forced the rollback segment to allocate a new extent. Although setting a value for the optimal parameter will not completely prevent you from having any rollback segment space management issues, it can help you limit the number and kind of space management issues you have.

Because of the manner in which rollback segments extend and shrink, the number of "Extends" in the previous script's output should always be more than the number of "Shrinks." For example, if the rollback segment started with a size less than its optimal setting, acquiring new extents would increment the "Extends" statistic value, but no "Shrinks" would be necessary. Once a rollback exceeds its optimal setting in size, it only shrinks at the end of a transaction—and that transaction may have forced multiple extensions.

As of Oracle7.2, you can use the **alter rollback segment** command to shrink rollback segments to a size of your choosing and at a time of your choosing. The rollback segments must always have a minimum of two extents. If you do not specify a size to shrink to, the rollback segment will shrink to its optimal size. In the following listing, the R01 rollback segment is shrunk back to its optimal size.

```
alter rollback segment R01 shrink;
```

Monitoring Rollback Segment Extent Size

To simplify the management of multiple rollback segment entries within a rollback segment, you should try to size the rollback segment so that each of its extents is large enough to support a typical transaction.

When a transaction's rollback segment entry cannot be stored within a single extent, the entry wraps into a second extent within the rollback segment. The extents within a rollback segment are assigned circularly, so a rollback segment entry can wrap from the last extent of the rollback segment to its first extent—as long as there is not an active rollback segment entry already in the first extent. If there is an active rollback segment entry already in the first extent, the rollback segment will extend.

You can query the V$ROLLSTAT view to see the number of wraps that have occurred in each rollback segment since the last time the database was started. If there have been no wraps in the rollback segment, then its extents are properly sized for the transactions it supports. If there is a non-zero value for the number of wraps, then you should re-create the rollback segments with larger extent sizes. We'll look at two different outputs from this query and tell you how to interpret what you see. First, here's the query:

```
REM   Rollback Segment Wraps Check
REM
column Name format A20
```

```
select Name, OptSize, Shrinks, AveShrink, Wraps, Extends
  from V$ROLLSTAT, V$ROLLNAME
 where V$ROLLSTAT.USN=V$ROLLNAME.USN;
```

Like the query for rollback segment extension, the script in the preceding listing queries statistics from V$ROLLSTAT along with the rollback segment names from V$ROLLNAME. The first sample output we'll look at from the query is shown in the following listing:

```
NAME                    OPTSIZE    SHRINKS  AVESHRINK      WRAPS    EXTENDS
-------------------- ---------- ---------- ---------- ---------- ----------
SYSTEM                                   0          0          0          0
R01                    10485760          4   41943040         41         32
R02                    10485760          2   44564480         26         17
```

As you can see, the sample query output shows that 67 wraps have occurred since the last time the database was started. Given the number of extensions that have occurred, the number of wraps is not surprising (because extensions usually require wraps). The extensions indicate that the rollback segments are handling larger transactions than they were designed for; and if the entire rollback segment cannot handle a transaction's rollback information, a single extent will not be able to hold it either. Thus, rollback segments that extend will frequently have high numbers of wraps.

The second sample output is shown in the following listing. This output is slightly modified from the preceding output. Notice that there are no extensions, but there are wraps.

```
NAME                    OPTSIZE    SHRINKS  AVESHRINK      WRAPS    EXTENDS
-------------------- ---------- ---------- ---------- ---------- ----------
SYSTEM                                   0          0          0          0
R01                    10485760          0          0         41          0
R02                    10485760          0          0         26          0
```

If there are wraps but no extensions, as shown in the preceding listing, the rollback segment has the proper optimal setting, but its extent sizes are too small. That is, the rollback segment is large enough to support its transactions without extending; however, the transaction entries require multiple extents within the rollback segment. If you have wraps with no extensions, then you should re-create your rollback segments using the same optimal setting but larger extent sizes.

Monitoring Extents

For versions of Oracle earlier than 7.3.3, we, as DBAs, had to keep track of how many extents had been allocated in a table or index. We feared that we would "blow extents" and receive one of the dreaded ORA-01650 through ORA-01659 errors, with the message "unable to extend..." Let's talk a bit about what values we see for the parameter maxextents and why there has been a problem with these values. Let's also talk about why we still should be monitoring what our maxextents are set to and what our actual extent values are.

When you create a default Oracle database, Oracle uses a block size of 2K. In an Oracle database, each extent in a segment has an associated row of header information at the beginning of that segment to enable Oracle to keep track of its location in the database. In versions of Oracle earlier than 7.3, the number of rows of header information a 2K block can hold is 121. Thus, for a 2K block size database, the maximum number of extents that you can have prior to version 7.3 of the RDBMS is 121. Now, if a 2K block size database can support 121 rows of header information and 121 maxextents per object, how many extents can a 4K database support? The answer is 249. For an 8K block size, the maximum number of extents is 505. As you increase the database block size, the number of maximum extents that you can have increases. Remember that we're talking about values for a database running a software version earlier than 7.3.

In version 7.3, the software has been modified to enable the header block to extend as well, so you can actually have as many extents as your operating system will support, and you can create your table with **maxextents unlimited** or any number you choose. **maxextents unlimited** is not actually unlimited. If you look at the Max_Extents column of DBA_TABLES for a table created with **maxextents unlimited**, you will see that it actually translates to 2,147,483,645, which for all intents and purposes *is* unlimited. If the tablespace does not have maxextents defined, and you do not specify a maxextents value on the storage clause when you create a table, the maxextents value on that table will be the default maximum extent limit based on the block size for that database. For example, let's create a tablespace in an 8K block size database as follows:

```
create tablespace MY_TS
datafile 'mydisk1:[Oracle.mydb]my_ts01.dbf' size 10M
default storage(initial 500k
                next 500k
                minextents 1)
online;
Tablespace created.
```

We have not specified a maxextents value. Now, let's create a table and see what the default value for maxextents will be.

```
create table MY_TAB (Ename varchar2(20), Empno number);
Table created.
```

Next, we'll select the values from USER_TABLES and see what our maxextents value is by default.

```
select Table_Name, Initial_Extent, Max_Extents
  from USER_TABLES
 where Table_Name = 'MY_TAB';

TABLE_NAME                     INITIAL_EXTENT MAX_EXTENTS
------------------------------ -------------- -----------
MY_TAB                                 524288         505
```

We see that the value for maxextents is equal to the default value for an 8K block size database.

To monitor the growth of tables in a database, you can use the following script:

```
prompt CHECKING FOR FRAGMENTED DATABASE OBJECTS:
prompt
column Owner noprint new_value Owner_Var
column Segment_Name format a30 heading 'Object Name'
column Segment_Type format a9 heading 'Table/Indx'
column Bytes format 999,999,999 heading 'Bytes Used'
column Extents format 999 heading 'No.'
break on Owner skip page 2
ttitle center 'Table Fragmentation Report' skip 2 -
  left 'creator: ' Owner_Var skip 2
select Owner,
       Segment_Name,
       Segment_Type,
       Bytes,
       Max_Extents,
       Extents
  from DBA_SEGMENTS
 where Extents > 12
   and Segment_Type = 'TABLE'
 order by Owner, Segment_Name, Segment_Type, Max_Extents
/
ttitle center 'Index Fragmentation Report' skip 2 -
  left 'creator: ' Owner_Var skip 2
select Owner,
       Segment_Name,
       Segment_Type,
       Bytes,
       Max_Extents,
       Extents
  from DBA_SEGMENTS
 where Extents > 12
   and Segment_Type = 'INDEX'
   and Owner not in ('SYS','SYSTEM')
 order by Owner, Segment_Name, Segment_Type, Max_Extents
/
```

In this script, we check for any table or index with a number of extents exceeding 12. You can, of course, set your threshold to whatever value makes sense for your environment. The idea is to keep track of those tables that are growing and may reach a point where they will exceed the amount of extents allocated for them. The results of running this script against a sample database are shown here:

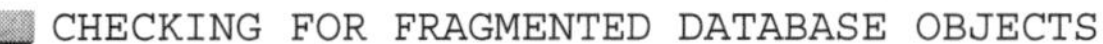

```
CHECKING FOR FRAGMENTED DATABASE OBJECTS:

                                     Table Fragmentation Report

creator: TEST

Object Name                    Table/Ind   Bytes Used MAX_EXTENTS  No.
------------------------------ --------- ------------ ----------- ----
MSG_IN                         TABLE      105,881,600        1000  584
MSG_OUT                        TABLE       38,666,240        1000  211

                                     Index Fragmentation Report

creator: TEST


Object Name                    Table/Ind   Bytes Used MAX_EXTENTS  No.
------------------------------ --------- ------------ ----------- ----
IDX_MSG_IN                     INDEX        2,867,200         505   67
IDX_MSG_OUT                    INDEX        1,925,120         505   43
IDX_MSG_OUT_2                  INDEX        3,072,000         505   71
SYS_C005595                    INDEX        1,269,760         505   30
SYS_C005598                    INDEX        1,720,320         505   40
```

As you can see, the tables MSG_IN and MSG_OUT have maxextents set to a number larger than the default. With version 7.3, Oracle began to allow the DBA to extend the maxextents past the former defaults for the database block size. The fact that the tables have such a high number of extents is an indication that the initial and next extents are set too low for the growth that these tables experience. When we look at the index portion of the report, we see two indexes whose names begin with SYS_C. When you create an index without specifying a name, Oracle will assign a name beginning with SYS_C followed by a number. While there is nothing wrong with allowing Oracle to name your index for you, it does make it difficult to quickly relate an index to the table to which it applies. In general, we recommend that you explicitly name all indexes when you create them and use some sort of naming convention that will allow you to quickly relate the index to its associated table.

Let's look at the script in a little more detail. SQL*Plus allows you to write scripts that create simple reports. The **prompt** command below echoes the line to whatever output you specify (either to the screen or spooled to a log file). The **column** command allows you to format the column and add a heading. The **new_value** option of the **column** command assigns the retrieved value to a variable, while the **noprint** option of the **column** command suppresses display of the data until the final report is printed.

```
prompt CHECKING FOR FRAGMENTED DATABASE OBJECTS:
prompt
column Owner noprint new_value Owner_Var
column Segment_Name format a30 heading 'Object Name'
column Segment_Type format a9 heading 'Table/Indx'
column Bytes format 999,999,999 heading 'Bytes Used'
column Extents format 999 heading 'No.'
```

The **break** command forces a break and a two-line skip when the owner changes. The **ttitle** command generates a top-of-page title on every page break. The first line of the page title will be centered, and then two lines will be skipped before the second line is displayed. The second line will be left-justified, and then another two lines will be skipped before the actual data of the report is displayed.

```
break on Owner skip page 2
ttitle center 'Table Fragmentation Report' skip 2 -
  left 'creator: ' Owner_Var skip 2
```

The **select** statement below uses the DBA_SEGMENTS view to pull the information from the data dictionary. This view contains information on every type of segment in the database. We will discuss the DBA_SEGMENTS view in greater detail in Chapter 6, along with some of the other DBA_ views we use most often. If you want to change this script to let you vary the number of extents you are checking for, change the 12 to &1, which will cause the script to prompt you for a value each time you run it.

The Bytes column value is the total number of bytes allocated to the segment.

```
select Owner,
       Segment_Name,
       Segment_Type,
       Bytes,
       Max_Extents,
       Extents
  from DBA_SEGMENTS
 where Extents > 12
   and Segment_Type = 'TABLE'
 order by Owner, Segment_Name, Segment_Type, Max_Extents
/
```

As an alternative, you can run the following script:

```
set feedback off;
set term off
set pagesize 60;
set newpage 0;
set linesize 80;
col Db_Name new_value instance
select 'INSTANCE NAME' description, Value Db_Name from V$PARAMETER
   where upper(Name) = 'DB_NAME'
/
ttitle center instance ' TABLESPACE/FILE/EXTENTS REPORT'
column Tablespace_Name format a15 heading 'TABLESPACE|NAME'
column Segment_Name format a20 heading 'TABLE|NAME'
column Extents format 99999 heading 'EXTENTS'
column Max_Extents format 99999 heading 'MAXEXTENTS'
column Owner format a10
column Segment_Type format a7 heading 'TABLE|TYPE'
break on Tablespace_Name skip 2 on report
spool check_extents.log
select Tablespace_Name,Segment_Name,Segment_Type, Owner, Extents, Max_Extents
from DBA_SEGMENTS
where Segment_Type not in ('CACHE','ROLLBACK','DEFERRED ROLLBACK')
and (Extents/decode(Max_Extents,0,1,Max_Extents))*100 > 25
order by Tablespace_Name,Owner,Segment_Name
/
spool off
exit
```

This version of the script will report on all segments (tables, indexes, temporary segments) with more than 25 percent of their maxextents already allocated. The **decode** statement in the **where** clause is used to make sure the equation does not do a divide by zero. This report output looks like the sample shown here:

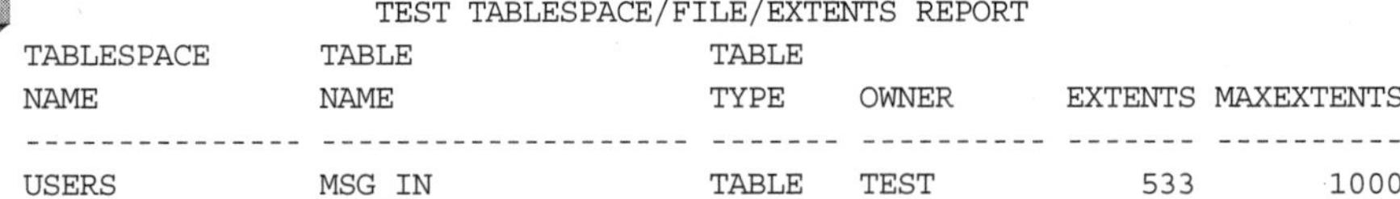

```
                   TEST TABLESPACE/FILE/EXTENTS REPORT
TABLESPACE      TABLE                TABLE
NAME            NAME                 TYPE    OWNER      EXTENTS MAXEXTENTS
--------------- -------------------- ------- ---------- ------- ----------
USERS           MSG_IN               TABLE   TEST           533       1000
```

Space Remaining

Although the scripts in the previous section will tell you how fragmented your tables and indexes are, and you can compare the outputs over several days or weeks to track how often your objects are extending, they won't tell you when your objects are likely to extend.

Why do you want to track the used space in your objects? Well, suppose all the objects in your tablespace were to extend at once. Do you have enough space free in the tablespace for this to happen, or will you run out of room and have your users running to you with space problems? Do you have a large enough extent free in your tablespace to hold the largest next extent in that tablespace?

One way to track all of this is to create a table to hold historical information about the objects and their storage characteristics. You can use this table for trending analysis, and you can run a daily report against it to warn you of objects close to extending. We use the following script to create a historical information table. We then initially fill the table with information about our largest, most frequently updated objects. We use the remaining scripts in this section to continue filling the table with daily statistics about the objects we want to track and to report on the contents. Oracle provides a package, DBMS_SPACE, which can be found in the /rdbms/admin directory under ORACLE_HOME. This package contains a procedure, UNUSED_SPACE, which reports on the amount of allocated space that has not yet been used for data.

```
create table EXTGROW
(Segname      VARCHAR2(81)    NOT NULL
,Segown       VARCHAR2(30)    NOT NULL
,Growdate     DATE            NOT NULL
,Segtype      VARCHAR2(17)
,Segtbs       VARCHAR2(30)
,Exts         NUMBER
,Nextext      NUMBER
,Tbsfree      NUMBER
,Hwm          NUMBER
,Totbytes     NUMBER
,Usedbytes    NUMBER
,Contigfree   NUMBER
,Freepct      NUMBER
,Tbsexts      NUMBER
)
tablespace TOOLS
storage (initial      819200
         next         819200
         minextents   10
         maxextents   505
         pctincrease  0
)
/
alter table EXTGROW add constraint EXTGROW_PK
      primary key (Segname, Segown, Growdate)
      using index tablespace TOOLS_IDX
      storage (initial     81920
               next        81920
               minextents  10
               maxextents  505
               pctincrease 0);
```

The rate at which this table will grow will depend on how many tables and indexes you want to track. Some of the information being stored is data about the tablespace the object resides in; the remainder is information about the object itself.

To fill the table initially, you can use the following script. It will prompt you for the name of the table and index owner. You can run the script multiple times if you have more than one user in your database that owns objects you want to track.

```
insert into EXTGROW (Segname, Segown, Growdate, Segtype, Segtbs, Exts,
                     Nextext, Tbsfree, Hwm, Totbytes, Usedbytes,
                     Contigfree, Freepct, Tbsexts)
       select   Segment_Name,Owner,
                to_date(to_char(sysdate-1,'YYYYMMDD'),'YYYYMMDD'),
                Segment_Type, Tablespace_Name,0,0,0,0,0,0,0,0,0
         from DBA_SEGMENTS
        where Owner = upper('&1')
          and Segment_Type in ('TABLE','INDEX')
/
```

To fill the table on a daily basis, run the script below. The script expects a date in YYYYMMDD format as input. This date is the date you are running the script, and the procedure assumes that there is data in the EXTGROW table for the prior day. We will explain the script in more detail below.

```
declare
   Total_Blocks        NUMBER;
   Total_Bytes         NUMBER;
   Unused_Blocks       NUMBER;
   Unused_Bytes        NUMBER;
   Lue_File_Id         NUMBER;
   Lue_Block_Id        NUMBER;
   Last_Used_Block     NUMBER;
   T_Name              EXTGROW.Segname%TYPE;
   Ts_Name             EXTGROW.Segtbs%TYPE;
   Hwm                 NUMBER;
   T_Exts              NUMBER;
   T_Own               EXTGROW.Segown%TYPE;
   N_Exts              NUMBER;
   T_Free              NUMBER;
   N_Ext_Bytes         NUMBER;
   L_Chunk             NUMBER;
   Db_Blk_Size         NUMBER;

cursor TABSPACE is
       select Table_Name,
              dt.Owner,
```

```
               dt.Tablespace_Name,
               dt.Next_Extent,
               Extents,
               dt.Blocks
          from DBA_TABLES dt, EXTGROW eg, DBA_SEGMENTS ds
         where Table_Name = Segname
           and dt.Owner=Segown
           and ds.Owner=Segown
           and Segment_Name = Segname
           and Growdate=to_date('&1','YYYYMMDD')-1;

cursor INDSPACE is
       select Index_Name,
               di.Owner,
               di.Tablespace_Name,
               di.Next_Extent,
               Extents
          from DBA_INDEXES di, EXTGROW eg, DBA_SEGMENTS ds
         where Index_Name = Segname
           and di.Owner=Segown
           and ds.Owner=Segown
           and Segment_Name =Segname
           and Growdate=to_date('&1','YYYYMMDD')-1;

begin

select Value
  into Db_Blk_Size
  from SYS.V_$PARAMETER
 where upper(Name) = 'DB_BLOCK_SIZE';

open TABSPACE;

loop
   fetch TABSPACE
    into T_Name,
         T_Own,
         Ts_Name,
         N_Ext_Bytes,
         T_Exts,
         Hwm;

    exit when TABSPACE%NOTFOUND;

DBMS_SPACE.UNUSED_SPACE(T_Own,T_Name,'TABLE',Total_Blocks, Total_Bytes,
Unused_Blocks, Unused_Bytes, Lue_File_Id, Lue_Block_Id, Last_Used_Block);
```

```
Hwm := Hwm*Db_Blk_Size;

select count(*),
       sum(Bytes),
       max(Bytes)
  into N_Exts, T_Free, L_Chunk
  from DBA_FREE_SPACE
 where Tablespace_Name = Ts_Name;

insert into EXTGROW (Segname, Segown, Growdate, Segtype, Segtbs, Exts,
                     Nextext, Tbsfree, Hwm, Totbytes, Usedbytes,
                     Contigfree,  Freepct, Tbsexts)
     values (T_Name, T_Own, to_date('&1','YYYYMMDD'), 'TABLE',Ts_Name,
             T_Exts, N_Ext_Bytes, T_Free, Hwm, Total_Bytes,
             (Total_Bytes-Unused_Bytes), L_Chunk,
             (Unused_Bytes/Total_Bytes)*100, N_Exts);

commit;

end loop;
close TABSPACE;

open INDSPACE;

loop
   fetch INDSPACE
    into T_Name,
         T_Own,
         Ts_Name,
         N_Ext_Bytes,
         T_Exts;
exit when INDSPACE%NOTFOUND;

DBMS_SPACE.UNUSED_SPACE(T_Own,T_Name,'INDEX',Total_Blocks, Total_Bytes,
                        Unused_Blocks, Unused_Bytes, Lue_File_Id,
                        Lue_Block_Id, Last_Used_Block);

select count(*),
       sum(Bytes),
       max(Bytes)
  into N_Exts, T_Free, L_Chunk
  from DBA_FREE_SPACE
 where Tablespace_Name = Ts_Name;

insert into EXTGROW (Segname, Segown, Growdate, Segtype, Segtbs, Exts,
```

```
                     Nextext, Tbsfree, Hwm, Totbytes, Usedbytes,
                     Contigfree,  Freepct, Tbsexts)
     values (T_Name, T_Own, to_date('&1','YYYYMMDD'), 'INDEX',Ts_Name,
             T_Exts, N_Ext_Bytes, T_Free, NULL, Total_Bytes,
            (Total_Bytes-Unused_Bytes), L_Chunk,
            (Unused_Bytes/Total_Bytes)*100, N_Exts);

commit;

end loop;
close INDSPACE;
end;
/
```

This script is used to fill the EXTGROW table with the information about the allocated and used space in each object named in the table for a date that you pass in as a parameter. PL/SQL code that is not stored in the database as a procedure or package is called an *anonymous PL/SQL block* and is recompiled each time it is run. If you are going to run this script more than once a day, it's a good idea to turn it into a stored procedure, so that Oracle can take advantage of the fact that the code in a stored procedure is already compiled and can be executed faster.

```
declare
   Total_Blocks         NUMBER;
   Total_Bytes          NUMBER;
   Unused_Blocks        NUMBER;
   Unused_Bytes         NUMBER;
   Lue_File_Id          NUMBER;
   Lue_Block_Id         NUMBER;
   Last_Used_Block      NUMBER;
   T_Name               EXTGROW.Segname%TYPE;
   Ts_Name              EXTGROW.Segtbs%TYPE;
   Hwm                  NUMBER;
   T_Exts               NUMBER;
   T_Own                EXTGROW.Segown%TYPE;
   N_Exts               NUMBER;
   T_Free               NUMBER;
   N_Ext_Bytes          NUMBER;
   L_Chunk              NUMBER;
   Db_Blk_Size          NUMBER;
```

The first section of the script defines variables to hold information being selected from the database and defines their data types. The interesting part of this section is the declaration for the T_Name, TS_Name, and T_Own variables. The variables are declared as TABLE_NAME.Column_Name%**TYPE**. By using the %**TYPE** operator, you tell Oracle to take the column definition from the database itself. If you decide to change the column definitions in the EXTGROW table, you will not have to change this script. The new column definitions will automatically be taken from the database.

```
cursor TABSPACE is
       select Table_Name,
              dt.Owner,
              dt.Tablespace_Name,
              dt.Next_Extent,
              Extents,
              dt.Blocks
         from DBA_TABLES dt, EXTGROW eg, DBA_SEGMENTS ds
        where Table_Name = Segname
          and dt.Owner=Segown
          and ds.Owner=Segown
          and Segment_Name = Segname
          and Growdate=to_date('&1','YYYYMMDD')-1;

cursor INDSPACE is
       select Index_Name,
              di.Owner,
              di.Tablespace_Name
              di.Next_Extent,
              Extents
         from DBA_INDEXES di, EXTGROW eg, DBA_SEGMENTS ds
        where Index_Name = Segname
          and di.Owner=Segown
          and ds.Owner=Segown
          and Segment_Name =Segname
          and Growdate=to_date('&1','YYYYMMDD')-1;
```

The two cursors are used to get some of the data from the data dictionary views DBA_TABLES, DBA_SEGMENTS, and DBA_INDEXES. The user table EXTGROW contains all the already-collected data for the objects at which you want to look. The section of the **where** clause that checks Growdate against the date you pass in looks for the names of tables or indexes that had data inserted for the prior day. If you want to run the script on a weekly basis, change the where clause on both cursors to

```
and Growdate=to_date('&1','YYYYMMDD')-7;
```

The information about the "high-water mark" (the boundary between used and unused space in a segment) is stored as a number of Oracle blocks, while all the other information about the space in a table or index is stored in bytes. The script selects the database block size from the V_$PARAMETER view so that high-water mark information can be converted to bytes.

```
begin

select Value
  into Db_Blk_Size
  from SYS.V_$PARAMETER
 where upper(Name) = 'DB_BLOCK_SIZE';
```

The first cursor loop reads through the EXTGROW table for all tables and selects information about the table from the DBA_TABLES and DBA_SEGMENTS data dictionary views. These views will be discussed in more detail in Chapter 6. They contain information about the storage parameters of the table, and the amount of space that has been allocated to the table, as well as the high-water mark of the table. The high-water mark is always in full blocks and therefore is not a true indicator of used space in the database. It is a rough guide to the used space, while the Oracle-supplied package DBMS_SPACE will provide an exact number of unused bytes in the table. You can then calculate the percentage of free space remaining. Once all the information about a table has been collected, it is inserted into the EXTGROW table and the next table is fetched from the cursor. When there are no more tables to process, the loop will exit and the cursor will be closed before the indexes are processed.

```
open TABSPACE;

loop
   fetch TABSPACE
    into T_Name,
         T_Own,
         Ts_Name,
         N_Ext_Bytes,
         T_Exts,
         Hwm;

    exit when TABSPACE%NOTFOUND;

DBMS_SPACE.UNUSED_SPACE(T_Own,T_Name,'TABLE',Total_Blocks, Total_Bytes,
Unused_Blocks, Unused_Bytes, Lue_File_Id, Lue_Block_Id, Last_Used_Block);

Hwm := Hwm*Db_Blk_Size;
```

```
select count(*),
       sum(Bytes),
       max(Bytes)
  into N_Exts, T_Free, L_Chunk
  from DBA_FREE_SPACE
 where Tablespace_Name = Ts_Name;

insert into EXTGROW (Segname, Segown, Growdate, Segtype, Segtbs, Exts,
                     Nextext, Tbsfree, Hwm, Totbytes, Usedbytes,
                     Contigfree,  Freepct, Tbsexts)
     values (T_Name, T_Own, to_date('&1','YYYYMMDD'), 'TABLE',Ts_Name,
             T_Exts, N_Ext_Bytes, T_Free, Hwm, Total_Bytes,
             (Total_Bytes-Unused_Bytes), L_Chunk,
             (Unused_Bytes/Total_Bytes)*100, N_Exts);

commit;

end loop;
close TABSPACE;
```

The second cursor loop reads through the EXTGROW table for all indexes and selects information about the index from the DBA_INDEXES and DBA_SEGMENTS data dictionary views. These views contain information about the storage parameters of the index and the amount of space that has been allocated to the index. Unlike tables, there is no high-water mark for indexes, and this column will be left empty (NULL) when the new row is inserted into EXTGROW. The Oracle-supplied package DBMS_SPACE will provide an exact number of unused bytes in the index. You can then calculate the percentage of free space remaining. Once all the information about an index has been collected, it is inserted into the EXTGROW table and the next index is fetched from the cursor. When there are no more indexes to process, the loop will exit and the cursor will be closed before the procedure exits.

```
open INDSPACE;

loop
   fetch INDSPACE
    into T_Name,
         T_Own,
         Ts_Name,
         N_Ext_Bytes,
         T_Exts;
exit when INDSPACE%NOTFOUND;

DBMS_SPACE.UNUSED_SPACE(T_Own,T_Name,'INDEX',Total_Blocks, Total_Bytes,
                        Unused_Blocks, Unused_Bytes, Lue_File_Id,
                        Lue_Block_Id, Last_Used_Block);
```

```
select count(*),
       sum(Bytes),
       max(Bytes)
  into N_Exts, T_Free, L_Chunk
  from DBA_FREE_SPACE
 where Tablespace_Name = Ts_Name;

insert into EXTGROW (Segname, Segown, Growdate, Segtype, Segtbs, Exts,
                     Nextext, Tbsfree, Hwm, Totbytes, Usedbytes,
                     Contigfree,  Freepct, Tbsexts)
     values (T_Name, T_Own, to_date('&1','YYYYMMDD'), 'INDEX',Ts_Name,
             T_Exts, N_Ext_Bytes, T_Free, NULL, Total_Bytes,
            (Total_Bytes-Unused_Bytes), L_Chunk,
            (Unused_Bytes/Total_Bytes)*100, N_Exts);

commit;

end loop;
close INDSPACE;
end;
/
```

Now that we've collected the information, we need to extract it in a readable form. The following SQL script will extract rows and format them, based on the criteria you pass in.

```
set pagesize 50 trimspool on linesize 250 verify off feedback off
set echo off term off
col Segname format a30 heading 'OBJECT'
col Segown format a10 heading 'OWNER'
col Segtype format a5 heading 'TYPE'
col Segtbs format a15 heading 'TABLESPACE'
col Exts format 9999 heading 'OBJEXTS'
col Nextext format 9,999,999,999 heading 'NEXT EXTENT'
col Tbsfree format 9,999,999,999 heading 'TOTAL TBS FREE'
col Hwm format 9,999,999,999 heading 'HIGHWATER MARK'
col Totbytes format 9,999,999,999 heading 'TOT ALLOC SPC'
col Usedbytes format 9,999,999,999 heading 'USED SPACE'
col Contigfree format 9,999,999,999 heading 'LARGEST FREE'
col Freepct format 999.99 heading '% FREE'
col Tbsexts format 9999 heading 'TBSEXTS'
compute sum of Nextext on Segtbs
break on report on Segtbs skip 1 on Tbsfree on Contigfree on Tbsexts on Segown
select Segtbs,
       Tbsfree,
       Contigfree,
       Tbsexts,
```

```
        Segown,
        Segname,
        Segtype,
        Hwm,
        Totbytes,
        Usedbytes,Exts,
        Nextext,
        Freepct
  from EXTGROW
 where Freepct <= &1
   and Growdate = to_date('&2','YYYYMMDD')
   and Segtbs like upper('%&3%')
 order by Segtbs, Segown, Segname

set concat +
spool spacerpt.log
/
exit
```

When you run this script, you will need to provide it with three parameters: the percentage of remaining free space to report on, the date you want to view (in YYYYMMDD format), and the tablespace you want to look at. If you want to see the data for all objects with 10 percent or less free space remaining, for May 24, 1999, and for all tablespaces, at the SQL*Plus command line you would type

```
@spacerpt 10 19990524 "%"
```

Sample output of this script is below. The amount of information being extracted is large, and the listing will wrap over several lines.

```
TABLESPACE      TOTAL TBS FREE  LARGEST FREE TBSEXTS OWNER      OBJECT                          TYPE
HIGHWATER MARK  TOT ALLOC SPC   USED SPACE OBJEXTS    NEXT EXTENT  % FREE
--------------- -------------- -------------- ------- ---------- ------------------------------ -----
-------------- -------------- -------------- ------- -------------- -------
USERS              603,635,712    66,314,240     327  TEST        IDX_MSGS_IN                   INDEX
                       327,680       327,680       8          40,960      .00
                                                                  IDX_MSGS_OUT                  INDEX
                     2,621,440     2,621,440      60          40,960      .00
                                                                  MSGS_IN                       TABLE
    44,998,656      14,049,280    14,049,280     332          40,960      .00
                                                                  MSGS_OUT                      TABLE
    15,351,808      52,510,720    52,428,800     224       1,048,576      .16
*************** ************** ************** ******* *************
                                                      -------------
sum                                                       1,171,456
```

Okay, now that we've shown you the script and the output, let's look a little more closely at what the script is doing and then at what the output of this script tells us.

The first section of the script sets up formatting information for the SQL*Plus report you are going to generate. The first two lines, the **set** commands, establish your SQL*Plus environment. The **pagesize** command tells Oracle how many lines to print per page. **Trimspool on** removes trailing blanks, and **linesize** sets the maximum number of characters per line. Since the script is asking for input parameters (the '&#' fields in the script), Oracle will prompt you for the value of the parameter and then list the old and new values. To stop this from happening, you can use the SQL*Plus **set** command **verify off** to tell Oracle not to prompt you and not to tell you what you entered. The last three commands control display. **Feedback off** tells Oracle not to display a row count, **echo** controls display of each command, and **term** controls display of the output. By turning **echo** and **term** off and spooling the output to a file, the file will contain a report without any extraneous lines.

```
set pagesize 50 trimspool on linesize 250 verify off feedback off
set echo off term off
```

The next set of lines in this section of the script sets up the headings and column formats for each row the script will display on the report. The **heading** parameter of the **col** (column) command changes the column heading from the column name itself to whatever you tell it to display. The **format** parameter sets up each column display. You can use it to set the width of each column and to insert commas and decimal points into numeric columns.

The last two lines of this section are used to add totals and breaks to the report. The **compute** command line tells Oracle to total the Nextext column for each tablespace. This will let you compare the total expansion with the amount of space left in the tablespace so you can tell whether you will have enough space if every object with that percentage of free space remaining were to expand at once. The **break** command does two things. First, it forces line breaks when the tablespace name or the owner within the tablespace changes. Second, it tells Oracle to suppress printing the tablespace name, tablespace free space, tablespace largest contiguous extent, number of extents in the tablespace, and owner name on each line if the values of these columns are not different from the ones on the prior line. This makes the output much more readable.

```
col Segname format a30 heading 'OBJECT'
col Segown format a10 heading 'OWNER'
col Segtype format a5 heading 'TYPE'
col Segtbs format a15 heading 'TABLESPACE'
col Exts format 9999 heading 'OBJEXTS'
col Nextext format 9,999,999,999 heading 'NEXT EXTENT'
col Tbsfree format 9,999,999,999 heading 'TOTAL TBS FREE'
col Hwm format 9,999,999,999 heading 'HIGHWATER MARK'
col Totbytes format 9,999,999,999 heading 'TOT ALLOC SPC'
col Usedbytes format 9,999,999,999 heading 'USED SPACE'
```

```
col Contigfree format 9,999,999,999 heading 'LARGEST FREE'
col Freepct format 999.99 heading '% FREE'
col Tbsexts format 9999 heading 'TBSEXTS'
compute sum of Nextext on Segtbs
break on report on Segtbs skip 1 on Tbsfree on Contigfree on Tbsexts on Segown
```

Finally, we're about to get the actual data! The **select** statement uses substitution variables instead of hard-coding values so that you don't have to continually edit the script when the date changes or when you want to see different percentages or tablespaces. We are firm believers in coding with parameters so that you only have to write the script once, and not go back and change it every time you, or the end user, needs to see something slightly differently.

If you pass in 100 for the first substitution variable (&1), you can see every table and index in the tablespaces you select for the date you select. The second variable is the date, and the script expects it in the format of YYYYMMDD, and concatenates the date to the name of the output log. By using this format, the output files will sort in date order. So that Oracle does not use the period to signify the end of the substitution variable, the script changes the concatenation character to a '+' before referencing the variable in the spool file name.

Oracle uses % as a wildcard, to match any value. By framing the &3 with %, you are telling Oracle to select any tablespace name that has the value of the third substitution variable anywhere in it. By passing in % as the third variable, you can select data for every tablespace.

The last "trick" in the script is the blank line between the end of the **select** statement and the **set concat** command. By inserting a blank line before you run the **select** statement with the /, you can enter SQL*Plus environment commands. If you didn't do this, you would have to put the **spool** command before the **select**, and the **select** statement would appear in your output listing.

```
select Segtbs,
       Tbsfree,
       Contigfree,
       Tbsexts,
       Segown,
       Segname,
       Segtype,
       Hwm,
       Totbytes,
       Usedbytes,Exts,
       Nextext,
       Freepct
  from EXTGROW
 where Freepct <= &1
   and Growdate = to_date('&2','YYYYMMDD')
   and Segtbs like upper('%&3%')
 order by Segtbs, Segown, Segname
```

```
set concat +
spool spacerpt_&2.log
/
exit
```

Now let's take a quick look at the output. There is a good deal of information on each line of the report, and each output line wraps onto two lines.

```
TABLESPACE      TOTAL TBS FREE  LARGEST FREE TBSEXTS OWNER      OBJECT                         TYPE
HIGHWATER MARK  TOT ALLOC SPC    USED SPACE OBJEXTS    NEXT EXTENT  % FREE
--------------- -------------- -------------- ------- ---------- ------------------------------ -----
-------------- -------------- -------------- ------- -------------- -------
USERS              603,635,712     66,314,240     327 TEST         IDX_MSGS_IN                    INDEX
                       327,680        327,680       8          40,960      .00
                                                                IDX_MSGS_OUT                   INDEX
                     2,621,440      2,621,440      60          40,960      .00
                                                                MSGS_IN                        TABLE
     44,998,656     14,049,280     14,049,280     332          40,960      .00
                                                                MSGS_OUT                       TABLE
     15,351,808     52,510,720     52,428,800     224       1,048,576      .16
*************** ************** ************** ******* *************
                                                        --------------
sum                                                         1,171,456
```

What can we tell from this report? The USERS tablespace has 603,635,712 bytes free, with the largest contiguous extent sized at 66,314,240. The tablespace is pretty fragmented, since the total free space is in 327 extents. This information is printed only on the first line because of the break commands we set, so it is easier to tell when there is a change.

None of the objects on this listing has a next extent larger than the largest free extent in the tablespace. The sum of the next extents for the percentage of free space remaining is 1,171,456 bytes, which will easily fit into both the total tablespace free space and the largest free extent in the tablespace. All of the objects show a very small percentage free, making them all likely to extend in the near future. This list may or may not show all the objects in the tablespace. The only way to make absolutely sure that you have enough space is to run the report and pass in 100 for the first substitution variable so that you see every object with 100 percent or less free space remaining.

Trace Files

When you have an internal error in a user session or background process, Oracle will create a trace file, to help in debugging and resolving the error. As the DBA, you can define where the trace files should be created and their maximum size, using the following init.ora parameters:

- MAX_DUMP_FILE_SIZE   Maximum size the trace file can become
- BACKGROUND_DUMP_DEST   Location for trace files created by the Oracle background processes
- USER_DUMP_DEST   Location for trace files created out of user sessions

Trace files created by the background processes will have the name of the background process that generated the trace file as part of the trace file name; those created by user processes will have the user process ID in the name of the trace file.

In general, it is a good idea to move the trace file directories from the default locations under the ORACLE_BASE directory tree to another disk. Trace files are not automatically purged and can grow quite large.

When a trace file is created due to an internal error, a line will be written into the alert log, with the Oracle error number and the name and location of the trace file. Check the meaning of the Oracle error, and if it is not due to programming or user error, call Oracle Technical Support for assistance in resolving the problem. They will generally ask you to send them the trace file for analysis.

We have included two sample trace files below. The first is from the user dump directory with an error code of 1013, which is caused by the user canceling the session. It is therefore not a problem that would have to be called into Support.

```
Dump file /db3/oracle/TEST/udump/TEST_ora_28495.trc
Oracle7 Server Release 7.3.4.3.0 - Production
With the distributed, replication and parallel query options
PL/SQL Release 2.3.4.3.0 - Production
ORACLE_HOME = /opt/app/oracle/product/7.3.4
System name:     SunOS
Node name:       TEST
Release:         5.6
Version:         Generic_105181-08
Machine:         sun4u
Instance name: TEST
Redo thread mounted by this instance: 1
Oracle process number: 561
Unix process pid: 28495, image: oracleTEST

*** 1999.05.21.15.03.00.000
*** SESSION ID:(86.27826) 1999.05.21.15.03.00.000
<<<<<<<<<<START PLSQL RUNTIME DUMP<<<<<<<<<<<<<
THIS IS AN INFORMATIONAL DUMP
..e.g., used for Bugs 227188 and 226937...
***Got ORA-1013 while running PLSQL***
PACKAGE BODY SYS.STANDARD:
library unit=90cd99d4 line=213 opcode=19 static link=0 scope=1
FP=8a84c0 PC=90cd7f30 Page=0 AP=8aa4cc ST=8a84e4
DL0=87da78 DL1=87da84 DPF=87da94 DS=90cd4f2c
   DON library unit variable list instantiation
------ ------------ ------------- -------------
     0     90cd99d4        87da9c        87b49c
     1     90cd99d4        87b580        87b49c
     2
```

```
   scope    frame
-------- --------
       2   8a84c0
       1        0
package variable  address      size
---------------- -------- --------
               0   87dac4       84
               1   87db18       84
               2   87db6c       84
               3   87dbc0        8
```

The second trace file shows a small section of a trace file from the background dump destination. This file shows a portion of an ORA-600 error that should be called in to Support for them to confirm whether this is a serious error.

```
Dump file /usr/app/oracle/admin/TEST/bdump/smon_TEST_9005.trc
Oracle7 Server Release 7.3.4.0.0 - Production
With the distributed and parallel query options
PL/SQL Release 2.3.4.0.0 - Production
ORACLE_HOME = /usr/app/oracle/product/7.3.4
System name:    TEST
Node name:      TEST
Release:        4.0
Version:        3.0
Machine:        4850
Instance name: TEST
Redo thread mounted by this instance: 1
Oracle process number: 6
Unix process pid: 9005, image: ora_smon_TEST

ksedmp: internal or fatal error
ORA-00600: internal error code, arguments: [3509], [2], [], [], [], [], [], []
Current SQL statement for this session:
SELECT FLEX_VALUE, FLEX_VALUE VALUE, DESCRIPTION DESCRIPTION, NVL(SUMMARY_FLAG,...
```

You can also generate trace files for tuning purposes, by setting **sql_trace** = TRUE, either in the init.ora or in the user session itself. These trace files are used by TKPROF to analyze the SQL statements. However, a severe performance impact comes along with setting **sql_trace** equal to TRUE for more than just a specific session on your system. We recommend that you either set this variable to TRUE only in a specific, monitored SQL session or set it to TRUE for the entire database for a very limited and controlled amount of time. You have to shut down and restart the database to set this variable to TRUE for the entire database, so you have double the impact. First, you have the impact of setting the variable to TRUE, and second, you have the impact of shutting down and restarting the database twice—once to enable **sql_trace** and the second time to turn it back off. You will definitely not want to run your database for an extended period of time with this variable set to TRUE. We discuss TKPROF in more detail in Chapter 11.

User Session Status

If you look in the V$SESSION view, you can tell the status of each user session in the database at that moment. The following script will return a count of sessions grouped by status in the database. Why do you want to check on these counts? You set an explicit or implicit limit to the number of sessions allowed in the database at any one time in your init.ora file by setting the parameter **sessions** to a value. If there are a large number of "KILLED" or "SNIPED" sessions in the database and that number does not go down over time, you are wasting the number of allowable sessions that you can have. The only way you can clear the number of sessions that are being counted is to shut down and restart the database.

```
select Status,count(*)
  from V$SESSION
 group by Status
/
```

The following listing is returned:

```
STATUS          COUNT(*)
-------- ---------------
ACTIVE                26
INACTIVE             160
KILLED                30
CACHED                 5
SNIPED                 3
```

The Status column values can be misleading. A value of INACTIVE does not mean the user process is not doing anything; it merely means that at the moment the **select** was run, the process was not executing a SQL statement. ACTIVE sessions are executing SQL, KILLED sessions are marked by Oracle to be killed and removed from the database, and SNIPED sessions are inactive and waiting for the client to do something. CACHED sessions have to do with Oracle*XA, an external interface that allows global transactions to be handled by a transaction manager other than Oracle. If the numbers of KILLED, SNIPED, and CACHED sessions do not change, or continually increase, there is a problem in the database and session slots are being unnecessarily used. You will have to shut down and restart the database to resolve this problem.

Monitoring Object Modifications

You can check on changes to database objects using the data dictionary views USER_OBJECTS or DBA_OBJECTS. Why do you care when objects were last changed? If you are running a production system, you want to control when changes are made and who makes them. You can use auditing to monitor who has made use of a privilege that changes an object, but auditing won't tell you which object was changed. The DBA_OBJECTS and USER_OBJECTS views contain a column called Last_DDL_Time. This column contains the time that the object was last modified. However, Oracle considers adding grants or an index a modification to the object, so this field doesn't really reflect the last time the object itself was changed. To find out the actual time an object was changed, you can look in the Timestamp column of the DBA_OBJECTS or USER_OBJECTS view. This field is VARCHAR2(75), so you will need to convert it to a date. Set up a batch job to execute once a day that runs the following SQL script:

```
col Owner              format a20
col Object_Name        format a30
col Timestamp          format a20
select Owner, Object_Name, Object_Type, Status, Timestamp
  from DBA_OBJECTS
 where SUBSTR(Timestamp,1,10) = TO_CHAR(sysdate-1,'YYYY-MM-DD')
 order by Owner, Object_Name
/
```

This script will list all objects that have changed since the prior day, in owner order. The status column is included because procedures, functions, and packages are objects and can become invalid when changed. Sample output from this report is shown here:

```
OBJECT_NAME                    OBJECT_TYPE   STATUS  TIMESTAMP
------------------------------ ------------- ------- --------------------
DBASE_TEMP                     TABLE         VALID   1999-05-08:15:20:42
TSPACE_TEMP                    TABLE         VALID   1999-05-08:15:15:12
IDX_MSG_IN                     INDEX         VALID   1999-05-08:10:01:00
IDX_MSG_OUT                    INDEX         VALID   1999-05-08:09:58:14
IDX_MSG_OUT_2                  INDEX         VALID   1999-05-08:09:58:18
SYS_C005595                    INDEX         VALID   1999-05-08:09:58:08
SYS_C005598                    INDEX         VALID   1999-05-08:10:00:56
TEMP_IN                        PACKAGE       VALID   1999-05-08:09:12:47
TEMP_IN                        PACKAGE BODY  INVALID 1999-05-08:09:32:59
```

Looking at the report above, you can see that the package TEMP_IN must have had errors in the package body compilation, since the status is still INVALID.

CHAPTER 5

General Database Considerations

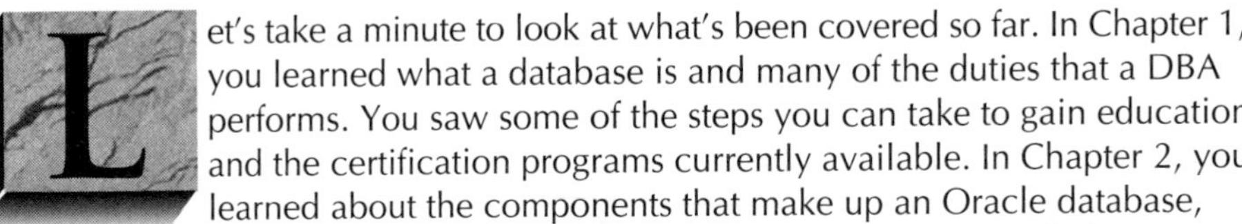

Let's take a minute to look at what's been covered so far. In Chapter 1, you learned what a database is and many of the duties that a DBA performs. You saw some of the steps you can take to gain education and the certification programs currently available. In Chapter 2, you learned about the components that make up an Oracle database, while in Chapter 3 you read about database installation, walked through the OFA approach to tablespace layout, and learned the steps to take immediately after your database is created. In Chapter 4, you were introduced to the monitoring tasks that you can perform on a daily basis to help you keep abreast of your database's health and well-being.

In this chapter, we'll look at some of the general database considerations and tasks that you can perform to help you maintain your database effectively. Since every object in your database is housed in a tablespace, we're going to spend quite a bit of time looking at tablespaces and the actions you can take to make them function optimally. We'll also cover the parameters you use the most for creating tables, indexes, views, roles, synonyms, and users, as well as some considerations for sizing those objects.

The Care and Feeding of Tablespaces

To get things rolling, let's pack a picnic lunch and go off to the zoo for a while. My, isn't the weather glorious? The sun is shining and the birds are singing—if not outside your window, then somewhere in the world! Ah. Here we are at the zoo. As we enter the zoo, there are wide expanses of land with fences around each one. Oh, look! There's Monkey Island with its moat of water around the outside and piles of rocks and trees for the monkeys to climb. The monkey over there is smiling at the guy with the camera as he takes his picture. How funny! To our right is the Feline House with the lions and tigers and panthers and other big cats. Let's walk in there for a minute. Wow! Look at how large that male lion is. Isn't he ferocious? The female looks almost playful sitting next to him. There's a panther in the cage next to them. Look at that tiger prowling around his cage. He's so sleek looking. It sure is a good thing they didn't put the lions and tigers together, isn't it? We suspect they would not get along well at all. Well, let's move on to the other areas. There's a mountain goat sitting on top of a huge rock near the top of that mountain to our left. There are antelope and giraffes and a reptile house, as well as seals and bears and an Amazon rain forest. Gee! Look at the size of that elephant. There is just too much to see in one day here, and our time to visit is just about up.

Wasn't that fun? Now, what in the world do animals in a zoo have to do with objects in tablespaces? So glad you asked! Let's review what we saw in the zoo. In some areas, there were wide expanses of land with several kinds of animals living happily together, while in other areas, there were cages with only one kind of animal in each cage. Antelope can live happily with giraffes and elephants, but lions would probably enjoy an antelope meal or two. The ideal would be to house each kind of animal in its own area with all of the space it needed to live safely and happily. In the next section, we'll apply these ideas to a database and show you how you can effectively place your objects.

Creating and Dropping a Tablespace

There are three actions that you can take in regard to a tablespace: create, alter, and drop. The majority of this chapter will deal with the second option—altering a tablespace. However, before we begin talking about maintaining and modifying tablespaces, we need to look at how you go about creating and removing a tablespace.

Creating a Tablespace

The command syntax to create or drop a tablespace is mapped out in the Oracle-supplied documentation, but the parameters may seem a bit confusing, so let's take a look at them now. Table 5-1 shows the parameters you can use in the **create tablespace** command.

Parameter	Definition
tablespace_name	The name assigned to the tablespace—should reflect the tablespace's functionality
datafile specifications:	
file location	The fully qualified directory path and file name
size	The total initial allocated size of the datafile
reuse	If the datafile exists, reuse the file instead of giving an error. The datafile must be the same size as defined in the **size** parameter
autoextend	Enable/disable Oracle's ability to automatically increase the size of the datafile. Can either be **off** or **on**. If **on** the additional parameters are **next:** number of bytes to increase file by each time **maxsize**: largest size to which the datafile can grow. Can be **unlimited**
minimum extent	Used to control fragmentation—shows the minimum extent size to be used

TABLE 5-1. *Create Tablespace Parameters*

Parameter	Definition
logging/nologging	Specifies whether redo log information is to be kept on objects in the tablespace
default storage	The amount of space to allocate for an object if no storage clause is supplied
initial	The amount of space to allocate for the first extent
next	The amount of space to allocate for the second and successive extents
minextents	The minimum number of extents to allocate
maxextents	The maximum number of extents to allocate—can be set to unlimited
pctincrease	The percentage of space to allocate for successive extents—based on the value of Next
freelist groups	Used with the Parallel Server option to specify the number of freelists for objects created in this tablespace without storage clauses
freelists	Specifies the number of freelists for objects created in this tablespace without storage clauses
optimal	Used only for rollback segments—shows the minimum amount of space to automatically shrink rollback segments to after they have extended beyond the optimal value
online/offline	Specifies the state in which the tablespace should initially be placed
permanent/temporary	Specifies whether the tablespace will hold objects or be used for temporary segments
extent management	
dictionary	Specifies that the extent management will be performed in the data dictionary
local	Specifies that some part of the tablespace has been set aside for a bitmap
plugged_in	Used with transportable tablespaces, indicates that a tablespace can be "plugged in" to a database (Oracle 8i only)

TABLE 5-1. *Create Tablespace Parameters* (continued)

Within the datafile parameters is the qualifier **reuse**. This qualifier can be used in place of a size specification in a tablespace creation statement. Here are a few rules associated with the **reuse** qualifier:

- If the file already exists, its size must match that of the **size** parameter. If no **size** parameter is specified, the size is assumed to be that of the existing datafile.
- If the file does not exist, Oracle ignores this clause and creates the file.
- You can omit this clause only if the file does not already exist. If you omit this clause, Oracle creates the file.

Now that you've seen the parameters, let's see if you can put them together and create a tablespace. First, to see what Oracle will supply as default values, create a tablespace without specifying anything but the required parameters:

```
create tablespace MYTAB
datafile 'd:\ora8i\oradata\orcl\mytab01.dbf'
    size 2M;
```

Now, you can use the DBA_TABLESPACES view to see what default values Oracle supplies.

```
select *
  from DBA_TABLESPACES
 where Tablespace_Name = 'MYTAB';

TABLESPACE_NAME    INITIAL_EXTENT  NEXT_EXTENT  MIN_EXTENTS
MAX_EXTENTS  PCT_INCREASE MIN_EXTLEN STATUS    CONTENTS  LOGGING
EXTENT_MAN ALLOCATIO PLU
------------------ -------------- ------------ ------------
------------ ------------ --------- --------- --------- ---------
---------- --------- ---
MYTAB                         10240         10240            1
         121            50          0 ONLINE    PERMANENT LOGGING
DICTIONARY USER      NO
```

By default, Oracle makes the initial and next extents five database blocks in size. The minimum extents are set to 1, while the maximum extents value is 121 (the old limit for a 2K block size database). The percent increase is set to 50, and the tablespace is placed online and available, but that parameter is listed with a column name of Status instead of **offline** or **online**. The tablespace is created as permanent, and objects can be created within it, but again, the parameter is listed with a column name of Contents instead of **temporary** or **permanent**. All changes to the tablespace are to be logged to the redo logs by default (the **logging** parameter is set). The data dictionary is to be used to do extent management (the default—newly available in Oracle8i), and the Allocation_Type is, therefore, the user. The final parameter—**plugged_in**—is used with transportable tablespaces in version 8i. We'll talk about transportable tablespaces in a later section of this chapter.

Dropping a Tablespace

To permanently remove a tablespace from your database, you can use the **drop tablespace** command. However, in order to really drop a tablespace, the tablespace must first be placed offline to ensure that no transactions are being performed while you are trying to remove the tablespace from the system. You must remember, too, that when you drop the tablespace from your database, you are only removing the entry information from the data dictionary; you are not removing the datafile from the operating system directory structure. Thus, the steps that you must take to drop a tablespace from your database are as follows:

1. Alter the tablespace offline so no transactions can be started while you are in the process of dropping the tablespace.
2. Issue the **drop tablespace** command. You must include the command phrase **including contents** if there are or have been any objects created in the tablespace. If the tablespace has never had an object in it, you do not need to specify this phrase.
3. Delete the datafile associated with the tablespace from the operating system.

Since no objects have been created in the MYTAB tablespace, you could drop this tablespace by issuing the following commands:

```
alter tablespace MYTAB offline;
drop tablespace MYTAB;
```

Next, create the tablespace and create a small table in the tablespace. Put a row of data into the tablespace.

```
create tablespace MYTAB
datafile 'd:\ora8i\oradata\orcl\mytab01.dbf' reuse;

create table MY_TABLE (Employee varchar2(20))
tablespace MYTAB;

insert into MY_TABLE
values ('ROSS');
```

```
alter tablespace MYTAB offline;
drop tablespace MYTAB;
drop tablespace MYTAB
*
ERROR at line 1:
ORA-01549: tablespace not empty, use INCLUDING CONTENTS option
```

Since the tablespace has an object in it, the **including contents** clause must be used as follows:

```
drop tablespace MYTAB including contents;
```

This time, the tablespace is dropped with no problem.

Placing Objects in Tablespaces

Let's take what you've seen at the zoo and apply the concepts to your database and tablespaces. All the objects in your tablespaces (tables, views, indexes, sequences, packages, procedures, etc.) would be most "happy" if each one was in its own tablespace. However, as with the zoo, that's not always possible in the real world. Imagine the waste of resources if you placed a 200-byte table alone on a 9-gigabyte disk. My, wouldn't your management like that? No! You are encouraged, by your management, to house objects together, with as little wasted space as possible.

Just as you would not put lions and tigers in the same confined area because they would attempt to dominate each other, you should not put table segments and index segments in the same tablespace. They could "fight" each other and cause disk contention. What else will you want to keep separate? As mentioned in Chapter 3, you will want to house rollback segments and temporary segments in separate tablespaces on separate disks. You will also want to place your control files, redo log files, and archive log files on separate disks.

Wouldn't it be wonderful to be able to start with a totally fresh and new database and begin to place objects and tablespaces from the beginning exactly where they should go? Unfortunately, you don't always have this luxury. More often than not, you will inherit a database that's already laid out, and not necessarily in the best manner. What can you do about a database whose objects are placed badly? Why, you can change it, of course.

Changing Your Tablespace Configuration

If you have inherited a database, how will you know whether it is laid out well or not? The first thing you can do is look at the current configuration. We'll be talking extensively about the DBA_ (pronounced "DBA underscore") views in Chapters 6, 7 and 8, but you'll need to look at some of them here to see the database layout.

The first view you can look at is the DBA_TABLESPACES view. This view will show you the overall information about the tablespaces that are currently in your

database and whether they are online and available or offline and unavailable.
To see the composition of the DBA_TABLESPACES view, you can use the following command. The results, from an Oracle8i database, are displayed following the command.

```
describe DBA_TABLESPACES;

 Name                                                    Null?    Type
 ------------------------------------------------------- -------- ------------
 TABLESPACE_NAME                                         NOT NULL VARCHAR2(30)
 INITIAL_EXTENT                                                   NUMBER
 NEXT_EXTENT                                                      NUMBER
 MIN_EXTENTS                                             NOT NULL NUMBER
 MAX_EXTENTS                                             NOT NULL NUMBER
 PCT_INCREASE                                                     NUMBER
 MIN_EXTLEN                                                       NUMBER
 STATUS                                                           VARCHAR2(9)
 CONTENTS                                                         VARCHAR2(9)
 LOGGING                                                          VARCHAR2(9)
 EXTENT_MANAGEMENT                                                VARCHAR2(10)
 ALLOCATION_TYPE                                                  VARCHAR2(9)
 PLUGGED_IN                                                       VARCHAR2(3)
```

We'll discuss the parameters shown here more completely in Chapter 6. Now that you know the composition of the view, you can select parts of the view to look at to gain information about the tablespaces in your database. You can look at the Tablespace Names And The Status Of Each Tablespace By Performing The Following Query:

```
select Tablespace_Name, Status
  from DBA_TABLESPACES;

TABLESPACE_NAME                STATUS
------------------------------ ---------
SYSTEM                         ONLINE
USERS                          ONLINE
RBS                            ONLINE
TEMP                           ONLINE
OEM_REPOSITORY                 ONLINE
INDX                           ONLINE
DATA                           ONLINE
RBS_2                          OFFLINE
TOOLS                          ONLINE

9 rows selected.
```

So, in this database, there are nine tablespaces, and all but one of them are online and available. The tablespace RBS_2 is offline and, therefore, unavailable for use. It's really great to know how many tablespaces you have and their names, but, looking at this report, you still don't have a clear picture of the location of each of the tablespaces on disks in your system.

You can use the DBA_DATA_FILES view, which shows you the names of the tablespaces that exist in your database, the datafiles that make up the tablespaces and their locations on disks, and the initial amount of space that's been allocated for each datafile. This view does not give you the status of each tablespace or the storage values assigned to the tablespace. Thus, both views are important and provide different pieces to help you build a complete picture of your tablespace configuration and composition. For now, you are interested in getting the location of each of the datafiles in each of the tablespaces. Here are both the script to use to see this information and the output from the command:

```
set pagesize 999
column File_Name format a45
select Tablespace_Name, File_Name
  from DBA_DATA_FILES;

TABLESPACE_NAME                FILE_NAME
------------------------------ ---------------------------------------
USERS                          C:\ORA8I\ORADATA\ORCL\USERS01.DBF
OEM_REPOSITORY                 C:\ORA8I\ORADATA\ORCL\OEMREP01.DBF
INDX                           G:\ORA8I\ORADATA\ORCL\INDX01.DBF
RBS                            D:\ORA8I\ORADATA\ORCL\RBS01.DBF
TEMP                           E:\ORA8I\ORADATA\ORCL\TEMP01.DBF
SYSTEM                         F:\ORA8I\ORADATA\ORCL\SYSTEM01.DBF
DATA                           G:\ORA8I\ORADATA\ORCL\DATA01.DBF
RBS_2                          D:\ORA8I\ORADATA\ORCL\RBS201.DBF
TOOLS                          E:\ORA8I\ORADATA\ORCL\TMP_USR01.DBF

9 rows selected.
```

The output shows that the tablespaces are on five different disks but with the same directory naming convention. Using the same naming convention for each database for each disk makes maintaining the database much easier. Under normal circumstances—that is, in a shop that follows a set of standards—if you know the name of one directory location for one of your files, you will be able to find the rest of the database files by a quick check of each disk for the same directory name. In an area where standards have not been followed, all bets are off. Datafiles may have been placed anywhere on the system. In that case, the only way you will be able to find the locations of the datafiles for your database is to query the DBA_DATA_FILES view, as shown above, but add an **order by** qualifier on the Tablespace_Name column.

Note that if you installed and are looking at the Oracle-supplied demonstration database, the tablespaces, as well as all of the other files associated with the database, will be on the same disk in the same directory. You should not be surprised to see this form of configuration for the demo database since Oracle doesn't know what disks you have available on your particular system. If, however, you see this layout (all of the tablespaces and support files on one disk) on your production system, you know you are in trouble.

A redundant array of inexpensive disks (RAID) can be configured in several different ways. The most common RAID sets are configured as follows:

- Disks configured with two or more disks logically joined together, over which the data is spread, known as *striping* and referred to as RAID-0
- Disks configured with one disk set up to match the other disk, known as *mirroring* and referred to as RAID-1
- A combination of mirroring and striping, referred to as RAID-0+1
- Disks configured with a *parity-check* system among a group of disks (usually RAID-3 or RAID-5)

In a parity-check system, the hardware decides how to distribute the data across disks and performs its own striping of data. In RAID-5, for example, each file is striped on a block-by-block basis across the disks in the mirroring group. A parity check is then written on another disk in the set so that if one disk is removed, its contents can be regenerated based on knowing the parity check and the contents of the rest of the mirrored set.

The system mirroring architecture can affect the distribution of database files across those disks. Disks that are mirrored on a one-to-one basis (RAID-1) can be treated as stand-alone disks. Disks that are part of a parity-check system (such as RAID-3 or RAID-5) must be considered as a set and can take advantage of the implicit striping.

It's important to talk frequently with your system administrator or systems group to obtain an understanding of how a RAID (if used) device is configured and how it will affect your database.

Let's put the tablespaces and their locations in a table format to more easily see the layout of tablespaces on disks:

Tablespace Name	Location
USERS	C:\ORA8I\ORADATA\ORCL\USERS01.DBF
OEM_REPOSITORY	C:\ORA8I\ORADATA\ORCL\OEMREP01.DBF
RBS	D:\ORA8I\ORADATA\ORCL\RBS01.DBF
RBS_2	D:\ORA8I\ORADATA\ORCL\RBS201.DBF
TEMP	E:\ORA8I\ORADATA\ORCL\TEMP01.DBF
TOOLS	E:\ORA8I\ORADATA\ORCL\TMP_USR01.DBF
SYSTEM	F:\ORA8I\ORADATA\ORCL\SYSTEM01.DBF
DATA	G:\ORA8I\ORADATA\ORCL\DATA01.DBF
INDX	G:\ORA8I\ORADATA\ORCL\INDX01.DBF

There, that's better. In the table above, you can see that the first rule of tablespace layout has been broken: the INDX tablespace is in the same directory, on the same disk, and therefore, on the same controller as the DATA tablespace. Since there are only five disks available for use with this database, the rest of the configuration is pretty good. The probability is that the USERS tablespace will not get much use and will not be in contention with the Oracle Enterprise Manager repository tablespace. In the listing earlier, the second rollback tablespace, RBS02, was listed as offline. If the rollback segment tablespaces are both on the same disk and online, this configuration might defeat the purpose of having two rollback tablespaces. The TOOLS and TEMP tablespaces are housed together, which might produce some contention depending on the objects that are stored in the TOOLS tablespace and their frequency of use. There is, however, no question that the DATA and INDX tablespaces, if used properly, will be in contention. Since there are only five disks available, where would it make sense to move either the DATA or the INDX tablespace? Hmm. You can use a V$ view (to be discussed more thoroughly in Chapters 9 and 10) to determine the amount of input and output (I/O) activity on each disk.

Using a V$ View to See Contention

Looking in Appendix C, you will see that there are several V$ views that, by name, might seem to be the view you would use to see the activity on your tablespaces. There's V$TABLESPACE, which only shows the tablespace name and number. No, that won't help here. There's V$DATAFILE, which shows all of the information about the composition of the datafile, such as its size and the tablespace with which it is associated. Strike two. Oh, there's V$FILESTAT, which shows physical reads, physical writes, and so on. Let's describe the view and see what's in it.

```
describe V$FILESTAT
 Name                                              Null?    Type
 ------------------------------------------------- -------- ----------
 FILE#                                                      NUMBER
 PHYRDS                                                     NUMBER
 PHYWRTS                                                    NUMBER
 PHYBLKRD                                                   NUMBER
 PHYBLKWRT                                                  NUMBER
 READTIM                                                    NUMBER
 WRITETIM                                                   NUMBER
 AVGIOTIM                                                   NUMBER
 LSTIOTIM                                                   NUMBER
 MINIOTIM                                                   NUMBER
 MAXIORTM                                                   NUMBER
 MAXIOWTM                                                   NUMBER
```

That's just the view we're looking for. There's only one problem. The datafile is displayed as a number and not as a name. Looking at V$DATAFILE_HEADER, you can see that there is a datafile number associated with each tablespace name entry. We can use the tablespace name from that view, coupled (or *joined*) with the V$FILESTAT view to get a picture of the amount of activity for each tablespace on a datafile-by-datafile basis. Using the following script, you can see the activity for each datafile on your system. Note that V$DATAFILE_HEADER does not exist in a version 7 database.

```
column Name format a34
column Tablespace_Name format a15
column File# format 999 head 'F#'
select a.File#, Name, Tablespace_Name, Phyrds, Phywrts, Phyblkrd, phyblkwrt
  from V$FILESTAT a, V$DATAFILE_HEADER b
 where a.File# = b.File#;
 F# NAME                               TABLESPACE_NAME    PHYRDS    PHYWRTS  PBLKRD PBLKWRT
--- ---------------------------------- --------------- --------- --------- ------- -------
  8 F:\ORA8I\ORADATA\ORC1\DATA01.DBF   DATA                    4         2       4       2
  6 F:\ORA8I\ORADATA\ORC1\INDX01.DBF   INDX                    4         2       4       2
  5 F:\ORA8I\ORADATA\ORC1\OEMREP01.DBF OEM_REPOSITORY         14        12      14      12
  3 F:\ORA8I\ORADATA\ORC1\RBS01.DBF    RBS                   132       333     132     333
  1 F:\ORA8I\ORADATA\ORC1\SYSTEM01.DBF SYSTEM               1716        12    3708      12
  4 F:\ORA8I\ORADATA\ORC1\TEMP01.DBF   TEMP                    4         2       4       2
  2 F:\ORA8I\ORADATA\ORC1\USERS01.DBF  USERS                  12         4       8       2
  7 F:\ORA8I\ORADATA\USER02.DBF        USERS                   6         2       6       2

8 rows selected.
```

The above output does not really reflect a heavily used system. You would expect DATA, INDX, RBS, and TEMP to have more physical disk activity. These figures are accumulated since the database was started. With figures this low, you can assume that either the database was just recently started or, as really is the case with this output, the database is a demonstration database and rarely used.

Based on the activity displayed here, you could move the DATA tablespace to the same disk as the USERS and OEM_REPOSITORY tablespaces and still have very little contention.

The above described script and output are purely for Oracle8i. Here is the same script translated for use with an Oracle7 database:

```
column File# format 9999
column File_Name format a40
column Tablespace_Name format a10
select a.File#, File_Name, Tablespace_Name, Phyrds, Phywrts, Phyblkrd,
       Phyblkwrt
  from V$FILESTAT a, DBA_DATA_FILES b
 where a.File# = b.File_Id;

FILE# FILE_NAME                                TABLESPACE  PHYRDS    PHYWRTS
----- ---------------------------------------- ---------- ------- ----------
  PHYBLKRD  PHYBLKWRT
---------- ----------
    1 MYDISK03\ORACLE\MYDB\SYSTEM01.DBF        SYSTEM       30418        254
     64305        254
    2 MYDISK17\ORACLE\MYDB\RBS01.DBF           RBS           1159      12584
      1159      12584
    3 MYDISK04\ORACLE\MYDB\TEMP01.DBF          TEMP             3      18781
        45      18781
    4 MYDISK16\ORACLE\MYDB\TOOLS01.DBF         TOOLS          222          0
       446          0
    5 MYDISK16\ORACLE\MYDB\USERS01.DBF         USERS           28         95
        28         95
    6 MYDISK01\ORACLE\MYDB\DATA01.DBF          DATA         51339        160
     85923        160
    7 MYDISK24\ORACLE\MYDB\IDX01.DBF           INDX          8145       1179
      8145       1179

7 rows selected.
```

In this example, the query has been run against a version 7.3.3.6 database. The amount of physical blocks read from the DATA tablespace is much higher than the amount of blocks written—an indication that more selects than inserts or updates are occurring in this database.

Moving the Contents of a Tablespace

In *The Oracle8i DBA Handbook*, Kevin Loney describes in great detail the ideal placement of tablespaces based on how many disks you have available. In this section, we'll just concentrate on how you move a tablespace from one disk to another. A tablespace can have one or more datafiles, so you want to be sure you know where all of the datafiles for a tablespace are located.

There are several approaches that you can use, including using the Oracle Enterprise Manager (OEM) tools, to move a tablespace's datafile(s) from one disk to another. Right now, we'll concentrate on the manual steps so that you can learn them. In Chapter 11, we'll talk more about the OEM and how to perform remote database administration.

To move a tablespace from one disk to another, the tablespace must first be placed offline. By placing the tablespace offline, you will ensure that no one is performing any transactions in the tablespace while you are trying to move it. However, while the tablespace is offline, no one can perform any work in it. Isn't that a dual-edged sword! Make sure you have let everyone who needs to know that the tablespace and its contents will be unavailable during the time you are moving it.

Here are the steps you will perform to move the tablespace from one disk to another:

1. From SQL*Plus, take the tablespace offline by issuing the command:

   ```
   alter tablespace <tablespace_name> offline;
   ```

2. From the operating system level, copy the tablespace's datafile(s) to its new location.

3. From SQL*Plus, rename the datafile to modify the location in the data dictionary:

   ```
   alter tablespace <tablespace_name>;
   rename datafile '<directory_name><file_name>' to
   '<new_directory_name><file_name>';
   ```

4. From SQL*Plus, put the tablespace online:

   ```
   alter tablespace <tablespace_name> online;
   ```

5. From the operating system level, remove the datafile(s) from the old directory.

On some operating systems, you can reverse steps 2 and 3, but on others, you cannot rename the datafile until an actual file exists in the new directory location. Therefore, we recommend that you make sure the file exists in its new location before you do the logical rename for the datafile.

Using these steps, you can move the DATA tablespace from the G disk to the C disk. The same steps are given next, without the step numbers, with the actual values filled in to move the DATA tablespace.

```
alter tablespace DATA offline;
Tablespace altered.
```

From the operating system, you can now copy the datafile(s) for the DATA tablespace from one disk to the other. On a Unix system, the command would look like the following:

```
cp /ora8i/oradata/orcl/data01.dbf /ora8i/oradata/orcl/data01.dbf
```

From a Windows NT system, you can copy and paste the file from one directory to the other or, at the DOS prompt, issue the **copy** command as follows:

```
Copy g:\ora8i\oradata\orcl\data01.dbf c:\ora8i\+oradata\orcl\data01.dbf
```

After the copy of the datafile(s) has been completed, from SQL*Plus, type the following commands to modify the data dictionary and put the tablespace back online:

```
alter tablespace DATA
rename datafile 'G:\ORA8I\ORADATA\ORCL\DATA01.DBF' to
'C:\ORA8I\ORADATA\ORCL\DATA01.DBF';
Tablespace altered.
alter tablespace DATA online;
Tablespace altered.
```

That was easy! The only step left is to go back to the operating system level and delete the datafile from the G disk. On a Windows NT system, you can use Microsoft Windows NT Explorer to select the file and delete it, or you can delete the file from the DOS prompt in a DOS operating system window. From a Unix system, you would use the following command:

```
rm /ora8i/oradata/orcl/data01.dbf
```

Resizing a Tablespace

Some of the authors love to go on cruises, and some of us have been on several different ones. The cruise lines seem to be in a contest to see who can entice you to eat more by offering food service 24 hours a day and making each food offering look incredibly delectable. By the end of a cruise, the salt air seems to have shrunk the clothes you brought, and you notice that they've become snugger (more snug? Okay, just plain tight!) than they were when you boarded the ship.

Marlene has a law about the expansion of things in general. Her law states that "given the opportunity, anything will expand to exceed any allocated amount of space." Actually, on thinking about it, Oracle may have written that law, since everything in an Oracle database seems, over time, to expand to exceed the given amount of space available. Therefore, one thing you must carefully monitor in your database is the amount of space each object is using. As objects grow, the amount of space available in their tablespace decreases. Eventually, if you do not take any action, a tablespace can fill to a point where there is not enough room to allocate another extent. In Chapter 4, we showed you a method for monitoring your table growth and determining whether you have enough space in your tablespace to accommodate every important object extending at the same time. Here, we'll show you how to add a datafile to your tablespace if there is not enough space available in your tablespace to support the extension of the object of interest.

There are several different actions you can take to help avoid this situation:

- Add one or more datafiles to the tablespace.
- Enable a mechanism called autoextend. (We'll discuss the advantages and disadvantages of using autoextend in a later section.)

Under what circumstances would you want to add a datafile to a tablespace? Let's say you have a production database with a table that has grown much faster than had been predicted. The tablespace that houses the table is rapidly running out of space, but it's the middle of a very busy work day and you cannot take the tablespace offline and rebuild it with more space right now. You can add a datafile to the tablespace to enable the table to continue to grow. If you do not take some kind of action before the tablespace reaches a point where it is unable to find any more usable space, the user attempting to perform work in the database who needs the space will not be able to perform that work. Anything that delays work in a database can be costly to a company. In cases where a company relies on electronic commerce—customers being able to buy things from an Internet website—the loss of revenue while a database or table is unavailable for any length of time can run into thousands of dollars.

Adding Space to a Tablespace

To add a datafile to a tablespace, you first must determine where the current datafile(s) for the tablespace are and how much room is available on the disk where you will be placing the new datafile. The script that we used earlier in this chapter to display the tablespace names and datafile locations can be used. To see how much space is available on the disk of interest, for a Unix system, you can use the command:

```
df -k
```

NOTE
*The **df –k** command may report that there is only a small amount of space available within a file system. There may be unallocated space on a disk. You should check with the system administrator or system group to see if there is any unallocated space. You may find that your Unix administrator does not place file systems on all drives; space is sometimes reserved for emergency use. This reserved space will not be shown via a **df** command.*

For a Windows NT system, from the Microsoft Windows NT Explorer, click on the disk of interest, and the amount of used and free space will be displayed at the bottom of the screen. You can also click the right mouse button while the disk is highlighted. Select the Properties option and a graph of the used and available disk space will be displayed.

On an OpenVMS system, you can display the used and free space by using the command:

```
$ show device <device_name>
```

Once you know the amount of available space on the disk, you must decide how big you should make the datafile to add to the tablespace. Using the scripts from Chapter 4, you can determine what size datafile the tablespace will need to support all of the objects expanding to a next extent at the same time. However, how big you can make your datafile may depend more on how much space is available for your use and less on the ideal size to which you would like to be able to expand the tablespace. If you have a tablespace that is filling rapidly, you may want to increase its size by a much larger amount than if your tablespace has been filling very slowly over a long period of time.

Let's say you have a tablespace that currently has 300 megabytes of space allocated to it. Your reports show you that 260 megabytes are currently being used. That leaves you 40 megabytes of free space in which to grow. That sounds like a lot of space, but it may not be. Your disk has over 3 gigabytes of space free. As you spend more time working with your database and applications, you begin to get a feel for what the "right" amount of space to allocate should be. Some of the questions that you will ask both yourself and your developers to determine how much space to add are as follows:

- How much space is available on the disk of interest?
- Is this disk dedicated to your Oracle database or is it shared with other applications and shared for other uses?
- How fast have the objects in the tablespace been expanding?
- Has there recently been a new object added that is growing rapidly?
- How many other tablespaces are located on the same disk?
- Are there tables that can have data either purged or removed to a history table?
- How much more space is needed to accommodate newly added objects?
- Should additional disk space be purchased to accommodate the addition of future objects?

In our scenario, we already have the first answer: 3 gigabytes of space are left. We'll fill in the rest of the answers by saying that the disk is a dedicated Oracle disk with only one other, very slow growing tablespace that has a great deal of growth room. The tablespace of interest has only just recently started to grow rapidly because a new table was added that is a huge data entry table. You have two choices under these circumstances. You can either add a large datafile to the tablespace or move the new table to its own tablespace and size the new tablespace to match the table's growth pattern. Since this section is devoted to enlarging a tablespace, we'll show you the steps to perform this task.

To keep round numbers, we'll arbitrarily choose to add another 400 megabytes of space to the tablespace to support the expansion of the new table. For this example, the tablespace name is USER_DATA, and the directory that the tablespace datafile is in is F:\ora8i\oradata\orcl\. The name of the original datafile is user01.dbf. To make it easier to recognize that the new datafile is associated with the USER_DATA tablespace and the user01.dbf datafile, you will want to name the new datafile user02.dbf. To add the space, all you need to do is submit the following command:

```
alter tablespace USER_DATA
add datafile 'F:\ora8i\oradata\orcl\user02.dbf' size 400M;
```

NOTE
Notice that no storage clause is specified. This is because we are just adding to the tablespace. The storage parameters used at tablespace creation still apply. It would have been possible to specify autoextend parameters to the added datafile.

If, as in this case, the datafile is being added to support a fast-growing table, you will want to monitor the tablespace to gauge how fast the new table is expanding.

Reducing the Size of a Tablespace

Now, let's look at the other side of the tablespace sizing coin—reducing the size of a tablespace. Why in the world would you ever want to "give space back"? Perhaps you initially sized a tablespace very large to accommodate a table for a data warehouse. The table is supposed to be very large. All of the other tables in the tablespace are very static tables and they will remain about the same size from now on. After all of the tables have been loaded, you find that the tablespace is only half full. There is a lot of space in the tablespace that will never be used—space that could be used by another tablespace or other object on the system. What can you do?

As of Oracle version 7.3, you have two choices. You can either use the **resize** command or you can rebuild the tablespace. We'll look at both options and let you decide which one you want to use. (Isn't it nice to have options to choose from and the knowledge to make a choice?)

First, you need to remember that what you are really resizing when you use the **resize** command is the datafile that supports the tablespace. You will, therefore, use a statement to alter the database to change the datafile size. In order for the command to work, the data within the datafile cannot exceed the reduced amount of space in the file. In earlier versions of Oracle, if you issue the **resize** command, Oracle will not verify that there is data in the area to be eliminated, but you will lose whatever data is below the cutoff point in the file and may end up corrupting data as well.

We'll use the USERS tablespace in our example. Let's take a look at the DBA_EXTENTS view joined with the DBA_FREE_SPACE view and see the complete map of the USERS tablespace. The script prompts you for the tablespace name and then retains the name you supply for the rest of the script's run (note the use of && in the first **where** clause and the use of & in the second one). The **undefine** command is used to ensure that there is no tablespace name assigned before you run the script. If you place the **undefine Tablespace_Name** command at the end of the script, the script will assume that the command is actually the input for the tablespace name prompt. If you run this script from a file, you can leave the final **undefine Tablespace_Name** in the script. However, if you cut this script out and paste it in to run it from SQL*Plus, leave the last **undefine Tablespace_Name** command off since Oracle will accept this command as the input for the tablespace name prompt.

```
Set term on echo off verify off pagesize 999
col Segment_Name format a30
col Blksize new_value blksz noprint
col Bytes format 999,999,999,999 heading 'BYTES'
col Blks format 999,999,999,999 heading 'END BLOCK'
select value Blksize
  from V$PARAMETER
 where Name like ('%db_block_size%');

undefine Tablespace_Name
select Segment_Name, File_Id, Block_Id, Block_Id+Blocks-1 BLKS, Blocks*&Blksz Bytes
  from DBA_EXTENTS
 where Tablespace_Name = upper('&&Tablespace_Name')
 union
select '****FREE****', File_Id, Block_Id, Block_Id+Blocks-1 BLKS, Blocks*&Blksz Bytes
  from DBA_FREE_SPACE
 where Tablespace_Name = upper('&Tablespace_Name')
order by 2,3;
undefine Tablespace_Name;
```

The output from the tablespace map is lengthy but worth looking at since you can learn a great deal from it. Here's the output:

```
SEGMENT_NAME                    FILE_ID  BLOCK_ID          END BLOCK       BYTES
------------------------------ --------- --------- ----------------- -----------
AQ$_QUEUE_TABLES                       2         2                 6      10,240
AQ$_QUEUE_TABLES_PRIMARY               2         7                11      10,240
AQ$_QUEUES                             2        12                16      10,240
SYS_LOB0000002430C00012$$              2        17                21      10,240
SYS_IL0000002430C00012$$               2        22                26      10,240
AQ$_QUEUES_PRIMARY                     2        27                31      10,240
AQ$_QUEUES_CHECK                       2        32                36      10,240
AQ$_SCHEDULES                          2        37                41      10,240
AQ$_SCHEDULES_PRIMARY                  2        42                46      10,240
AQ$_SCHEDULES_CHECK                    2        47                51      10,240
DEF$_AQCALL                            2        52                56      10,240
SYS_LOB0000002576C00025$$              2        57                61      10,240
SYS_IL0000002576C00025$$               2        62                66      10,240
SYS_C00740                             2        67                71      10,240
DEF$_AQERROR                           2        72                81      20,480
DEF$_TRANORDER                         2        82                86      10,240
SYS_LOB0000002586C00025$$              2        87                91      10,240
SYS_IL0000002586C00025$$               2        92                96      10,240
SYS_C00743                             2        97               101      10,240
DEF$_ERROR                             2       102               106      10,240
```

```
DEF$_ERROR_PRIMARY                  2      107          111      10,240
DEF$_DESTINATION                    2      112          116      10,240
DEF$_DESTINATION_PRIMARY            2      117          121      10,240
DEF$_CALLDEST                       2      122          126      10,240
DEF$_CALLDEST_PRIMARY               2      127          131      10,240
DEF$_CALLDEST_N2                    2      132          136      10,240
DEF$_DEFAULTDEST                    2      137          141      10,240
DEF$_DEFAULTDEST_PRIMARY            2      142          146      10,240
DEF$_LOB                            2      147          151      10,240
SYS_LOB0000002604C00003$$           2      152          156      10,240
SYS_IL0000002604C00003$$            2      157          161      10,240
SYS_LOB0000002604C00004$$           2      162          166      10,240
SYS_IL0000002604C00004$$            2      167          171      10,240
SYS_LOB0000002604C00005$$           2      172          176      10,240
SYS_IL0000002604C00005$$            2      177          181      10,240
DEF$_LOB_PRIMARY                    2      182          186      10,240
DEF$_LOB_N1                         2      187          191      10,240
DEF$_TEMP$LOB                       2      192          196      10,240
SYS_LOB0000002613C00001$$           2      197          201      10,240
SYS_IL0000002613C00001$$            2      202          206      10,240
SYS_LOB0000002613C00002$$           2      207          211      10,240
SYS_IL0000002613C00002$$            2      212          216      10,240
SYS_LOB0000002613C00003$$           2      217          221      10,240
SYS_IL0000002613C00003$$            2      222          226      10,240
DEF$_PROPAGATOR                     2      227          231      10,240
DEF$_PROPAGATOR_PRIMARY             2      232          236      10,240
DEF$_ORIGIN                         2      237          241      10,240
DEF$_PUSHED_TRANSACTIONS            2      242          246      10,240
DEF$_PUSHED_TRAN_PRIMARY            2      247          251      10,240
DEPT                                2      252          256      10,240
PK_DEPT                             2      257          261      10,240
EMP                                 2      262          266      10,240
PK_EMP                              2      267          271      10,240
BONUS                               2      272          276      10,240
SALGRADE                            2      277          281      10,240
ACCOUNT                             2      282          286      10,240
RECEIPT                             2      287          291      10,240
SQLPLUS_PRODUCT_PROFILE             2      292          296      10,240
REPCAT$_REPCAT                      2      297          301      10,240
REPCAT$_REPCAT_PRIMARY              2      302          306      10,240
REPCAT$_FLAVORS                     2      307          311      10,240
REPCAT$_FLAVORS_UNQ1                2      312          316      10,240
REPCAT$_FLAVORS_GNAME               2      317          321      10,240
REPCAT$_FLAVORS_FNAME               2      322          326      10,240
REPCAT$_REPSCHEMA                   2      327          331      10,240
REPCAT$_REPSCHEMA_PRIMARY           2      332          336      10,240
REPCAT$_SNAPGROUP                   2      337          341      10,240
I_REPCAT$_SNAPGROUP1                2      342          346      10,240
REPCAT$_REPOBJECT                   2      347          351      10,240
REPCAT$_REPOBJECT_PRIMARY           2      352          356      10,240
REPCAT$_REPOBJECT_GNAME             2      357          361      10,240
REPCAT$_REPCOLUMN                   2      362          366      10,240
REPCAT$_REPCOLUMN_PK                2      367          371      10,240
REPCAT$_REPCOLUMN_UK                2      372          376      10,240
REPCAT$_KEY_COLUMNS                 2      377          381      10,240
REPCAT$_KEY_COLUMNS_PRIMARY         2      382          386      10,240
REPCAT$_GENERATED                   2      387          391      10,240
REPCAT$_REPGEN_PRIMARY              2      392          396      10,240
```

```
REPCAT$_GENERATED_N1                2        397             401       10,240
REPCAT$_REPPROP                     2        402             406       10,240
REPCAT$_REPPROP_PRIMARY             2        407             411       10,240
REPCAT$_REPPROP_DBLINK_HOW          2        412             416       10,240
REPCAT$_REPPROP_KEY_INDEX           2        417             421       10,240
REPCAT$_REPCATLOG                   2        422             426       10,240
REPCAT$_REPCATLOG_PRIMARY           2        427             431       10,240
REPCAT$_REPCATLOG_GNAME             2        432             436       10,240
REPCAT$_DDL                         2        437             441       10,240
REPCAT$_DDL                         2        442             446       10,240
REPCAT$_REPGROUP_PRIVS              2        447             451       10,240
REPCAT$_REPGROUP_PRIVS_UK           2        452             456       10,240
REPCAT$_REPGROUP_PRIVS_N1           2        457             461       10,240
REPCAT$_PRIORITY_GROUP              2        462             466       10,240
REPCAT$_PRIORITY_GROUP_PK           2        467             471       10,240
REPCAT$_PRIORITY_GROUP_U1           2        472             476       10,240
REPCAT$_PRIORITY                    2        477             481       10,240
REPCAT$_PRIORITY_PK                 2        482             486       10,240
REPCAT$_COLUMN_GROUP                2        487             491       10,240
REPCAT$_COLUMN_GROUP_PK             2        492             496       10,240
REPCAT$_GROUPED_COLUMN              2        497             501       10,240
REPCAT$_GROUPED_COLUMN_PK           2        502             506       10,240
REPCAT$_CONFLICT                    2        507             511       10,240
REPCAT$_CONFLICT_PK                 2        512             516       10,240
REPCAT$_RESOLUTION_METHOD           2        517             521       10,240
REPCAT$_RESOL_METHOD_PK             2        522             526       10,240
REPCAT$_RESOLUTION                  2        527             531       10,240
REPCAT$_RESOLUTION_PK               2        532             536       10,240
REPCAT$_RESOLUTION_STATISTICS       2        537             541       10,240
REPCAT$_RESOLUTION_STATS_N1         2        542             546       10,240
REPCAT$_RESOL_STATS_CONTROL         2        547             551       10,240
REPCAT$_RESOL_STATS_CTRL_PK         2        552             556       10,240
REPCAT$_PARAMETER_COLUMN            2        557             561       10,240
REPCAT$_PARAMETER_COLUMN_PK         2        562             566       10,240
REPCAT$_AUDIT_ATTRIBUTE             2        567             571       10,240
REPCAT$_AUDIT_ATTRIBUTE_PK          2        572             576       10,240
REPCAT$_AUDIT_COLUMN                2        577             581       10,240
REPCAT$_AUDIT_COLUMN_PK             2        582             586       10,240
REPCAT$_FLAVOR_OBJECTS              2        587             591       10,240
REPCAT$_FLAVOR_OBJECTS_PK           2        592             596       10,240
REPCAT$_FLAVOR_OBJECTS_FG           2        597             601       10,240
REPCAT$_REFRESH_TEMPLATES           2        602             606       10,240
REPCAT$_REFRESH_TEMPLATES_PK        2        607             611       10,240
REPCAT$_REFRESH_TEMPLATES_U1        2        612             616       10,240
REPCAT$_USER_AUTHORIZATIONS         2        617             621       10,240
REPCAT$_USER_AUTHORIZATIONS_PK      2        622             626       10,240
REPCAT$_USER_AUTHORIZATIONS_U1      2        627             631       10,240
REPCAT$_TEMPLATE_OBJECTS            2        632             636       10,240
SYS_LOB0000011791C00005$$           2        637             641       10,240
SYS_IL0000011791C00005$$            2        642             646       10,240
REPCAT$_TEMPLATE_OBJECTS_PK         2        647             651       10,240
REPCAT$_TEMPLATE_OBJECTS_U1         2        652             656       10,240
REPCAT$_TEMPLATE_OBJECTS_N1         2        657             661       10,240
REPCAT$_TEMPLATE_PARMS              2        662             666       10,240
SYS_LOB0000011804C00004$$           2        667             671       10,240
SYS_IL0000011804C00004$$            2        672             676       10,240
REPCAT$_TEMPLATE_PARMS_PK           2        677             681       10,240
```

```
REPCAT$_TEMPLATE_PARMS_U1         2        682              686       10,240
REPCAT$_OBJECT_PARMS              2        687              691       10,240
REPCAT$_OBJECT_PARMS_PK           2        692              696       10,240
REPCAT$_USER_PARM_VALUES          2        697              701       10,240
SYS_LOB0000011818C00004$$         2        702              706       10,240
SYS_IL0000011818C00004$$          2        707              711       10,240
REPCAT$_USER_PARM_VALUES_PK       2        712              716       10,240
REPCAT$_USER_PARM_VALUES_U1       2        717              721       10,240
REPCAT$_TEMPLATE_SITES            2        722              726       10,240
REPCAT$_TEMPLATE_SITES_PK         2        727              731       10,240
REPCAT$_TEMPLATE_SITES_U1         2        732              736       10,240
REPCAT$_RUNTIME_PARMS             2        737              741       10,240
SYS_LOB0000011841C00003$$         2        742              746       10,240
SYS_IL0000011841C00003$$          2        747              751       10,240
REPCAT$_RUNTIME_PARMS_PK          2        752              756       10,240
****FREE****                      2        757            1,536    1,597,440

151 rows selected.
```

Now, let's look at the output. You can see every object that exists in the USERS tablespace. Most of the objects have been allocated five blocks. You can figure the block allocation by subtracting the current Block_Id value from the previous Block_Id value. The Bytes column also shows the allocation by bytes, but if you divide the bytes by your database block size, you will see that the value is just the blocks times the database block size.

The amount of free space left at the end of the datafile is almost 1.6 megabytes. For this example, let's say that the objects in this tablespace are not going to grow at all and that you really need to recover some of the extra space for another object. The only other piece of information you need is the total size that was allocated for the tablespace. You can find that information easily by querying the DBA_DATA_FILES view as follows:

```
select Tablespace_Name, Bytes
  from DBA_DATA_FILES
 where Tablespace_Name = 'USERS';

TABLESPACE_NAME                    BYTES
------------------------------ ---------
USERS                            3145728
```

As you can see, the allocated size for the datafile is 3 megabytes. If you have more than one datafile, only the last datafile can be reduced in size, so you want to look at the size for that datafile. For this example, you'll reduce the size of the datafile for the USERS tablespace by 1 megabyte. The parameters that Oracle expects are the datafile name and the size you want the datafile to be after the resize. Therefore, if you have a 3-megabyte datafile that you want to reduce by 1 megabyte, the value that you will supply for the resize option will be 2 megabytes—the size you want the file to be after the command is executed. If there is data beyond the limit that you specify, Oracle will return an error. The command to reduce the size of the tablespace is as follows:

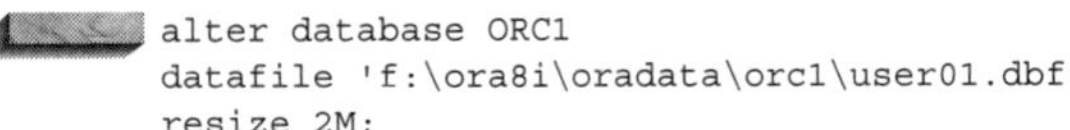

```
alter database ORC1
datafile 'f:\ora8i\oradata\orc1\user01.dbf'
resize 2M;
```

A Neat Tablespace Status Script

There are times when you want to see the general status of all of your tablespaces:

- How much space was allocated
- How much space (generally) has been used
- How much space is remaining
- The smallest and largest available, contiguous amount of space in each tablespace
- The number of extents in each tablespace that have been allocated

Here's a really neat script to show you this information:

```
set pagesize 70
set feedback off
set numwidth 12
compute sum of Bytes on report
compute sum of Bytes on Tablespace_Name
break on Tablespace_Name skip 2
column One noprint
column Two heading 'Space type' format a20
column Bytes format 9,999,999,990
column Tablespace_Name format a18
set termout off
set echo off
set head on
spool ts_space.txt
select 1 One,
       Tablespace_Name, 'Max available: ' Two, sum(Bytes) Bytes
  from
       DBA_DATA_FILES
 group by
       Tablespace_Name
 union
select 2 Two,
       Tablespace_Name, 'Allocated: ',
       nvl(((sum(Bytes) + decode(Tablespace_Name, 'SYSTEM',2048,1024)) * -1),0)
  from
       DBA_EXTENTS
 group by
       Tablespace_Name
 order by
```

```
       2, 1;
clear computes
clear breaks
column Tb heading 'Frag' format 9,990
column Sm heading 'Small' format 9,999,999,990
column Lg heading 'Large' format 9,999,999,990
rem
select
       Tablespace_Name, sum(Bytes) Bytes, count(Blocks) Tb, min(Bytes) Sm,
       max(Bytes) Lg
  from
       DBA_FREE_SPACE
 group by
       Tablespace_Name;
spool off
```

The output from this script, found in the ts_space.txt file, follows:

```
TABLESPACE_NAME    Space type                    BYTES
------------------ -------------------- --------------
INDX               Max available:            2,097,152
******************                      --------------
sum                                          2,097,152

OEM_REPOSITORY     Max available:            5,242,880
                   Allocated:               -1,895,424
******************                      --------------
sum                                          3,347,456

RBS                Max available:           41,943,040
                   Allocated:              -12,442,624
******************                      --------------
sum                                         29,500,416

SYSTEM             Max available:          146,800,640
                   Allocated:             -142,141,440
******************                      --------------
sum                                          4,659,200

TEMP               Max available:            2,097,152
******************                      --------------
sum                                          2,097,152

USERS              Max available:            3,145,728
                   Allocated:               -1,547,264
******************                      --------------
sum                                          1,598,464

TABLESPACE_NAME             BYTES   Frag          Small          Large
------------------ -------------- ------ -------------- --------------
INDX                    2,095,104      1      2,095,104      2,095,104
OEM_REPOSITORY          3,346,432      1      3,346,432      3,346,432
RBS                    29,499,392     30        256,000      4,923,392
SYSTEM                  4,659,200     13         30,720      3,706,880
TEMP                    2,095,104      1      2,095,104      2,095,104
USERS                   1,597,440      1      1,597,440      1,597,440
```

The first portion of the output shows the amount of allocated space in each tablespace in the database, the amount of used space, and the amount of space remaining. The second portion of the output shows the amount of available space, the number of allocated extents, the smallest amount (or chunk) of contiguous space, and the largest amount (or chunk) of contiguous space left in that tablespace. If you ever have a tablespace fail to extend when you know there is still more than enough space left in the tablespace, run this set of scripts to verify that the largest available chunk of space is large enough to handle the next extent size for the tablespace. Chances are, you will find that, although there is enough "space" in the tablespace, there is not enough contiguous space to support the next extent size.

Enabling Autoextend for a Tablespace

At the beginning of this chapter in the "Creating a Tablespace" section, we showed the parameters for the autoextend option. When we talked about resizing a tablespace later in this chapter, we again mentioned this option. We said then that we would talk more about this parameter later. Well, "later" has finally arrived!

What Autoextend Is

Before we look at how to enable or disable this feature, let's talk a bit about what the feature actually does. When you enable autoextend, you are telling Oracle that you want the datafile to be able to allocate more space if it is running too low on space to be able to allocate a next extent for an object. Gee, that sounds wonderful, doesn't it? You can enable autoextend on a tablespace and never have to worry about the tablespace being unable to create a next extent. In theory, this feature really *is* wonderful. However, there is a potential problem associated with letting a tablespace's datafile grow unbounded. A problem that you can encounter deals with the actual space available on the disk. Let's say autoextend is enabled with no upper limit placed on the amount of space that the tablespace can consume. There is a very real probability that, eventually, the tablespace or combination of tablespaces on a disk will "devour" all of the available space—just as that lion we saw at the zoo would probably, eventually, devour the antelope. As a proactive DBA, you want to monitor and have control over the growth of tablespaces on your system. The last thing you want is to have a process or multiple processes fail because a disk runs completely out of space.

Now, let's look at a situation where autoextend can be used to your advantage. One of the authors was supporting a data warehouse conversion effort. The original database was located in an Oracle Rdb database. The database was being converted to Oracle Enterprise Server. There was no real way to predict how much more or less space would be taken in the new database as the conversion and data-loading processes were performed. The solution that was chosen by management was to enable autoextend for the tablespaces in which the data was being loaded. This solution worked very well for a while. Unfortunately, the **pctincrease** parameter was initially set to the Oracle default value (50%), and all the tablespaces overextended at about the same time. The application came to a screeching halt when the disk supporting the tablespaces ran out of space. The solution—to move some of the tablespace datafiles to another, larger disk—took quite a while to perform because the files had become so large that the process of copying the files from one disk to another was very time consuming. Even though this particular application ran into problems using the feature, there are times when autoextend may be a viable solution.

To see if autoextend has been enabled for a tablespace datafile, you can look in the DBA_DATA_FILES view in Oracle8 and 8i. In earlier versions (7.3), you will need to look in the FILEXT$ view.

Autoextend Parameters

The **autoextend** clause can be specified for a datafile either when you issue the command **create tablespace** or by using the **alter database datafile...** command. As shown earlier in Table 5-1, the parameters for the **autoextend** clause are **off** or **on**, with additional parameters for the **on** option. The parameter **on** enables autoextending, while the parameter **off** disables the automatic extension of a datafile. By default, if you do not specify this clause, **autoextend** is set to **off**. If you use either **create tablespace... autoextend off** or **alter database datafile... autoextend off**, you disable **autoextend** if it is turned on. When **off** is specified, the parameters **next** and **maxsize** are automatically set to zero. When you use either **create tablespace... autoextend on** or **alter database datafile... autoextend on**, values for **next** and **maxsize** must be specified. The **next** parameter specifies, in bytes, the size of the next increment of disk space to be automatically allocated to the datafile when more extents are required. You can use **K** for kilobytes or **M** for megabytes to specify the size. The default is one data block, which is pretty small. If you let the size for the next extent default to one database block, you could run out of extents really quickly, especially if the block size is the default (2K) and **maxextents** is set to 121 (the default for a 2K database block size). The parameter **maxsize** is used to define how large the datafile can grow, that is, how much total disk space the datafile can use. You have the choice of specifying a number or the parameter **unlimited**. In a case like the data warehouse conversion described earlier, when you do not know how large the datafile needs to grow, the **unlimited** parameter can be used. We do recommend caution if you use the autoextend feature at all. Our recommendation is not to use this feature unless you have a really good business reason to do so.

Another danger of using autoextend is that the datafile might try to grow beyond the size of a file supported by the OS. For example, Solaris 2.5.1 can only support a file up to 2GB in size.

If you are working on a Unix system, you need to remember that most Unix systems define a maximum file size in the userid definition. Autoextend can fail because the "max file size" associated with the oracle userid was not set to the maximum allowed. The "max file size" is usually detected when creating the database for the first time.

Temporary vs. Permanent Tablespaces

Within Oracle, as of version 7.3, you can define a tablespace as either temporary or permanent. By default, all tablespaces are created as permanent. A tablespace that is defined as temporary can be used only for sort operations. Objects such as tables and indexes cannot be stored in a tablespace that has been defined as temporary.

When you create a user in your database, you designate a default tablespace where the user's objects will be stored if he or she does not specify a tablespace name in the create statement. You also designate a temporary tablespace that will be used for the user's sort operations. Even if you do not define a tablespace as temporary, any tablespace that is identified as a user's temporary tablespace should never be used to store any objects. If you have an application in which a great many sorts are being performed, you might consider creating a separate tablespace for that application and modifying the application schema to point to that tablespace for sort operations. You will gain performance benefits from placing the tablespace on a different controller and defining the tablespace as temporary.

All operations that use sorts, such as joins, index builds, ordering (**order by**), computations of aggregates (**group by**), and the **analyze** command, will benefit by using tablespaces designated as temporary. Oracle processes its management operations differently against these tablespaces than it does against the ones that are permanent. Research has shown that the following two statements are true:

1. If a tablespace is created with the type temporary, Oracle will not allow creation of permanent objects such as tables, indexes, and so on, in the tablespace. Oracle will return an error if any attempt is made to create any objects. This ensures that such tablespaces are used only for their real purpose as temporary tablespaces.

2. If you try to alter a tablespace that is of type permanent to type temporary, and the tablespace already contains any permanent objects such as tables, indexes, and so on, then the create statement will return an error. Only when you clean up the tablespace either by dropping or moving the objects, will Oracle allow you to change the type to permanent.

As a DBA, you will often be asked to investigate problems and verify that technical statements made in a meeting or elsewhere are correct. Let's see if you can prove the two statements listed above. We'll walk you through an approach that you can apply to many different situations that require investigation. At the end of the investigation, we'll summarize the steps taken to prove the two statements. In a real investigation, you should have a pad of paper and a pen next to you at all times, and as you take each action, you write down exactly what you did. In this way, you will have a complete set of documentation at the completion of your investigation.

Do the Groundwork

The first thing you'll need to do is verify your current environment so you will know the parameters with which you are starting. You want to see some of the current values for your tablespaces and the Contents column status. To do this, you'll use the DBA_TABLESPACES view. To get all of the output to fit, with each row taking up no more than one line, you'll need to do some column formatting. Generally, you can either do the math to calculate how large each column needs to be to fit on one line or you can experiment with setting different format sizes until you get the output to fit and still be meaningful. For this example, we experimented until the output looked nice and fit correctly for the amount of space we have here. Obviously, the format we show will not be big enough for a column with a maximum size set to unlimited.

```
describe DBA_TABLESPACES
 Name                                                  Null?    Type
 ----------------------------------------------------- -------- -------------
 TABLESPACE_NAME                                       NOT NULL VARCHAR2(30)
 INITIAL_EXTENT                                                 NUMBER
 NEXT_EXTENT                                                    NUMBER
 MIN_EXTENTS                                           NOT NULL NUMBER
 MAX_EXTENTS                                           NOT NULL NUMBER
 PCT_INCREASE                                          NOT NULL NUMBER
 MIN_EXTLEN                                                     NUMBER
 STATUS                                                         VARCHAR2(9)
 CONTENTS                                                       VARCHAR2(9)
 LOGGING                                                        VARCHAR2(9)

set pagesize 999
column Tablespace_Name format a15 heading 'Tablespace Name'
column Initial_Extent format 999999 heading 'Initial'
column Next_Extent format 9999999 heading 'Next'
column Min_Extents format 9999 heading 'MinX'
column Max_Extents format 9999 heading 'MaxX'
column Min_Extlen format 9999 heading 'MinL'
column Pct_Increase format 999 heading 'Pct'
column Status format a6 heading 'Status'
```

```
column Contents format a9 heading 'Contents'
column Logging format a7 heading 'Logging'
select *
  from DBA_TABLESPACES;

Tablespace Name Initial      Next  MinX  MaxX  Pct  MinL Status Contents  Logging
--------------- ------- -------- ----- ----- ---- ----- ------ --------- -------
SYSTEM           10,240   10,240     1   121   50     0 ONLINE PERMANENT LOGGING
USERS            10,240   10,240     1   121   50     0 ONLINE PERMANENT LOGGING
RBS              10,240   10,240     1   121   50     0 ONLINE PERMANENT LOGGING
TEMP             10,240   10,240     1   121   50     0 ONLINE PERMANENT LOGGING
```

Hey, wait a minute! There's something different here. The description of the DBA_TABLESPACES view and the contents are very different from the description and contents that were displayed at the beginning of the chapter in the "Placing Objects in Tablespaces" section. What's going on here?

This is a graphic example of the way the Oracle data dictionary can change from version to version. The descriptions and contents of the DBA_TABLESPACES view shown at the beginning of this chapter were produced from an Oracle8i database, while the example shown here is from an Oracle8.0.5 database. There are three fewer parameters in this version than in the 8i version, and the number of tablespaces is very different. You must always be careful to determine which database you are in before you begin any work. It is easy to believe that you are in one database on one machine when you are really in a different database on the same or a different machine. Okay, that's enough preaching. Back to our exercise.

Looking at the tablespace listing, you can see that all of the tablespace's Contents values are set to permanent—even the TEMP tablespace, which we already know is being used for temporary sorts.

Alter the Tablespace to Type Temporary

Go ahead and alter the TEMP tablespace to be of type temporary.

```
alter tablespace TEMP temporary;
Tablespace altered.
```

You'll want to do a check to make sure the tablespace is now marked as temporary.

```
select *
  from DBA_TABLESPACES;

Tablespace Name Initial      Next  MinX  MaxX  Pct  MinL Status Contents  Logging
--------------- ------- -------- ----- ----- ---- ----- ------ --------- -------
SYSTEM           10,240   10,240     1   121   50     0 ONLINE PERMANENT LOGGING
USERS            10,240   10,240     1   121   50     0 ONLINE PERMANENT LOGGING
RBS              10,240   10,240     1   121   50     0 ONLINE PERMANENT LOGGING
TEMP             10,240   10,240     1   121   50     0 ONLINE TEMPORARY LOGGING
```

You can see that the command worked. The TEMP tablespace is now marked as type temporary. Gee, isn't this fun? Since you were able to change the tablespace type, you can assume there were no objects stored in the TEMP tablespace, but go ahead and verify that this is the case by selecting from the DBA_SEGMENTS view. Since you feel pretty confident that there are no objects in the tablespace, you don't really need to do much more than select one column from the view.

```
select Segment_Name
  from DBA_SEGMENTS
 where Tablespace_Name = 'TEMP';
no rows selected
```

So far, so good! But you haven't yet proved either of the two statements you set out to prove. However, you've set the stage to begin the proof. You know the environment and the exact condition of the TEMP tablespace.

Prove Statement Number 1

The first statement says you cannot create objects in a tablespace that is marked as type temporary. You have a tablespace that fits the description, so you will now try to create an object in that tablespace.

```
create table TESTTEMP
tablespace TEMP
as select *
     from MYSCHEMA.DEPARTMENT;
                    *
ERROR at line 3:
ORA-02195: Attempt to create PERMANENT object in a TEMPORARY tablespace
```

Oracle returns a clear error indicating that you cannot create permanent objects in a tablespace that was declared as type temporary. Cool! You've proven statement number 1 with very little effort. You just used a logical and thorough approach.

Prove Statement Number 2

Statement 2 says you can't change a tablespace to type temporary if any objects exist in the tablespace. To prove this statement, you'll want to take a tablespace whose type is permanent, create an object in it, and then try to modify the tablespace type. Let's stick with using the TEMP tablespace because you already know the state and contents (or lack of contents) in this tablespace.

To begin the proof for statement 2, change the tablespace type back to permanent:

```
alter tablespace TEMP permanent;
Tablespace altered.
```

Verify that the tablespace is now of type permanent:

```
select *
  from DBA_TABLESPACES;

Tablespace Name  Initial      Next  MinX  MaxX  Pct  MinL Status Contents  Logging
--------------- -------  -------- ----- ----- ---- ----- ------ --------- -------
SYSTEM            10,240   10,240     1   121   50     0 ONLINE PERMANENT LOGGING
USERS             10,240   10,240     1   121   50     0 ONLINE PERMANENT LOGGING
RBS               10,240   10,240     1   121   50     0 ONLINE PERMANENT LOGGING
TEMP              10,240   10,240     1   121   50     0 ONLINE PERMANENT LOGGING
```

You will now create an object in the tablespace. You should have no problem doing this since there is no restriction on creating objects in permanent tablespaces as long as you have the privileges and quota necessary to do so.

```
create table TESTTEMP tablespace TEMP
as select *
     from MY_SCHEMA.DEPARTMENT;
Table created.
```

As expected, no problem. Okay, to recap where you are. You have a tablespace with a type permanent and one object created—a table named TESTTEMP. You will want to verify that the table exists in the tablespace, so the select statement can be very simple. You'll just verify the names of any tables that have a tablespace named TEMP.

```
select Owner, Table_Name, Tablespace_Name
  from DBA_TABLES
 where tablespace_name = 'TEMP';

OWNER          TABLE_NAME  TABLESPACE_NAME
-------------- ----------- ---------------
SYSTEM         TESTTEMP    TEMP
```

Okay, the table's there. Statement 2 says you cannot alter a tablespace to type temporary if any objects exist in the tablespace. The next step will prove or disprove this statement.

```
alter tablespace TEMP temporary;
alter tablespace TEMP temporary
*
ERROR at line 1:
ORA-01662: tablespace 'TEMP' is non-empty and cannot be made temporary
```

This proves you cannot alter a tablespace to type temporary if any objects exist in the tablespace. To be completely thorough, you could go ahead and drop the table and then alter the tablespace to type temporary, but you did that at the beginning of your investigation so it would be redundant to do it again. Good job!

The Steps You Took

As promised when you began the proof of the statements, here is a step-by-step list of the actions and rules that you followed:

1. Lay the groundwork by verifying your current environment as a starting point for your investigation.
2. Make one change at a time and verify the results of each change.
3. Once your environment is established, begin proving one piece at a time. Don't give up too easily. Don't be afraid to try several different approaches to prove or disprove the statement.
4. Keep track of the steps you have taken by documenting as you go along to ensure that you have not missed something.
5. As you go through your proof, keep your environment consistent by using the same tablespace (or objects) for the entire set of proofs so that you know at every step your environmental status.

Transportable Tablespaces

Here's an interesting question for you to ponder: is there ever a situation in which you will want to move a tablespace or subset of tablespaces from one database to another? The wise DBA will, of course, answer, "Yes." If you're not feeling particularly wise today, that's okay, because we'll explain some of the situations in which you might want to perform this task.

Rationales for Moving a Subset of a Database

One situation that you might already have thought about is when you want to move a subset of the database from your production environment back to a development or test/quality assurance area. In the case of a test/QA database, you start out with an exact replica of your production system. Some application code testing has been done, and a subset of the database has been damaged or radically changed by the test. You have very limited time to return the database to its prior configuration. A database rebuild is too time consuming, and you are absolutely sure that the subset of tablespaces from production can be moved to the test database without leaving the test database in a questionable state.

Another situation in which you might want to move one tablespace or a subset of tablespaces is if you have multiple development activities taking place at the same time and each one requires a separate, but identical, environment. You could create several separate schemas in several databases and populate them all by moving the same tablespace from one schema to another.

A third scenario would be one in which you want to remove a tablespace from one database entirely and place it in another database. For this situation, you might have an application that was originally placed with one or more other applications in a database. This new application is not "getting along well" with the other applications. Perhaps the new application is growing much more rapidly than expected or the availability requirements for the new application have changed and it must either remain up for longer periods of time or be shut down intermittently. The new requirements might dictate that this application be moved to a separate, isolated database.

Possible Approaches

If you want to move part of a database to another database, how are you going to do it? Think for a moment about the possible problems involved and the amount of work you might have to perform to accomplish this task. There could be more than one schema in a given tablespace, so you can't export a specific user schema and import it to move the tablespace. It would be cumbersome and time consuming to rebuild the entire database just to move one tablespace. Well, before you give yourself a brain cramp thinking about the problems involved, we'll tell you that, as of version 8i, Oracle supplies a facility to make this job fairly easy.

Let's talk a little bit first about the phrase *point-in-time recovery*. The phrase implies that the database cannot be recovered up to the point at which it failed. The only means of ensuring that the database is in a consistent state is to recover to a point in time before the failure. Point-in-time recovery will usually involve some data loss. Based on the concepts used in the tablespace point-in-time recovery option that became available in version 8.0, the transportable tablespace feature enables you to move a subset of an Oracle database from one database to another. You can clone (make an exact copy of) a tablespace and "plug it into" another database, or you can "unplug" a tablespace from one database and relocate the tablespace or database subset to another database.

In the first situation mentioned earlier, you did not have much time to clone the tablespace(s) from the production database back to the test/QA database. Moving data using the transportable tablespace facility can be substantially faster than exporting and importing or unloading and reloading the data. Why is this approach so much faster? When you export and import data, you must first drop and rebuild the tablespace(s) involved. The rebuild and export-import processes can be very time consuming. Moving the indexes associated with the tables in the tablespace(s) can also take time. By using the transportable tablespace feature, you need only copy the datafiles that are associated with the tablespace(s) and move the tablespace metadata. The indexes can be moved as well, saving the rebuild time that you would normally have to use after importing or data loading.

In version 8.1.5, there are some rules that you must follow to use the transportable tablespace feature:

- The databases must have the same data block size.
- The databases must have the same character set.
- The databases must be on compatible platforms from the same hardware vendor.
- A tablespace cannot be transported to a target database in which a tablespace with the same name already exists.

In version 8.1.5, transportable tablespaces do not support

- Snapshot/replication
- Function-based indexes
- Scoped REFs
- Domain indexes (a new type of index provided by extensible indexing)
- 8.0-compatible advanced queues with multiple recipients

How Transportable Tablespaces Work

The whole idea behind transportable tablespaces is to quickly move the tablespace datafiles and the tablespace metadata from one database to another. In order to copy or move a tablespace, you must first declare the tablespace as read-only and then export the tablespace metadata. You import the metadata to the target database and copy the tablespace's datafile(s) over to the new location.

Oracle provides some parameters that you can use to perform the tablespace metadata operations. In the Export utility, the parameters **transport_tablespace** and **tablespaces** are used; the first designates that the transportable tablespace facility is to be used, and the second provides a list of one or more tablespaces to be moved. You must first set the tablespace(s) to read-only:

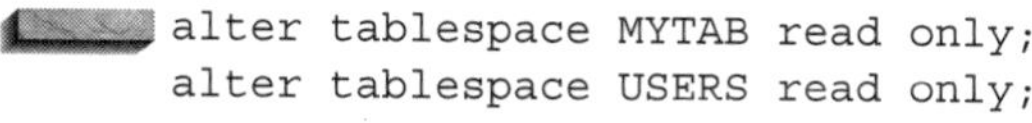

```
alter tablespace MYTAB read only;
alter tablespace USERS read only;
```

Next, you perform an export of the tablespace metadata by using the following parameters for the export:

```
transport_tablespace=y
tablespaces=(MYTAB,USERS)
```

In this example, the **transport_tablespace** parameter is set from its default of "n" to "y" to indicate that the tablespace metadata is to be exported. The **tablespaces** parameter indicates that the metadata for the tablespaces MYTAB and USERS is to be captured.

Once the tablespaces' datafile(s) are copied to their new location, the Import utility is run to move the tablespace metadata into the new database. The parameters that you use to move the tablespace metadata into the new databases match the Export utility parameters with the following additional parameters:

- The **datafiles** parameter to tell Oracle the names and locations of the datafiles for the tablespaces
- The **tts_owners** parameter to tell Oracle the names of the users/schemas that own the data

The Import utility parameters could look like the following:

```
transport_tablespace=y
tablespaces=(MYTAB,USERS)
datafiles=(d:\ora8i\oradata\newdb\mytab01.dbf,d:\ora8i\oradata\newdb\users01.dbf)
tts_owners=(MYAPP,USER01)
```

In this example, the parameters tell the Import utility that the locations for the tablespaces specified will be in the NEWDB directory and that the owners of the schema areas are to be MYAPP and USER01.

Documenting Your Database

If a disaster were to occur today, would you know where every one of your files in each of your databases was? Could you be sure that the list of files you have today will be current and valid next week? Here is a script that you can run from a nightly batch or cron job that will produce a report of the location of all your database files. You can set it up to run for each of your databases. We recommend that you set up the job and have it print the results to a printer so you will have a hard-copy document of your file locations on a daily basis to use for disaster recovery and database documentation.

```
set pages 999
col File_Name format a45
col Tablespace_Name format a20
col Bytes format 9999999999
col Blocks format 9999999999
col Member format a38
col Group# format 99999
set head off feedback off termout off
col Name format a10
```

```
column Dbname new_value xdb noprint
column Today new_value tdy noprint
select substr(Sysdate,1,9) Today
  from DUAL
/
select Value Dbname
  from V$PARAMETER
 where Name = 'db_name'
;
spool &tdy..&xdb
select 'Datafile Information for '||Name||' - '||Sysdate
  from V$DATABASE, DUAL;
prompt
prompt
set head on feedback on termout on
select *
  from V$DATABASE;
prompt
prompt
select a.Group#, a.Member, b.Bytes
  from V$LOGFILE a, V$LOG b
 where a.Group# = b.Group#;
prompt
prompt
col Value heading 'CONTROL FILE INFO'
select Value
  from V$PARAMETER
 where Name like '%control%';
prompt
prompt
select Tablespace_Name, File_Name, Bytes
  from DBA_DATA_FILES
 order by 2,1;
spool off
exit
```

This script creates a file with a name in the form of DD-MON-YY.<database_name>, such as 10-OCT-98.MYDB, and produces a report like the following:

```
Datafile Information for MYDB - 09-OCT-98
NAME       CREATED            LOG_MODE     CHECKPOINT_CHANGE# ARCHIVE_CHANGE#
---------- -----------------  ------------ ------------------ ---------------
MYDB       11/21/97 08:22:17  NOARCHIVELOG              14274           14144
1 row selected.
GROUP# MEMBER                                         BYTES
------ -------------------------------------- -----------
     1 MYDISK01:[ORACLE.MYDB]ORA_LOG1.RDO         3145728
     2 MYDISK01:[ORACLE.MYDB]ORA_LOG2.RDO         3145728
     3 MYDISK01:[ORACLE.MYDB]ORA_LOG3.RDO         3145728
3 rows selected.
CONTROL FILE INFO
-----------------------------------------
MYDISK38:[ORACLE.MYDB]ORA_CONTROL1.CON, MYDISK39:[ORACLE.MYDB]ORA_CONTROL2.CON,
MYDISK40:[ORACLE.MYDB]ORA_CONTROL3.CON
1 row selected.
```

```
TABLESPACE_NAME      FILE_NAME                                      BYTES
-------------------- ---------------------------------------- -----------
MY_TS                MYDISK41:[ORACLE.MYDB]MY_TS01.DBF           10485760
SYSTEM               MYDISK01:[ORACLE.MYDB]ORA_SYSTEM.DBF       629145600
RBS                  MYDISK702:[ORACLE.MYDB]RBS01.DBF           314572800
TEMP                 MYDISK703:[ORACLE.MYDB]TEMP01.DBF          314572800
TOOLS                MYDISK704:[ORACLE.MYDB]TOOLS01.DBF         157286400
USERS                MYDISK704:[ORACLE.MYDB]USERS01.DBF         157286400
6 rows selected.
```

You will also want to include the location of archive logs (if archive logging is used) and the location of the init.ora parameter file. As we mentioned in Chapter 4, the alert log will include any nondefault init.ora settings that were enabled at database startup. You will want to capture them as well.

Creating Objects in a Database

At the beginning of this chapter, you saw the parameters that you can use when you create a tablespace. In this section, you will see the parameters that you use the most for the objects you will be called upon most often to create—tables, indexes, views, roles, synonyms, and users.

Creating Tables

There are two schools of thought about the duties of a DBA when it comes to dealing with the creation of objects. One school of thought goes by these general principles:

- The developers create all of the objects as they are needed for the new application.
- The DBA creates all public synonyms, as required, for the new application.
- The DBA gives the developer privileges on the development system only as each privilege is required.
- For production, the DBA creates the new database and the required schemas for the new application.
- For production, the developers create all of the objects for the new application and populate the new database.
- Optionally, for production, the new database is created by the DBA and populated by an export from the development database.

The other school of thought goes by these principles:

- The DBA is handed the object creation requirements for each object during the development phase of the project.
- The DBA creates scripts for each object's creation.
- The DBA runs the scripts to create all of the objects in both the development and production environments.
- The DBA controls the creation of all objects, roles, and grants, and assists with all data loading.

In the second scenario, the DBA has much more control of the development and production environments, as well as much more work and responsibility for object sizing and creation. Both schools of thought are valid for different company cultures. Since you may end up working in a company whose approach to application development requires you to be deeply involved in object creation, we are going to show you the parameters available and explain how each works for the objects that you will most likely be called upon to create.

Let's start with tables since every form of data is stored in one kind of table or another and there are several different kinds of tables to deal with. The list of table types for Oracle 8i consists of the following:

- **Relational table** The basic, most common table in a database, which can now be global and/or temporary as well as permanent
- **Partitioned tables** Used to spread a large table over a set of smaller tables for ease of maintainability and more efficient data retrieval
- **Advanced Queue tables** Used to integrate a message-queuing system within the database
- **Index-Organized tables (also called Index-Only)** Used to store index columns as a table to aid in faster data retrieval
- **Nested tables** Used to store multiple columns of data within one column of a table
- **Object tables** Used to enable the creation of object types that more closely represent their composition in the real world

Since this is a basic book, we are going to concentrate on the basic table creation parameters.

Relational Table Creation Parameters

In Chapter 2, we talked about creating a simple table, but we really didn't show you all of the parameters available for table creation. Let's look at them now. Table 5-2 shows the list of table creation parameters, a brief description of each one, and, where applicable, the default value for the parameter.

Parameter	Description	Default Value
Table	Name of the table	n/a
Column	Name of the column	n/a
Default	Specifies a default value for the column if no value is supplied during data insertion	n/a
Column_ref_constraint	Specifies a reference to another table's column constraint to apply to this column	n/a
Column_constraint	Specifies an integrity constraint as part of the column definition	n/a
Datatype	Specifies the type of data—number, character, large object type, etc.	n/a
Table_Constraint	Specifies a constraint definition for the entire table	n/a
Table_Ref_Constraint	Specifies a reference to another table's constraint to apply to this table	n/a
Tablespace	The tablespace in which the table is to be placed	The owner's specified default tablespace
Logging/NoLogging	Specifies whether the object information is to be tracked in the redo log file	Logging

TABLE 5-2. *Relational Table Parameters*

Parameter	Description	Default Value
Pctfree	Specifies the percentage of free space to be retained in each data block of the table for future updates to the table's rows	Range is 1–99, default is 10%
Pctused	Specifies the minimum amount of used space that Oracle maintains for each data block of the table	Range is 1–100, default is 40%
Initrans	Specifies the initial number of transaction entries allocated within each data block allocated to the table	Range is 1–255, default is 1 (for cluster, or index is 2)
Maxtrans	Specifies the maximum number of concurrent transactions that can update a data block allocated to a table—does not apply to queries	Range is 1–255, default is a function of the data block size
Storage Clause	Same parameters as for a tablespace	

TABLE 5-2. *Relational Table Parameters* (continued)

In order to create a table in your own schema, you must have the **create table** privilege and quota on the tablespace in which you are creating the table. If, as is usually the case for a DBA, you need to create a table in another schema, you will need to have the **create any table** privilege and either quota on the tablespace in which the table will be created or the **tablespace unlimited** privilege, which lets you create objects in any tablespace in the database.

Creating a Complex Table

Now that you have all of the basic parameters for creating a table, let's see how many of them you can use in one table creation statement—just for practice. Here's the assignment. You need to create a table that will hold information about the primates in the zoo we visited earlier in this chapter.

```
create table ZOO.PRIMATES
(Code           varchar2(3) not null
    constraint Primates_PK
      primary key
```

```
,Description     varchar2(250)     not null
,Location        varchar2(30)      not null
,Date_of_birth   date         not null
,Status          varchar2(3)
,Name            varchar2(10)     not null
,Date_Acquired   date
,Cage_Num        number(8,2)
,Coloring        varchar2(3)
    constraint Chk_Color_Type
         check(Coloring in ('brn','blk','red','tan','bld'))
)
 tablespace ZOO_DATA
   parallel (degree 1 instances 1)
    pctfree 10
    pctused 40
   initrans 1
   maxtrans 255
    logging
    storage
(   initial 73728
       next 1048576
 minextents 1
 maxextents 500
pctincrease 0
  freelists 1
   freelist groups 1);
```

Well, you certainly used most of the basic parameters. Good job! Of course, in the real world, your goal is not to see how many parameters you can use but to make sure the creation script is as thorough as it needs to be so the table is created clearly and effectively. You do not have to list the parameters anywhere that the default values will be used. We do, however, recommend that you try to use a consistent approach to coding your creation scripts. Therefore, you may decide to include all of the basic parameters in each script—even the default ones—to ensure that you do not accidentally miss a parameter that you need.

Now, let's see what you've got in the table creation script. You are creating a table in the ZOO schema called PRIMATES. The primary key is the Code column. There are several informational columns and a check constraint on the color of the animal. The animal's color can only be black, brown, red, tan, or blonde. No other color will be permitted. The tablespace is ZOO_DATA. For the next several parameters listed, the default values are used. The storage clause has been filled in with **initial** and **next** values. The **minextents** value is the default, while the **maxextents** value has been set to 500. The **pctincrease** has been set to 0, and the rest of the parameters are default values.

Creating Indexes

An index is used to help retrieve data quickly from the database. As we said in Chapter 2 in the "Indexes" section, without indexes, each time you wanted to retrieve information, Oracle would have to perform a full table scan of the data and look at each and every row in each table of interest. How time consuming!

If you have a commonly used query that just retrieves two columns of a table containing a large volume of information, you can create an index on those two columns. Oracle will look in the index for the information you want instead of walking through every complete row of the table. Much quicker!

As with tables, you can create different forms of indexes on each of the different table types. For this chapter, we will look at the basic index creation parameters that you will use the most.

Index Creation Parameters

Table 5-3 shows the basic parameters that you can use to create an index on a relational table.

Parameter	Description	Default Value
Unique	Specifies that the value of the column(s) in the index must be unique	Non-unique
Bitmap	Specifies that the index will be a bitmap rather than a B-Tree index—used with low cardinality columns	B-Tree
Schema	Specifies the name of the index owner	The creator's schema
Index_Name	Specifies the name of the index	n/a
Cluster Index Clause	Specifies that the index is to be built on a cluster and lists the cluster attributes	n/a
Table Index Clause	Specifies the table on which the index is to be built, includes any alias for the table name, index_expression_list, whether the index is local or global (for partitioned indexes)	Defaults are the index creator's schema, no alias, and global

TABLE 5-3. *Index Creation Parameters*

Parameter	Description	Default Value
Index Expression List	Specifies either the column(s) on which the index is based or an expression list to create a function-based index	For a regular index, 32 columns max; for a bitmap index, 30
ASC/DESC	Specifies whether the index is to be created in ascending or descending order	Ascending
Physical Attribute List	Same as for a table: pctfree, pctused, initrans, maxtrans, storage_clause	
Logging/ Nologging	Specifies whether the object information is to be tracked in the redo log file	Logging
Online	Specifies whether the index is to be made immediately available	Online
Compute Statistics	Specifies whether statistics are to be generated for the index	
Tablespace	Specifies the tablespace in which the index is to be stored	Default tablespace of the index creator
Compress/ Nocompress	Used to eliminate repeated occurrences of key values	Nocompress
Nosort	Specifies that the values are to be inserted in ascending order—Oracle does not have to sort the rows on insertion	n/a
Reverse	Stores the bytes of the index in reverse order, excluding the row ID—cannot be used with Nosort	n/a

TABLE 5-3. *Index Creation Parameters* (continued)

To create an index, you will need either the **create index** or **create any index** privilege and quota on the tablespace in which the index will be created or the **tablespace unlimited** privilege.

Creating an Index on the PRIMATES Table

Now that you have the parameters, let's see if you can use them to create an index on the PRIMATES table you created earlier in the table creation section. It turns out that the animal's name, date of birth, and status have been heavily queried lately and the query response time has been really slow because a full table scan is being used. To help speed up the query, you need to add an index to these columns. The order in which the information is being queried is Status, Date_Of_Birth, and Name. Although the status (living or dead) and the date of birth are not unique by themselves (since many different animals could have been born on the same date), if you add the animal's name— which will never be the same as that given to any other animal born the same day—the combination of columns becomes unique. Thus, you can create a unique index on the combination of the three columns, even though you could not create a unique index on any one of the columns by itself.

```
create unique index PRIMATES_IDX1
         on ZOO.PRIMATES(Status,Date_Of_Birth,Name)
 Tablespace ZOO_INDEX
    logging
    pctfree 10
   initrans 2
   maxtrans 255
    storage
(   initial 52630
       next 1024000
 minextents 1
 maxextents 350
pctincrease 0
);
```

In this example, a unique index PRIMATES_IDX1 is created on the ZOO.PRIMATES table using the ZOO_INDEX tablespace. As you can see, the storage and other parameters are used in the same basic manner as the table creation parameters. However, for an index creation, **initrans** must be set to a value of at least 2 instead of 1.

Creating Views

There are often times that you will need to create a view either to join parts of several tables together more rapidly or to hide information from one or more columns in a table. Hide information? Why would you want to do that? There will be times when you do not want specific column names to be known to the general users. Employment information is a good example of data you might need to hide. If users do not know there is a Salary column in the PAYROLL table, they will be much less likely to try to see the information or will have a much harder time seeing the data. You could have a table called PAYROLL with columns that all employees should be able to see, such as the number of hours they work each week or the number of vacation or sick leave hours they have accrued. You can create a view called PAYROLL_V that contains the columns you want them to see while excluding other columns.

To create a view in your own schema, you need the **create view** privilege; to create a view in another user's schema, you need the **create any view** privilege.

As we have done in the other creation sections, let's first look at the available basic parameters, and then you can create a view using them.

View Creation Parameters

Table 5-4 shows the parameters available for creating a basic view. Once you have the list of view creation parameters, you can create a view.

Parameter	Description	Default
Create or Replace	Specifies whether this is a new view creation or a modification to an already existing view	Create
Force/Noforce	Specifies whether to create the view even if there are creation errors (such as an underlying column that does not currently exist)	Noforce
Schema	The name of the schema that will own the view	Creator's schema
View_Name	Specifies the name of the view	n/a
Alias	Specifies the alias to use for each expression in the view—the number of aliases must match the number of expressions used in the view	Oracle will derive the alias from the expression name
As (subquery)	Specifies columns and rows on which the view is based	n/a
With_clause	Specifies one or more constraints: "with read only", with "check option" constraint (name for check constraint)	n/a

TABLE 5-4. *View Creation Parameters*

Creating a Basic View

For this exercise to be meaningful, you will create a view on the PAYROLL table called PAYROLL_EMP_V that will include the columns Employee_Name, Vacation_Accrued, and Sick_Accrued. You do not want the employee to be able to change anything, so you will enforce a read-only constraint. Okay, take a stab at it.

```
create or replace view PAYROLL_EMP_V
as select Employee_Name, Vacation_Accrued, Sick_Accrued
     from PAYROLL
with read only;
```

Employees will see the information that you have made available without being able to modify the information.

Creating Synonyms

Synonyms are often referred to as nicknames or shortcuts or alternatives for the syntax object_owner.object_name. Synonyms can be created for tables, views, procedures, packages, materialized views, sequences, stored functions, Java class schema objects, and even for other synonyms.

Synonyms are very powerful constructs because they let you reference an object without having to know exactly who owns the object or where the object is located in the database. For example, you could have a table named PRIMATES owned by the schema ZOO. Every time you refer to the table, you need to use the construct ZOO.PRIMATES so there will be no question of which table you are referencing. If you create a synonym for the table, you can reference the table PRIMATES without using the qualifier ZOO.

To create a synonym in your own schema, you must have the **create synonym** privilege. You need **create any synonym** to create a synonym for another user's schema. To create a public synonym, you need the **create public synonym** privilege.

Let's take a look at the parameters available for synonym creation.

Synonym Creation Parameters

Table 5-5 shows the parameters you can use to create a synonym.

To create a synonym that is only available to someone connected directly to your schema—that is, a private synonym—you do not need to use **create private synonym** because a private synonym is the default.

Now, it's time to create a synonym or two.

Parameter	Description	Default
Public	Specifies whether the synonym is to be seen by all users	Private
Synonym_Name	Specifies the name of the synonym	n/a
For	Specifies the object for which the synonym is created	n/a
Dblink	Specifies the full or partial database link to create a synonym for an object on a remote database	n/a

TABLE 5-5. *Synonym Creation Parameters*

Creating Private and Public Synonyms

The first synonym you will create is a very basic private synonym for the ZOO.PRIMATES table. This should be easy, so take a moment to think of what your syntax will be.

```
create synonym PRIMATES
   for ZOO.PRIMATES;
```

See? We told you that would be easy.

Now, you can get a bit more complex. Try to create a public synonym called APES for the ZOO.PRIMATES table.

```
create public synonym APES
   for ZOO.PRIMATES;
```

That wasn't too bad, now was it? What have you learned from this exercise? The most important lesson in this creation statement is that the synonym name does not have to match the underlying object's name. If a user wanted to select the primate's name from the ZOO.PRIMATES table, he could just use the following syntax:

```
select Name
  from APES;
```

Isn't that much easier than the fully qualified select statement that follows?

```
select Name
  from ZOO.PRIMATES;
```

Also, it's a much more secure approach because the user does not know who owns the table or what the real table name is.

Creating Roles

The last group of parameters you will examine in this chapter is the one associated with creating roles. We talked at length about roles in Chapter 2, so we'll just remind you here that a role is a set of privileges that can be granted to one or more users. Roles make the administration of users much easier while helping to further secure your database objects. You can easily add or remove privileges from a role and affect every user who has been granted that role.

Role Creation Parameters

You only need to know a few parameters to create a role. Table 5-6 shows the parameters.

There are two forms of roles: those that are automatically enabled and accessible when a user connects to the database and those that are enabled and accessible through the command **set role**. The **set role** command is usually issued by an application on behalf of the user, and, generally, a password or external operating system authentication is required to enable the role.

To create a role, you need the **create role** privilege.

Privilege	Description	Default
Role_Name	Specifies the name of the role	n/a
Not Identified	Specifies that there is no password required for the role	Not Identified
Identified	Specifies that the command **set role** must be used to enable and access the role	
Identified By Password	Specifies a password to be used to enable and access the role	n/a
Identified Externally	Specifies that operating system authentication is to be used to enable and access the role	n/a

TABLE 5-6. *Role Creation Parameters*

Creating Two Types of Roles

This time, your task is to create two roles—one that requires no identification and one that does. The syntax for the role creation statements should be pretty straightforward, so take a moment to think about it. First, create a role that requires no identification:

```
create role MY_ROLE;
```

Next, create a role that requires a password, and specify the password required:

```
create role MY_PWROLE identified by NEEDAPASSWORD;
```

In order to access the privileges assigned to the role MY_PWROLE, the user must use the **set role** command using the following syntax:

```
set role MY_PWROLE identified by NEEDAPASSWORD;
```

Creating Users

One task you'll be called upon to perform most frequently is creating users in your database. There are really two connotations to the term *users*. The connotation you are probably most familiar with is the term applied to a person who logs on to your database to perform work. The other connotation is the reference to an application schema area where the objects for an application are housed. Either way, you will be creating users on your system.

As we have done with the other objects, we will show the parameters first, and then you will have a chance to try your hand at creating a few different users.

User Creation Parameters

Table 5-7 shows the parameters for creating a user.

To create a user, you must have the **create user** privilege. In order for a user to connect to a database, the user must have the **create session** privilege.

The **default role** parameter shown in Table 5-7 is a new parameter introduced in version 8.1.5. Unfortunately, it does not work yet. However, in later releases, it should be available and will be wonderful. Once this new parameter is available, you will be able to assign roles to users as you create them. For now, though, you should create a role that contains the **create session** privilege (and any others that you want all users to have by default) and grant that role whenever you create a new user.

Now, let's see if you can create a user or two.

Parameter	Description	Default
User Name	Specifies the name of the user	n/a
By Password	Specifies the password for the account	n/a
Externally	Specifies that operating system authentication is to be used	n/a
Globally as	Specifies that the user is to be a "global" user and specifies the name to identify the user	n/a
Default Tablespace	Specifies where objects created by the user are to be stored if no tablespace value is given	SYSTEM
Temporary Tablespace	Specifies the temporary tablespace for the user's sort operations	SYSTEM
Quota <amount> On <tablespace>	Specifies the quota a user is to have in an integer amount (K or M) and the tablespace on which the quota is applied	No quota assigned
Profile	Specifies the name of a profile for the user	Default profile
Default Role—all, except, none	Specifies the default role for the user—can assign "all roles," "all roles except" a specified role, or no default roles	None
Password Expire	Specifies that the password is to expire at a certain time	Not expired
Account Lock/Unlock	Specifies whether the account is to be initially locked and inaccessible or unlocked	Unlocked

TABLE 5-7. *User Creation Parameters*

Creating a User with Roles and Privileges

The first user for you to create will be yourself! How generous will you be with your roles and other parameters? Take a minute to think about what you would like to have as your default tablespace, your temporary tablespace, and so on, and then start coding.

```
     create user <Put_Your_Name_Here>
identified by <Put_Your_Password_Here>
   default tablespace USERS
 temporary tablespace TEMP
   profile DBA_PROFILE;
```

For security purposes, Oracle will store passwords in an encrypted form. If you select the password column from DBA_USERS, you will see an encrypted password.

Since the **default roles** feature isn't available yet, in order to give yourself roles, you'll have to use a separate command. Once this feature is working, you will be able to assign roles to a user as you create him or her. Okay, go ahead and give yourself the Oracle-supplied roles CONNECT, RESOURCE, and DBA.

```
grant CONNECT,RESOURCE,DBA
   to <Put_Your_Name_Here>;
```

Can't you just feel the power? Of course, you can also implicitly create a user by writing a **grant** statement with the following syntax:

```
grant CONNECT,RESOURCE,DBA
   to NEW_USER
identified by PASS1;
```

The problem with using this syntax is that you will then have to perform an **alter user** command in order to assign a default tablespace, temporary tablespace, and all of the other parameters that you want the user to have. We do not recommend that you use the implicit form of user creation since it's too easy to miss modifying a default parameter that you really want changed.

PART II

The World of Views

CHAPTER 6

Mapping the Database

ave you ever been frustrated when you asked how to spell a word and your folks said, "Look it up in the dictionary." Well, gee, how can you look it up to see how to spell it if you don't know how to spell it in the first place! Right? We still feel that way! Anyhow, over a period of years, you learned how to use a dictionary effectively; even for words you don't know how to spell. You should now feel pretty comfortable with the idea of "looking it up."

Throughout the prior chapters, we've used and made reference to the data dictionary views that Oracle provides, which contain information about the composition of the database (the metadata). In this and the next two chapters, you'll learn how you can use the data dictionary views, specifically the DBA_ views (pronounced "DBA underscore"), to help you in your daily work. Now, let's get started.

The Data Dictionary Views

Oracle has provided a set of dictionary views for you to use to look up information about various areas of interest in the data dictionary. A specific naming convention is associated with the dictionary views and three different categories of views, as follows:

- USER_ views
- ALL_ views
- DBA_ views

The naming convention gives you a hint as to what information you can see in each of these categories of views. When users look at the USER_ views, they see only the objects that are owned specifically by each of them. When you look at the ALL_ views, you see the objects to which you have access that are owned by yourself or other users. The DBA_ views are available to users with DBA privileges and show both more information and information about every object in the database. They are a superset of the USER_ and ALL_ views.

In the next few chapters, we are going to concentrate on the most commonly used DBA_ views and explain them in more detail, grouping them by the way we use them. In this chapter, we'll concentrate on the physical world of the database, looking at how we organize and store the data in the database. Next, in Chapter 7, we'll take a look at the information we store and use about the users of the database. Finally, in Chapter 8, we'll investigate the DBA_ views that help us to manage the logical database world—tables and the associated indexes, constraints, views, and so on. For a complete list of all the default DBA_ views available in

Oracle8i, look in Appendix B. You can create other useful DBA_ views by running some of the catxxxxx.sql and dbmsxxxx.sql scripts located in your rdbms/admin directory. We've already told you about the catalog.sql and catproc.sql scripts, used to set up the basic DBA_ views. You can run catblock.sql to create the DBA_ views to look at locks and locking in your database, or run catdbsyn.sql to create private synonyms for the DBA_ views. The dbmsxxxx.sql scripts create packages that you can use to manipulate your database environment. Just a few of the ones we use often are

- **dbmsotpt.sql** Stored procedures to write informational lines to the screen
- **dbmspipe.sql** Stored procedures to pass information out to and in from programs running at your operating system level
- **dbmspool.sql** Stored procedures to display information about objects in the shared pool

The DBA_ Views

As a DBA with full privileges on the system, you can use the DBA_ views to see the complete information about objects in the database. But how do you know what the data dictionary view names are? Or if you get a new version of the RDBMS, how will you know what's been added or what's changed? Good questions!

In Oracle7.3.4.3 there are 93 views that start with DBA_, in Oracle8.0.5 there are 118 views, and in Oracle8.1.5 there are 165. What does this mean? Well, for one thing, it means that Oracle did a lot of work enhancing the database between versions. And it means there are a lot of new views for you to learn about that have been created to support the new features for each new version. So we're back to the question of how do you know what's been added.

Oracle provides a view (yes, another one!) called DICTIONARY. If you do a **describe** on this view, you'll see that it lists table names and comments about these tables. In reality, the contents of DICTIONARY are all views. This view contains descriptions of all the data dictionary views and the V$ views that we will discuss in Chapters 9 and 10. If you've done as we've suggested in the earlier chapters, you will have a test database for each new version of Oracle you've installed. You can do a **select Table_Name from DICTIONARY** in both your current database and the test database, and then compare the two lists to see what's new (assuming that one database is a different version than the other).

Okay, that tells you what's new. How do you know what's been changed? Unfortunately, that's not quite as easy. We're going to repeat something we've said before and will continue to say: you are going to have to read the documentation. For every DBA_ view that you use frequently, take a few minutes and read through the new documentation on that view. Oracle may have added new columns (as they did to the DBA_DATA_FILES view between versions 7.x and 8.0), or they may have changed the default values for some of the columns in the views. The only way you can be sure is to read the documentation.

Before we begin talking about the individual views, let's take a quick look at the ones we'll be discussing in this chapter. Table 6-1 contains a list of the views along with a short description of each one.

Although this list is in alphabetical order, we'll talk about the views in logical groups, as they relate to each other. And now, on to the DBA_ views we use most often. Throughout the chapters, we will mark columns that are new in Oracle8.0 with * and those new in Oracle8i with **.

DBA_TABLESPACES

In Chapter 5 we spent a good deal of time talking about tablespaces and how to manage them. As we showed you several times in Chapter 5, the view DBA_TABLESPACES contains information and descriptions of all the tablespaces in the database. In this and the next few sections, we're going to show you how to find out more detailed information about your database's physical layout and how you can combine these views with others to find out more about the layout of your database. Table 6-2 contains a list of all the columns in this view and what they represent.

View	Description
DBA_DATA_FILES	Information about database datafiles
DBA_EXTENTS	Extents composing all segments in the database
DBA_FREE_SPACE	Free extents in all tablespaces
DBA_FREE_SPACE_COALESCED	Statistics on coalesced space in tablespaces
DBA_OBJECTS	All objects in the database
DBA_ROLLBACK_SEGS	Description of rollback segments
DBA_SEGMENTS	Storage allocated for all database segments
DBA_TABLESPACES	Description of all tablespaces

TABLE 6-1. *DBA_ Views in Chapter 6*

Column	Description
TABLESPACE_NAME	Tablespace name
INITIAL_EXTENT	Default initial extent size
NEXT_EXTENT	Default incremental extent size
MIN_EXTENTS	Default minimum number of extents
MAX_EXTENTS	Default maximum number of extents
MIN_EXTLEN*	Minimum extent size for the tablespace
PCT_INCREASE	Default percent increase for extent size
STATUS*	Tablespace status: ONLINE, OFFLINE, or READ ONLY
CONTENTS*	Tablespace contents: PERMANENT or TEMPORARY
LOGGING*	Default logging attribute
EXTENT_MANAGEMENT**	Extent management tracking: DICTIONARY or LOCAL
ALLOCATION_TYPE**	Type of extent allocation in effect for this tablespace
PLUGGED_IN**	YES—the tablespace is plugged in; NO—it is not plugged in

TABLE 6-2. *DBA_TABLESPACES View for 8i (* = new to Oracle8.0, ** = new to Oracle8i)*

As we discussed in Chapter 5, tablespaces allow you to group your objects logically. All indexes can be stored in one tablespace, tables in another, rollback segments in a third, and so on. And you can create multiple tablespaces for different applications or for different classes of data within a single application.

By segregating your data into different tablespaces on different disks, you can decrease contention on the disks and help to improve performance. Even if you do not currently have enough disks to spread out the tablespaces and datafiles the way you would like to, you can still separate them now and move the underlying datafiles when you get more disk space. It is much easier and faster to take a tablespace offline and move the datafiles than it is to export and import data into new tablespaces, especially if you are using referential constraints in your application.

Now let's look a little more closely at what information Oracle provides in this view. The first set of columns in the view deal with the default storage for any objects created in this tablespace. Initial_Extent, in combination with Min_Extents, determines how much space Oracle will allocate when you create an object in this tablespace. If you have an initial extent size of 8192000 (1000 blocks in a database with an 8K block size), and minimum extents of 5, how many blocks will Oracle allocate when you create an object without a storage clause? If you said 5000 blocks, you're absolutely right.

We've talked about Max_Extents, Next_Extent, and Pct_Increase in earlier chapters. These values determine the size the object can grow to, by limiting the number of extents and by determining how large each succeeding extent will be. As a rule of thumb, you should specify a percent increase of zero. If you want SMON to automatically coalesce free space in the tablespace, specify a very small percent increase on the tablespace—say, a percent increase of one—and make very sure you specify a zero percent increase when you create any object in the tablespace. Oracle will default the percent increase to 50 if you do not specify a value when you create the tablespace, and a percent increase of 50 can create fragmentation and space problems.

Min_Extlen is a new parameter for Oracle8. As a DBA, you should be concerned about tablespace fragmentation. If the objects you place in your tablespace have extent sizes that are not multiples of each other, your tablespace can become very fragmented as these objects are dropped or truncated. Eventually, you can end up with a tablespace that has lots of free space, but all of it will be unusable because the extent sizes are not multiples. The space in the tablespace will end up looking like a moth-eaten coat, and the free extents will be too small to be usable. Min_Extlen lets you set a minimum extent size for the objects in that tablespace, and all objects that are created must have extent sizes that are multiples of this minimum.

Before we move on to the other columns in the DBA_TABLESPACES view, let's take a look at an illustration of how Min_Extlen enforces uniform extent size in a tablespace. First let's create a test tablespace and specify minimum extents of 5 and a minimum extent length of 204800. Since this database has a 2K block size, we're saying that any object allocated in this tablespace will have to be a multiple of 100 blocks.

```
create tablespace TESTTBS
datafile 'd:\orant\database\tst1orcl.ora'
size 15M
default storage(initial 409600 next 409600 minextents 5 maxextents 500
pctincrease 0) minimum extent 204800
/
select *
  from DBA_TABLESPACES
 where Tablespace_Name ='TESTTBS';
```

```
TABLESPACE INITIAL_EXTENT NEXT_EXTENT MIN_EXTENTS MAX_EXTENTS PCT_INCREASE MIN_EXTLEN STATUS
---------- -------------- ----------- ----------- ----------- ------------ ---------- ---------
CONTENTS  LOGGING
--------- ---------
TESTTBS          409600      409600           5         500            0     204800 ONLINE
PERMANENT LOGGING
```

Okay, now let's create two tables. We'll create the first one with no storage clause at all. We'll just let it take the defaults from the tablespace.

```
create table MYTESTTAB
(Name varchar2(30)
,ID   number
)
tablespace TESTTBS
/
```

If you check the DBA_SEGMENTS view (we'll talk about it in more detail later in this chapter), you'll see that Oracle has allocated 5 extents for the table (Extents) and that the actual space allocated is 2048000 bytes, even though the initial extent is only 409600.

```
select Segment_Name, Tablespace_Name, Bytes, Blocks,
       Extents, Initial_Extent, Next_Extent, Min_Extents, Max_Extents
  from DBA_SEGMENTS
 where Segment_Name ='MYTESTTAB';

SEGMENT_NAME    TABLESPACE      BYTES    BLOCKS   EXTENTS INITIAL_EXTENT
--------------- ---------- --------- --------- --------- --------------
NEXT_EXTENT MIN_EXTENTS MAX_EXTENTS
----------- ----------- -----------
MYTESTTAB       TESTTBS      2048000      1000         5         409600
     409600           5         500
```

Now let's create a second table, this time specifying only the initial extent size and making sure it is not a multiple of the minimum extent size. What do you think Oracle will do in this case?

```
create table MYTESTTAB2
(Name  varchar2(30)
,ID    number)
tablespace TESTTBS
storage (initial 5000)
/
```

Checking the DBA_SEGMENTS view again, we see

```
select Segment_Name, Tablespace_Name, Bytes, Blocks,
       Extents, Initial_Extent, Next_Extent, Min_Extents, Max_Extents
  from DBA_SEGMENTS
 where Segment_Name ='MYTESTTAB2';

SEGMENT_NAME    TABLESPACE      BYTES    BLOCKS   EXTENTS INITIAL_EXTENT
--------------- ---------- --------- --------- --------- --------------
NEXT_EXTENT MIN_EXTENTS MAX_EXTENTS
----------- ----------- -----------
MYTESTTAB2      TESTTBS      1843200       900         5           6144
     409600           5         500
```

That's interesting. The initial extent is not the one you specified, and the actual number of bytes allocated is the minimum extent size (100 blocks) plus four more extents at the next extent size of 200 blocks, for a total of 900 blocks. But why does the initial extent show 6144 when that number is not used in the allocation? Well, you specified 5000 bytes for an initial extent. Since 5000 is not a multiple of the database block size, Oracle rounded up to the next highest multiple of 2K, or 6144 bytes (3 blocks). But you also had a minimum extent length of 100 blocks on this tablespace. So even though Oracle lists the initial extent as 6144 bytes, it really allocates the minimum, or 100 blocks, as the initial extent. Then the next and minimum extents specifications on the tablespace come into the equation, and you get the remaining four of five extents allocated at 200 blocks, or the next extent size. We'll look more closely at the extents allocated when we talk about the DBA_EXTENTS view later in this chapter.

The remaining columns were added to the view with the introduction of Oracle8. Status lets you know whether the tablespace is online, offline, or read-only. An offline tablespace is part of the database but cannot be accessed by any user. A read-only tablespace is one that you can only select from. Contents tells you whether the contents of the tablespace are permanent or temporary. As we said in Chapter 5, if the contents of a tablespace are temporary, you cannot have any objects in that tablespace. Oracle will use that tablespace for temporary segments for sorting and will not drop these temporary segments once the sort operation is done. This can improve the performance of your application if it does a lot of sorting, since the temporary segments will not have to be allocated for each sort.

Logging has to do with whether the DML (Data Manipulation Language) and DDL (Data Definition Language) operations are written to the redo logs. Why would you *not* want to log something? Well, sometimes it's faster to re-create an object than to recover it from the log files. It is usually faster to re-create an index than it is to do recovery to restore it.

The last three columns were introduced in Oracle8i. Extent_Management and Allocation_Type have to do with whether you opt to use the data dictionary to manage your tablespace extents. If you decide to manage your tablespaces yourself, you can then specify either to have uniform extents (extents all the same size) or to have Oracle manage the extent sizes. Plugged_In refers to transportable tablespaces and was discussed in detail in Chapter 5.

DBA_DATA_FILES

The DBA_DATA_FILES data dictionary view, described in Table 6-3, holds the information about the physical files that make up the tablespaces and the database.

Datafiles are the foundation of the database. Without the physical files, there is nowhere to place the data. This view can be used to see the layout of your files on disk, and it can quickly show you if you have put datafiles from "competing"

Column	Description
FILE_NAME	Name of the database file
FILE_ID	ID of the database file
TABLESPACE_NAME	Name of the tablespace to which the file belongs
BYTES	Size of the file in bytes
BLOCKS	Size of the file in Oracle blocks
STATUS	File status: AVAILABLE or INVALID
RELATIVE_FNO*	Relative file number
AUTOEXTENSIBLE*	Autoextensible indicator
MAXBYTES*	Maximum file size in bytes
MAXBLOCKS*	Maximum file size in blocks
INCREMENT_BY*	Autoextension increment
USER_BYTES**	Corresponding number of bytes
USER_BLOCKS**	Number of blocks that can be used by the data

TABLE 6-3. *DBA_DATA_FILES View for 8i*

tablespaces (such as table and index tablespaces) on the same disks, as we discussed in Chapter 5. In combination with other data dictionary views, you can see the fragmentation within your datafiles and tablespaces, as in the scripts we use for daily monitoring that we discussed in Chapter 4.

The columns File_Name and File_ID both contain unique information. No datafile name can be repeated, and no File_ID (assigned by Oracle) can be either. So why does Oracle have both columns, when each one is unique? Well, the underlying database tables that these views are built on have indexes on them so that Oracle can return the information to you quickly. In general, it's a better idea to index a numeric column than it is to index a character column. So even though both columns are unique, and there is some extra space "wasted" to store the File_ID, ORACLE includes that column to improve performance. We'll see this repetition of unique columns in other data dictionary views as well.

The File_ID column is a number, unique within the database, that identifies the datafile. Oracle's documentation will refer to this number as the *absolute file number*. The absolute file number is used as a foreign key in other data dictionary views, notably DBA_FREE_SPACE, DBA_EXTENTS, and DBA_ROLLBACK_SEGS. These views can be joined to the DBA_DATA_FILES view to provide more information about the fragmentation, object allocation, and rollback segments in your database. When we talk about those views later in this chapter, we'll give you some examples of how to combine them.

The Bytes and Blocks columns define the total size of the datafile. When you create a tablespace or add another datafile to an existing tablespace, you must give Oracle the size of the datafile. This is the amount of space that will be initially allocated at the operating system level for this datafile. Unless you have turned autoextend on for this datafile, this is the maximum size the datafile will be. Blocks are always defined in Oracle blocks.

Status refers to whether the datafile is available or invalid. A datafile is invalid if that file in the tablespace was dropped. Why would you drop a datafile? Suppose you have a corrupted datafile, and you do not have a valid backup of that file so you cannot perform media recovery. The database will not open, as the files are not consistent. Oracle will allow you to mount the database and alter the database to drop the datafile. You use the statement:

```
alter datafile '<datafile_name>' offline drop;
```

When you issue this statement, you are telling Oracle that you will drop the associated tablespace as soon as you can. Once you have issued this statement and opened the database, you will not be able to do anything else with the tablespace to which the datafile belongs except drop it. You will not even be able to alter the tablespace offline because Oracle already views it as offline. If you check the Status column of that datafile before you drop the tablespace, it will be INVALID.

The remaining columns are new to Oracle8 and 8i. Relative_Fno is the relative file number for the datafile within that particular tablespace. While the File_ID is the absolute (or unique) file number within your database, the relative file number is unique only within a tablespace. So several tablespaces can have datafiles with the same Relative_Fno, but the File_ID of each of these datafiles will be different. For the first 1023 datafiles in the database, the relative file number will be the same as the absolute file number. Once you have more than 1024 datafiles in your database, Oracle begins to reuse the relative file numbers across different tablespaces. You cannot have more than 1024 datafiles in a single tablespace. Oracle has added the Relative_Fno column to all the DBA_ views that contain both the datafile's File_ID and the tablespace name.

Autoextensible, Max_Bytes, Max_Blocks, and Increment_By all refer to the ability to automatically extend the size of a datafile. Prior to Oracle8, if you had turned on autoextend for a datafile, the only way to see any of the autoextend information was to join DBA_DATA_FILES to the table SYS.FILEXT$. This table was only created if autoextend had ever been turned on for any datafile; so you would get errors trying to see autoextend information if you had never turned autoextend on. In Oracle8, the information was incorporated directly into the DBA_DATA_FILES view. For backward compatibility, Oracle still creates the SYS.FILEXT$ table if you turn on autoextend.

Autoextensible is a YES/NO flag to indicate whether the datafile can automatically extend. Max_Bytes and Max_Blocks are the maximum size the file can extend to, in both bytes and Oracle blocks. Increment_By is the amount to extend each time the datafile needs more space, expressed in Oracle blocks.

If you allow Oracle to create the default database as part of the installation of Oracle8, be sure to check the Autoextensible column for the datafiles that are created. Several of the tablespaces are created with autoextend on, and you should know which ones they are and disable autoextend where appropriate.

The query below selects all information about the datafiles in the SYSTEM tablespace.

```
select *
  from DBA_DATA_FILES
 where tablespace_name ='SYSTEM';
```

There are two datafiles in the SYSTEM tablespace. The first one can autoextend, the second cannot. Each time the first one extends, Oracle will allocate another 5210 Oracle blocks (in this case 1M, as this database has a 2K block size) of physical disk space, up to a maximum allocation of 200M for the datafile. If Oracle attempts to autoextend the datafile and cannot get the physical space, the transaction causing the extend will fail.

```
FILE_NAME                         FILE_ID TABLESPACE_NAME      BYTES    BLOCKS
------------------------------ --------- --------------- --------- ---------
STATUS     RELATIVE_FNO AUT  MAXBYTES MAXBLOCKS INCREMENT_BY
--------- ------------ --- --------- --------- ------------
D:\ORANT\DATABASE\SYS1ORCL.ORA          1 SYSTEM            62914560     30720
AVAILABLE             1 YES 209715200    102400         5120

D:\ORANT\DATABASE\SYS0ORCL.ORA          5 SYSTEM            52428800     25600
AVAILABLE             5  NO         0         0            0
```

User_Bytes and User_Blocks are new to Oracle8i and are used to define how much space the data can take up in a datafile. The values are displayed in both byte and block format. To better understand how the values for User_Bytes/User_Blocks work, let's take a look at the entry for the OEM_REPOSITORY tablespace in our Oracle8i demonstration database. We happen to know that this tablespace has an existing repository and, therefore, objects in it.

```
FILE_NAME
----------------------------------------------------------------------
  FILE_ID TABLESPACE_NAME                      BYTES    BLOCKS STATUS
--------- ------------------------------ --------- --------- ---------
RELATIVE_FNO AUT  MAXBYTES MAXBLOCKS INCREMENT_BY USER_BYTES
------------ --- --------- --------- ------------ ----------
```

```
USER_BLOCKS
-----------
D:\ORA8I\ORADATA\ORC1\OEMREP01.DBF
        5 OEM_REPOSITORY                    10485760       5120 AVAILABLE
           5 YES 157286400     76800           2560   10483712
       5119
```

Okay, we see that the total number of blocks available in this tablespace is 5120, with 5119 blocks available for data. Therefore, we can assume that the one block that is not available is being held (reserved) by Oracle for some other use. Hmm. Do you wonder how much space has been allocated so far in this datafile? Just out of curiosity, let's take a look. We'll use the DBA_SEGMENTS view (we'll talk about it in more depth later in this chapter) to get the total number of bytes and blocks that have been allocated for objects currently in the OEM_REPOSITORY tablespace.

```
select sum(Bytes), sum(Blocks)
  from DBA_SEGMENTS
 where Tablespace_Name = 'OEM_REPOSITORY';

SUM(BYTES) SUM(BLOCKS)
---------- -----------
   8259584        4033
```

If you look back at the values in User_Bytes and User_Blocks compared to Bytes and Blocks allocated, it's pretty obvious that neither set of values reflects any space that is being used in the datafile by current data; only the limits that have been set.

DBA_FREE_SPACE

The DBA_FREE_SPACE view, described in Table 6-4, contains information about the free extents in your datafiles.

Column	Description
TABLESPACE_NAME	Name of the tablespace containing the extent
FILE_ID	ID number of the file containing the extent
BLOCK_ID	Starting block number of the extent
BYTES	Size of the extent in bytes
BLOCKS	Size of the extent in Oracle blocks
RELATIVE_FNO*	Relative file number of the first extent block

TABLE 6-4. *DBA_FREE_SPACE View for 8i*

We've told you how to find out about the total space in your database by looking at the DBA_DATA_FILES dictionary view. Before we discuss the used space, let's take a look at the unused, or "free," space. The DBA_FREE_SPACE view has an entry for every unused extent in every datafile in every tablespace. However, if two contiguous extents have been freed at different times, Oracle does not combine them in the view. If you do a select for every extent in this view, and you have a lot of free extents in your database, you will get a very long, very unreadable list. In Chapter 4, we gave you a script that reads through the DBA_FREE_SPACE view and identifies contiguous extents and reports on them as if they were a single extent.

The Tablespace_Name, File_ID, and Relative_Fno columns in this view have the same meaning as the columns in the DBA_DATA_FILES view we looked at in the previous section. All of them are used to uniquely designate the tablespace and datafile within the tablespace in which the free extents reside. The Block_ID column contains the starting block number of the extent within the datafile. Block numbers are unique within datafiles but are not unique throughout the database. The Bytes and Blocks column are the number of bytes and Oracle blocks in the free extent. Bytes will always be a multiple of Blocks.

Why would you want to look at this view? By joining this view to the DBA_DATA_FILES data dictionary view, you can get a picture of not only how much space is available in your database by datafile, but also how fragmented your datafiles are. As we showed you in Chapter 4, it is possible to have a good deal of space free and still not have enough space for your objects to extend because that free space is very fragmented. The script below shows you a summary of the free space in your database.

```
select a.Tablespace_Name, b.File_Name, Sum(a.Bytes) Freespace,
       Count(*) Extcnt, b.Bytes, max(a.Bytes) largest,
       min(a.Bytes) smallest
  from DBA_FREE_SPACE a, DBA_DATA_FILES b
 where a.Tablespace_Name=b.Tablespace_Name
   and a.File_ID=b.file_ID
 group by a.Tablespace_Name, b.File_Name, b.Bytes
/
```

The output of this script, run against a sample database, is below.

```
TABLESPACE_NAME FILE_NAME                        FREESPACE     EXTCNT    LARGEST   SMALLEST
--------------- ---------------------------- ---------- ---------- ---------- ----------
TESTAPP1        /ORADATA1/TEST/test1_1.dbf    5730680832         11 5726126080     327680
TESTAPP2        /ORADATA2/TEST/test2_1.dbf    6066520064          6 6064226304     327680
TESTAPP1IDX1    /ORADATA3/TEST/tstidx1_1.dbf  3795550208         42 3721560064      32768
TESTAPP1IDX1    /ORADATA3/TEST/tstidx1_2.dbf  6838206464        100 6142017536      32768
TESTAPP2IDX1    /ORADATA4/TEST/tstidx2_1.dbf  9750331392         63 9242312704      32768
RBS             /ORADATA5/TEST/rbs01.dbf      1834991616          7 1785184256   24903680
SYSTEM          /ORADATA6/TEST/sys01.dbf       463650816          5  419020800     147456
TEMP            /ORADATA5/TEST/temp01.dbf       33406976          2   23756800    9650176
```

What can you tell from the output above? Let's see. The TESTAPP1 tablespace has a large quantity of free space left, and that space is in 11 extents, with the smallest extent being fairly large. So it's not too badly fragmented. However, the TESTAPP1IDX1 tablespace, with 142 extents in two datafiles, is pretty badly fragmented. The smallest free extent is fairly small, while the largest is almost the same size as the total free space. This probably means that the majority of the free extents are very small, and, unless they are contiguous, they may not be usable when the objects in the tablespace need to extend.

By monitoring the free space in your tablespaces, you can get a feel for the growth patterns of the objects within your database. Why would you want to track that? Well, let's say you know the free space in tablespace TESTAPP1 almost never varies. Then, one day you see that there is almost no free space left. You know that something has changed in the application or the system and that you should investigate the change and either add another datafile before the tablespace runs out of space or move a new, fast-growing object to a separate tablespace. Once you've found the problem, you can tell your boss that you noticed the change in tablespace free space; found out what was causing the sudden loss of space in the tablespace; and have taken action to ensure that this tablespace does not run out of space in the future. What a great way to be a proactive DBA!

DBA_FREE_SPACE_COALESCED

The DBA_FREE_SPACE_COALESCED view, described in Table 6-5, contains information about the coalesced space in the database and is new in Oracle8.0.

Why do you want to coalesce the free space in your tablespaces? If you have many contiguous free extents, you are experiencing fragmentation, and, when Oracle needs to allocate another extent, you can experience a performance impact as the database searches for extents large enough to allocate. If no extent large enough is available, Oracle will attempt to coalesce the free space to find a suitable extent. If you set the default storage parameter for percent increase on your tablespaces to a non-zero value, SMON will automatically coalesce the free space in your tablespace. However, since the temporary and rollback segment tablespaces usually have a percent increase of zero, SMON will never coalesce them. Alternatively, as of Oracle7.3, you can manually coalesce your tablespaces, regardless of the percent increase. To manually coalesce a tablespace, you use the command

```
alter tablespace <tablespace_name> coalesce;
```

So how do you determine whether you need to coalesce the tablespace? You can certainly look into the DBA_FREE_SPACE view we discussed in the prior section and list all the free extents and search to see if any of them are contiguous. If you have a lot of extents, that's going to be a very tedious process. However, as of Oracle8, the new data dictionary view, DBA_FREE_SPACE_COALESCED, makes determining whether or not you need to coalesce much simpler.

Column	Description
TABLESPACE_NAME*	Name of tablespace
TOTAL_EXTENTS*	Total number of free extents in tablespace
EXTENTS_COALESCED*	Total number of coalesced free extents in tablespace
PERCENT_EXTENTS_COALESCED*	Percentage of coalesced free extents in tablespace
TOTAL_BYTES*	Total number of free bytes in tablespace
BYTES_COALESCED*	Total number of coalesced free bytes in tablespace
TOTAL_BLOCKS*	Total number of free Oracle blocks in tablespace
BLOCKS_COALESCED*	Total number of coalesced free Oracle blocks in tablespace
PERCENT_BLOCKS _COALESCED*	Percentage of coalesced free Oracle blocks in tablespace

TABLE 6-5. *DBA_FREE_SPACE_COALESCED View for 8i*

The Total_Extents and Total_Bytes columns in this view are the same information we derived from the DBA_FREE_SPACE view, by doing a **count(*)** and **sum(Bytes)**. One important difference to note is that while the information in the DBA_FREE_SPACE view is stored by datafile, the information in this view is by tablespace. So for the TESTAPP1IDX1 tablespace in the example in the prior section, you would have to sum the numbers for the two datafiles to come up with the information in the DBA_FREE_SPACE_COALESCED view.

The Extents_Coalesced column shows you the number of extents that have no neighboring free extents. Percent_Extents_Coalesced is the percentage of the tablespace's free extents that are coalesced. In general, you want this number to be as close to 100 as possible. Bytes_Coalesced is the number of free bytes that were coalesced. If this number does not match the Total_Bytes, then the tablespace has some extents that can be coalesced, either by SMON (if the percent increase is non-zero) or manually, by issuing the command **alter tablespace <tablespace name> coalesce**.

If you look at the sample output below, only one tablespace has extents that could be coalesced.

```
select Tablespace_Name, Total_Extents, Extents_Coalesced
  from DBA_FREE_SPACE_COALESCED;

TABLESPACE_NAME                 TOTAL_EXTENTS EXTENTS_COALESCED
------------------------------ ------------- -----------------
SYSTEM                                      5                 5
RBS                                         7                 4
TESTAPP1                                   11                11
TESTAPP2                                    6                 6
TEMP                                        2                 2
TESTAPP1IDX1                              142               142
TESTAPP2IDX1                               63                63
```

To see which tablespaces you will have to manually coalesce, you can join the DBA_TABLESPACES view with the DBA_FREE_SPACE_COALESCED view, as we do below.

```
select a.Tablespace_Name, Percent_Blocks_Coalesced, Pct_Increase
  from DBA_TABLESPACES a, DBA_FREE_SPACE_COALESCED b
 where a.Tablespace_Name = b. Tablespace_Name
/

TABLESPACE_NAME PERCENT_BLOCKS_COALESCED PCT_INCREASE
--------------- ------------------------ ------------
SYSTEM                               100           50
TESTAPP1                             100            0
TESTAPP2                             100            0
TESTAPP1IDX1                         100            0
TESTAPP2IDX1                         100            0
RBS                                   90            0
TEMP                                 100            0
```

As we might have suspected, since the number of Total_Extents did not match the Extents_Coalesced from the prior query, the RBS tablespace is not completely coalesced. While it is generally good practice to coalesce fragmented tablespaces, if you have sized your rollback segments so that all the Next_Extents are the same size, it is not necessary to coalesce this tablespace, since Oracle will always find extents of the proper size.

You should notice also that only the SYSTEM tablespace has a non-zero percent increase. This means the DBA for this database must have manually coalesced the other tablespaces. You can set up a job, to run during off-peak hours, that will coalesce all tablespaces in your database.

DBA_SEGMENTS

The DBA_SEGMENTS view, described in Table 6-6, contains information about storage allocated for all database segments.

Column	Description
OWNER	Username of the segment owner
SEGMENT_NAME	Name of the segment
PARTITION_NAME*	Object partition name
SEGMENT_TYPE	Type of segment
TABLESPACE_NAME	Name of the tablespace containing the segment
HEADER_FILE	ID of the file containing the segment header
HEADER_BLOCK	ID of the block containing the segment header
BYTES	Size in bytes of the segment
BLOCKS	Size in Oracle blocks of the segment
EXTENTS	Number of extents allocated to the segment
INITIAL_EXTENT	Size in bytes of the initial extent of the segment
NEXT_EXTENT	Size in bytes of the next extent to be allocated to the segment
MIN_EXTENTS	Minimum number of extents allowed in the segment
MAX_EXTENTS	Maximum number of extents allowed in the segment
PCT_INCREASE	Percent by which to increase the size of the next extent to be allocated
FREELISTS	Number of process freelists allocated to this segment
FREELIST_GROUPS	Number of freelist groups allocated to this segment
RELATIVE_FNO*	Relative file number of the segment header
BUFFER_POOL*	Name of the default buffer pool for the appropriate object

TABLE 6-6. *DBA_SEGMENTS View for 8i*

So far in this chapter, we've talked about the physical world of the database in large terms, describing the tablespaces and datafiles and the space in them. Now we're going to talk a little about the things that go into the datafiles and use up that space.

Every object in the database that can take up space is called a *segment.* You can see the storage information about the segment by querying the DBA_SEGMENTS view. Every segment is created in a tablespace and, in Oracle8, may also be created in a partition. Each table, index, rollback segment, and so on, will have an Initial_Extent that defines the size of the first chunk of blocks allocated for that segment. The Next_Extent, in combination with the Pct_Increase defined, will determine the size of each succeeding chunk that is allocated. Well, almost. We saw earlier in this chapter, in the section on DBA_TABLESPACES, that the initial and next extents requested in the storage clause may not actually be the amount of space allocated for that segment, since Oracle will round the bytes allocated up to a multiple of a database block. And, even then, if the tablespace has a minimum extent length defined, the initial and next extent values stored in this view may not reflect the sizes of the extents allocated. So why look at this view if the information may not be accurate? In Chapter 3, in the section on the Tablespace Default Storage clause, we showed you how to calculate what the size of the segment should be, based on the Initial_Extent, Next_Extent, Pct_Increase, and number of extents allocated (the Extents column). If the segment is not the size you think it should be, you, as a proactive DBA, should be looking to see why it isn't. The fastest way to know if things are not quite the size you expect them to be is to look at the values in the DBA_SEGMENTS view.

In addition, with version 8, Oracle gives you the ability to decide in which buffer pool within the SGA to place the segment, by specifying the Buffer_Pool when the segment is created or altered. The buffer pools determine whether the data blocks of this segment are retained in memory or flushed as they are no longer needed. Why keep the data blocks in memory? Let's go back to the XYZ Company for a moment. They have a list of products they manufacture, and each product has a product code attached to it. Every time an order is placed, the person taking the order has to look up the product code for that product in the table. If that table is kept in memory, the lookup will be much faster. The other side of this is that the customer information probably does not have to stay in memory, because it is not likely that the customer will call back several times in a single day to place orders.

You can use the script below to check how close the segments in your database are to reaching their maximum extents.

```
select Owner, Tablespace_Name, Segment_Name, Extents, Max_Extents,
       (Extents/Max_Extents)*100 UsedPct
  from DBA_SEGMENTS
 where Owner not in ('SYS','SYSTEM')
   and Segment_Type not in ('ROLLBACK','DEFERRED ROLLBACK','TEMPORARY')
```

```
 order by Tablespace_Name, Owner, Extents
/

OWNER       TABLESPACE SEGMENT_NAME     EXTENTS MAX_EXTENTS  USEDPCT
----------  ---------- --------------- --------- ----------- --------
JAMES       TESTTBS    TEST1                    5         500    1.000
RACHEL      TESTTBS    ABC                      5         500    1.000
MY_SCHEMA   USER_DATA  PRIMATES                 1         500     .200
MY_SCHEMA   USER_DATA  PRIMATES_PK              1         121     .826
QC_USER     USER_DATA  FREESP                   1         121     .826
QC_USER     USER_DATA  TOY                      1         121     .826
QC_USER     USER_DATA  STUDENT                  1         121     .826
QC_USER     USER_DATA  CUSTOMERS_SJ             1         121     .826
QC_USER     USER_DATA  PRIMATES_PK              1         121     .826
QC_USER     USER_DATA  CUSTOMERS_PA             1         121     .826
QC_USER     USER_DATA  ABC                      1  2147483645     .000
QC_USER     USER_DATA  ABC1                     1         121     .826
QC_USER     USER_DATA  VIEW_TEMP                1         121     .826
QC_USER     USER_DATA  PRIMATES                 1         500     .200
```

It seems that none of the segments is close to reaching their maximum extents, which is good. But wait a minute. One of the segments has a very unusual Max_Extents of 2147483645. What's that all about? Well, starting with version 7.3, Oracle added a new feature to the storage clause—the ability to create a segment with a **maxextents unlimited** sub-clause. Since Oracle has to store some number in the Max_Extents column, they chose 2147483645, which is the numeric value of 2GB. Anytime you see a segment with a Max_Extents value of 2147483645, you know that it has actually been created with **maxextents unlimited**.

DBA_EXTENTS

The DBA_EXTENTS view, described in Table 6-7, lists the extents composing all segments in the database.

In the prior section, we looked at DBA_SEGMENTS and the storage allocation parameters you define when you create a segment. The DBA_EXTENTS view is a more detailed look at the segments, with information about each extent that has been allocated for a particular segment. What is an extent? An *extent* is a contiguous number of data blocks allocated for storing data.

The information in the DBA_EXTENTS view is a road map of the segment. There is a parent-child relationship between the DBA_SEGMENTS and DBA_EXTENTS views, with one row in DBA_EXTENTS for every extent allocated to the segment. Each row contains the Segment_Name, Owner, Segment_Type, and Tablespace_Name, which in combination can be used to link the rows in the DBA_EXTENTS view back to the DBA_SEGMENTS view. Other columns in this view are the Extent_ID, unique within the segment, indicating the order in which that extent has been allocated; the File_ID

Column	Description
OWNER	Owner of the segment associated with the extent
SEGMENT_NAME	Name of the segment associated with the extent
SEGMENT_TYPE	Type of the segment
TABLESPACE_NAME	Name of the tablespace containing the extent
EXTENT_ID	Extent number in the segment
FILE_ID	Name of the file containing the extent
BLOCK_ID	Starting block number of the extent
BYTES	Size of the extent in bytes
BLOCKS	Size of the extent in Oracle blocks
RELATIVE_FNO*	Relative file number of the first extent block
PARTITION_NAME*	Object partition name (Set to NULL for nonpartitioned objects)

TABLE 6-7. *DBA_EXTENTS View for 8i*

and Block_ID, which locate the extent within the datafile; and the Bytes and Blocks columns, which are the amount of space allocated for this extent, expressed in both bytes and database blocks.

Why drilldown to this level of detail? As we discussed in Chapter 4, as a proactive DBA, you need to monitor not only the number of extents allocated to a segment, but also the size and growth of these extents. If you have set a non-zero percent increase for a segment, you will want to keep a close eye on the last extent size allocated, so that you can ensure there is enough space in the tablespace for the next extent to be allocated when needed.

Another reason to check on the number of extents in a segment has to do with the way Oracle releases extents back to the database when you drop or truncate a table or index. As the extents are released, information about the extent is removed from an internal used-extent table and added to an internal free-extent table. Releasing a lot of extents causes a lot of activity at the data dictionary level. So if you have a lot of extents allocated to the segment, it won't cause a performance impact when you access the data, unless you try to release that space. We know of a DBA who had to drop a table with 10,000 extents. He was patient and waited it out until the bitter end—ten hours later!

Let's take a look at a segment with more than one extent:

```
select *
  from DBA_SEGMENTS
 where Segment_Name ='TSTTAB'
/

OWNER      SEG_NAME   PART_NAME  SEG_TYP TBS_NAME   HDR_FILE HDR_BLK
    BYTES     BLOCKS   EXTENTS
---------- ---------- ---------- ------- ---------- -------- -------
--------- --------- ---------
INIT_EXT NEXT_EXT MIN_EXT MAX_EXT PCT_INCR FREELISTS FREEL_GRPS REL_FNO
BUFF_POOL
-------- -------- ------- ------- -------- --------- ---------- -------
----------
JAMES      TSTTAB                TABLE   TESTTBS           6    1902
  2048000       1000         5
  409600   409600       5     500        0          1          1       6
DEFAULT

select *
  from DBA_EXTENTS
 where Segment_Name = 'TSTTAB'
/

OWNER   SEG_NAME   PART_NAME  SEG_TYP TBS_NAME   EXT_ID FILE_ID BLK_ID
    BYTES     BLOCKS REL_FNO
------- ---------- ---------- ------- ---------- ------ ------- ------
--------- --------- -------
JAMES   TSTTAB                TABLE   TESTTBS         0       6   1902
   409600       200       6
JAMES   TSTTAB                TABLE   TESTTBS         1       6   2102
   409600       200       6
JAMES   TSTTAB                TABLE   TESTTBS         2       6   2302
   409600       200       6
JAMES   TSTTAB                TABLE   TESTTBS         3       6   2502
   409600       200       6
JAMES   TSTTAB                TABLE   TESTTBS         4       6   2702
   409600       200       6
```

Did you notice anything about this segment? If you look at the Block_ID column in the select from the DBA_EXTENTS view, you see that the blocks are contiguous. This is an unusual occurrence in an active database, so why did it happen? Checking the DBA_SEGMENTS information, you can see that the minimum extents value is 5. So all the extents were allocated at the same time. If your tablespace is very fragmented, you may still see the extents placed all over the tablespace, wherever Oracle can find the room for them.

DBA_ROLLBACK_SEGS

The DBA_ROLLBACK_SEGS view, described in Table 6-8, contains information about the rollback segments available to the database.

Have you ever rearranged the furniture in your living room and then decided the change made the room look terrible and put everything back where it originally was? When you make changes to the data in the database, Oracle keeps a copy of the old version of the data in case you change your mind and want to put everything back the way it was. To do this, Oracle uses a special database object called a *rollback segment* to store the old versions of the data blocks. In addition, Oracle uses the information in a rollback segment to present a consistent picture of

Column	Description
SEGMENT_NAME	Name of the rollback segment
OWNER	Owner of the rollback segment
TABLESPACE_NAME	Name of the tablespace containing the rollback segment
SEGMENT_ID	ID number of the rollback segment
FILE_ID	ID number of the file containing the segment header
BLOCK_ID	ID number of the block containing the segment header
INITIAL_EXTENT	Initial extent size in bytes
NEXT_EXTENT	Secondary extent size in bytes
MIN_EXTENTS	Minimum number of extents
MAX_EXTENTS	Maximum number of extents
PCT_INCREASE	Percent increase for extent size
STATUS	Rollback segment status
INSTANCE_NUM*	Rollback segment owning parallel server instance number
RELATIVE_FNO*	Relative file number of the segment header

TABLE 6-8. *DBA_ROLLBACK_SEGS View for 8i*

the original data to other users, so that you don't stop everyone from working if you start to make changes and then go out to lunch! Until you commit your changes, anyone else trying to access that data will read the changed blocks from the rollback segments.

Because rollback segments store copies of data blocks, they also take up physical space in the database. Oracle's special DBA_ view DBA_ROLLBACK_SEGS lets you quickly see the information about your rollback segments. Most of the information in this view can be extracted from the data dictionary by querying the DBA_SEGMENTS and DBA_EXTENTS views we discussed earlier in this chapter. As you can see from the select statement and results below, a rollback segment, like any other segment, has a Segment_Name, Owner, Initial_Extent, Next_Extent, Min_Extent, Max_Extent, and Pct_Increase defined. Also like any other segment, it is created and takes up space in a tablespace, shown in the Tablespace_Name column. Unlike other segments, a rollback segment has a unique Segment_ID column, which can be joined to the Usn column of the V$ROLLSTAT view (which will be discussed in detail in Chapter 10) to give you dynamic information about your rollback segments. In addition, a rollback segment must have a minimum of at least two extents and a percent increase of zero. The first of the extents allocated for a rollback segment is the *header block* and is used by Oracle to store information that tracks the transactions accessing this rollback segment and the extents the transaction is using. In the File_ID and Block_ID columns, Oracle maintains information about the location of the header block.

```
select Segment_Name, Tablespace_Name, Owner, Initial_Extent,
       Next_Extent, Min_Extents, Max_Extents, Pct_Increase
  from DBA_ROLLBACK_SEGS
/

SEGMENT_NAME TABLESPACE      OWNER  INIT EXT NEXT EXT MIN EXT MAX EXT PCTINC
------------ -------------- ------ -------- -------- ------- ------- ------
SYSTEM       SYSTEM          SYS       51200    51200       2     121      0
RB_TEMP      SYSTEM          SYS      102400   102400       2     121      0
RB1          ROLLBACK_DATA   SYS       51200    51200       2     121      0
RB2          ROLLBACK_DATA   SYS       51200    51200       2     121      0
RB3          ROLLBACK_DATA   SYS       51200    51200       2     121      0
RB4          ROLLBACK_DATA   SYS       51200    51200       2     121      0
RB5          ROLLBACK_DATA   SYS       51200    51200       2     121      0
RB6          ROLLBACK_DATA   SYS       51200    51200       2     121      0
RB7          ROLLBACK_DATA   SYS       51200    51200       2     121      0
RB8          ROLLBACK_DATA   SYS       51200    51200       2     121      0
RB9          ROLLBACK_DATA   SYS       51200    51200       2     121      0
RB10         ROLLBACK_DATA   SYS       51200    51200       2     121      0
RB11         ROLLBACK_DATA   SYS       51200    51200       2     121      0
RB12         ROLLBACK_DATA   SYS       51200    51200       2     121      0
```

So you can get the same storage information from DBA_ROLLBACK_SEGS that you can from DBA_SEGMENTS. Why create a separate view? Unlike any other type of segment, a rollback segment can be created with a status of ONLINE or OFFLINE and, if you are using Oracle's Parallel Server, can be owned by an individual instance (the Instance_Num column).

What's the difference between ONLINE and OFFLINE, and how is the status set? A rollback segment that is online is one that is available for the database to use. There will be information about your online rollback segments in the V$ROLLSTAT and V$ROLLNAME views, which you can use to tune the performance of your database. To bring an existing rollback segment online, you can either specifically list it in your init.ora or config.ora using the parameter **rollback_segments** or bring it online using the command **alter rollback segment <rollback segment name> online**. When you create a rollback segment, it is created as offline by default, but you can override this on the **create** command line.

Rollback segments that are listed in one of the initialization parameter files are considered private rather than public. A *private* rollback segment is available only to the instance that names it in the parameter file, while a *public* one is available to any instance. The only time there is a difference between private and public rollback segments is when you are using Oracle Parallel Server. If you are using OPS, each instance can create both private rollback segments that can only be seen by that instance and public rollback segments that are available to all the instances. You identify rollback segments as private by naming them in your init.ora using the **rollback_segments** parameter. No two instances can identify the same rollback segments as private.

In the listing below, two of the rollback segments are in the tablespace SYSTEM. When you create a database, Oracle automatically creates a rollback segment named SYSTEM and reserves it for its own use. Before you can create any tablespaces, you must create a second rollback segment. Since no other tablespaces are available, that rollback segment is created in the SYSTEM tablespace as well. Once you create a separate tablespace for your rollback segments and then create the rollback segments themselves, it is a good idea to take that second rollback segment offline and keep it offline—but do not drop it, since you may need to use it at some later time. Rollback segments expand and can fragment your SYSTEM tablespace if you leave them in it and online. You should not list the SYSTEM rollback segment in the **rollback_segments** parameter list because you do not want any process but Oracle's to access the SYSTEM rollback segment.

Some of the rollback segments in this database are online and some are offline. Why would you want to keep several rollback segments available but offline? Suppose you have an unusual load on your system, and you see that your online rollback segments are heavily used, growing in size and causing the users to wait. You can immediately bring the offline segments online and make them available to Oracle. Additionally, the offline rollback segments reserve disk space in the tablespace. If you find that your rollback segments are expanding and you need to add space quickly to the tablespace, you can drop the offline rollback segments and return some free space to your rollback tablespace without having to add another datafile.

```
select Segment_Name, Owner, Tablespace_Name, Status, Instance_Num
  from DBA_ROLLBACK_SEGS
/

SEGMENT_NAME OWNER  TABLESPACE     STATUS     INSTANCE_NUM
------------ ------ -------------- ---------- -------------
SYSTEM       SYS    SYSTEM         ONLINE
RB_TEMP      SYS    SYSTEM         OFFLINE
RB1          SYS    ROLLBACK_DATA  ONLINE
RB2          SYS    ROLLBACK_DATA  ONLINE
RB3          SYS    ROLLBACK_DATA  ONLINE
RB4          SYS    ROLLBACK_DATA  ONLINE
RB5          SYS    ROLLBACK_DATA  ONLINE
RB6          SYS    ROLLBACK_DATA  ONLINE
RB7          SYS    ROLLBACK_DATA  ONLINE
RB8          SYS    ROLLBACK_DATA  OFFLINE
RB9          SYS    ROLLBACK_DATA  OFFLINE
RB10         SYS    ROLLBACK_DATA  OFFLINE
RB11         SYS    ROLLBACK_DATA  OFFLINE
RB12         SYS    ROLLBACK_DATA  OFFLINE
```

DBA_OBJECTS

The DBA_OBJECTS view, described in Table 6-9, contains information about the objects in the database.

What is an object? In simple terms, an object is anything that a user can own. Wait a minute, how is that different from a segment? Well, a segment is an object that takes up physical space in the database; but there are other types of objects, such as views, synonyms, sequences, and stored programs, that can be owned by a user but don't take up physical space. So all segments are objects, right? Not exactly. There are two special types of segments—temporary segments and rollback segments—that take up space in the database but do not appear in a list of object types. These segments cannot be directly accessed by any user and so are not considered objects.

Okay, now that we've confused you just a bit, let's take a look at the DBA_OBJECTS view and see if we can make things a bit clearer. When you look at the columns in the view, you see that, like segments, objects have an Object_Name, Owner, and Object_Type. Unlike segments, however, there is no tablespace

Column	Description
OWNER	Username of the owner of the object
OBJECT_NAME	Name of the object
SUBOBJECT_NAME*	Name of the sub-object (for example, partition)
OBJECT_ID	Object number of the object
DATA_OBJECT_ID*	Object number of the segment that contains the object
OBJECT_TYPE	Type of the object (for example, TABLE, INDEX)
CREATED	Timestamp for the creation of the object
LAST_DDL_TIME	Timestamp for the last DDL change (including GRANT and REVOKE) to the object
TIMESTAMP	Timestamp for the specification of the object
STATUS	Status of the object
TEMPORARY*	Can the current session only see data that it places in this object itself?
GENERATED*	Was the name of this object generated by the system?
SECONDARY**	Is this a secondary object created as part of icreate for domain indexes?

TABLE 6-9. *DBA_OBJECTS View for 8i*

associated with the object. Think about a synonym. A synonym is merely another name for something and doesn't take up space. If it doesn't take up space, it doesn't need a tablespace. The Object_ID, like the IDs in some of the other DBA_ views, is a number that uniquely identifies this object.

There are three dates associated with an object. Created is the date the object was created. Last_DDL_Time is the date of the last DDL change to the object, and Timestamp is the last time someone changed the object. Hmm, isn't that the same thing? No, not quite. Timestamp will be updated only when the object itself is changed, such as changing the definition of a view; while Last_DDL_Time will be updated then as well, but will also be updated when a grant or revoke is done on the object. One of the authors spent a few worried hours trying to figure out why it seemed as if everything in her database had been changed overnight before she realized what the difference was between the two columns! She had granted access to all the objects to a new user.

Status is either VALID or INVALID. In the case of objects that are stored programs or views, the status will be INVALID if the program does not compile properly or if an object that the stored program accesses is changed. If you want to find all the stored programs that are invalid, you can run the following script:

```
select Owner Oown, Object_Name Oname, Object_Type Otype
  from DBA_OBJECTS
 where Object_Type in
     ('PROCEDURE','PACKAGE','FUNCTION','TRIGGER','PACKAGE BODY','VIEW')
   and Owner not in ('SYS','SYSTEM')
   and Status != 'VALID'
 order by 1,4,3,2
/

OOWN       ONAME           OTYPE
---------- --------------- ---------------
ORDSYS     ORDIMG_PKG      PACKAGE BODY
QC_USER    INSTRIG         TRIGGER
```

The column Generated is new in Oracle8 and indicates that the object name has been created by Oracle itself. Object names created by Oracle begin with 'SYS_', and, while there is nothing wrong with letting Oracle create the name of the object, it is generally not a good idea to do so. When you generate object names yourself, you can create meaningful names that link the objects together, such as PK_<tablename> for the primary key of a table. This allows you to quickly see object relationships. Let's take a look at an example of an Oracle-generated name.

First, you will create a new table and add a primary key to it, without giving a name to the primary key constraint.

```
create table TESTGEN (
Id      number,
Name    varchar2(20),
Address varchar2(30));

Table created.

alter table TESTGEN add primary key(Id);

Table altered.
```

Next, you'll look in the DBA_CONSTRAINTS view to see what name the primary key constraint was given.

```
select Constraint_Name
  from DBA_CONSTRAINTS
 where Table_Name = 'TESTGEN'
   and Constraint_Type = 'P'
 ;
```

```
CONSTRAINT_NAME
------------------------------
SYS_C00841
```

That's not a particularly meaningful name. It doesn't tell you what the constraint is or to which table the constraint applies. Finally, take a look at the Generated column for the table and the constraint.

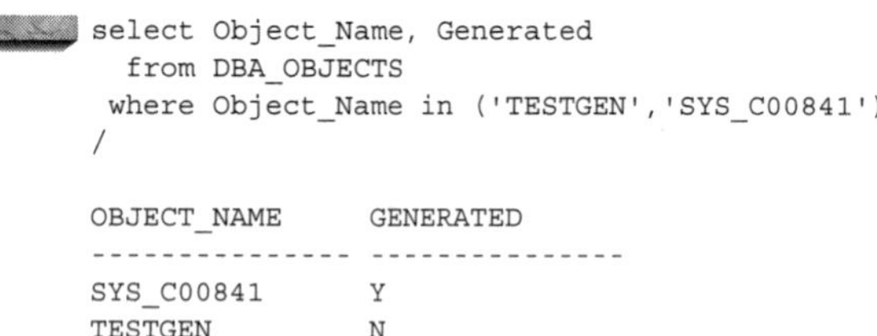

```
select Object_Name, Generated
  from DBA_OBJECTS
 where Object_Name in ('TESTGEN','SYS_C00841')
/

OBJECT_NAME     GENERATED
--------------- ---------------
SYS_C00841      Y
TESTGEN         N
```

Since you let Oracle name the constraint, the Generated column is Y, while the table that you explicitly named has a Generated column of N. At this time, Oracle uses the naming convention of prefixing all names it generates with 'SYS_C'. This convention may change in future releases, and if it does, you will still be able to use the new column Generated to find out which objects have been named by Oracle.

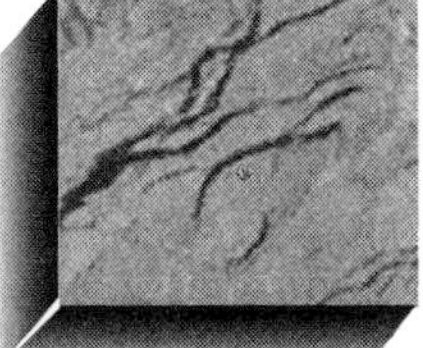

CHAPTER 7

The Users' World

n the previous chapter, we described the DBA_ data dictionary views that relate to the physical world of the database: the tablespaces and datafiles, the rollback segments, the segments and extents, and the objects. While all this information is useful, you still need to know who can access your database and use the space in it. In this chapter we are going to examine how you can see the information about the users who have been created within your database and the privileges those users have been granted.

The User Information Views

Before we begin talking about the individual views, let's just take a quick look at the ones we'll be discussing. Table 7-1 contains a list of the views we'll review in this chapter, along with a short description of each.

Although this list is in alphabetical order, we'll talk about the views in logical order and as they relate to each other. In the tables throughout the chapter, we will mark columns new to Oracle8.0 with a single asterisk (*) and those new in Oracle8i with double asterisk (**).

Now, let's see who's been able to get into your database and what they can do once they've gotten in.

DBA_USERS

DBA_USERS contains the list of all users who can access your database. Table 7-2 shows the columns in this view and what the columns represent.

View	Description
DBA_PROFILES	Display all profiles and their limits
DBA_ROLES	All roles that exist in the database
DBA_ROLE_PRIVS	Roles granted to users and roles
DBA_SYS_PRIVS	System privileges granted to users and roles
DBA_TAB_PRIVS	All grants on objects in the database
DBA_TS_QUOTAS	Tablespace quotas for all users
DBA_USERS	Information about all users of the database

TABLE 7-1. *DBA_ User Information Views*

Column	Description
USERNAME	Name of the user
USER_ID	ID number of the user
PASSWORD	Encrypted password
ACCOUNT_STATUS*	Indicates whether the account is locked, expired, or unlocked
LOCK_DATE*	Date the account was locked if account status was locked
EXPIRY_DATE*	Date of expiration of the account
DEFAULT_TABLESPACE	Default tablespace for data
TEMPORARY_TABLESPACE	Default tablespace for temporary segments
CREATED	User creation date
PROFILE	User resource profile name
INITIAL_RSRC_CONSUMER_GROUP**	The initial resource consumer group for the user
EXTERNAL_NAME*	User external name

TABLE 7-2. *DBA_USERS View for 8i (* = new to Oracle8.0, ** = new to Oracle8i)*

Let's take a look at the columns we use most often. Username is self-explanatory—that's the account name users will enter when they log on to the database. It can be made up of characters (letters of the alphabet), numbers, and the special characters: underscore (_), dollar sign ($), or pound sign (#). The username must begin with an alphabetic character unless you surround the name with double quotation marks ("). In general, Oracle recommends that you do not use the pound or dollar sign in a username—and so do we. The "Schema Object Names and Qualifiers" section in the *Oracle8 SQL Reference Guide* contains a complete set of the rules on choosing usernames.

The User_ID is the unique identifier for that user and is made up of numbers (a mix of numbers 0–9). Hmm, that makes it sound like you can create two users with the same username as long as they have different User_ID numbers. Let's try to do that and see what happens.

```
create user RACHEL identified by TEST
default tablespace USERS
temporary tablespace TEMP;

User created.

create user RACHEL identified by TEST2
default tablespace USERS
temporary tablespace TEMP;
create user RACHEL identified by TEST2
            *
ERROR at line 1:
ORA-01920: user name 'RACHEL' conflicts with another user or role name
```

No, that doesn't work. There was no way to tell Oracle what the User_ID number should be. Oracle assigned the number itself. So why does Oracle have both columns, when each one is unique? Well, the underlying database tables on which these views are built have indexes on them so that Oracle can return the information to you quickly. In general, it's better to index a numeric column than it is to index a character column. So even though both columns are unique, and there is some extra space "wasted" to store the User_ID, Oracle includes that column to improve performance.

Default_Tablespace and Temporary_Tablespace are columns we've talked about before. When a user creates an object and doesn't specify a tablespace in which to create it, Oracle will create the object in the tablespace that you have assigned as the default. The temporary tablespace for a user is the tablespace that Oracle uses when a SQL statement requires sorting. Statements that require sorting are index creation statements and statements with joins, group by clauses, order by clauses, and distinct clauses. If you don't specify a default tablespace or temporary tablespace for a user when you create the user, Oracle will use the SYSTEM tablespace. If you then grant that user the ability to create objects in his or her default tablespace, the user will be able to create objects in SYSTEM. As we've said before, the SYSTEM tablespace should only contain objects that belong to the user SYS, to help keep it from getting fragmented and to ensure that there is always room for the data dictionary tables to grow. You should always specify a default and temporary tablespace for each new user you create, even when you know the user will never own any objects. Over time, requirements have a habit of changing.

You can check to see if any users were created in the SYSTEM tablespace with the following query:

```
select Username, Default_Tablespace, Temporary_Tablespace
  from DBA_USERS
 where Default_Tablespace = 'SYSTEM'
```

```
    or Temporary_Tablespace = 'SYSTEM'
/
```

The results of that query are below.

```
USERNAME          DEFAULT_TABLESPACE    TEMPORARY_TABLESPACE
---------------- --------------------- ---------------------
SYS               SYSTEM                SYSTEM
PROD_OWNER        SYSTEM                SYSTEM
```

In general, no user should have a temporary tablespace of SYSTEM, not even SYS. Sorting in the SYSTEM tablespace will fragment the tablespace, and when the data dictionary tables need to extend, Oracle may not be able to find an extent large enough. In addition, we've said that no user other than SYS should have a default tablespace of SYSTEM because of fragmentation issues. The user PROD_OWNER has SYSTEM as both the default and temporary tablespaces. You can change both of these tablespace values for a user while the database is up and active using the **alter user** command. However, making the change will only affect the location of any new objects. Existing objects that were created in the SYSTEM tablespace will not be moved. To relocate existing objects, you will have to export the user's objects, change the default tablespace, drop the objects, create an empty version of the object in the new default tablespace, and import the user's objects, specifying the **ignore=y** parameter on the import command. We recommend you make sure that all users are created with their default and temporary tablespaces declared properly from the beginning so that you do not have the extra work involved in correcting the tablespace declarations later.

The Password column contains the encrypted password for that account. Going back to the user you created earlier, here's what the password for the RACHEL user entry looks like:

```
select Username, Password
  from DBA_USERS
 where Username like 'RACHEL';

USERNAME                        PASSWORD
------------------------------ ------------------------------
RACHEL                          DE0E2C8587E4087E
```

Remember, when the user RACHEL was created, you used the password TEST. As you can see, the output from the Password column doesn't look anything like the word TEST!

In Oracle versions prior to 8.0 (when Oracle introduced password protection, history, and expiration), you could extract a user's encrypted password, change that password and log in, and then restore the original encrypted password using the "identified by values" clause of the **alter user** command. Why would you want to do that? Well, suppose you wanted to make absolutely sure that no one could access the userid that owned all your production tables, unless you wanted to make changes yourself. You could create the user with a password that could not be used:

```
create user prod_owner identified by values 'no access';
User created.

select Password
  from DBA_USERS
 where Username = 'PROD_OWNER';

PASSWORD
------------------------------
no access
```

Wow! The actual value that you told Oracle to store as the password is displayed instead of an encrypted one. Since the password is stored in the database exactly as you entered it and not as an encrypted value, there is no way for someone to figure out the unencrypted value of that password, and no one can log in as that user—not even you. Now, let's say you want to make changes to the objects in that schema. How are you going to get in if there is no unencrypted password for you to type? Well, you can either make changes from an account that has DBA privileges or has been granted the "any" privileges (**alter any table**, **create any table**, **create any index**, etc.). You can also change the password so that you can log in as the production user directly and then change it back when you are done. If you do not take advantage of Oracle's password expiration and history features, you can still use this method to protect your passwords—a very handy feature to know about. If you do use the history and expiration features, when you go to reset the password after using the account, you will not be able to, because the password has already been used once within the history and expiration times.

Okay, since we've begun talking about the new password features, let's discuss the Account_Status, Lock_Date, and Expiry_Date columns, which all pertain to the new password features in Oracle8. Account_Status tells you whether users can access their accounts and if they can't, why they can't. Lock_Date is the date an account was locked, because the user failed to enter the correct password *x* number of times (you can set the number of allowable attempts in the user's profile). Expiry_Date is the date the account password expired. You can set a grace period during which users can log in with the old password before being forced to change it. Let's take a look at one of the users and see what her Account_Status is.

```
select Username, Account_Status, Lock_Date
  from DBA_USERS
 where Account_Status != 'OPEN'
/
```

```
USERNAME                       ACCOUNT_STATUS                     LOCK_DATE
------------------------------ -------------------------------- ---------
RACHEL                         LOCKED(TIMED)                      16-JUL-99
```

Oh dear, it looks like RACHEL is not going to be able to access her account. You can clear the locked status and allow her to access the database again using the command

```
alter user RACHEL account unlock;
```

The remaining two columns in the DBA_USERS view are Created, which is the date you created this user account, and Profile, which is the Oracle user profile to use when checking the resource limits placed on this user. Hmm, we see a connection here to the next DBA_ view we'll talk about, DBA_PROFILES.

DBA_PROFILES

The DBA_PROFILES view contains information about all profiles that have been defined in the database. By default, when you create an Oracle database in versions 7 and 8, Oracle creates a profile named DEFAULT. Table 7-3 shows all the columns in this view and what they represent.

Why do we need profiles? Profiles define limits on groups of system resources (those with a Resource_Type of KERNEL) and, in Oracle8, define password restrictions (those limits with a Resource_Type of PASSWORD). So for different users, you can set up different limits. In order for Oracle to apply the limits you set in the profiles you create, you must first set **resource_limit** to TRUE in your init.ora file.

Perhaps you want to limit the amount of time the payroll clerks can be connected without pressing a key. Or perhaps you want to limit the number of times a user can log in and open concurrent sessions. You can define the limit of IDLE_TIME or the limit SESSIONS_PER_USER in the default profile. But what if you

Column	Description
PROFILE	Profile name
RESOURCE_NAME	Resource name
RESOURCE_TYPE*	Resource type
LIMIT	Limit placed on this resource for this profile

TABLE 7-3. *DBA_PROFILES View for 8i*

want to give different types of users different limits? You may want to limit the idle time for a clerk, but you probably don't want to limit the idle time for the CEO of your company. Like the roles we discussed in Chapter 2, Oracle allows you to set up multiple profiles and assign each one to one or more users. By default, each new user created in your database is assigned the DEFAULT profile. If you want a user to be assigned a specific profile, you tell Oracle the profile to use when you issue the **create user** command. We'll talk more about assigning profiles a bit later in this section.

You can also define password limits with a profile. With Oracle8, you can now limit the number of times a user can try to log in before the account is locked, the number of password changes that must occur before a password can be reused, along with a number of other password-specific limits.

So how do you create a profile and how do you use it? A sample profile create statement for Oracle8 is

```
create profile CLERK_PROFILE limit
    sessions_per_user 2
            idle_time 10
failed_login_attempts 3
         connect_time 60;
```

In this example, the CLERK_PROFILE profile specifies limits for

- Number of sessions a user can have (2)
- Amount of time the process can be idle (10 minutes)
- Number of times a user can attempt to connect without the correct password (3)
- Total amount of time the user can be connected to the database (60 minutes)

You can then assign that profile to a user with the statement:

```
alter user RACHEL profile CLERK_PROFILE;
```

Now, let's see what happens when RACHEL logs in and enters the wrong password three times. On each of the first three attempts, an error message indicating an invalid username or password is returned. On the fourth try, it doesn't matter what password is entered; the account is now locked, and the DBA must unlock that account, unless the Password_Lock_Time has been set so that the account will automatically unlock after the specified amount of time has passed.

```
connect RACHEL/BADPSWD
ERROR:
ORA-01017: invalid username/password; logon denied
connect RACHEL/BADPSWD
ERROR:
ORA-01017: invalid username/password; logon denied
connect RACHEL/BADPSWD
ERROR:
ORA-01017: invalid username/password; logon denied
connect RACHEL/TEST
ERROR:
ORA-28000: the account is locked
```

Now that you've seen what the profiles are and what you can use them for, how do you see which profile limits are assigned to which user? Remember the Profile column in DBA_USERS? You're going to join the two views together and see what you get. Any limit that you have not specifically mentioned in your **create profile** statement will keep the same value as it has in the DEFAULT profile. Although you can change the values of the profile limits for the DEFAULT profile, we recommend you don't. Any value you change that is not specifically overridden in your other profiles will take on the new value in those other profiles as well.

```
select Username, Resource_Name, Limit
  from DBA_USERS, DBA_PROFILES
 where DBA_USERS.Profile != 'DEFAULT'
   and Limit != 'DEFAULT'
   and DBA_USERS.Profile = DBA_PROFILES.Profile
/

USERNAME   RESOURCE_NAME                    LIMIT
---------- -------------------------------- ----------
RACHEL     FAILED_LOGIN_ATTEMPTS            3
RACHEL     SESSIONS_PER_USER                2
RACHEL     IDLE_TIME                        10
RACHEL     CONNECT_TIME                     60
```

You've just managed to find the nondefault profile settings for a user! And you've seen how you can join two of the DBA_ views to extract and combine information. For a complete listing of the profile limits for your version of Oracle, you can check the SQL reference manual, in the "Create Profile" section.

DBA_ROLES

The DBA_ROLES view contains information about all the roles that have been defined in the database. When you create an Oracle database in versions 7 or 8, Oracle creates several default roles. Table 7-4 shows the columns in this view and what they represent.

Column	Description
ROLE	Role name
PASSWORD_ REQUIRED	Indicates whether the role requires a password to be enabled

TABLE 7-4. *DBA_ROLES View for 8i*

In versions of Oracle prior to Oracle6, there were only three roles available for assignment to users:

- **CONNECT** Gives the user the ability to access the database
- **RESOURCE** Gives the user the ability to create objects and use space in the database
- **DBA** Gives the user the ability to do anything in the database

In fact, these roles did not exist as roles, but were a set of privileges, defined and stored within the Oracle kernel, that you could grant to a user. With Oracle's version 6, true roles were introduced. By Oracle7.x, the DBA received the ability to combine groups of system and object privileges, and to create customized roles to fit the needs of the applications that resided in the database.

If you do a select from an Oracle8.1.5 database, you see the roles that have been created by default.

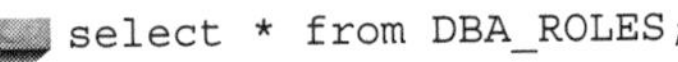

```
select * from DBA_ROLES;

ROLE                           PASSWORD
------------------------------ --------
CONNECT                        NO
RESOURCE                       NO
DBA                            NO
AQ_ADMINISTRATOR_ROLE          NO
SELECT_CATALOG_ROLE            NO
EXECUTE_CATALOG_ROLE           NO
DELETE_CATALOG_ROLE            NO
IMP_FULL_DATABASE              NO
EXP_FULL_DATABASE              NO
RECOVERY_CATALOG_OWNER         NO
AQ_USER_ROLE                   NO
SNMPAGENT                      NO
HS_ADMIN_ROLE                  NO
```

Depending on which products you install, you may see other default roles.

Notice that CONNECT, RESOURCE, and DBA still exist. Oracle retains these roles for backward compatibility but does not guarantee they will always be there. The predefined roles may change from version to version, and, as with the DBA_ views themselves, you should always check to see what new roles have been added and what roles have been removed.

One thing to remember is that the role RESOURCE grants the privilege **unlimited tablespace** to a user. With this privilege, users can create objects in tablespaces that are not their default tablespace and that they have no quota on. *Quota* is the amount of space a user can use in a tablespace. We'll discuss quota in more detail a bit later when we look at the DBA_TS_QUOTAS view.

The Password column indicates whether a password must be entered when a user or application enables a role. If a password is required, users will need to supply the password when they enable the role for their session via the **set role** command. There is one exception to this. If a role that requires a password is granted to a user as his default role, that role will be enabled when he logs on to the database, and he will not need to supply a password. You can see which roles are enabled for your session with the SQL statement:

```
select * from SESSION_ROLES;
```

You can create a role if you have been granted either the **create role** privilege or if you have been granted a role that has been granted this privilege. To create a role:

```
create role TESTROLE;
```

To add privileges to the role, you can grant each privilege to that role. Let's say you want the TESTROLE role to have the **create role** privilege. You'd just need to grant that privilege as follows:

```
grant CREATE ROLE to TESTROLE;
Grant succeeded.
```

Now, if you grant the TESTROLE to a user, that user will be able to create roles in the database.

DBA_ROLE_PRIVS

In the previous section you've seen how to find roles that exist in the database. The DBA_ROLE_PRIVS view tells you which users or roles have been granted these roles, and what administrative privileges have been granted for the role. Table 7-5 shows the columns in this view and what they represent.

Column	Description
GRANTEE	Grantee name—user or role receiving the grant
GRANTED_ROLE	Granted role name
ADMIN_OPTION	Grant was made with the ADMIN option
DEFAULT_ROLE	Role is designated as a DEFAULT ROLE for the user

TABLE 7-5. *DBA_ROLE_PRIVS View for 8i*

Once a role has been created, it must be granted to a user or other role before it can be used. The DBA_ROLE_PRIVS view allows you to see what roles have been granted. The Grantee column is the username or role that has the ability to access this role. You cannot grant roles in a circular fashion. That means, if you create a role called CLERK and another role called MANAGER, you can grant the role CLERK to MANAGER, but once you have done that, you cannot grant MANAGER to CLERK, since that would have the MANAGER role referencing itself.

Granted_Role is the same as the Role column in the DBA_ROLES view, and Admin_Option means that the user who has been granted this role can grant it in turn to others. Default_Role means that when the user logs in to the database, this role will automatically be enabled.

To see which roles have been granted to a user and whether they are automatically enabled, you can type

```
select Grantee, Granted_Role, Default_Role
   from DBA_ROLE_PRIVS
  where Grantee not in ('SYS','SYSTEM')
  order by Grantee;

GRANTEE                   GRANTED_ROLE                    DEF
--------------------      ------------------------------  ---
DBA                       DELETE_CATALOG_ROLE             YES
DBA                       EXECUTE_CATALOG_ROLE            YES
DBA                       EXP_FULL_DATABASE               YES
DBA                       IMP_FULL_DATABASE               YES
DBA                       SELECT_CATALOG_ROLE             YES
DBSNMP                    CONNECT                         YES
DBSNMP                    RESOURCE                        YES
DBSNMP                    SNMPAGENT                       YES
EXP_FULL_DATABASE         EXECUTE_CATALOG_ROLE            YES
EXP_FULL_DATABASE         SELECT_CATALOG_ROLE             YES
IMP_FULL_DATABASE         EXECUTE_CATALOG_ROLE            YES
```

```
IMP_FULL_DATABASE     SELECT_CATALOG_ROLE              YES
JAMES                 CONNECT                          YES
JAMES                 RESOURCE                         YES
JAMES                 TESTROLE                         YES
MY_SCHEMA             CONNECT                          YES
RACHEL                CONNECT                          YES
RACHEL                TESTROLE                         NO
```

Both RACHEL and JAMES have been granted the role TESTROLE, but RACHEL cannot use the privileges from that role until she enables the role for her session. JAMES will automatically inherit any privileges from that role when he logs on and will not have to enter a password if that role has a password.

If you want to see whether any roles that require passwords have been granted to anyone, you can join the DBA_ROLES and DBA_ROLE_PRIVS table as follows:

```
select Grantee, Granted_Role
  from DBA_ROLES a, DBA_ROLE_PRIVS b
 where a.Role = b.Granted_Role
   and a.Password_Required='YES';

GRANTEE               GRANTED_ROLE
--------------------- ------------------------------
RACHEL                TESTROLE
JAMES                 TESTROLE
```

DBA_SYS_PRIVS

The next view, DBA_SYS_PRIVS, shows you which system-level privileges have been granted to which users or roles. System-level privileges are those that allow you to manipulate the database environment, either by creating, dropping, or altering objects within the database. Table 7-6 shows the columns in this view and what they represent.

Column	Description
GRANTEE	Grantee name—user or role receiving the grant
PRIVILEGE	System privilege
ADMIN_OPTION	Grant was made with the ADMIN option

TABLE 7-6. *DBA_SYS_PRIVS View for 8i*

Once again, we advise you to check the number and type of system privileges available in each new version of the database. As Oracle adds new features, new privileges are added to manage them. While you may not need to use all the new features and privileges available to you, a smart DBA will at least be aware that they exist and know how each one works.

Okay. So how do you find out all the system privileges that a user has been granted? If you do a **select** from the view, you get the following:

```
select *
  from DBA_SYS_PRIVS
 where Grantee ='JAMES';

GRANTEE                  PRIVILEGE                                ADM
------------------------ ---------------------------------------- ---
JAMES                    UNLIMITED TABLESPACE                     NO
```

Hmm. That doesn't make sense. We saw earlier that JAMES has the CONNECT, RESOURCE, and TESTROLE roles granted to him. He should have some privileges associated with these roles, as well as the privilege **unlimited tablespace**. In fact, he does, but he inherits the rest of his privileges from the roles. So to truly see what privileges he has, you also have to look for the privileges that are granted to the roles he has been granted.

One thing to note, before we show you how to extract the privileges that have been granted to both JAMES and the roles, is that this user has been granted **unlimited tablespace**. As we've said before, this system privilege allows a user to create an object in *any* tablespace, including SYSTEM, even if he doesn't have quota on that tablespace. Oracle automatically grants this privilege when you grant RESOURCE to a user. If we are beginning to sound like a broken record about this, you must assume that we think it's a pretty important and dangerous situation. We do! In general, a much better idea is to create your own roles and assign the privileges you want them to have, rather than to use the predefined roles of CONNECT and RESOURCE. We feel even more strongly about not assigning the DBA role to anyone who does not warrant having total control over your database.

Now, to see the privileges that have been granted to JAMES and the roles he has been granted, you can run the following:

```
select b.Grantee, b.Privilege
  from DBA_ROLE_PRIVS a, DBA_SYS_PRIVS b
 where a.Grantee=b.Grantee and a.Grantee='JAMES'
 union
select b.Grantee, b.Privilege
  from DBA_ROLE_PRIVS a, DBA_SYS_PRIVS b
 where a.Granted_Role=b.Grantee and a.Grantee='JAMES'
/
```

```
GRANTEE                    PRIVILEGE
-------------------------- ----------------------------------------
CONNECT                    ALTER SESSION
CONNECT                    CREATE CLUSTER
CONNECT                    CREATE DATABASE LINK
CONNECT                    CREATE SEQUENCE
CONNECT                    CREATE SESSION
CONNECT                    CREATE SYNONYM
CONNECT                    CREATE TABLE
CONNECT                    CREATE VIEW
JAMES                      UNLIMITED TABLESPACE
RESOURCE                   CREATE CLUSTER
RESOURCE                   CREATE PROCEDURE
RESOURCE                   CREATE SEQUENCE
RESOURCE                   CREATE TABLE
RESOURCE                   CREATE TRIGGER
RESOURCE                   CREATE TYPE
TESTROLE                   CREATE ANY TABLE
```

That's better! The union of the two separate queries is necessary because you are trying to extract not just the privileges granted directly to JAMES but also the privileges granted to the roles he has been granted. This script will work only for the user and the roles that user has been directly granted. If any of the roles granted to the user have also had roles granted to them, the privileges from those roles will not appear in this listing. Huh? What does that really mean? Well, earlier, we said that a role can be assigned to another role. We used the example of the CLERK role being assigned to the MANAGER role. If JAMES is now granted the MANAGER role and the script is run, the privileges that the CLERK role contains will not show up in the listing because this script will not show the privileges of a role granted to a role. To find those privileges, you must run the script again and substitute one of the role names for JAMES.

There is something interesting in the output of this script though. While in older versions of Oracle the CONNECT privilege only allowed the user to connect to the database, it now gives the user privileges to create objects. So JAMES inherits the ability to create tables from both the CONNECT and RESOURCE roles. Of course, if JAMES does not have the RESOURCE role and its explicit grant of **unlimited tablespace**, he will not be able to create any tables unless he also has an allocation of quota on a tablespace in which his table will reside.

If you look closely, you'll see a privilege is "missing." Which one is it? Well, CONNECT and RESOURCE both give you the ability to create a table, but what about indexes? The **create table** privilege implicitly gives users the ability to create an index on any table they create, so it does not have to be explicitly granted. To create an index on a table in someone else's schema, you would need to have the **create any index** privilege granted.

DBA_TS_QUOTAS

The DBA_TS_QUOTAS view, described in Table 7-7, gives you information about each tablespace and the users that have the ability to allocate space within that tablespace.

We've talked a little about quota on tablespaces. Now it's time to explain what that really means. What is quota? It's the amount of physical space within a tablespace that a user can allocate for objects.

When you create a user, you define the default tablespace for that user. Unless you also assign quota on that tablespace to a user, she cannot create objects in the tablespace. You can also assign quota on tablespaces that are not the default tablespace for that user.

The columns Max_Bytes and Max_Blocks indicate the maximum amount of space the user can allocate in the tablespace. Bytes and Blocks are the already allocated space. Both Blocks and Max_Blocks are in Oracle blocks. A value of –1 in Max_Bytes and Max_Blocks means there is no limit to the space the user can allocate (up to the total available space in the tablespace).

Let's look at a couple of examples. In the first, you are going to see only what the quotas are for the various users in your database.

```
select Username, Tablespace_Name, Max_Bytes
  from DBA_TS_QUOTAS;

USERNAME   TABLESPACE_NAME MAX_BYTES
---------- --------------- ---------
QC_USER    USER_DATA         1048576
MY_SCHEMA  USER_DATA              -1
RACHEL     TESTTBS           2097152
JAMES      USER_DATA         2097152
```

Only one user can allocate as much space as is available in the tablespace. The others all have limits. Wait a minute. Doesn't JAMES have **unlimited tablespace**? Why does he show up in this list? JAMES has the ability to override any quota assignment because he has **unlimited tablespace**, but he will still show up in this list if he has been granted any quota on a specific tablespace. In other words, he has been granted quota on the USER_DATA tablespace but will actually be able to create objects beyond the amount of space that he's been given because the **unlimited tablespace** privilege will override the quota specified.

Column	Description
TABLESPACE_NAME	Tablespace name
USERNAME	User with resource rights on the tablespace
BYTES	Number of bytes charged to the user
MAX_BYTES	User's quota in bytes, or –1 if no limit
BLOCKS	Number of Oracle blocks charged to the user
MAX_BLOCKS	User's quota in Oracle blocks, or -1 if no limit

TABLE 7-7. *DBA_TS_QUOTAS View for 8i*

In the second example, we're going to use both the DBA_TS_QUOTAS view as well as the DBA_USERS view to find all the users who have quota on a tablespace that is not their default tablespace and see how much of that quota they've already used.

```
select a.Username, Tablespace_Name, Max_Bytes, Bytes
  from DBA_TS_QUOTAS a
 where Tablespace_Name not in (select Default_Tablespace
                                 from DBA_USERS b
                                where b.Username = a.Username)
/

USERNAME   TABLESPACE_NAME MAX_BYTES     BYTES
---------- --------------- --------- ---------
RACHEL     TESTTBS           2097152   2048000
```

It seems that RACHEL has quota of 2M on the tablespace TESTTBS and has already used 2,048,000 bytes of that quota. If she tries to allocate more than 49,152 bytes more in the TESTTBS tablespace, she will get an error. You can use this view to see who is using up the space within your tablespaces.

DBA_TAB_PRIVS

The DBA_TAB_PRIVS view, described in Table 7-8, gives you information on all grants on all objects in the database.

Column	Description
GRANTEE	User to whom access was granted
OWNER	Owner of the object
TABLE_NAME	Name of the object
GRANTOR	Name of the user who performed the grant
PRIVILEGE	Table privilege
GRANTABLE	Privilege is grantable

TABLE 7-8. *DBA_TAB_PRIVS View for 8i*

The DBA_TAB_PRIVS view sounds like it has information on the table privileges, right? Well, in this case, the "TAB" is a bit misleading, since this view actually contains access information on all objects in the database. What is an object? A simple answer is that an object is anything that a user can own. We've already seen the DBA_OBJECTS view in Chapter 6 and discussed how you can use it. Although you can grant privileges on most objects, there are several exceptions. Indexes, triggers, and synonyms are considered objects, but they are not accessible in and of themselves. If you are granted access to a table, you automatically have access to the indexes and triggers on that table. Oracle will execute a trigger if it applies to the action you are taking on the table, and will modify or access an index on that table if necessary. A synonym is just an alias and, as such, requires no privileges to use it.

As newer versions of Oracle are released, new types of objects may be added to the database. Once again, we stress that with each new release, you should read through the documentation and, if possible, build a test database to try things out.

The column Grantee refers to the user who has been given this privilege. Owner is the owner of the object itself. Table_Name refers to the object name, while Grantor is the user actually doing the grant. Privilege is the access being granted, and Grantable determines whether the user who has received this privilege can, in turn, grant it to someone else. Because Oracle allows the owner of an object to give another user the right also to grant access, this view needs both the Owner and Grantor columns to show who granted the access.

So, now that you know what objects are and what the columns in the view refer to, what kind of access can you grant? If you perform a query for privileges available in an 8.1.5 database, you get the following:

```
select distinct Privilege
  from DBA_TAB_PRIVS;

PRIVILEGE
----------------------------------------
ALTER
DELETE
EXECUTE
INDEX
INSERT
READ
REFERENCES
SELECT
UPDATE
```

You can grant nine different privileges to a user in Oracle8.1.5. In fact, the **read** privilege is a new privilege as of Oracle8.0, and it refers to the ability to read an operating system–level directory and the files within it.

What do the other privileges mean? The **execute** privilege refers to packages, procedures, functions, and libraries and allows the user who has this privilege to do exactly that—execute the object. This allows you, as the DBA, to maintain tighter security on your database. Rather than grant access to all the tables and views in the database, you can grant access only to the user who will create the packages and procedures that access the tables, and then that user can grant **execute** on his stored program to everyone else. While a user is executing a stored program, she has the access privileges that the owner of the stored program has and can access the tables through the program, without needing access in her own right.

Select, **insert**, **update**, and **delete** are the Data Manipulation Language (DML) privileges that allow a user to actually retrieve or affect the data in the database. **Alter**, **index**, and **references** are Data Definition Language (DDL) privileges that allow the user to alter the structure of the table, create an index on that table, or create a referential constraint on the table.

Now let's see how we can use this view, along with the DBA_OBJECTS view, to see what privileges have been granted by a user. The select statement below looks for all the privileges that have been granted on all tables owned by the user RACHEL.

```
select *
  from DBA_TAB_PRIVS
 where Table_Name in (select Object_Name
                        from DBA_OBJECTS
                       where Owner = 'RACHEL'
                         and Object_Type = 'TABLE')
 order by Table_Name, Grantee;
```

```
GRANTEE    OWNER      TABLE_NAME GRANTOR    PRIVILEGE  GRA
---------- ---------- ---------- ---------- ---------- ---
JAMES      RACHEL     TESTTAB    RACHEL     ALTER      NO
JAMES      RACHEL     TESTTAB    RACHEL     INSERT     NO
JAMES      RACHEL     TESTTAB    RACHEL     REFERENCES NO
JAMES      RACHEL     TESTTAB    RACHEL     UPDATE     NO
JAMES      RACHEL     TESTTAB    RACHEL     SELECT     NO
JAMES      RACHEL     TESTTAB    RACHEL     DELETE     NO
JAMES      RACHEL     TESTTAB    RACHEL     INDEX      NO
MY_SCHEMA  RACHEL     TESTTAB    QC_USER    SELECT     NO
QC_USER    RACHEL     TESTTAB    RACHEL     SELECT     YES
MLT        RACHEL     TESTTAB    RACHEL     INSERT     NO
```

If we look at the output of that select statement, we see that RACHEL has granted all privileges on the table to JAMES, but has only granted **insert** on the table to MLT. In addition, QC_USER has been granted **select** on the table, along with the ability to pass that privilege on. MY_SCHEMA has been granted the **select** privilege on TESTTAB by QC_USER, not by RACHEL.

Let's see what happens when RACHEL revokes the **select** privilege from QC_USER.

```
revoke select on TESTTAB from qc_user;

select *
  from DBA_TAB_PRIVS
 where Table_Name in (select Object_Name
                        from DBA_OBJECTS
                       where Owner = 'RACHEL'
                         and Object_Type = 'TABLE')
 order by Table_Name, Grantee;


GRANTEE    OWNER      TABLE_NAME GRANTOR    PRIVILEGE  GRA
---------- ---------- ---------- ---------- ---------- ---
JAMES      RACHEL     TESTTAB    RACHEL     ALTER      NO
JAMES      RACHEL     TESTTAB    RACHEL     DELETE     NO
JAMES      RACHEL     TESTTAB    RACHEL     INSERT     NO
JAMES      RACHEL     TESTTAB    RACHEL     UPDATE     NO
JAMES      RACHEL     TESTTAB    RACHEL     INDEX      NO
JAMES      RACHEL     TESTTAB    RACHEL     SELECT     NO
JAMES      RACHEL     TESTTAB    RACHEL     REFERENCES NO
RAC        RACHEL     TESTTAB    RACHEL     INSERT     NO
```

Gee. Not only did QC_USER lose the ability to select from TESTTAB, but so did MY_SCHEMA!

A very important point to remember about granting a privilege to a user **with grant option** is that if the owner of the table later revokes the privilege from the first user, any other user who has received the privilege from the user will lose the privilege. Is that clear enough? Let's just walk through a quick example to make sure, since this is a really important point to remember.

To set the stage, you have three users: A, B, and C. User A owns a table named MYTAB and grants user B **insert** and **update** privileges on MYTAB with grant option. User B then grants the **insert** privilege on MYTAB to user C. Later, user B leaves the project, and, without thinking about the impacts, user A revokes the **insert** and **update** privileges on MYTAB from user B. User C is now out of luck, because the **insert** privilege to MYTAB is also removed from user C.

CHAPTER 8

Logical Data Description

In the previous two chapters, we described the DBA_ data dictionary views that relate to the physical world of the database and the users who can access this world. In this chapter, we're going to talk about the way your corporate data is logically laid out and stored, in tables and indexes, views and constraints. The DBA_ views we'll be talking about in this chapter are like a road map or atlas. You can use these views to "drive" from one location to another, gathering information along the way about the data stored in the database. As with the physical world views, the logical data map shows the structure of the data and not the data itself.

Logical Data Views

Before we begin talking about the individual views, let's take a quick look at the ones we'll be discussing. Table 8-1 contains a list of the views we'll review in this chapter, along with a short description of each.

As with the previous chapters, we will mark columns new to Oracle8.0 with * and those new to Oracle8i with **.

DBA_TABLES

A table is the basic logical building block for the database. The physical representation of a table is a segment, but while a segment and the extents that make

View	Description
DBA_CONSTRAINTS	Constraint definitions on all tables
DBA_CONS_COLUMNS	Information about accessible columns in constraint definitions
DBA_INDEXES	Description for all indexes in the database
DBA_IND_COLUMNS	Columns composing indexes on all tables and clusters
DBA_SYNONYMS	All synonyms in the database
DBA_TABLES	Description of all relational tables in the database
DBA_TAB_COLUMNS	Columns of user's tables, views, and clusters
DBA_VIEWS	Description of all views in the database

TABLE 8-1. *DBA_ Logical Data Views*

up a segment define the space that a table takes up within the datafiles, a table and its columns represent the actual information you are storing within the database.

DBA_TABLES contains descriptions of all the relational tables in the database. If you use the **analyze** command when viewing the table, the view will also contain statistics that the Cost Based Optimizer can use when choosing an execution plan. We'll talk more about the Cost Based Optimizer in Chapter 11. Table 8-2 shows the columns in this view and what the columns represent.

Column	Description
OWNER	Owner of the table
TABLE_NAME	Name of the table
TABLESPACE_NAME	Name of the tablespace containing the table
CLUSTER_NAME	Name of the cluster, if any, to which the table belongs
IOT_NAME*	Name of the index organized table, if any, to which the overflow entry belongs
PCT_FREE	Minimum percentage of free space in a block
PCT_USED	Minimum percentage of used space in a block
INI_TRANS	Initial number of transactions
MAX_TRANS	Maximum number of transactions
INITIAL_EXTENT	Size of the initial extent in bytes
NEXT_EXTENT	Size of secondary extents in bytes
MIN_EXTENTS	Minimum number of extents allowed in the segment
MAX_EXTENTS	Maximum number of extents allowed in the segment
PCT_INCREASE	Percentage increase in extent size
FREELISTS	Number of process freelists allocated to this segment
FREELIST_GROUPS	Number of freelist groups allocated to this segment
LOGGING*	Whether logging is enabled (YES or NO)
BACKED_UP	Has table been backed up since last modification?

TABLE 8-2. *DBA_TABLES View for 8i (* = new to Oracle8.0, ** = new to Oracle8i)*

Column	Description
NUM_ROWS	Number of rows returned by the **analyze** command
BLOCKS	Number of blocks below the high-water mark
EMPTY_BLOCKS	Number of empty (never used) data blocks in the table
AVG_SPACE	Average available free space in the table
CHAIN_CNT	Number of chained rows in the table
AVG_ROW_LEN	Average row length, including row overhead
AVG_SPACE_FREELIST_BLOCKS*	Average free space of all blocks on a freelist
NUM_FREELIST_BLOCKS*	Number of blocks on the freelist
DEGREE	Number of query servers used for a full table scan
INSTANCES	Number of instances across which the table is to be scanned
CACHE	Whether the table is to be cached in the buffer cache
TABLE_LOCK*	Whether table locking is enabled or disabled
SAMPLE_SIZE*	Sample size used in analyzing this table
LAST_ANALYZED*	Date of the most recent time this table was analyzed
PARTITIONED*	Whether this table is partitioned
IOT_TYPE*	If this is an index organized table, then IOT_TYPE is IOT or IOT_OVERFLOW. If this is not an index organized table, then IOT_TYPE is NULL
TEMPORARY*	Whether the table is temporary
NESTED*	Is the table a nested table?
BUFFER_POOL*	Name of the default buffer pool for the appropriate object
ROW_MOVEMENT**	Whether partitioned row movement is enabled or disabled

TABLE 8-2. *DBA_TABLES View for 8i (* = new to Oracle8.0, ** = new to Oracle8i)* (continued)

Column	Description
GLOBAL_STATS**	Are the statistics calculated without merging underlying partitions?
USER_STATS**	Were the statistics entered directly by the user?
DURATION**	If temporary table, then duration is sys$session or sys$transaction, else NULL
SKIP_CORRUPT**	Whether skip corrupt blocks is enabled or disabled
TABLE_TYPE*	Type of the table if the table is a typed table (removed in 8i)
PACKED*	If the table is a typed table, does it store objects in packed format? (removed in 8i)
SECONDARY	Is this table object created as part of icreate for domain indexes?
MONITORING	Whether to gather statistics for the number of rows altered by DML statements

TABLE 8-2. *DBA_TABLES View for 8i (* = new to Oracle8.0, ** = new to Oracle8i)* (continued)

Each table is uniquely defined by a combination of Owner and Table_Name. Multiple users can have tables with the same name, and these tables do not need to be identical.

Because tables do take up physical space, they are created with a storage clause. The Tablespace_Name column has the information about the tablespace that contains this table. The Initial_Extent, Next_Extent, and Pct_Increase columns all have to do with the sizing of the first and all subsequent extents within the table, while Min_Extents and Max_Extents contain information about the initial and maximum size of the table. These columns have been discussed in greater detail in Chapter 6 in the section on the DBA_TABLESPACES view.

Init_Trans and Max_Trans deal with the number of concurrent transactions that can access each data block in the table at a time. Once the Max_Trans number of transactions is accessing the data block, any other users attempting to access the block will have to wait. The Freelists column is the number of process freelists for that table. A *process freelist,* also known as a freelist, is simply a list of free data blocks within the extents within the table. The default for this column is 1. Once you have established the freelist value for a table, it cannot be changed dynamically. In other words, once you've set the value, you're stuck with it. The only way to change this value is to drop and re-create the table with a larger freelist size declared. The Freelist_Groups column is used mainly with the Oracle Parallel Server and is the number of freelists to be created for use by the various instances that are part of the Parallel Server. We'll talk more about freelists in Chapters 10 and 12. Again, as with the freelist value, the only way to change the Freelist_Groups value is to drop and re-create the table.

Pct_Free is the percentage of the block that should be reserved for overflow on updates. If you have a table that is rarely updated, or where the columns are static sizes, you can set Pct_Free to a very low number. Pct_Used determines when Oracle will begin inserts into the block again. Pct_Used is not checked until the block has first reached the Pct_Free number. If you have set Pct_Free to 10, then when the block is 90 percent full, Oracle stops inserting new rows into it. If you have also set Pct_Used to 70, Oracle will begin inserting rows into the block again once it is less than 70 percent used.

The Num_Rows, Blocks, Empty_Blocks, Avg_Space, Chain_Cnt, Avg_Row_Len, Sample_Size, and Last_Analyzed columns are all filled when you analyze a table. The Cost Based Optimizer uses the information stored in these columns to determine the best way to access the data in the table.

```
select Num_Rows, Blocks, Empty_Blocks, Avg_Space,
       Chain_Cnt, Avg_Row_Len, Sample_Size, Last_Analyzed
  from DBA_TABLES
 where Table_Name='EXTGROW'
/

 NUM_ROWS    BLOCKS EMPTY_BLOCKS AVG_SPACE CHAIN_CNT AVG_ROW_LEN
SAMPLE_SIZE LAST_ANAL
--------- --------- ------------ --------- --------- -----------
----------- ---------
       15         1         3998      1036         0          59
          0 15-AUG-99
```

In the output to this query, you can see that there are 15 rows stored in the EXTGROW table. The rows are only using one block of space, and there are 3998 empty blocks available. By analyzing a table, you can gather important information about that table's current state and its potential for running out of space.

The User_Stats column, introduced in Oracle8i, indicates whether the optimizer statistics have been inserted by the user. Why would you want to insert your own statistics? Well, if you don't have enough room in your test database to keep a complete copy of production, your testing can be inaccurate. If you can insert the production statistics, even if you don't have all the production data, you can get a more accurate gauge of what the performance will be.

Buffer_Pool, added in Oracle8.0, determines whether the data blocks of this table are retained in memory or flushed as they are no longer needed. With version 8, Oracle introduced the concept of multiple buffer pools. You can assign a table to one of three buffer pools: KEEP, RECYCLE, or DEFAULT. The size of these buffer pools is set in the init.ora file by the parameters **buffer_pool_keep**, **buffer_pool_recycle**, and **db_block_buffers**. Tables assigned to the KEEP buffer pool will have their data blocks kept in memory, while those assigned to the RECYCLE buffer pool will have their data blocks flushed from memory more quickly. Data blocks in the DEFAULT buffer pool will be kept or flushed based on their position in the LRU list.

Cache indicates whether the table is to be cached in the buffer cache. A cached table has its data blocks placed at the most recently used end of the LRU list in the buffer cache when a full table scan is performed. This keeps the data in the table in the SGA longer and is useful for small lookup tables. We'll talk about the LRU list and buffer cache in Chapter 10.

Logging has to do with whether the creation of the table (and any indexes created because of table constraints) and subsequent direct-load changes to the table are logged to the redo logs. Although you can improve performance by not logging changes, you will have to rebuild the indexes if you need to do recovery. Tables that are cached cannot have logging turned off.

The Degree column is used in conjunction with the parallel query option and specifies the number of query servers to use when doing parallel queries on the table.

DBA_TAB_COLUMNS

DBA_TAB_COLUMNS contains information on the columns of all tables, views, and clusters in the database. If you analyze the table, both the DBA_TABLES and DBA_TAB_COLUMNS views will also contain statistics that the Cost Based Optimizer can use to determine the execution plan. Table 8-3 shows the columns in this view and what the columns represent.

Column	**Description**
OWNER	Owner of the table, view, or cluster
TABLE_NAME	Table, view, or cluster name
COLUMN_NAME	Column name
DATA_TYPE	Datatype of the column
DATA_TYPE_MOD*	Datatype modifier of the column
DATA_TYPE_OWNER*	Owner of the datatype of the column
DATA_LENGTH	Length of the column in bytes
DATA_PRECISION	Decimal precision for NUMBER datatype; binary precision for FLOAT datatype; NULL for all other datatypes

TABLE 8-3. *DBA_TAB_COLUMNS View for 8i*

Column	Description
DATA_SCALE	Digits to right of decimal point in a number
NULLABLE	Does column allow NULL values?
COLUMN_ID	Sequence number of the column as created
DEFAULT_LENGTH	Length of default value for the column
DATA_DEFAULT	Default value for the column
NUM_DISTINCT, LOW_VALUE, HIGH_VALUE, DENSITY, NUM_NULLS	These columns remain for backward compatibility with Oracle7. This information is now in the {TAB|PART}_COL_STATISTICS views.
NUM_DISTINCT	Number of distinct values for the column
LOW_VALUE	Smallest value for the column, expressed in hexadecimal notation for the internal representation of the first 32 bytes of the value
HIGH_VALUE	Highest value for the column, expressed in hexadecimal notation for the internal representation of the first 32 bytes of the value
DENSITY	Density of the column (a measure of how distinct the values are)
NUM_NULLS	Number of NULL values in the table for this column
NUM_BUCKETS*	Number of buckets in histogram for the column
LAST_ANALYZED*	Date of the most recent time this column was analyzed
SAMPLE_SIZE*	Sample size used in analyzing this column
CHARACTER_SET_NAME*	Name of the character set: CHAR_CS, NCHAR_CS
CHAR_COL_DECL_LENGTH*	Declaration length of character type column
GLOBAL_STATS**	Are the statistics calculated without merging underlying partitions?
USER_STATS**	Were the statistics entered directly by the user?
AVG_COL_LEN**	Average column length in bytes

TABLE 8-3. *DBA_TAB_COLUMNS View for 8i* (continued)

The DBA_TABLES view gives you the storage and physical layout of the table, while the DBA_TAB_COLUMNS view gives you the layout of the information stored within the table. Information about each column of your table is stored in a single row within this view. Even the columns of the view itself are stored within this view!

The Owner, Table_Name, and Column_Name columns make up the unique key of this view. It's possible for the same table name to be owned by different users, or for the column names to be reused between tables. In fact, an easy way to show that the column contains the same information between tables, for a foreign key relationship, is to use the same name. Column_ID is used to indicate the order of the column within the table.

This view contains the descriptions and formats for the information you can store in your table. The Data_Type column defines the type of data that can be stored. Data_Types include VARCHAR2, CHAR, DATE, NUMBER, LONG, and in Oracle8.x, BLOB, CLOB, LOB, and user-defined datatypes. Each datatype that can be stored also has an associated Data_Length. Dates are always stored in 7 bytes; numbers are stored in a maximum of 22 bytes. Data_Precision and Data_Scale contain information about numeric columns where you have defined the size of the column instead of accepting the Oracle default of 38 digits. Data_Precision is the maximum total length of data in that column, including the decimal places. Data_Scale is the number of decimal places to store for that numeric column. Why would you want to define numbers with precision and scale? If you know that the value in the column can never be larger than three digits, such as a person's age, you can ensure that no one enters a number larger than that by specifying the column as NUMBER(3). If users attempt to enter a four-digit number into that column, they will get an error. Data_Type_Mod and Data_Type_Owner contain information about the user-defined datatype.

Columns can be defined as null or not null. Not null columns must either have data entered into them during an insert or update or have a default value assigned. The Nullable column in DBA_TAB_COLUMNS indicates whether the column can contain null values. Data_Default and Default_Length will only have data in them if you have assigned a default value to the column, and they contain the default value for the column and the length of the default. Why assign defaults? Let's suppose you are building a database for a veterinarian. One of the tables will contain information about the pet owners. One of the columns in this table is Number_Pets. Since pet owners come to the veterinarian because they have at least one pet, you can set a default of 1 for this column. That way, the doctor's staff only has to enter information in that column if the client has more than one pet.

The Num_Distinct, Low_Value, High_Value, and Density columns are filled when you analyze the table. This information is used by the Cost Based Optimizer to determine which query path to use when you access the table. As of Oracle8.x, the information in these columns is also stored in the DBA_TAB_COL_STATISTICS view, and these columns are kept in DBA_TAB_COLUMNS for backward compatibility to Oracle7. The User_Stats column, new in Oracle8i, indicates whether the statistical information has been entered by the user or generated by the **analyze** command as explained in the previous view.

Now let's look at a **create table** statement and see how the table definitions are stored within the view.

```
create table qc_user.PRIMATES
(Code  varchar2(3) not null
     constraint Primates_PK
        primary key
,Description varchar2(250) not null
,Location  varchar2(30) not null
,Date_Of_Birth date  not null
,Status  varchar2(3)
,Name  varchar2(10) not null
,Date_Acquired date
,Cage_Num  number(8,2)
,Coloring  varchar2(3)
    constraint Chk_Color_Type
         check(Coloring in ('brn','blk','red','tan','bld'))
,Gender char(1) default 'U' not null
)
/

select Column_Name, Data_Type, Data_Length, Data_Precision,
       Data_Scale, Nullable, Column_ID, Default_Length
  from DBA_TAB_COLUMNS
 where Table_Name='PRIMATES'
   and Owner='QC_USER'
/

COLUMN_NAME          DATA_TYPE  LENGTH PRECISION SCALE NULL   ID DEF LENGTH
-------------------- ---------- ------ --------- ----- ---- ---- ----------
CODE                 VARCHAR2        3                 N       1
DESCRIPTION          VARCHAR2      250                 N       2
LOCATION             VARCHAR2       30                 N       3
DATE_OF_BIRTH        DATE            7                 N       4
STATUS               VARCHAR2        3                 Y       5
NAME                 VARCHAR2       10                 N       6
DATE_ACQUIRED        DATE            7                 Y       7
CAGE_NUM             NUMBER         22         8     2 Y       8
COLORING             VARCHAR2        3                 Y       9
GENDER               CHAR            1                 N      10          4
```

Hmm. The Cage_Num column was defined as NUMBER(8,2). Yet it shows with a Data_Length of 22. That is the maximum number of bytes that column can possibly take to store values. Like VARCHAR2 columns, the value of Data_Length is the maximum size of the column, not the actual number of bytes it will take up. LONG columns, which have no real length definition, will have a Data_Length of 0. The Gender column was created with a default, so there is a Default_Length for that column.

DBA_VIEWS

A view is a mask laid over a table or set of tables to define or restrict the columns users see when they access the database. Views can be on single tables or on joins of multiple tables.

Think of that ever-popular horse costume people wear at parties. It's actually made of two parts, the front half filled by one person, the back by another. Yet when it is put together, you see a single picture, a whole. Views can be used to create a single, simpler picture of the tables in your database and to make ad hoc queries and general coding easier for the end users and programmers. We'll show you some examples a little later in this section.

DBA_VIEWS contains the text of all views in the database. Table 8-4 shows the columns in this view and what the columns represent.

Oracle stores a view as a select statement. Views can be owned by anyone who has been given the **create view** privilege and can be named anything that Oracle will accept as a valid object name. The Owner and View_Name columns contain

Column	Description
OWNER	Owner of the view
VIEW_NAME	Name of the view
TEXT_LENGTH	Length of the view text
TEXT	View text
TYPE_TEXT_LENGTH*	Length of the type clause of the typed view
TYPE_TEXT*	Type clause of the typed view
OID_TEXT_LENGTH*	Length of the WITH OID clause of the typed view
OID_TEXT*	WITH OID clause of the typed view
VIEW_TYPE_OWNER*	Owner of the type of the view if the view is a typed view
VIEW_TYPE*	Type of the view if the view is a typed view

TABLE 8-4. *DBA_VIEWS View for 8i*

this information and make up the unique identifier for a view. The Text column contains the actual SQL statement that will be executed when the view is accessed. This column is stored as a LONG datatype, so the Text_Length column contains the true size of the select statement in bytes. With Oracle8, users were given the ability to create user-defined object types, and the remaining columns in the DBA_VIEWS view contain information about views created with user-defined object types.

Why use views? Why not just let the programmers write the complicated queries wherever they need them? Well, remember that if the SQL statement being executed is identical to one already stored in the SGA, Oracle will not have to develop a new execution plan, which improves performance. But if the statement is even slightly different, with an extra space or a column capitalized or lowercase, Oracle sees it as a different statement and will have to reprocess it. For very complicated queries, it's easy to code the query slightly differently and have it reprocessed.

Also, we believe strongly in modular programming and in making everyone's life easier when working on an application. If that complicated query changes, it's much simpler to change it in only one place, the view definition, than it is to go and find every program that contains that query and fix them all. Plan ahead and look like a hero!

There are other reasons to use views, even on single tables. Let's look at the XYZ Company. They have decided to implement a new system that allows employees to update some of their own personnel information. You can now log on to the system and change the number of dependents you want to list for your tax withholdings or change your address. The table that contains that information has the following structure:

```
desc EMP_INFO

Name                            Null?    Type
------------------------------- -------- ----
EMPID                                    NUMBER
LAST_NAME                                VARCHAR2(30)
FIRST_NAME                               VARCHAR2(30)
MID_INIT                                 VARCHAR2(1)
ADDRESS1                                 VARCHAR2(30)
ADDRESS2                                 VARCHAR2(30)
ADDRESS3                                 VARCHAR2(30)
ZIPCODE                                  VARCHAR2(9)
SALARY                                   NUMBER(9,2)
DEPENDENTS                               NUMBER(2)
MARITAL_STATUS                           VARCHAR2(1)
```

What are the problems you can see if you give the employees access to the table itself? Hmm, we wouldn't want to let employees change their salary, or see someone else's salary, and we wouldn't want to let anyone change information for any other employee. So, how do you prevent them from doing this? If you said, "Use a view," congratulations, you've been paying attention! You can create the following view, and grant select and update access on the view to the employees.

```
create view UPD_EMP_INFO
as
select Empid, Last_Name, First_Name, Mid_Init,
       Address1, Address2, Address3, Zipcode,
       Dependents, Marital_Status
  from Emp_Info
 where Empid=USER;
```

The only column missing from this view is the Salary column. Notice the where clause. Oracle has built-in functions that return system values to you. We've used one of these, SYSDATE, before in some of the queries we've shown you. The USER function returns the Oracle userid of the session currently logged on. This view assumes that employees log on to the system using their employee ID. Grant **select** and **update** to this view to public, create a public synonym, and you are now ready to allow the employees to update everything but their salary.

First, let's look at what is in the table; then we'll take a look at what the view returns when we log on and select from it. We're going to attempt to update some of the information as well.

```
select *
  from EMP_INFO
/

EMPID  LAST_NAME       FIRST_N M ADDRESS1           ADDRESS2
ADDRESS3           ZIPCODE      SALARY DEPENDENTS M
------ -------------- ------- - ------------------ ------------------
------------------ --------- --------- ---------- -
  1234 Carmichael      Rachel    1010 All Star Way  New York NY
                   10000        100000          0 W
  2345 Theriault       Marlene L 222 Dream Street   Washington, DC
                   20000        150000          0 D
  3456 Viscusi         James     1234 Racing Avenue Philadelphia PA
                   30000        125000          0 M

connect 3456/3456
Connected.

select *
  from UPD_EMP_INFO;
```

```
EMPID  LAST_NAME  FIRST_NAME M ADDRESS1            ADDRESS2
ADDRESS3 ZIPCODE   DEPENDENTS M
------ ---------- ---------- - ------------------- ---------------
-------- --------- ---------- -
  3456 Viscusi    James        1234 Racing Avenue   Philadelphia PA
         30000              0 M

update UPD_EMP_INFO
   set Dependents=4;

1 row updated.

select *
  from UPD_EMP_INFO;

 EMPID LAST_NAME  FIRST_NAME M ADDRESS1            ADDRESS2
ADDRESS3 ZIPCODE   DEPENDENTS M
------ ---------- ---------- - ------------------- ---------------
-------- --------- ---------- -
  3456 Viscusi    James        1234 Racing Avenue   Philadelphia PA
         30000              4 M
```

James can only see part of his own information, and he can update it. What happens when he tries to select information about another employee or attempts to update his salary?

```
select *
  from UPD_EMP_INFO
 where Empid=1234;

no rows selected

update UPD_EMP_INFO set Salary=200000;
update UPD_EMP_INFO set Salary=200000
                        *
ERROR at line 1:
ORA-00904: invalid column name
```

Perfect! You've protected the information you want to protect and allowed the employee to update only the information you wanted.

We've shown you how and why to use a view for a single table. Now let's take a look at an example of using a view to join multiple tables.

```
create or replace view order_report
as
select /*+ FIRST_ROWS */
       L.Order_Number Order_Number,
       L.Last_Name||', '||L.First_Name Customer,
       L.Order_Status Order_Status,
       L.Billto_State,
       L.Shipto_State,
       P.Orig_Order_Date Orig_Order_Date,
       P.Payment_Type
```

```
  from PAYMENT_INFO P,
       PURCHASE_LOG L
 where P.Order_Number = L.Order_Number
/
```

In this view, you are joining two tables together, selecting information from both, and joining them on the Order_Number column in each table. Views cannot be optimized, but you can include hints to direct the optimizer in the select statements that make up the view. In this view, the FIRST_ROWS hint has been specified, telling Oracle to choose the optimizer plan that will return the first row as quickly as possible. Let's see what gets stored in DBA_VIEWS.

```
select Text
  from DBA_VIEWS
 where View_Name = 'ORDER_REPORT'
/

TEXT
-----------------------------------------------------
select /*+ FIRST_ROWS */
       L.Order_Number Order_Number,
       L.Last_Name||', '||L.First_Name Customer,
       L.Order_Status Order_Status,
       L.Billto_State,
       L.Shipto_State,
       P.Orig_Order_Date Orig_Order_Date,
       P.Payment_Type
  from PAYMENT_INFO P,
       PURCHASE_LOG L
 where P.Order_Number = L.Order_Number
```

Looks familiar, doesn't it? Oracle will store the SQL statement that will be executed when you query the view. Now, since all the DBA_ views *are* views, they should also be in the DBA_VIEWS table, right? Let's see if we can find the underlying SQL statement for the DBA_VIEWS view itself.

```
select Text
  from DBA_VIEWS
 where View_Name='DBA_VIEWS'
/

TEXT
--------------------------------------------------------------------------
select u.name, o.name, v.textlength, v.text, t.typetextlength, t.typetext,
       t.oidtextlength, t.oidtext, t.typeowner, t.typename
from sys.obj$ o, sys.view$ v, sys.user$ u, sys.typed_view$ t
where o.obj# = v.obj#
  and o.obj# = t.obj#(+)
  and o.owner# = u.user#
```

Isn't it easier to type **select * from DBA_VIEWS** than all of the above? As we said, using views to hide multiple table joins makes life easier on your programmers and end users, and especially on you!

DBA_INDEXES

DBA_INDEXES contains descriptions for all indexes in the database. If you analyze the index or the table the index is on, the view will also contain statistics on the data distribution that the Cost Based Optimizer can use. Table 8-5 shows the columns in this view and what the columns represent.

The DBA_INDEXES view contains one row for every index on every table in the database. The Owner, Index_Name, Table_Owner, and Table_Name columns contain information about the ownership of the index and the table to which it

Column	Description
OWNER	Username of the owner of the index
INDEX_NAME	Name of the index
INDEX_TYPE*	Type of index
TABLE_OWNER	Owner of the indexed object
TABLE_NAME	Name of the indexed object
TABLE_TYPE	Type of the indexed object
UNIQUENESS	Uniqueness status of the index: UNIQUE or NONUNIQUE
COMPRESSION**	Enabled or disabled
PREFIX_LENGTH**	Number of columns in the prefix of the key used for compression
TABLESPACE_NAME	Name of the tablespace containing the index
INI_TRANS	Initial number of transactions
MAX_TRANS	Maximum number of transactions
INITIAL_EXTENT	Size of initial extent
NEXT_EXTENT	Size of secondary extents

TABLE 8-5. *DBA_INDEXES View for 8i*

Column	Description
MIN_EXTENTS	Minimum number of extents allowed in the segment
MAX_EXTENTS	Maximum number of extents allowed in the segment
PCT_INCREASE	Percentage increase in extent size
PCT_THRESHOLD*	Threshold percentage of block space allowed per index entry
INCLUDE_COLUMN*	User column ID for last column to be included in index organized table top index
FREELISTS	Number of process freelists allocated to this segment
FREELIST_GROUPS	Number of freelist groups allocated to this segment
PCT_FREE	Minimum percentage of free space in a block
LOGGING*	Logging attribute
BLEVEL	B-Tree level: depth of the index from its root block to its leaf blocks. A depth of 0 indicates that the root block and leaf block are the same
LEAF_BLOCKS	Number of leaf blocks in the index
DISTINCT_KEYS	Number of distinct keys in the index
AVG_LEAF_BLOCKS_PER_KEY	Average number of leaf blocks per key
AVG_DATA_BLOCKS_PER_KEY	Average number of data blocks per key
CLUSTERING_FACTOR	A measurement of the amount of (dis)order of the table this index is for
STATUS	State of the index: DIRECT LOAD, VALID, or INPROGS (a DDL operation on the domain index is in progress)
DOMIDX_STATUS**	Reflects the status of the domain index. A NULL value means the specified index is not a domain index. A value of VALID means the index is a domain index and the index does not have any errors. If the value of this column is IDXTYP_INVLD, it means the index type corresponding to this domain index is invalid

TABLE 8-5. *DBA_INDEXES View for 8i* (continued)

Column	Description
DOMIDX_OPSTATUS**	Reflects the status of an operation that was performed on the domain index. A value of NULL indicates that the specified index is not a domain index. A value of VALID specifies that the index does not have any errors. A value of FAILED indicates that the operation performed on the domain index failed with an error
FUNCIDX_STATUS**	A value of NULL indicates a non-function-based index. ENABLED indicates the function-based index is enabled. DISABLED indicates the function-based index is disabled
NUM_ROWS*	Number of rows in this index
SAMPLE_SIZE*	Size of the sample used to analyze this index
LAST_ANALYZED*	Timestamp for when this index was last analyzed
DEGREE*	Number of threads per instance for scanning the index. NULL if PARTITIONED=NO
INSTANCES*	Number of instances across which the indexes are to be scanned. NULL if PARTITIONED=NO
PARTITIONED*	Indicates whether this index is partitioned. Set to YES if it is partitioned
TEMPORARY*	Can the current session only see data that it placed in this object itself?
GENERATED*	Was the name of this index system generated?
SECONDARY*	Is the index object created as part of icreate for domain indexes?
BUFFER_POOL*	Name of the default buffer pool for the appropriate object
USER_STATS**	Were the statistics entered directly by the user?
DURATION**	The duration
PCT_DIRECT_ACCESS**	If index on IOT, then this is percentage of rows with Valid guess

TABLE 8-5. *DBA_INDEXES View for 8i* (continued)

Column	Description
ITYP_OWNER	Index Type owner. Used with Oracle Data Cartridge Interface
ITYP_NAME	Index Type name. Used with Oracle Data Cartridge Interface
PARAMETERS	Parameter string used for domain indexes. Used with Oracle Data Cartridge Interface
GLOBAL_STATUS	Specifies that the partitioning of the index is user defined and is not equipartitioned with the underlying table. By default, nonpartitioned indexes are global indexes

TABLE 8-5. *DBA_INDEXES View for 8i* (continued)

refers. It is possible for a user who does not own the table to create an index on a table, if he has been given the **create any index** privilege. It is not possible for two different users to create an index with the same columns on the same table. Oracle ensures that only one index is created per combination of columns. Even though you can do it, it is not a good idea to have an index on a table owned by a user who is not the table owner. If another user attempts to access the table, she will not have access to that index. There is no way to create a synonym for an index.

The Table_Type column distinguishes between tables that are simple tables and those that are parts of clustered tables. Index_Type is a new column as of Oracle8 and contains information on the type of index. Indexes can be clustered indexes or normal indexes as well as bitmap indexes. *Bitmap indexes,* which were introduced in Oracle7.3, store the rowids associated with a key value as a bitmap. In Oracle7.3, the only way to tell if an index is a bitmap index is to check the Uniqueness column. In Oracle8, that information was moved to its own column, and the Uniqueness column indicates whether the index has been created as a unique index. *Unique indexes* are those where the only acceptable values in the columns are nulls or a unique combination of the columns making up the index.

Tablespace_Name, Ini_Trans, Max_Trans, Initial_Extent, Next_Extent, Min_Extents, Max_Extents, Pct_Increase, Pct_Free, Freelists, and Freelist_Groups all pertain to the storage allocation parameters for the index and have been discussed in detail in Chapter 6 in the section on the DBA_TABLESPACES view.

Logging has to do with whether the creation of the index and subsequent direct-load changes to the index are logged to the redo logs. Although you can improve performance by not logging changes, you will have to rebuild the indexes if you need to do recovery. Thus, if you are going to disable logging of index information, you must be sure that you can re-create the index correctly should you need to do so.

Blevel, Leaf_Blocks, Distinct_Keys, Avg_Leaf_Blocks_Per_Key, Avg_Data_Blocks_Per_Key, and Clustering_Factor all contain information that can be used by the Cost Based Optimizer to determine whether this index should be used to improve the performance of a query. If you have not analyzed the index or the table that the index is built on, there will be no data in these columns if your database is Oracle8.0 or a prior version. With Oracle8.0, the columns Num_Rows, Sample_Size, and Last_Analyzed were added to this view to help you better evaluate the statistics it holds. As of Oracle8i, you can insert your own statistics about the index into these views, and this is flagged in the User_Stats column.

Buffer_Pool, added in Oracle8.0, determines whether the data blocks of this index are retained in memory or flushed as they are no longer needed. Generated indicates whether the name of the index was created by the system or by the user.

With Oracle8i, users can create a function-based index. In earlier versions of the database, when you had an index on a character column, you could not be sure if the data in the column was stored in uppercase, lowercase, or some combination. You had to use a function on the column in the where clause to force it to a particular case. As soon as you used the function, Oracle would no longer use the index on that column. A *function-based index* is created with the function as part of the index, so you no longer have to add it to the where clause, and the index can be used for searches. If you use a function-based index, you must analyze the table and the index or Oracle will not be able to use the index. The column Funcidx_Status indicates whether the index is a function-based index and the status of the index if it is.

Let's take a look at a table and the indexes on that table.

```
describe SKU_ATTR

Name                            Null?    Type
------------------------------- -------- ----
SKU_ID                          NOT NULL NUMBER(38)
PRODUCT_ID                      NOT NULL NUMBER(38)
NAME_ID                                  NUMBER(38)
NAME                                     VARCHAR2(18)
VALUE_ID                                 NUMBER(38)
VALUE                                    VARCHAR2(18)
LST_UPD_DT                               DATE
UPD_CD                                   CHAR(1)

select Owner, Index_Name, Table_Owner, Table_Name, Table_Type,
       Uniqueness,Tablespace_Name, Initial_Extent, Next_Extent,
```

```
       Min_Extents, Max_Extents,Pct_Increase
  from DBA_INDEXES
 where Table_Name = 'SKU_ATTR';

OWNER     INDEX_NAME     TABLE_OWNER TABLE_NAME     TYPE  UNIQUENES
-------- ------------  ----------- ------------ ----- ---------
 TABLESPACE INITIAL NEXT_EXT MIN_EXT MAX_EXT PCT_INCR
 ---------- ------- -------- ------- ------- --------
QC_USER  SKU_ATTR_IDX1 QC_USER     SKU_ATTR      TABLE UNIQUE
 CATINDEX    8388608  8388608      1      249        0

QC_USER  XIF8SKU_ATTR  QC_USER     SKU_ATTR      TABLE NONUNIQUE
 CATINDEX    8388608  8388608      1      249        0

QC_USER  XIE1SKU_ATTR  QC_USER     SKU_ATTR      TABLE NONUNIQUE
CATINDEX     8388608  8388608      1      249        0
```

This table has three indexes, only one of which is unique, but you cannot tell which columns are indexed by looking at this view. We'll show you how to see the indexed columns in the next section on the DBA_IND_COLUMNS view.

DBA_IND_COLUMNS

Now that you know the indexes on the tables in your database, wouldn't it be helpful to know which columns in the table are indexed? You should know which columns are indexed and, for indexes with multiple columns, where the columns are in the column list. The optimizer will use an index for a query where possible, by checking the columns in the where clause to see if they are part of an index. However, if the column is in the middle of a concatenated index, and the leftmost columns in that index are not part of the where clause, Oracle will not use the index. You should examine the queries in your application that are either taking a long time to complete or doing full table scans to see if you can rewrite the query to take advantage of an existing index or add an index to improve the performance.

DBA_IND_COLUMNS contains descriptions of the columns composing the indexes on all tables and clusters in the database. Table 8-6 shows the columns in this view and what the columns represent.

The Index_Owner, Index_Name, Table_Owner, and Table_Name columns contain information about the ownership of the index and the table it refers to and can be linked back to the DBA_INDEXES view. Column_Name is the name of the column in the table, Column_Position is the position of the column in the column list for the index, and Column_Length is the default length of the column. With Oracle8i, you can now specify whether the column should be sorted in ascending or descending order.

Column	Description
INDEX_OWNER	Index owner
INDEX_NAME	Index name
TABLE_OWNER	Table or cluster owner
TABLE_NAME	Table or cluster name
COLUMN_NAME	Column name or attribute of the object type column
COLUMN_POSITION	Position of column or attribute within index
COLUMN_LENGTH	Indexed length of the column or attribute
DESCEND**	Y/N; Y if this column is sorted in descending order

TABLE 8-6. *DBA_IND_COLUMNS View for 8i*

A sample of the indexes on a table and the columns in the indexes from an Oracle7.3.4 database is below.

```
select *
  from DBA_IND_COLUMNS
 where Table_Name = 'SKU_ATTR'
 order by Index_Name, Column_Position
/

OWNER    INDEX_NAME     TABLE_OWNER TABLE_NAME COL_NAME   POSITION LENGTH
-------- -------------- ----------- ---------- ---------- -------- ------
QC_USER  SKU_ATTR_IDX1  QC_USER     SKU_ATTR   SKU_ID            1     22
QC_USER  SKU_ATTR_IDX1  QC_USER     SKU_ATTR   PRODUCT_ID        2     22
QC_USER  SKU_ATTR_IDX1  QC_USER     SKU_ATTR   NAME_ID           3     22
QC_USER  XIE1SKU_ATTR   QC_USER     SKU_ATTR   LST_UPD_DT        1      7
QC_USER  XIF8SKU_ATTR   QC_USER     SKU_ATTR   PRODUCT_ID        1     22
```

You can see that the Product_ID is indexed twice. Because it is in the middle of the column list for the first index, any query that specifies only the Product_ID will not make use of the SKU_ATTR_IDX1 index. The DBA for this system has determined that performance will be improved if an additional index is added on this column alone.

Don't create indexes just because the column is mentioned in a where clause. If the column does not have very discriminating data, such as a gender column, a regular index on that column will likely not be used by Oracle, although a gender column is an ideal candidate for a bitmapped index. While the more combinations of columns you have indexes for can help in querying data, remember that when you insert, update, or delete data, all the indexes on a table will also be modified. You can seriously degrade performance by having too many indexes. One of the authors had an application in which a query on the test database took 6 minutes, while the same query on the production database took 30 minutes. The test database had been refreshed from the production database, so the data being queried was identical. After some research, she found that there was an index on the production table that did not exist in the test database. She dropped the index, and the production query took 6 minutes! The additional index was not a very discriminating index, and Oracle was using it instead of one that had more unique characteristics. This is a perfect example of how an index can sometimes negatively impact performance. Always check the execution plan when you are having a performance problem to see which, if any, indexes are being used. We'll tell you how to create and read the execution plan in detail in Chapter 11.

Be cautious when deciding to add bitmap indexes. A bitmap index on a table that is very update intensive or on a column where new values are added frequently can actually hurt rather than help performance. You cannot do row-level locking with bitmap indexes, so the entire table will be locked until the update, insert, or delete completes.

DBA_CONSTRAINTS

Constraints are restrictions on the contents of the columns of a table or view. DBA_CONSTRAINTS lists all constraints in the database. Table 8-7 shows the columns in this view and what the columns represent.

You can use *referential integrity constraints*—primary and foreign keys—as a means of ensuring that the data in your database is consistent across tables. A referential integrity constraint defines a relationship between columns in one or more tables. *Primary key constraints* require the data in that column or combination of columns to be a unique combination in the table and not be null. *Unique constraints* require that the data be a unique combination, but will allow you to insert null values. *Foreign key constraints* can only refer to columns defined as either primary key constraint columns or unique key constraint columns. When we refer to the tables in a referential integrity relationship, we call the primary/unique key table the *parent table* and the table with the foreign key defined on it the *child table*. Referential integrity guarantees that when you try to insert a value into the child table, the corresponding value already exists in the parent table.

At the XYZ Company, you would not want to be able to insert an order for a product not in your production line. A foreign key constraint on the orders table, referencing the product code column in the orders table back to the product code primary key column in the products table ensures that any product you list on the order is in the products table.

Column	Description
OWNER	Owner of the table
CONSTRAINT_NAME	Name associated with constraint definition
CONSTRAINT_TYPE	C (check constraint on a table) P (primary key) U (unique key) R (referential integrity) V (with check option on a view) O (with read-only, on a view)
TABLE_NAME	Name associated with table with constraint definition
SEARCH_CONDITION	Text of search condition for table check
R_OWNER	Owner of table used in referential constraint
R_CONSTRAINT_NAME	Name of unique constraint definition for referenced table
DELETE_RULE	Delete rule for a referential constraint: CASCADE / NO ACTION
STATUS	Enforcement status of constraint: ENABLED or DISABLED
DEFERRABLE*	Indicates whether the constraint is deferrable
DEFERRED*	Indicates whether the constraint was initially deferred
VALIDATED*	Indicates whether all data obeys the constraint: VALIDATED, NOT VALIDATED
GENERATED*	Indicates whether the name is system generated
BAD*	Creating this constraint should give ORA-02436; rewrite it before the year 2000
RELY**	If set, this flag will be used in the optimizer
LAST_CHANGE*	Indicates when the constraint was last enabled or disabled

TABLE 8-7. *DBA_CONSTRAINTS View for 8i*

Just to confuse things a bit, you can create what is called a *self-referring constraint.* A self-referring constraint is one where the parent and child tables are the same table. Hmm, let's look at a simple example to make this easier to understand. Let's suppose you are working on the reporting structure for a large company. The company has several divisions, each of which has a department code. Each division is made up of several departments that also have their own department code. You need to show the relationship between the departments and the division to which they belong. The DEPARTMENT table has two columns, Department_Code and Department_Name. The Department_Code column has been defined as the primary key for this table. If you add a third column, Division, you can create a self-referring constraint on Division that points back to Department_Code. This will prevent anyone from updating a department with a division that does not already exist in the DEPARTMENT table. Let's look at how you would create this.

```
create table DEPARTMENT
(Department_Code    varchar2(5)
,Department_Name    varchar2(30)
,Division           varchar2(5)
)
/

Table created.

alter table DEPARTMENT add constraint DEPARTMENT_PK
primary key (Department_Code)
/

Table altered.

alter table DEPARTMENT add constraint DVISION_FK
 foreign key (Division) references DEPARTMENT
/

Table altered.
```

Now that you've created the table, the primary key, and the self-referencing foreign key, let's see what happens as you insert data into the table.

```
insert into DEPARTMENT values('10000','Division 1',null);

1 row created.
```

Wait a second! How were you able to insert a row into the DEPARTMENT table when you didn't give a Division value? Look back at how you created the DEPARTMENT table. Because you didn't specify **not null** when you created the Division column, Oracle automatically created it to allow null values. When you insert a null into the table, the null value is not checked for the foreign key constraint. So you can enter all the division codes you will need by giving them a null value for Division. Now insert two more rows, one with a Division that matches the one you just inserted and one row with a Division code that does not exist yet.

```
insert into DEPARTMENT values('10001','Accounting','10000');

1 row created.

insert into DEPARTMENT values('20001','Data Operations','20000');
insert into DEPARTMENT values('20001','Data Operations','20000')
            *
ERROR at line 1:
ORA-02291: integrity constraint (QC_USER.DVISION_FK) violated - parent
key not found
```

In this case, because you had a value in the Division column, Oracle checked the value against the values in the Department_Code column. The first row you inserted had an existing Division code, but the second one did not, and Oracle returned an error indicating that.

Oracle will automatically create indexes on the columns you define as unique or primary key constraint columns. However, indexes are not created on the columns in a foreign key constraint, and you should create those indexes yourself. In Oracle7.3 and later, if there is no index on the foreign key column, Oracle will lock the entire child table when you change the contents of the foreign key column in the parent table. Without an index, it is possible therefore to lock out all other users of the child table while one user updates a record in the parent table. This is not a terrific situation, especially if that user goes out to lunch before committing that update!

You can, if you want, write all the relationship checks into your application and not use the referential integrity constraints provided by Oracle. So why use the constraints? Although using the referential integrity constraints does make some maintenance difficult for a DBA, you still should use them. Without the constraints, it's possible for someone to bypass the application and insert inconsistent data into the tables. We'd rather spend a little extra time occasionally on maintenance than have to explain to an irate customer why we didn't ship the nonexistent product we let him order. And if the application is coded incorrectly, allowing you to insert data into the child table before the parent table insert is done, or delete from the parent table before the child rows have been deleted, the referential integrity constraint tells Oracle to return an error and protects the integrity of your data.

Check constraints ensure that the data being inserted into a column meets certain conditions. If you have a well-defined, limited set of possible values for the column, check constraints are a good idea. As an example, a gender column in an employee database is an excellent candidate for a check constraint. Any column that must have data in it can be defined with a special check constraint, the NOT NULL constraint.

You can also create constraints on views. A *read-only constraint* on a view flags that view as one that you cannot update, insert into, or delete from. A *check option constraint* on a view limits any inserts or updates to rows that the view itself can select. So if you create a view on an employee table that limits rows selected to those of the employee looking at the view, a check option constraint would prevent that employee from updating information about another employee. Let's go back to the UPD_EMP_INFO view you created earlier and re-create it now, with a check option constraint.

```
create view UPD_EMP_INFO
as
select Empid, Last_Name, First_Name, Mid_Init,
       Address1, Address2, Address3, Zipcode
       Dependents, Marital_Status
  from Emp_Info
 where Empid=USER
  with check option constraint LIMIT_ACCESS
/
create public synonym UPD_EMP_INFO for qc_user.UPD_EMP_INFO
/
grant select, update on UPD_EMP_INFO to public
/
```

If we look in DBA_CONSTRAINTS, we can see the constraint there.

```
select Constraint_Name, Constraint_Type
  from DBA_CONSTRAINTS
 where Table_Name = 'UPD_EMP_INFO'
/

CONSTRAINT_NAME                C
------------------------------ -
LIMIT_ACCESS                   V
```

Now let's log on as one user and try to update the data for a different user.

```
connect 3456/3456
Connected.
update UPD_EMP_INFO set Dependents=5 where Empid=1234;

0 rows updated.
```

The check option constraint prevents any unauthorized updates.

The Owner of a constraint on a table will always be the table owner. The Constraint_Type column lists the type of constraint, as defined above. If the constraint is a check constraint, the Search_Condition column contains the conditions to evaluate. A foreign key constraint will have the R_Owner and R_Constraint_Name defined, indicating the primary or unique key constraint to which the foreign key constraint refers.

Delete_Rule defines what happens to the rows in the foreign key table when a row is deleted from the primary or unique key table. If the Delete_Rule column is CASCADE, then all rows in the child table with the foreign key column that matches the value being deleted from the parent table will also be deleted. If the Delete_Rule column is NO ACTION, Oracle will return an error message indicating that there are foreign key columns that depend on this value, and the delete of the row in the primary key table will fail.

The Deferrable and Deferred columns refer to a new feature in Oracle8, allowing you to delay the constraint checking to the end of the transaction, rather than have it checked as each row is inserted or updated. This allows you to insert a child record and then the parent record.

Let's look at the constraints for one user.

```
select Table_Name, Constraint_Name, Constraint_Type, Search_Condition,
       R_Owner, R_Constraint_Name
  from DBA_CONSTRAINTS
 where Owner='QC_USER'
/

TABLE      CONSTRAINT_NAME  C SEARCH_CONDITION     R_OWNER    REF CONSTR
---------- ---------------- - -------------------- ---------- -------------
PRIMATES   CHK_COLOR_TYPE   C Coloring in ('bro','
                              blk','red','tan','bl
                              d')
PRIMATES   PRIMATES_ANIM_FK R                      MY_SCHEMA  PRIMATES_PK
PRIMATES   PRIMATES_PK      P
PRIMATES   SYS_C00827       C CODE IS NOT NULL
PRIMATES   SYS_C00828       C DESCRIPTION IS NOT
                              NULL
PRIMATES   SYS_C00829       C LOCATION IS NOT NULL
PRIMATES   SYS_C00830       C DATE_OF_BIRTH IS NOT
                               NULL
```

This user has constraints on only one table. Four of the constraints are the special NOT NULL constraint. There is a check constraint on the column Coloring that limits the values to those listed in the Search_Condition. Trying to insert any other value will cause an error. The table has a primary key constraint defined and a foreign key constraint that refers to a table and constraint owned by another user.

But what columns are these constraints defined on? For that information, we need to look at the DBA_CONS_COLUMNS view in the next section.

DBA_CONS_COLUMNS

In the prior section, we discussed the DBA_CONSTRAINTS view. Constraints are created against columns in a table or view. DBA_CONSTRAINTS gives you some information about the constraint, but it does not tell you which columns are part of the constraint itself and what order they are in. The data in the DBA_CONS_ COLUMNS view contains the information you need to fully understand the constraint.

DBA_CONS_COLUMNS contains information about the columns in the constraint definitions. Table 8-8 shows the columns in this view and what the columns represent.

Owner is the owner of the constraint, Constraint_Name is the name of the constraint, and Table_Name is the name of the table the constraint is defined on. All of these will match the corresponding columns in the DBA_CONSTRAINTS view. The Column_Name is the column the constraint is defined on, and Position refers to the position of the column within the constraint. For single column constraints, Position will always be 1.

DBA_CONS_COLUMNS will contain information on primary key constraints, foreign key constraints, and check constraints. However, for check constraints, the Search_Condition column in DBA_CONSTRAINTS will contain the column name, so the information in DBA_CONS_COLUMNS will not give you any more information.

Now, let's go back to the example from the previous section. We know that the owner of the constraint is QC_USER, the table the constraints are defined on is called PRIMATES, and there are several check constraints, as well as a primary key

Column	Description
OWNER	Owner of the constraint definition
CONSTRAINT_NAME	Name associated with the constraint definition
TABLE_NAME	Name associated with table with constraint definition
COLUMN_NAME	Name associated with column or attribute of the object type column specified in the constraint definition
POSITION	Original position of column or attribute in definition

TABLE 8-8. *DBA_CONS_COLUMNS View for 8i*

constraint and a foreign key constraint, defined on this table. Let's see what more we can find out. Because we know that we won't get any additional information about check constraints from this view, we're going to skip them by joining DBA_CONS_COLUMNS to DBA_CONSTRAINTS and eliminating any Constraint_Type of C.

```
select a.Owner, a.Constraint_Name, a.Table_Name,
        Constraint_Type, Column_Name, Position
  from DBA_CONS_COLUMNS a, DBA_CONSTRAINTS b
 where a.owner='QC_USER'
   and a.Table_Name ='PRIMATES'
   and b.Owner=a.Owner
   and b.Constraint_Name=a.Constraint_Name
   and b.Constraint_Type != 'C'
 order by a.Constraint_Name, Position
/

OWNER      CONSTRAINT_NAME   TABLE      C COLUMN_NAME     POSITION
---------- ----------------- ---------- - --------------- --------
QC_USER    PRIMATES_ANIM_FK  PRIMATES   R CODE                   1
QC_USER    PRIMATES_PK       PRIMATES   P CODE                   1
```

We have two constraints—one is a primary key constraint, the other is a foreign key constraint. Both of them are on the same column.

DBA_SYNONYMS

What is a synonym, and why or when would you want to use one? A *synonym* is a mask for another object—a way of referring to the object with the name of your choosing. If you need to select from a table owned by someone else, you could write the select statement as

```
select * from <other_owner>.<table_name>;
```

Of course, that starts to get annoying after a while, and what do you do if the owner of the table changes? Finding and correcting all references to this table in your code is time consuming, and we can almost guarantee that you will miss at least one.

Okay, now that we've discouraged you, how can you avoid this problem? Oracle provides a construct called a synonym, which allows you to mask the real name and owner of an object and refer to it by a constant, even if the owner or name of the object changes. Synonyms can be *private*, available only to the owner of the synonym, or *public*, available to any user in the database. To create a synonym, you use the following SQL:

```
create [public] synonym <synonym_name>
        for <owner>.<object_name>[@<database_link>];
```

If you include the word *public*, you must have the **create public synonym** privilege or you will get an error. You only need to include the database link clause if the object you want to reference is not in the local database.

DBA_SYNONYMS lists all synonyms in the database. Table 8-9 shows the columns in this view and what the columns represent.

So, what information does Oracle store about a synonym? The DBA_SYNONYMS view contains the Owner of the synonym and the Synonym_Name. If a synonym is a public synonym, the Owner column will contain the value PUBLIC. The columns named Table_Owner and Table_Name are misleading, as you can have a synonym for any object that you can access. So you can create synonyms for procedures, functions, views, packages, as well as tables. The Db_Link column contains the name of the database link if the synonym refers to an object in a remote database.

How does Oracle decide whether to use the synonym or use an object you own yourself? Oracle first checks to see if you own an object with the name you've used. If you do, then that object is the one Oracle will use. If not, Oracle then checks to see if you have a private synonym with that name, and if you do, the object referenced by your private synonym is used. Finally, if neither of these is true, Oracle checks to see if there is a public synonym with that name and accesses the

Column	Description
OWNER	Username of the owner of the synonym
SYNONYM_NAME	Name of the synonym
TABLE_OWNER	Owner of the object referenced by the synonym
TABLE_NAME	Name of the object referenced by the synonym
DB_LINK	Name of the database link referenced in a remote synonym

TABLE 8-9. *DBA_SYNONYMS View for 8i*

object referenced by the public synonym if it exists. Only if none of these is true do you get an error that the object does not exist.

How can you make use of this hierarchy? Let's suppose you have a copy of your production database in your development database. One of your programmers wants to test changes to a stored procedure. Other people are working and testing, so they need the original version of this stored procedure. If you've set up synonyms for everyone for all the objects or, if you use roles, you've set up public synonyms for the objects, then the application can be coded to just reference the name of the stored procedure. The programmer who is testing can create a private synonym pointing to his version of the stored procedure. Any test he makes will use his stored procedure, but anyone else working in the database will use the original version.

Let's use an example to make this a bit clearer. We'll start out assuming the following:

1. The application schema owner is PROD_OWNER.
2. PROD_OWNER has a stored procedure named VALIDATE_HOLIDAY.
3. JAMES has his own version of VALIDATE_HOLIDAY.
4. Marlene needs to use JAMES's new version of VALIDATE_HOLIDAY in her own testing.

When you set up the application in the database, you ran the following SQL:

```
create public synonym VALIDATE_HOLIDAY
   for PROD_OWNER.VALIDATE_HOLIDAY;
```

If you then select from DBA_SYNONYMS and DBA_OBJECTS, you see

```
select *
  from DBA_SYNONYMS
 where Table_Name = 'VALIDATE_HOLIDAY'
/

OWNER      SYNONYM_NAME       TABLE_OWNER     TABLE_NAME         DB_LINK
---------- ------------------ --------------- ------------------ ----------
PUBLIC     VALIDATE_HOLIDAY   PROD_OWNER      VALIDATE_HOLIDAY

select Owner, Object_Name, Object_Type
  from DBA_OBJECTS
 where Object_Name = 'VALIDATE_HOLIDAY'
/

OWNER      OBJECT_NAME          OBJECT_TYPE
---------- -------------------- ---------------
PUBLIC     VALIDATE_HOLIDAY     SYNONYM
```

```
JAMES      VALIDATE_HOLIDAY     PROCEDURE
PROD_OWNER VALIDATE_HOLIDAY     PROCEDURE
```

Now let's see who sees what. The hierarchy says that if you own an object, you will see your version of it, even if there is a public synonym for it. So JAMES sees his version of the stored procedure. Since there is a public synonym available for the version owned by PROD_OWNER, MARLENE sees the version owned by PROD_OWNER.

How can MARLENE test with the version owned by JAMES? Well, she can make a copy of JAMES's version in her own schema, and then she will see her own version. But if JAMES makes changes to his version, he's going to have to remember to tell MARLENE, and she's going to have to make another copy each time. Hmm, that doesn't sound like a good thing. Instead, if you run the statement

```
create synonym MARLENE.VALIDATE_HOLIDAY
   for JAMES.VALIDATE_HOLIDAY;
```

to create a synonym for MARLENE that points to JAMES's version, based on the hierarchy that private synonyms are resolved before public ones, MARLENE will see JAMES's version. Of course, JAMES will also have to give MARLENE permission to execute his stored procedure or she won't be able to use the procedure.

```
select *
  from DBA_SYNONYMS
 where Table_Name = 'VALIDATE_HOLIDAY'
/

OWNER      SYNONYM_NAME       TABLE_OWNER     TABLE_NAME         DB_LINK
---------- ------------------ --------------- ------------------ ----------
PUBLIC     VALIDATE_HOLIDAY   PROD_OWNER      VALIDATE_HOLIDAY
MARLENE    VALIDATE_HOLIDAY   JAMES           VALIDATE_HOLIDAY
```

CHAPTER 9

Using the V$ Views

By now, you should be pretty comfortable with the concepts behind a view. You know that a view is like the difference between looking through a camera lens at a very narrowed scene or looking at an entire panorama. You learned about how views are used to combine columns from more than one table and how they are used to hide columns, table names, and locations from users. In Chapters 6, 7, and 8, you learned about the Oracle data dictionary views called the DBA_ views. The DBA_ views help you to monitor the contents of the database and the locations of objects.

In this and the next chapter, you will learn about the views that Oracle has provided to help you see your database statistics—both the overall statistics and, more specifically, its performance. The views, commonly referred to as the V$ views (pronounced "Vee dollar"), are used to hide the Oracle dynamic tables from you while providing you with a way to monitor your database and its performance.

Wait a minute. What's the difference between the DBA_ views and the V$ views? Aren't they basically the same? Well, no. The DBA _ views are referred to by Oracle documentation as "Static Data Dictionary" views, while the V$ views are referred to as "Dynamic Performance" views because they record real-time values that show the current state of the database. In other words, the DBA_ views show you the status and composition of the data dictionary, while the V$ views help you to see how your database is performing. V$ views can provide you with the following information:

- Insights into areas of database contention
- Amounts of data being read or written to or from disk
- Statistical information, such as the last time a datafile header was changed or the summary information for the SGA
- Values used for database recovery

There are some columns in a few of the V$ views that will not be populated with values unless the parameter **timed_statistics** is set equal to TRUE in the init.ora parameter file. For the majority of operating systems, there is little performance impact in setting this parameter to TRUE. However, there are still some operating systems that show performance degradation with this parameter enabled. When you enable it on your system for the first time, be very careful to monitor the performance impact. If you notice an impact, enable the parameter only for short, controlled periods of time while you gather your database information. You can also change **timed_statistics** dynamically by using the **alter system** command. This way, the database does not have to be shut down and restarted. This is useful if you only want to have **timed_statistics** active for short periods of time.

Keep in mind, too, that the contents and descriptions of the V$ views can change from version to version, so do not rely on them to be the same when you change versions of the RDBMS. As we've said before, check the documentation that comes with the new release for changes between versions. We'll try to point out areas where changes in the V$ view composition can cause you headaches.

General V$ View Information

When you create a database, the first script you run after the database exists is the catalog.sql script. Here is a small section of the catalog.sql script for version 8.1.5:

```
rem Load PL/SQL Package STANDARD first, so views can depend upon it
@@standard
remark
remark   FAMILY "FIXED (VIRTUAL) VIEWS"
remark

create or replace view v_$dlm_misc as select * from v$dlm_misc;
drop public synonym v$dlm_misc;
create public synonym v$dlm_misc for v_$dlm_misc;
grant select on v_$dlm_misc to select_catalog_role;

create or replace view v_$dlm_latch as select * from v$dlm_latch;
drop public synonym v$dlm_latch;
create public synonym v$dlm_latch for v_$dlm_latch;
grant select on v_$dlm_latch to select_catalog_role;

create or replace view v_$dlm_convert_local as select * from v$dlm_convert_local;
drop public synonym v$dlm_convert_local;
create public synonym v$dlm_convert_local for v_$dlm_convert_local;
grant select on v_$dlm_convert_local to select_catalog_role;
```

From the comments in this little snippet of the script, you can see that Oracle breaks the V$ views into families. There are 49 families listed in this version of the script. How many are in the catalog.sql script on your system? Should you care? You probably don't care, but a great way to become familiar with both the composition of the catalog.sql script and the different families of V$ views is to find out. We'll leave you to explore catalog.sql on your own. Just keep in mind that the script is the origin of the V$ views (and the data dictionary views in version 8.0 and higher).

The V$ views act as a central repository of information and enable you to gather statistics over time about your database. They show the state of the database, objects, performance, backups, user processes, memory areas, and so on. New global views have been created to accommodate the Oracle Parallel Server. They are basically the same as the V$ views but were created to ensure identification of parallel databases and multiple instances. For parallel databases, a column is added for the instance ID (Inst_ID) so that each instance connecting to a database can be tracked and identified.

A Look at the V$ Views

Now that you've had a chance to see where the V$ views come from, let's see what the DICTIONARY view has to say about them. Since the DICTIONARY view only shows the name and not much description, we'll only show a short piece of the listing here. You will find the complete list of V$ views and a brief description of each one in Appendix C.

There are 171 V$ views, not counting the global GV$ views, in version 8.1.5; 141 V$ views in version 8.0.5; and only 96 V$ views in version 7.3.3.6. Let's take a look at the first five V$ views listed in the DICTIONARY view:

```
set pagesize 999
column Table_Name format a29
column Comments format a49 wrap word
select Table_Name, Comments
  from DICTIONARY
 where Table_Name like 'V$%';

TABLE_NAME                    COMMENTS
----------------------------- ------------------------------------------
V$ACCESS                      Synonym for V_$ACCESS
V$ACTIVE_INSTANCES            Synonym for V_$ACTIVE_INSTANCES
V$AQ                          Synonym for V_$AQ
V$AQ1                         Synonym for V_$AQ1
V$ARCHIVE                     Synonym for V_$ARCHIVE
```

As we said, the comments are not very helpful. The one interesting thing about the comments is that they give you a clue to the real names of each of the views. So, the V$ view names that you will be working with are really synonyms for slightly different views owned by SYS. Wow! Talk about hiding information!

In this chapter and the next one, we are going to present the V$ views that we use the most. As we did with the DBA_ views, we will list the views individually, explain them, and show some output from each. Where applicable, we will list the groups of views that you can join together to get more complete information and show you the output from the joined views. The convention that was used in the preceding three chapters (6, 7, and 8) will be used in these two chapters (9 and 10): columns that are new in Oracle8.0 will be identified with a single asterisk (*) and columns that are new in 8i with a double asterisk (**).

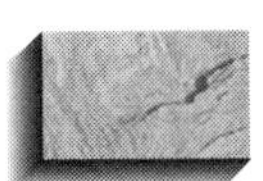

NOTE
An account with DBA privileges is normally used to query the V$ views.

The Levels of V$ Views

There are two levels of V$ views: instance-level and session-level views. The instance-level views contain information about the instance as a whole. They record statistics from the time the database is started until it is shut down. We have further broken down the instance-level views into two categories: those that provide vital information but can't be influenced by changes in init.ora parameters (referred to here as *static* V$ views) and those that can be influenced by changes (referred to here as *active* V$ views). Some of the active views have session-level counterparts. For example, there is a V$SYSSTAT view that lists basic information about the system statistics and a V$SESSTAT view that lists information about a specific session. Some of the values in the active instance-level views are cumulative—they are collected from the time the database starts up. In Chapter 10, we'll tell you about the active V$ instance-level and associated session-level views that we use most.

Let's take a minute to look at some of the differences between a static and an active V$ view. When you want to look at the system global area (SGA) values, for example, there are two SGA views you can use. One of these views, V$SGA, records the summary information about the SGA. This information will remain constant until you shut down the database. On database startup, if an init.ora parameter, such as **shared_pool_size**, has been changed, the SGA space in memory will be a different size than it was previously. If you make changes dynamically to any of the init.ora parameters that affect the allocation of resources within the SGA, the summary information will remain the same, even though the allocation of resources within the SGA may have changed. So according to our definition, V$SGA would be a static view because the dynamic changes in the init.ora are not reflected in the data the view displays until the database has been shut down and restarted.

The other view, V$SGASTAT, records the dynamic changes to SGA values as various resources are allocated or deallocated. Therefore, we'd define V$SGASTAT as an active view. Are you beginning to get the picture? We hope so.

Lookup Tables or Views

Some of the V$ views are actually *lookup tables* that provide a translation of a number to a character value. For example, V$DBFILE contains the name of each datafile and its corresponding number. The file f:/ora8i/oradata/rbs01.dbf might have the number 6 assigned to it. In other views that reference this file (f:/ora8i/oradata/rbs01.dbf), only the number (6) will be used. Therefore, if you want to see the information about this datafile with its name—which is much more meaningful to us—you will use the V$DBFILE view to look up the file number and provide the actual file name.

Just to make sure you understand how a lookup table works, let's say you work for a school that offers several different subjects, such as geometry, algebra, calculus, English, French, Spanish, biology, chemistry, history, geology, and so on. The school uses a computerized system to keep track of what courses each student is taking and the grade that each student earns for each course. You can use several different approaches to store the course names and grades. However, you've decided that the most efficient storage approach is to assign a number to each course and just store the course number each time a reference is needed. Good choice!

You could decide to use a scheme in which all courses will be assigned a three-digit number and each type of course will begin with a different number. All language courses will start with a 1, all mathematics courses will start with a 2, and so on. To take the example a step further, you've set up a table like Table 9-1 to keep track of what number is assigned to which course.

Table 9-1 does not reflect all of the courses that your school offers but should give you an idea of what we are trying to illustrate. Now, instead of having to list each course each time you need to reference it, you can just use the course number.

Course	**Number**
English	110
Spanish	111
Latin	112
French	113
Geometry	210
Algebra	211
Trigonometry	213
Calculus	214
Biology	310
Chemistry	311

TABLE 9-1. *School Courses and Their Associated Numbers*

If you are creating a report, you will want to list the course name to make the report more meaningful. At the time you create the report, you will use the course number to look up the translation for the course name. You've just created and used a lookup table! You will find several lookup tables within the DBA_ and V$ views.

The Static, Instance-Level V$ Views

The instance-level views that we use most often and have dubbed as static V$ views are shown in Table 9-2. We're going to explore these views thoroughly in this chapter. Do keep in mind that these are not all of the static V$ views but only the ones we use frequently and are our favorites. You'll find a complete list, with a brief description of each view, in Appendix C.

Note that only one view included here is new for Oracle8/8i—V$DATAFILE_HEADER.

V$DATABASE

The V$DATABASE view provides general information about the database. Table 9-3 shows the columns in the V$DATABASE view and a brief description of each one.

View	Description
V$DATABASE	Shows the database-specific information
V$DATAFILE	Datafile information from the control file
V$DATAFILE_HEADER*	Shows the datafile header information
V$DBFILE	Contains the datafile number and datafile name
V$FIXED_TABLE	Lists the fixed objects: X$ tables, GV$ global views, and V$ views. In Oracle 8i, there are 612 entries in this view
V$INSTANCE	Shows the instance-specific information
V$PARAMETER	Lists each of the parameters in the database along with a description and information, such as whether it is modifiable or not
V$SGA	Contains summary information on the SGA

TABLE 9-2. *Instance-Level V$ Views*

Column	Description
DBID*	The database ID—calculated when the database is created and stored in all file headers
NAME	Name of the database
CREATED	Creation date
LOG_MODE	Archive log mode: NOARCHIVELOG or ARCHIVELOG
CHECKPOINT_ CHANGE#	Last System Change Number (SCN) checkpointed
ARCHIVE_CHANGE#	Last SCN archived
RESETLOGS_CHANGE#*	Change number at open resetlogs
RESETLOGS_TIME*	Timestamp of open resetlogs
PRIOR_RESETLOGS_CHANGE#*	Change number at prior resetlogs
PRIOR_RESETLOGS_TIME*	Timestamp of prior resetlogs
CONTROLFILE_TYPE*	CURRENT/STANDBY/CLONE/BACKUP/ CREATED: STANDBY indicates database is in standby mode, CLONE indicates a clone database, BACKUP/CREATED indicates database is being recovered using a backup or created control file. A **standby database activate** or **database open after recovery** changes the type to CURRENT
CONTROLFILE_CREATED*	Control file creation timestamp
CONTROLFILE_SEQUENCE#*	Control file sequence number incremented by control file transactions
CONTROLFILE_CHANGE#*	Last change number in backup control file. Set to NULL if the control file is not a backup
CONTROLFILE_TIME*	Last timestamp in backup control file. Set to NULL if the control file is not a backup

TABLE 9-3. *V$DATABASE View for 8i (* = new to Oracle8.0, ** = new to Oracle8i)*

Column	Description
OPEN_RESETLOGS*	NOT ALLOWED/ALLOWED/REQUIRED: indicates whether the next database to be opened allows or requires the resetlogs option
VERSION_TIME*	The version time
OPEN_MODE**	Open mode information. Shows whether the database is set to READ WRITE or READ ONLY

TABLE 9-3. *V$DATABASE View for 8i (* = new to Oracle8.0, ** = new to Oracle8i)* (continued)

Now let's look at the columns we tend to use most often. Until version 8, the database identification number was hidden in the control file and could not easily be seen. The Dbid column displays this value. The Name column is self-explanatory but vital. The Log_Mode column tells you whether archive logging has been enabled, while the Archive_Change# shows you the last archive log number that was used. The Open_Mode column, new in Oracle 8i, shows whether the database is in READ WRITE mode or in READ ONLY mode. You will care about the mode of the database if you are going to use the transportable tablespace 8i feature described in Chapter 5. The control file information is important to you if you need to perform recovery on your database, since you can view the V$ information even if the database is started and mounted but not opened.

The Open_Mode parameter shows you whether the data in the datafile can be modified (mode would be READ WRITE if it can be) or only queried or looked at (mode would be READ ONLY).

The output from this view looks like this:

```
select *
  from V$DATABASE;

     DBID NAME                                   CREATED
--------- ------------------------------------ ---------
RESETLOGS_CHANGE# RESETLOGS PRIOR_RESETLOGS_CHANGE# PRIOR_RES
----------------- --------- ----------------------- ---------
LOG_MODE     CHKPNT_CHG# ARCHIVE_CHANGE# CONTROL CONTROLFI
------------ ----------- --------------- ------- ---------
CONTROLFILE_SEQUENCE# CONTROLFILE_CHANGE# CONTROLFI OPEN_RESETL
--------------------- ------------------- --------- -----------
```

```
VERSION_T OPEN_MODE
--------- ----------
998532885 ORC1                                          28-MAY-99
           137639 28-MAY-99                                 1 01-MAR-99
NOARCHIVELOG      1575727        1535229 CURRENT 28-MAY-99
                  3870            1575727 18-JUL-99 NOT ALLOWED
28-MAY-99 READ WRITE
```

From this listing, you can see that the database was created on May 28, 1999. But the time set for Prior_Res (prior reset logs) is March 1, 1999. Huh? How could that be? Where did that date come from, and how can it be earlier than the date on which the database was created? Under normal circumstances, you would expect the database creation date to match or be earlier than the prior reset log date, and you'd be right. But the database we are looking at is the demonstration database that Oracle creates and then bundles to ship with their software. When you choose to create the demo database, Oracle unbundles this database and places the files on your system, opens the database, and runs the environment scripts (catalog.sql, catproc.sql, etc.). So, in reality, this database was created in March of 1999 on an Oracle Corporation computer and then unbundled and placed on our computer in May of 1999. If you look carefully at some of the listings in the following sections, you'll see this March 1 date again, because many of the datafiles associated with this database were created in the default database supplied with the Oracle software.

Now that we have the date straight, there seem to be a lot of columns dealing with something called resetlogs. What does the clause *resetlogs* mean? Resetlogs is a command clause used in several different commands. It or its counterpart *noresetlogs* can be used when you issue the command **alter database** to either **open** the database after recovery, create a standby control file, or **backup controlfile to trace**. Resetlogs resets the current log sequence number to 1 and discards any redo information that has not been applied during recovery of the database. By resetting the redo log sequence number, you ensure that any unapplied redo will never be used. Thus, any changes that are in the redo log but not in the database will be discarded. You will use this clause when you've performed an incomplete database recovery. We'll talk more about this clause in Chapter 13 when we talk about database recovery. For now, let's get back to the contents of the V$DATABASE view.

The database has been named orc1, and archive log mode has not been enabled. The database is in read/write mode and was last opened on July 17, 1999. The next time the database is opened, the resetlogs clause cannot be used.

V$DATAFILE

Looking at the columns of the V$DATAFILE view, you might be tempted to ask, "What do I need to look at in this view that isn't in the DBA_DATA_FILES view?" That's a great question, and the answer is, "Quite a bit." When you look at the

DBA_DATA_FILES view, you are looking at the datafile information from the database's perspective. When you look at the V$DATAFILE view, you are seeing information from the control file's perspective. The V$DATAFILE information in some ways overlaps the DBA_DATA_FILES data.

There are several columns that you might find of interest in this V$ view. Before we start looking at the columns individually, let's look at all of the columns to see what they contain. Table 9-4 shows the columns and a very brief description of each one.

There are several "last number" values with timestamps that you may need to know if you are trying to determine the last time a datafile was changed. Two

Column	Description
FILE#	File identification number
STATUS	Type of file (system or user) and its status. Values: OFFLINE, ONLINE, SYSTEM, RECOVER, SYSOFF (an offline file from the SYSTEM tablespace)
ENABLED	Describes how accessible the file is from SQL. The values can be DISABLED, READ ONLY, READ WRITE, and UNKNOWN
CHECKPOINT_CHANGE#	SCN at last checkpoint
CHECKPOINT_TIME*	Timestamp of the checkpoint number
UNRECOVERABLE _CHANGE#*	Last unrecoverable change number made to this datafile. This column is always updated when an unrecoverable operation completes
UNRECOVERABLE_TIME*	Timestamp of the last unrecoverable change
BYTES	Current size in bytes; 0 if inaccessible
CREATE_BYTES	Size when created, in bytes
NAME	Name of the file
CREATION_CHANGE#*	Change number at which the datafile was created
CREATION_TIME*	Timestamp of the datafile creation

TABLE 9-4. *V$DATAFILE View for 8i*

Column	Description
TS#*	Tablespace number
RFILE#*	Tablespace relative datafile number
LAST_CHANGE#*	Last change number made to this datafile. Set to NULL if the datafile is being changed
LAST_TIME*	Timestamp of the last change
OFFLINE_CHANGE#*	Offline change number of the last offline range. This column is updated only when the datafile is brought online
ONLINE_CHANGE#*	Online change number of the last offline range
ONLINE_TIME*	Online timestamp of the last offline range
BLOCKS*	Current datafile size in blocks; 0 if inaccessible
BLOCK_SIZE*	Block size of the datafile
PLUGGED_IN**	Describes whether the tablespace is plugged in. The value is 1 if the tablespace is plugged in and has not been made read/write, 0 if not

TABLE 9-4. *V$DATAFILE View for 8i* (continued)

different forms of status values tell the status of the datafile: the Status column and the Enabled column. The Status column values in an Oracle8i database are offline, online, system, recover, sysoff (an offline file from the SYSTEM tablespace). The Enabled column tells whether you can perform the following tasks through SQL commands: write to the datafile, read from it; or it tells you whether SQL interaction has been disabled or the SQL interaction availability is unknown.

You can see the size, in bytes, when the datafile was originally created. This value is meaningful if you've enabled autoextend and want to get a feel for how quickly or slowly the file is growing. You can compare the original datafile size with the current size by multiplying the Blocks column by the database block size.

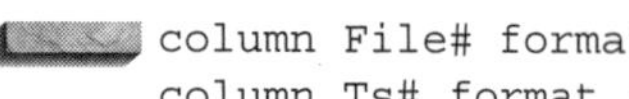

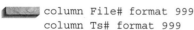

```
column File# format 999
column Ts# format 999
column Rfile# format 99999
column Checkpoint_Change# heading 'CHKPNT_CHG#' format 99999999
column Creation_Change# heading 'CREATE_CHG#' format 999999999
```

```
column Name format a35
select *
  from V$DATAFILE;

FILE# CREATE_CHG# CREATION_  TS# RFILE# STATUS  ENABLED    CHKPNT_CHG#
----- ----------- --------- ---- ------ ------- ---------- -----------
CHECKPOIN UNRECOVERABLE_CHANGE# UNRECOVER LAST_CHANGE# LAST_TIME
--------- --------------------- --------- ------------ ---------
OFFLINE_CHANGE# ONLINE_CHANGE# ONLINE_TI     BYTES    BLOCKS
--------------- -------------- --------- --------- ---------
CREATE_BYTES BLOCK_SIZE NAME                                PLUGGED_IN
------------ ---------- ----------------------------------- ----------
    1           4 01-MAR-99    0      1 SYSTEM  READ WRITE     1575727
18-JUL-99                1515097 15-JUL-99
         137638         137639 28-MAY-99 146800640     71680
           0       2048 D:\ORA8I\ORADATA\ORC1\SYSTEM01.DBF           0

    2        4385 01-MAR-99    1      2 ONLINE  READ WRITE     1575727
18-JUL-99                      0
         137638         137639 28-MAY-99   3145728      1536
           0       2048 D:\ORA8I\ORADATA\ORC1\USERS01.DBF            0

    3        4394 01-MAR-99    2      3 ONLINE  READ WRITE     1575727
18-JUL-99                      0
         137638         137639 28-MAY-99  41943040     20480
           0       2048 D:\ORA8I\ORADATA\ORC1\RBS01.DBF              0

    4        4403 01-MAR-99    3      4 ONLINE  READ WRITE     1575727
18-JUL-99                      0
         137638         137639 28-MAY-99   2097152      1024
           0       2048 D:\ORA8I\ORADATA\ORC1\TEMP01.DBF             0

    5        4413 01-MAR-99    4      5 ONLINE  READ WRITE     1575727
18-JUL-99                      0
         137638         137639 28-MAY-99  10485760      5120
           0       2048 D:\ORA8I\ORADATA\ORC1\OEMREP01.DBF           0

    6        4422 01-MAR-99    5      6 ONLINE  READ WRITE     1575727
18-JUL-99                      0
         137638         137639 28-MAY-99   2097152      1024
           0       2048 D:\ORA8I\ORADATA\ORC1\INDX01.DBF             0

    7      364956 04-JUN-99    6      7 ONLINE  READ WRITE     1575727
18-JUL-99                      0
              0              0             2097152      1024
     2097152       2048 D:\ORA8I\ORADATA\ORC1\MYTAB01.DBF            0

    8     1453906 09-JUL-99    7      8 ONLINE  READ WRITE     1575727
```

```
18-JUL-99                    1454359 09-JUL-99
                  0                  0                31457280       15360
    31457280         2048 D:\ORA8I\ORADATA\ORC1\CCDAT01.DBF                      0

    9       1453915 09-JUL-99     8        9 ONLINE   READ WRITE       1575727
18-JUL-99                              0
                  0                  0                20971520       10240
    20971520         2048 D:\ORA8I\ORADATA\ORC1\CCIDX01.DBF                      0

   10       1453923 09-JUL-99     9       10 ONLINE   READ WRITE       1575727
18-JUL-99                              0
                  0                  0                31457280       15360
    31457280         2048 D:\ORA8I\ORADATA\ORC1\TEST01.DBF                       0

   11       1555437 17-JUL-99     0       11 SYSTEM   READ WRITE       1575727
18-JUL-99                              0
                  0                  0                    4096           2
        4096         2048 D:\ORA8I\ORADATA\ORC1\SYSTEM02.DBF                     0
```

V$DATAFILE_HEADER

The V$DATAFILE_HEADER view is new in version 8.0 and has some interesting information about each of the datafiles in the database. Table 9-5 shows the columns and a brief description of each.

Until version 8.0 and the inclusion of the V$DATAFILE_HEADER view, there was almost no way to successfully see any information about a datafile header. This view displays these important pieces of information:

- Status of the datafile (online or offline), in the Status column
- Whether any errors occurred when the datafile was brought online, in the Error column
- Whether the datafile needs recovery, in the Recover column
- The Oracle version of the header block (v6, v7, v8, or unknown), in the Format column
- The current size of the datafile (in bytes and in blocks), in the Bytes or Blocks column

Column	Description
FILE#	Datafile number (from control file)
STATUS	ONLINE/OFFLINE (from control file)
ERROR	NULL if the datafile header read and validation were successful. If the read failed, the rest of the columns are NULL or may display invalid data. If there is an error, then usually the datafile must be restored from a backup before it can be recovered or used
FORMAT	Indicates the format for the header block. The possible values are 6, for Oracle version 6 7, for Oracle version 7 8, for Oracle version 8 0, which indicates the format could not be determined (for example, the header could not be read)
RECOVER	File needs media recovery: YES/NO
FUZZY	File is fuzzy: YES/NO
CREATION_CHANGE#	Datafile creation change number
CREATION_TIME	Datafile creation timestamp
TABLESPACE_NAME	Tablespace name
TS#	Tablespace number
RFILE#	Tablespace relative datafile number
RESETLOGS_CHANGE#	Resetlogs change number
RESETLOGS_TIME	Resetlogs timestamp
CHECKPOINT_CHANGE#	Datafile checkpoint change number
CHECKPOINT_TIME	Datafile checkpoint timestamp
CHECKPOINT_COUNT	Datafile checkpoint count
BYTES	Current datafile size in bytes
BLOCKS	Current datafile size in blocks
NAME	Datafile name

TABLE 9-5. *V$DATAFILE_HEADER View for 8i*

Here are two entries from the V$DATAFILE_HEADER view showing the information for the SYSTEM tablespace datafile:

```
col Error format a10
col Tablespace_Name format a15
select *
  from V$DATAFILE_HEADER
 where Tablespace_Name = 'SYSTEM';

FILE# STATUS  ERROR         FORMAT REC FUZ CREATION_CHANGE#
----- ------- ---------- --------- --- --- ----------------
CREATION_ TABLESPACE_NAME        TS#     RFILE# RESETLOGS_CHANGE#
--------- --------------- ---------- ---------- -----------------
RESETLOGS CHECKPOINT_CHANGE# CHECKPOIN CHECKPOINT_COUNT      BYTES
--------- ------------------ --------- ---------------- ---------
   BLOCKS NAME
--------- ------------------------------------------
    1 ONLINE                         8 NO                      4
01-MAR-99 SYSTEM                       0          1            137639
28-MAY-99            1575727 18-JUL-99                1321 146800640
    71680 D:\ORA8I\ORADATA\ORC1\SYSTEM01.DBF

   11 ONLINE                         8 NO                 155543
17-JUL-99 SYSTEM                       0         11            137639
28-MAY-99            1575727 18-JUL-99                  11      4096
        2 D:\ORA8I\ORADATA\ORC1\SYSTEM02.DBF
```

Even if the query had not specified a name in the Tablespace_Name column, you can be sure the datafiles listed here are for the SYSTEM tablespace (note the names of the datafile with the nomenclature system01.dbf and system02.dbf) because a standard file-naming convention has been used in this database.

V$DBFILE

The V$DBFILE view is a lookup table (or view). As we talked about earlier in the section "Lookup Tables or Views," one column of the view is used to translate a value from a short representation, such as a number, to a much longer representation, such as a name.

In this case, the File# column is very short, while the Name column can be much longer. In all of the other views that need to reference the datafile, the File# will be used. When the actual file name is needed (for a report or other translation), you can use a lookup into this view to resolve the name. Table 9-6 shows the columns in the V$DBFILE view.

Column	Description
FILE#	File identifier
NAME	Name of file

TABLE 9-6. *V$DBFILE View for 8i*

In our Oracle-supplied demonstration database for 8i, here are the values for the V$DBFILE view:

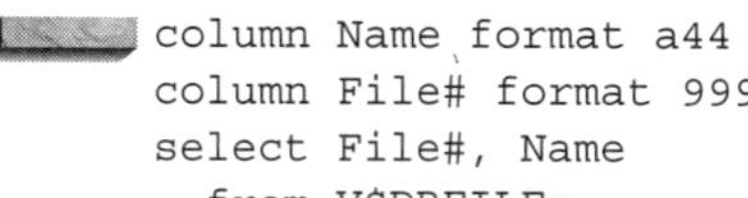

```
column Name format a44
column File# format 999
select File#, Name
  from V$DBFILE;

FILE# NAME
----- --------------------------------------------
    2 D:\ORA8I\ORADATA\ORC1\USERS01.DBF
    5 D:\ORA8I\ORADATA\ORC1\OEMREP01.DBF
    6 D:\ORA8I\ORADATA\ORC1\INDX01.DBF
    3 D:\ORA8I\ORADATA\ORC1\RBS01.DBF
    4 D:\ORA8I\ORADATA\ORC1\TEMP01.DBF
    1 D:\ORA8I\ORADATA\ORC1\SYSTEM01.DBF
    7 D:\ORA8I\ORADATA\ORC1\MYTAB01.DBF
    8 D:\ORA8I\ORADATA\ORC1\CCDAT01.DBF
    9 D:\ORA8I\ORADATA\ORC1\CCIDX01.DBF
   10 D:\ORA8I\ORADATA\ORC1\TEST01.DBF
   11 D:\ORA8I\ORADATA\ORC1\SYSTEM02.DBF
```

There's something different about the output from this query compared to the output from the V$DATAFILE and the V$DATAFILE_HEADER queries. Can you see what it is? In the other two queries, even though no **order by** qualifier is given, the file numbers are displayed in order. In the V$DBFILE query, no **order by** qualifier is given and the file numbers appear to be displayed out of order. There's a lesson to be learned here. If you want to be sure the numbers you are displaying will always be in a specific order, you must be sure to put in a clause to specify that order. People tend to get very upset when numbers are unexpectedly displayed out of sequence.

V$FIXED_TABLE

The V$FIXED_TABLE view displays all the names of the dynamic tables, views, and derived views that are contained in the database. The V$FIXED_TABLE view contains information on X$ tables, V$ views, and GV$ views and is the easiest way for you to find out the name of an X$ dynamic table. You will probably not need to use this view very often, but it's important that you can identify it and its contents. Table 9-7 shows the columns in this view.

Because there are 612 objects listed in this view and 256 of them are X$ tables, we are going to show you the output from a very limited subset of the X$ tables here.

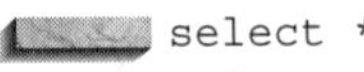

```
select *
  from V$FIXED_TABLE
 where Type = 'TABLE'
   and Table_Num between 0 and 10;

NAME                                   OBJECT_ID TYPE  TABLE_NUM
-------------------------------------- --------- ----- ---------
X$KQFTA                                4.295E+09 TABLE         0
X$KQFVI                                4.295E+09 TABLE         1
X$KQFVT                                4.295E+09 TABLE         2
X$KQFDT                                4.295E+09 TABLE         3
X$KQFCO                                4.295E+09 TABLE         4
X$KSLLT                                4.295E+09 TABLE         5
X$KSLLD                                4.295E+09 TABLE         6
X$KSLED                                4.295E+09 TABLE         7
X$KSLES                                4.295E+09 TABLE         8
X$KSLEI                                4.295E+09 TABLE         9
X$KSLLW                                4.295E+09 TABLE        10
```

Column	Description
NAME	Name of the object
OBJECT_ID	Identifier of the fixed object
TYPE	Object type: TABLE, VIEW
TABLE_NUM	Number that identifies the dynamic performance table if it is of type TABLE

TABLE 9-7. *V$FIXED_TABLE View for 8i*

You can see that the names of the X$ tables listed here are not very meaningful or obvious. Although it's close to impossible to guess what each of the dynamic tables listed here contains, many of the views have more meaningful names. We suggest you list the contents of the V$FIXED_TABLE view and explore the tables and views it contains. Remember that you must not in any way attempt to modify any of the dynamic tables or views. That would be a very quick way to compromise the integrity of your database!

If you try to use the **describe** command on an X$ table and you are not connected as "sys" or "internal," you will be told that the object does not exist. In other words, Oracle keeps the X$ tables well hidden. If you want to see the composition of an X$ table, first, you must be connected as internal, and if you know the name of an X$ table, you can select it and see its contents. A bit of caution is recommended when trying to view any of the X$ tables, as they can contain many thousands of rows (or more). We've found that doing a count of the number of rows contained in a table is a good practice to follow before selecting the data from that table. That's a great general rule to follow for any queries you do!

V$INSTANCE

The V$INSTANCE view provides general information about each instance that is connected to your database. This view has changed dramatically in version 8. In version 7, there were only two columns: Key and Value. The Key column showed the name of the state variable, and the Value column showed the actual state value. As you can see from Table 9-8, the view has been modified to reflect much more information for version 8. Table 9-8 shows the columns for the most current version of the V$INSTANCE view.

There will be times when an application is coded with a detached process running. The detached process makes a connection to your database and maintains that connection indefinitely. There are many valid reasons to have an application process do this. However, a problem arises when you need to shut down your database. You won't be able to perform a normal shutdown because the application process is running and the database will wait until all processes have disconnected before the shutdown is completed. There are two ways to solve this problem. You can make it a policy always to do a **shutdown immediate**, or you can have your developers use the V$INSTANCE view to determine whether your database is waiting to shut down by checking the Shutdown_Pending column. If this column value changes from NO to YES, the application can be coded to automatically

Column	Description
INSTANCE_NUMBER*	Instance number used for instance registration. Corresponds to INSTANCE_NUMBER initialization parameter
INSTANCE_NAME*	Instance name
HOST_NAME*	Name of the host machine
VERSION*	RDBMS version
STARTUP_TIME*	Time when instance was started up
STATUS*	Current status of the database. Can be STARTED/MOUNTED/OPEN: STARTED after startup nomount; MOUNTED after startup mount or alter database close; OPEN after startup or after database open
PARALLEL*	YES/NO in parallel server mode
THREAD#*	Redo thread opened by the instance
ARCHIVER*	STOPPED/STARTED/FAILED: FAILED means the archiver failed to archive a log last time but will try again within five minutes
LOG_SWITCH_WAIT*	Event the log switch is waiting for. Can be ARCHIVE LOG/CLEAR LOG/CHECKPOINT Note that if ALTER SYSTEM SWITCH LOGFILE is hung, but there is room in the current online redo log, then value is NULL
LOGINS*	ALLOWED/RESTRICTED
SHUTDOWN_PENDING*	YES/NO
DATABASE_STATUS**	The status of the database

TABLE 9-8. *V$INSTANCE View for 8i*

disconnect from the database. You will, of course, have to give the application user the privilege to select from this view.

```
column Instance_Number heading 'INST#' format 9999
column Host_Name format a12
column Version format a9
column Thread# format 9999999
 select *
  from V$INSTANCE;

INST# INSTANCE_NAME    HOST_NAME    VERSION   STARTUP_T STATUS  PAR  THREAD#
----- ---------------- ------------ --------- --------- ------- --- --------
ARCHIVE LOG_SWITCH_ LOGINS     SHU DATABASE_STATUS
------- --------------------- --- -----------------
    1 orcl             THERIML1-PC2 8.1.5.0.0 28-JUN-99 OPEN    NO         1 STOPPED
ALLOWED                NO  ACTIVE
```

If you are running the Parallel Server option, the instance name may not match your database name. Therefore, you can join the V$DATABASE and V$INSTANCE views together to view both the instance and database name, as follows:

```
select Instance_Name, Name
  from V$INSTANCE, V$DATABASE;

INSTANCE_NAME    NAME
---------------- ------------------------------------
orcl             ORC1
```

Did you notice something interesting about this query? Even though we did the select from two different views, we do not have a join clause. That's because we know there is only one row in each of these views. If you join two tables or views that have a single row in them, you do not have to provide a join clause.

Okay, so in this particular case, the names match. They may not always match, and this is a handy way to determine whether they do. Notice, though, that if a SQL statement was querying for a match of the two names, you would have to use either the **upper** or **lower** function to actually get the names to match, since one is stored in uppercase and the other is in lowercase. Very interesting!

V$PARAMETER

The V$PARAMETER view stores all of the database parameters. In earlier versions of Oracle, this view contained only the parameter number, parameter name,

Column	Description
NUM	Parameter number
NAME	Parameter name
TYPE	Parameter type: 1 = Boolean; 2 = string; 3 = integer
VALUE	Parameter value
ISDEFAULT	Whether the parameter value is the default
ISSES_MODIFIABLE*	TRUE/FALSE: TRUE indicates the parameter can be changed with **alter session**; FALSE indicates the parameter cannot be changed with **alter session**
ISSYS_MODIFIABLE*	IMMEDIATE/DEFERRED/FALSE: IMMEDIATE indicates the parameter can be changed with **alter system**; DEFERRED indicates the parameter cannot be changed until the next session; FALSE indicates the parameter cannot be changed with **alter system**
ISMODIFIED*	Indicates how the parameter was modified. If an **alter session** was performed, the value will be MODIFIED. If an **alter system** (which will cause all the currently logged-in sessions' values to be modified) was performed, the value will be SYS_MODIFIED
ISADJUSTED*	Indicates that Oracle adjusted the input value to a more suitable value (for example, the parameter value should be prime, but the user input a nonprime number, so Oracle adjusted the value to the next prime number)
DESCRIPTION*	A descriptive comment about the parameter

TABLE 9-9. *V$PARAMETER View for 8i*

parameter type, and associated group. Now, as you can see in Table 9-9 which shows the columns for the V$PARAMETER view, there are many more columns with helpful information.

In our Oracle8i demonstration database, there are 195 parameters. We'll only look at the first few. You should take the time to do a select of all the parameters and look at what they do.

```
column Value format a7
column Description format a53
select *
  from V$PARAMETER
 where Num < 20;

      NUM NAME                                   TYPE
--------- ------------------------------------ ---------
VALUE ISDEFAULT ISSES ISSYS_MOD ISMODIFIED ISADJ
----- --------- ----- --------- ---------- -----
DESCRIPTION
-----------------------------------------------------
        9 processes                                  3
59    FALSE     FALSE FALSE     FALSE      FALSE
user processes

       10 sessions                                   3
69    TRUE      FALSE FALSE     FALSE      FALSE
user and system sessions

       11 timed_statistics                           1
FALSE TRUE      TRUE  IMMEDIATE FALSE      FALSE
maintain internal timing statistics

       12 timed_os_statistics                        3
0     TRUE      FALSE IMMEDIATE FALSE      FALSE
internal os statistic gathering interval in seconds

       13 resource_limit                             1
FALSE TRUE      FALSE IMMEDIATE FALSE      FALSE

master switch for resource limit

       14 license_max_sessions                       3
0     TRUE      FALSE IMMEDIATE FALSE      FALSE
maximum number of non-system user sessions allowed

       15 license_sessions_warning                   3
0     TRUE      FALSE IMMEDIATE FALSE      FALSE
warning level for number of non-system user sessions

       18 cpu_count                                  3
1     TRUE      FALSE FALSE     FALSE      FALSE
number of cpu's for this instance
```

This view is most valuable for letting you quickly see

- Which parameter values are still the default and which ones have been changed in the init.ora parameter file
- Which parameters can be changed dynamically
- Which parameters have been changed
- Whether the parameter was changed by an **alter session** or **alter system** command

If the parameter was changed with the **alter session** command, the value will only be visible and usable by that specific session. If the parameter was changed using **alter system**, the value will be visible systemwide.

V$SGA

The V$SGA view displays the summary statistics for the allocation of space in the system global area. Table 9-10 shows the columns in the V$SGA view.

The V$SGA view gives you a feel for the total amount of memory that has been allocated to the SGA and how Oracle has divided that memory. Let's look at the memory allocation for the Oracle8i default demonstration database:

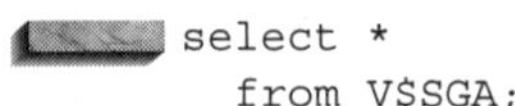

```
select *
  from V$SGA;

NAME                                      VALUE
----------------------------------- ----------
Fixed Size                                65484
Variable Size                          19521536
Database Buffers                       16777216
Redo Buffers                              73728
```

Column	Description
NAME	SGA component group
VALUE	Memory size in bytes

TABLE 9-10. *V$SGA View for 8i*

To see the total real memory allocation for the current SGA, you can select the sum of the Value column, as follows:

```
select sum(Value) from V$SGA;

SUM(VALUE)
----------
  36437964
```

From this listing, you can see that the total SGA for this instance is 36 megabytes. In the next chapter, you'll see the counterpart view, V$SGASTAT, which shows the breakdown of the SGA by parameter instead of the summary values that V$SGA gives you. Both views are valuable.

CHAPTER 10

The Instance-Level Dynamic V$ Views

hen you decide to watch television, you can choose which program you want to watch, but you have no direct control over what programs are available for viewing. In the same vein, there are V$ views that you influence and others that you can't. In Chapter 9, you learned about the general information, instance-level views—the ones that are important but over which you have little noticeable effect. In this chapter, you will learn about the views Oracle has provided to help you see activity in the database that you can influence.

We are going to examine these instance-level views extensively. As we mentioned in Chapter 9, there are session-level counterparts to some of the V$ views. In the case where a session-level counterpart exists, we'll point it out and, in some cases, explain it as well.

V$ Views Used for Tuning

Just as a coach monitors his ball team and has the players modify their actions to help improve how they play, you can use some of the V$ views to monitor your database to help give you insights into how to improve your database's performance.

In almost every case, poor database performance centers around the fact that there is some form of contention for resources on your system. Poor performance can almost always be tracked back to a process waiting for a resource that another process is using. The trick is to determine what resource is being waited for and see if you can find a way to eliminate contention for it. This is not always easy to do, but we'll try to help by showing you the areas you can monitor and suggesting actions you can take to help eliminate contentions on your system. In order for you to use the V$ views, you will need some background knowledge about the structures you are looking at. We've tried to provide the needed background before going into in-depth explanations of the views. Further tuning information is presented in a whole different way in Chapter 12.

Some Interesting Instance-Level V$ Views

The instance-level views we use most often and are going to explore in detail in this chapter are shown in Table 10-1. As we did in the DBA_ views chapters, we are listing them in alphabetical order here but will look at them in logical groups where appropriate.

To be consistent with the other view chapters, we will indicate columns that are new in Oracle8.0 with * and columns that are new in Oracle8i with **. Again, since these views are predominantly used to help you tune your system, the discussion about each view will deal primarily with tuning issues and solutions.

View	Description
V$FILESTAT	Lists the information on file read/write statistics
V$LATCH	Lists statistics for nonparent latches and summary statistics for parent latches
V$LIBRARYCACHE	Contains statistics about library cache performance and activity
V$LOCK	Lists the locks currently held by the Oracle server and outstanding requests for a lock or latch
V$LOCKED_OBJECT	Lists all locks acquired by every transaction on the system
V$PROCESS	Contains information about the currently active processes
V$ROLLSTAT	Lists the names of all online rollback segments
V$ROLLNAME	Lists the rollback segment number and its corresponding name
V$ROWCACHE	Shows statistics for data dictionary activity
V$SGASTAT	Contains detailed information on the system global area
V$STATNAME	Lists the name of the statistic
V$SYSSTAT	Contains basic instance statistics
V$SYSTEM_EVENT	Contains information on total waits for an event
V$WAITSTAT	Lists block contention statistics. Values are updated for this only when **timed_statistics** are enabled through the init.ora parameter file

TABLE 10-1. *Instance-Level V$ Views Used for Database Tuning*

V$FILESTAT

The V$FILESTAT view is used to gain information about activity on each file in the database. The columns are shown in Table 10-2. All columns whose names end in TIM or TM will contain a zero if you have not set **timed_statistics** to TRUE in your init.ora file.

Column	Description
FILE#	Number of the file
PHYRDS	Number of physical reads done
PHYWRTS	Number of times DBWR is required to write
PHYBLKRD	Number of physical blocks read
PHYBLKWRT	Number of blocks written to disk; this may be the same as PHYWRTS if all writes are single blocks
READTIM	Time (in hundredths of a second) spent doing reads
WRITETIM	Time (in hundredths of a second) spent doing writes
AVGIOTIM	The average time (in hundredths of a second) spent on I/O
LSTIOTIM	The time (in hundredths of a second) spent doing the last I/O
MINIOTIM	The minimum time (in hundredths of a second) spent on a single I/O
MAXIOWTM	The maximum time (in hundredths of a second) spent doing a single write
MAXIORTM	The maximum time (in hundredths of a second) spent doing a single read

TABLE 10-2. *V$FILESTAT View for 8i (* = new to Oracle8.0, ** = new to Oracle8i)*

We mentioned in Chapter 5 that in most databases setting the parameter **timed_statistics** to TRUE was necessary to obtain values for some V$ view columns. V$FILESTAT is a prime example of a view with several columns that will have a zero value if this parameter is set to FALSE.

This view is generally joined to the V$DBFILES view described in Chapter 9 as follows:

```
set pagesize 100;
set space 1
column pbr format 99999999 heading 'Physical|Blk Read'
column pbw format 999999 heading 'Physical|Blks Wrtn'
column pyr format 999999 heading 'Physical|Reads'
column Readtim format 99999999 heading 'Read|Time'
column Name format a38 heading 'DataFile Name'
column Writetim format 99999999 heading 'Write|Time'
```

```
ttitle center 'Tablespace Report' skip 2
compute sum of f.Phyblkrd, f.Phyblkwrt on report
select fs.Name name,f.Phyblkrd pbr,f.Phyblkwrt pbw,f.Readtim,f.Writetim
  from V$FILESTAT f, V$DBFILE fs
 where f.File# = fs.File#
 order by fs.Name;

                                    Tablespace Report

                                          Physical  Physical      Read     Write
DataFile Name                             Blk Read Blks Wrtn      Time      Time
---------------------------------------- --------- --------- --------- ---------
/devora01/oradata/mydb/mydbev01.dbf        3064223     16382     49069     55495
/devora02/oradata/mydb/devtest01.dbf          1763         8        36        17
/qaora/oradata/mydb/pre_indexes01.dbf         1924        28       157        78
/qaora/oradata/mydb/pre_indexes02.dbf         7377      3368      2450      7204
/qaora/oradata/mydb/pre_sample_data01.dbf     1578         0        34         0
/qaora/oradata/mydb/pre_sample_data02.dbf    73340        51      2214       187
/qaora/oradata/mydb/pre_sample_data03.dbf     1784       695       270      1441
/qaora/oradata/mydb/des2000_01.dbf          215397         0      3341         0
/testora/oradata/mydb/rbs01.dbf                110    272553       133   1300607
/testora/oradata/mydb/system01.dbf          180180     30560      6716     83373
/testora/oradata/mydb/temp01.dbf                 0        18         0        83
/testora/oradata/mydb/tools01.dbf           104501     70036     13867    322179
/testora/oradata/mydb/users01.dbf           435678        31      6908        96
```

The output from this report shows the amount of activity on each datafile in the database. If there are several datafiles on the same disk with high read or write activity and performance is slow, you could move one or more of the datafiles to a different, less busy disk. The output above was obtained from a Unix system. If your output comes from a Windows NT system, files may appear to be on different drives but, in reality, they could be on a partition of the same physical drive.

V$LATCH

At the back of one of the authors' houses is a fenced area with a lawn and a garden. The fence that surrounds the yard has a gate. The gate has a metal closure on it, commonly referred to as a latch. The latch on that gate helps to discourage people from coming into the garden to take any of the vegetables (except, of course, for the gardener, who always takes one or two tomatoes when he comes in to mow the grass). The latch on the gate is there to keep the gate shut and protect the garden, but people are periodically invited in to visit. While the gardener is bringing his (very large) lawn mower in and out of the garden, access to the garden is temporarily blocked. No one else can fit through the gate.

Latches in the database are used to prevent access to Oracle's internal memory structures while a process is accessing them. This action is necessary to ensure that the structure remains in a consistent state while it is being accessed. When a process needs to access an internal structure, it "takes out a latch" on that structure. Once a latch has been taken against a structure, like the lawn mower blocking the gate, no other process can interact with that structure until the current latch is released.

Latches are generally held for a very brief amount of time, but if several processes are trying to access the same structure at the same time, contention will occur. Each process is contending for the same resource at the same time. Like the people we see waiting in line for refreshments at a movie theater, some processes will be willing to wait for the latch to become available, while others will be unwilling to wait and will go off to continue processing without having acquired what they initially came to get.

V$LATCH, combined with the lookup table V$LATCHNAME (see Chapter 9 for more information on lookup tables), provides information on the different types of latches and their status. Table 10-3 shows the composition of V$LATCH. In Oracle8i, the Sleep5 through Sleep11 columns (marked with a plus sign (+)) have been kept for compatibility with earlier versions and are no longer used. That would imply that either willing-to-wait requests no longer sleep more than four times or that after four sleep cycles, there's just too much overhead generated to continue incrementing different column counters. (This is pure speculation on our part but fun to think about. We're open to your suggestion on why these columns are no longer used.)

There are different types of latches with which different types of actions are associated. A latch can be requested in either a willing-to-wait or an immediate category. Let's take a look at the actions that occur with each of these categories of latches.

If the latch that is requested with a *willing-to-wait* state is not available, the requesting process will wait for a short time and try to obtain the latch again. The process will keep waiting and requesting over again until the latch becomes available and the process can obtain it. Each time a willing-to-wait latch request is successful, the Gets column value is incremented. If the process that is willing to wait does not get the latch on the initial attempt, the Misses column value is incremented. Once the process has made its initial request, the Sleeps column value will show how many times the process waited and requested the latch.

In the case of an *immediate* latch, if the latch is not available, the process making the request does not wait but continues on, much like the impatient refreshment stand customer who tries to break into the line and push ahead of others. If he succeeds, he gets his refreshments. If the crowd won't let him push his way in, he goes off to watch the movie without acquiring his popcorn and soft drink. The Immediate_Gets column shows the number of successful immediate requests for each latch, while the Immediate_Misses column shows the number of unsuccessful immediate requests for each latch.

Column	Description
ADDR	Address of latch object
LATCH#	Latch number
LEVEL#	Latch level
NAME	Latch name
GETS	Number of times obtained a wait
MISSES	Number of times obtained a wait but failed on the first try
SLEEPS	Number of times slept when wanted a wait
IMMEDIATE_GETS	Number of times obtained without a wait
IMMEDIATE_MISSES	Number of times failed to get without a wait
WAITERS_WOKEN	How many times a wait was awakened
WAITS_HOLDING_LATCH	Number of waits while holding a different latch
SPIN_GETS	Gets that missed first try but succeeded on spin
SLEEP1	Waits that slept 1 time
SLEEP2	Waits that slept 2 times
SLEEP3	Waits that slept 3 times
SLEEP4	Waits that slept 4 times
SLEEP5+	Waits that slept 5 times
SLEEP6+	Waits that slept 6 times
SLEEP7+	Waits that slept 7 times
SLEEP8+	Waits that slept 8 times
SLEEP9+	Waits that slept 9 times
SLEEP10+	Waits that slept 10 times
SLEEP11+	Waits that slept 11 times

TABLE 10-3. *V$LATCH View for 8i*

In Oracle8i, there are 142 latches with 12 different levels, but there are only a few latches that you can directly control or have an effect on. These are the latches that you will spend time monitoring and tuning. The areas of contention that you can affect are

- Redo copy latch
- Redo allocation latch
- LRU latch
- Freelist

Of course, before you turn your attention to latch contention, you should already have addressed buffer size and file I/O (see V$FILESTAT above). Having said that, let's examine each of these latch types and talk about what you can do to help reduce contention, should you find it.

Redo Copy Latch and Redo Allocation Latch

The redo copy latch is the first one on our list and works in conjunction with the redo allocation latch, so we'll look at both of these latch types now. When a process goes to write information to the redo log buffer, it first obtains a redo copy latch. Next, since space is required in which to write the entry, a redo allocation latch is used. As its name implies, a redo allocation latch allocates space in the log buffer for writing the entry. There is only one redo allocation latch to ensure that the writes are done sequentially to the redo log buffer. If the amount of space needed to write the entry is smaller than a preset value, the write can occur under the redo allocation latch. If the amount of space needed is bigger than the preset size, the write is done under the redo copy latch. Once space has been allocated, if the write has not been performed, the redo allocation latch passes the address of the allocated space to the copy latch. The redo allocation latch is released, and the redo copy latch performs the actual write. Once the write is completed, the redo copy latch is released. If your computer has multiple CPUs, your redo log buffer can have multiple redo copy latches. If your computer has one CPU, there should be no redo copy latches. The redo allocation latch will perform all of the copies. To look at the redo log buffer activity, you can use the following query:

```
column Name format a20
select ln.Name, Gets, Misses, Immediate_Gets, Immediate_Misses
  from V$LATCH l, V$LATCHNAME ln
 where ln.Name in ('redo allocation', 'redo copy')
```

```
   and ln.Latch# = l.Latch#;

NAME                          GETS    MISSES IMMEDIATE_GETS IMMEDIATE_MISSES
-------------------- --------- --------- -------------- ----------------
redo allocation               1647        38              0                0
redo copy                       24         0          19876                2
```

From this output, you can calculate the ratio of Misses/Gets and Immediate Misses to the sum of Immediate_Misses plus Immediate_Gets. If you have a ratio of greater than 1 percent, you have contention on your system. If you decide to code the ratio calculations, be sure to use a **decode** clause so that you won't try to divide by zero. Let's see what the figures above show about this system. First, you divide the Misses by the Gets to get the percentage of Misses to Gets:

%Misses = Misses/Gets
%Misses = (38/1647) * 100
%Misses = 2.3%

Hmm. That value is over 1 percent, so you can see redo allocation latch contention on this system. We'll talk about what actions you can take to help remove this contention in just a minute. For now, let's look at the percentage of Immediate_Misses.

%Immediate_Misses = Immediate_Misses/(Immediate_Gets + Immediate_Misses)
%Immediate_Misses = (2/(2 + 19876)) * 100
%Immediate_Misses = .01006%

That's much less than 1 percent, so no problem there!

There are two init.ora parameters that you can use to affect redo log buffer writes: **log_small_entry_max_size** and **log_simultaneous_copies**. When a process goes to write to the redo log buffer and take out a redo allocation latch, the value for **log_small_entry_max_size** is checked to see if the redo allocation latch can perform the write. If the amount to be written is smaller than the value for this parameter, the redo allocation latch can write. For redo allocation latch contention, you can reduce the value for **log_small_entry_max_size**, which will force more writes to be performed by the redo copy latch. For redo copy latch contention, you can increase the number for **log_simultaneous_copies**.

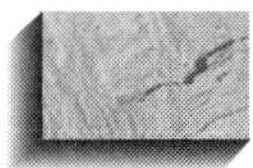

NOTE
In Oracle8i, these parameters are obsolete, so you won't find them in the database.

You can look in V$PARAMETER in versions 8.0 and 7.3 to see the value that is currently assigned to each of these parameters as follows:

```
column Name format a45
column Value format a15
select Name, Value
  from V$PARAMETER
 where upper(Name) like '%LOG_S%';

NAME                                          VALUE
--------------------------------------------- --------------
log_small_entry_max_size                      80
log_simultaneous_copies                       0
```

LRU Latch

The next type we'll look at is LRU latches. In Chapter 12, we'll talk more about Oracle's least recently used (LRU) algorithm, but let's lay some groundwork here. With LRU latches, you are looking at what happens when you perform a query that causes data to be read into the buffer cache. LRU latches control the replacement of buffers in the buffer cache. Right. Now, what does *that* mean? Let's look at a common scenario to see.

You perform query X, not a full table scan, asking just to look at data. Query X is processed and the results loaded into the data buffer cache. Marlene comes along and performs the same query (X). Since the results are already in the data buffer cache, Oracle can present the results much faster with much less processing overhead. You continue working and execute several other queries (Y, Z, A, B, and C), as does Marlene. The results from query X are slowly moved to the least recently used end of the data buffer cache. Now, you perform query D, but there is no room in the data buffer cache to store the results. The LRU latch begins its duties and starts to search the least recently used list for candidate blocks to remove to make room for the new query's results. Query X's results are flushed from the data buffer cache, and query D's results are moved to the most recently used end of the list. Why did we exclude full table scans? Because a full table scan will examine blocks and just continue on, there is no need to store them in the most recently used (MRU) end of the buffer; so they are immediately moved to the LRU end of the list to be reused more rapidly.

Now, let's see what happens to the query result that's moved down toward the LRU end of the list. That's simple! When that query is reexecuted, the results are moved back up to the MRU end, and processing continues. There's certainly a big shuffling act going on there!

To see the overall ratio for LRU latch contention, use the query:

```
select Sleeps / Gets ratio
  from V$LATCH
 where Name = 'cache buffers lru chain';

RATIO
---------
.00128546
```

To see the specific LRU latch statistic, use

```
select l.Name, ((Sleeps/Gets) * 100) "LRU Hit%"
  from V$LATCH l, V$LATCHNAME ln
 where ln.Name in ('cache buffers lru chain')
   and ln.Latch# = l.Latch#;

NAME                                                                LRU Hit%
----------------------------------------------------------------    ----------
cache buffers lru chain                                              .0051284
```

By default, Oracle sets the number of LRU latches to half the number of CPUs on the system (rounded up to the next whole number) with a minimum of one. Each LRU latch, by default, controls a minimum of 50 blocks, but a more realistic amount would be 100. As with all other latches, your goal is to reduce contention among the server processes and to balance the number of latches with the number of CPUs on the system. In a single CPU system, adding more LRU latches may not be beneficial since the limit on how many processes the CPU can manage at any given time still remains. The init.ora parameter **db_block_lru_latches** determines the number of LRU latches to allocate per instance. If contention is high, increase **db_block_lru_latches**. If you have Sleeps, also increase this parameter. The maximum number of LRU latches you should have is the lower of these two numbers:

number of CPUs * 6
number of db_block_buffers / 50

Remember that the CPU utilization is a factor to consider when deciding how many LRU latches you set.

Freelist

As the name implies, *freelists* are used to track the blocks that are available for inserts to the database, just as the hostess at a restaurant keeps track of the tables available for seating diners. If many processes are attempting to insert data to the same table, contention for the same freelist can occur. However, you cannot dynamically set the number of freelists for an object. The only way you can affect the freelist value for an object is at the segment level, by dropping and rebuilding the object with a higher value for the **freelists** keyword.

Since evaluation of freelist contention is done using V$WAITSTAT and V$SYSTEM_EVENT, we'll talk more about freelists a bit later in this chapter.

Other latch views of interest are V$LATCH_HOLDER, V$LATCHNAME (a lookup table), V$LATCH_CHILDREN, V$LATCH_MISSES, and V$LATCH_PARENT. See Appendix C for a brief description of each of these views.

V$LIBRARYCACHE

When you walk into your local library (yep, just like Chapter 2, we're back in the library again!), you expect to find many different types of reading material. You'll see books, maps, newspapers, encyclopedias, and other reference materials, as well as videotapes, music CDs, and so forth. You can use the materials available in the library since they are there for everyone to share. Although they are all in one central building, the first time you go to get a specific book, it might take you a while to look up its location in the card or online catalog and locate the book on its shelf. Once you've found the book, you do not have to look up its location again or map your route to the shelf but can go straight to it if you want to use it again. Because you know where to look for it, you can access the book in question quickly.

Likewise, when a SQL statement is presented to Oracle for processing for the first time, Oracle must go through several steps to process the query. Since the beginning of version 7, SQL cursors can be shared; this means more than one process can execute the same SQL statement that is stored in memory. Note, however, that the Oracle parser must see the code as identical before it will reuse code stored in the library cache. Once Oracle has processed the statement and stored its execution plan for reuse, if the same statement is presented again, Oracle can execute the statement with much less processing. In other words, Oracle knows "where the book is on the shelf" and can go directly to it. SQL and PL/SQL statements are stored in the library cache. Remember, though, that the statement truly must be identical, down to spaces and upper- and lowercase letters, for Oracle to reuse it. Watch out for applications that use dynamic SQL. It's possible for an "identical" SQL statement to be reparsed every time because the statement is dynamically generated.

To aid in tuning the library cache, Oracle supplies the V$LIBRARYCACHE view. Table 10-4 shows the columns for this view.

Column	Description
NAMESPACE	The library cache namespace
GETS	The number of times a lock was requested for objects of this namespace
GETHITS	The number of times an object's handle was found in memory
GETHITRATIO	The ratio of GETHITS to GETS
PINS	The number of times a PIN was requested for objects of this namespace
PINHITS	The number of times all of the metadata pieces of the library object were found in memory
PINHITRATIO	The ratio of PINHITS to PINS
RELOADS	Any PIN of an object that is not the first PIN performed since the object handle was created, and which requires loading the object from disk
INVALIDATIONS	The total number of times objects in this namespace were marked invalid because a dependent object was modified
DLM_LOCK_REQUESTS	The number of GET requests lock instance locks
DLM_PIN_REQUESTS	The number of PIN requests lock instance locks
DLM_PIN_RELEASES	The number of release requests PIN instance locks
DLM_INVALIDATION_REQUESTS	The number of GET requests for invalidation instance locks
DLM_INVALIDATIONS	The number of invalidation pings received from other instances

TABLE 10-4. *V$LIBRARY_CACHE View for 8i*

The library cache is another shared memory structure. This memory structure is part of the shared pool and is the most important of the shared pool structures to tune. A least recently used (LRU) algorithm is used to manage the cache. Obviously, if a statement is already in the library cache, it can be reused quickly. Thus, one of the goals in tuning the library cache is to reduce the number of SQL statements that must be reparsed. Another goal is to make sure there is enough space in the library cache to hold the majority of SQL statements. If the library cache is full and a new statement must be inserted, Oracle will age out (remove) the oldest statement in the cache. If Oracle has to steadily age out and reparse statements, performance will suffer.

Some Terminology

To understand the values that the V$LIBRARYCACHE view is showing you, we must define some terms. *Gets* are the number of lookups for objects in the namespace. Each time a statement is presented to Oracle for execution, Oracle checks to see if the statement is already stored. That counts as one get. There are eight different types of items in the library cache for which statistics are kept: the SQL area, consisting of SQL statements and PL/SQL blocks; Table/Procedure; Body; Trigger; Index; Cluster; Object; and Pipe. Each row in the V$LIBRARYCACHE view reflects one of these item types, and the types are stored in the Namespace column. *Pins* reflect the number of executions for each of these areas. *Reloads* are the number of times statements had to be reparsed in order to be executed. If a statement was aged out of the cache, or an object referenced by the statements was invalidated (changed in some way), the statement must be reparsed to be reexecuted.

The V$SGASTAT view, described later in this chapter, can be used to show the way in which shared pool areas have been allocated. You can use this view to determine whether you have enough space allocated in the shared pool.

To see the values that pertain to performance in the V$LIBRARYCACHE view, you can use the following query:

```
column Namespace format a8
column Gets format 99999
column Pins format 999999
column Reloads format 99999
column Gethits format 9999999
select Namespace, Gets, Gethits, round((Gethitratio * 100),2) GetRatio,
       Pins, Pinhits, round((Pinhitratio * 100),2) PinRatio, Reloads relds
   from V$LIBRARYCACHE;

NAMESPAC   GETS   GETHITS  GETRATIO     PINS   PINHITS  PINRATIO  RELDS
-------- ------ --------- --------- ------- --------- --------- ------
SQL AREA   1414      1328     93.91     3824      3642     95.24      8
TABLE/      333       262     78.67      496       363     73.18      0
PROCEDURE
```

```
BODY              4          2          50          4          2          50          0
TRIGGER           0          0         100          0          0         100          0
INDEX            29          0           0         29          0           0          0
CLUSTER         131        126       96.18        178        173       97.19          0
OBJECT            0          0         100          0          0         100          0
PIPE              0          0         100          0          0         100          0
```

The Gethitratio determines the percentage of parse calls that find a cursor to share. The value is derived from Gethits divided by Gets. This ratio should be in the high 90s. A lower Gethitratio indicates that there is room to tune the SQL code.

Now, let's look at Reloads and Pins. Reloads should never be more than 1 percent of Pins. The ideal is to have zero reloads, but that's very difficult to achieve. Here's how to check the Reloads to Pins:

```
select sum(Pins) "Executions", sum(Reloads) "Cache Misses",
       sum(Reloads)/sum(Pins)
  from V$LIBRARYCACHE;

Executions Cache Misses SUM(RELOADS)/SUM(PINS)
---------- ------------ ----------------------
      8632            7             .00081094
```

If the Reloads to Pins ratio is greater than 1 percent, increase the init.ora parameter **shared_pool_size**.

V$LOCK

There are locks everywhere we look. We use key locks for the doors in our houses, offices, and almost everywhere. We use combination locks with chains to protect our bicycles and padlocks to protect the contents of storage sheds. Different kinds of locks are everywhere, and the different types of locks offer different degrees of protection for the things we value. I might give you a copy of my house key so you can come in to water my plants while I am on vacation (thank you very much!), but I will probably not give you a copy of the key to my safe deposit box at my bank. Oracle uses the same locking concepts to protect your data in the database.

Earlier, we talked about the different types of latches in an Oracle system. Now, we're talking about locks. What's the difference? Well, a latch is a form of low-level locking used to protect a memory structure, while a lock is normally used to protect a data structure. A latch is usually held for a very brief amount of time, while a lock can be held continuously until a commit or rollback takes place.

The Oracle server automatically manages locks. Oracle's locking policy is to try to apply the least restrictive lock needed to protect data consistency while allowing the highest amount of data availability to all processes. If you are performing a query, Oracle will not place a lock on the structure you are looking at. If, however, you are inserting, updating, or deleting data, Oracle will use a lock to protect the structure from anyone else trying to do something to it while you're manipulating it.

There are several different kinds of locks. You can monitor them using the V$LOCK view. Before we start looking at all of the different types of locks and when they are used, let's look at the composition of the V$LOCK view, as seen in Table 10-5.

Now we can talk about the various types of locks and how Oracle uses some of them.

Lock Levels

There are three levels at which a structure may be locked (shown with their type): at a single row level (TX), at the partition level (TM), or at the table level (TM). There are Data Manipulation Language (DML) locks used to protect data at either the row, partition, or table level and Data Dictionary Language (DDL) locks used to protect the dictionary definition of an object such as a table or view. There are internal locks and latches used to protect memory structures (as you saw earlier). These

Column	Description
ADDR	Address of lock state object
KADDR	Address of lock
SID	Identifier for session holding or acquiring the lock
TYPE	Type of lock (see the section "Number and Types of Locks" for system lock types)
ID1	Lock identifier number 1 (depends on type)
ID2	Lock identifier number 2 (depends on type)
LMODE	Lock mode in which the session holds the lock: 0 None, 1 Null (NULL), 2 Row-S (SS), 3 Row-X (SX), 4 Share (S), 5 S/Row-X (SSX), 6 Exclusive (X)
REQUEST	Lock mode in which the process requests the lock: 0 None, 1 Null (NULL), 2 Row-S (SS), 3 Row-X (SX), 4 Share (S), 5 S/Row-X (SSX), 6 Exclusive (X)
CTIME	Time since current mode was granted
BLOCK	The lock is blocking another lock

TABLE 10-5. *V$LOCK View for 8i*

locks are entirely automatic. There are distributed locks that are used to ensure that structures remain consistent across more than one instance. These are *instance-level* rather than transaction-level locks. And there are parallel cache management (PCM) locks used with shared server configurations. Used to lock one or more data blocks in the SGA, these locks are held at the memory, data-block level. They do not lock rows.

A lock can be either exclusive or shared. Queries are always allowed on a structure, even a locked one, but other activities may be prevented. In exclusive mode, the data structure remains locked, preventing the resource from being shared with any other transaction until the lock is released. If you are performing an update of a row in a table, no one else will be able to modify that specific row until you have issued either a rollback or commit command. Until you commit your change, Oracle will present a consistent view of that row as it appeared before you started to change it. For example, you issue the statement:

```
update EMPLOYEE
   set Salary = Salary * 2
 where Employee_Num = 123456;
```

If Jim tries to perform an update on the same row, he'll be forced to wait until you've either committed your change or rolled it back. In the meantime, anyone else who looks at the salary for employee number 123456 will see the old salary value. That's data consistency at work.

With shared locks, more than one transaction can hold a shared lock on a structure at the same time since shared locks are set at the table level for DML transactions. You issue the statement:

```
update EMPLOYEE
   set Salary = Salary * 2
 where Employee_Num = 123456;
```

At the same time, Jim issues the statement:

```
update EMPLOYEE
   set Salary = Salary * 2
 where Employee_Num = 654321;
```

The two transactions will update rows in the same table at the same time with no problem.

Number and Types of Locks

As we said earlier in this section, there are three different levels of DML locks. A table-level lock (TM type) is set for any DML statement that modifies a table, such as

insert, **update**, **delete**, **select...for update**, and **lock table**. The table lock protects the structure of the table from any DDL statement that would conflict with the transaction. A row-level lock (TX type) is automatically acquired for each row that is modified by a statement using **insert**, **update**, **delete**, and **select...for update**. This lock keeps anyone else from modifying the same row at the same time, as we illustrated.

A DML transaction will get at least two locks: a shared table lock (TM type) and an exclusive row-level lock (TX type). Internally, when a transaction goes to modify a row, Oracle turns a byte on in the row header pointing to the internal transaction lock (ITL) slot used by that transaction. At the row level, a lock mode can only be exclusive. If you are dealing with a partition table, the transaction will acquire a table partition lock for each required partition as well as a table lock.

The following tables show the various user and system locks and their types. The type column values for user locks are

Lock	Type
TM	DML enqueue
TX	Transaction enqueue
UL	User supplied

The type column values for system locks are

Lock	Type
BL	Buffer hash table instance
CF	Control file schema global enqueue
CI	Cross-instance function invocation instance
CU	Cursor bind
DF	Datafile instance
DL	Direct loader parallel index create
DM	Mount/startup db primary/secondary instance
DR	Distributed recovery process
DX	Distributed transaction entry
FS	File set
HW	Space management operations on a specific segment
IN	Instance number

Lock	Type
IR	Instance recovery serialization global enqueue
IS	Instance state
IV	Library cache invalidation instance
JQ	Job queue
KK	Thread kick
LA .. LP	Library cache lock instance lock (A..P = namespace)
MM	Mount definition global enqueue
MR	Media recovery
NA..NZ	Library cache pin instance (A..Z = namespace)
PF	Password file
PI, PS	Parallel operation
PR	Process startup
QA..QZ	Row cache instance (A..Z = cache)
RT	Redo thread global enqueue
SC	System commit number instance
SM	SMON
SN	Sequence number instance
SQ	Sequence number enqueue
SS	Sort segment
ST	Space transaction enqueue
SV	Sequence number value
TA	Generic enqueue
TS	Temporary segment enqueue (ID2 = 0)
TS	New block allocation enqueue (ID2 = 1)
TT	Temporary table enqueue
UN	Username
US	Undo segment DDL
WL	Being-written redo log instance

The Enqueue Mechanism

Oracle maintains all locks as *enqueues*. The enqueue mechanism keeps track of users waiting for locks that are held by others and the lock mode these users require. The enqueue mechanism also keeps track of the order in which users requested the locks. Let's say there are three users (Marlene, Rachel, and Jim—in that order) who want to update the same row of a table at the same time. All three users will get the shared table lock, but only Marlene gets the row lock because Marlene made the first request. The table-locking mechanism keeps track of who holds the row lock and who is waiting for it. The init.ora parameters **dml_locks** and **enqueue_resources** control the number of locks available for an instance.

Table-Level Lock Modes

There are five basic table lock modes within an Oracle system. For DML transactions, some lock modes are automatically assigned. Each lock mode has a different level of restrictiveness that will be used to determine the modes on the table that other transactions can obtain. Table 10-6 shows the five different lock modes. In some entries, you will see two different values used in parenthesis. This

Mode	Description
Row exclusive (RX or SX)	The least restrictive of the locks. Allows other transactions to **insert**, **update**, **delete**, or lock other rows in the same table. Prohibits **lock table...in exclusive mode**
Row share (RS or SS)	Allows other transactions to **insert**, **update**, **delete**, or lock other rows in the same table. Prohibits **lock table** commands with the following options: **in share mode**, **in exclusive mode**, and **in share exclusive mode**
Share (S)	Explicitly acquired through the **lock table...in...mode** command. Allows other transactions only to **select...for update**. Prohibits other modifications on the table
Share row exclusive (SRX or SSX)	Explicitly acquired; more restrictive than a share lock
Exclusive (X)	The most restrictive lock. Only a single transaction can lock a table in X mode

TABLE 10-6. *Table Lock Modes from Least to Most Restrictive*

is because different Oracle documentation shows the notations for lock mode differently. We wanted you to see both versions.

Here's a sample output from V$LOCK:

```
column Sid format 99999
column Block format 9999999
select *
  from V$LOCK;

ADDR     KADDR       SID TY       ID1        ID2      LMODE   REQUEST     CTIME
  BLOCK
-------- -------- ----- -- --------- --------- --------- --------- ---------
-------
8C13807C 8C13808C      6 TS 1.342E+09         0         3         0    436120
       0
8C1380B0 8C1380C0      4 RT         1         0         6         0    436476
       0
8C1380E4 8C1380F4      2 MR        21         0         4         0    436476
       0
8C138118 8C138128      2 MR        20         0         4         0    436476
       0
8C13814C 8C13815C      2 MR        15         0         4         0    436476
       0
8C138180 8C138190      2 MR        14         0         4         0    436476
       0
8C1381B4 8C1381C4      2 MR        13         0         4         0    436476
       0
8C1381E8 8C1381F8      2 MR        12         0         4         0    436476
       0
8C13821C 8C13822C      2 MR        11         0         4         0    436476
       0
8C138250 8C138260      2 MR         9         0         4         0    436476
       0
8C138284 8C138294      2 MR         8         0         4         0    436476
       0
8C1382B8 8C1382C8      2 MR         7         0         4         0    436476
       0
8C1382EC 8C1382FC      2 MR         6         0         4         0    436476
       0
8C138320 8C138330      2 MR         5         0         4         0    436476
       0
8C138354 8C138364      2 MR         4         0         4         0    436476
       0
8C138388 8C138398      2 MR         3         0         4         0    436476
       0
8C1383BC 8C1383CC      2 MR         2         0         4         0    436476
       0
8C1383F0 8C138400      2 MR         1         0         4         0    436476
       0
0A0AD970 0A0ADA44     13 TX    196625       181         6         0         9
       0
04CE2008 04CE201C     13 TM     10922         0         3         0         9
       0
```

```
8B08F100 8B08F114     20 TM       2144         0         3         0         1
       0
8B08F16C 8B08F180     20 TM       2337         0         3         0         1
       0
00860230 008602E0     20 TX     196624    135448         6         0         1
       0
8C138458 8C138468     20 TM       2204         0         4         0         1
       0
8B08F1D8 8B08F1EC     20 TM       2184         0         3         0         1
       0
```

Let's see. We have five different types of locks displayed in this listing: TS, RT, MR, TM, and TX. Referring back to the tables of locks, you can see that TS, which is a system lock and has an ID2 of zero, is a temporary segment enqueue lock. The RT is also a system lock and is a redo thread global enqueue. The MRs are all system media recovery locks, which are okay because this listing was taken while a database load was taking place. Finally, Sid numbers 13 and 20 are users using DML enqueue and transaction enqueue locks. For the user locks with TX mode, the ID1 column will show the rollback segment number and slot number, while for TM mode, the same column will show the Object_Id being modified. Pretty interesting! A quick way to detect whether one lock is blocking another is to check for a "1" in the block column.

DDL Locks

When you issue a statement like **drop table** or **alter table**, you are affecting the underlying structure of the table, and therefore, an exclusive DDL lock will be taken out during the period of time that your statement is processing. There are two other types of DDL locks: shared DDL locks used in **create procedure** and **audit** statements, and breakable parse locks, which are held on each object in the SQL shared pool. DDL locks rarely cause contention on the system because they are held and released so quickly. However, you should be aware that DDL locks exist, and for exclusive locks (used for **create**, **alter**, and **drop** commands), a user cannot get an exclusive lock on a table if any other user holds any level of lock. Thus, if a user has issued a statement that has not been committed or rolled back, and you go to alter that table, your command will fail.

Detecting Lock Contention

In the last section we saw the output from a **select...from** for the V$LOCK view. Once you have the table number from this listing, you can determine the table name by using the V$LOCK view and the DBA_OBJECTS view discussed in Chapter 6. Running the following script, you can see the user and table names.

```
column Object_Name format a20
column Owner format a10
```

```
select Owner, Object_Id, Object_Name, Object_Type, V$LOCK.Type
  from DBA_OBJECTS, V$LOCK;

OWNER      OBJECT_ID OBJECT_NAME          OBJECT_TYPE        TY
---------- --------- -------------------- ------------------ --
SYS               11 I_USER#              INDEX              MR
SYS               10 C_USER#              CLUSTER            MR
SYS                9 I_FILE#_BLOCK#       INDEX              MR
SYS                8 C_FILE#_BLOCK#       CLUSTER            MR
SYS                7 I_TS#                INDEX              MR
SYS                6 C_TS#                CLUSTER            MR
SYS                5 CLU$                 TABLE              MR
SYS                4 TAB$                 TABLE              MR
SYS                3 I_OBJ#               INDEX              MR
SYS                2 C_OBJ#               CLUSTER            MR
SYS               12 FET$                 TABLE              MR
RACHEL         10922 EMPLOYEE             TABLE              TM
```

There is another, Oracle-provided way that you can check for lock contention on your system. If you suspect lock contention is a problem, you can use the script utllockt.sql in the ORACLE_HOME/rdbms/admin directory and run it as SYSTEM. The script creates a list in tree order of the session holding a lock and the users waiting for that lock. From the comments section of the script, here is a sample of the script output:

```
WAITING_SESSION   TYPE MODE REQUESTED    MODE HELD         LOCK ID1 LOCK ID2
----------------- ---- ----------------- ----------------- -------- --------
8                 NONE None              None              0        0
   9              TX   Share (S)         Exclusive (X)     65547    16
      7           RW   Exclusive (X)     S/Row-X (SSX)     33554440 2
      10          RW   Exclusive (X)     S/Row-X (SSX)     33554440 2
```

You should run $ORACLE_HOME/rdbms/admin/catblock.sql prior to running the above query since catblock.sql is not called from catproc.sql.

There are some problems with this script. For one thing, you can't easily tell who is holding the lock and blocking others. Also, if you look at the script for utllockt.sql, you will see that a table is created each time the script is run and then dropped at the end of the script. Since locks are taken out when you create a table, the script may get caught in the lock contention problem and add to it. To solve this problem, you can create the table and modify the utllockt.sql script so it will not create or drop this table when the script is run. You will, instead, need to change the code in the script to truncate the table before the next insert is performed so that old data will be removed.

that solves problem two. What about problem one—the fact that we can't tell who owns the process that is blocking? There is an easy way to solve this problem. You can use the V$LOCKED_OBJECT view, which we are going to talk about next.

V$LOCKED_OBJECT

In the previous section, we looked at locks and the V$LOCK view. To get more information about the processes that are holding locks, Oracle has provided a view called V$LOCKED_OBJECTS. This view has remained unchanged from Oracle7.3 forward. Table 10-7 shows the columns for V$LOCKED_OBJECT.

The most valuable information is the Oracle username and the operating system username. The Locked_Mode tells us what type of lock is being held currently or being requested. Let's run utllockt.sql and look at a locking situation on our system.

```
WAITING_SESSION      LOCK_TYPE         MODE_REQUESTED MODE_HELD      ID1     ID2
-------------------- ----------------- -------------- -------------- ------- -----
11                   None              None           None           0       0
   12                Transaction       Exclusive      Exclusive       196612 181
```

In this example, we've created a *deadlock* contention situation (which Oracle cleared out itself over time by killing off process 12, the requestor who caused the lock problem). A deadlock occurs when two or more users wait for data that is locked by each other. Oracle will arbitrarily decide which of the two user processes to kill, so you should always look for and fix code that can cause deadlocks.

Column	Description
XIDUSN	Undo segment number
XIDSLOT	Slot number
XIDSQN	Sequence number
OBJECT_ID	Object ID being locked
SESSION_ID	Session ID
ORACLE_USERNAME	Oracle username
OS_USER_NAME	OS username
PROCESS	OS process ID
LOCKED_MODE	Lock mode

TABLE 10-7. *V$LOCKED_OBJECT View for Oracle8i*

Let's see what V$LOCKED_OBJECT shows under these circumstances.

```
select *
  from V$LOCKED_OBJECT;

   XIDUSN    XIDSLOT     XIDSQN OBJECT_ID SESSION_ID ORACLE_USERNAME
--------- --------- --------- --------- ---------- ---------------------
OS_USER_NAME                      PROCESS    LOCKED_MODE
------------------------------ --------- -----------
        3         4         0     19762         11 MARLENE
MYMACHINE-PC\marlene1            301:298          3

        0         0       181    196612         12 RACHEL
OTMACHINE-PC\rachel1             295:257          3
```

Looking back at the output from the utllockt.sql script in this section and comparing it to the output from this query, you can see that MARLENE has not acquired a lock yet and RACHEL is holding an exclusive lock.

More importantly, if there is contention due to locking on your system, you now have the information you need to call the person who is holding the lock and ask him either to commit or rollback his session. As a last resort, you will need to kill the blocking session. You will need to determine both the Sid and the Serial# of the blocking process. You already have the Sid, but you still need the Serial#. To obtain the Serial#, you can query V$SESSION. Although we'll talk more about V$SESSION later, let's finish this conversation by performing the query to obtain the Sid and Serial# and "kill off RACHEL." The query you need to execute to obtain the Sid and Serial# is

```
select Sid, Serial#, Username
  from V$SESSION
 where Username = 'RACHEL';

      SID   SERIAL# USERNAME
--------- --------- ------------------------------
       12        43 RACHEL
```

Because users can have multiple sessions in the database, verify the Sid is the same as the one you have from V$LOCKED_OBJECT. Here is the command you can use to kill a session

```
REM alter system kill session 'Sid, Serial#';
REM
alter system kill session '12,43';
```

V$PROCESS

By itself, V$PROCESS provides some interesting information about each process that is active in an Oracle database. The columns that compose the V$PROCESS view are shown in Table 10-8.

Column	Description
ADDR	Address of process state object
PID	Oracle process identifier
SPID	Operating system process identifier
USERNAME	Operating system process username. Any Two-Task user coming across the network has "-T" appended to the username
SERIAL#	Process serial number
TERMINAL	Operating system terminal identifier
PROGRAM	Program in progress
BACKGROUND	Value of 1 for a background process; NULL for a normal process
LATCHWAIT	Address of latch the process is waiting for; NULL if none
LATCHSPIN	Address of latch the process is being spun on; NULL if none

TABLE 10-8. *V$PROCESS View in Oracle8i*

The interesting columns in this view are Pid, Spid, and Username. You will often be called upon to determine "which user is doing what to whom." Knowing that the V$PROCESS view exists and can supply a key into the "whom" portion can really help.

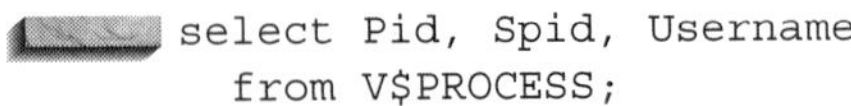

```
select Pid, Spid, Username
  from V$PROCESS;

      PID SPID      USERNAME
--------- --------- ------------
        1
        2 110       SYSTEM
        3 237       SYSTEM
        4 163       SYSTEM
        5 85        SYSTEM
        6 44        SYSTEM
        7 189       SYSTEM
        8 255       SYSTEM
        9 271       SYSTEM
       10 272       SYSTEM
       11 273       SYSTEM
       12 316       SYSTEM
       13 300       SYSTEM
       14 282       SYSTEM
```

To make the output more meaningful, you'll have to use another view, V$SESSION. Let's look at this view now.

V$SESSION

Remember we said at the beginning of this chapter that we would show you session-level views as seemed appropriate? Well, here comes one of those times. The V$PROCESS view, coupled with the V$SESSION view, can help you determine what's going on in the sessions in your database. Therefore, let's take a look at the V$SESSION view now.

Table 10-9 shows you more than you probably would ever want to know about each session on your system.

One word of caution about V$SESSION. The session numbers are reused as one session logs off the system and another session connects, so you may end up looking at two different sessions if you check something and then go back ten minutes later to look again.

Now, let's join V$SESSION with V$PROCESS and see what additional information you can obtain. We'll just look at a few specific sessions for this query,

Column	Description
SADDR	Session address
SID	Session identifier
SERIAL#	Session serial number. Used to identify uniquely a session's objects. Guarantees that session-level commands are applied to the correct session objects if the session ends and another session begins with the same session ID
AUDSID	Auditing session ID
PADDR	Address of the process that owns this session
USER#	Oracle user identifier
USERNAME	Oracle username

TABLE 10-9. *V$SESSION View for Oracle8i*

Column	Description
COMMAND	Command in progress (last statement parsed)
OWNERID	The column contents are invalid if the value is 2147483644. Otherwise, this column contains the identifier of the user who owns the migratable session. For operations using Parallel Slaves, interpret this value as a four-byte value, the low-order two bytes of which represent the session number and the high-order bytes, the instance ID of the query coordinator
TADDR	Address of transaction state object
LOCKWAIT	Address of lock waiting for; NULL if none
STATUS	Status of the session: ACTIVE (currently executing SQL), INACTIVE, KILLED (marked to be killed), CACHED (temporarily cached for use by Oracle*XA), SNIPED (session inactive, waiting on the client)
SERVER	Server type: DEDICATED, SHARED, PSEUDO, NONE
SCHEMA#	Schema user identifier
SCHEMANAME	Schema username
OSUSER	Operating system client username
PROCESS	Operating system client process ID
MACHINE	Operating system machine name
TERMINAL	Operating system terminal name
PROGRAM	Operating system program name
TYPE	Session type
SQL_ADDRESS	Used with SQL_HASH_VALUE to identify the SQL statement currently being executed

TABLE 10-9. *V$SESSION View for Oracle8i (continued)*

Column	Description
SQL_HASH_VALUE	Used with SQL_ADDRESS to identify the SQL statement currently being executed
MODULE	Contains the name of the currently executing module as set by calling the DBMS_APPLICATION_INFO. SET_MODULE procedure
MODULE_HASH	The hash value of the above MODULE
ACTION	Contains the name of the currently executing action as set by calling the DBMS_APPLICATION_INFO.SET_ACTION procedure
ACTION_HASH	The hash value of the above action name
CLIENT_INFO	Information set by the DBMS_APPLICATION_INFO. SET_CLIENT_INFO procedure
FIXED_TABLE_SEQUENCE	This contains a number that increases every time the session completes a call to the database and there has been an intervening select from a dynamic performance table. This column can be used by performance monitors to monitor statistics in the database. Each time the performance monitor looks at the database, it only needs to look at sessions that are currently active or have a higher value in this column than the highest value that the performance monitor saw the last time. All the other sessions have been idle since the last time the performance monitor looked at the database
ROW_WAIT_OBJ#	Object ID for the table containing the ROWID specified in ROW_WAIT_ROW#

TABLE 10-9. *V$SESSION View for Oracle8i (continued)*

Column	Description
ROW_WAIT_FILE#	Identifier for the datafile containing the ROWID specified in ROW_WAIT_ROW#. This column is valid only if the session is currently waiting for another transaction to commit and the value of ROW_WAIT_OBJ# is not –1
ROW_WAIT_BLOCK#	Identifier for the block containing the ROWID specified in ROW_WAIT_ROW#. This column is valid only if the session is currently waiting for another transaction to commit and the value of ROW_WAIT_OBJ# is not –1
ROW_WAIT_ROW#	The current ROWID being locked. This column is valid only if the session is currently waiting for another transaction to commit and the value of ROW_WAIT_OBJ# is not –1
LOGON_TIME	Time of logon
LAST_CALL_ET	The last call
PDML_STATUS	If ENABLED, the session is in a PARALLEL DML enabled mode. If DISABLED, PARALLEL DML enabled mode is not supported for the session. If FORCED, the session has been altered to force PARALLEL DML
PDDL_STATUS	If ENABLED, the session is in a PARALLEL DDL enabled mode. If DISABLED, PARALLEL DDL enabled mode is not supported for the session. If FORCED, the session has been altered to force PARALLEL DDL
PDML_ENABLED	This column has been replaced by a combination of PDML_ENABLED and PDML_STATUS. See above

TABLE 10-9. *V$SESSION View for Oracle8i (continued)*

Column	Description
FAILOVER_TYPE	NONE if failover is disabled for this session, SESSION if client is able to failover its session following a disconnect, and SELECT if client is able to failover selects in progress as well
FAILOVER_METHOD	NONE if failover is disabled for this session, BASIC if client reconnects following a disconnect, PRECONNECT if the backup instance is able to support all connections from every instance that it is backup for
FAILED_OVER	TRUE if running in failover mode and have failed over, otherwise FALSE
PREV_SQL_ADDRESS	Used with PREV_HASH_VALUE to show the address of the previous SQL statement that was executed
PREV_HASH_VALUE	Used with PREV_SQL_ADDRESS to show the address of the SQL statement that was previously executed
RESOURCE_CONSUMER_GROUP	Name of the session's current resource consumer group

TABLE 10-9. *V$SESSION View for Oracle8i (continued)*

but you can remove the line "and Spid between 280 and 320" to view all of the session information for your database.

```
set linesize 80
set pagesize 999
column Username heading "Oracle Uname" format a12
column Osuser heading "Rmt Username" format a20 wrap
column Process heading "Rmt PID"
column Machine heading "Rmt System" format a18
column Program heading "Remote Program" format a20
column Spid heading "Local PID"
column Sid format 99999
column Serial# format 99999
select b.Username, b.Osuser, b.Process, b.Machine, a.Spid, b.Program,
       b.Sid, b.Serial#
  from V$PROCESS a,V$SESSION b
```

```
 where a.Addr = b.Paddr
   and Spid between 280 and 320
/

Oracle Uname Rmt Username         Rmt PID   Rmt System         Local PID
------------ -------------------- --------- ------------------ ---------
Remote Program          SID SERIAL#
------------------- ------ -------
RACHEL       MYSYSTEM\myuseracct  310:314   MYNET1\MYSYSTEM    316
SQLPLUSW.EXE              9    1602
MARLENE      MYSYSTEM\myuseracct  317:133   MYNET1\MYSYSTEM    300
SQLPLUSW.EXE             11    1398
JAMES        MYSYSTEM\myuseracct  299:278   MYNET1\MYSYSTEM    282
SQLPLUSW.EXE             13    1563
```

If you want to shut down your database normally (not using the **immediate** or **abort** option), you can use the above query to gain the information you need to remove active sessions other than the detached processes and your own session from the database. Armed with this information, you can contact the people who are active in your database, issue a **kill** command from the database level, and also be able to kill the process at the operating system level should you need to. (Sometimes, just killing a session does not automatically stop the associated process at the operating system level, and you must interactively kill the OS process as well.)

We talked about lock contention earlier in the V$LOCK section. V$SESSION provides information on the row and table participating in a lock contention. Let's see how. In this example, we've created a lock contention situation. You can use the following query to determine the Owner and Object_Name by joining the V$SESSION view with the DBA_OBJECTS view described earlier in this book. Here's the query you can use:

```
column Object_Name format a20
column Object_Type format a10
column Owner format a15
select Row_Wait_Obj# obj#, Row_Wait_File# file#, Row_Wait_Block# block#,
       Row_Wait_Row# row#, Sid, Object_Name, Owner, Object_Type
  from V$SESSION, DBA_OBJECTS
 where Row_Wait_Obj# = Object_Id
   and Row_Wait_Obj# > 0;

OBJ#      FILE#     BLOCK#    ROW#      SID       OBJECT_NAME
--------- --------- --------- --------- --------- ---------------
OWNER      OBJECT_TYP
---------- ----------
    10922         2       263         0        12 EMPLOYEE
RACHEL     TABLE
```

The Row_Wait_Obj# is the object number in the database that uniquely identifies the table (in this case) where contention is occurring. You can easily see who owns the table and that it is, indeed, a table.

We'll leave the other contents of the V$SESSION view as an exercise for you to explore yourself.

V$ROLLSTAT

As we said in Chapter 4, rollback segments are used to store undo or before-change information. If a transaction must be rolled back to its content before the change, the information stored in the rollback segment will be used for this purpose. Transactions are assigned to rollback segments in a circular manner, and the faster a user acquires the rollback header and rollback data block, the better. Table 10-10 shows the columns of the V$ROLLSTAT view.

Column	Description
USN	Rollback segment number
EXTENTS	Number of extents in rollback segment
RSSIZE	Size in bytes of rollback segment
WRITES	Number of bytes written to rollback segment
XACTS	Number of active transactions
GETS	Number of header gets
WAITS	Number of header waits
OPTSIZE	Optimal size of rollback segment
HWMSIZE	High-water mark of rollback segment size
SHRINKS	Number of times the size of a rollback segment decreases
WRAPS	Number of times rollback segment is wrapped
EXTENDS	Number of times rollback segment size is extended
AVESHRINK	Average shrink size
AVEACTIVE	Current size of active extents, averaged over time
STATUS	Rollback segment status
CUREXT	Current extent
CURBLK	Current block

TABLE 10-10. *V$ROLLSTAT View in Oracle8i*

There are many different areas of information contained in this view that you will find interesting. To see how your rollback segments are performing (how much traffic they are getting and how often they are extending and shrinking), you can use the following script:

```
column Name format a7
column Extents format 999 heading 'Extents'
column Rssize format 999,999,999 heading 'Size in|Bytes'
column Optsize format 999,999,999 heading 'Optimal|Size'
column Hwmsize format 99,999,999 heading 'High Water|Mark'
column Shrinks format 9,999 heading 'Number of|Shrinks'
column Wraps format 9,999 heading 'Number of|Wraps'
column Extends format 999,999 heading 'Number of|Extends'
column Rownum noprint
select Name, Rssize, Optsize, Hwmsize, Shrinks, Wraps, Extends
from V$ROLLSTAT, V$ROLLNAME
where V$ROLLSTAT.Usn = V$ROLLNAME.Usn
order by Rownum;

              Size in       Optimal  High Water Number of Number of Number of
Name            Bytes          Size        Mark   Shrinks     Wraps   Extends
------- ------------ ------------ ----------- --------- --------- ---------
SYSTEM        733,184                  733,184         0         0         0
R01        21,295,104   20,971,520  64,958,464         5        63        41
R02        21,295,104   20,971,520  21,295,104         0        19         0
R03        21,295,104   20,971,520  21,295,104         0         5         0
R04        21,295,104   20,971,520  21,295,104         0        16         0
R05        21,295,104   20,971,520  21,295,104         0        13         0
R06        21,295,104   20,971,520  21,295,104         0         8         0
R07        21,295,104   20,971,520  21,295,104         0         5         0
```

Each time a rollback segment adds another extent (Extends), wraps around to the first extent (Wraps), or returns to its optimal size (Shrinks), Oracle has to perform the work of tracking the action. The overhead involved in extends, wraps, and shrinks can impact system performance. You will use the V$ROLLSTAT view (joined to the V$ROLLNAME view to resolve the rollback segment names) to see the value for **optimal** that's been established for the rollback segments (stored in the Optsize column) by performing the query:

```
select Name, Optsize
  from V$ROLLSTAT s, V$ROLLNAME n
 where s.Usn = n.Usn;

NAME                              OPTSIZE
------------------------------ ---------
SYSTEM
RB1                                512000
RB2                                512000
RB3                                512000
RB4                                512000
RB5                                512000
RB6                                512000
RB7                                512000
RB8                                512000
RB9                                512000
```

In this example, there is no optimal size set for the SYSTEM rollback segment, and all of the other segments have an optimal size of 512K. If you have a high number of Extends, consider re-creating your rollback segments with a larger initial and next extent size. If you have a high number of Wraps, re-create your rollback segments with a larger minimum extent size.

You can also derive the average of Waits to Gets by using the following query:

```
set head off;
select 'The average of Waits to Gets is '||
       round((sum(Waits) / sum(Gets)) * 100,2)||'%'
  from V$ROLLSTAT;

The average of Waits to Gets is 0%
```

If the ratio of Waits to Gets is more than 1–2 percent, consider creating more rollback segments. If you have enough disks and controllers and you are seeing high rollback segment activity, you can increase the rollback segment tablespaces to two or more sets on different disks using separate controllers with several rollback segments spread evenly over them.

V$ROLLNAME

In the previous query under V$ROLLSTAT, the view was joined to the V$ROLLNAME table to resolve the rollback segments' names. V$ROLLNAME is a lookup table and contains the columns shown in Table 10-11.

In both views, the column you use to join the views to resolve the rollback segment name is called Usn. Therefore, you must distinguish the names by fully qualifying the value—you know, using the view name coupled with the column name, as in V$ROLLSTAT.Usn. If you don't use this form of qualification, Oracle will return an error about being unable to resolve the column name.

Column	Description
USN	Rollback (undo) segment number
NAME	Rollback segment name

TABLE 10-11. *V$ROLLNAME View for Oracle8i*

V$ROWCACHE

V$ROWCACHE provides you with insights into the performance of the dictionary cache. Each user who connects to the database, and every data request that user makes, references the data dictionary. The data dictionary cache is an area of the shared pool that contains data dictionary information in memory. Table 10-12 shows the columns of this view.

Column	Description
CACHE#	Row cache ID number
TYPE	Parent or subordinate row cache type
SUBORDINATE#	Subordinate set number
PARAMETER	Name of the initialization parameter that determines the number of entries in the data dictionary cache
COUNT	Total number of entries in the cache
USAGE	Number of cache entries that contain valid data
FIXED	Number of fixed entries in the cache
GETS	Total number of requests for information on the data object
GETMISSES	Number of data requests resulting in cache misses
SCANS	Number of scan requests
SCANMISSES	Number of times a scan failed to find the data in the cache
SCANCOMPLETES	For a list of subordinate entries, the number of times the list was scanned completely
MODIFICATIONS	Number of inserts, updates, and deletions
FLUSHES	Number of times flushed to disk
DLM_REQUESTS	Number of DLM requests
DLM_CONFLICTS	Number of DLM conflicts
DLM_RELEASES	Number of DLM releases

TABLE 10-12. *V$ROWCACHE View in Oracle8i*

In Oracle version 6, the greatest performance improvement you could make was to modify the values for each of the data dictionary parameters (referred to as "dc underscore parameters"). In version 7, they became internal parameters, and you can no longer directly tune or affect them. You can, however, influence the amount of resource they get by increasing the value for the init.ora parameter **shared_pool_size**. The object is to keep as much of the data dictionary information in memory as possible.

The values stored in the V$ROWCACHE view reflect activity since the database was started. Therefore, a database that was just started will have values that do not reflect the true activity of the system. You will want to wait at least an hour or two after starting the database to look at this view's contents.

When an Oracle database starts, Oracle loads definitions into the cache. Therefore, the Getmisses column should never be equal to 0. However, the Gets column, which shows the total number of requests for an item, could be 0. We have taken this into account by adding a really small value to the Gets column when performing the ratio computation. Here's a look at a way to determine the hit ratio of each data dictionary cache item using the V$ROWCACHE view. The sample query was performed on a very quiet system. Normally, you want the percentage of misses to be below 15 percent.

```
column Parameter format a20
select Parameter, Gets,
       Getmisses, round(Getmisses / (Gets+0.000000000001) * 100,2)
pctmisses
from V$ROWCACHE;

PARAMETER              GETS GETMISSES PCTMISSES
-------------------- ------ --------- ---------
dc_free_extents        1550        96      6.19
dc_used_extents          40        20        50
dc_segments              65        37     56.92
dc_tablespaces          109         3      2.75
dc_tablespace_quotas      0         0         0
dc_files                  0         0         0
dc_users                 55        15     27.27
dc_rollback_segments   1707        28      1.64
dc_objects              426        73     17.14
dc_global_oids            0         0         0
dc_constraints            0         0         0
dc_object_ids           231        33     14.29
dc_synonyms              19         6     31.58
dc_sequences              3         2     66.67
```

```
dc_usernames                80          4          5
dc_database_links            0          0          0
dc_histogram_defs            0          0          0
dc_outlines                  0          0          0
dc_profiles                  3          1      33.33
dc_users                     0          0          0
dc_sequence_grants           0          0          0
dc_histogram_data            0          0          0
dc_user_grants              28         13      46.43
```

V$SGASTAT

The system global area (SGA), which is sometimes referred to as the shared global area, is a memory structure that is highly tunable. The SGA is composed of three memory structures: database buffers, shared pool, and redo log buffers. The shared pool also consists of three structures: the library cache, data dictionary cache, and user global area (UGA). A cache miss (not finding the needed information in memory) on the data dictionary or library cache is much more expensive than a database buffer cache miss. If the cache is too small, Oracle must dedicate resources to managing the limited space (like a juggler who must keep at least one of many balls constantly in the air because he does not have enough space in his hands to hold all of them at once). If there is not enough space, CPU resource is consumed, and you see contention on the system for resources.

V$SGASTAT is used to display information about the sizes of all the structures in the SGA. Table 10-13 shows the columns for V$SGASTAT.

There are two different values in the SGA—dynamic and static. The static values will remain the same from the point in time when the database is started to the time

Column	Description
NAME	SGA component name.
BYTES	Memory size in bytes.
POOL*	Designates the pool in which the memory in the NAME column resides. Value can be **large pool**, meaning memory is allocated from the large pool,or **shared pool**, meaning memory is allocated from the shared pool.

TABLE 10-13. *V$SGASTAT View for Oracle8i*

when it is shut down. The dynamic values will change over time. Some values, like free memory, will change from moment to moment. To determine which ones are dynamic (if you really want to know), you can spool a listing to a file of the values and run a second listing of the same output about five minutes later. By comparing them, you can see which values are changing and which ones are not.

Here's a list of the values in our sample database:

```
select *
  from V$SGASTAT;

POOL        NAME                                     BYTES
----------- ---------------------------------------- ---------
            fixed_sga                                    65484
            db_block_buffers                          16777216
            log_buffer                                   65536
shared pool free memory                               13913100
shared pool miscellaneous                               341552
shared pool PLS non-lib hp                                2096
shared pool State objects                               134920
shared pool transaction_branches                        368000
shared pool Checkpoint queue                             73764
shared pool KGK heap                                     17568
shared pool db_files                                    426280
shared pool latch nowait fails or sle                    36000
shared pool DML locks                                    34800
shared pool ktlbk state objects                          32100
shared pool fixed allocation callback                      320
shared pool db_handles                                   42952
shared pool enqueue_resources                            96768
shared pool PL/SQL MPCODE                                25128
shared pool trigger inform                                 180
shared pool table columns                                15736
shared pool PL/SQL DIANA                                282072
shared pool KGFF heap                                     9160
shared pool distributed_transactions-                   180152
shared pool dlo fib struct                               40980
shared pool SYSTEM PARAMETERS                            57024
shared pool dictionary cache                            190368
shared pool message pool freequeue                      124550
shared pool KQLS heap                                   172036
shared pool character set memory                         31196
shared pool db_block_buffers                           1114112
shared pool library cache                               437612
shared pool transactions                                 66000
shared pool sql area                                    375252
shared pool processes                                    44368
shared pool sessions                                    136896
```

```
shared pool java static objs                                   37208
shared pool VIRTUAL CIRCUITS                                  105912
shared pool event statistics per sess                         217488
shared pool db_block_hash_buckets                             262360
shared pool file # translation table                           65572
```

To obtain the total allocated size of the SGA, you can do a sum of the Bytes column:

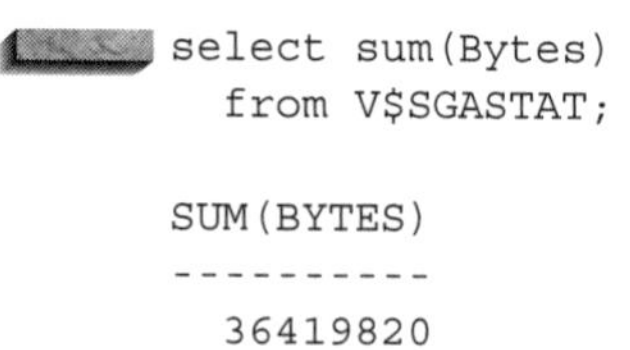

```
select sum(Bytes)
  from V$SGASTAT;

SUM(BYTES)
----------
  36419820
```

Sizing the SGA correctly is an important step in tuning your system. V$SGASTAT can help you determine the amount of space being used currently and how that space is allocated. If you increase any of the following init.ora parameters, you will change the size allocated for the SGA: **shared_pool_size**, **log_buffers**, **db_block_buffers**, **processes**, **open_cursors**, **java_pool_size**, **large_pool_size**. Also, be aware that a change you make to one parameter may have a "ripple" effect and influence the size of another parameter.

V$STATNAME

A fundamental question must be asked when you examine both the V$STATNAME view and the V$SYSSTAT view. That question is, "Why does the V$STATNAME view exist at all?" That's a great question! Looking at the two column listings (Tables 10-14 and 10-15), the only difference between the two views is that the V$SYSSTAT view contains a value for each entry. Take a moment to look at the two tables and ponder the existence of the V$STATNAME view.

Column	Description
STATISTIC#	Statistic number
NAME	Statistic name
CLASS	Statistic class: 1 (User), 2 (Redo), 4 (Enqueue), 8 (Cache), 16 (OS), 32 (Parallel Server), 64 (SQL), 128 (Debug)

TABLE 10-14. *V$STATNAME View for Oracle8i*

In earlier versions of Oracle, the V$SYSSTAT view did not contain a Name column, so the V$STATNAME view was used as a lookup table to resolve the value for the statistic name. The V$SYSSTAT view has now been denormalized to contain the statistic name, so a join no longer needs to be performed between these two views, reducing the query's overhead cost. So, why is the V$STATNAME view still around?

Okay, we won't keep you in suspense any longer. There is a third view, V$SESSTAT, that still relies on V$STATNAME to provide the resolution of each statistic's name. The only columns in the V$SESSTAT view are Sid, Statistic#, and Value. Thus, V$STATNAME still serves an important function (and we've very sneakily slipped a bit of discussion about a V$ session view into this section).

Notice the Class column and the values listed in its description. The eight different classes of statistics provide a wonderful map for you. You can use the Class column to see exactly which statistics are valuable for different areas of tuning. For instance, there are 24 statistics in the Oracle8i version of the view that pertain to users and 24 that pertain to redo. We'll look more at the values in the next section, but let's just take a quick, preview peek at the statistic names for the redo statistics.

```
column Name format a30
select *
  from V$STATNAME
 where Class = 2

STATISTIC# NAME                                CLASS
---------- ------------------------------ ---------
        98 redo entries                            2
        99 redo size                               2
       100 redo buffer allocation retries          2
       101 redo wastage                            2
       102 redo writer latching time               2
       103 redo writes                             2
       104 redo blocks written                     2
       105 redo write time                         2
       106 redo log space requests                 2
       107 redo log space wait time                2
       108 redo log switch interrupts              2
       109 redo ordering marks                     2
```

In this case, the statistic numbers for each member of the Class are all consecutive. However, that is really rarely the case. Most of the statistic classes are mixed together.

Well, guess we've "beaten" this view to death! Let's go on to a really interesting view packed full of fascinating information.

V$SYSSTAT

V$SYSSTAT provides a wealth of information about the performance of your database. Before we begin to examine all of the statistics that you can obtain from this view, we'll look at the composition of it. Table 10-15 shows the V$SYSSTAT columns.

As we said in the previous section on V$STATNAME, the only difference between the two views is the Value column. Let's perform the same query that we did earlier and see what the values are for the redo statistics (Class 2).

```
select *
  from V$SYSSTAT
 where Class = 2;

STATISTIC# NAME                              CLASS      VALUE
---------- ------------------------------ --------- ---------
        98 redo entries                          2       153
        99 redo size                             2     36492
       100 redo buffer allocation retries        2         0
       101 redo wastage                          2     10124
       102 redo writer latching time             2         0
       103 redo writes                           2        40
       104 redo blocks written                   2        94
       105 redo write time                       2       166
       106 redo log space requests               2         0
       107 redo log space wait time              2         0
       108 redo log switch interrupts            2         0
       109 redo ordering marks                   2         0
```

Column	Description
STATISTIC#	Statistic number
NAME	Statistic name
CLASS	Statistic class: 1 (User), 2 (Redo), 4 (Enqueue), 8 (Cache), 16 (OS), 32 (Parallel Server), 64 (SQL), 128 (Debug)
VALUE	Statistic value

TABLE 10-15. *V$SYSSTAT View for Oracle8i*

Well, there doesn't seem to be much activity for redo logs on this system. You'll want to look closely at the ratio between the redo log space requests and redo entries to determine whether there is redo contention on your system. This value should not be greater than 1 in 5000. The init.ora parameter **log_buffer** (stored in bytes) will influence this statistic. A larger **log_buffer** size will decrease redo log I/O, but if you increase this parameter, do so slowly and in increments of about 5 percent or 10 percent at a time until the ratio is stable. A modest increase can significantly enhance throughput. Keep in mind that **log_buffer** size must be a multiple of the operating system block size.

As we said at the beginning of this section, there is a wealth of statistics stored within the V$SYSSTAT view that can provide you with insights into tuning your database. An area of great interest for tuning is the buffer cache (an area of the SGA that stores a copy of Oracle database blocks in memory). You can use the V$SYSSTAT view to determine whether there is excessive parsing and execution of SQL code going on in your system. Here is a set of scripts using V$SYSSTAT to determine and display your system's buffer cache hit ratio. To obtain the output we show here, you must run the script from a file with its output going to an output file; otherwise, you will see all of the SQL queries displayed on the screen.

```
set head off echo off termout off verify off feedback off
column xn1 format a50
column xn2 format a50
column xn3 format a50
column xv1 new_value xxv1 noprint
column xv2 new_value xxv2 noprint
column xv3 new_value xxv3 noprint
column d1 format a50
column d2 format a50
spool hit_ratio.txt
prompt HIT RATIO:
prompt
prompt Values Hit Ratio is calculated against:
prompt
select lpad(Name,20,' ')||'  =  '||Value xn1, Value xv1
  from V$SYSSTAT
 where Statistic# = 38
/
select lpad(Name,20,' ')||'  =  '||Value xn2, Value xv2
  from V$SYSSTAT
 where Statistic# = 39
/
```

```
select lpad(Name,20,' ')||'  =  '||Value xn3, Value xv3
  from V$SYSSTAT
 where Statistic# = 40
/
set pages 60
select 'Logical reads = db block gets + consistent gets ',
lpad('Logical Reads = ',24,' ')||to_char(&xxv1+&xxv2) d1
from DUAL
/
select 'Hit Ratio = (logical reads - physical reads) / logical reads',
lpad('Hit Ratio = ',24,' ')||
round( (((&xxv2+&xxv1) - &xxv3) / (&xxv2+&xxv1))*100,2 )||'%' d2
from DUAL
/
spool off
```

If you've run this script from a file and spooled the output to a second file, the second file contains

```
HIT RATIO:
Values Hit Ratio is calculated against:

       db block gets   =  951743
       consistent gets  =  704525
       physical reads  =  51671

Logical reads = db block gets + consistent gets

      Logical Reads = 1656268

Hit Ratio = (logical reads - physical reads) / logical reads

            Hit Ratio = 96.88%
```

Note the use of the hard-coded values for "Statistic#." This script must be checked against each new version of Oracle because the statistic numbers can, and often do, change between versions. In a database where the major application is predominantly forms based, there should be a very high hit ratio. In a database where interaction is more direct, you might see a hit ration of 80 percent as acceptable. If the hit ratio is low, you will want to increase the **shared_pool_size** parameter value in your init.ora parameter file.

Another valuable area of information that you can gain from V$SYSSTAT is the volume of sorts that Oracle is performing in memory as opposed to having to sort to disk. Ideally, all sorting operations will be performed in memory, because the overhead of having to place sort values on disk and then retrieve them into memory is costly.

Normally, sort operations (**order by**, **group by**, etc.) are performed in the user's process global area (PGA). However, if there is not enough memory available in this area to hold the sort values, Oracle will shift the sorting operation into the area designated as the user's temporary tablespace. The sorts performed in this area will be done to disk. You can see how many sorts are being performed, how many are in memory, and how many are to disk by executing the query:

```
column Name format a30
select Name, Value
  from V$SYSSTAT
 where Name like 'sort%';

NAME                                         VALUE
---------------------------------------- ---------
sorts (memory)                              168700
sorts (disk)                                    25
sorts (rows)                               1077000
```

In this database, the ratio of sorts performed in memory to sorts performed to disk is

ratio of sorts = round((25 / 168700) * 100,3)
ratio of sorts = 0.015%

Of course, there has not been a particularly high volume of sorts performed, but the statistic looks good. You would like to see a ratio of less than 1 percent of sorts to disk. So, if the sorts to disk are high, what can you do about it? There are two parameters that influence the amount of space each user has available for sort operations: **sort_area_size** and **sort_area_retained_size**. By default, these parameters are set much lower than they should be for anything but the lightest of OLTP transaction traffic. If your ratio of sorts is high, try to determine the average sized sort on your system and increase the **sort_area_size** parameter to that value. If you have an environment where the volume of sorts is high, you can set the **sort_area_retained_size** to a fraction of the **sort_area_size**. The user's sort process will initially allocate the **sort_area_retained_size** amount and grow to the **sort_area_size** limit. Just increasing the **sort_area_size** on one system we worked with improved the ratio dramatically.

V$SYSTEM_EVENT

We've said that contention—users waiting for resources on your system—is at the center of performance tuning. The V$SYSTEM_EVENT view gives you a tool to help you quickly identify those areas of contention. Before we show you how to use this view, look at Table 10-16 to see the view's composition.

A great place to begin investigating where problems lie in your system's performance is by gathering information from the views V$SYSTEM_EVENT,

Column	Description
EVENT	The name of the wait event
TOTAL_WAITS	The total number of waits for this event
TOTAL_TIMEOUTS	The total number of timeouts for this event
TIME_WAITED	The total amount of time waited for this event, in hundredths of a second
AVERAGE_WAIT	The average amount of time waited for this event, in hundredths of a second

TABLE 10-16. *V$SYSTEM_EVENT View for Oracle8i*

V$SESSION_EVENT, and V$SESSION_WAIT. Each view gives you a different insight into whether you have performance problems and where they really are. The V$SYSTEM_EVENT view gives you a high-level perspective of the database wait events, while the V$SESSION_EVENT view gives you a more detailed perspective on a session-by-session level. Keep in mind, though, that the V$SESSION_EVENT view will give you statistics on a session basis only while that session is active. Sessions are given a session ID number for the period of time that they are connected to the database. If a session disconnects, a new session may be assigned the old session's ID. Thus, you must look at V$SESSION_EVENT interactively to gather meaningful information.

A script that you can use to look at the system wait events in order of impact is

```
col Event format a37 heading 'Event'
col Total_Waits format 99999999 heading 'Total|Waits'
col Time_Waited format 9999999999 heading 'Time Waitd|In Hndrds'
col Total_Timeouts format 999999 heading 'Timeout'
col Average_Wait heading 'Average|Time' format 999999.999
set pages 999
select *
  from V$SYSTEM_EVENT
 where Time_Waited > 0
   and Event not in('pmon timer','smon timer','rdbms ipc message',
   'parallel dequeue wait','virtual circuit','SQL*Net message from client',
   'client message','Null event','dispatcher timer')
 order by Time_Waited desc
/
                                         Total          Time Waitd       Average
Event                                    Waits Timeout   In Hndrds          Time
------------------------------------- -------- ------- ----------- -----------
db file sequential read                1368816       0      875970        .640
db file scattered read                  479104       0      609420       1.272
```

```
db file parallel write                         27857       1      104577      3.754
log file switch (checkpoint                     1024     645       81086     79.186
incompleted)
log file parallel write                        23377       1       46002      1.968
log file sync                                  18733       1       35011      1.869
buffer busy waits                              28200      30       12315       .437
enqueue                                          194      14       11178     57.619
control file sequential read                     128       0         843      6.586
library cache pin                                  7       2         784    112.000
control file parallel write                     1855       0         455       .245
file identify                                     30       0         317     10.567
direct path read                                  48       0          89      1.854
db file single write                              12       0          78      6.500
log file single write                             10       0          38      3.800
refresh controlfile command                        1       0          27     27.000
process startup                                    1       0          23     23.000
file open                                         84       0          18       .214
checkpoint completed                               1       0          16     16.000
direct path write                                 24       0           9       .375
instance state change                              1       0           6      6.000
db file parallel read                              1       0           5      5.000
```

Looking at the output above, you would probably want to look at disk file access and log file switches that are not completing in a timely manner before you examined free buffer waits or enqueue. One thing to note is that "db file sequential read" actually refers to index accesses, while "db file scattered read" refers to full table scans.

Once you have examined the overall system, you can use the V$SESSION_EVENT view to drilldown to a finer-grain level to identify the session or sessions that might be experiencing resource contention.

```
col Sid format 9999 heading 'Sess|ID'
col Event format a30 heading 'Event'
col Total_Waits format 99999999 heading 'Total|Waits'
col Time_Waited format 9999999999 heading 'Time (ms)|Waited'
col Average_Wait heading 'Ave (ms)|Time' format 999999.999
set pages 999
select Sid, Event, Total_Waits, Time_Waited, Average_Wait
  from V$SESSION_EVENT
 where Sid = &Sid
 order by Time_Waited desc, Event
/
```

Using V$SESSION, described earlier in this chapter, you can identify sessions on your system. For a Financials application user whose Sid is 8, the output from our V$SESSION_EVENT query looks like the following:

```
 Sess                                    Total   Time (ms)    Ave (ms)
   ID Event                              Waits      Waited        Time
----- ------------------------------ --------- ----------- -----------
    8 SQL*Net message from client        20964     4127008     196.862
    8 log file switch (checkpoint          269       21496      79.911
      incomplete)
```

```
8 log file sync                         4149       7778        1.875
8 enqueue                                 15       1246       83.067
8 buffer busy waits                        6        854      142.333
8 log file switch completion              21        752       35.810
8 db file sequential read                789        596         .755
8 write complete waits                    11         26        2.364
8 latch free                             168         12         .071
8 free buffer waits                        1         10       10.000
8 log buffer space                         3         10        3.333
8 SQL*Net message to client            20965          0         .000
8 SQL*Net more data to client             16          0         .000
8 control file sequential read             2          0         .000
```

Again, you can see that incomplete log file switches have caused some waits for this session—a reconfirmation that this is an area of potential concern. Thus, by using first the V$SYSTEM_EVENT view and then the V$SESSION_EVENT view, you can quickly determine which sessions are waiting for resources on your system.

V$WAITSTAT

Earlier in this chapter, we looked at V$ROLLSTAT to determine the rate at which rollback segments are extending and shrinking. V$WAITSTAT can be used to help monitor for rollback segment contention. Table 10-17 shows the V$WAITSTAT columns.

There are 14 rows in the V$WAITSTAT view in Oracle8i. Each row shows a different candidate for contention. However, these figures are total number of waits for a resource and may not, in themselves, give you a complete picture of the actual object that has a contention problem. This is especially true in the case of freelists. You may be able to see that there is contention for freelists on your system, but the overall value will not tell you which table or index has the problem.

Column	Description
CLASS	Class of block
COUNT	Number of waits by this OPERATION for this CLASS of block
TIME	Sum of all wait times for all the waits by this OPERATION for this CLASS of block

TABLE 10-17. *V$WAITSTAT View for Oracle8i*

In the case of rollback segments, the V$WAITSTAT view will give you a much clearer picture of whether you have enough rollback segments and whether they are large enough to support the transaction activity for your system. Let's take a look at the output from the V$WAITSTAT view and see what it can tell you.

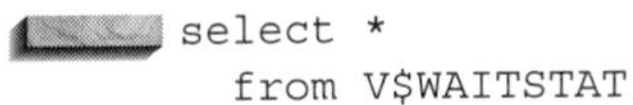

```
select *
  from V$WAITSTAT;

CLASS                  COUNT      TIME
------------------ --------- ---------
data block               218       176
sort block                 0         0
save undo block            0         0
segment header             0         0
save undo header           0         0
free list                  0         0
system undo header         0         0
system undo block          0         0
undo header              126        82
undo block                 0         0
```

In this output, you see that there is contention for undo header in our sample database. If you see contention for undo header, you generally do not have enough rollback segments to support the workload on your system. If you see contention on the undo blocks, increase the size of the rollback segments or use larger extents.

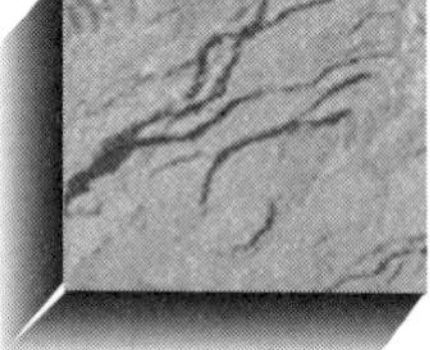

PART III

Oracle Tools and Performance

CHAPTER 11

Oracle-Supplied Tools

y goodness, look at the stars tonight! Aren't they beautiful? The night is so clear and just cool enough to be pleasant. Let's do a bit of stargazing before we go any further. Hmm, what will we use to look more closely at the stars? Oh, you say that you have a pair of binoculars? That will be great. We have a telescope we can set up, too. There! That should do it. We can now do some stargazing with our eyes, your binoculars, or our telescope. If we were really intent on examining the stars more closely, we could even go to an observatory and look through their telescope, the one that's much more powerful than ours. There are many products that you could buy to enhance your ability to see the stars well.

As you can see from our stargazing experience, there are many different ways that you can look at something and many different tools that you can use to "do the job." Some tools will give you a more in-depth view than others or show you different aspects of the object that you are trying to view. There are even additional products that you can buy to enhance your ability to see into one area or another. This is all true of an Oracle database as well.

In this chapter, we are going to explore several different Oracle-supplied tools that you can use to see into your database. We will highlight the ways that you can generate a report using these tools and give an overview of what each tool provides. We'll look first at SQL*Plus and how to use its commands to obtain formatted reports of your database activity. Next, we'll talk about the Oracle optimizers and how they work. We'll discuss the tools Explain Plan and TKPROF and the information they provide. Finally, we'll highlight the Oracle8i version of the Oracle Enterprise Manager (OEM) and the sights you can see using this tool. There are three additional-cost options associated with OEM, and we'll touch very lightly on them. So, let's get started with a look at SQL*Plus.

Things You Need to Know About SQL*Plus

In the beginning, back around version 2.0, Oracle supplied a tool called the User Friendly Interface (UFI, pronounced "youfee"), which you could use to execute commands and see into the database. As database products became more popular, standards were written, and slowly, all of the database manufacturers began to adopt a standard database language called Structured Query Language or SQL (pronounced "seequel"). Oracle Corporation then developed the program called SQL*Plus to allow you to manipulate SQL commands and PL/SQL blocks as well as to perform a number of calculations and reporting functions.

SQL*Plus is provided with every current version of the database. Although there are a great many excellent third-party tools available that allow you to query the database and give you a graphical interface as well, SQL*Plus is still a valuable tool.

First, it's free. Second, it allows you to develop ad hoc queries and reports quickly and easily.

Oracle provides you with a statement buffer so that you can edit the command you just issued to modify the format or the output. You are also provided with commands to set up your environment and format your reports. With the release of Oracle8i, Oracle is replacing the Server Manager tool with SQL*Plus as the means to do database startup and shutdown for many platforms. Therefore, it's a good idea to become familiar with this tool.

Throughout the previous chapters, we've included some of the various SQL*Plus commands without really going into detail on what they are and how they work. It's time now for us to give you a short overview of what you can do with SQL*Plus. As was true with views in the previous section of this book, we can't include every command available, but we're going to "hit the highlights" and include some of the ones we use most often.

Accessing SQL*Plus

Before we can tell you about the commands we use within SQL*Plus, we need to help you get into the tool itself. From the command line on non-Windows-based platforms, you start SQL*Plus by typing

```
sqlplus <username>/<password>
```

If you were going to connect to the HR database as a user named JAMES with the password THEBEST, at the command line, you'd type

```
sqlplus james/thebest@hr
```

You can leave off the username and/or the password, and Oracle will prompt you for them. The advantage of this is that anyone looking over your shoulder will not be able to see your password when you type. Also, it avoids the added security risk (with Unix) that someone may view your .history file to try and get your Oracle password. You can connect to a remote database using a SQL*Net or Net8 connect string. For Windows-based platforms, you access SQL*Plus from the Start menu, and a window will pop up with prompts for username, password, and connect string. If you are connecting to your default database, no connection string is necessary.

When you log on to your computer, the operating system runs a script or set of scripts (autoexec.bat for PCs, .profile or .login for Unix, login.com for VMS) to set up your environment. Oracle also runs scripts to set up your SQL*Plus environment. If you have commands that you want executed for every user who accesses SQL*Plus, such as changing the prompt to show which database they have logged onto, you put these commands in a global login script, called glogin.sql. This script should be placed in the ORACLE_HOME/sqlplus/admin directory on non-Windows platforms and in the

ORACLE_HOME/plus*xx* directory for Windows-based platforms, where *xx* is the version of SQL*Plus. The environment commands you place in this script will be executed for every user who logs on to the database via SQL*Plus. You can put SQL, PL/SQL, and SQL*Plus commands in this script.

Just as your system administrator might have certain environment variables she wants set every time you log on to the server, you may have environment variables that you want set only for your own session. You set them by creating your own version of the login script and accessing it after the global login script has been run. You can do the same within SQL*Plus, setting up a customized environment just for yourself. To set up this environment, you need to create a login.sql file and place it either in the local directory from which you access SQL*Plus or in a directory that is part of an operating system–dependent path. Oracle will look first for glogin.sql and execute it if it is found, and then it will look for the login.sql file and execute it. As with the glogin.sql file, you can put SQL, PL/SQL, and SQL*Plus commands in the login.sql file.

Here is a sample glogin.sql file:

```
--
--   SQL*Plus Global Login startup file.
--
--   This is the global login file for SQL*Plus.
--   Add any sqlplus commands here that are to be
--   executed when a user invokes sqlplus
--   Used for the SHOW ERRORS command
column Line/Col format A8
column Error    format A65  WORD_WRAPPED
set term on echo on
set numwidth 10
set pagesize 10
set linesize 132
```

And a sample login.sql file:

```
My personal login.sql
--
set numwidth 9
set linesize 100
set pagesize 24
col User new_value usernm
set term off echo off
select User from DUAL;
set sqlprompt &usernm>
set term on echo on
```

When you first log in with these two scripts, you will see

```
SQL> set pagesize 10
SQL> Input truncated to 16 characters
set linesize 132
SQL> set numwidth 9
SQL> set linesize 100
SQL> set pagesize 24
SQL> col User new_value usernm
SQL> set term off echo off
QC_USER>
```

The prompt has been changed to the username of the user logging in to SQL*Plus, and some of the global environmental settings have been overridden. One thing to note about the glogin.sql and login.sql scripts is that they are only executed when you first log in to SQL*Plus. If you reconnect to another user from within SQL*Plus itself, without going back to the operating system, the scripts will not be reexecuted.

Okay, now that you know how to get into SQL*Plus, let's go inside and see what you can do once you get there! Remember that while we are going to separate the commands into the following different areas, many of the commands are used in all of these areas.

- Commands that establish your environment
- Information-gathering commands
- Report generation commands

Environment Commands

In the previous section, we showed you some of the commands you can include in the various login scripts. Let's take a look at these commands, as well as a few others, and see what they actually do.

```
--
--   SQL*Plus Global Login startup file.
--
--   This is the global login file for SQL*Plus.
--   Add any sqlplus commands here that are to be
--   executed when a user invokes sqlplus
--   Used for the SHOW ERRORS command
column Line/Col format A8
column Error    format A65  word_wrapped
set term on echo on
```

```
set numwidth 10
set pagesize 10
set linesize 132
```

In the global login script, we first use the SQL*Plus command **column** and its associated subcommands **format** and **word_wrapped**. The **column** command lets you define the attributes of a column in a query result. The **format** subcommand tells Oracle how to format the display of the column. The column named Line/Col will be displayed with 8 characters, while the column named Error will be displayed with 65 characters on the line. If the value of the column is greater than 65, the data within the column will wrap to the next line. The **word_wrapped** subcommand tells Oracle to left-justify each new line and to remove any initial blanks, tabs, or newline characters on each line. A variation of the **word_wrapped** subcommand is the **wrapped** subcommand, which tells Oracle either to wrap the data onto a new line or truncate it at the column width. You can also change the heading of a column using the **heading** subcommand. For example, you might feel that the column Name would be more meaningful if it was displayed as "EMPLOYEE NAME." You would use the **column** command as follows to change the heading:

```
column Name heading 'EMPLOYEE NAME'
```

We'll see the **column** command quite a bit as we explore our most-used SQL*Plus commands. Before we move on though, we have one more thing to explain. If you were looking very closely, you saw the line

```
column Line/Col format A8
```

Huh? How did the / get into the column name? Here's the trick. When you create an object, Oracle automatically changes the name of the object to all uppercase letters before storing it. So even if you type

```
create table lowercase_table (
first_column varchar2(10),
second_column number);
```

Oracle will actually store the name of the table as LOWERCASE_TABLE and the column names as FIRST_COLUMN and SECOND_COLUMN in all the data dictionary tables. But if you enclose the name of the object in quotation marks, like this

```
create table "lowercase_table" (
"first_column" varchar2(10),
"second/column" number);
```

you tell Oracle to store the name exactly as you have written it. So you can create object names with special characters in them (like the Line/Col column) and with mixed-case names. A word of caution though. Most people and third-party systems rely on the "all uppercase" convention, so use this trick sparingly.

The **set** command has a number of subcommands that can be used with it. Here, we are using the **termout** and **echo** commands, and enabling them. **Termout** controls the display of the output generated by commands, while **echo** controls whether each command in a script file is listed as it is executed. Turning them both on means that you will see all the commands as well as their output. Hmm, did you notice something here? Although the actual command name is **termout**, in the script it is referred to as "term." Many of the SQL*Plus commands have abbreviated forms, and the only way to tell if they do (and what they are) is to read the manual.

In the login.sql script, we use the **column** command again, this time with another subcommand, **new_value**. Here, it is used to specify a local variable that will "hold" the value of that column so we can use it later. In this script, we are telling Oracle to save the value of the User column so we can reuse it. User is a system-defined environment variable that Oracle fills with the username you used to log in with. To get the value, you can select it from the DUAL pseudo-table, which really just fills in values from either memory or the operating system. Finally, we use another **set** subcommand, **sqlprompt**, to change the default prompt of SQL to the username.

```
My personal login.sql
--
set numwidth 9
set linesize 100
set pagesize 24
col User new_value usernm
set term off echo off
select User from DUAL;
set sqlprompt &usernm>
set term on echo on
```

The other **set** subcommands we are using here are **numwidth**, **pagesize**, and **linesize**. **Numwidth** defines the default display width of numeric columns. If you do not override the default numwidth, either by explicitly setting the column width with the **column... format...** command or by issuing another **set numwidth** command, any numeric column will be displayed using the default numwidth. If the value to be displayed is less than the default number of characters, Oracle will fill in spaces. If it is greater than the default, but there is enough room, Oracle will display the value using exponential format. Finally, if the value is greater than the default, and there is not enough room to display using exponential format, Oracle will fill the display with #, to indicate that the value has overflowed the column width. Let's take a look at an example of this.

```
SYSTEM>set numwidth 10
SYSTEM>select File_Name, Bytes
  2      from DBA_DATA_FILES
  3     where Tablespace_Name = 'SYSTEM';

FILE_NAME                           BYTES
------------------------------ ----------
D:\ORANT\DATABASE\SYS1ORCL.ORA   62914560
D:\ORANT\DATABASE\SYS0ORCL.ORA   52428800

SYSTEM>set numwidth 7
SYSTEM>select File_Name, Bytes
  2    from DBA_DATA_FILES
  3   where Tablespace_Name = 'SYSTEM';

FILE_NAME                        BYTES
------------------------------ -------
D:\ORANT\DATABASE\SYS1ORCL.ORA 6.3E+07
D:\ORANT\DATABASE\SYS0ORCL.ORA 5.2E+07


SYSTEM>set numwidth 5
SYSTEM>select File_Name, Bytes
  2    from DBA_DATA_FILES
  3   where Tablespace_Name = 'SYSTEM';

FILE_NAME                      BYTES
------------------------------ -----
D:\ORANT\DATABASE\SYS1ORCL.ORA #####
D:\ORANT\DATABASE\SYS0ORCL.ORA #####
```

The **pagesize** subcommand defines the number of lines of output that will be displayed before a page break is inserted and the headers are repeated. You can use this subcommand to format your screen display or to format the number of lines on a report, as you will see a bit later in the "Reporting Commands" section. In addition, there is a neat trick you can use **pagesize** for. If you issue the command **set pagesize 0**, Oracle will remove all page breaks from your output, as well as any column headings that would normally be displayed. Why is this useful? Well, while Oracle provides you with the SQL*Loader utility to load flat-file data into the database, there is no such utility to extract flat-file data. So you can use SQL*Plus and the **set pagesize 0** command to generate an ASCII list of the rows of your table or tables. We use it as part of our backup strategy, to make sure we list every file in the database that should be backed up. The flat file of file names that we generate is used as input to our backup scripts. That way, we never have to worry that we forgot to update the backups when we add a new datafile to the database!

The **linesize** subcommand defines how wide the display will be before Oracle wraps the line to the next line. Depending on whether you are displaying to the screen or printing in different orientations, you may want to make it larger or smaller. The default value is 80; the maximum value is operating system dependent.

A few other environment commands you should know about are listed here:

- **show** Just as **set** defines some of the environment variables, **show** displays the current settings of your environment. In addition to all the variables defined by **set**, you can display the page titles, username, errors, and error codes, as well as the Oracle release.
- **clear** Clears the SQL buffer, any breaks and compute settings, and the screen display.
- **define** Allows you to define local variables. If you have a constant that you want to use, such as a carriage return that you want to include in various displays, you can use the **define** command to set the value.
- **undefine** Just as you use **define** to set values, you use **undefine** to clear the values of variables. **Undefine** can also be used to clear the values of implicitly defined variables. To define an implicit variable, use the & character before the variable name, and Oracle will prompt you for a value.
- **set arraysize** Tells Oracle the number of rows to return in a single call to the database. While the maximum value is 5000, setting the array size to greater than 100 usually has no additional effect on performance. The larger the array size setting, the more memory Oracle will need for each fetch.
- **set maxdata** Sets the maximum total row width that SQL*Plus can process. It is used in conjunction with the **arraysize** command, and the larger the value of maxdata, the lower the array size should be set. (This is no longer supported in 8.0 but still can be set using the **set** command.)
- **set autocommit** Controls when Oracle commits pending changes to the database. If you set this to on, Oracle will automatically issue a commit after each successful insert, update, delete, or PL/SQL block. The default value is off, which means you must manually commit your changes by issuing the **commit** command.
- **set pause** Controls the scrolling of output to your screen. Setting pause on will cause the screen display to stop and wait for you to press ENTER before displaying the next page.

- **set colsep** Defines the text to be displayed between columns. You can use this to set off columns. This sets the value to be displayed between all columns.
- **set recsep** Just as **colsep** defines the separator string to be displayed between columns, **recsep** defines the line to be displayed between each row of output.
- **set timing** Used to collect and display data on the amount of computer resources used to run one or more commands or blocks of PL/SQL or SQL code. **Timing** collects data for an elapsed period of time, saving the data on commands run during the period in a timer. To delete all timers, you use the **clear timing** command.

Information-Gathering Commands

Now that the environment has been set up, let's see what you can do to get information about the results of SQL commands you've run as well as the definitions of objects within your database.

Wouldn't it be great if you could get trace information about the SQL statements you're running, as you run them? Guess what! You can, by using some of the informational commands available in SQL*Plus.

The **set autotrace** command and its subcommands allow you to gather performance tuning information on the queries that you run. In order to effectively use this command, you should have been granted the PLUSTRACE role. To create the PLUSTRACE role, you must run the script plustrce.sql found in your ORACLE_HOME/sqlplus/admin directory as SYS. If you attempt to run this script as SYSTEM, you will get error messages that the table or view does not exist. The file contains the following commands:

```
set echo on

drop role plustrace;
create role plustrace;

grant select on v_$sesstat to plustrace;
grant select on v_$statname to plustrace;
grant select on v_$session to plustrace;
grant plustrace to dba with admin option;

set echo off
```

You will also need to create the PLAN_TABLE table in your schema. To create this table, run the utlxplan.sql script that can be found in the ORACLE_HOME/

rdbms/admin directory. Once you've created this table, you can then turn tracing on and have the trace files created in the user dump destination defined for this database.

The subcommands of the **set autotrace** command are

- **off** This is the default and means that no tracing information will be generated.
- **on** This version of the **autotrace** command displays the most detailed information, containing the query output, the optimizer execution path, and the SQL statement execution statistics.
- **traceonly** This version of the **autotrace** command displays the same information as **set autotrace on**, except that the query output itself is suppressed.
- **on explain** This version of the **autotrace** command displays only the optimizer execution path.
- **on statistics** This version of the **autotrace** command displays only the SQL statement execution statistics.

Other commands give you information either about your database or about what is going on within your session. The **show errors** command will display the compilation errors of any procedure, function, or package that you attempt to create or compile. In the example below, an error within the procedure prevents it from compiling. The error message that is returned, however, is not very explicit. By using the **show errors** command, you can retrieve more information about the error, which can help you to debug the problem quickly.

```
SYSTEM>create procedure qc_user.validate_date
  2  as valdate date;
  3  begin
  4  select sydate into valdate from DUAL;
  5  end;
  6  /

Warning: Procedure created with compilation errors.

SYSTEM>show errors
Errors for PROCEDURE QC_USER.VALIDATE_DATE:

LINE/COL ERROR
-------- -----------------------------------------------------------
4/1      PL/SQL: SQL Statement ignored
4/8      PLS-00201: identifier 'SYDATE' must be declared
```

In the listing above, the **show errors** command returns two rows. The first tells you that line 4 of the procedure contains a SQL statement that has been ignored because of an error. The second tells you what the error on that line is. The information retrieved by the **show errors** command can also be queried from the DBA_ERRORS view.

If you just type **show errors** at the prompt, SQL*Plus will display the errors for the most recently created or altered stored procedure. To display the errors for a particular stored program, use the expanded form of the command:

```
show errors <type> <stored program name>
```

You can display the errors for functions, procedures, packages, package bodies, and triggers.

The next SQL*Plus informational command can be used in conjunction with the **show errors** command to retrieve the line that has an error, so that you can review the problem and correct it. The **list** command, with a line number, will display the individual line. If you do not supply a line number, the entire SQL statement will be displayed. To continue the example above:

```
SYSTEM>list 4
  4* select sydate into valdate from DUAL;
SYSTEM>
```

At this point, you can edit the line, using the **change** command, and retry the compilation.

Hmm, this seems to be a good time to talk briefly about the **change** command. The **change** command is a single-line editor, which allows you to substitute a new character string for the existing one. You type the **change** command, followed by a nonalphanumeric separator character, then the string you want to replace, the same separator character, and finally, the new string. To correct the problem above, you would type

```
SYSTEM>change /sydate/sysdate
  4* select sysdate into valdate from DUAL;
SYSTEM>
```

You can now reexecute the command, and it will compile. When you use the **change** command, the default will be the last line you entered. In our example, the line we modified is the fourth line in a list of six lines used. Let's go back to the command before this last one to see how we told Oracle which line we wanted to edit.

```
SYSTEM>list 4
  4* select sydate into valdate from DUAL;
SYSTEM>
```

See! We first told Oracle to display the fourth line in our listing. The asterisk next to a number indicates the line Oracle is currently pointing to. In this case, the 4 has an asterisk after it, so we know Oracle is pointing to the correct line. Now, let's do this exercise again using a bit of "shorthand." Since we already know where our error is in this example, we'll go right to the problem line:

```
SYSTEM> 4
  4*   select sydate into valdate from DUAL;
SYSTEM> c/sydate/sysdate
  4*   select sysdate into valdate from DUAL;
SYSTEM> l
  1  create procedure qc_user.validate_date
  2      as valdate date;
  3   begin
  4  select sysdate into valdate from DUAL;
  5     end;
  6* /
```

There are three things of interest in this listing. We did not use the subcommand **list** for the line number but merely typed in the number of the line we wanted Oracle to point to. We did not type the full command **change** but used only its abbreviated form. Finally, we again used the abbreviated form of a command (**list**) to ask Oracle to list the entire set of commands in our procedure. Oh, look at the line Oracle is now pointing to. Yep, it's line 6.

If you find that the SQL in your list contains multiple errors, single-line editing can be rather tedious. The SQL*Plus command allows you to edit your SQL statements using an editor. This can be done via **define _editor = edt**. Within Unix, you could use the vi editor, and NT's default editor is Notepad. Also, within Unix, setting the environment variable **editor** has the same effect.

The final information-gathering command we want to talk about is the **describe** command. This command is used to display information about tables and views. Suppose you want to create a report on the information in one of your tables? (We'll tell you how to create reports in the next section.) Before you can begin to format your report, you'd need to know what information is in your table, right? By doing a **describe** on the table, you can see what the column names are, how wide the columns are, and which of the columns must not be null.

```
SYSTEM>describe EXTGROW
 Name                            Null?    Type
 ------------------------------- -------- ----
 SEGNAME                         NOT NULL VARCHAR2(81)
 SEGOWN                          NOT NULL VARCHAR2(30)
 GROWDATE                        NOT NULL DATE
 SEGTYPE                                  VARCHAR2(17)
```

```
SEGTBS                                  VARCHAR2(30)
EXTS                                    NUMBER
NEXTEXT                                 NUMBER
TBSFREE                                 NUMBER
HWM                                     NUMBER
TOTBYTES                                NUMBER
USEDBYTES                               NUMBER
CONTIGFREE                              NUMBER
FREEPCT                                 NUMBER
TBSEXTS                                 NUMBER
```

Looking at this, you know that you will probably have to reformat some of the columns or the report won't fit on one line. Okay, now that we know what the EXTGROW table looks like, let's see how we'd run a report on the information in this table.

Reporting Commands

One of the things you want when creating a report is for the report to be readable. It doesn't matter how good the information you are including is, if the report has lines wrapping all over the place, no one is going to use it. SQL*Plus has a number of report formatting commands to help you create readable, informative reports.

We're going to create a report on the EXTGROW table, building the report section by section as we explain the commands we are using. Let's start by defining the display environment.

```
set pagesize 50 trimspool on linesize 250 verify off feedback off
set echo off term off
```

Some of these commands we've discussed in earlier sections. We've decided to set the number of lines per page to 50 and the number of characters on each line to at most 250. We've also decided not to display the commands to the screen and not to display the output to the screen. By turning **echo** and **term** off and spooling the output to a file, the file will contain a report without any extraneous lines. Notice that we did not use five separate commands preceded by the keyword **set**, but we ran the five commands together in one line. You can group your **set** commands like this to save space.

We are using several new **set** subcommands for this report. The subcommand **trimspool on** tells Oracle that trailing blanks on the output line should be trimmed off, so that if the line does not fill all 250 characters we defined for linesize, we won't get blanks filling in the empty spaces. If you use a variable name prefixed by an ampersand (&) in Oracle, you will be prompted for the value of the variable and will see the old and new values of this variable. By using the **verify off** subcommand, you tell Oracle not to prompt you and not to tell you what you entered. The **feedback off** subcommand tells Oracle not to display a row count at the end of the report.

The next section of the report prompts for the values to use later in the where clause of the select statement.

```
accept free_pct prompt 'Enter maximum percentage free: '
accept grow_date prompt 'Enter date to report on: '
accept tbsname prompt 'Enter tablespace to report on: '
```

The **accept** command, with its subcommand **prompt**, lets you create a report that is somewhat dynamic, as the contents are determined at runtime by the values input when you run the script. You could also prompt the user for the values by simply using the variable name with & in front of it at the point in the script where you need the value, but when you do that, you cannot choose the prompting text. The **accept** command allows you to request the information with a prompt that is clearer to the user.

We've seen and explained the **column** command in earlier sections of this chapter. However, we're using some new subcommands here, and they need to be explained. The **format** subcommand allows you to format numeric data as well as alphanumeric data. When you format a numeric column, you can have Oracle display the number with commas and periods as well as minus and plus signs. The *SQL*Plus Reference Manual* has a complete list of all the possible format masks for numeric columns. The other column subcommand we are using is **heading**. We mentioned this subcommand earlier when we first talked about the **column** command, but we didn't tell you very much about it. By default, if you do not specify a heading for a column, Oracle will use the name of the column as the heading, displaying it in all capitals, with underscores if they are in the name. Also by default, Oracle will truncate the column heading name to the number of characters you have defined in the **format** subcommand, or the length of the column itself if you don't define a format. This can lead to a somewhat ambiguous set of headings, and you can use the **heading** subcommand to override the default headings and have your report display more meaningful names.

```
col Segname format a30 heading 'OBJECT'
col Segown format a10 heading 'OWNER'
col Segtype format a5 heading 'TYPE'
col Segtbs format a15 heading 'TABLESPACE'
col Exts format 9999 heading 'OBJEXTS'
col Nextext format 9,999,999,999 heading 'NEXT EXTENT'
col Tbsfree format 9,999,999,999 heading 'TOTAL TBS FREE'
col Hwm format 9,999,999,999 heading 'HIGHWATER MARK'
col Totbytes format 9,999,999,999 heading 'TOT ALLOC SPC'
col Usedbytes format 9,999,999,999 heading 'USED SPACE'
col Contigfree format 9,999,999,999 heading 'LARGEST FREE'
col Freepct format 999.99 heading '% FREE'
col Tbsexts format 9999 heading 'TBSEXTS'
```

The next two commands work in conjunction with each other. The **compute** command tells Oracle what computation to make and when. The computation is displayed every time the **break** command takes effect. In this example, you are not only telling Oracle to sum up the Nextext column and display the sum every time the Segtbs column changes value, but also suppressing the printing of the Segtbs column until the value changes. In addition, the total sum will be displayed at the end of the report. Any break location that does not have an action associated with it by a **compute** command will not actually cause a break, but will suppress the printing of the column information until the information changes. In this example, Oracle will only print the values of the Tbsfree, Contigfree, Tbsext, and Segown columns when their contents change from the last time they were displayed. The Segtbs column will also print only once per value; but in addition, when the value changes, the sum of the Nextexts will be displayed, because of the **compute** command, and a blank line will be inserted into the report, because of the **skip 1** clause.

```
compute sum of Nextext on Segtbs
break on report on Segtbs skip 1 on Tbsfree on Contigfree on Tbsexts on Segown
```

Careful use and combination of the **break** and **compute** commands can make for a very complex, very readable report.

The final section of the script contains the actual query statement as well as the final formatting commands for the output.

```
select Segtbs,  Tbsfree,  Contigfree,  Tbsexts, Segown,  Segname,
       Segtype,  Hwm,  Totbytes,  Usedbytes, Exts,  Nextext,  Freepct
  from EXTGROW
 where Freepct <= &free_pct
   and Growdate = to_date('&grow_date','YYYYMMDD')
   and Segtbs like upper('%&tbsname%')
 order by Segtbs, Segown, Segname

set concat +
spool spacerpt_&grow_date.log
```

Oracle normally uses a period to terminate a substitution variable—any variable name prefixed by &. Another useful feature of SQL*Plus is the double ampersand (&&). It is used to avoid being prompted for a value multiple times when that value occurs in several places within the report or query.

If you didn't reset the concatenation symbol, the **spool** command, which tells Oracle the name of the file to write the output to, would create a file named spacerpt_<growdate>log, with no extension. The **set concat** command tells Oracle that for the next command, you are replacing the concatenation symbol of a period with the symbol in the **set concat** command. This allows you to create an output file named spacerpt_<growdate>.log.

Now, let's take another look at the script, all in one piece, and look at the results when we run this script.

```
set pagesize 50 trimspool on linesize 250 verify off feedback off
set echo off term off
accept free_pct prompt 'Enter maximum percentage free: '
accept grow_date prompt 'Enter date to report on: '
accept tbsname prompt 'Enter tablespace to report on: '
col Segname format a30 heading 'OBJECT'
col Segown format a10 heading 'OWNER'
col Segtype format a5 heading 'TYPE'
col Segtbs format a15 heading 'TABLESPACE'
col Exts format 9999 heading 'OBJEXTS'
col Nextext format 9,999,999,999 heading 'NEXT EXTENT'
col Tbsfree format 9,999,999,999 heading 'TOTAL TBS FREE'
col Hwm format 9,999,999,999 heading 'HIGHWATER MARK'
col Totbytes format 9,999,999,999 heading 'TOT ALLOC SPC'
col Usedbytes format 9,999,999,999 heading 'USED SPACE'
col Contigfree format 9,999,999,999 heading 'LARGEST FREE'
col Freepct format 999.99 heading '% FREE'
col Tbsexts format 9999 heading 'TBSEXTS'
compute sum of Nextext on Segtbs
break on report on Segtbs skip 1 on Tbsfree on Contigfree on Tbsexts on Segown
select Segtbs,  Tbsfree,  Contigfree,  Tbsexts, Segown,  Segname,
       Segtype,  Hwm,  Totbytes,  Usedbytes, Exts,  Nextext,  Freepct
  from EXTGROW
 where Freepct <= &free_pct
   and Growdate = to_date('&grow_date','YYYYMMDD')
   and Segtbs like upper('%&tbsname%')
 order by Segtbs, Segown, Segname

set concat +
spool spacerpt_&grow_date.log
/
TABLESPACE       TOTAL TBS FREE   LARGEST FREE TBSEXTS OWNER
OBJECT                           TYPE HIGHWATER MARK  TOT ALLOC SPC
USED SPACE     OBJEXTS    NEXT EXTENT  % FREE
--------------- -------------- -------------- ------- ----------
------------------------------ ----- --------------  --------------
-------------- ------- -------------- -------
USERS              603,635,712     66,314,240     327 TEST
IDX_MSGS_IN                      INDEX                      327,680
       327,680       8          40,960     .00

IDX_MSGS_OUT                     INDEX                    2,621,440
     2,621,440      60          40,960     .00

MSGS_IN                          TABLE     44,998,656    14,049,280
    14,049,280     332          40,960     .00

MSGS_OUT                         TABLE     15,351,808    52,510,720
    52,428,800     224       1,048,576     .16
************** ************** *************** *******
                        **************
                        --------------
sum                          1,171,456
```

Unfortunately, the listing is so wide that it will still wrap from one line to the next. However, you can imagine just how unreadable the report would be if the repeated column values were not suppressed! If you print this file using the landscape orientation of your printer, the rows will appear on a single line each, because we reset the line size to a wide enough value.

There are several other SQL*Plus commands you can use to make your reports more sophisticated. The **ttitle** command and the associated **btitle** command allow you to set a header and footer for each page. You can set a variable to contain the date, using the **new_value** subcommand of the **column** command, and insert that into the header or footer on the page. Notice that we added yet another subcommand to the **column** command, the **noprint** subcommand. This command tells Oracle not to display the results of the query. We use that to set the value of the variable today_date that we will use later in the report.

```
btitle off
ttitle off
set pagesize 10 linesize 30 heading off
col today new_value today_date noprint
select Sysdate today from DUAL;

ttitle center 'Tablespace Listing'
btitle left 'Page: ' format 999 sql.pno right today_date
select Tablespace_Name from DBA_TABLESPACES;

      Tablespace Listing
SYSTEM
USER_DATA
ROLLBACK_DATA
TEMPORARY_DATA
TESTTBS
Page:    1           05-SEP-99
```

The SQL*Plus commands **repheader** and **repfooter**, new in Oracle8.0, use the same variables and subcommands as **ttitle** and **btitle**, but they are displayed only once per report, rather than once on each page. You can use them to create a title page and end page for your reports.

The last commands we want to talk about are subcommands to the **set** command:

- **serveroutput** Controls whether to display the output of stored procedures or PL/SQL blocks in SQL*Plus. PL/SQL programs display output via the Oracle-supplied dbms_output package. You must issue the command **set serveroutput on** to see the results of calls to dbms_output from your PL/SQL program.

- **newpage** Sets the number of blank lines printed before the top title on a page. A zero value will put a formfeed at the beginning of every page.
- **embedded** Controls where each report begins on a page. Setting **embedded** to off forces each report to start at the top of a new page. If you want reports to print immediately after one another, set embedded to on.

About the Optimizer, Explain Plan, TKPROF, and Autotrace

In the first part of this chapter, we looked at SQL*Plus and how to use various commands to generate a report. In that discussion, you were gathering report information directly from the database with no regard for how long your report query might take to run. Let's consider for a moment the impact on your database if your report query took several hours or days to run because a needed index or set of indices was missing. The probability is that your system would show an overall degradation in performance while this badly written query was running. Eventually, you'd probably have to interactively stop the query and try to figure out what was causing it to take so long. How would you go about your investigation to determine what was wrong with your query? Well, step right up lady or gentleman, we've got just the tool for you! However, before we can tell you about the tool you can use to determine your query's performance, we need to explain the tools Oracle uses to decide how your query will be executed. So, enter the optimizer.

The Optimizer

Jim, one of the authors of this book, owns a home built just after World War II. Although he and his family love their house, its age and all of the other maintenance tasks associated with any house force him to plan at least half of any Saturday on chores. Usually these jobs require trips to hardware stores or supply houses to pick up items needed for that day's job. As far as the jobs go:

- Some jobs could take a few minutes (like fixing a leaky faucet).
- Some chores can take hours of continuous effort (like yard work).
- Some tasks could require small bits of sustained effort with large gaps of downtime (like a small painting project where time is needed for the paint to dry between coats).

Since no two sets of chores are ever the same, every Saturday morning, Jim performs some very careful deliberation over that second cup of coffee. After making a list of all the chores and errands for the day, Jim must order the list in the most efficient way possible. He must get all the necessary materials to have on hand before each job starts and must order the start of each job so it can overlap with other jobs to ensure the entire list can be done as quickly as possible.

Now, imagine that you are faced with sorting out that same kind of problem every time someone asks you a question! Imagine that each time you were asked a question, you had to go through the conscious process of deciding how you would access the information in your head and order that information in a way that the answer made sense to the questioner. And, since you are having a conversation, you can't spend a lot of time thinking about how you are going to answer that other person who is expecting you to respond as quickly as possible.

The Oracle optimizer faces this situation each time someone submits a SQL statement. In a traditional procedural programming language, when you make a request for data, you specify which files to open and in what order. Since SQL is a nonprocedural language, each time any type of Data Manipulation Language (DML) statement, such as a **select, insert, update**, or **delete**, is executed, Oracle has to determine the best way to retrieve the data. And just to make things more interesting, it has to figure out how to retrieve that data quickly enough so that overall response time is not unduly affected. Phew, what a job!

Cost-Based vs. Rule-Based Optimization

The part of Oracle that is responsible for determining how to retrieve the answer to your DML statement is called the *optimizer*. Oracle has two different optimizers that can be used to determine how to get the answer to any SQL statement, the Rule Based Optimizer (RBO) and the Cost Based Optimizer (CBO). The job of the optimizer is to break down a SQL statement into individual components and determine the fastest way to access the data and return the answer. It does this by first understanding which tables are involved in a SQL statement and finding all the available access paths to that data. An *access path* is a fancy name for a method that Oracle can use to get to the data.

Access paths break down into two general methods—either using an index or by accessing the data directly from the table. If more than one table is involved, the optimizer has to figure out which join method to use. A *join method* is the name for the different algorithms the optimizer can call on to combine two different tables. If you have had some introductory programming classes, you might remember two different approaches that you can use to join one set of data to another. One approach is called a *nested loop*, where you pick one row of a table and then loop through the other table trying to find any matches. The other approach is called a *sort-merge*, where both tables are sorted into the same order and the results are compared to find matches. Don't worry too much about the terminology now; we'll discuss access paths and join methods more when we talk about the two different optimizers Oracle has available for query processing.

What is important to remember is that the output of the optimizer is the query plan. The *query plan* is the set of instructions the optimizer puts together on how to access the data and, if necessary, join together multiple tables most efficiently. Let's go back to Jim's list of Saturday chores and see how it relates to the Oracle optimizer's activities. The optimizer has produced a list of materials to gather (determined the access path) and has decided how to do the chores (determined which join method to use and in what order), all in much less time than it took Jim to drink his coffee! Not a bad moment's work at all.

Now, let's take a look at the two different approaches the Oracle optimizer can use to create its query plan.

Rule Based Optimizer

As the name implies, the Rule Based Optimizer is based on a fixed set of instructions that the optimizer can use as guidelines when building a query plan for a SQL statement. These rules tell the optimizer how to value one access path over another when trying to determine the quickest approach to get to or join your data. On the surface, this might look like the easiest way to create an optimizer. Unfortunately, Oracle has set up its optimizer to make some assumptions that can cause problems. You see, the rules are determined by ranking the access paths to the data. That means Oracle has created an approach that says one method of access is always better than another method. The assumptions about which path is more efficient as built into the ranking of the rules does not take into account how much effort or resource it will take to use a particular access path.

In Oracle, the RBO is biased toward index operations. This means Oracle will always favor the use of an index-based access plan over a table scan when using the RBO. We have all been taught that indexes are the fastest way to get data, but, while this sounds good in theory, it can be another story entirely in practice.

To illustrate this point with the RBO, let's assume you have a table called EMPLOYEE with 1000 rows of data. You have an index on the Employee_Id column. Now suppose you need to get the data on a single employee, and you know the employee's number. Naturally, the optimizer would use the index and then read the table, retrieving the data very quickly.

Now, if you take the same table and index and try to access a range of employees from the table, the RBO will still favor the use of an index, even though the rows needed to satisfy the query might be scattered across all the data blocks in the table. In this case, for each row accessed, the query plan would force a read of the index first and then a read of the table for each row of data, when scanning across all the table data blocks might be the more efficient approach. Because the optimizer is biased toward using indexes, it would not consider the number of reads required to obtain the information and would not choose the table scan as the more efficient plan, even though it really is the best approach to use.

A summary of the rules the RBO uses is covered in the list below. Each entry is an example of an access method. The list shows the assumptions implicit in how the RBO values one access path over another. Oracle will try to find these access paths in descending order. The rule-based access path ranking order is as follows:

1. Single row by rowid
2. Single row by cluster join
3. Single row by hash cluster key with unique or primary key
4. Single row by unique or primary key
5. Cluster join
6. Hash cluster key
7. Indexed cluster key
8. Composite key (entire key)
9. Single-column indexes (single index or index merge)
10. Bounded range search on indexed columns (including key prefix)
11. Unbounded range search on indexed columns (including key prefix)
12. Sort-merge join
13. Max or min of indexed column
14. Order by on indexed columns
15. Full table scan

Looking at the list, the first entry is considered the fastest way to get data from the database, by selecting a single row of information using a specific, known rowid. Remember that the Rowid column is present for each entry in the database. If your SQL statement contains a Rowid value and fetches on one, the RBO will choose the plan that reflects rule number one. Notice that the RBO is geared to choose a full table scan as the very last resort.

The RBO has not been enhanced since version 7.0 of Oracle. If you take a look at the list above, you might notice that some of the new functionality introduced in later versions of Oracle7 and Oracle8 (for example, hash joins) are not included in the list of rules. Therefore, these features will not be considered when Oracle creates a query plan. Currently, there are no plans to enhance the Rule Based Optimizer to include these new features.

As you will see in the next section, one of the bigger benefits of using the Cost Based Optimizer is that it takes advantage of all the new features and continues to be enhanced (and improved) over time.

Cost Based Optimizer

The Cost Based Optimizer (CBO) is as aptly named as the Rule Based Optimizer. In this case, the optimizer starts to take into account the relative resource "cost" of one access path over another when considering how to build the query plan. Returning to our example of Saturday morning errands, let's assume for a moment that you were planning your travel route from one location to another. If you were creating the list of rules to follow (like the RBO), you might make a series of rules that were biased toward riding on main highways. Your assumption would be that driving on a main highway would always be the fastest way to get from place to place. That would bias your choice to get to main highways as quickly as possible and stay on them as long as you possibly could (similar to the RBO's bias of always using an index).

However, if you were aware of the traffic flow in the area, understood when the main highways would be busy, and, perhaps, knew some shortcuts, you might be able to determine a faster route by making some more informed decisions. You would be able to balance the amount of time it takes to travel on a little-used back road instead of a crowded highway and begin to guess how long each would take so you could choose the fastest path. Similarly, the CBO is able to make decisions by assessing the amount of resources each access path would take for any given table, and not just blindly following a set of rules.

The best way to summarize the theory behind this approach is to say that the CBO attempts to take into account the relative cost of each table or index access and join operation when building the query plan. The cost calculation takes into account an estimate of CPU operations, network accesses, and disk accesses for any operation. Using statistics kept in the data dictionary, the CBO is able to make the estimates for any table in the database. The CBO can then use this number when comparing different choices for accessing data from a table and, by comparing the relative costs, pick the operation with the lower cost, which should equate to creating the most efficient query plan. However, things are not as simple as they sound!

In practice, the CBO first examines each table involved in a SQL statement and determines the least costly way to access each table, whether that is by an index access if there is an index on the column or, as a worst case, by a full table scan. The optimizer then computes a relative cost for each table access and saves that information. It then begins to compute the cost of joining pairs of tables together using different join methods at its disposal. The difference between the CBO and the RBO is that the RBO will join tables based only on the access path ranking. After finding the cheapest cost for the first pair, it computes the cost of joining the next table to that result. When it has computed the cost of joining all the tables together, it saves that cost as a baseline and starts again, running through the tables in a different order. Obviously, the more complex the SQL statement, the more possible permutations the optimizer has to explore. In most cases, for a complex query, the optimizer is able to examine thousands of combinations in less than a second! Imagine thinking through all of the possible ways you can get from your house to work and back in less than a second.

The CBO's success in picking a plan comes from its ability to evaluate the computed cost factor of each part of a SQL statement and use that cost as a gauge of the amount of resources that operation will take. But the CBO needs to understand more than just the types of access methods available to it when building a query plan. It needs to have information on the type and distribution of data in the tables or indexes. Oracle provides the **analyze** command to gather statistics on objects within the database. Analyze gathers data by reading some or all of the data in an object and saving the information needed to understand the data distribution, such as the highest and lowest values in the column, the number of rows in the object, and the number of blocks in the object.

An abbreviated version of the **analyze** command syntax for a table is as follows (the complete version is available in the *Oracle SQL Reference Manual*).

```
analyze table <tablename> {estimate | compute} statistics
```

The interesting thing to note here is the end phrase about **estimate** or **compute statistics**. Rather than force the **analyze** command to review every row in each block of a table, you can allow the **analyze** command to sample some portion of the table to build its statistics. Since the optimizer is using statistical representations of the data to build its cost, it just needs to have a representative sample of the data to use when making its decisions.

How much of a sample is needed depends in part on the distribution of the data in your database. Some studies have shown that a sampling rate of as little as 5 percent can give the optimizer enough information to compose an optimal plan. However, this is another case where "your mileage may vary"!

We suggest you start by analyzing your data with an estimation factor of 20 percent. If the operation completes within a reasonable time frame and performance on your system is acceptable, then leave well enough alone. If you need to reduce the amount of time the **analyze** operation takes because of its overall impact on system performance, reduce the amount of information gathered. To do this, you can first take a look at some of the statistics kept in your tables using the DBA_TABLES view and compare the statistics with both samples to see how much they have changed. See Chapter 8 for information about the DBA_TABLES view.

You can also monitor the performance of selected SQL statements in your database. A sudden change for the worse may indicate a change in the plan created by the optimizer based on your statistics. If you find that you are often tuning SQL statements and the optimizer is not choosing the best plans, you can increase the amount of data sampled with **analyze** in the hope that more information will give the optimizer enough data to pick a better plan. Keep in mind, though, if the sampling rate is greater than 50 percent, the **analyze** command will read all the data in the table, which is also the definition of a **compute statistics**.

NOTE
*Never run the **analyze** command directly against the SYS schema. When some of the tables in that schema are analyzed, it will cause performance problems.*

If your application does need to access some tables in the data dictionary and you are using the Cost Based Optimizer, you can analyze SYS by using the package dbms_utility.analyze_schema, which is designed to avoid some of the problems that could occur when analyzing SYS. This package is also handy for analyzing all the objects in any schema.

Keep in mind that statistics on tables can get old very quickly if there are a lot of inserts and updates being performed. If the CBO is using out-of-date statistics, it can come up with an inefficient plan. You'll be able to spot this problem when a query that was taking a few minutes seems to slow to a snail's pace. A user is sure to complain that the report only took 6 minutes last week and is now taking 20. You can avoid this situation by setting up an automated job to run the **analyze** command on the most heavily used areas once a week, or more or less frequently based on your system's performance. Keep in mind that when you are using partitioned tables, if a partitioned table is analyzed, all of the partitions in the table are also analyzed unless the action is aimed at a specific partition or subpartition.

With the information provided by the **analyze** command, the CBO is able to do some calculations at the time any SQL statement is being optimized. When we discussed the Rule Based Optimizer, in our example we mentioned the possibility that using an index might be more costly if many rows needed to be returned from a table. Looking at that same example using the Cost Based Optimizer, the CBO would be able to make some calculation on how many rows would be returned based on the fact that we were asking for a range of data in the SQL statement's where clause. Because the CBO is driven more by resource cost than rules, it would be more likely to understand the potential number of blocks involved and pick a table scan as the optimal path for that query.

Limitations to a Cost-Based Approach

There are some limitations and drawbacks to a cost-based approach. When the CBO is working to optimize a query, it only has the information stored in the data dictionary as its model, not the actual data itself. So, for example, although the highest and lowest values for each column are stored, under normal circumstances the optimizer does not have any information on the distribution of the data in the column. To resolve this dilemma, the optimizer assumes that all data is distributed evenly within a column. While this might make sense in some cases, consider as an example the names listed in a telephone directory. The size of the result set is considerably different if you query on all the people with a last name beginning with the letter *S* and compare that to all the people with the last name beginning with *Z*! Yet the CBO would consider the queries to be the same cost when making its computations.

To overcome this limitation, Oracle introduced a special feature called the histogram. A *histogram* is a set of statistics on a table that gives the optimizer additional information on the distribution of the data in the particular column. To illustrate this point, imagine that Oracle was saving the distribution of data for each column as a yardstick. Normally, the only information in the data dictionary is the values at each end of the stick—the high and low values for a column. When Oracle creates a histogram, it is filling in the gaps on that yardstick, doing some additional work to put some regularly spaced marks on the hypothetical yardstick and determine what the values are at each mark. Using the **size** keyword of the **analyze** command, we determine how many marks we want made across the stick, called *buckets*, to a maximum of 254. The difference between a conventional measuring stick and the one in our example is that although the marks are distributed evenly, the values assigned to the marks are based on the actual distribution of the data. So if we were creating a histogram on the last name in the phone book, there would be several marks starting with the letter *S* and perhaps only one or two for the letter *Z*. By using this "stick," the CBO now has a better idea of the distribution of the data in the column and will be able to make a more informed choice of access path.

There are some maintenance and space concerns in the data dictionary when using histograms, so they should only be used when the distribution of the data is very skewed.

Setting the Optimizer in Your Environment

So, how do you set the optimizer for your instance? This being Oracle, there are several ways to do so, of course! Globally, the optimizer is set in the init.ora parameter file using the **optimizer_mode** parameter. By default, the value is set to the Cost Based Optimizer, but you can select several different values for this parameter: CHOOSE, FIRST_ROWS, ALL_ROWS, and RULE. Let's look at each of these value options more closely.

CHOOSE This is the default setting, and the wording is significant. Above, we mentioned that the default optimizer is the CBO, but the optimizer will only use the cost-based method if certain conditions are met. First, if there are any statistics on at least one of the tables involved, Oracle will use the CBO. This fact is sometimes the cause of very poor SQL statements!

You see, if Oracle uses the CBO and does not have statistics for a table, it will substitute a set of default values to perform the cost calculations. As you can guess, the values are only placeholders and do not represent the actual data distribution in your table. Thus, it's often a case of "garbage in, garbage out," and the plan that the optimizer creates with these default values will most likely not be the best plan available. If you are going to use CHOOSE for the **optimizer_mode** parameter, plan to analyze all of the tables in your database frequently enough to capture the changes to data distribution. With this setting, if there are no statistics on any table involved in the SQL statement, Oracle will use the Rule Based Optimizer.

FIRST_ROWS This setting invokes the CBO, and, as such, all the guidance about statistics listed above still applies. However, this instruction biases the CBO to produce query plans that will produce the first set of data from a SQL statement as quickly as possible, even at the expense of producing a plan that would take a longer time overall. In other words, we are optimizing for best response time. This setting is good in environments where you are working with transactions that interface with users directly. In this case, we may want to get some data right to the users quickly (say to an Oracle Forms screen), where they can look at it, while the rest of the result set is built in the background.

ALL_ROWS The opposite of FIRST_ROWS, this directs the optimizer to build the most efficient plan for returning all the data as quickly as possible. In this case, we are optimizing for best throughput. This is the default behavior of the optimizer with the CHOOSE setting.

RULE This is the setting for the Rule Based Optimizer, as we discussed earlier in this section.

Individualizing the Optimizer Settings

Besides directly invoking the optimizer by a parameter placed in the init.ora file, you can change the optimizer during your individual session by using the following syntax:

```
alter session set optimizer_mode <one of the four values listed above>
```

As well as explicitly setting the **optimizer_mode** parameter, you can invoke the CBO by using a hint. A *hint* is a direction that can be given to the Cost Based Optimizer to use a specific access method, join order, optimizer goal, or table order. In fact, **rule**, **all_rows**, and **first_rows** are all examples of hints. Hints are added to SQL statements using the comment syntax along with the + sign (see the example below). We'll discuss hints more in the section "Cost Based Optimizer Tuning."

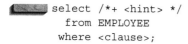

```
select /*+ <hint> */
  from EMPLOYEE
 where <clause>;
```

The CBO will also be invoked if parallel operations are enabled in the instance by any means, either through the use of global parameters in the initialization file or by setting the default degree of parallelism for a table.

New Optimization Features in Oracle8i

When we discussed getting statistics for the CBO, we reviewed the **analyze** command. With Oracle8i, a new package, DBMS_STATS, has been introduced. This package is intended to replace the use of the **analyze** command for gathering statistics, and it introduces some performance enhancements and new features. For example, the problem that has always plagued DBAs is the question of when to analyze data, because scanning the tables to gather the required data can impact other users' performance. As rows are inserted, deleted, or changed, the statistics that the optimizer uses become outdated and need to be refreshed. The problem is that until the latest version of Oracle, you had no way of knowing how far out of sync the statistics in the data dictionary were from the actual data, and you would just run **analyze** on a regular schedule. Running **analyze** on a table is expensive in terms of computational power and disk access. Usually it is scheduled to run at low usage periods on the system. In a system that has a lot of usage during the day and night, it can sometimes be difficult to find the time to run this job without impacting users. With Oracle8i, you can flag individual tables for monitoring. Flagging a table for monitoring can be done at table creation time or by using the **alter table** command. It signals Oracle to keep track of the amount of change activity against a table. The DBMS_STATS package can now read the results of this flag and be set to update only the statistics for those tables that Oracle has flagged as "stale," removing the need to rebuild statistics for tables that have not changed much since the last run. In addition, statistics-gathering improvements have been made to enable the information to be gathered in parallel and to reduce the amount of I/O required when only sampling data from a table.

Plan stability is another new optimization feature in Oracle8i that allows you to attempt to preserve a given SQL statement's execution plan by using stored outlines. A *stored outline* is a collection of hints for a SQL statement saved in the data dictionary. This is an important distinction to draw, as the outline does not save the query plan itself. When an outline is used to build the query plan of a SQL statement, those hints are fed directly to the optimizer, enforcing such things as table order, join order, and access method. This implies that any statement using a stored outline will necessarily use the Cost Based Optimizer. We will touch on hints more in the section "Cost Based Optimizer Tuning." The importance of this feature is that for the first time you can tune a SQL statement and then save the query plan. This allows you to change parameters that would affect the optimizer or to upgrade the database without worrying as much about how those changes will affect the performance of well-tuned statements in your application.

Explain Plan

Being able to "see" the execution plan that Oracle has created is most helpful in effectively tuning SQL statements. Oracle provides a command called **explain plan** that you can run to display the path the optimizer will use when the SQL is executed. **Explain plan** will evaluate the steps in a query plan and place one row for each step into a table called the PLAN_TABLE.

To use **explain plan**, first the parameter **timed_statistics** must be set to TRUE in the init.ora parameter file and the database stopped and restarted to enable this parameter. After version 7.0, the same parameter can also be set using the **alter system** command syntax. Note that enabling this tuning parameter has a minimal effect on the performance of the system. Next, the PLAN_TABLE must be created. As we mentioned in the section on SQL*Plus, Oracle provides a script, utlxplan.sql, located in the /ORACLE_HOME/rdbms/admin/ directory on a Unix or Windows NT system, which you can use to create this table.

To determine the execution plan of a query, preface the query with

```
explain plan set Statement_Id = 'TEST' for…
```

and then enter the SQL statement. The query will not actually be run until its execution plan has been written to the PLAN_TABLE. The same Statement_Id value should be used each time, but the PLAN_TABLE should be emptied before each use. To empty that table, use either **delete from** or **truncate**. Once the query has been executed, query the PLAN_TABLE to see the execution plan by using

```
 select lpad(' ',2*Level)||Operation||' '||Options||' '||Object_Name q_plan
   from PLAN_TABLE
  where Statement_Id = 'TEST'
connect by prior Id = Parent_Id
    and Statement_Id = 'TEST'
  start with Id = 1;
```

The plan is executed from inside out and from top to bottom. As a brief illustration of how Explain Plan works, the Oracle-supplied tables EMP and DEPT in the SCOTT schema will be used:

```
explain plan set Statement_Id = 'TEST' for
 select Ename, Empno, b.Deptno
 from EMP a, DEPT b
 where a.Deptno = b.Deptno;
```

The execution plan for this statement is

```
QPLAN
-------------------------------
NESTED LOOPS
  TABLE ACCESS FULL EMP
  INDEX UNIQUE SCAN PK_DEPT
```

A unique index scan will be performed on the primary key of the DEPT table, which should provide faster query processing. As queries are evaluated and tuned successfully, performance should improve. In some cases, just placing an index on a table to change a full table scan to an index scan can reduce query time from hours to minutes or even seconds.

The SQL Trace Facility (TKPROF)

Oracle provides the SQL trace facility known as TKPROF for gaining insight into SQL query processing. TKPROF is used to format output from a trace file into a more readable form. To activate the facility, you must

- Ensure that the init.ora parameter **timed_statistics** is set to TRUE.
- Determine the location for USER_DUMP_DEST, where the output trace file will be located.
- Ensure that the parameter **max_dump_file_size** is set large enough to store the entire amount of output that will be generated.

From the SQL*Plus user session, you can issue the following statement to let Oracle know that a trace file should be generated for the session.

```
alter session set sql_trace = true;
```

This will create a trace file that would give all but the most seasoned programmer eyestrain. Therefore, TKPROF was created to decode that trace into a more readable form. You can also use the procedure DBMS_SESSION.SET_SQL_TRACE to activate the SQL trace facility. If you wanted to enable the facility for the entire database (which we heartily suggest that you *not* do since it could degrade performance substantially for the system), the init.ora parameter **sql_trace** can be set to TRUE and the database shut down and restarted.

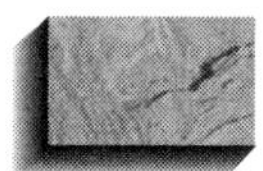

NOTE
*Setting **timed_statistics** to TRUE will have little performance impact, but **sql_trace** set to TRUE for the system can have great negative impact.*

Like Explain Plan, TKPROF lets you see the execution plan for a statement or set of statements issued during a session in which **sql_trace** was set to TRUE. However, TKPROF also provides much more information, as you can see from the list of parameters displayed when just the command TKPROF is issued.

As an example, from the Oracle-supplied user SCOTT identified by TIGER, the following session was run:

```
alter session set sql_trace = true;
Session altered.
select Ename, Empno, b.Deptno
 from EMP a, DEPT b
 where a.Deptno = b.Deptno;
(output deleted to conserve space)
```

From the DOS prompt on a Windows NT system running v8.1.5 from the d:\ora8i\admin\orc1\udump directory, TKPROF was run with the following command line:

```
tkprof ora00174.trc t.txt explain=scott/tiger
```

This follows the syntax: **tkprof** *inputfile outputfile* **explain**=*username/password.* The following output (with some excess blank lines removed in order to conserve space) was produced. Notice how much work Oracle does before the actual statement is processed.

```
TKPROF: Release 8.1.5.0.0 - Production on Tue Sep 7 10:43:31 1999
(c) Copyright 1999 Oracle Corporation. All rights reserved.
Trace file: ORA00174.TRC
Sort options: default
********************************************************************************
count    = number of times OCI procedure was executed
cpu      = cpu time in seconds executing
elapsed  = elapsed time in seconds executing
disk     = number of physical reads of buffers from disk
query    = number of buffers gotten for consistent read
current  = number of buffers gotten in current mode (usually for update)
rows     = number of rows processed by the fetch or execute call
```

```
********************************************************************************
alter session set sql_trace = true

call     count       cpu    elapsed       disk      query    current        rows
------- ------  -------- ---------- ---------- ---------- ----------  ----------
Parse        0      0.00       0.00          0          0          0           0
Execute      1      0.00       0.13          0          0          0           0
Fetch        0      0.00       0.00          0          0          0           0
------- ------  -------- ---------- ---------- ---------- ----------  ----------
total        1      0.00       0.13          0          0          0           0

Misses in library cache during parse: 0
Misses in library cache during execute: 1
Optimizer goal: CHOOSE
Parsing user id: SYS
********************************************************************************
select con#,obj#,rcon#,enabled,nvl(defer,0)
from
 cdef$ where robj#=:1

call     count       cpu    elapsed       disk      query    current        rows
------- ------  -------- ---------- ---------- ---------- ----------  ----------
Parse        1      0.00       0.02          0          0          0           0
Execute      2      0.00       0.02          0          0          0           0
Fetch        3      0.00       0.00          0          4          0           1
------- ------  -------- ---------- ---------- ---------- ----------  ----------
total        6      0.00       0.04          0          4          0           1

Misses in library cache during parse: 1
Misses in library cache during execute: 1
Optimizer goal: CHOOSE
Parsing user id: SYS   (recursive depth: 1)
********************************************************************************
select con#,type#,condlength,intcols,robj#,rcon#,match#,refact,nvl(enabled,0),
  rowid,cols,nvl(defer,0),mtime
from
 cdef$ where obj#=:

call     count       cpu    elapsed       disk      query    current        rows
------- ------  -------- ---------- ---------- ---------- ----------  ----------
Parse        1      0.00       0.00          0          0          0           0
Execute      2      0.00       0.00          0          0          0           0
Fetch        5      0.01       0.01          0          9          0           3
------- ------  -------- ---------- ---------- ---------- ----------  ----------
total        8      0.01       0.01          0          9          0           3

Misses in library cache during parse: 1
Misses in library cache during execute: 1
Optimizer goal: CHOOSE
Parsing user id: SYS   (recursive depth: 1)
********************************************************************************
select intcol#,nvl(pos#,0),col#
from
 ccol$ where con#=:1

call     count       cpu    elapsed       disk      query    current        rows
------- ------  -------- ---------- ---------- ---------- ----------  ----------
Parse        1      0.00       0.00          0          0          0           0
```

```
Execute      3      0.00       0.00          0          0          0          0
Fetch        6      0.00       0.01          1         12          0          3
------- ------  -------- ---------- ---------- ---------- ----------  ----------
total       10      0.00       0.01          1         12          0          3

Misses in library cache during parse: 1
Misses in library cache during execute: 1
Optimizer goal: CHOOSE
Parsing user id: SYS   (recursive depth: 1)
********************************************************************************
select Ename, Empno, b.Deptno
  from SCOTT.EMP a, SCOTT.DEPT b
 where a.Deptno = b.Deptno

call     count       cpu    elapsed       disk      query    current        rows
------- ------  -------- ---------- ---------- ---------- ----------  ----------
Parse        1      0.04       0.10          0          0          0          0
Execute      1      0.00       0.00          0          0          0          0
Fetch        2      0.00       0.03          2          4          4         14
------- ------  -------- ---------- ---------- ---------- ----------  ----------
total        4      0.04       0.13          2          4          4         14

Misses in library cache during parse: 1
Optimizer goal: CHOOSE
Parsing user id: SYS

Rows     Row Source Operation
-------  ---------------------------------------------------
     14  NESTED LOOPS
     15   TABLE ACCESS FULL EMP
     14   INDEX UNIQUE SCAN (object id 10921)
********************************************************************************

OVERALL TOTALS FOR ALL NON-RECURSIVE STATEMENTS

call     count       cpu    elapsed       disk      query    current        rows
------- ------  -------- ---------- ---------- ---------- ----------  ----------
Parse        1      0.04       0.10          0          0          0          0
Execute      2      0.00       0.13          0          0          0          0
Fetch        2      0.00       0.03          2          4          4         14
------- ------  -------- ---------- ---------- ---------- ----------  ----------
total        5      0.04       0.26          2          4          4         14

Misses in library cache during parse: 1
Misses in library cache during execute: 1
OVERALL TOTALS FOR ALL RECURSIVE STATEMENTS

call     count       cpu    elapsed       disk      query    current        rows
------- ------  -------- ---------- ---------- ---------- ----------  ----------
Parse        3      0.00       0.02          0          0          0          0
Execute      7      0.00       0.02          0          0          0          0
Fetch       14      0.01       0.02          1         25          0          7
------- ------  -------- ---------- ---------- ---------- ----------  ----------
total       24      0.01       0.06          1         25          0          7

Misses in library cache during parse: 3
Misses in library cache during execute: 3
```

```
     2  user  SQL statements in session.
     3  internal SQL statements in session.
     5  SQL statements in session.
     0  statements EXPLAINed in this session.
********************************************************************************
Trace file: ORA00174.TRC
Trace file compatibility: 7.03.02
Sort options: default

       1  session in tracefile.
       2  user  SQL statements in trace file.
       3  internal SQL statements in trace file.
       5  SQL statements in trace file.
       5  unique SQL statements in trace file.
      78  lines in trace file.
```

Demystifying the TKPROF Output

In the preceding example, we ran TKPROF with the **explain** option. That produces a copy of each SQL statement, the query plan, and the execution statistics for each statement. Reviewing the output, we see that the statistics for each SQL statement are decoded in a common fashion. For each statement, TKPROF creates a table of values from the trace file that give some insight into how the statement was processed. In the points below, we cover some of the highlights most useful for SQL tuning.

- The Count column shows the number of times a statement was parsed, executed, or fetched in the time measured by the trace.
- The Cpu column records the CPU time in seconds for all parse, execute, or fetch calls attributed to it.
- The Elapsed column shows the elapsed time in seconds for all parse, execute, or fetch calls. Subtracting the CPU column from this value shows the amount of time the statement had to wait for some resource. When tuning, this gives you some insight into where to focus your efforts (on the work being done or the delays affecting the statement).
- The Disk column shows the number of data blocks physically read from disk for all parse, execute, or fetch calls.
- The Query column shows the number of buffers retrieved in consistent read mode for all parse, execute, or fetch calls. The sum of the Query and Current columns is the total number of buffers accessed by the statement.
- The Rows column is the number of output rows processed by the SQL statement. For **select** statements, the number of rows returned appears for the fetch step. For **update**, **delete,** and **insert** statements, the number of rows processed appears for the execute step.

As you can see from this example, you can obtain much more information about your session if you use TKPROF. If all you want is a quick insight into the execution plan of a query, Explain Plan is an excellent tool.

For a more in-depth view of multiple queries, use TKPROF. There's one other thing to consider when using TKPROF with the **explain** option. TKPROF will parse the query and report the plan back to you at the time TKPROF was run. It does not guarantee to show you the plan from the time the trace file was created. So it is possible that you are seeing a different plan than one that is in the trace file. If at all possible, make sure you are using the same session-level parameters and the same statistics when decoding a trace file with TKPROF. Also, remember that when you run the same statement a second time, your statement has already been stored in the library cache, so the processing time will be reduced. This can skew your statistics.

There are extra-cost Oracle-supplied and third-party vendor tools available to assist you in analyzing explain plans. These are a great time saver for both experienced and less experienced DBAs.

Autotrace

In the SQL*Plus section earlier in this chapter, we looked at the **autotrace** command, which provides an easy way to explain the query path of a SQL statement. We're going to revisit this option now to show you a little different perspective on it. Using the options documented below, you can easily view the query plan chosen by the optimizer in a readable format. You can also use the trace function of this command to examine such information as the number of reads it took to resolve a query, or the number of sort operations that were required to return the data. This gives you a "quick and dirty" way to examine an individual SQL statement to see if it is perhaps the cause of a performance problem and worth some additional investigation. We showed you the syntax for this command earlier. Now, let's look at some examples of what you can do with it.

As we mentioned earlier, you must grant the PLUSTRACE role to anyone who will be using **autotrace**. Remember, too, that the SQL statement is always executed before Oracle produces and displays its explain plan and statistics.

In the first example, we use the **set autotrace** command to execute the query and view the explain plan.

```
set autotrace on explain
select count(*)
  from DEPT;

COUNT(*)
----------
         4
```

```
Execution Plan
----------------------------------------------------------
0      SELECT STATEMENT Optimizer=CHOOSE
1    0   SORT (AGGREGATE)
2    1     TABLE ACCESS (FULL) OF 'DEPT'
```

The first column of the output is basically a count of steps within the explain plan and is of little significance. The second column is helpful since it shows the order in which the steps of the explain plan are executed—the highest number is executed first. If two or more numbers of the same value are displayed, the order is from top to bottom.

In the above example, TABLE ACCESS (FULL) of 'DEPT' is the first step in the explain plan, followed by SORT (AGGREGATE). Thus, the above plan tells you that all of the rows from DEPT are read and then counted via the SORT AGGREGATE algorithm.

We can also look at the trace output for the same query. Notice how quickly you can tell how many reads, consistent reads, and sorts the SQL statement required. High values for the "reading" indicators or for sorting are sometimes clues that a query could be tuned further.

```
set autotrace trace statistics
select count(*)
  from DEPT;

Statistics
----------------------------------------------------------
134       recursive calls
4         db block gets
19        consistent gets
9         physical reads
0         redo size
563       bytes sent via SQL*Net to client
653       bytes received via SQL*Net from client
4         SQL*Net roundtrips to/from client
2         sorts (memory)
0         sorts (disk)
1         rows processed
```

Tuning SQL

Tuning any area of a system is the art of ensuring that the "work" is being done as efficiently as possible and with as little delay as possible. Ideally, the perfectly tuned system is using all components of the physical hardware (CPU, disk, network, memory) to 100 percent capacity with no delays waiting for resources. This is, of course, a total fantasy! All resources in a system are constrained by some type of bottleneck, usually waiting for some other resource to free up or another operation to complete. We will explore response time and tuning more completely in Chapter 12, but it is useful to touch on it here as a basis for a discussion on SQL tuning.

Although we may be in danger of making a gross oversimplification, when tuning almost any system, eventually all roads lead to the application code as a source of the bottleneck. As we discussed earlier, SQL is a nonprocedural language, and the optimizer determines how the data will be retrieved, joined, and sorted before it is presented to the user. Explain Plan, TKPROF, and **autotrace** all give you some insight into how the optimizer is treating the statement and how much resource is being used. Tuning the SQL then becomes the art of making sure the optimizer has picked the most efficient plan possible. You can either change the query plan, give the optimizer additional information by using histograms, or add indexes to support a SQL statement (although that has its own pitfalls as well).

When you suspect a problem in the SQL code (again, refer to Chapter 12 for more details on how to narrow down exactly where any potential bottleneck might be), you must first isolate the statements causing the problem. Oracle does provide a V$ view that you can use to isolate a potentially poorly performing SQL statement. That view is V$SQL. The output from the view can be sorted to show you how often a particular query is being run or how many resources are needed (in terms of database buffer reads). Two queries are illustrated below to show you how to use V$SQL.

When deciding which query to tune, look at the output of both statements. Tuning a query that uses a lot of resources but is only executed once a day may not be as profitable as tuning a query that uses only a few resources but is executed many thousands of times during the day. This incremental improvement can often provide more overall value to your system by reducing the amount of resources used through the entire day and making those resources available for other users.

Use the following queries on V$SQL to retrieve the SQL statements that have a number of disk accesses greater than some user-supplied number. The Sql_Text column shows the actual statement being executed.

```
select Disk_Reads, Executions, Disk_Reads/Executions, Sql_Text
  from V$SQL
 where Disk_Reads > {some number};
```

The second query on V$SQL that you can use follows. This time, we are looking for the most frequently executed statement by ordering on the Executions column.

```
select Disk_Reads, Executions, Disk_Reads/Executions, Sql_Text
  from V$SQL
 where Executions != 0
 order by 2;
```

The choices available for tuning are very dependent on the optimizer you are using. Tuning SQL statements is an art unto itself, and many excellent books and courses are offered on the subject. Here, as a start, we will try and provide some basic tips for changing the access path of a query. With the Explain Plan facility to review the query plan chosen by the optimizer and **autotrace** and TKPROF to see how many resources a query is using, you can use these tips and see how they change the optimizer's access path decisions. As there are no hard-and-fast rules for getting to the optimal plan, the best advice is to experiment and see if you can change the plan in your favor.

Rule Based Optimizer Tuning

Because the RBO is heavily biased toward indexes and cannot take advantage of newer performance enhancements available to the optimizer, most of the changes revolve around forcing the optimizer to use or ignore a specific index. Force the optimizer to ignore an index when you see that it has to loop through the same table using an index many times, perhaps doing more reads than it needs to do.

Sometimes the RBO is doing a table scan to get just a few rows of data. This type of access is usually an indicator that an index would be helpful. Be cautious about adding indexes too freely. When an update or insert is done to the indexed column, both the index and table must be updated. Too many indexes could slow down these operations to the table to the point where their performance would become unacceptable. As with all tuning, deciding whether to use an index or not is a balancing act!

To change the access path of the Rule Based Optimizer, you can

- Drop or add indexes on columns.
- Disable indexes by concatenating NULL or adding 0 to indexed columns.
- Change the order of the tables in the **from** clause.

Keep in mind that for the RBO, the order of execution is right to left in the **from** clause.

Cost Based Optimizer Tuning

When tuning SQL that has a query plan generated through the CBO, the first thing to review is the age and quality of the statistics. If the statistics are not up-to-date, the optimizer does not have the information it needs to create a proper query plan.

The DBA_TABLES view (DBA_TAB_COLUMNS in Oracle7) has a column called Last_Analyzed that will show the last date statistics were gathered for this table (although it does not show the sampling rate).

While the methods outlined above for tuning the Rule Based Optimizer can be effective when dealing with the CBO, tuning the CBO is done primarily through the use of hints. One of the most common problems encountered with using hints is that Oracle does not report an error if the hint is used incorrectly. If the hint is syntactically incorrect, the optimizer will ignore it and create a query plan as normal. You'll be given no warning that your hint has been ignored.

Hints are a very powerful tuning tool because you can use them to override the optimizer's choice of query plan with your own. This facility takes into account the fact that you, as the DBA or application developer, may know more about the tables or distribution of data than the optimizer can, based on the statistics available to it. While we cannot classify all the available hints here, they break down into the following categories:

- Hints to change the optimization approach for a SQL statement (RULE, CHOOSE, FIRST_ROWS, ALL_ROWS). These hints are general guidelines and will affect the construction of the entire query plan.
- Hints to change the access path for a table accessed by the statement. Here we can tell the optimizer to use or ignore specific indexes.
- Hints to change the join order for a join statement. For example, the **ordered** hint allows us to specify the exact order of table joins in the query plan.
- Hints to use a specific join operation. Here we can direct the optimizer to specific programmatic algorithms to use when joining two tables. As of Oracle8i, those methods include nested loop, sort-merge, hash join, semi-join and anti-join.

Another factor that globally influences the optimizer is setting certain initialization parameters. Table 11-1 shows a list of these parameters as a reference. Complete documentation of each of them is available in the Oracle Server Reference manual. When you are tuning the database, remember that changes to these parameters will change the query plan created by the Cost Based Optimizer. If you notice a sudden change in the plans created by the CBO, ensure that these values have not changed. As noted earlier, the plan stability feature will protect the SQL that you have tuned from being affected by changes in these values. The list shown in Table 11-1 is from an 8.1.5 database.

Parameter	Description
always_anti_join	Sets the type of anti-join that the Oracle server uses
always_semi_join	Sets the type of semi-join that the Oracle server uses
bitmap_merge_area_size	Specifies the amount of memory used to merge bitmaps retrieved from a range scan of an index. Default value is 1MB
create_bitmap_area_size	Specifies the amount of memory allocated for bitmap creation. The default value is 8MB
db_file_multiblock_read_count	Used for multiblock I/O and specifies the maximum number of blocks read in one I/O operation during a sequential scan
hash_area_size	Specifies the maximum amount of memory, in bytes, to be used for hash joins
hash_join_enabled	Specifies whether the optimizer should consider using a hash join as a join method
hash_multiblock_io_count	Specifies how many sequential blocks a hash join reads and writes in one I/O
optimizer_features_enabled	Allows you to change the init.ora parameters that control the optimizer's behavior
optimizer_index_caching	Lets the user adjust the behavior of the CBO to select nested-loop joins more often
optimizer_index_cost_adj	Lets the user tune the optimizer behavior for access path selection to be more or less index-friendly
optimizer_max_permutations	Lets the user limit the amount of work the optimizer spends on optimizing queries with large joins
optimizer_mode	Specifies the behavior of the optimizer: RULE, CHOOSE, FIRST_ROWS, or ALL_ROWS

TABLE 11-1. *Initialization Parameters Used for SQL Tuning*

Parameter	Description
optimizer_percent_parallel	Specifies the amount of parallelism that the optimizer uses in its cost functions. The default of 0 means that the optimizer chooses the best serial plan
optimizer_search_limit	Specifies the maximum number of tables in a query block for which the optimizer will consider join orders with Cartesian products
partition_view_enabled	If set to TRUE, the optimizer prunes (or skips) unnecessary table accesses in a partition view
sort_area_size	Specifies the maximum amount, in bytes, of memory to use for a sort

TABLE 11-1. *Initialization Parameters Used for SQL Tuning* (continued)

Using the Oracle Enterprise Manager (OEM)

Until now, we've shown you tools that you access from either SQL*Plus or your operating system command line. Now, it's time to look at a tool that can only be accessed using a Windows environment on a PC, either Windows95, Windows98, or Windows NT. This tool set was introduced in version 7 and has been released for no extra cost, with a different version number, for each release of the Oracle RDBMS. For example, Oracle8.0.3 was released with Oracle Enterprise Manager version 1.5, Oracle8.0.5 was released with OEM 1.6, while Oracle8i has been released with OEM 2.0.4. For this book, we are going to focus on the features offered in the OEM version 2.0.4 release because it is compatible with the earlier Oracle releases from Oracle7.3 forward and offers the richest set of options currently available. There are three extra-cost enhancement packages that you can purchase to use with the OEM. We will look very briefly at them as well.

The Oracle Enterprise Manager tool set is a GUI tool that offers you a way to manage your databases from one central PC. New with OEM 2.0.4, is the ability for several DBAs to connect to the same OEM repository. This important feature ensures that you and your fellow DBAs will be able to work in concert to manage databases remotely while not interfering with each other's jobs. Up until this version of OEM, only one DBA could connect to a repository. You either had to have your own environment on your own PC or only one person could use the tool at a time.

Along with the problem of keeping each OEM repository safe came the problem of identifying who had made a change to a specific database and when that change was made. There was no way to maintain an audit trail of database changes.

But, what is a repository and what are the basic features that you can use with this tool set? Let's take a little closer look at the OEM. Since documentation of the installation, configuration, and management of the OEM could easily fill an entire book by itself and we have a limited number of pages available here, we are only going to give you a very brief overview of the tool set.

OEM Basic Features

Several components make up the OEM. A set of screens, called the OEM *console*, let you manage databases. The OEM uses a set of tables that are stored in a database to hold information for the tool's use. These tables are referred to as the *repository*. There are many Java programs that you interact with to perform different areas of database administration. Some of these programs are referred to as *wizards* that guide you through an activity, such as creating a user or tablespace in your database.

When you initially log on to the OEM console, four sections are displayed at once: the Navigator, the Group option, the Job Scheduler, and the Event Scheduler. Figure 11-1 shows the OEM console screen with all four options available.

The Navigator enables you to quickly view all of your databases and their composition in a tree-structure format. Using the Group option, you can create a view of several databases and perform tasks on all of the databases in the group at the same time. You can even scan in a background of your office or corporate layout and place the databases graphically on the background to show you where each database is located. Oracle supplies several graphical, geographical maps that you can use by default, such as a map of the United States and one of Europe.

Among the features within OEM is the Job Scheduler, which you can use to set up jobs to run either once immediately, once at a prescheduled time, or on a specific, recurring schedule. You could, for example, schedule your backup job to run on a nightly basis.

The fourth feature available from the OEM console is the Event Scheduler. We've stressed throughout this book the need for you to be a proactive DBA. In theory, the Event Scheduler enables you to set up jobs that will watch for specific problems to occur in your database. We say "in theory" because with the basic OEM tool supplied by Oracle, you can only set up one event to run automatically—InstanceUpDown. This event periodically checks to see if your database is available and notifies you when it is not. In order to have an effective set of events to monitor, you must either write your own events using a language called TCL (pronounced "tickle") or purchase one of the Oracle extra-cost packages, the DBA Diagnostic pack.

As we'll discuss in Chapter 13 on database backup and recovery, in Oracle8.0, a new utility called the Recovery Manager (RMAN) was introduced. The OEM

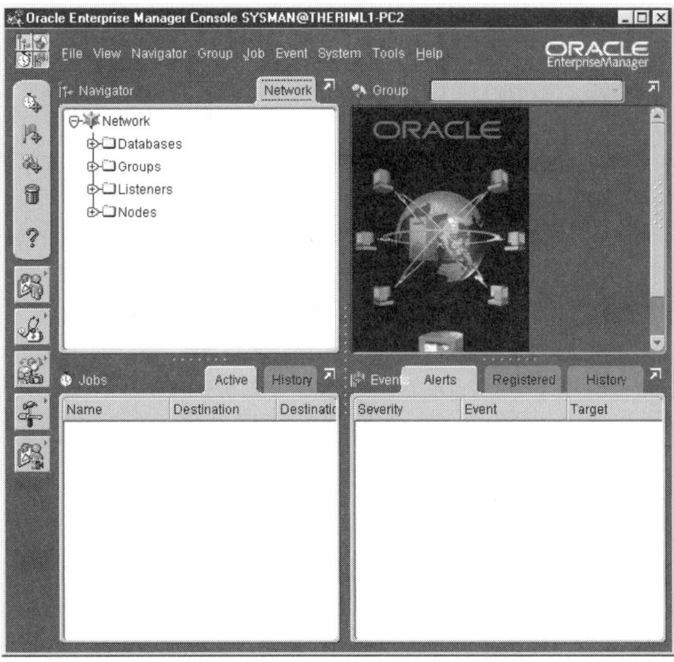

FIGURE 11-1. *The Oracle Enterprise Manager initial console screen*

provides a graphical interface to RMAN. Because it is new with Oracle8, this feature is not available with earlier versions of OEM.

If you want to perform prescheduled jobs or tasks other than looking at statistical information about your database, you will need to configure a process called the Intelligent Agent to run on each machine that has a database of interest. You can only configure one Intelligent Agent per machine, no matter how many different databases are available from that machine. The Intelligent Agent supports communication between the databases on that machine and the central OEM console. In earlier versions of OEM, the console had to be running and visible before scheduled jobs could be run correctly. In the latest version of OEM, the console can be closed and scheduled jobs will still run.

From the console, you can view the makeup of, and administer to, different databases on one or more nodes at once. There are several database administration options that you can use from either the OEM console or as separate options from the Windows Start | Programs menu. With the release of Oracle8.0.4, you can have separate Oracle homes on a PC for each different version of Oracle. When you install the OEM tool set, you will install it in its own directory structure. Therefore, you will have a separate option in the Windows Start | Programs menu for OEM.

Database Administration OEM Options

There are five options available from OEM version 2.0.4 for database administrators:

- **Oracle Security Manager** Used to create users, roles, and profiles. The **create like** option enables you to create a user, role, or profile exactly like another one. Using this option, you can add one or more privileges to a user or role, and you can assign a profile to a user.
- **Oracle Storage Manager** Used to manage tablespaces, datafiles, rollback segments, and redo log groups. From this option, you have the ability to create, create like, remove, and show dependency for each of these object types. You can also perform backup or recovery operations and exports, imports, or data loads.
- **SQL*Plus Worksheet** Used to run SQL queries, create scripts, view and execute your previous command, and view the history of commands that you have issued from your session.
- **Oracle Instance Manager** Used to start, stop, and view the status of your database. From this option, you can enable or disable archive log mode. You can modify a stored init.ora parameter file, view the sessions connected to your database and interactively stop one or more of them, and view in-doubt transactions on your system. You can also enable or disable restricted access to the database through this option.
- **Oracle Schema Manager** Used to create, create like, remove, and manage Oracle objects clusters, database links, functions, indexes, package bodies, packages, procedures, refresh groups, sequences, snapshot logs, snapshots, synonyms, triggers, and views. In addition, objects new in Oracle8.*x* such as arrays, Java source code, object types, queue tables, and table types can be managed with the Schema Manager. You can also perform exports, imports, and data loads from this option.

Extra-Cost Packs

For an additional fee, you can purchase one or more of the three additional OEM packs that Oracle has developed as add-ons for this product. They are the Change Management pack, the Performance Tuning pack, and the Diagnostic pack.

With the Change Management pack, you can analyze the impact and complex dependencies associated with application change and automatically perform upgrades. The Change Management pack enables you to investigate and track changes, define and plan changes, evaluate the impact a change has on the system, and then implement the change. You can keep a history of the changes and synchronize objects and schemas within different databases. Thus, you can perform a comparison of your production and development databases and synchronize the development database to match the production one.

Using the Diagnostic pack, you can perform advanced database monitoring, diagnosis, and planning. You can track resource usage to help you plan your future resource needs. Oracle supplies a wide array of customized performance charts with this pack, and you can use the pack to identify and remove lock contention. The pack can be configured to perform many different event monitoring tasks that can be set up to send email, or even page you if a preestablished resource threshold is reached.

With the Performance Tuning pack, you can identify and tune major database and application bottlenecks. The pack discovers tuning opportunities and generates the analysis and scripts necessary to help you tune your database. Using the Performance Tuning pack, you can obtain execution plans and tune your application's SQL statements.

CHAPTER 12

Server Performance

Years ago, one of the authors was involved in a theater group that put on four plays or musicals a year. The group was made up of volunteers who got together once or twice a week and rehearsed. When a new play was chosen and the group began to practice, things were pretty rough. The players didn't know their lines or cues, and they didn't know where to stand or where they were supposed to walk to, and so on. Over time, with lots of rehearsals, the performance became very polished, and on opening night, the group generally put on a pretty professional production within the appropriate time constraints. Well, okay, no one in the audience ever threw rotten tomatoes, so we guess the productions were a success.

Another of the authors was into motorcycle riding and racing. He spent a great deal of time and money modifying his hardware to produce motorcycles that ran just a fraction of a second faster than the competitors' bikes.

What do the people who participated in these two hobbies have in common? Well, they both dealt with improving performance. In the first example, members of the theater group worked steadily to improve the way they did things by keeping track of how smoothly their production was going. There was always room for improvement, and they were continuously trying to enhance their performance—trying to say their lines more smoothly, have their props in the correct places in a timely manner, and so on. They proactively took steps to make their product better each time they rehearsed. The motorcyclist was more reactive. During the course of each race, if he was winning, he just kept going and did not pay much attention to how the bike was running. However, if he was behind, he would be constantly making mental notes to himself. As soon as that particular race was over, he'd make adjustments to the bike that he hoped would give him that extra edge he needed to succeed—meet his performance requirements. He might even try to make minor adjustments during the race to help improve his position. In other words, the biker reacted to how the bike performed and either made changes or left the bike alone based on how the bike was running in each race.

Like the member of the theater group, your goal in performance management should be to work most of the time as a proactive DBA—taking measurements and making adjustments to help you tune your database effectively. However, there will be times when you will not be able to avoid having to react to a situation—becoming a reactive DBA. This chapter is intended to help you be as proactive as possible in the performance tuning arena while supplying the tools you need to effectively react to emergency situations.

Understanding Performance Management

Invariably, as a DBA you will at some point be faced with questions about the performance of your system. If you're lucky, the questions posed to you will be detailed and will give you a good basis for your investigation! For example, a user may come to you and say, "Yesterday, I ran my report and it took 4 minutes. Today, I ran my report and it took 20 minutes. What's going on?" Sometimes the questions are a little less specific. In fact, they could be as generic as "Why is the system so slow?" Inevitably, no matter how specific the question is, the next question is a constant: "What are you going to do to make it faster?" Using questions is a great approach to guiding you through performance tuning. The questions help you get a clear understanding of the problems your users are facing and give you objectives to fulfill. Of course, if you can figure out the answers before the questions are ever asked, you will be well ahead of the game.

In this chapter, you'll see the topic of performance tuning from several angles. First, we'll define what we mean by performance tuning and discuss some steps to prepare you and your users to answer the questions listed above—before they are asked. In case you have been forced to turn to this chapter because you already have a performance problem and you want some tips on how to fix it, we'll provide some questions that will help you isolate the problem. We'll finish with a discussion of commonly encountered performance problems and some tips for detecting and correcting them.

A common example will be used to illustrate some of the points we want to make in this chapter. So, for now, you are the brand-new Oracle DBA of the XYZ Company. Congratulations on your new job! XYZ has been producing widgets for years, with many aspects of production and distribution controlled by legacy code. (You can translate *legacy code* to mean that the software is old and does not perform well and should have been rewritten years ago.) XYZ has decided to migrate to a new application that will use Oracle as its engine. The new code will tie the manufacturing and product distribution directly to the reporting and planning applications. Your job is to manage the new Oracle database. Although there are many areas to consider in a scenario such as this, we will focus on the performance tuning aspects in this chapter. Good luck and don't panic!

Although tuning a system is still more of an art than a science, our goal is to give you a systematic approach to use throughout the database and software development life cycle. This approach will help to minimize the effect of performance issues in your shop and provide some strategies for handling performance issues as they develop later, during day-to-day activities. Most importantly, a solid process that covers the fundamentals will improve your efficiency, thereby reducing your stress level when dealing with tuning issues. Let's take a look at some concepts that will be used often in this chapter.

The 80/20 Rule

In general, the suggestions here will follow a principle well known to you in everyday life. The 80/20 rule, conceived by Vilfredo Pareto, will be used as the basis for your approach to tuning a database. The 80/20 rule says that a minority of causes, inputs, or efforts usually produces a majority of the results, outputs, or rewards. In other words, you want to look for the things that take the least amount of effort but achieve significant tuning results.

If you are starting out with the development of a brand-new system, you can achieve the 80/20 rule by doing as much work as possible up front—in the design phase. By designing the application and database effectively from the start, much of the database performance will already be enhanced.

You must define and set realistic expectations between your management and your developers and users. There are times when expectation setting is the most effective performance tuning tool. If the absolutely fastest startup time your users can ever obtain is a three-second response time, then setting their expectation to the fact that they will have a three-second startup time is the way to go. If your management is not willing or able to enhance a system with enough resources to effectively support the user requirements, setting expectations may be your only real approach.

Just now, we mentioned response time as the amount of time that it might take for an application to be loaded into memory and an initial screen to be displayed for user interaction. In reality, the majority of your tuning efforts will be to try to help improve the response time of one area of the database or another. In the next sections, we'll take a closer look at what the term *response time* means and the actions you can take to improve it.

What Is Response Time?

In general terms, response time can be described by the following formula:

Response Time = Service (or Work) Time + Wait Time

Let's see if we can break this formula down into meaningful terms. By service (or work) time, we mean the amount of time it takes the database to respond to a request or perform an actual amount of work. By wait time, we mean the amount of time the user or process is waiting for an action or amount of work to be completed. Thus, if either service time or wait time is high, the total response time will be affected.

Okay, so now that you know the formula for computing response time, how do you get the figures you need to see your database's response time? By using the Oracle database dynamic views, you can calculate the total service time and the total wait time within the Oracle database. We'll show you exactly how to determine your database's response time during our discussion of reactive performance tuning later in this chapter. The response time that you determine will always be less than or equal to the actual response time that the end user will see. The difference is due to external forces—delays in other layers of the system, such as the network or other components or tiers in the application. While you should not ignore the other components of your system, you have more control over your database and can first make sure you eliminate any problems there.

You must realize that when you are asked to improve the response time, you are really being asked to tune a system. The system consists of all the components between the users and the database. These components include but are in no way limited to

- The network
- The client (PC or browser)
- Any number of middle-tier servers
- The operating systems for the database server and any of their middle tiers

All of these pieces work together to satisfy a request to the database. Obviously, we are not going to cover all of these areas here, but it is important to be aware of these other considerations when tuning. Although our focus is primarily on the database server, you must realize that the best tuning gains can sometimes come from other areas.

Where's the Problem?

Even when focusing strictly on the database component, most performance issues do not originate directly from the database server, so the question you need to ask yourself is "Where *is* the problem?"

In reality, most performance problems originate from the application because of design issues or coding problems. Thus, most performance improvements can be achieved by making changes in the application. Given this reality, why is the main focus usually on the database? Generally, the database is a victim of its own capabilities. Administrators and users tend to focus on the database because it supplies easy access to a wealth of statistics on its performance. In addition, application tuning may not be simple or straightforward. Applications are designed around business rules and processes. It is sometimes impossible, or extremely difficult, to find algorithms that match both the business need and optimal performance on the database. However, information from the database can be used to pinpoint these types of issues.

Another reason for turning to the database instead of the application code for answers may relate more to cost than anything else. Finding out that a poorly designed application has already been implemented, either internally by a project team or externally through special consultants, is not a discovery that most organizations will happily accept. Necessary changes will incur greater costs that will not be welcomed by the manager whose budget is going to be impacted.

If management is resistant to forcing application changes, what can you do? Here's where expectation setting comes in (again). Make sure your management realizes that you can do only so much to improve database performance when poor application design is at fault.

There are some areas in which you can try to improve performance, and we'll talk about them next.

Response Time vs. Throughput

When discussing performance and tuning problems, remember that the primary goal can be either one of the following (or both): improve response time or improve throughput. We've already talked a bit about response time but haven't, as yet, mentioned throughput. *Throughput* is the number of transactions being processed within a given amount of time.

For example, if you have a pipe with a one-half inch diameter into which you are putting marbles (and, please, don't ask us why you might want to put marbles into a pipe), you might be able to get 12 marbles into the pipe. If, however, you have a pipe with a one and one-half inch diameter, you might be able to put 24 or more marbles into it. Your throughput has increased because you've increased the capacity of your pipe.

Okay. With this definition of throughput in mind, let's look at the two goals mentioned above.

Improving Response Times

Improving response times normally means you can either improve the service time or the wait time. Usually the improvement is driven by the need to have some individual transactions finish faster. The obvious way to begin to improve response time is by tuning the component with the largest time.

For example, if the service time (the time we spend actually running on the CPU) is 20 percent of the total response time, then the remaining 80 percent of the response time must be due to some kind of delay in processing or wait time (total response time = 20 percent work time + 80 percent wait time). If you spend all your efforts tuning elements that affect only the amount of CPU used by the transaction, you will not make much of a difference in the transaction's overall response time! Even if you reduce the amount of work done in this transaction by 50 percent, that would only translate to a 10 percent reduction in the overall response time (because you are only tuning 20 percent of the overall equation). However, if you focus your efforts on the delay time, which is a larger component of the response time in our example, the same 50 percent improvement would get you a 40 percent increase in response time and make your users that much happier.

Improving Throughput

Improving throughput can be a bit more complicated. Throughput improvement is usually driven by the need to complete more transactions in the same time frame and with the same system resources (like trying to stuff more marbles into that pipe without increasing the diameter). Looking at a database-oriented problem, if an application is running out of available CPU time on the system, you need to reduce the service time. A simple but expensive way to correct the problem would be to add more or faster components, for example, more disks or more or faster CPUs. Another possibility would be to have each batch process or user process do more work during each CPU cycle. You could achieve this goal by reducing the wait time of the process, thus improving the overall response time. By reducing the wait time and increasing the amount of work performed during each CPU cycle, each process will complete each transaction quicker. Over time, more transactions can actually be done without changing the available resource.

Determining the Performance Benefit

Whether you tackle response time or throughput, or both, you must identify the percentage of performance improvement desired. As an example, a user may require a 30 percent response time or throughput improvement. Your normal reaction when faced with the requirement is to look for any ratios that seem to be "bad." Trying to improve these so-called bad ratios without considering how much the change will contribute to the overall performance of the system will usually fail to improve things noticeably.

Although rewriting an application or purchasing hardware may be expensive, determining the performance benefit before weighing the cost is also important. So how can you use the concepts we've just discussed in order to proactively avoid performance problems? To understand your options, you must first understand the business or corporate objectives that your database supports. In the next section, you'll learn more about determining and supporting your corporation's objectives.

Understanding the Critical Business Transactions

We've already mentioned several areas in which you may need to set both management's and users' expectations about how the database or applications will perform. We've also mentioned throughput as the number of transactions completed over a specific amount of time. We've talked about some of the factors that influence both response time and throughput.

For you to be able to set realistic tuning goals, you must understand the composition of your critical business transactions, the underlying objectives of your company, and who the appropriate people to define the issues and objectives are.

Looking at Transactions

In our discussion of throughput, we've been a bit remiss about what we mean by a transaction. So, here goes. A *transaction* is defined in Oracle terms as the work done between two commit statements. This definition is a little narrow for our discussion. In our case, a transaction is any unit of work that is required as a part of the application. This could be as simple as a single SQL statement, or any series of statements, or the generation of a complete report. In fact, for the discussion here, any unit of work that needs to be executed against the database can be thought of as a transaction.

Busy databases will have millions of transactions executed against them during the course of a workday. The trick is to determine which of those transactions need to be completed within a certain period of time and which of them, if not completed in time, will have an impact on the business. Let's say your boss requests a report at XYZ, and the report runs a few minutes longer than it takes him to get a cup of coffee. He complains about the database being slow. Is this situation as critical as the shipping department not being able to fill orders and ship product on time? While both situations may be critical to your career as a DBA, the inability to ship a product is usually going to have a more lasting impact on your (and your company's) future than your boss having to wait a few seconds more for his report. Of course, if the report that your boss is waiting for is going to determine your company's entire future existence, the report may take precedence.

So we will define a *critical business transaction* as a consistent unit of work that, when executed against the database, must be completed in a specific period of time under the expected workload. Further, there is some significant negative consequence or impact if the transaction does not complete in the specified time.

These transactions and their day-to-day performance will become your yardstick for measuring the health of your system.

Tongue-in-cheek comments about bosses aside, defining the transactions that need to complete in a specific window should be the first step in tuning. As Steven Covey states in his book *7 Habits of Highly Effective People*, one of the things we need to do is "Begin with the end in mind." In your case, that means you need to understand which transaction's performance is most important to your users. In addition, you need to set some goals with your users in terms of how fast they need the system to perform. Beware the answer, "As fast as it can!" That answer is an open-ended invitation to tune a database forever.

By understanding what criteria make your business successful, you can work with your users to understand and set a standard of performance for the database. Once you have achieved that performance, you can use those transactions as a benchmark to gauge the performance of your system over time.

The following questions, along with their explanations, should provide some guidance on how to isolate the critical business transactions in your system. We'll refer back to them when we look further at XYZ's new manufacturing system.

Examining the Application Flow

Let's return to your job at the XYZ Company. Yes, it's time to get back to work! The current legacy system is used on the manufacturing floor to keep track of the amount of raw material coming into the plant and the total number of widgets created. A different function in the system captures the customer's order and is used in the creation of a packing list and shipping labels. Purchasing uses the data from the order entry component to determine when they should reorder needed material to keep the widget manufacturing line running with minimal inventory in-house. Accounting uses the order data to generate sales reports and projections. Both departments use the same reports on a daily and weekly basis, with some additional reports run monthly, quarterly, and at the end of the year.

The new system will have some additional features. An analysis component for the planning and forecasting department to develop what-if scenarios is being included. The reports from the new component will be run on an as-needed basis, using queries designed by the users. The new system will now also keep track of the intermediate products that go into the manufacture of a widget and track those as separate inventory items. Figure 12-1 shows the various departments that depend on the database, with the legacy system's tasks identified by the letter *L*. The new system area is shown in Figure 12-1 with a designation of *N*.

Since the majority of the work in this system is being done in interactive, short processes, you would classify this as an OLTP system with some additional

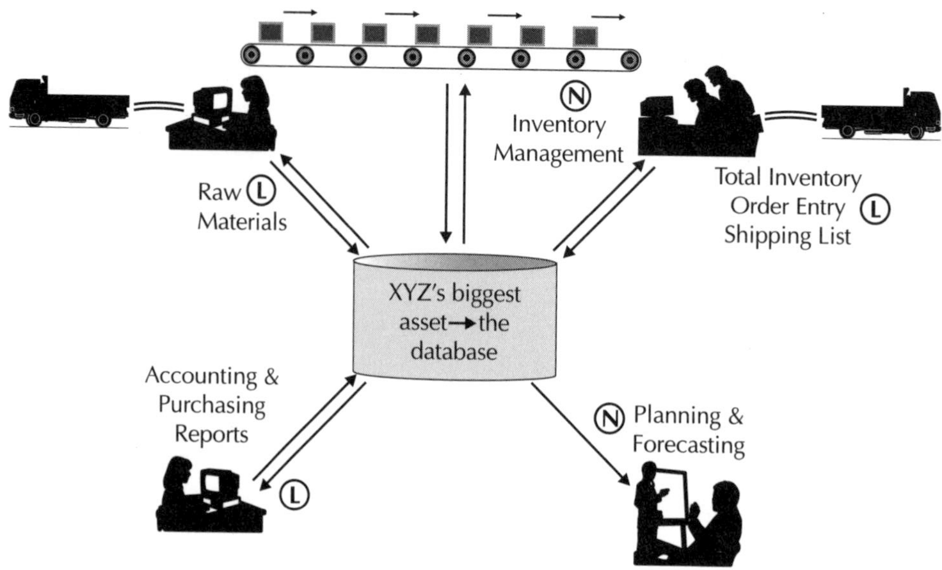

FIGURE 12-1. *Various departments of the XYZ Company. Transactions marked with an Ⓛ are from the legacy system, and new transactions are marked with an Ⓝ*

reporting components. From the above description, you can determine some transactions that are a part of this application, as follows:

- **Order entry** Completion of an order in the system.
- **Inventory management** Entry of raw inventory and completed products into the database. In the new system you have the added requirement of tracking a widget during its assembly process.
- **Shipping** Creation of a packing and shipping list from a completed order.
- **Analysis** Reports are run by the purchasing and sales departments, usually overnight in a specific batch window. In the new system, the planning department will need to run its own reports against the data.

Each of these areas contains candidate critical business transactions.

Identifying Expected Response Times

The next step in the process of identifying the critical business transactions in the system is to determine the expected time in which these transactions should complete and the consequences if these transactions do not complete in the given amount of time. In an ideal world, this information will be available to you from design specifications or knowledge of the system or perhaps even from your intuition. Since you live in the "real" world, it is more likely that you will have to go and find this information yourself! Surprisingly and unfortunately, the information you are trying to obtain can be difficult to get. At this point, your users become one of your most valuable resources.

For any system, old or new, the users will be able to provide you with a wealth of information on what areas or applications they perceive are running slowly. More to the point, they will be able to tell you about the transactions they do in the current system on a daily basis. This information will give you insights into where to focus your efforts. Fortunately, you have some other data available that will be very valuable to you as well.

Back at your job at XYZ, assuming things were running smoothly in the current application and system performance is acceptable, you have the baseline for the performance of the new system—at least for those functions that are currently implemented. For new systems and additions to existing systems, determining the baseline time will take you back to negotiating with the users.

In our example, the time it takes to enter an order into the system and the time it takes to create a shipping and packing list are critical transactions that you have been doing all along. The transactions required to create the documents must run fast enough to ensure they are not a bottleneck in the shipping process. You can determine a baseline value by examining the existing system.

An Online Transaction Processing Situation

You can also see that in the manufacturing environment, the new requirement of checking partially completed widgets in and out of inventory during the assembly process is a transaction that will occur many times throughout the day. This transaction will have to complete fast enough to ensure that no delays in the assembly process occur. From talking to the users and studying the systems, you can determine something about the transactions themselves. All of these transactions will be relatively short inserts or updates to the database and will be done interactively. As we mentioned earlier, these types of transactions describe an OLTP system.

The other transactions mentioned here could have an impact on the business as well. Cataloging the inventory used in the manufacturing process must be done in a timely fashion. However, this process will most likely not be done online (interactively)

Isolating Critical Business Transactions

What is the purpose of the application?

You need to understand all of the critical transactions to ensure that changes made to one part of the system do not have an adverse effect on other components. For example, adding an index to support rapid access to data for an online user can result in an unacceptable slowdown of a batch report. By understanding these dependencies, you will be able to better deal with how your changes affect the overall system. An understanding of your system's critical business transactions will help you to balance any trade-offs that you make in favor of the transactions that are most important to your customers.

What is the transaction mix of this system? Is it primarily OLTP, batch, data warehouse queries, or a mixture? Is the mixture different at different times of the day?

Understanding the transaction mix will further refine what types of tuning will be most effective. For example, varying requirements on a system depending on time of day might suggest creating different database server init.ora files with settings that favor either batch or online processing and then shutting down and restarting the database with the appropriate init.ora file each time the processing type is changed. Different system types and their processing performance implications are as follows:

Online transaction processing (OLTP): Systems used mainly for online transaction processing are characterized as high throughput, insert/update-intensive systems. They have a constantly growing database and a high number of concurrent users. Major concerns for this type of system are appropriate indexes, the size of the shared pool, well-tuned SQL statements, and pinned packages.

Batch data processing: Most of the batch data processing modules move large amounts of data entered by OLTP users. Primary concerns in a batch data processing environment are the amount of memory reserved for sorting records; the temporary tablespace, which is used for sorts that do not fit into memory; the number and size of rollback segments; and the required transaction throughput. Transactions for this type of system can sometimes be handled more efficiently using table scans and parallel processing.

Decision support systems (DSS), data warehouse, reporting systems: Reports tend to sort large amounts of data, and their requirements are similar to those of batch processes. Poorly written reports can consume huge amounts of memory and CPU. Frequent concerns for this type of system are temporary tablespaces, the efficiency of the SQL statements, and the transaction throughput.

What is the transaction profile on a daily basis? Does the profile change for end of the month, end of the quarter, or end of year processing?

This information will allow you to determine whether there are any special requirements outside of normal daily processing that you need to account for during system design. Building this information in a time-line graph could provide you with some insight on how to redistribute transaction activity at peak times to other points of the day when system usage is not as high. The following questions will help create a complete picture of the processing on the system.

- What is the batch window?
- Are all batch processes started at the same time? Can they be distributed?
- What is the backup window?
- If there is an online window, are reports or large queries being run at the same time?
- Are large delete/insert batch jobs running? (The tables and indexes associated with these objects can become fragmented.)

What components of the stack are a part of this application? Is the architecture client-server, three-tier, or n-tier?

This question will define which technology areas are a part of this system. For example, running Oracle applications on a PC client introduces the PC as both a potential bottleneck and a place for performance improvement. Additionally, understanding that a three-tier architecture is more vulnerable to poor network performance may suggest the network as a candidate for more detailed analysis.

as part of the day-to-day work. You can verify this at XYZ with your users. Keep in mind that your realization that the cataloging of inventory is not an interactive process does not give you license to let the transaction run slowly, but it probably is not the first place to concentrate your tuning efforts. If this form of transaction processing runs so slowly that it starts to infringe on the time you need for backups or maintenance, you may want to start tuning here.

Another consideration is the human factor. At XYZ, users at terminals enter the inventory manually. You can see another facet of setting goals for tuning based on the users' interaction with the application. In reality, the inventory data entry may not require any more responsiveness than is required to keep the user productive. However, a user who sits for more than a few seconds waiting to perform a repetitive task is bound to be dissatisfied with the performance of the system, even if the responsiveness is meeting the business need. Keep the user's idle time in mind, since we'll discuss this more in the section "Defining a Service-Level Agreement" later in this chapter.

A Batch Processing Situation

The existing sales and marketing department reports will most likely not be time critical. You will, of course, need to verify this supposition with the users. In your system, the sales and marketing reports are static reports that are run the same way each month. The only change in each month's run is the value for each input variable. The reports are run overnight and away from the peak usage time of the system. Thus, you gain some advantages in your efforts to tune them. The reports can be written and tuned with supporting indexes and hints, as we discussed in Chapter 11. The response time for running these reports is bounded only by the window of time it takes to run the reports in a batch mode. The only restriction you face is ensuring that the report runs do not interfere with your overnight maintenance window. In other words, you must ensure that the reports are completed before you begin your nightly database maintenance tasks. At this point, your system behaves more like a decision support system, where you would be optimizing more for the long-running transactions.

Potentially Unbounded Queries

The planning department requirement is another matter entirely. Their expectation to allow their users to run ad hoc queries during the day can have serious consequences for the performance of the system. Because the queries will be undefined and, therefore, not tunable, you cannot predict their effect on the system. Unfortunately, this is another all-too-common problem when developing systems. You may not have enough data to determine the impact of a requirement on a new system or a design change on an existing system.

The inability to predetermine the effect of some kinds of queries on your system is one of the strongest arguments you can use for building a test system with live data, as close to the production data and production load as possible. As a DBA responsible for the performance of your system, you will want to make sure that time to test the impacts of various forms of queries is built into the development cycle of your project. If you can't build performance testing into the development cycle, you won't be able to accurately confirm that the system will meet its performance and design targets. This really is an example of the old adage "you can pay me now or pay me later." If you are not given the opportunity to test and verify the system up front, you may face major performance problems later. Some of these problems could be inherent in the system design and will not be easily corrected once the system "goes live."

Defining a Service-Level Agreement

Earlier, when we talked about a user's idle time, we mentioned the term *service-level agreement* but didn't really explain it. Let's talk about this term and its meaning now.

A service-level agreement is a set of expectations upon which you and your users agree regarding the performance of the system. The agreement should be for specific transactions in your system and should specify exactly how you are going to measure the result set. We have talked about setting expectations with your users on system performance in concrete terms. With the use of service-level agreements, you really are trying to move from the art of performance to a definable science.

Asking questions like "What are the expected transaction rates and completion rates for the critical business transactions on this system?" and "How do you measure performance?" (in terms the users can understand) not only gives you the starting point to make agreements with your users on how the system should perform, but also gives you concrete objectives to work toward when tuning.

Setting Up Measurement Generation

How the result set is measured is less important than agreeing on a way to implement the measurement process. One suggestion for measuring the performance of transactions that do not alter the data is to set up transactions in a script and execute that script at various times of the day during all kinds of system load. Collect statistics just before you start to run the script and just after the run so you can gauge the impact of the run on your system. You can then compare the results of each run and begin to get a feel for how your system is responding during specific periods of time and over time. The collection of measurement data will allow you to understand whether the system is meeting the users' performance expectations. Additionally, you can examine the statistical data for trends in performance.

For example, a trend toward longer response times could be correlated to an increase in the number of users on the system, allowing you to forecast when the system will no longer be able to meet the current expectations. The detailed statistics you collect can help you to justify to your management the building of a maintenance window for database reorganizations or table rebuilds. You can also use the statistics to predict when your well-tuned system will no longer be able to meet user requirements, justifying the purchase of additional hardware, network equipment, and so on.

Additionally, you can see sudden changes in performance (ideally, they will be positive ones due to your activities!). If the change is negative and the reason is unknown, the data approach will let you pinpoint a smaller range of time to examine the system and find the answer to the question "What changed?"

Data that does alter data can be measured using the same type of methodology by having the users record the transaction completion times during their normal workday. Although having your users record their processing times is a little less automated and more prone to errors, this gets users involved in the process of performance tuning, which may help make them allies instead of adversaries.

One of the authors was receiving complaints from users that the system seemed to slow down noticeably during the day. She had the users write down the times during the day when they felt the system slowed down noticeably, and from their reports, she determined that a performance problem was occurring at about the same time every day. Investigation showed that a batch job was being run about that time daily. The batch job was rescheduled to run two hours later in the day (during lunchtime, when most of the data entry people were away from their terminals), and the performance improvement and the users' perception of the improved performance was dramatic.

Overall, the statistical data that you gather becomes the yardstick for measuring the performance of your system. One advantage of using this method is that you and your users have agreed on what you are measuring and what units you are using to do the measurements.

The following questions provide some guidance in constructing a service-level agreement if one does not exist:

- How many transactions should be completed per minute?
- How many users should be connected to the system at peak time?
- How many concurrent processes should be running at peak time?
- What times of day are considered for online usage only?
- What is the batch processing window?

- What is the expected response time for an online process?
- How much system resource should be available during peak time? Define the margin of error.

The Initial Steps Summarized

Let's look back in on our XYZ example. In the first stage of performance analysis, before the system goes live, you have taken the time to meet with your users and understand the type of system and the transactions that will be most prevalent. You understand that your system is a mix of OLTP and DSS, with some ad hoc queries thrown in. You've discussed the most common transactions that will be run on the system and identified them as the critical business transactions (CBTs). After identifying the CBTs, you were able to work with your users and, for most of those transactions, identify how long each transaction should take and when it will normally be run. You were not really able to do this for your new ad hoc planning department transaction. You were also able to define the day-to-day workload characteristics of the system and define your maintenance and availability windows. Based on the CBT and the workload definition, you worked with the users to build a test system with representative data and test the response time. Also, you set up your test transactions in a script that will allow you to repeat the exact transactions over and over and to monitor the response time of the CBTs over time. This allows you to stop any trends in reduced response time before they become problems. You've really done a great job!

Diagnosing a Problem

Now that we have talked about the "right" way to design and build for performance, let's talk about the way it really happens! More often than not, the first time you are introduced to performance tuning is when there is a problem and the users are looking to you for help. In Chapter 11, we talked about the tuning of specific SQL statements for better performance. Here, we will look at the overall system and give you some steps to use in determining where your performance problem may be located. After that, we will discuss isolating a problem in the database using some of the Oracle V$ tables (explained more fully in Chapters 9 and 10).

Quick Hits: How to Spend the First Five Minutes

Let's return to your job as the DBA at XYZ. Let's assume for the moment that you came into the job well into the development cycle and were not able to set up any proactive measures in advance. Whether you put those measures in place or not, at some point, you will get a call from your user community telling you that the database is "slow." What you do in the first few minutes after that phone call will determine how much work (and stress) you will have to deal with to resolve the complaint. Yes, we're now going to talk about reactive performance tuning.

Talking to the Users

The first thing you need to do is define the problem clearly with the users. Defining the problem clearly, early in the process is a large step forward in finding the solution, much in the same way that we discussed using service-level agreements and critical business transactions during the proactive tuning process. Done correctly, your talk with the users will provide both of you a clear understanding of the goal to be accomplished, which helps both sides to stay focused and understand how to prioritize the steps that must be taken to solve the problem. You'll be asking questions that should provide some clues about which parts of your overall system are good candidates to investigate further. For this discussion, we'll assume that more than one user is reporting a problem.

When defining the problem, get the users to state the problem clearly. Ask them for specifics. First, get them to tell you what they mean by slow and what they are comparing that against. How are they measuring the response time? What were they running at the time? How were they running it? You need to move users from telling you about generic slowness in their workstations to a specific application (perhaps even a specific transaction) that is running slowly. Often, a generic complaint about slow response time can be refined to something more specific. If it can't, that tells you something as well. We'll discuss the implications of a vague complaint that can't be refined as we go.

Your discussion with the users should be kept open ended, but the desired outcome is to guide the users to an explanation of the specific issues. Your conversation might also start to provide clues to the location of the bottleneck that is causing the problem. For example, the users may feel that the entire system is slow or slower than it has been. This information is helpful because it may indicate that the problem is one that affects all transactions, such as a problem with the client interface or the network. Also, understanding the characteristics of the beginnings of the problem can provide some information. If the onset of the problem has been gradual, then either data fragmentation issues or an increase in system usage could cause the slowdown over time. A more sudden onset points to a specific environmental change such as a system upgrade or version change. The rate that the problem occurs can also provide some clues as to the true cause of the problem. A problem that occurs intermittently can perhaps be related to another environmental factor that changes with the same frequency. Often, the initial conversation alone is enough for you to determine exactly where the problem is occurring and to proceed directly to tuning.

At this point, users may present you with multiple problems, all of which are extremely urgent in their eyes. If this is the case, you must work with them to define which issue is the most critical and prioritize the work on that basis. Remember, all of the problems are important, but some are more important than others. Helping users to understand and build that prioritized list and then solving their problems in a systematic manner will give your users confidence that you are taking steps to get them back on track in a logical, well thought out manner and that you are taking their complaints seriously. Also, as you solve each problem on the list, your users will be able to share in that sense of accomplishment with you!

Asking the Right Questions

In this section, we'll look at a collection of questions you can use to help isolate the problem that is slowing down your system. For each problem presented to you, ask the questions given here. Understanding the environmental factors (time of occurrence, number of users affected) should also give more indications of the nature of the problem. But these questions will usually provide enough information to develop a hypothesis and possible cause, giving you some thoughts on where to start tuning.

What, specifically, is underperforming?

We touched on this a bit earlier, but by way of further explanation, this is where you need to understand exactly what the users were doing at the time performance degraded. What transaction were they running? What specific variables did they enter (if any)? At what time did the system start running slowly? Did they run the application/transaction any differently than they usually do? If so, what did they do differently?

This discussion alone may be enough to get users thinking about what is different now from what they have done in the past. Capturing this information now will be helpful later, when you need to test and see if you have corrected the problem.

What is the nature of the problem?

What is the system doing that it shouldn't be doing? What isn't the system doing that it should be doing? Here, you are trying to isolate the problem definition based on examining the expectation of performance, both positive and negative.

Is the problem occurring with specific users or at specific locations? (If yes, where is or isn't the problem occurring?)

These questions will help you determine whether physical location is a component of the problem. For example, you might find out that all the users in a particular remote site are having a sudden performance slowdown, but users in other remote sites or locally are not experiencing any problems. This not only defines the problem nicely, but also gives you good reason to believe that the problem is outside of the application (and database) entirely. This might also point you to a specific user who is having a problem. A user whose permissions and synonyms are set up incorrectly might be pointing to the wrong version of the data.

Can the problem be isolated to a specific component?

This question relates to the previous question. You are trying to determine whether a distinction can be drawn between a place where the problem is occurring and a place where it is not. One example of isolating the specific component that is a problem would be testing clients on a different part of the network or eliminating the network entirely. If the performance problem still occurs after running the application directly connected to the server, then you have eliminated the network as a possible suspect. Conversely, if the problem is reduced or eliminated when you run the application directly on the server, you have narrowed down your culprit. At this point, you as the DBA may need to be creative in thinking about other places or ways that you can run the application.

Are any third-party tools causing a load on the servers or network?

By the time you ask this question, you are beginning to look outside of your system to see if some other application's load has changed. This is not the question you would expect users to answer when you are doing your initial assessment. This question is one for you to file away in the back of your mind if the other questions do not produce any good starting points.

Are specific transactions slow? Are those transactions slow when they are run in an isolated environment?

Here, you are trying to isolate the application code as a potential cause for the problem. If users can point to a specific transaction as the problem and the transaction is always slow, regardless of the system load at the time of execution, then you may have found your culprit and can begin the exercise of tuning the SQL. You will need to make sure that when you are trying to isolate the transaction, you take into account any triggers or related events that might occur during the execution of a front-end process. If you have a SQL statement that responds quickly when run from SQL*Plus but runs slowly from inside the application, you will need to see if there are any triggers or functions that are being run as a result of the SQL. An underlying trigger or function may be slowing the process down.

Has this problem always occurred? If not, when did it start? Are there any correlated events?

Here, you need to make a distinction between *day-one* deviations and deviations over time. A day-one deviation is one that occurred the first time the transaction was executed. In other words, the process is slow and has always been slow! Before you begin any type of tuning, this is a time when examining the users' expectations is worthwhile. Assuming the expectations are realistic, you can then begin tuning. There is no magic formula for determining "realistic" expectations, nor are there any good general guidelines. Each system hardware configuration and application design will be different and will produce different results.

If a problem occurs after the system was performing in an acceptable manner, examining the time between when performance was acceptable and when it became unacceptable should help pinpoint some event that is related to the change. At least you will have narrowed down the search.

Does the problem occur consistently?

Problems that can be consistently reproduced are less likely to be related to some external event, while problems that do not occur consistently may be related to an external event.

If the problem is intermittent, is there a pattern?

Again, you are trying to establish some connection to another cause outside of the specific transaction that seems to be causing the problem.

Is the rate of the problem getting better, worse, or staying consistent?

This question will help isolate whether transaction volume or overall system load is influencing the problem. If the onset of the problem was gradual and measurements over time show that the problem is getting worse, you can try to map the deterioration to an increase in users or a need to do some maintenance on some objects that may have grown or become disorganized over time.

How many users or locations are affected?

Here, you are trying to draw some distinctions between where the problem is occurring and where it is not occurring. You might determine from this question that only a single user is affected (perhaps a workstation problem). You may find that a group of users are affected—perhaps an index was dropped on a table that is used by all sales department users in their reports; or all the users on the second floor are affected, but everyone else is fine. Or you might find that all users are affected, and you will begin the search for the problem directly with a global component like the database itself.

How much functionality is affected?

This is another question that will help users to isolate whether a specific transaction is the problem. Here, if users tell you all the transactions are running slowly in the sales application, you might ask them to run something in the marketing application, if possible, to see if that application area is slow as well.

Evaluating the Answers for the XYZ Company

Well, back to work you go. In your conversations with the users reporting slow response time at XYZ, you found that all functions related to the new order entry, inventory, and shipping system were slow at points throughout the business day. You verified that all users were affected (no difference between sites on the LAN or WAN, most likely ruling out the network as a bottleneck).

You found that all transactions were slow at these times and that no specific transaction was involved. With this information, you ruled out any specific SQL as the cause and increased your suspicion that the problem is systemic in nature. The facts you have gathered give you a reason to check with the system administrators to see if there have been any changes on the system.

When you asked about the rate of the problem, you found out that it was intermittent and inconsistent. Also, the problem just started happening "a few days ago." An event that is happening outside of the user's application but still in the overall system may be the offender. You now have a time frame to narrow down your investigation of any changes or errors.

You have spoken to the users about how quickly the transactions should complete. Since you did not get the chance to build your baseline of critical business transactions (as we discussed in the proactive sections earlier in this chapter) and the slowdown is occurring in varying transactions, you do not have a baseline of performance to work toward. You could use this opportunity to ask the users to focus on a few transactions and record the times for the transactions when performance is good and bad. This gives you a chance to work with the users to determine critical business transactions. Gathering data about when the performance is bad will also give you information on the rate of the problem.

You tried to discuss the ordering of transactions to deal with first (prioritizing), but could not because of the intermittent nature of the problems and the transactions affected.

Where to Look First: Tuning Within the Database Server

You have now gone through the set of questions to try and isolate a possible cause. You have put in a call to the system administrator to see if there were any system changes that could have impacted performance. Now, you are ready to begin your investigation into the database. You will be investigating the database at the system level, although these techniques apply to the session level, too. Where appropriate, we will show you the session-level statements as well. How do you know whether to look at the system or session level?

Looking at the System/Instance Level

If sessions on your system log on or off the database frequently, you will want to perform your investigation at the instance or system level. You will obtain a general overview of what could be wrong with the instance. Use the V$SYSSTAT and V$SYSTEM_EVENT views, discussed briefly in Chapter 10, to look into what is occurring over the entire database.

Looking at the Session Level

If sessions stay connected to the database over a long period of time, looking at the session level is more beneficial. You will be able to perform direct measurement of response times by looking at the session level. Use the V$SESSTAT and V$SESSION_EVENT views, discussed briefly in Chapter 10, to drilldown into the activities of each user.

Setting the init.ora Parameter timed_statistics

To properly analyze the performance within Oracle, you will want to set the init.ora parameter **timed_statistics** to TRUE. On most platforms, this feature introduces a small (maximum of 2–3 percent) impact on performance, but returns the much greater benefit of more detailed statistics to use when diagnosing performance bottlenecks. Many sources of tuning information recommend disabling **timed_statistics** due to perceived overhead (which was larger on some older operating systems), but tuning a system without this information becomes an almost impossible task. Note that, as of Oracle7.3, you can dynamically change the setting of **timed_statistics** while the database is up by issuing one of the following two commands:

```
alter system set timed_statistics = TRUE (for all users. DBA privileges required)
alter session set timed_statistics = TRUE (for this session only)
```

Calculating the Total Response Time

Earlier in this chapter, we talked about what total response time is and mentioned that you can use the V$ views to determine your system's response time, but we didn't show you how to actually determine this value. In this section, we'll cover how to retrieve the relevant statistics from the Oracle performance tables that you need in order to calculate total response time.

To restate the original response time formula:

Response Time = Service (or Work) Time + Wait Time

Now let's look at how to determine each of the values needed.

Calculating Service (or Work) Time

The service time is equal to the statistic "CPU used by this session," which is shown through entries in the V$SYSSTAT or V$SESSTAT view. You select this event. Use the lookup table V$STATNAME to help you find the correct statistic number for "CPU used by this session" for each platform and release. This event represents the total amount of CPU time used.

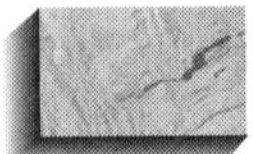

NOTE
V$SYSSTAT does not include CPU used by the Oracle background processes, and V$SESSTAT doesn't show the amount of CPU used per Oracle background process.

The SQL statement to run at either instance or session level is shown below. The first query is used to determine the instance-level service time value.

```
select a.Value "Total CPU Time"
 from V$SYSSTAT a
 where a.Name = 'CPU used by this session';

Total CPU Time
--------------
        408153
```

For the session-level query shown next, you must join the view V$SESSTAT with V$STATNAME in order to obtain the value for the CPU.

```
select a.Sid, a.Value "Total CPU Time"
  from V$SESSTAT a, V$STATNAME b
 where a.Statistic# = b.Statistic#
```

```
   and b.Name = 'CPU used by this session'
 order by Sid;

      SID  Total CPU Time
--------- ---------------
        1             222
        2              25
        3              57
        4             155
        5             457
        6             296
        7            1443
        8              60
        9            1362
       11            2503

10 rows selected.
```

Now that you know the amount of service or work time, you will need to obtain the amount of wait time to complete the formula.

Calculating Wait Time

The wait time is recorded through entries in V$SYSTEM_EVENT or V$SESSION_EVENT by summing the time waited for all the events excluding those waited for due to the foreground process and all background waits. We can ignore the following wait events:

- client message
- dispatcher timer
- KXFX: execution message dequeue – Slaves
- KXFX: Reply Message Dequeue – Query Coord
- Null event
- parallel query dequeue wait
- parallel query idle wait - Slaves
- pipe get
- PL/SQL lock timer
- pmon timer
- rdbms ipc message

- slave wait
- smon timer
- SQL*Net message from client
- virtual circuit status
- WMON goes to sleep

Here's the query you will use to collect the total wait time from the instance level, note that this query does include the entire list above:

```
select sum(Time_Waited) "Total Time Waited"
  from V$SYSTEM_EVENT
 where Event not in ('pmon  timer', 'smon  timer', 'rdbms ipc  message', 'parallel
dequeue wait', 'virtual circuit', 'SQL*Net message from client', 'client message',
'NULL event');

Total Time Waited
-----------------
          2771194
```

For the session-level query, you would use the following:

```
select Sid, sum(Time_Waited) "Total Time waited"
  from V$SESSION_EVENT
 where Event != 'SQL*Net message from client'
 group by Sid;

      SID Total Time Waited
--------- -----------------
        1            218329
        2               104
        3               358
        4                72
        5               654
        6              2488
        9              3284
       11                80
8 rows selected.
```

Tuning to Change Overall Response Time

Now that you have the data for either the instance or session, you can decide how to best direct your tuning efforts by examining the area that is taking the highest percentage of time. The next step involves further examination of the largest component of the response time equation. Keep in mind that once all this data has been gathered, the problem may not be at the database level at all, but only manifesting itself there.

Decomposing CPU Time

If CPU usage contributes the most to total response time, you will need to break the value down further into detailed segments to properly understand the problem. CPU time basically falls into three categories:

- Parse time CPU
- Recursive CPU usage
- Other CPU

Let's look at each of these categories individually.

Parse Time CPU

This parameter reports the amount of CPU used for parsing SQL statements and consists of four components: parse count, execute count, session cursor cache count, and session cursor cache hits. We'll look at each of these components briefly.

Generally, parse time CPU should not exceed 10 percent to 20 percent of the total CPU. A high value for parse time CPU can be a strong indication that an application has not been well tuned (or an older version of Forms, such as 4.0 or below, is still being used). High parse time CPU usually indicates that the application is either spending too much time opening and closing cursors or is not using bind variables. Check the following statistics from V$SYSSTAT or V$SESSTAT:

- **Parse count** Total number of hard and soft parses. A hard parse occurs when a SQL statement has to be loaded into the shared pool. In this case, Oracle has to allocate memory in the shared pool and parse the statement. A soft parse is recorded when Oracle checks the shared pool for a SQL statement and finds a version of the statement that it can reuse. An application using dynamic SQL may have a high parse count. Dynamic SQL statements usually have a one-to-one ratio for the execute count (see next item).

In version 8.0 and above, the number of soft parses is available as a separate statistic.

- **Execute count** Total number of executions of Data Manipulation Language (DML) and Data Definition Language (DDL) statements.

- **Session cursor cache count** Total size of the session cursor cache for the session (in V$SESSTAT) or the total size for all sessions (in V$SYSSTAT).
- **Session cursor cache hits** Number of times a statement did not have to be reopened and reparsed, because it was still in the cursor cache for the session.

From these statistics, the percentage of parses versus executes can be calculated (parse count / execute count). If this ratio is higher than 20 percent, consider the following:

- Ensure that the application is using bind variables. By using bind variables, it is unnecessary to reparse SQL statements with new values before reexecuting. It is significantly better to use bind variables and parse the SQL statement once in the program. It will also reduce resource contention within the shared pool.
- If applications open/reparse the same SQL statements and the value of "session cursor cache hits" is low compared to the number of parses, it may be useful to increase the number of cursor cache hits for the session. Increasing the init.ora parameter **session_cached_cursors** will set aside additional memory for this purpose. This will reduce the number of hard parses by holding a copy of the parsed SQL statement in a cache. If no hit ratio improvement results, lower this number to conserve memory and reduce cache maintenance overhead.

Recursive CPU Usage

This value includes the amount of CPU used for executing row cache statements (data dictionary lookup) and PL/SQL programs. If recursive CPU usage is high relative to the total CPU, check for the following:

- Determine whether much PL/SQL code (triggers, functions, procedures, packages) is executed. Stored PL/SQL code always runs under a recursive session, so it is reflected in recursive CPU time and will skew this value. Consider optimizing any SQL coded within those program units. This activity can be determined by querying V$SQL.
- Examine the size of the shared pool and its usage, and possibly, increase the SHARED_POOL_SIZE. This can be determined by monitoring V$SQL and V$SGASTAT.

In the next section, we'll show you a script to extract the different kinds of CPU values.

Other CPU

This last category is composed of CPU time that will be used for tasks such as looking up buffers, fetching rows or index keys, and so on. Generally, "other CPU" should represent the highest percentage of CPU time out of the total CPU time used. Also look in V$SQL to find SQL statements that have a high number of BUFFER_GETS per execution and/or a high number of physical reads per execution. Investigation of these "gets" (especially the first) will help to reduce the remaining, or other, CPU time. The following SQL statement will find the overall SQL usage:

```
select a.Value "Total CPU",
       b.Value "Parse CPU",
       c.Value "Recursive CPU",
       a.Value - b.Value - c.Value "Other"
  from V$SYSSTAT a, V$SYSSTAT b, V$SYSSTAT c
 where a.Name = 'CPU used by this session'
   and b.Name = 'parse cpu time'
   and c.Name = 'recursive cpu';
```

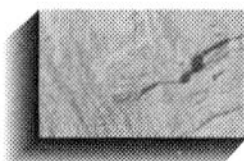

NOTE
The descriptors in V$SYSSTAT may change between versions.

In the next query, you'll be looking for the CPU usage per session. In that query, you're using the Statistic# column instead of a meaningful name. Before you run that query, you can use the following select statement to see the names of the values you'll be selecting when you look for the CPU usage per session. Since Oracle may change the Statistic# value associated with a statistic name from version to version, you should double-check the statistic names and Statistic# values for the version you are on before you run the query.

```
select Statistic#, Name
  from V$STATNAME
 where Statistic# in (12,162,8);

STATISTIC# NAME
---------- ------------------------------------------------------------
         8 recursive cpu usage
        12 CPU used by this session
       162 parse time cpu
```

The following SQL statement will show the CPU usage per session. The most interesting thing about this query is that it is joining against the same V$ view several times. Therefore, you will see a separate set of values for each of the joins, with the same session ID (SID) shown many times. The results set can be very large depending on the number of sessions that are running when you perform the query. Therefore, we are going to narrow our select to one SID. We'll arbitrarily pick session ID number 11.

```
select distinct a.Sid, a.Value "Total CPU",
       b.Value "Parse CPU",
       c.Value "Recursive CPU",
       a.Value - b.Value - c.Value "Other CPU"
 from  V$SESSTAT a, V$SESSTAT b, V$SESSTAT c
 where a.Statistic# = 12
   and b.Statistic# = 162
   and c.Statistic# = 8
   and a.Sid = 11
/

      SID Total CPU Parse CPU Recursive CPU Other CPU
--------- --------- --------- ------------- --------
       11        27         0             0       27
       11        27         0             8       19
       11        27         1             0       26
       11        27         1             8       18
       11        27         2             0       25
       11        27         2             8       17
       11        27        17             0       10
       11        27        17             8        2
```

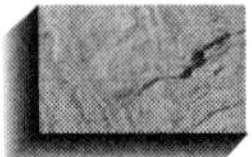

NOTE
The descriptors in V$SYSSTAT may change between versions.

Improving the CPU time will help to improve the throughput.

Decomposing Wait Time

If wait time is the largest contributor to total response time, you can decompose it into detailed segments to further understand the problem. To correctly identify the events contributing the highest amounts of wait time, query the view V$SYSTEM_EVENT and order the events by Time_Waited in descending order:

```
col Event format a30
select *
  from V$SYSTEM_EVENT
 where Event not in ('pmon timer', 'smon timer', 'rdbms ipc message', 'parallel
dequeue wait', 'virtual circuit', 'SQL*Net message from client', 'client message',
'Null event')
 order by Time_Waited desc;
EVENT                          TOTAL_WAITS TOTAL_TIMEOUTS TIME_WAITED AVERAGE_WAIT
------------------------------ ----------- -------------- ----------- ------------
dispatcher timer                        36             36      221221    6145.0278
virtual circuit status                  72             72      221217    3072.4583
```

```
db file sequential read              1502         0      2461     1.638482
library cache pin                       5         1       589        117.8
db file scattered read                359         0       578    1.6100279
rdbms ipc reply                         7         0       508    72.571429
file open                              83         0       367    4.4216867
control file sequential read          137         0       275    2.0072993
control file parallel write           754         0       169    .22413793
file identify                          29         0       131    4.5172414
log file parallel write                43         0        73    1.6976744
log file sequential read               11         0        32    2.9090909
reliable message                        1         0        17           17
buffer busy waits                       1         0        14           14
refresh controlfile command             5         0         9          1.8
db file single write                   11         0         2    .18181818
db file parallel write                  2         0         2            1
log file single write                  10         0         1           .1
direct path read                       44         0         1    .02272727
log file sync                           3         0         1    .33333333
direct path write                      22         0         0            0
instance state change                   1         0         0            0
SQL*Net message to client             129         0         0            0
SQL*Net more data to client             1         0         0            0
SQL*Net break/reset to client           2         0         0            0
```

If you get all zeros in the Time_Waited and Average_Wait columns, check to see if the parameter **timed_statistics** is set to TRUE in your init.ora parameter file.

The output from V$SYSTEM_EVENT has been ordered to show the events that are the greatest contributors to the amount of time waited. From the event descriptions, you can take appropriate actions to correct any performance problems that you've identified. However, for the purpose of this book, the following discussion covers the primary events that usually contribute the greatest amount of wait time.

Buffer Busy Waits

A high buffer busy waits event value can be caused by either of the following situations:

- Multiple sessions requesting the same block (one or more sessions are waiting for a process to read the requested block into the buffer cache)
- Multiple sessions waiting for a change to complete for the same block (only one process at a time can write to the block, so other processes have to wait for that buffer to become available)

If buffer busy waits is high, determine which blocks are being accessed concurrently and whether the blocks are being read or changed. You can use the V$SESSION_WAIT and V$WAITSTAT views. V$SESSION_WAIT will show the file number, block number, and ID (where ID represents the status of the buffer busy wait event). V$WAITSTAT will show the block classes and the number of times waited for each. Different actions may be taken for each block class to alleviate contention. Tuning priorities should be oriented toward the classes that contribute the highest wait time percentage.

Segment Header Waits

Each segment has one segment header block. There are basically two types of segments: data and index. The following is a brief discussion on causes for segment header block contention based on the data structures they contain.

If you see a high insert rate on a table with insufficient transaction freelists that results in a bottleneck, the solution is to increase the number of freelists. Unfortunately, a segment's freelists cannot be increased dynamically. The segment must be dropped and recreated with a higher value for freelists. On single-CPU machines, the CPU manages one process at a time so the system may not benefit greatly from an increase in freelists. However, adding freelists on a single-CPU machine may ensure that the processor is used more efficiently. For databases running in exclusive mode, this recommendation may also circumvent the issue of a small block size constraining the number of available freelists.

If you observe Oracle constantly inserting new entries into the extent map within the segment header because extent sizes are too small, increase the size of each extent. Although Oracle7.3 and later versions allow an object to have unlimited extents, a small number of very large extents is better than a large number of small extents.

Data Block Waits

The data block class is used to store data (index or table data). Let's look at some reasons for data block waits:

- Multiple sessions could be requesting the same block from disk.
- Multiple sessions are going after rows in the same block because it contains so many rows.
- Multiple sessions are trying to insert into the same block because there is only one freelist (or insufficient freelists).

In the first case (this could actually happen for each block class), only one session will do the read from disk, and the other sessions will be waiting for the block to be placed into the buffer cache. The cause of this problem could be that the buffer cache is too small to keep the current working set in memory. Enlarging the buffer cache (**db_block_buffers**) can help. Another option is to use buffer pools to reduce the number of buffers an object can occupy in the buffer cache. For example, you may effectively limit the number of buffers that a randomly accessed large table can occupy in the buffer cache by placing it in the recycle pool. Several new types of buffer pools were introduced in Oracle8.

If multiple sessions are going after rows in the same block because it contains so many rows, reduce the number of rows per block by modifying the pctfree/pctused settings. This is a "space for time" trade-off. The table will use more space, but buffer busy waits will be reduced.

Finally, adding multiple freelists to the object will increase the number of heads of freelists; thus the contention point can be distributed over the freelists, reducing the number of buffer busy waits. The only way to add more freelists, though, is to export the object, drop and re-create it with the appropriate number of freelists, and then import the data.

Finding the Buffer Cache Size

The memory area referred to as the buffer cache or buffer pool is specified by two init.ora parameters:

- **db_block_buffers** Number of blocks
- **db_block_size** Block size

As a rule of thumb, the buffer cache should be about 2.5 percent of the size of the database. Thus, if your total amount of data is 1GB and your block size is 4K, a good starting point would be to set the number of buffers to 5200. The main concept of the buffer cache is to hold data that has been read by previous queries. The assumption is that it's likely these blocks will be needed again.

When a query executes, Oracle will check to see if the data block is in the cache. If it is, that block will be used (a cache hit); if it's not, the query will have to fetch data from disk. The new blocks will be stored in the buffer cache. Eventually there will be no more room in the buffer cache to hold new blocks. When this happens, the DBWR background process will flush blocks out of the buffer cache to make room for the new blocks that must be brought into the cache from disk. A block that has been updated is marked as a dirty block and will be written to disk the next time DBWR is activated.

DBWR also uses an algorithm called LRU (least recently used) to clear some space in the cache. The LRU algorithm basically means the blocks in the cache that have not been accessed for the longest time will be removed. Blocks read into the cache via full table scans automatically get placed at the end of the LRU chain to avoid filling the entire cache with unnecessary data from one query. The flushing event is also triggered when a checkpoint occurs.

Cache hits are good for performance and are measured in terms of a hit ratio. Hit ratios can be measured at system or session level. Generally speaking, the higher the ratio the better. OLTP applications should aim for a hit ratio of better than 90 percent, while for batch applications, a cache hit ratio of around 60 percent to 70 percent is acceptable. To measure the hit ratio for the system, the following query can be used:

```
select trunc((1 -(sum(decode(Name,'physical reads',value,0)) /
       (sum(decode(Name,'consistent gets',value,0)) +
       (sum(decode(Name,'db block gets',value,0)))))
       ) * 100 ) "Buffer Hit Ratio"
  from V$SYSSTAT
 where Statistic# in (38,39,40);

Buffer Hit Ratio
----------------
              98
```

To get a breakdown of the buffer hit ratio at session level, execute the following query:

```
select a.Username,
      avg((b.Consistent_Gets + b.Block_Gets - b.Physical_Reads) *100 /
      (b.Consistent_Gets + b.Block_Gets)) "Buffer Hit Ratio"
  from  V$SESSION a, V$SESS_IO b
 where a.Sid = b.Sid
   and (b.Consistent_Gets + b.Block_Gets) > 0
   and  Username is not null
 group by Username;

USERNAME                       Buffer Hit Ratio
------------------------------ ----------------
AMRDEV                               99.9325682
AMRTEST                              99.5589174
FWKDEV                               89.1736861
FWKTEST                              93.8428192
QDBA                                 99.0275177
SYSTEM                               85.8736059
```

Freelist Block Waits

This statistic measures contention for "freelist group" blocks. Some documentation and tuning scripts claim that waits on this block class indicate that the number of freelists need to be increased for some objects. Most databases that run in exclusive mode see zero waits on this block class because their DBAs do not create objects with freelist groups. Otherwise, the reasons and solutions for freelist block waits are similar to those of segment header waits. See that earlier section for details.

Db File Scattered Read

This wait event usually indicates some type of multiblock I/O operation (full table scans or fast full index scans in Oracle7.3 and higher). The number of data blocks read per I/O operation is determined by the init.ora parameter **db_file_multiblock_read_count** (which can be changed dynamically as of Oracle7.3).

Check V$FILESTAT to see which files have done scans:

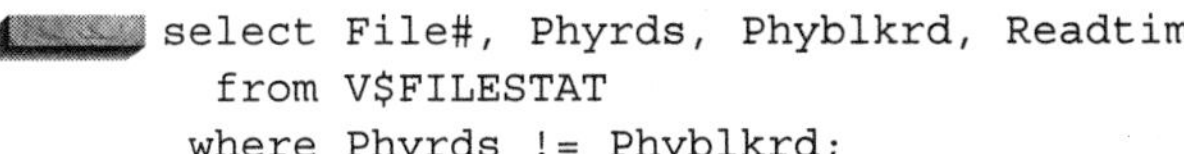

```
select File#, Phyrds, Phyblkrd, Readtim
  from V$FILESTAT
 where Phyrds != Phyblkrd;

    FILE#    PHYRDS  PHYBLKRD   READTIM
--------- --------- --------- ---------
        1      1790      3850         0
        4        24       110         0
```

If phyrds is close to phyblkrd, then single block reads are occurring. If that is not the case, full scans or range scans are happening on that file. To reduce the cost of a db file scattered read, check the file placement on each disk, the number of disks, and the stripe size per disk. To reduce the amount of db file scattered reads, check for missing indexes on the object where the scan is happening, or check the SQL statement that is executing the scan.

Db File Sequential Read

This event occurs for single block reads (like index lookup). The normal way to reduce this event is to examine the amount and cost of the I/Os that are being performed. You can normally reduce the amount of I/Os and make each I/O faster by taking a combination of the following actions:

- Increase **db_block_buffers**.
- Reduce physical reads per execute for SQL statements.

It is likely that the buffer cache is too small. Increasing the number of buffers will have a positive effect on the buffer cache hit ratio. Even a small increase in the buffer cache hit ratio can have a dramatic effect if the buffer cache is large.

In the proactive tuning section, we discussed how tuning the application could have a big impact on the overall performance of the system. One of the biggest wait components of the SQL statement execution is the I/O. Finding the SQL statement with the highest number of disk reads per execution is a good start. Although you can use a SQL statement to "dump" all of the Sql_Text along with all of the Disk_Reads information, we recommend that you perform this search in two steps. First, determine the highest range of disk reads per execution that are being performed on your system, and then look at the SQL for those specific queries that are doing the high volume. Here's the first query to run:

```
select Disk_Reads, Executions, Disk_Reads/Executions
  from V$SQL
 where Executions != 0
 order by Disk_Reads desc;

DISK_READS EXECUTIONS DISK_READS/EXECUTIONS
---------- ---------- ---------------------
       969          4                242.25
       927          1                   927
       671          4                167.75
       487          1                   487
       216          1                   216
       137          2                  68.5
       114         12                   9.5
        58          1                    58
        53          1                    53
        44          1                    44
        30         84             .35714286
        26         18             1.4444444
        20         30             .66666667
        18         18                     1
        17         30             .56666667

15 rows selected.
```

Alternatively, you could order the query by the Disk_Reads/Executions column, since the row ordering shown here could potentially put a well-tuned query that is executed the most toward the top of the output list. In other words, you could have a situation where a well-tuned query does a small amount of disk I/O each time it's run, but it's run so frequently that it could show up with both a high execution count and a high disk I/O count. The way the output is currently shown, you would end up with this query very high on your list. If you order by reads per execution, you would have a very low count for the same query. Either approach in the query output order is fine as long as you pay primary attention to the reads per execution values.

The output you see here has been cut way back to conserve space but should give you an idea of what you are looking for from this query. Just for this example, let's look at the SQL statements that generated the three highest values for disk reads per execution.

```
select Disk_Reads, Executions, Disk_Reads/Executions, Sql_Text
  from V$SQL
 where Disk_Reads > 600;

DISK_READS EXECUTIONS DISK_READS/EXECUTIONS
---------- ---------- ---------------------
SQL_TEXT
-----------------------------------------------------------------------------------------------
       671          4                167.75
select i.obj#, i.flags, u.name, o.name from sys.ind$ i, sys.obj$ o, sys.user$ u where
(bitand(i.flags, 256) = 256 or bitand(i.flags, 512) = 512) and o.obj#=i.obj# and o.owner#=u.user#

       927          1                   927
select distinct i.obj# from sys.idl_ub1$ i where i.obj#>=:1 and i.obj# not in (select d.p_obj# from
sys.dependency$ d)

       969          4                242.25
select i.obj#, i.flags, u.name, o.name     from sys.indpart$ i, sys.obj$ o, sys.user$ u, ind$ idx
where  bitand(i.flags, 512) = 512 and o.obj#=idx.obj# and           o.owner# = u.user# and
idx.obj#=i.bo#
```

Once the SQL statement with the highest reads per execution has been identified, it is good to have a quick look at the number of executions (or the total number of reads that the SQL statement has done). You will want to verify that the SQL statement being tuned is significant to the application instead of being one that is executed only once or at night, for example, in a batch job. You can also use the same query to identify the SQL statements that are executed most:

```
select Disk_Reads, Executions, Disk_Reads/Executions, Sql_Text
  from V$SQL
 where Executions != 0
 order by 2;
```

Of the 112 rows displayed for this query, the highest two values are presented here:

```
DISK_READS EXECUTIONS DISK_READS/EXECUTIONS
---------- ---------- ---------------------
SQL_TEXT
-----------------------------------------------------------------------------------------------
        30         84             .35714286
select obj#,type#,ctime,mtime,stime,status,dataobj#,flags,oid$ from obj$ where owner#=:1 and name=:2
and namespace=:3 and(remoteowner=:4 or remoteowner is null and :4 is null)and(linkname=:5 or
linkname is null and :5 is null)and(subname=:6 or subname is null and :6 is null)

         7       2900             .00241379
select job from sys.job$  where next_date < sysdate  and (field1 = :1 or field1 = 0) order by
next_date, job
```

By tuning the SQL, you can significantly improve the overall performance of your system. Tuning SQL statements is addressed in Chapter 11.

Reducing the Cost of I/Os

Each time Oracle has to process an I/O, there's a resource cost and wait time cost that must be paid. To help reduce the cost of I/Os, you can do the following:

- Increase the I/O speed.
- Check the wait time for each disk.

Faster disks can make a big difference. Also, using more disks to spread the I/O to different disks is the easiest and most consistent way to reduce I/O bottlenecks. The drawbacks are the cost of more or faster disks and the time it takes either to move datafiles from older, slower disks to newer, faster ones or to reconfigure the datafiles across the added disks.

You will be trying to find the disks with the highest wait time. Once you have identified them, check to see what objects reside on those disks. You may need to physically redistribute the data to reduce the wait times.

In order to determine which file may be causing a problem for I/O, you can use V$FILESTAT. Examine the ratio of Readtim (amount of time spent reading) and Phyrds (total number of reads) per file:

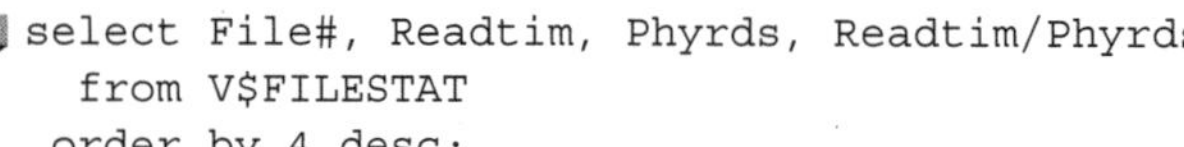

```
select File#, Readtim, Phyrds, Readtim/Phyrds
  from V$FILESTAT
 order by 4 desc;

FILE#      READTIM    PHYRDS     READTIM/PHYRDS
---------  ---------  ---------  --------------
        3         93         34       2.7352941
        1       2809       1757       1.5987479
        2         11         10             1.1
        4          0         24               0
        5          0          4               0
        6          0          4               0
        7          0          4               0

7 rows selected.
```

By showing the rows in descending order, the worst read time is always at the top of the list. To obtain the name of the file that has the worst read time, you can look it up in the V$DBFILE lookup table (explained in Chapter 9).

Look at the file with the highest read percentage out of the total reads and the highest read times. If the average cost per I/O is high, you may need to redistribute the I/O. If you are using a Windows NT system, be sure to check whether the drive numbers you are looking at are different drives or just logical drives representing partitions of the same disk. You can use the NT Disk Administrator tool to determine the physical drive on which each partition exists.

Free Buffer Waits

Free buffer waits may be caused by the session's scanning the buffer cache for a free buffer. If there are none available, a foreground process must wait for dirty buffers to be written to disk. Check for the following statistics in V$SYSSTAT and V$SESSTAT:

- **Free buffer inspected** The number of dirty and pinned buffers skipped before a free buffer is found
- **Free buffer requested** The number of buffers requested to store data by all sessions
- **Dirty buffers inspected** The number of dirty buffers (buffers that need to be flushed to disk before they can be reused by sessions)

The following formula will calculate the average number of buffers that a session is scanning at the end of an LRU to find a free buffer:

Average Number of Buffers Scanned = Free Buffer Inspected / Free Buffer Requested

This is, unfortunately, one of the areas in which you will have to make some manual calculations. You can select the values from V$SYSSTAT or V$SESSTAT, but then you will need to manually perform the math to get the average number of buffers that are being scanned. The query that you can use to obtain the values is as follows:

```
column Name format a30
select Statistic#, Name, Value
  from V$SYSSTAT
 where Name like 'free%'
    or Name like 'dirty%';

STATISTIC# NAME                                VALUE
---------- ------------------------------ ---------
        47 free buffer requested               3931
        48 dirty buffers inspected                0
        51 free buffer inspected                  0
```

If the average number is close to zero, a process can find a buffer on average very quickly.

Latch Free Waits

With a high number of latch free waits, you will need to determine which latch is being requested the most. Two of the most highly contended latches are the shared pool latch and the library cache latch. Each of these latches can be held for a long time. There can also be a great deal of contention for the redo allocation latch. The redo allocation latch is used for allocating space in the log buffer when foregrounds need to write redo records.

All of these latches are potential points of contention. In the case of the library cache latches and shared pool latch, the number of "latch gets" occurring is influenced directly by the amount of activity in the shared pool, especially parse operations. Anything that can minimize the number of latch gets and, indeed, the amount of activity in the shared pool is helpful to both performance and scalability.

First, you can use V$LATCH to determine the latch with the highest sleep count:

```
select Name, Sleeps
  from V$LATCH
 where Sleeps > 0
 order by Sleeps
/
```

Since V$LATCH only shows the parent latch, check V$LATCH_CHILDREN to determine which child latch (if any) has the most contention:

```
select Name, Sleeps
  from V$LATCH_CHILDREN
 where Name = <latch name>
   and Sleeps > <minimum base>
order by Sleeps
/
```

Depending on the latch type, you can make many different changes. Let's take a look at the type of latch and the changes that you can make.

SHARED POOL LATCH AND LIBRARY CACHE LATCH Every time an application makes a parse call for a SQL statement and the parsed representation of the statement is not in the shared SQL area, Oracle parses and allocates space for the SQL in the library cache. The shared pool and library cache latches protect these operations. Once the SQL area becomes fragmented and available memory is reduced, the single-threaded shared pool latch may become a bottleneck. Contention for these latches can be achieved by increasing sharing of SQL and reducing parsing by keeping cursors open between executions.

CACHE BUFFER HASH CHAIN LATCH Each hash chain latch protects a hash chain composed of a number of buffer headers, which, in turn, point to the buffer itself. This latch is acquired every time a buffer is queried or updated. The number of latches defaults to prime (0.25 x db_block_buffers). There could be a large number of latches, so you must add the clause "where sleeps > <*some number*>" to filter out most of the latches. Find the latch with the highest number of sleeps. Once you've found it, find the buffers that are protected by that latch. Here's the script to accomplish this task:

```
select Hladdr, Dbafil, Dbablk
    from X$BH b, V$LATCH_CHILDREN l
    where l.Name = (latch_name)
    and l.Addr  = Hladdr
    and Sleeps >= <maxsleeps>;
```

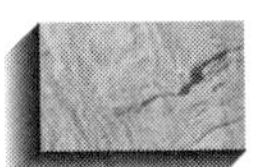

NOTE
Use the column File# instead of Dbafil in Oracle8.

When the Dbafil and Dbablk values are found, check DBA_EXTENTS to see what the object name and type is. Here is the code:

```
select Segment_Name, Segment_Type
  from DBA_EXTENTS
 where File = <file>
   and <block> between Block_Id and Block_Id + Blocks - 1;
```

Log File Sync

Log file sync happens at commit time when a foreground process is waiting for the LGWR to complete. If the LGWR process is too active, too much redo latch contention can occur. Another reason for a "small average redo write size" could be that LGWR is unable to piggyback many commits. The whole system may not be very busy, resulting in LGWR waking up immediately (when posted) and writing the redo for a session. Thus, the next session may have to wait for this write to complete before its redo will be written. The maximum I/O size for the redo writer is also port specific. The normal values can range from 64K to 128K.

Enqueue

V$SYSSTAT/V$SESSTAT will show some interesting information here:

- **Enqueue gets** The number of enqueue "get" operations that are performed. For example, getting the ST lock will count as an enqueue get.
- **Enqueue converts** The number of enqueue convert operations that are performed. For example, converting an enqueue from S (shared) mode to X (exclusive) mode.

- **Enqueue releases** Most enqueues that are obtained are then released. This means the number of conversions will be minimal or nonexistent on most systems.
- **Enqueue waits** The number of times a session tried to get an enqueue but could not get one right away (this is true for enqueue gets and enqueue conversions). Some tuning sources state that if the enqueue waits are high, **enqueue_resources** need to be increased. This is incorrect. Waits just indicate that an enqueue could not be granted. If **enqueue_resources** are depleted, an appropriate message indicating the need to increase resources is returned immediately.
- **Enqueue deadlocks** Indicates the number of deadlocks detected for the session or the number of ORA-60 errors returned to the session.
- **Enqueue timeouts** If an enqueue could not be granted, the session will have to wait (enqueue waits). Within this wait, there can be several timeouts.

Look in V$LOCK or V$SESSION_WAIT to see what the enqueue sessions are currently waiting on:

```
select *
  from V$SESSION_WAIT
 where Event = 'enqueue';
```

Join V$SESSION_WAIT with V$SESSION with V$SQL to find the current SQL statement and object for this session. Using the SID (Session_ID) from V$SESSION_WAIT, you can find the SQL statement waiting for an enqueue:

```
select a.Sid, a.Username, b.Sql_Text
  from V$SESSION a, V$SQL b
 where Sid = <sid value>
   and a.User# = b.Parsing_User_Id;
```

Write Complete Waits

When a buffer is being written, it cannot change until the buffer is flushed to disk. The most common reason for this is frequent checkpointing. Normally, a hot buffer will stay at the most recently used end of the LRU, and the chance that it will be written is small.

Checkpointing occurs normally because of small redo log files or a low default setting for the log_checkpoint_interval.

SQL*Net More Data from Client/SQL*Net More Data to Client

When the application design is not judged a culprit, sometimes the network can be responsible for most of the wait time (or latency). *Network latency* is defined by the time it takes to gain access to a particular network device accompanied by the time it takes to transmit the data to the next device in the network. This latency can vary greatly based on the type of network, the opportunity to transmit on the network (bandwidth utilization), and distance traveled. Once the network has been created, however, the latency for each network packet that is being sent can vary. Thus, optimizing the performance of an application on a network can be done in two ways: by reducing the number of network packets or by reducing the latency (reducing the cost per packet).

To reduce the number of network packets:

- Bundle packages into bundled and/or deferred Oracle calls.
- Use array operations.
- Use a different session layer protocol (HTTP instead of SQL*Net or Net8 as in Web server–based applications).

To reduce the latency (reduce the cost per packet):

- Use Gigabit Ethernet in the backbone or data center.
- Use ATM or SONAT for the wide area network.

Solving the Problem at XYZ Company

Back at XYZ, you were able to run the queries to determine the components of your response time equation. You found that you were spending 85 percent of the time working and the remainder waiting for some resource. Further investigation showed that a majority of the CPU time was in the "other" category, related to application usage.

You then checked to see what SQL was running during one of the slowdown periods and found queries running related to the new planning department application. You have found the source of the problem! Good job! Now, your options are

- Work with the planning department to tune the queries and educate the staff on SQL tuning (reducing service time).
- If possible and the business requirements allow it, queue these queries for execution during off-peak hours or to another system specifically designed for their reporting needs.

Common Causes of Performance Problems

Some causes of performance problems that you will find when you are working either proactively or reactively on tuning will be design-time issues. You will have little control over these issues. There are other causes that you'll have more access to and control over, and we'll discuss some of these in the following sections.

Application and Database Design Faults

The designer may have designed the application with inherent bottlenecks, such as a sequence table that becomes a single-threaded choke point. You will see this design problem show up in many ways. In the sequence table example, you might see errors in the alert log signifying deadlocks or find that a particular block is being accessed frequently. You'd see this as a higher overall wait time in your transactions.

A bad design is difficult to correct the further you are in development of the system. Although we can provide you with tips, there is no easy way to see if your particular design will perform well. Thus, the best advice that we can give you is to test the system as heavily as possible during the development cycle.

Inefficient Datafile Layout and Storage Configuration

As the database grows in size, and when it is under high loads, I/O contention may indicate deficiencies in I/O distribution, striping, and object layout plans. In Chapter 5, we discussed identifying deficiencies in I/O distribution. The problem is relatively easy to fix by moving the more frequently accessed datafiles to different, less busy disks if possible.

Inappropriate db_block_size for the Application

The database block size can be defined only once—at database creation time. The block size determines how much information will be paged into memory with each read. Since physical reads are the most expensive operation, the size of the block can have a great deal of impact on the performance of the system. However, there is a balance to be struck. Bringing in too much information at one time can cause a problem by flushing other needed data out of the database block buffers too quickly. Therefore, you must put thought into your **db_block_size** decision before you build your database.

The default block size, 2K, is usually too small for all but the simplest of applications. A good rule of thumb is to make the block size either 4K or 8K for applications that are mostly OLTP, and 8K or higher for applications that are mostly batch. You can identify problems with a block size that is too small by delays in the application response time due to the need to read data into the buffers more frequently. You'll be able to identify problems with too large a block size by the amount of time it takes to read data into the buffer and by problems getting needed latches on block headers.

Inappropriate Settings for Database Objects

Some values for the database objects, if set incorrectly, can impact performance. Let's look at them now.

Inittrans

The inittrans value controls the amount of space set aside in the Oracle block header for DML transactions to register the fact that they are modifying a particular block. The default value for inittrans is 1. Any other transactions that want to modify the block will have to allocate additional space for their control information during their transaction.

Maxtrans

The maxtrans header limits the total number of transactions that can access a block. The default value for maxtrans is usually 255, but it depends somewhat on the block size and space available in the block.

Freelists

Freelists are the lists of free blocks within the segment. How space is managed in data blocks is controlled by the pctfree and pctused settings. The pctfree parameter determines how much of the block is reserved for the growth of rows that are already in the data block. The pctused parameter determines at what threshold a block can be released back to the freelist. The freelist can be a source of contention for systems that have a large amount of updates. Contention will show up in the V$SYSTEM_WAIT or V$SESSION_WAIT view. Careful choice of these parameters based on the type of application you are running can reduce the amount of activity on the freelist and the amount of unused storage in a block.

Unsuitable Sizing and Number of Rollback Segments

Contention for the rollback segments will show up in the V$SYSTEM_WAIT or V$SESSION_WAIT view for any of the following waits: undo header, undo block, system undo header, system undo block. If the values of these waits are greater than

1 percent of the total number of reads done in your system, consider adding more rollback segments.

Poor Application Design

As we've said before, poorly designed applications are usually the major cause of performance issues on your system. Let's look more closely at some of the issues involved with poor application design.

Poorly Tuned Application Code

Nothing will reduce the overall performance of a system faster than bad application SQL! Monitor the V$SQL view for application code that is running overlong or requires many disk reads. Tips for detecting and tuning poorly written SQL are discussed in Chapter 11. A quick fix can sometimes be found in the statistics used to generate the query plan. Problems could be caused by out-of-date or nonexistent statistics with the Cost Based Optimizer (CBO). If the optimizer does not have the most up-to-date statistics, there is a greater chance that the plan will be less than optimal.

Shared Pool Issues

Performance will be improved by minimizing fragmentation in the shared pool and reducing the amount of time required to parse a SQL statement. Parsing is the work done by the database to validate the SQL statement and generate the query plan used for execution. One way to reduce parsing is to make sure you can reuse existing parsed statements as much as possible. Sharing SQL statements in the shared pool will help to ensure that Oracle will reuse existing parsed statements.

You can force more reuse of statements by making sure the statements are the same. For a SQL statement to be the same, everything about that SQL statement needs to be the same, including the capitalization and spacing. Sharing SQL cuts down on the time that any individual statement executes by reducing or eliminating the time needed to parse the statement, thus reducing the number of hard parses. (We discussed hard parses earlier in the section "Decomposing CPU Time.")

Bind variables are another factor that can influence SQL statement reuse. Bind variables allow parameters to be passed to the statement at execution time and make the statement more likely to be reused. There are some trade-offs when using bind variables though. The CBO will need to make assumptions that may be incorrect about data distribution. However, appropriate hints can help to overcome the CBO's incorrect assumptions.

Initialization Parameters

Some of the initialization parameters have great impact on the performance of your system. Let's take a look at them now.

OPTIMIZER_MODE The value for **optimizer_mode** in the init.ora file tells the database server which optimizer setting to use when generating an execution plan. The setting RULE invokes the Rule Based Optimizer, which will heavily favor the use of indexes. The setting CHOOSE will invoke the Cost Based Optimizer if statistics exist on any one of the tables involved in the SQL statement. FIRST_ROWS will invoke the CBO for any query, using default statistics for any table that does not have them. This setting will tend to produce plans that favor the return of rows quickly, even if the overall execution is a little longer than optimal. ALL_ROWS will behave the same as FIRST_ROWS with regard to the optimizer and statistics, but will favor producing the optimal plan.

The biggest "gotcha" here is the statistics when using the CBO. If the statistics are out of date and do not reflect the true distribution of data in the tables, the query plans will likely be suboptimal. These statistics are created and maintained by the **analyze** command. You need to remember that session-level parameters and hints can override the optimizer mode setting.

SHARED_POOL_SIZE The **shared_pool_size** variable controls the size of the memory area used for parsing and executing SQL statements. In general, a large number of hard parses indicates that you need more memory for your system (although sharing SQL statements, as noted above, also influences that value). As with all memory parameters, this value should not be increased to the point where swapping of memory pages occurs at the operating system level.

SORT_AREA_SIZE This parameter controls the amount of memory allocated to each process in the Process Global Area (PGA) for any sorting activity (for Multi-Threaded Server (MTS), this memory is allocated in the shared pool). When a process needs more memory than is available for a sort operation, disk space must be allocated in the temporary tablespace. The **sort_area_size** is a value that will need to be tuned depending on the transaction mix of the application. An indicator that this memory might need to be increased (if available physical memory allows) would be a high ratio of sorts to disk, as seen in the V$SYSSTAT view. Changes to **sort_area_size** should be done cautiously, since this value impacts all sessions.

To see the values for sorts on your system, you can use the following query:

```
column Name format a30
column Value format 999999999999
select a.Name, Value
  from V$STATNAME a, V$SYSSTAT
 where a.Statistic# = V$SYSSTAT.Statistic#
   and a.Name in ('sorts (disk)','sorts (memory)','sorts (rows)')
```

```
NAME                                          VALUE
-------------------------------- ---------------
sorts (memory)                                 6095
sorts (disk)                                      4
sorts (rows)                                  15049
```

From this output, you can see that very few sorts are being performed to disk.

SORT_DIRECT_WRITES Setting the correct value for this parameter can improve system performance of sorting, or overall performance if sorting is a large part of the system load. This parameter can be set to TRUE, which tells the server to allocate some additional memory for sorting outside the buffer cache. A process will gain the benefit of some additional memory if **sort_direct_writes** is set to TRUE because the process can use the additional memory for sorting but does not need to incur the cost of buffer cache management. Setting **sort_direct_writes** to TRUE stops pages from being flushed from the buffers that might be needed by another process.

DB_BLOCK_BUFFERS This parameter is expressed in database blocks and controls how much memory is available in the buffer cache for data blocks.

DB_FILE_MULTI_BLOCK_READ_COUNT This parameter controls the number of blocks read into the buffer cache in a single read during a full table scan. Oracle will read this many blocks into the cache from the first block needed, on the assumption that this read ahead to populate the buffer cache will be more efficient than single block reads (it usually is!). On most ports of Oracle, there is a limit of 64K total for **db_file_multi_block_read_count** times **db_block_size**, although on some ports, such as newer versions of Solaris, the maximum value is larger.

Oracle Redo Logs

Sometimes, you will see waits in the system due to a high redo log switch rate. Redo logs that are sized too small will cause frequent checkpoints, which cause a flush of all committed data buffers to disk from the data cache. A spike in writes to your datafiles and a delay in the processing of other statements while the checkpoint completes can occur. You can tune the number of checkpoints with the checkpoint_process variable. Remember, though, that when Oracle comes to the physical end of any log, a log switch will occur, which will force a checkpoint.

There are trade-offs here as well. If you set the redo logs very large with an equally large checkpoint interval, when a thread switch does occur, Oracle will need a longer amount of time to write the redo information to disk. Also, the length of time between checkpoints has implications in the amount of time that you will need for recovery in the event of a database failure.

PART IV

Database Protection

Backup and Recovery

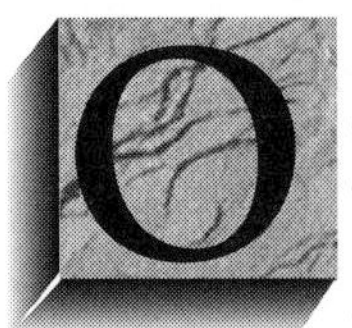
ne of the authors is an avid recreational walker who participates in an organized walking sport called Volksmarching. There's a saying among the walking group members that goes, "There are only two kinds of walkers in the world: those who have gotten lost on a trail and those who will." We'd like to paraphrase that statement and make it: There are only two kinds of DBAs in the world: those who have had a database crash and those who will!

Throughout this book, we've made references to backing up and recovering your database. As you've probably noticed, we tend to be very opinionated about some areas of database administration. Well, backups are another topic that we're very opinionated about. We believe that there are very few good reasons *not* to back up your database or parts of it. You see, we've all suffered more than one catastrophic experience with a "downed production database" in our lives, and we'd like to share with you the lessons that we've learned from these experiences.

As an Oracle DBA, you have a responsibility to ensure that data within your database is protected and recoverable. Oracle provides several tools to enable you to perform these duties. For years, DBAs have relied on utilities like export and import and the manual implementation of online or offline files-level backups to protect their systems. With the introduction of Oracle8, some new features and utilities have been added to provide new options and, hopefully, improve the way the backup tasks can be performed.

With the advent of Internet commerce, databases that are maintained with high availability have become more prevalent. The need to keep a database available seven days a week, 24 hours a day has created a demand for third-party vendors to supply viable solutions. Oracle's answer to this requirement is to provide a standby database. We'll look closely at how to implement a standby database using Oracle only since we feel that third-party vendor solutions are outside the scope of this book.

In this chapter, we'll talk about the considerations involved in preparing your disaster recovery strategies, and we'll provide you with an overview of the current tools that are available for helping you protect your systems.

About Backups

If you own an automobile, you probably have a spare tire in the trunk. Why? Well, to ensure that, should you get a flat tire on a dark road in the middle of the night coming home from work, you'll be able to change that tire and continue home safely. (We won't even go into why you might be coming home late at night from work!) In other words, you have a contingency strategy. You have the tools you need to implement your strategy: a spare tire, a jack, a tire iron, and some lubricant to put on the lug nuts to help loosen them up. You know the basic procedures to change a tire, or you have a manual that can guide you through the process. You might never have that flat tire, but at least you are prepared in case of an emergency. And, of course, the probability is that if you were not prepared, disaster would surely strike.

In the same way, we're suggesting you prepare in advance for the possibility that your database will experience some problem that could cause a loss of data to your system. As cited in the *Oracle8 Backup and Recovery Handbook*, by Rama Velpuri and Anand Adkoli (Osborne/McGraw-Hill, 1998), the IEEE defines four different categories of outages that can occur on a system:

- Physical
- Design (software bug)
- Operations
- Environment

Let's think about what constitutes an outage of each type. Physical outages are hardware failures: a disk, controller, or CPU goes bad. Equipment ages. There's no way of getting around that fact. Each piece of equipment has an expected life span. Most computer equipment we've seen seems to fail well before the manufacturer's designated life span date. If a disk is beginning to go bad, signs of this problem may show up as corrupted blocks in your database. In that case, Oracle will give you ample warning that a problem is brewing by issuing an ORA-000600 error with an appropriate set of arguments. (Oracle Support will be able to tell you what the arguments of a 600 error mean.) By letting your systems operations people know that you have found a corrupted block error in the database, they may be able to track down what's going wrong on the system—a disk or a controller going bad—before the problem reaches catastrophic proportions.

Most operating systems provide hardware error reporting tools. System administrators regularly check reports produced by these tools. The reports give details of both permanent and temporary errors. A sign of a disk going bad is a steady increase in the number of temporary errors. You can ask the system administrator to forward these reports to you so that you can monitor for temporary errors as well. Your alert logs, as discussed in Chapter 4, can also provide indications of disk access problems. Watch for errors that end with a number in the 600 range.

Design outages occur when software code fails. We generally refer to these outages as software bugs and/or viruses. The problem code can come from your software vendor (Oracle-delivered executables, for example), from your in-house applications developers, or from shareware or freeware code downloaded from an Internet site.

Operations outages are always caused by a human being. For example, a person accidentally issues an incorrect command using a privileged account in your production database and truncates a table, or someone walks out to a machine in your computer room and pulls a disk out of a slot because she thinks the disk has failed. She inadvertently pulls out the wrong disk. Oops!

Environmental outages are generally disasters caused by nature: lightning strikes, fires, floods, and so on. Having a storage area off-site that contains the most current backups and a hard-copy listing of what's in the backups could save your company huge volumes of downtime. If warranted, you can have a contract with your hardware vendor that states the equipment that will be replaced and the time frame in which the new hardware will be made available to you and your systems group. Having an off-site location where equipment can be placed that will still enable connection to your network is also recommended. If your computer room burns to the ground, how fast will your company be able to recover its systems and be back in business?

Any of these outages can strike your facility at any time. It's your job to be prepared for them beforehand. Remember, too, that there is no one correct answer to the question, "What should I do to protect *my* systems?" Only you and your management can determine the correct answer for your company.

Backup Considerations

You must answer many questions before you can determine what backup approach is right for your environment. You'll first need to determine how much downtime is acceptable. In a test environment, it might be acceptable for your database to be down for a day or two. In a shop that is running a Web-based business that must be accessible 24 hours a day, 7 days a week, 365 days a year, a two-hour outage might result in hundreds of thousands of dollars in lost revenue and would be unacceptable. How do you make this determination? Well, truthfully, you are probably not the person who will decide. You see, many different cost factors play into how long a database outage can be tolerated, and even your immediate management might not be able to make that decision. The cost of a database outage can be measured by several factors:

- Amount of data loss that can be tolerated
- Cost of salaries for people who will not be able to work unless the database is available
- Number of orders that may be lost because customers can't reach your database
- Number of customers who will never come back to your site because they can't reach your database
- Expense of the equipment that's required to implement a specific disaster recovery strategy

- Number of hours it will take to perform a complete database recovery
- Cost of training for one or more people to perform a database recovery

Each of these areas requires a decision that can normally only be made by the people who allocate and authorize money for expenditures in your company. All you can really do is raise the issues and make suggestions on what the costs of a catastrophic outage will be, what equipment is required to implement each backup scenario, and what your recommendations are.

When presenting options to management, always put things in terms of money. For example, you can say something like, "This is how much we would lose if the system is unavailable for, say, four hours, and these are the costs of implementing the recovery options." Management understands money talk! Do not put too much technical detail in a report aimed at management. It will only annoy them. Save technical talk for the senior technicians.

To be able to express your concerns and recommendations competently, you must learn the options available for protecting your company's data from harm. In the next several sections, we'll explore the various backup options and how each one is used.

Offline Database Backups

An *offline database backup,* also referred to at times as a *cold backup, image backup,* or *files-level backup,* derives its name from the fact that the database is shut down to perform this action. You must ensure that no processes are active within the database when you attempt to shut down the database. A good shutdown procedure will include verification that all processes have been stopped before a **shutdown normal** command (the Oracle recommended command) is performed. With the use of Oracle Enterprise Manager (OEM) to enable remote database management, an Intelligent Agent is attached to your database at all times. If you are using OEM and have an active Intelligent Agent on your system, you will use a **shutdown immediate** command instead. The only time a **shutdown immediate** command will not complete is when a deadlock situation is present in your database at the time the command is issued. If a deadlock situation exists, the **shutdown abort** command must be used to shut the database down completely. (See Chapter 10 for more information about deadlocks.) Under normal conditions, however, you should never have to issue a **shutdown abort** command.

Performing an Offline Backup

Once the database is shut down, each file that makes up the database is copied either to another disk or to tape. You should be sure to include all datafiles, redo logs, control files, and the init.ora file when you perform the files-level backup.

There are many different system-dependent utilities that you can use to perform the actual backup of the files. Among them are

- **UNIX** OBACKUP, TAR, DD, FBACKUP, or CPIO
- **VMS** BACKUP
- **Windows NT** Backup Manager or OCOPY
- **MAC** GUI Finder to copy to disk, third-party software such as Dantz Retrospect
- **OS/2** Standard DOS/OS2 copy
- **NetWare** NetWare NBACKUP utility, third-party software
- **MVS** DFDSS or IDCAMS using EXPORT (not REPRO)

After the files-level copy process is completed, you can restart the database. Once the copy is completed, if a disaster occurs, the database can be recovered to the condition it was in when the copy was made. Thus, if you make your file copies at midnight on Monday and your database crashes at noon on Tuesday, all transactions that were performed in your database from Monday at midnight until Tuesday at noon will be lost. Performing an offline backup by itself is like taking a photograph of your database as it is at one particular moment. The database condition is frozen at the point in time when the database was shut down. This is a very important factor to keep in mind as you begin to plan your backup strategies.

Besides the possibility of data loss, a disadvantage of performing a files-level copy of your database is that it is very difficult, though not impossible, to recover one or more individual tables easily because you are making copies of the entire contents of each datafile and not each specific table.

Used in conjunction with archive log mode (we'll talk more about that in just a minute), the database can be recovered to a **point in time** later than the point at which the cold backup was performed. Also, if archive log mode has been enabled on your system, you have the option of continuing to restore the database (applying archive logs to the database) until you specifically cancel the recovery operation, called **until cancel**.

Enabling Archive Log Mode

If you think about a video recorder, you know that you can record a message to your grandmother wishing her a happy birthday. You rewind the tape and send it off to her. She receives the tape and plays through your message and is delighted to hear both your good wishes and your voice. In fact, she's so excited by your thoughtful recording that she calls in all of her neighbors and plays the tape over and over for anyone who will listen. Keep Grandma and her tape recording in mind as we discuss the concepts behind enabling archive log mode on your system.

We've mentioned the term archive log mode in a few other chapters, but we haven't really talked about what that means or how to enable it. What better time to talk about this feature than now? We've talked about redo log files and their use in an Oracle database. When you enable archive log mode, you tell Oracle that as each redo log file fills up, you want an exact copy of that filled redo log file to be copied to one or more disk locations. In Oracle7.3, you can only have archive logs copied to one location. In Oracle8.0, you can have them copied to two locations, and in Oracle8i, you can have them copied to up to five different locations on different disks and even to a remote site.

Why would you want to copy redo log files? Well, we've mentioned before that Oracle writes to the redo log files in a circular fashion. When a redo log file fills up, Oracle switches over and begins writing to the next redo log file. Once Oracle has filled the entire set of redo log files, it starts over at the first one and overwrites the contents of that redo log file. If you save the contents of a redo log file by archiving it before Oracle begins to overwrite the old data, you can "roll forward" through the file, replaying the transactions, much like Grandma can rewind that tape of yours and bore her neighbors over and over again.

Let's go back to our scenario of performing your files-level backups at midnight on Monday and losing the database at noon on Tuesday, 12 hours later. If you have archive log mode enabled on your system, you've been making copies of each of the redo log files as they filled up. You have a complete set of all the transactions that occurred on your system over the last 12 hours. You can literally play through the archive log files and recover your database up to the last committed transaction, if you want to, or you can play through the archive log files to a specific point in time or to a specific archive log file number.

When you perform a database recovery and play through the archive logs on the system, you are actually said to be restoring the database to a point in the future. Hmm, what does that really mean? Well, the files that make up your database were copied at midnight on Monday. If you must perform a database recovery on Tuesday at noon, you are restoring your database to a point in time much later than Monday midnight, or to a point in time beyond when the original backup was made. But if you restore the files from last night, the redo log files and control files are from last night too. How will Oracle know that you want to restore to a time in the future? Great question!

Before you restore your files from last night's backup, you save the current redo log files and control files to a safe place where they will not be overwritten by last night's files. You can then restore the files from the backup and replace the older log files from your backup with the current saved ones. At this point, if you attempt to start the database, Oracle will look at the current control file and redo log files and see that their checksums do not match the information in the restored files. Oracle will tell you that your database needs recovery, and you can then tell Oracle to begin playing through the archived log files to recover the database.

An important factor to keep in mind if you are considering using backups that copy the physical datafiles as your only method of backups is that the entire database will be unavailable to users while you are performing database recovery.

Many different backup and recovery scenarios are discussed in the *Oracle8 Backup and Recovery Handbook* mentioned earlier. For a really complete picture of backup and recovery, we highly recommend this book.

Online Database Backups

Online database backups are essential for a 24 x 7 environment. They derive their name from the fact that the database remains up and running while the backup is performed. Essentially, you perform the same files-level copies of the datafiles and control files, but you do not back up the redo log files. Archive log mode must be enabled so that Oracle knows the database is recoverable. Online backups are also known as *hot backups*.

While with an offline backup you must back up all the files of the database at once, with an online backup you can back up some or all of the files at any one time. The smallest unit you can back up is a tablespace. To begin an online backup of a tablespace's datafile(s), you put the tablespace into backup mode by issuing the command

```
alter tablespace <ts_name> begin backup;
```

There are some procedures that you must follow if effective hot backups are to be made:

- Be sure to take the tablespace out of backup mode by issuing the command **alter tablespace <ts_name> end backup** once you complete the file copies of each tablespace's datafiles.
- Archive the current redo log file by completing a log switch. You will use the **alter system switch logfile;** command.
- Capture all archived redo logs that have been created from the time the backup was started through the time the backup is completed.
- Back up the control file using the **alter database backup controlfile to <filespec>;** command, where the **filespec** parameter is the complete directory path and file name of the location where you want the control file written.

As with offline backups, individual tables cannot easily be recovered. Unlike offline backups, the database can be recovered to a point in time or until you cancel the recovery. During normal database operations, only the changed information of a transaction is written to the redo log file and archived log files. However, during the time that the **alter tablespace begin backup** command is in effect, the entire block containing changed data is written to the log files. Thus, the volume of log files generated can become quite large if there are a lot of changes going on in your system while online backups are being performed. Therefore, Oracle recommends that you perform online backups during periods when less DML is occurring on the system.

As of Oracle8i, if you are using the Oracle-supplied Recovery Manager (RMAN), you will not have to manually place the tablespaces in and out of backup mode. Oracle will handle these actions automatically for you. We'll talk more about RMAN later in this chapter.

Logical Database Backups (Exports)

Let's take a second to go back to Grandma and your tape recording. By now, she's played that tape so often that her friends and neighbors are avoiding her. Poor thing! The concept of making a copy of something that you can replay over and over again can be applied both to files-level backups and to an Oracle-supplied utility called *export*.

An export, like an offline backup, is actually a snapshot in time. Instead of making a copy of the datafiles that reside on your system, you make a binary copy of the objects and their data as they exist within your database. In other words, when you export your entire database, you make a copy of each individual table, index, view, synonym, package, procedure, trigger, and so on, that makes up your database. The export file can be read by another utility called *import* that enables you to restore your database to the point in time that the export was performed.

Unlike an online or offline backup with archive log mode enabled, you cannot restore a database using the import utility to a time in the future. In other words, there is no way to apply archive log files to an import to bring it to another point in time beyond when the export was made.

One of the major advantages of making an export file of your database is that you can easily restore one or more tables or an entire schema if you need to. If you've been careful to keep each application's database structure in its own specific tablespace, you can recover only one schema without affecting other applications in your database.

Types of Exports

There are several types of export that you can perform:

- **Full** A complete database export
- **Owner** A complete schema or user export
- **Tables** A single table or set of tables within one or more schemas

In **full** mode, the complete database is exported. Here's what happens during a full database export: Oracle reads the entire data dictionary and writes the data dictionary language (DDL) commands needed to re-create the entire database to the export dump file. The export dump file, with a default name of expdat.dmp, includes definitions for all tablespaces, all users, and all of the objects, data, and privileges in their schemas. If you need to re-create the complete database, you can use the dump file from your full export to perform this task.

In **owner** mode, Oracle reads the data dictionary and exports the specified user's objects, as well as the data within those objects. Oracle will include all of the grants and indexes created by the user on the user's objects in the export file. However, if there are any grants and/or indexes that were created by users other than the owner, they are not included in a user mode export.

In **tables** mode, one or more tables are exported. You tell Oracle which table or tables you want exported and Oracle places the table's structure, indexes, and grants in the export file along with its data, based on the parameters that you specify. You can use **tables** mode to export the full set of tables owned by a user (by specifying the schema owner, but no table names). You can also specify partitions of a table to export.

There are also several different forms of export that can be performed using the parameter **inctype**:

- **Complete** Captures a full database export
- **Incremental** Captures the changes made from the last incremental export forward
- **Cumulative** Captures the changes made since the last full export was performed

In all of the above cases, **full=y** must be used. The **inctype** parameter lets you export only those tables that have changed since the last export was performed. Keep in mind, though, that if any row in a table has changed, the entire table will be exported using an **incremental** or **cumulative** export. Hmm, does that mean that if just one block in each table in your database has changed since the last export, the entire database is going to be exported, even though you specified **incremental**? Yep! That's exactly what it means. Thus, you may not save much space or time performing an export using the **inctype** parameter. Well, then, why use it at all? The advantage of using **inctype** is that Oracle will keep track of your export activity automatically if you use this parameter. If you do not want the information to be stored in your database, you can set the parameter **record=n**. The information about an export that has been performed using **inctype** can be seen from the views:

- **SYS.INCEXP** Shows the objects in specific exports

- **SYS.INCFIL** Contains the incremental and cumulative export information
- **SYS.INCVID** Displays the ExpID and is used to determine the next ExpID

To see the full list of the available export parameters, you can issue the command **exp help=y** at the operating system command prompt. Figure 13-1 shows an actual screen print of the output of the command, and Table 13-1 explains each of the commands and their meanings in Oracle8i. As we have with previous chapters, we'll mark the commands that are new in 8.0 with a * and commands that were added in 8i with a **.

Before you can perform an export of a database, the database must be up and opened. Export files are very portable, and you can use them to move or copy a database from one system to another. However, the process of exporting an entire database can be very slow and may not be feasible for very large databases. An interesting point to keep in mind is that the export process will identify any data

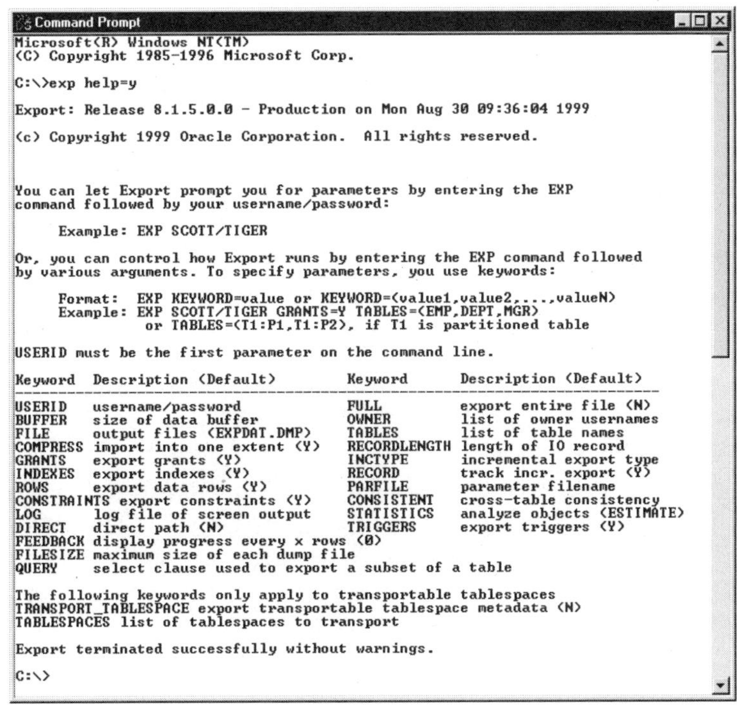

```
Command Prompt
Microsoft(R) Windows NT(TM)
(C) Copyright 1985-1996 Microsoft Corp.

C:\>exp help=y

Export: Release 8.1.5.0.0 - Production on Mon Aug 30 09:36:04 1999

(c) Copyright 1999 Oracle Corporation.  All rights reserved.


You can let Export prompt you for parameters by entering the EXP
command followed by your username/password:

     Example: EXP SCOTT/TIGER

Or, you can control how Export runs by entering the EXP command followed
by various arguments. To specify parameters, you use keywords:

     Format:  EXP KEYWORD=value or KEYWORD=(value1,value2,...,valueN)
     Example: EXP SCOTT/TIGER GRANTS=Y TABLES=(EMP,DEPT,MGR)
               or TABLES=(T1:P1,T1:P2), if T1 is partitioned table

USERID must be the first parameter on the command line.

Keyword  Description (Default)        Keyword      Description (Default)
--------------------------------------------------------------------------
USERID   username/password            FULL         export entire file (N)
BUFFER   size of data buffer          OWNER        list of owner usernames
FILE     output files (EXPDAT.DMP)    TABLES       list of table names
COMPRESS import into one extent (Y)   RECORDLENGTH length of IO record
GRANTS   export grants (Y)            INCTYPE      incremental export type
INDEXES  export indexes (Y)           RECORD       track incr. export (Y)
ROWS     export data rows (Y)         PARFILE      parameter filename
CONSTRAINTS export constraints (Y)    CONSISTENT   cross-table consistency
LOG      log file of screen output    STATISTICS   analyze objects (ESTIMATE)
DIRECT   direct path (N)              TRIGGERS     export triggers (Y)
FEEDBACK display progress every x rows (0)
FILESIZE maximum size of each dump file
QUERY    select clause used to export a subset of a table

The following keywords only apply to transportable tablespaces
TRANSPORT_TABLESPACE export transportable tablespace metadata (N)
TABLESPACES list of tablespaces to transport

Export terminated successfully without warnings.

C:\>
```

FIGURE 13-1. *Export command screen output for Oracle8i*

Keyword	Description
USERID	Username/password of the account running the export. If this is the first parameter after the **exp** command, this keyword does not have to be specified
BUFFER	Size of the buffer used to fetch data rows. The default is system dependent; this value is usually set to a high value (> 64,000)
FILE	Name of the export dump file
FILESIZE**	Maximum size for an export dump file. If multiple files are listed in the **file** entry, the export will be directed to those files based on the **filesize** setting
COMPRESS	Y/N flag to indicate whether export should compress fragmented segments into single extents. This affects the **storage** clauses that will be stored in the export file for those objects
GRANTS	Y/N flag to indicate whether grants on database objects will be exported
INDEXES	Y/N flag to indicate whether indexes on tables will be exported
ROWS	Y/N flag to indicate whether rows should be exported. If this is set to N, only the DDL for the database objects will be created in the export file
CONSTRAINTS	Y/N flag to indicate whether constraints on tables are exported
FULL	Set to Y to perform a **full** database export
OWNER	List of database accounts to be exported. User exports of those accounts may then be performed
TABLES	List of tables to be exported. Table exports of those tables may then be performed
RECORDLENGTH	Length, in bytes, of the dump export file record. Usually left at the default value unless you are going to transfer the export file between different operating systems
INCTYPE	Type of export being performed (valid values are **complete** (default), **cumulative**, and **incremental**). The export types are described in the text

TABLE 13-1. *Export Parameters for Oracle8i (* = new in Oracle8.0, ** = new in Oracle8i)*

Keyword	Description
DIRECT*	Y/N flag to indicate whether a direct export should be performed. A direct export bypasses the buffer cache during the export, generating significant performance gains for the export process
RECORD	Y/N flag for incremental exports. Indicates whether a record will be stored in data dictionary tables recording the export
PARFILE	Name of a parameter file to be passed to export. This file may contain entries for all of the parameters listed here
STATISTICS	Indicates whether **analyze** commands for the exported objects should be written to the export dump file. Valid values are **compute**, **estimate** (the default), and **n**. In earlier versions of Oracle, this parameter was called **analyze**
CONSISTENT	Y/N flag to indicate whether a read-consistent version of all exported objects should be maintained. This is needed when tables that are related to each other are being modified by users during the export process
LOG	Name of a file to which the log of the export will be written
FEEDBACK	Number of rows after which to display progress during table exports. The default value is 0, so no feedback is displayed until a table is completely exported
POINT_IN_TIME_RECOVER*	Y/N flag used to signal Oracle if you are exporting metadata for use in a tablespace point-in-time recovery. This is an advanced recovery technique
RECOVERY_TABLESPACES*	Tablespaces whose metadata should be exported during a tablespace point-in-time recovery
QUERY**	Where clause that will be applied to each table during the export
TRIGGERS**	Include triggers in the export file
TRANSPORT_TABLESPACE**	Set to Y if you are using the **pluggable tablespace** option available as of Oracle8i. Use in conjunction with the **tablespaces** keyword
TABLESPACES**	Tablespaces whose metadata should be exported during a tablespace move

TABLE 13-1. *Export Parameters for Oracle8i (* = new in Oracle8.0, ** = new in Oracle8i)* (continued)

block corruption—it will do this by failing. Another way to identify data block corruption is to use the command **analyze table validate structure** on each table.

Several new parameters have been added in Oracle8.0 and 8i. Among them are **point_in_time_recover** and **recovery_tablespaces**, which are used together to recover one or more tablespaces to a specific point in time, and **transportable_tablespace** and **tablespaces**, which are used together to move a tablespace from one database to another. See Chapter 5 for more information about transportable tablespaces. While the ability to export an individual table has always been present, now the ability to export a specific partition within a table has been added, using the construct **tables=T1.P1**, where T1 is the table name and P1 is the partition designation.

The parameter **compress=y** tells Oracle to add up all of the allocated space in a table and modify the **initial** value for the table creation statement in the export dump file to reflect the current total allocated space. Huh? That really does sound confusing, doesn't it?

We've talked about fragmentation frequently in this book. One way to reduce fragmentation in a table is to rebuild the table with all of its extents compressed into one larger extent. To accomplish defragmenting a table, you export the table with **compress=y**, drop the table from the database, re-create the table, and import the table's contents back into the database. When Oracle re-creates the table from the commands in the export dump file, the **initial** extent value will be the sum of all the allocated space that was in the table before the export was performed. Let's say the table has five extents and you want to compress it. Each of the five extents has 512000 bytes allocated. However, only 204800 bytes of each extent have data in them, and there are no used bytes in the last extent (512000 free bytes). When you issue the parameter **compress=y**, you would expect Oracle to calculate how much space is actually used within the table and set the **initial** extent value to match the results of that calculation.

Well, Oracle doesn't work that way! Oracle will simply add up all of the allocated space (512000 bytes per extent times five extents) and allocate 2560000 bytes as the **initial** extent for the **create table** statement in the export dump file. So, when you perform the import operation, Oracle will place the data in approximately the first 819200 bytes of the table extent and about 1740800 bytes of the space will be empty.

The **consistent** parameter tells Oracle whether to keep track of any changes that are occurring while the export is taking place. If you use **consistent=y**, you will need to make sure that you have a really large rollback segment available for the export to use. You see, while Oracle is performing the export, as each table is exported, a copy of the table is stored in the rollback segment. Now, as each additional table is exported, Oracle checks to see if any changes that would affect the current table have been made to the prior exported tables. Remember we said earlier that Oracle exports the object information from the data dictionary. The data dictionary stores table names in alphabetical order:

```
select Table_Name
  from DBA_TABLES
 where Owner = 'ROSS';

TABLE_NAME
------------------------------
ACCOUNTING
BONUSES
DEPTMENT
EMPLOYEE
RECEIPTS
SALARY
```

In this schema, there is a dependency between the DEPTMENT and the EMPLOYEE tables. Because Oracle exports alphabetically, DEPTMENT will be exported before EMPLOYEE. Okay, so Oracle is exporting the EMPLOYEE table and someone makes a change to the DEPTMENT table. There's no problem in the current database, but if you must recover the tables from the export, they are now going to be inconsistent. If you use the parameter **consistent=y**, the change in the DEPTMENT table will be noticed during the export and a correction will be made. Because Oracle has to be constantly checking the status of tables that depend on each other, the export will take much more time to perform and, as we said, could require a very large rollback segment. Therefore, we recommend that instead of using this parameter for a full database export, you break your export into two or more processes and just export specific tables that must be kept consistent in one export process. For tables where data consistency is not an issue, you can then export them much more quickly with much less resource requirement.

The Import Utility

It's four o'clock in the afternoon (on a Friday, of course!), and you get a call from one of your developers saying that he "accidentally" dropped a table in the development database and he's got to get it back really *fast*. As luck would have it, this table already exists in the production database and can be used to replace the lost table in development. How are you going to perform the task of moving a copy of the production table into the development database? Actually, you should be able to do this pretty easily.

Oracle provides a utility called import that you can use to recover database structures and data from an export file. The first step you would take to recover the lost development table would be to export a copy of the table from production. Since the table has already been dropped in development, you would just import that table into the correct user's schema. Any indexes and constraints associated with the table will be carried over in the export file. Pretty cool!

As with export, you can list the parameters associated with the import utility by issuing the command **imp help=y** at an operating system command line. Figure 13-2 shows a screen print of the output from this command, and Table 13-2 shows a listing of the commands and their definitions.

If you have performed a full database export, you can use the **imp** command in conjunction with the parameters **show=y log=<filename>** to create a file containing the entire contents of the export file. Although the commands displayed in the file look like executable commands, they are not formatted correctly to be run. They can, however, be used to document your database.

The keyword **indexfile**, on the other hand, will produce a file that is executable. This file will contain the commands to create every index contained in the export file. The associated table creation statements will also be included in the file, but they will be "remmed" out (each line is preceded by "rem" to indicate that it is a remark and should not be executed). Using **indexfile** is a great way to see the

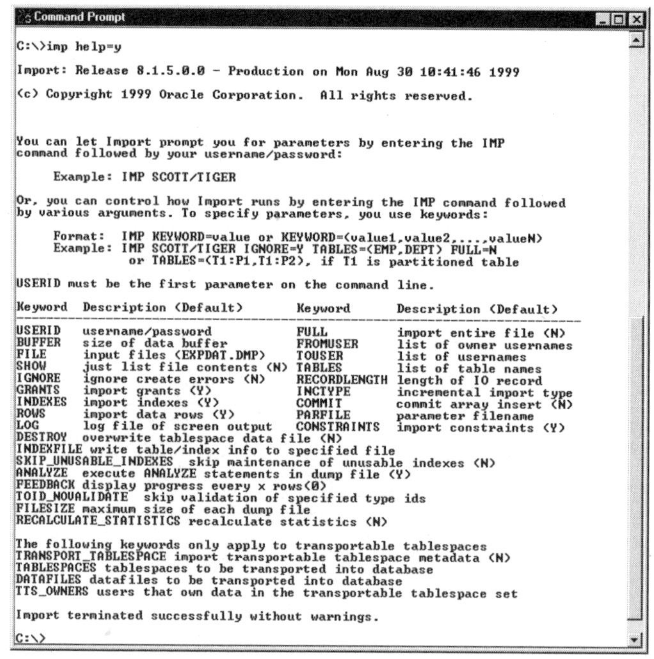

```
Command Prompt
C:\>imp help=y

Import: Release 8.1.5.0.0 - Production on Mon Aug 30 10:41:46 1999

(c) Copyright 1999 Oracle Corporation.  All rights reserved.


You can let Import prompt you for parameters by entering the IMP
command followed by your username/password:

     Example: IMP SCOTT/TIGER

Or, you can control how Import runs by entering the IMP command followed
by various arguments. To specify parameters, you use keywords:

     Format:  IMP KEYWORD=value or KEYWORD=(value1,value2,...,valueN)
     Example: IMP SCOTT/TIGER IGNORE=Y TABLES=(EMP,DEPT) FULL=N
               or TABLES=(T1:P1,T1:P2), if T1 is partitioned table

USERID must be the first parameter on the command line.

Keyword  Description (Default)       Keyword      Description (Default)
--------------------------------------------------------------------------
USERID   username/password           FULL         import entire file (N)
BUFFER   size of data buffer         FROMUSER     list of owner usernames
FILE     input files (EXPDAT.DMP)    TOUSER       list of usernames
SHOW     just list file contents (N) TABLES       list of table names
IGNORE   ignore create errors (N)    RECORDLENGTH length of IO record
GRANTS   import grants (Y)           INCTYPE      incremental import type
INDEXES  import indexes (Y)          COMMIT       commit array insert (N)
ROWS     import data rows (Y)        PARFILE      parameter filename
LOG      log file of screen output   CONSTRAINTS  import constraints (Y)
DESTROY  overwrite tablespace data file (N)
INDEXFILE write table/index info to specified file
SKIP_UNUSABLE_INDEXES  skip maintenance of unusable indexes (N)
ANALYZE  execute ANALYZE statements in dump file (Y)
FEEDBACK display progress every x rows(0)
TOID_NOVALIDATE  skip validation of specified type ids
FILESIZE maximum size of each dump file
RECALCULATE_STATISTICS recalculate statistics (N)

The following keywords only apply to transportable tablespaces
TRANSPORT_TABLESPACE import transportable tablespace metadata (N)
TABLESPACES tablespaces to be transported into database
DATAFILES datafiles to be transported into database
TTS_OWNERS users that own data in the transportable tablespace set

Import terminated successfully without warnings.

C:\>
```

FIGURE 13-2. *Import command screen output for Oracle8i*

Keyword	Description
USERID	Username/password of the account running the import. If this is the first parameter after the **imp** command, this keyword does not have to be specified
BUFFER	Size of the buffer used to fetch data rows. The default is system dependent; this value is usually set to a high value (>100,000)
FILE	Name of the export dump file to be imported
SHOW	Y/N flag to specify whether the file contents should be displayed rather than executed
IGNORE	Y/N flag to indicate whether the import should ignore errors encountered when issuing **create** commands. This is used if the objects being imported already exist
GRANTS	Y/N flag to indicate whether grants on database objects will be imported
INDEXES	Y/N flag to indicate whether indexes on tables will be imported
CONSTRAINTS	Y/N flag to indicate whether constraints on tables will be imported
ROWS	Y/N flag to indicate whether rows should be imported. If this is set to N, only the DDL for the database objects will be executed
FULL	Y/N flag; if set to Y, the full export dump file is imported
FROMUSER	List of database accounts whose objects should be read from the export dump file (when **full=n**)
TOUSER	A list of database accounts into which objects in the export dump file will be imported. **fromuser** and **touser** do not have to be set to the same value
TABLES	List of tables to be imported
RECORDLENGTH	Length, in bytes, of the export dump file record. Usually left at the default value unless you are going to transfer the export file between different operating systems
INCTYPE	Type of import being performed (valid values are **complete** (default), **cumulative**, and **incremental**)

TABLE 13-2. *Import Parameters for Oracle8i*

Keyword	Description
COMMIT	Y/N flag to indicate whether import should **commit** after each array (whose size is set by BUFFER). If this is set to N, then import will **commit** after every table is imported. For large tables, **commit=n** requires equally large rollback segments
PARFILE	Name of a parameter file to be passed to import. This file may contain entries for all of the parameters listed here
INDEXFILE	This very powerful option writes all of the **create table**, **create cluster**, and **create index** commands to a file, rather than running them. All but the **create index** commands will be commented out. This file can then be run (with slight modifications) after importing with **indexes=n**. It is very useful for separating tables and indexes into separate tablespaces
CHARSET	Character set to use during the import for v5 and v6 (obsolete but retained)
POINT_IN_TIME_ RECOVER*	Y/N flag to indicate whether the import is part of a tablespace point-in-time recovery (removed for 8i)
DESTROY	Y/N flag to indicate whether the **create tablespace** commands found in dump files from full exports will be executed (thereby destroying the datafiles in the target database)
LOG	Name of a file to which the log of the import will be written
SKIP_UNUSABLE_ INDEXES*	Y/N flag that indicates whether import should skip partition indexes marked as "unusable." You may wish to skip the indexes during import and manually create them later to improve index creation performance
ANALYZE*	Y/N flag to indicate whether import should execute the **analyze** commands found in the export dump file
FEEDBACK	Number of rows after which to display progress during table imports. The default value is 0, so no feedback is displayed until a table is completely imported
TIOD_ NOVALIDATE**	Enables import to skip validation of specified object types. This option is generally used with cartridge installs. One or more object types can be specified

TABLE 13-2. *Import Parameters for Oracle8i* (continued)

Keyword	Description
FILESIZE**	Maximum dump size that was specified on export if the parameter FILESIZE was used on export
RECALCULATE_ STATISTICS**	Y/N flag to indicate whether optimizer statistics should be generated
TRANSPORTABLE_ TABLESPACE**	Y/N flag to indicate that transportable tablespace metadata is to be imported into the database
TABLESPACES**	Name or list of names of tablespaces to be transported into the database
DATAFILES**	List of datafiles to be transported into the database
TTS_OWNER**	Name or list of names of owners of data in the transportable tablespace

TABLE 13-2. *Import Parameters for Oracle8i* (continued)

storage parameters for both your tables and indexes. The output file can also be modified, before it is run to create indexes, to change the tablespace location and/or the storage parameters of the indexes in your database.

The Oracle8 Recovery Manager

As any person who has ever worked on a craft can tell you, there are many different ways to complete a project, but it's infinitely easier to do if you have the right tools. When it comes to backup and recovery, there are many different approaches that you can use to implement your disaster recovery strategy and an array of tools to select from.

As of version 8.0, Oracle offers a new backup and recovery tool known as the Recovery Manager (RMAN). RMAN provides flexibility in backing up an entire database, individual tablespaces, or datafiles. You can perform backup and recovery interactively by issuing line-mode commands, or RMAN provides automated backup and recovery wizards through the Oracle Enterprise Manager (OEM) Graphical User Interface.

To set up RMAN in Oracle8.0, you must create a recovery catalog (a repository that keeps track of the RMAN backup locations, dates, and files). You can either have a recovery catalog or enable RMAN to store recovery information in each database's control files. With a recovery catalog, the database in which you house the recovery catalog must be readily accessible. You will have to determine a backup and recovery strategy for the recovery catalog as well. You won't want to store the recovery catalog in a database on which you may have to perform recovery, because if the database is inaccessible, the recovery catalog will be unavailable as well. In Oracle8i, the recovery information is stored automatically in the database control files and can be obtained from them.

RMAN supports two types of backup: a *backup set* and an *image copy*. Backup sets can contain either datafiles (a datafile backup set) or archive logs (an archive log backup set). Only one type of file can be stored in a backup set, but many files of the same type can be stored within each set. Often, the backup sets are written to tape. However, one set may not fit completely on one tape. Thus, if you are going to make backup sets and write them directly to tape, you may need to make several tapes available for the backup operations. Backup sets can be created on disk and later stored to tape. Therefore, you could keep the latest copy of the database backup sets on disk and the older sets on tape.

RMAN provides three possible levels of backup: full, cumulative, and incremental (doesn't that sound like export?). The difference in the backups is the number of database blocks that are saved. In a full or "level 0" datafile backup, every block that has ever been changed within a datafile is backed up. A cumulative or "level 1" datafile backup will capture all of the blocks that have been changed since the last full datafile backup. The most significant new backup option is the incremental or "level 2" datafile backup. This option enables you to capture only the blocks that have changed in the datafile since the most recent cumulative or full backup. If you use this new facility, you will reduce the amount of storage space required for backups. The amount of time required to perform a recovery should also be reduced.

If recovery is required and the backup set is currently on tape, you will have to extract the backup set from the tape before performing the recovery operations. You see, when the backup set is stored to tape, it is stored in a compressed format. In order to be used during recovery, the backup set must be uncompressed and placed in a format that Oracle can read and understand. During a recovery, RMAN can perform the operations required to restore the backup set from tape back to disk. The assumption is, of course, that there will be enough space on the disks to support the restoration of the needed files. Thus, you will have to insure, before you begin a recovery operation, that there really is enough space to restore the backup set.

You can actually perform up to four levels of incremental backups. Level 1 could be monthly, while level 2 could be weekly and level 3 daily, and so on. Each set of weekly incremental backups would replace the other six daily backups, and each level 1 monthly would replace the four weekly backups. If you are storing the backups on disk, you can reuse the disk space on a rotating basis. You are free to decide what each level of backup will contain and how frequently each level is replaced.

You can also use RMAN to make image copies. An image copy is a copy of a single file (like a files-level backup). The beauty of an image copy is that you can either use it in a restore scenario or directly by renaming a datafile within the database to the image copy. That means if you've made an image copy of a datafile and then have to recover the file, you could just issue the **alter tablespace rename datafile** command and replace the bad file with the good one. This is a very rapid way to recover a datafile, but you would be restoring the file to the point in time that the image copy had been made and not to the current moment. You could potentially run into a problem with inconsistent data using this approach. The only time this approach makes sense is if you are absolutely sure the image copy contains a table or tables that are not usually changed or that all of the tables that depend on each other for data consistency are in the same datafile.

An image copy must be performed to disk, so the amount of disk space required must be taken into consideration if you use this form of backup. Image copies can be made from archive logs, datafiles, or control files, but each image copy can contain only one individual file.

Standby Database

Several chapters ago, we talked about a little theater group that staged several plays and musicals a year. To ensure that the show could go on, the cast always included several actors and actresses as understudies for the people who held the lead roles. The understudies "stood by" to replace the leads at a moment's notice.

Over the course of time, many DBAs have come to realize that with the need for critical databases to be constantly available, a better approach to database recoverability is to have a *standby database*. When Oracle Corporation first unveiled the standby database concept in version 7.3, it was a very immature feature. You see, a standby database in Oracle7.3 is an *inaccessible* duplicate of your primary database. You cannot use the standby database for queries or in any way unless you are activating it for disaster recovery.

The standby database runs in constant recovery mode, so you only need to recover the archive logs that have not yet been applied. You will lose the data in the current redo log files as well as the data in any archive log that has not been transferred to the secondary machine. Enhancements in 8i make it possible to open the standby database in a read-only mode and then return it to standby status. The ability to use the database in read-only mode provides the option of using the standby for decision-support system types of activities. Once you return the database to standby mode, you will have to apply all the archived redo logs that have been created since you put the database into read-only mode.

Any action written to the redo logs must be propagated to the standby database, such as datafile resizing or tablespace status changes. This includes adding new datafiles. If you can perform an online backup and copy the datafile to the standby site before the redo is applied, you will have no interruption in your recovery process. Otherwise, recovery will fail because you are missing the newly added datafile, and you will have to manually run the command to add the datafile and then restart recovery.

Changes to datafile names and any action that affects the redo log configuration are not propagated and may invalidate the standby database. You can also invalidate the standby database by doing SQL*Loader Direct Path loads in **unrecoverable** mode or by issuing **create table/create index as unrecoverable** statements. These actions are not written to the redo logs and cannot be propagated to the standby database. Data blocks affected by these actions are marked logically corrupt at recovery time (when the archive logs are applied at the standby database), and any redo activity to these objects that appears subsequent to the unrecoverable action will also be ignored during application of the log files.

As with online backups and archive logs, there is always the possibility of corrupted archive logs. If any archive log has corruption in it, you will have to re-create the standby database. Once you failover to your standby database, you cannot return it to standby mode. Until you create a new standby database, you will have no contingency options.

Implementing a Standby Database

Setting up a standby database takes a little planning. To implement a standby database, you must be running your primary database in archive log mode. You will need a second computer with at least the same amount of disk storage as your primary machine. The configuration does not need to be identical, but it must be totally separate and distinct from your primary database. If the configuration is not identical, application of your archive logs may take longer, and you will operate in a degraded mode if you need to switch over to the standby database. In an ideal world, no other application will be running on the same machine as your standby database.

To create the standby database, follow these steps:

1. Back up (either online or offline) your primary database. If you are using an online backup, make sure to back up all your archive log files as well.
2. Create the control file for the standby database.
3. Archive your current redo logs.
4. Transfer the backed up data files, the archive logs, and the standby control file to your secondary machine.
5. On the secondary machine, start up the instance using the NOMOUNT clause.
6. Mount the database as standby.
7. Begin recovering the standby database.

Once you have created the standby database, you need to maintain and keep it up-to-date with your primary database. To do this, you will need to continually transfer the archive logs as they are generated on the primary machine and apply them to the standby database. The transfer and application of the archive logs should be automated so that your possible data loss from lost archive logs and your downtime while you finish recovering are minimized. Again, changes in 8i allow the archive logs to be generated directly to the remote system, automating the transfer of archive logs to the standby system for you.

If you make a structural change to the primary database (add a datafile, move a datafile, drop a tablespace), you will need to copy the new datafile over before redo for that datafile is applied to the standby database. If you do not apply these changes prior to recovery, the recovery will fail, and you will have to manually make the change and restart recovery at your standby site.

Failing Over to the Standby Database

If you're lucky, when you need to failover, you'll have the luxury of archiving your online redo logs and copying any remaining archive logs over to your standby database site. This type of failover, a "graceful switchover," is not sanctioned by Oracle for disaster recovery since you cannot count on having the time to do this. In reality, you probably won't even get a warning that you need to move to your standby database until after the primary site has become inaccessible.

In that case, you're going to lose data. Anything that hasn't been archived and copied over is lost forever. To minimize the loss, you can run a batch job that automatically archives your online logs every *x* minutes. You'll have some performance impact, and you will possibly waste lots of space in your archive logs, but you *will* minimize data loss. You might consider remotely mounting your archive directory disk to your standby machine (called NFS-mounting) to minimize the time it takes to get the archive logs to the other machine. If you do use an NFS-mounted disk approach, make sure you do one of the following:

- Have a job running to copy the archive logs to a local disk the instant they appear on the NFS-mounted one
- Have the NFS-mounted disk be a local disk to the standby machine so that you won't lose any archive logs that haven't been copied when the primary site goes down

Remember too that if the NFS-mounted disk is local to your standby machine and you lose either the disk or the standby machine, your ARCH process will hang because it has nowhere to write the archive logs.

Once you know you have to failover to the standby database, you will need to perform the following steps:

1. Finish recovering all remaining archive logs. The more up-to-date your standby processing is, the less time you will have to spend recovering the final archive logs.
2. Activate the standby database.
3. Modify your tnsnames.ora file as necessary, start up your listener and, depending on the redundancy and failover you have built into your network, notify your users to connect to the new database server. Use of an Oracle Names Server will reduce the amount of manual editing needed to move your users to the secondary site.

As you can see, moving to a contingency site using a standby database is a fairly simple process. Once you have moved to the standby site, however, you are exposed to loss of that site until you create a standby database again.

Returning to Your Primary Site

Depending on distance, staffing, and cost, you can leave the original standby site as your new primary and create the new standby database back at the original primary. In terms of speed and reduction of lost data, this is the optimal solution. If you have the option available, you only need to follow the steps outlined above to build a standby database at your former primary site.

Unfortunately, standby sites are usually standby for a reason. They run as either lights-out or reduced staff data centers, and leaving the primary database there is not an option. In that case, returning to your original configuration becomes a bit more of a problem for you.

To return normal processing to your primary location, first build a standby database at the primary site. You may need to run your primary database at the standby site for a short time, until you reach a period of very low or no activity that will allow you to "fail back" to your primary site with no loss of data. Once you reach a point where you can activate the standby database at your primary site with little or no loss of data, you will need to run through the same steps as the failover to standby and then, once again, re-create your standby database at your secondary site. By following this approach, "coming home" can not only be time consuming but also leave you exposed at several points in time to loss of data and/or no contingency at all.

Recovery Options

There are many different ways that you could recover a database. The ways to recover an entire database are

- As a snapshot in time (from export)

- To a point in time (from files-level backups + archive logs)
- Until Cancel (from files-level backups + archive logs)
- By maintaining a standby database

For an entire tablespace (from files-level backups), you can restore one or more data files. From an export, an entire database, one or more schemas, or one or more tables can be restored. Using the import option **indexfile=<file_name>**, you can obtain a script to build an index or set of indices from an export file.

There are two types of recovery: online, with the database open, and offline, with the database closed. From an online recovery within the database, the commands **recover tablespace...** and/or **recover datafile...** can be used in tablespace recovery. From outside the database, the import utility can be used to recover tables, schemas, or the entire database from an export file.

For an offline recovery from sqldba or the Server Manager (svrmgrl), you can use the command **startup mount** to mount the database but not open it. You can then recover the SYSTEM tablespace as well as perform recovery on the entire database. From this position, if a tablespace has been corrupted and you are absolutely sure the tablespace can be rebuilt, the datafiles associated with that tablespace can be altered offline using the sub-command **offline drop** and the database opened. The tablespace will be "untouchable" and must be dropped immediately. Great caution should be used when applying this technique, and you should contact Oracle Support before proceeding with this plan since possible repercussions could occur, such as further severe database corruption.

Testing Your Strategy

Like our friends in the little theater group, before a disaster has ever occurred on your system, we recommend that you "rehearse" (test and "play through") every imaginable form of database loss that is practical and possible for you to stage. You can use that private little database we keep telling you to build to practice your backup and recovery strategies. One of the authors had to work on a Sunday to support an application upgrade. Having nothing better to do while she waited for the upgrade to be completed, she staged and practiced many different forms of disaster recovery (and kept notes of her actions and their results). One week after the application went into full production, a disk failed. The disk contained the SYSTEM tablespace's datafile and one copy of the control file. Having just played through and documented this specific failure, she was able to explain in detailed steps what needed to be done and how to perform recovery of the database. Within two and a half hours, the disk had been rebuilt by the systems operations team, and the database had been recovered with no loss of data. Being prepared and knowing what the commands were saved the day.

In a presentation on backup and recovery strategies that we once attended, the presenter talked about going out into the computer room and "pulling the plug" on a database disk to practice recovery procedures. If that approach seems a little too harsh or risky, there are ways to stage the loss of a SYSTEM or non-SYSTEM tablespace by renaming the associated datafiles. You should also practice the recovery of a non-SYSTEM tablespace with active rollback segments, redo logs—both online and archived, static or dynamic user tables, and control files.

Recommendations

Below is a list of recommendations that you may want to consider. These recommendations are geared to help you ensure protection of the Oracle databases on your system.

- Size redo logs according to operational requirements.
- Keep multiple redo log members for each log group—on different disks, or use hardware mirroring.
- Have at least three copies of the control file—on different disks under different controllers.
- Operate in archive log mode.
- Keep archive logs on different disks than redo log files.
- Keep a second copy of archive logs on tape (if possible, to a dedicated tape drive).
- If space permits, keep the backup of the data files and all associated redo log files on disk on the system (saves time in restoring).
- Perform exports before files-level backups, which will catch data block corruption.
- Use the **analyze table validate structure** command to catch any data block corruption.
- Perform exports while the database is in restricted mode, or use **consistent=y** for tables that contain dependencies.
- Keep a complete set of object-creation scripts outside the database to re-create tables, indexes, views, constraints, and grants.
- Keep a copy of the control file create script.
- Take a backup of the database any time you change the structure.

- Periodically test your recovery strategy to ensure that it works.
- Keep a copy of your backups off-site.
- Keep a copy of the Oracle source software off-site.

Additionally, for Oracle8:

- Determine where the Recovery Manager repository will be maintained—preferably in a database by itself.
- Ensure an effective backup/recovery strategy for the Recovery Manager repository.
- Test your recovery strategy to ensure that it works!

PART V

Appendixes

APPENDIX A

Glossary

resented here is a set of brief definitions of the major terms you will encounter in this book. Every attempt has been made to ensure that all of the important terms have been included.

Access path The method that Oracle can use to get to the data. Access paths break down into two general methods—either using an index or accessing the data directly from the table. If more than one table is involved, the optimizer has to figure out which join method to use. *See also* Join method.

Alert log A file that is created when the database is created to track specific types of database interactions. The alert log contains information about each database startup and shutdown, each parameter that is not a default database value, each log thread switch, any database errors, and any data dictionary language commands that were used to alter the structure of the database.

Application One or more computer programs used to perform work on behalf of a business.

Applications DBA A DBA who works closely with application developers to assist in creating the structures within a database that are necessary to support an application.

ARCH The archiver background process. Used by Oracle to copy redo log files to one or more separate disks or tape drives to provide redundancy and help ensure database recovery. Required for online database backups and standby databases.

Architectural DBA A DBA whose primary function is to design and model the database structures for a system. This type of DBA should have a good understanding of the business processes to which the application is geared and the effect the processes have on both the flow and state of the data.

Archive log A file created by the archiver process that contains a copy of a redo log file. In Oracle7.3, archive logs can be copied to one location. In Oracle8.0, archive logs can be copied to two locations, and in Oracle8i, they can be copied to up to five different locations on different disks and even to a remote site.

Archive log mode A database state in which backups of the datafiles can be taken while the database is open. Databases must be in archive log mode to be recoverable to a point-in-time past the time of the backup.

Backup The process of copying one or more database files for protection of the data and recovery of the database. Can be used in the database recovery process in the event of a failure/disaster. *See also* Backup, logical database and Backup, physical database.

Backup, logical database A method of storing database objects in an external file. The export (*see* Export) utility is used to perform this backup and can only be run when the database is up. The recovery process is performed via the import utility (*see* Import).

Backup, physical database A method of directly copying Oracle datafiles to a backup media. Physical backups can be either online or offline.

Backup plan A plan describing the procedures that will be used to back up and recover a database.

Backup set Used in conjunction with the Recovery Manager. Can contain either datafiles (a datafile backup set) or archive logs (an archive log backup set). Only one type of file can be stored in a backup set, but many files of the same type can be stored within each set. Often, the backup sets are written to tape.

Batch A group of rows returned in a single call to the database. Used with the **set arraysize** command, the maximum value is 5000. Setting the array size to greater than 100 usually has no additional effect on performance. The larger the array size setting, the more memory Oracle will need for each fetch.

Batch job *See* Batch process.

Batch process A procedure submitted to an operating system utility to perform work automatically. Can be scheduled to run immediately, once at a specified time, or repeatedly on a scheduled basis.

Before image A copy of data before any changes have been made.

Bit The smallest unit of data in a computer. A bit has a single binary value, either 0 or 1.

Bit-mapped index Introduced in Oracle7.3. A bit-mapped index stores the rowids associated with a key value as a bitmap. These indexes should only be built on columns with a low number of different values (*see* Low cardinality values).

Block Composed of bytes; the bytes are grouped together, usually in 512 bytes of operating system space per operating system block. *See also* Database block size.

Buckets Used in conjunction with a histogram to describe the distribution of data across a column in a table.

Byte Eight contiguous bits starting on any addressable boundary. A byte can be used to store one ASCII character. *See also* Bit.

Cache An amount of space reserved in memory in which data can be stored.

Check constraint Ensures that the data being inserted into a column meets certain conditions.

Check option constraint Placed on a view. Limits any inserts or updates to rows that the view itself can select.

Child table The table on which the foreign key is defined. *See also* Parent table.

Cold backup *See* Offline database backup.

Column An individual compartment in which a specific type of information is stored within a table. A column's definition will describe the type and size of the particular data that will be stored within it.

CONFIG.ORA A secondary configuration file used to store instance-specific, nondefault parameters.

Configuration files Used to store nondefault Oracle parameters. *See also* CONFIG.ORA and INIT.ORA.

Constant A variable whose value is preassigned and retained throughout the execution of a software program.

Constraint A mechanism used to ensure that data is consistent within a table or across tables.

Cost Based Optimizer *See* Optimizer, Cost Based.

CPU A computer central processing unit.

Data DBA A person who determines the composition and management of data within a database. Often, this person is involved with data loading and data cleansing operations.

Data type The designation used to describe a specific data element.

Database A collection of information, electronically stored in one location, used to manipulate data in a logical way.

Database Administrator (DBA) A person who creates, configures, and oversees the maintenance of a database.

Database block size The DBA-designated size of an Oracle block declared when creating a database and used for information storage. The default number of bytes in an Oracle database block is 2048, which is a very small block size by today's standards. Normally, the designated database block size will be at least 4096 bytes or higher. *See also* Block.

Database migration The act of creating a new database under the new Oracle software version, making a copy of the old database, and putting that copy into the new database within the new version.

Database upgrade The act of shutting down the current database under the old Oracle software version, starting it up under the new Oracle software version, and immediately running configuration scripts to convert the database to the new Oracle software version.

Datafile The physical file used to store database information. Tablespaces are composed of datafiles.

DBWR (DBW0) The Oracle background process responsible for managing the contents of the data block buffer cache and the dictionary cache. The DBWR process reads blocks from datafiles and stores them in the SGA. The DBWR process also performs batch writes of changed blocks back to the datafiles.

Deadlock contention A situation that occurs when two or more users wait for data that is locked by each other. Oracle will arbitrarily decide which of the two user processes to kill.

Declaration (of variables) A mechanism used to describe the composition of a variable. *See also* Data type.

Detached processes The five or more processes that, along with the SGA, make up an Oracle instance. Each process has its own functionality and preassigned tasks.

Directory The general area in which information is stored on a computer. There can be many different directories on a computer and several different levels of directories within a single directory.

Enqueue A mechanism that keeps track of users waiting for locks that are held by others and the lock mode these users require. The enqueue mechanism also keeps track of the order in which users requested the locks.

Export An Oracle-supplied utility that enables the capture of a table, set of tables, complete schema, set of schemas, or entire database as a snapshot in time. Instead of making a copy of the datafiles that reside on the system, a binary copy of the objects and their data as they exist within the database is made.

Extent A contiguous allocation of database blocks. An extent is dedicated to a specific table, cluster, index, temporary segment, or rollback segment. An extent is created whenever a segment is created or a current segment is not large enough to hold information that is being inserted.

File(s) The area in which information is stored within a directory.

File extension The ending names used to differentiate one form of file from another. Standard extensions are used for Oracle files, such as .ora to represent a parameter file, .exe to indicate an executable file, .dbf to designate a datafile.

File number, absolute The number identifying a datafile that is unique to the entire database.

File number, relative The number identifying a datafile that is unique within the tablespace.

Files-level backup *See* Offline database backup.

Foreign key constraint Refers only to columns defined as either primary key constraint columns or unique key constraint columns. Data values entered into these columns must already exist in the referenced columns.

Freelists Used to track the blocks that are available for inserts to the database.

Full table scan The action of examining every row in a table to gather information to fulfill a query.

Function A procedure that always returns a single value to the caller.

Function-based index Created with the function as part of the index.

Grant The action a DBA takes to assign a privilege to a user or role.

Header block The first of the extents allocated for a rollback segment. The header block is used by Oracle to store information that tracks the transactions accessing the specific rollback segment and the extents the transaction is using.

Hint A direction that can be given to the Cost Based Optimizer to use a specific access method, join order, optimizer goal, or table order. *See also* Optimizer, Cost Based.

Histogram A set of statistics on a table that gives the optimizer additional information on the distribution of the data in the particular column of interest.

Hot backups *See* Online database backups.

Icon A symbol used to represent an object. On a Windows NT system, the directory indicators are file folder icons. Icons are frequently used in GUI applications.

Image backup *See* Offline database backup.

Image copy Used in conjunction with the Recovery Manager. A copy of a single file (like a files-level backup). Can be used either in a restore scenario or directly, by renaming a datafile within the database to the image copy.

Import An Oracle-supplied utility that enables the restoration of objects stored within an export file. Provides an easy way to restore one or more tables within a database.

Index A structure used to improve the speed of information retrieval in a database.

INIT.ORA A parameter file used by Oracle to define nondefault values for variables.

Installation *See* Software installation.

Instance Composed of a set of background processes and memory structures that access a set of database files. It is possible for a database to be accessed by multiple instances.

Join (tables or views) The act of combining parts of two or more tables or views to produce a complete picture of the information of interest.

Join method The name for the different algorithms the Oracle optimizer can call on to combine two different tables. Two of the different approaches available to join one set of data to another are nested loop and sort-merge. In a nested loop, one row of a table is selected, and then the process loops through the other table trying to find any matches. Using a sort-merge, both tables are sorted into the same order, and then the results are compared to find matches.

Latch A form of low-level locking used to protect a memory structure. A latch is usually held for a very brief amount of time.

Latches, immediate state A latch that is requested with an immediate state will try to obtain the latch once. If unsuccessful, the process will not wait but will continue on.

Latches, willing-to-wait state A latch that is requested with a willing-to-wait state will wait for a short time and try to obtain the latch again. The process will keep waiting and requesting over again until the latch becomes available and the process can obtain it.

LGWR This background process is responsible for managing the writes of the contents of the redo log buffer to the online redo log files. The writes are performed in batches and contain the most up-to-date status of the data within the database.

LISTENER.ORA The primary file used to supply a SQL*Net2 or Net8 listener with configuration information.

Lock A mechanism normally used to protect a data structure. Can be held continuously until a commit or rollback occurs.

Locks, instance level Distributed locks used to ensure that structures remain consistent across more than one instance.

Locks, transaction level Used to ensure that a structure remains consistent while a transaction, such as an update, is performed.

Lookup table A table or view used to resolve a number into a meaningful name.

Low cardinality values In a table, a column that has a low number of different values, such as a gender column that has two different options—Male and Female—has low cardinality values. Bit-mapped indexes should be built only on this type of column.

Metadata Information about the database structure.

Mirroring The act of maintaining an exact copy of a file on a separate disk from the original file.

Net8 An Oracle-supplied utility to enable communication from a computer to a central database or from one database to another. *See also* SQL*Net2.

Offline database backup A backup performed while the database is shut down to ensure that no processes are active within the database. Also known as cold backup, image backup, and files-level backup.

Online database backup Essential for an environment that operates 24 hours, 7 days a week. It derives its name from the fact that the database remains up and running while the backup is performed. The same files-level copies of the datafiles and control files are performed, but the redo log files are not backed up. Archive log mode must be enabled so that Oracle knows the database is recoverable. Also known as hot backups.

Optimal (parameter for rollback segment) A value that is declared when a rollback segment is created to provide Oracle with a specific minimum size to which a rollback segment can be reduced.

Optimal Flexible Architecture (OFA) An approach, created by Cary Millsap, that describes the optimal way to locate files of an Oracle database on disks, defines the naming conventions to be used for files, and identifies the names and contents of directories used to house an Oracle database and software system.

Optimizer The part of Oracle that is responsible for determining how to retrieve the answer to a DML statement. The optimizer is used to break down a SQL statement into individual components and determine the fastest way to access the data and return the answer. It does this by first understanding which tables are involved in a SQL statement and choosing the best available access path to that data.

Optimizer, Cost Based Takes into account the relative resource "cost" of one access path over another when considering how to build the query plan. *See also* Access path and Query plan.

Optimizer, Rule Based Uses a fixed set of instructions as guidelines when building a query plan for a SQL statement. These rules tell the optimizer how to value one access path over another when trying to determine the quickest approach to get to or join data.

Oracle Certified Professional (OCP-DBA) Program The prescribed course of study and set of tests created by Oracle Education and administered by Sylvan Learning Centers to establish a DBA's basic knowledge of the Oracle products.

Oracle Enterprise Manager (OEM) A graphical user interface (GUI) tool that enables management of remote databases from one central personal computer.

Oracle Enterprise Manager console An application that enables interface with the Oracle Enterprise Manager tool set.

Oracle Enterprise Manager repository A set of tables that are stored in a database to hold information for the Oracle Enterprise Manager tool.

Oracle software A group of programs designed to enable the creation and interaction with an Oracle relational database.

Package Made up of combinations of procedures and functions, packages allow the grouping of related functions, procedures, and cursors as a single program unit.

Parent table The primary/unique key table. The table with the foreign key defined on it. *See also* Child table.

Parse The Oracle-performed act of examining a SQL statement to enable an execution plan to be created.

Personal Digital Assistant (PDA) A hand-held device used for personal information storage.

Physical I/O The act of reading information from or writing information to a physical disk.

PMON The background process that cleans up behind failed user processes. PMON is responsible for releasing the lock and making it available to other users.

Primary key constraint Requires that the data in a particular column or combination of columns be a unique combination in the table and not be null.

Private synonym A synonym that is available only to the owner of the synonym.

Privilege The ability to perform a specific action within a database. Granted to a user or role.

Procedures Several forms of stored programs, all of which are written in PL/SQL and stored within the database. Each type of program can take input and return output. Functions always return a single value to the caller, while procedures can return none, one, or more values.

Process A job started by the operating system that can be used to run one or more computer programs.

Process freelist Also known as a freelist, this is a list of free data blocks within the extents within the table.

Program A collection of computer commands assembled in one file that enables work to be performed on a computer.

Public synonym A synonym that is available to any user in the database.

Query A statement presented to a database to obtain information. The query will always begin with the command word **select**.

Query plan The set of instructions the optimizer puts together on how to access the data and, if necessary, join together multiple tables most efficiently.

Quota An allotment of space assigned to a user or process on a computer system.

RAID A redundant array of inexpensive disks used to enable the storage of data in a protected fashion.

Readme documentation One or more files supplied with computer software that provide additional information that may have been written after the official documentation was published.

Read-only constraint Placed on a view to flag that view as one you cannot update, insert into, or delete from.

RECO The background process used to resolve failures in distributed databases.

Recovery The act of replacing damaged or deleted database files with backed up copies.

Recovery Manager (RMAN) An Oracle-supplied utility to enable backup and recovery of a database in an easy, automatic manner.

Recovery plan A defined approach containing procedures to be used when a database recovery must be performed. *See also* Backup plan.

Redo log A collection of the changes made to a database.

Referential integrity constraints Primary and foreign keys. A referential integrity constraint defines a relationship between columns in one or more tables.

Relational Database Management System (RDBMS) A set of programs designed to manage and manipulate data in the fastest, most efficient manner.

Reloads The number of times statements had to be reparsed in order to be executed. If a statement was aged out of the cache, or an object referenced by the statements was invalidated (changed in some way), the statement must be reparsed to be reexecuted. The action of reparsing a statement is counted as a reload.

Revoke The action a DBA takes to remove a privilege from a user or role.

Rollback segment Used to capture the image of data before it is changed to provide read integrity. Queries, performed against the data while it is being changed, will return the before-image version of the data.

Rollback segment, private Explicitly acquired when a database is opened, these rollback segments are available only to the first instance that acquires them.

Rollback segment, public Available for use by any instance, these rollback segments can be acquired for a pool of rollback segments, if available.

Row An area of a table that stores one complete, individual set of information. Can comprise one or more columns of information and is identified by a unique identification number within a table and within the database. In Oracle versions earlier than 8.0, the row identification number contains six bytes; in Oracle8, the row identification number contains ten bytes.

Rule Based Optimizer *See* Optimizer, Rule Based.

Schema An area designated within a database in which an application's objects are stored.

Segment A collection of extents that make up a single table, index, temporary segment, or rollback segment. *See also* Extent.

Self-referring constraint A constraint in which the parent and child tables are the same table.

Session A connection to the database including the memory area as well as the access privileges allocated to a specific user.

Shared pool or shared SQL pool Used to store the data dictionary cache and the library cache. Within the library cache is information about statements that have been run against the database. The shared pool contains the execution plans and parse trees for SQL statements run against the database. The second time an exact replica of a SQL statement is presented, the statement can be run much more quickly because the execution plan is already stored and available.

SMON The system monitor background process. Used to perform system tasks for an Oracle database, such as conducting instance recovery as needed, eliminating transactional objects that are no longer needed, coalescing adjacent tablespace free space.

Snapshot A picture of a table or set of tables that is captured at a point in time. Snapshots are copies of data in one database that have been copied to another database.

Snapshot, complex Created by selecting information from multiple tables with subqueries or "group by" clauses. *See also* Snapshot, simple.

Snapshot fast refresh A simple snapshot can be refreshed with changes to the data only.

Snapshot full refresh The data in a complex snapshot has to be completely copied to the remote database.

Snapshot refresh The act of updating a snapshot with the most current information available.

Snapshot, simple Created by selecting information from a single table or a simple set of tables that are joined together. *See also* Snapshot, complex.

Software A collection of computer programs designed to enable a user to accomplish a specific set of tasks.

Software installation The act of placing a complete set of software in a directory structure.

Software migration The act of creating a separate directory structure for the new Oracle software version's files. There will be two (or more) copies of Oracle software on the system at one time in completely separate directories.

Software upgrade The act of overwriting the old Oracle software version's files with the new version's files.

SQL*Net2 An Oracle-supplied communications package that enables a remote client to communicate with a central Oracle database.

SQL*Plus An Oracle-supplied utility to enable a user to insert, update, remove, or view information in a database.

Standby database In Oracle7.3, an inaccessible duplicate of the primary database. Cannot be used for queries or in any way unless you are activating it for disaster recovery. The standby database runs in constant recovery mode, so only the archive logs that have not been applied yet need to be recovered. In Oracle8i, can be used as a read-only database and switched over to a standby database to resynchronize the data. The ability to use the database in read-only mode provides the option of using the standby for decision-support system types of activities.

Stored outline A collection of hints for a SQL statement saved in the data dictionary. *See also* Hints.

Stored program or procedure One or more PL/SQL scripts stored directly in the database for ease of access.

Striping The act of combining two or more disks into a logical, single disk for data storage and information protection.

Structured Query Language (SQL) An ANSI standard language used to interact with a database.

Synonym Masks or hides the real name and owner of an object. Sometimes referred to as an alias.

System Global Area (SGA) Holds the most commonly requested structural information about the database and facilitates the transfer of information between users. The SGA is comprised of the data block buffer cache and the dictionary cache, the redo log buffer, and the shared SQL pool, which is comprised of a context area and a program global area.

System Identification Number (SID) Generally, a name used to differentiate between instances and to ensure the correct processes, and in turn the correct data, are being manipulated.

Systems DBA A DBA who oversees and performs database administration for a set of databases on a system.

Table The logical unit of storage for a specific collection of data. Made up of columns, a table is used to store rows of information.

Tablespace The logical storage area for one or more objects in a database.

Technical Action Report (TAR) An identification number assigned by Oracle Support, describing a problem that has been encountered with an Oracle product or database.

TNSNAMES.ORA A file that contains connection information describing the locations of databases. Configured to be used with the SQL*Net2 or Net8 listener.

Transportable tablespaces A mechanism that enables a tablespace to be relocated to another database. This is a new feature in Oracle8i.

Trigger Used to capture or verify information or load other tables with data as needed.

Unique constraint Requires that the data be a unique combination, but will allow you to insert null values.

Unique index An index in which the only acceptable values are nulls or a unique combination of one or more columns.

Unix A form of operating system available through several different hardware vendors. There are many different "flavors" of Unix including SCO, Linux, HP-UX, Compaq, and AIX. Each flavor of Unix will require slightly different database installation and configuration procedures.

Unix Process ID A unique identification number assigned to a Unix operating system process.

Upgrade *See* Software upgrade.

User A person who performs work on a system or database.

View A combination of columns from one or more tables that enable a user to see selected portions of database information while preventing access to other sensitive areas.

Willing-to-wait state *See* Latches, willing-to-wait.

Wizard A Java program that guides the user through performing a task. In Oracle8i, many Java wizards are used to assist the DBA in performing various database administration tasks, such as database backup and recovery, and network configuration.

Oracle8.1.5 DBA Views

he DBA_ views for Oracle8.1.5 are listed with brief descriptions here. Views discussed in Chapters 6, 7, and 8 are cross-referenced with the chapter number in which they appear.

DBA_2PC_NEIGHBORS Contains information about incoming and outgoing connections for pending transactions.

DBA_2PC_PENDING Contains information about distributed transactions awaiting recovery.

DBA_ALL_TABLES Displays descriptions of all tables (object tables and relational tables) in the database.

DBA_ANALYZE_OBJECTS Lists analyze objects.

DBA_ASSOCIATIONS Lists user-defined statistics information.

DBA_AUDIT_EXISTS Lists audit trail entries produced by AUDIT NOT EXISTS and AUDIT EXISTS.

DBA_AUDIT_OBJECT Contains audit trail records for all objects in the system.

DBA_AUDIT_SESSION Lists all audit trail records concerning CONNECT and DISCONNECT.

DBA_AUDIT_STATEMENT Lists audit trail records concerning GRANT, REVOKE, AUDIT, NOAUDIT, and ALTER SYSTEM statements.

DBA_AUDIT_TRAIL Lists all audit trail entries.

DBA_BLOCKERS Lists all sessions that have someone waiting on a lock the session holds, but that are not themselves waiting on a lock.

DBA_CATALOG Lists all database tables, views, synonyms, and sequences.

DBA_CLU_COLUMNS Lists mappings of table columns to cluster columns.

DBA_CLUSTER_HASH_EXPRESSIONS Lists hash functions for all clusters.

DBA_CLUSTERS Contains descriptions of all clusters in the database.

DBA_COL_COMMENTS Lists comments on columns of all tables and views.

DBA_COL_PRIVS Lists all grants on columns in the database.

DBA_COLL_TYPES Displays all named collection types in the database, such as VARRAYs, nested tables, object tables, and so on.

DBA_CONS_COLUMNS Contains information about accessible columns in constraint definitions. (Chapter 8)

DBA_CONSTRAINTS Contains constraint definitions on all tables. (Chapter 8)

DBA_CONTEXT Lists all context namespaces information.

DBA_DATA_FILES Contains information about database files. (Chapter 6)

DBA_DB_LINKS Lists all database links in the database.

DBA_DDL_LOCKS Lists all DDL locks held in the database and all outstanding requests for a DDL lock.

DBA_DEPENDENCIES Lists dependencies to and from objects. Dependencies on views created without any database links are also available.

DBA_DIM_ATTRIBUTES Represents the relationship between a dimension level and a functionally dependent column. The table that the level columns are in must match the table of the dependent column.

DBA_DIM_CHILD_OF Represents a 1:n hierarchical relationship between a pair of levels in a dimension.

DBA_DIM_HIERARCHIES Represents a dimension hierarchy.

DBA_DIM_JOIN_KEY Represents a join between two dimension tables. The join is always specified between a parent dimension level column and a child column.

DBA_DIM_LEVEL_KEY Represents a column of a dimension level. The position of a column within a level is specified by KEY_POSITION.

DBA_DIM_LEVELS Represents a dimension level. All columns of a dimension level must come from the same relation.

DBA_DIMENSIONS Represents dimension objects.

DBA_DIRECTORIES Provides information on all directory objects in the database.

DBA_DML_LOCKS Lists all DML locks held in the database and all outstanding requests for a DML lock.

DBA_ERRORS Lists current errors on all stored objects in the database.

DBA_EXP_FILES Contains a description of export files.

DBA_EXP_OBJECTS Lists objects that have been incrementally exported.

DBA_EXP_VERSION Contains the version number of the last export session.

DBA_EXTENTS Lists the extents that make up all segments in the database. (Chapter 6)

DBA_FREE_SPACE Lists the free extents in all tablespaces. (Chapter 6)

DBA_FREE_SPACE_COALESCED Contains statistics on coalesced space in tablespaces. (Chapter 6)

DBA_IND_COLUMNS Contains descriptions of the columns that make up the indexes on all tables and clusters. (Chapter 8)

DBA_IND_EXPRESSIONS Lists functional index expressions on all tables and clusters.

DBA_IND_PARTITIONS Describes, for each index partition, the partition-level partitioning information, the storage parameters for the partition, and various partition statistics determined by ANALYZE.

DBA_IND_SUBPARTITIONS Describes, for each index subpartition that the current user owns, the partition-level partitioning information, the storage parameters for the subpartition, and various partition statistics determined by ANALYZE.

DBA_INDEXES Contains descriptions for all indexes in the database. (Chapter 8)

DBA_INDEXTYPE_OPERATORS Lists all the operators supported by index types.

DBA_INDEXTYPES Lists all the index types.

DBA_JOBS Lists all jobs in the database.

DBA_JOBS_RUNNING Lists all jobs in the database that are currently running.

DBA_LIBRARIES Lists all the libraries in the database.

DBA_LOB_PARTITIONS Displays the LOBs contained in tables accessible to the user.

DBA_LOB_SUBPARTITIONS Displays partition-level attributes of LOB data subpartitions.

DBA_LOBS Displays the LOBs contained in all tables.

DBA_LOCK_INTERNAL Contains a row for each lock or latch that is being held and one row for each outstanding request for a lock or latch.

DBA_LOCKS Lists all locks or latches held in the database and all outstanding requests for a lock or latch.

DBA_METHOD_PARAMS Contains a description of method parameters of types in the database.

DBA_METHOD_RESULTS Contains a description of method results of all types in the database.

DBA_MVIEW_AGGREGATES Represents the grouping functions (aggregated measures) that appear in the SELECT list of an aggregated materialized view.

DBA_MVIEW_ANALYSIS Represents the materialized views that potentially support query rewriting and have additional information that is available for analysis by applications. This view excludes any materialized view that references a remote table or that includes a reference to a nonstatic value such as SYSDATE or USER.

DBA_MVIEW_DETAIL_RELATIONS Represents the named detail relations that are either in the FROM list of a materialized view, or that are indirectly referenced through views in the FROM list. Inline views in the materialized view definition are not represented in this table.

DBA_MVIEW_JOINS Represents a join between two columns in the WHERE clause of a materialized view.

DBA_MVIEW_KEYS Represents the named detail relations that are either in the FROM list of a materialized view, or that are indirectly referenced through views in the FROM list. Inline views in the materialized view definition are not represented in this table.

DBA_NESTED_TABLES Displays descriptions of the nested tables contained in all tables.

DBA_OBJ_AUDIT_OPTS Lists auditing options for all objects owned by a user.

DBA_OBJECT_SIZE Lists the sizes, in bytes, of various PL/SQL objects.

DBA_OBJECT_TABLES Displays descriptions of all object tables in the database.

DBA_OBJECTS Lists all objects in the database. (Chapter 6)

DBA_OPANCILLARY Lists ancillary information for operator bindings.

DBA_OPARGUMENTS Lists argument information for operator bindings.

DBA_OPBINDINGS Lists operator bindings.

DBA_OPERATORS Lists operators.

DBA_OUTLINE_HINTS Lists the set of hints that make up the outlines.

DBA_OUTLINES Lists information about outlines.

DBA_PART_COL_STATISTICS Contains column statistics and histogram information for all table partitions.

DBA_PART_HISTOGRAMS Contains the histogram data (endpoints per histogram) for histograms on all table partitions.

DBA_PART_INDEXES Lists the object-level partitioning information for all partitioned indexes.

DBA_PART_KEY_COLUMNS Describes the partitioning key columns for all partitioned objects.

DBA_PART_LOBS Describes table-level information for partitioned LOBs, including default attributes for LOB data partitions.

DBA_PART_TABLES Lists the object-level partitioning information for all the partitioned tables.

DBA_PARTIAL_DROP_TABS Describes tables that have partially dropped tables.

DBA_PENDING_TRANSACTIONS Gives information about unresolved transactions (either due to failure or if the coordinator has not sent a commit/rollback).

DBA_POLICIES Lists policies.

DBA_PRIV_AUDIT_OPTS Describes current system privileges being audited across the system and by user.

DBA_PROFILES Displays all profiles and their limits. (Chapter 7)

DBA_QUEUE_SCHEDULES Describes the current schedules for propagating messages.

DBA_QUEUE_TABLES Describes the names and types of the queues in all of the queue tables created in the database.

DBA_QUEUES Describes the operational characteristics for every queue in a database.

DBA_RCHILD Lists all the children in any refresh group.

DBA_REFRESH Lists all the refresh groups.

DBA_REFRESH_CHILDREN Lists all of the objects in refresh groups.

DBA_REFS Describes the REF columns and REF attributes in object type columns of all the tables in the database.

DBA_REGISTERED_SNAPSHOT_GROUPS Lists all the snapshot repgroups at this site.

DBA_REGISTERED_SNAPSHOTS Retrieves information about remote snapshots of local tables.

DBA_REPCAT_REFRESH_TEMPLATES This view is used with Advanced Replication.

DBA_REPCAT_TEMPLATE_OBJECTS This view is used with Advanced Replication.

DBA_REPCAT_TEMPLATE_PARMS This view is used with Advanced Replication.

DBA_REPCAT_TEMPLATE_SITES This view is used with Advanced Replication.

DBA_REPCAT_USER_AUTHORIZATIONS This view is used with Advanced Replication.

DBA_REPCAT_USER_PARM_VALUES This view is used with Advanced Replication.

DBA_REPCATLOG This view is used with Advanced Replication.

DBA_REPCOLUMN This view is used with Advanced Replication.

DBA_REPCOLUMN_GROUP This view is used with Advanced Replication.

DBA_REPCONFLICT This view is used with Advanced Replication.

DBA_REPDDL This view is used with Advanced Replication.

DBA_REPGENERATED This view is used with Advanced Replication.

DBA_REPGENOBJECTS This view is used with Advanced Replication.

DBA_REPGROUP This view is used with Advanced Replication.

DBA_REPGROUPED_COLUMN This view is used with Advanced Replication.

DBA_REPKEY_COLUMNS This view is used with Advanced Replication.

DBA_REPOBJECT This view is used with Advanced Replication.

DBA_REPPARAMETER_COLUMN This view is used with Advanced Replication.

DBA_REPPRIORITY This view is used with Advanced Replication.

DBA_REPPRIORITY_GROUP This view is used with Advanced Replication.

DBA_REPPROP This view is used with Advanced Replication.

DBA_REPRESOL_STATS_CONTROL This view is used with Advanced Replication.

DBA_REPRESOLUTION This view is used with Advanced Replication.

DBA_REPRESOLUTION_METHOD This view is used with Advanced Replication.

DBA_REPSITES This view is used with Advanced Replication.

DBA_RGROUP Lists all refresh groups.

DBA_ROLE_PRIVS Lists roles granted to users and roles. (Chapter 7)

DBA_ROLES Lists all roles that exist in the database. (Chapter 7)

DBA_ROLLBACK_SEGS Contains descriptions of rollback segments. (Chapter 6)

DBA_RSRC_CONSUMER_GROUP_PRIVS Lists all resource consumer groups and the users and roles to which they have been granted.

DBA_RSRC_CONSUMER_GROUPS Lists all resource consumer groups that exist in the database.

DBA_RSRC_MANAGER_SYSTEM_PRIVS Lists all the users and roles that have been granted system privileges pertaining to the resource manager.

DBA_RSRC_PLAN_DIRECTIVES Lists all resource plan directives that exist in the database.

DBA_RSRC_PLANS Lists all resource plans that exist in the database.

DBA_RULESETS Lists information about rule sets.

DBA_SEGMENTS Contains information about storage allocated for all database segments. (Chapter 6)

DBA_SEQUENCES Contains descriptions of all sequences in the database.

DBA_SNAPSHOT_LOG_FILTER_COLS Lists all filter columns (excluding PK cols) being logged in the snapshot logs.

DBA_SNAPSHOT_LOGS Lists all snapshot logs in the database.

DBA_SNAPSHOT_REFRESH_TIMES Lists snapshot refresh times.

DBA_SNAPSHOTS Lists all snapshots in the database.

DBA_SOURCE Contains source of all stored objects in the database.

DBA_STMT_AUDIT_OPTS Contains information that describes current system auditing options across the system and by user.

DBA_SUBPART_COL_STATISTICS Lists column statistics and histogram information for table subpartitions.

DBA_SUBPART_HISTOGRAMS Lists the actual histogram data (endpoints per histogram) for histograms on table subpartitions.

DBA_SUBPART_KEY_COLUMNS Lists subpartitioning key columns for tables (and Local indexes on tables) partitioned using the Composite Range/Hash method.

DBA_SYNONYMS Lists all synonyms in the database. (Chapter 8)

DBA_SYS_PRIVS Lists system privileges granted to users and roles. (Chapter 7)

DBA_TAB_COL_STATISTICS Contains column statistics and histogram information in the DBA_TAB_COLUMNS view.

DBA_TAB_COLUMNS Contains information that describes columns of all tables, views, and clusters. (Chapter 8)

DBA_TAB_COMMENTS Contains comments on all tables and views in the database.

DBA_TAB_HISTOGRAMS Lists histograms on columns of all tables.

DBA_TAB_PARTITIONS Describes, for each table partition, the partition-level partitioning information, the storage parameters for the partition, and various partition statistics determined by ANALYZE.

DBA_TAB_PRIVS Lists all grants on objects in the database. (Chapter 7)

DBA_TAB_SUBPARTITIONS Describes, for each table subpartition, its name, name of the table and partition to which it belongs, and its storage attributes.

DBA_TABLES Contains descriptions of all relational tables in the database. (Chapter 8)

DBA_TABLESPACES Contains descriptions of all tablespaces. (Chapter 6)

DBA_TEMP_FILES Contains information about database temp files.

DBA_TRIGGER_COLS Lists column usage in all triggers.

DBA_TRIGGERS Lists all triggers in the database.

DBA_TS_QUOTAS Lists tablespace quotas for all users. (Chapter 7)

DBA_TYPE_ATTRS Displays the attributes of types in the database.

DBA_TYPE_METHODS Describes methods of all types in the database.

DBA_TYPES Displays all abstract data types in the database.

DBA_UNUSED_COL_TABS Contains a description of all tables containing unused columns.

DBA_UPDATABLE_COLUMNS Contains a description of columns that are updatable by the database administrator in a join view.

DBA_USERS Lists information about all users of the database. (Chapter 7)

DBA_USTATS Contains information about the current user.

DBA_VARRAYS Lists the text of views accessible to the user.

DBA_VIEWS Contains the text of all views in the database. (Chapter 8)

DBA_WAITERS Lists all sessions that are waiting on a lock as well as the session that is blocking them.

APPENDIX C

Oracle8.1.5 V$ Views

his appendix contains the list of V$ views available in Oracle8.1.5 along with a short description of what the view displays. Views discussed in Chapters 9 and 10 are cross-referenced with the chapter number in which they appear.

V$ACCESS Displays objects in the database that are currently locked and the sessions that are accessing them.

V$ACTIVE_INSTANCES Maps instance names to instance numbers for all instances that have the database currently mounted.

V$AQ Describes statistics for the queues in the database.

V$ARCHIVE Contains information on redo log files in need of archiving. Each row provides information for one thread. This information is also available in V$LOG. Oracle recommends that you use V$LOG.

V$ARCHIVE_DEST Describes, for the current instance, all the archive log destinations, their current value, mode, and status.

V$ARCHIVED_LOG Displays archived log information from the control file, including archive log names. An archive log record is inserted after the online redo log is successfully archived or cleared (name column is NULL if the log was cleared). If the log is archived twice, there will be two archived log records with the same THREAD#, SEQUENCE#, and FIRST_CHANGE#, but with a different name. An archive log record is also inserted when an archive log is restored from a backup set or a copy.

V$ARCHIVE_PROCESSES Provides information about the state of the various ARCH processes for the instance.

V$BACKUP Displays the backup status of all online datafiles.

V$BACKUP_ASYNC_IO Displays backup set information from the control file. A backup set record is inserted after the backup set is successfully completed.

V$BACKUP_CORRUPTION Displays information about corruptions in datafile backups from the control file. Note that corruptions are not tolerated in the control file and archived log backups.

V$BACKUP_DATAFILE Displays backup datafile and backup control file information from the control file.

V$BACKUP_DEVICE Displays information about supported backup devices. If a device type does not support named devices, then one row with the device type and a null device name is returned for that device type. If a device type supports named devices, then one row is returned for each available device of that type. The special device type DISK is not returned by this view because it is always available.

V$BACKUP_PIECE Displays information about backup pieces from the control file. Each backup set consists of one or more backup pieces.

V$BACKUP_REDOLOG Displays information about archived logs in backup sets from the control file. Note that online redo logs cannot be backed up directly; they must be archived first to disk and then backed up. An archive log backup set can contain one or more archived logs.

V$BACKUP_SET Displays backup set information from the control file. A backup set record is inserted after the backup set is successfully completed.

V$BACKUP_SYNC_IO Displays backup set information from the control file. A backup set record is inserted after the backup set is successfully completed.

V$BGPROCESS Describes the background processes.

V$BH This is a Parallel Server view. This view gives the status and number of pings for every buffer in the SGA.

V$BUFFER_POOL Displays information about all buffer pools available for the instance. The "sets" pertain to the number of LRU latch sets.

V$BUFFER_POOL_STATISTICS Displays information about all buffer pools available for the instance. The "sets" pertain to the number of LRU latch sets.

V$CACHE This is a Parallel Server view. This view contains information from the block header of each block in the SGA of the current instance as related to particular database objects.

V$CACHE_LOCK This is a Parallel Server view. V$CACHE_LOCK is similar to V$CACHE, except for the platform-specific lock manager identifiers. This information may be useful if the platform-specific lock manager provides tools for monitoring the PCM lock operations that are occurring.

V$CIRCUIT Contains information about virtual circuits, which are user connections to the database through dispatchers and servers.

V$CLASS_PING Displays the number of blocks pinged per block class. Use this view to compare contentions for blocks in different classes.

V$COMPATIBILITY Displays features in use by the database instance that may prevent downgrading to a previous release. This is the dynamic (SGA) version of this information, which may not reflect features that other instances have used and may include temporary incompatibilities (like UNDO segments) that will not exist after the database is shut down cleanly.

V$COMPATSEG Lists the permanent features in use by the database that will prevent moving back to an earlier release.

V$CONTEXT Lists set attributes in the current session.

V$CONTROLFILE Lists the names of the control files.

V$CONTROLFILE_RECORD_SECTION Displays information about the control file record sections.

V$COPY_CORRUPTION Displays information about datafile copy corruptions from the control file.

V$DATABASE Contains database information from the control file. (Chapter 9)

V$DATAFILE Contains datafile information from the control file. (Chapter 9)

V$DATAFILE_COPY Displays datafile copy information from the control file.

V$DATAFILE_HEADER Displays datafile information from the datafile headers. (Chapter 9)

V$DBFILE Lists all datafiles making up the database. This view is retained for historical compatibility. Use of V$DATAFILE is recommended instead. (Chapter 9)

V$DBLINK Describes all database links (links with IN_TRANSACTION = YES) opened by the session issuing the query on V$DBLINK. These database links must be committed or rolled back before being closed.

V$DB_OBJECT_CACHE Displays database objects that are cached in the library cache. Objects include tables, indexes, clusters, synonym definitions, PL/SQL procedures and packages, and triggers.

V$DB_PIPES Displays the pipes that are currently in this database.

V$DELETED_OBJECT Displays information about deleted archived logs, datafile copies, and backup pieces from the control file. The only purpose of this view is to optimize the recovery catalog resync operation. When an archived log, datafile copy, or backup piece is deleted, the corresponding record is marked deleted.

V$DISPATCHER Provides information on the dispatcher processes.

V$DISPATCHER_RATE Provides rate statistics for the dispatcher processes.

V$DLM_ALL_LOCKS This is a Parallel Server view. V$DLM_ALL_LOCKS lists information of all locks currently known to lock manager that are being blocked or blocking others.

V$DLM_CONVERT_LOCAL Displays the elapsed time for the local lock conversion operation.

V$DLM_CONVERT_REMOTE Displays the elapsed time for the remote lock conversion operation.

V$DLM_LATCH V$DLM_LATCH is obsolete. See V$LATCH for statistics about DLM latch performance.

V$DLM_LOCKS This is a Parallel Server view. V$DLM_LOCKS lists information of all locks currently known to lock manager that are being blocked or blocking others.

V$DLM_MISC Displays miscellaneous DLM statistics.

V$DLM_RESS V$DLM_RESS is a Parallel Server view. It displays information of all resources currently known to the lock manager.

V$ENABLEDPRIVS Displays which privileges are enabled. These privileges can be found in the table SYS.SYSTEM_PRIVILEGES_MAP.

V$ENQUEUE_LOCK Displays all locks owned by enqueue state objects. The columns in this view are identical to the columns in V$LOCK. For more information, see V$LOCK.

V$EVENT_NAME Contains information about wait events.

V$EXECUTION Displays information on parallel execution.

V$FALSE_PING V$FALSE_PING is a Parallel Server view. This view displays buffers that may be getting false pings—that is, buffers pinged more than ten times that are protected by the same lock as another buffer that pinged more than ten times. Buffers identified as getting false pings can be remapped in "GC_FILES_TO_LOCKS" to reduce lock collisions.

V$FAST_START_SERVERS Provides information about all the recovery slaves performing parallel transaction recovery.

V$FAST_START_TRANSACTIONS Contains information about the progress of the transactions that Oracle is recovering.

V$FILE_PING Displays the number of blocks pinged per datafile. This information in turn can be used for determining access patterns to existing datafiles and deciding new mappings from datafile blocks to PCM locks.

V$FILESTAT Contains information about file read/write statistics. (Chapter 10)

V$FIXED_TABLE Displays all dynamic performance tables, views, and derived tables in the database. Some V$ tables (for example, V$ROLLNAME) refer to real tables and are therefore not listed. (Chapter 9)

V$FIXED_VIEW_DEFINITION Contains the definitions of all the fixed views (views beginning with V$). Use this table with caution. Oracle tries to keep the behavior of fixed views the same from release to release, but the definitions of the fixed views can change without notice. Use these definitions to optimize your queries by using indexed columns of the dynamic performance tables.

V$GLOBAL_BLOCKED_LOCKS Displays global blocked locks.

V$GLOBAL_TRANSACTION Displays information on the currently active global transactions.

V$HS_AGENT Identifies the set of HS agents currently running on a given host, using one row per agent process.

V$HS_SESSION Identifies the set of HS sessions currently open for the Oracle server.

V$INDEXED_FIXED_COLUMN Displays the columns in dynamic performance tables that are indexed (X$ tables). The X$ tables can change without notice. Use this view only to write queries against fixed views (V$ views) more efficiently.

V$INSTANCE Displays the state of the current instance. This version of V$INSTANCE is not compatible with earlier versions of V$INSTANCE. (Chapter 9)

V$INSTANCE_RECOVERY Used to monitor the mechanisms that implement the user-specifiable limit on recovery reads.

V$LATCH Lists statistics for nonparent latches and summary statistics for parent latches. That is, the statistics for a parent latch include counts from each of its children. (Chapter 10)

V$LATCHHOLDER Contains information about the current latch holders.

V$LATCHNAME Contains information about decoded latch names for the latches shown in V$LATCH. The rows of V$LATCHNAME have a one-to-one correspondence to the rows of V$LATCH.

V$LATCH_CHILDREN Contains statistics about child latches. This view includes all columns of V$LATCH plus the CHILD# column. Note that child latches have the same parent if their LATCH# columns match.

V$LATCH_MISSES Contains statistics about missed attempts to acquire a latch.

V$LATCH_PARENT Contains statistics about the parent latch. The columns of V$LATCH_PARENT are identical to those in V$LATCH.

V$LIBRARYCACHE Contains statistics about library cache performance and activity. (Chapter 10)

V$LICENSE Contains information about license limits.

V$LOADCSTAT Contains SQL*Loader statistics compiled during the execution of a direct load. These statistics apply to the whole load. Any SELECT against this table results in "no rows returned," since you cannot load data and do a query at the same time.

V$LOADTSTAT Contains SQL*Loader statistics compiled during the execution of a direct load. These statistics apply to the current table. Any SELECT against this table results in "no rows returned," since you cannot load data and do a query at the same time.

V$LOCK Lists the locks currently held by the Oracle server and outstanding requests for a lock or latch. (Chapter 10)

V$LOCK_ACTIVITY This is a Parallel Server view. It displays the DLM lock operation activity of the current instance. Each row corresponds to a type of lock operation.

V$LOCK_ELEMENT This is a Parallel Server view. There is one entry in V$LOCK_ELEMENT for each PCM lock that is used by the buffer cache. The name of the PCM lock that corresponds to a lock element is {'BL', indx, class}.

V$LOCKED_OBJECT Lists all locks acquired by every transaction on the system. (Chapter 10)

V$LOCKS_WITH_COLLISIONS This is a Parallel Server view. Use this view to find the locks that protect multiple buffers, each of which has been either force-written or force-read at least ten times. It is very likely that those buffers are experiencing false pings due to being mapped to the same lock.

V$LOG Contains log file information from the control files.

V$LOGFILE Contains information about redo log files.

V$LOGHIST Contains log history information from the control file. This view is retained for historical compatibility. Use of V$LOG_HISTORY is recommended instead.

V$LOGMNR_CONTENTS Contains log history information.

V$LOGMNR_DICTIONARY Contains log history information.

V$LOGMNR_LOGS Contains log information.

V$LOGMNR_PARAMETERS Contains log information.

V$LOG_HISTORY Contains log history information from the control file.

V$MLS_PARAMETERS This is a Trusted Oracle Server view that lists Trusted Oracle Server–specific initialization parameters. For more information, see your Trusted Oracle documentation.

V$MTS Contains information for tuning the Multi-Threaded Server.

V$MYSTAT Contains statistics on the current session.

V$NLS_PARAMETERS Contains current values of NLS parameters.

V$NLS_VALID_VALUES Lists all valid values for NLS parameters.

V$OBJECT_DEPENDENCY Can be used to determine what objects are depended on by a package, procedure, or cursor that is currently loaded in the shared pool. For example, together with V$SESSION and V$SQL, it can be used to determine which tables are used in the SQL statement that a user is currently executing. For more information, see V$SESSION and V$SQL.

V$OBSOLETE_PARAMETER Lists obsolete parameters. If any value is true, you should examine why.

V$OFFLINE_RANGE Displays datafile offline information from the control file.

V$OPEN_CURSOR Lists cursors that each user session currently has opened and parsed.

V$OPTION Lists options that are installed with the Oracle server.

V$PARALLEL_DEGREE_LIMIT_MTH Displays all available parallel degree limit resource allocation methods.

V$PARAMETER Lists information about initialization parameters. (Chapter 9)

V$PING This is a Parallel Server view. The V$PING view is identical to the V$CACHE view but only displays blocks that have been pinged at least once. This view contains information from the block header of each block in the SGA of the current instance as related to particular database objects.

V$PQ_SESSTAT Lists session statistics for parallel queries. Note: This view will be obsoleted in a future release.

V$PQ_SLAVE Lists statistics for each of the active parallel execution servers on an instance. Note: This view will be replaced/obsoleted in a future release by a new view called V$PX_PROCESS.

V$PQ_SYSSTAT Lists system statistics for parallel queries. Note: This view will be replaced/obsoleted in a future release by a new view called V$PX_PROCESS_SYSSTAT.

V$PQ_TQSTAT Contains statistics on parallel execution operations. The statistics are compiled after the query completes and only remain for the duration of the session. It displays the number of rows processed through each parallel execution server at each stage of the execution tree. This view can help determine skew problems in a query's execution. Note: This view will be renamed V$PX_TQSTAT in a future release.

V$PROCESS Contains information about the currently active processes. While the LATCHWAIT column indicates what latch a process is waiting for, the LATCHSPIN column indicates what latch a process is spinning on. On multiprocessor machines, Oracle processes will spin on a latch before waiting on it. (Chapter 10)

V$PROXY_ARCHIVEDLOG Contains descriptions of archived log backups that are taken with a new feature called Proxy Copy. Each row represents a backup of one archived log.

V$PROXY_DATAFILE Contains descriptions of datafile and control file backups that are taken with a new feature called Proxy Copy. Each row represents a backup of one database file.

V$PWFILE_USERS Lists users who have been granted **sysdba** and **sysoper** privileges as derived from the password file.

V$PX_PROCESS Contains information about the sessions running parallel execution.

V$PX_PROCESS_SYSSTAT Contains information about the sessions running parallel execution.

V$PX_SESSION Contains information about the sessions running parallel execution.

V$PX_SESSTAT Contains information about the sessions running parallel execution.

V$QUEUE Contains information on the multithread message queues.

V$RECOVER_FILE Displays the status of files needing media recovery.

V$RECOVERY_FILE_STATUS Contains one row for each datafile for each **recover** command. This view contains useful information only for the Oracle process doing the recovery. When Recovery Manager directs a server process to perform recovery, only Recovery Manager is able to view the relevant information in this view. V$RECOVERY_FILE_STATUS will be empty to all other Oracle users.

V$RECOVERY_LOG Lists information about archived logs that are needed to complete media recovery. This information is derived from the log history view, V$LOG_HISTORY. For more information, see V$LOG_HISTORY. V$RECOVERY_LOG contains useful information only for the Oracle process doing the recovery. When Recovery Manager directs a server process to perform recovery, only Recovery Manager is able to view the relevant information in this view. V$RECOVERY_LOG will be empty to all other Oracle users.

V$RECOVERY_PROGRESS Can be used to track database recovery operations to ensure that they are not stalled, and also to estimate the time required to complete the operation in progress.

V$RECOVERY_PROGRESS is a subview of V$SESSION_LONGOPS.

V$RECOVERY_STATUS Contains statistics of the current recovery process. This view contains useful information only for the Oracle process doing the recovery. When Recovery Manager directs a server process to perform recovery, only Recovery Manager is able to view the relevant information in this view. V$RECOVERY_STATUS will be empty to all other Oracle users.

V$REQDIST Lists statistics for the histogram of MTS dispatcher request times, divided into 12 buckets, or ranges of time. The time ranges grow exponentially as a function of the bucket number.

V$RESERVED_WORDS Gives a list of all the keywords that are used by the PL/SQL compiler. This view helps developers to determine whether a word is already being used as a keyword in the language.

V$RESOURCE Contains resource name and address information.

V$RESOURCE_LIMIT Displays information about global resource use for some of the system resources. Use this view to monitor the consumption of resources so that you can take corrective action, if necessary.

V$ROLLNAME Lists the names of all online rollback segments. It can only be accessed when the database is open.

V$ROLLSTAT Contains rollback segment statistics.

V$ROWCACHE Displays statistics for data dictionary activity. Each row contains statistics for one data dictionary cache.

V$ROWCACHE_PARENT Displays information for parent objects in the data dictionary. There is one row per lock owner and one waiter for each object. This row shows the mode held or requested. For objects with no owners or waiters, a single row is displayed.

V$ROWCACHE_SUBORDINATE Displays information for subordinate objects in the data dictionary.

V$RSRC_CONSUMER_GROUP Displays data related to the currently active resource consumer groups.

V$RSRC_CONSUMER_GROUP_CPU_MTH Shows all available resource allocation methods for resource consumer groups.

V$RSRC_PLAN Displays the names of all currently active resource plans.

V$RSRC_PLAN_CPU_MTH Shows all available CPU resource allocation methods for resource plans.

V$SESSION Lists session information for each current session.

V$SESSION_CONNECT_INFO Displays information about network connections for the current session.

V$SESSION_CURSOR_CACHE Displays information on cursor usage for the current session. Note: The V$SESSION_CURSOR_CACHE view is not a measure of the effectiveness of the SESSION_CACHED_CURSORS initialization parameter.

V$SESSION_EVENT Lists information on waits for an event by a session.

V$SESSION_LONGOPS Displays the status of certain long-running operations. It provides progression reports on operations using the columns SOFAR and TOTALWORK.

V$SESSION_OBJECT_CACHE Displays object cache statistics for the current user session on the local server (instance).

V$SESSION_WAIT Lists the resources or events for which active sessions are waiting.

V$SESSTAT Lists user session statistics. To find the name of the statistic associated with each statistic number (STATISTIC#), see V$STATNAME.

V$SESS_IO Lists I/O statistics for each user session.

V$SGA Contains summary information on the system global area. (Chapter 9)

V$SGASTAT Contains detailed information on the system global area. (Chapter 10)

V$SHARED_POOL_RESERVED Lists statistics that help you tune the reserved pool and space within the shared pool.

V$SHARED_SERVER Contains information on the shared server processes.

V$SORT_SEGMENT Contains information about every sort segment in a given instance. The view is only updated when the tablespace is of the TEMPORARY type.

V$SORT_USAGE Describes sort usage.

V$SQL Lists statistics on shared SQL area without the GROUP BY clause and contains one row for each child of the original SQL text entered.

V$SQL_BIND_DATA Displays the actual bind data sent by the client for each distinct bind variable in each cursor owned by the session querying this view if the data is available in the server.

V$SQL_BIND_METADATA Displays bind metadata provided by the client for each distinct bind variable in each cursor owned by the session querying this view.

V$SQL_CURSOR Displays debugging information for each cursor associated with the session querying this view.

V$SQL_SHARED_MEMORY Displays information about the cursor shared memory snapshot. Each SQL statement stored in the shared pool has one or more child objects associated with it. Each child object has a number of parts, one of which is the context heap, which holds, among other things, the query plan.

V$SQLAREA Lists statistics on shared SQL area and contains one row per SQL string. It provides statistics on SQL statements that are in memory, parsed, and ready for execution.

V$SQLTEXT Contains the text of SQL statements belonging to shared SQL cursors in the SGA.

V$SQLTEXT_WITH_NEWLINES Identical to the V$SQLTEXT view except that, to improve legibility, V$SQLTEXT_WITH_NEWLINES does not replace newlines and tabs in the SQL statement with spaces.

V$STATNAME Displays decoded statistic names for the statistics shown in the V$SESSTAT and V$SYSSTAT tables. For more information, see V$SESSTAT and V$SYSSTAT.

V$SUBCACHE Displays information about the subordinate caches currently loaded into library cache memory. The view walks through the library cache, printing out a row for each loaded subordinate cache per library cache object.

V$SYSSTAT Lists system statistics. To find the name of the statistic associated with each statistic number (STATISTIC#), see V$STATNAME. (Chapter 10)

V$SYSTEM_CURSOR_CACHE Displays information similar to the V$SESSION_CURSOR_CACHE view except that this information is systemwide. For more information, see V$SESSION_CURSOR_CACHE.

V$SYSTEM_EVENT Contains information on total waits for an event. (Chapter 10)

V$SYSTEM_PARAMETER Contains information on system parameters.

V$TABLESPACE Displays tablespace information from the control file.

V$TEMPFILE Displays tempfile information.

V$TEMPORARY_LOBS Displays temporary LOBs.

V$TEMP_EXTENT_MAP Displays the status of each unit for all temporary tablespaces.

V$TEMP_EXTENT_POOL Displays the state of temporary space cached and used for a given instance. Note that loading of the temporary space cache is lazy, and instances can be dormant. Use GV$TEMP_EXTENT_POOL for information about all instances.

V$TEMP_PING This view displays the number of blocks pinged per datafile. This information in turn can be used for determining access patterns to existing datafiles and deciding new mappings from datafile blocks to PCM locks.

V$TEMP_SPACE_HEADER Displays aggregate information per file per temporary tablespace regarding how much space is currently being used and how much is free as per the space header.

V$TEMPSTAT Contains information about file read/write statistics.

V$THREAD Contains thread information from the control file.

V$TIMER Lists the elapsed time in hundredths of seconds. Time is measured since the beginning of the epoch, which is operating-system specific, and wraps around to zero again whenever the value overflows four bytes (roughly 497 days).

V$TRANSACTION Lists the active transactions in the system.

V$TRANSACTION_ENQUEUE Displays locks owned by transaction state objects.

V$TYPE_SIZE Lists the sizes of various database components for use in estimating data block capacity.

V$VERSION Lists version numbers of core library components in the Oracle server. There is one row for each component.

V$WAITSTAT Lists block contention statistics. This table is only updated when timed statistics are enabled. (Chapter 10)

Index

Symbols

A

D

E

G

H

I

N

O

P

Q

R

S

T

U

X

Get Your **FREE** Subscription to Oracle Magazine

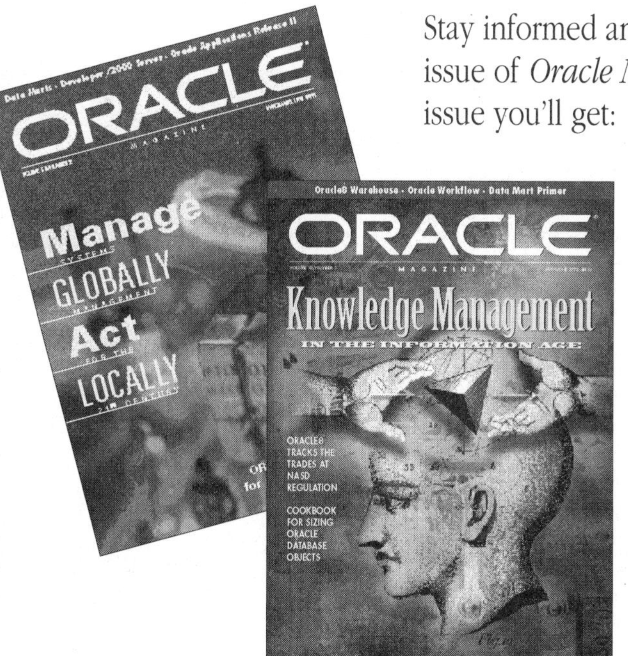

Stay informed and increase your productivity with every issue of *Oracle Magazine*. Inside each FREE, bimonthly issue you'll get:

- Up-to-date information on Oracle Data Server, Oracle Applications, Network Computing Architecture, and tools
- Third-party news and announcements
- Technical articles on Oracle products and operating environments
- Software tuning tips
- Oracle customer application stories

Three easy ways to subscribe:

1 **MAIL** Cut out this page, complete the questionnaire on the back, and mail it to: *Oracle Magazine,* P.O. Box 1263, Skokie, IL 60076-8263.

2 **FAX** Cut out this page, complete the questionnaire on the back, and fax it to **+ 847.647.9735.**

3 **WEB** Visit our Web site at **www.oramag.com.** You'll find a subscription form there, plus much more!

If there are other Oracle users at your location who would like to receive their own subscription to *Oracle Magazine,* please photocopy the form and pass it along.

☐ YES! Please send me a FREE subscription to Oracle Magazine.

☐ NO, I am not interested at this tim

If you wish to receive your free bimonthly subscription to *Oracle Magazine,* you must fill out the entire form, sign and date it (incomplete forms cannot be processed or acknowledged). You can also subscribe at our Web site at **www.oramag.com/html/subform.html** or fax your application to *Oracle Magazine* at **+847.647.9735.**

SIGNATURE (REQUIRED) ✓ ____________________ **DATE** __________

NAME ____________________ TITLE ____________________

COMPANY ____________________ E-MAIL ADDRESS ____________________

STREET/P.O. BOX ____________________

CITY/STATE/ZIP ____________________

COUNTRY ____________________ TELEPHONE ____________________

You must answer all eight questions below.

1 What is the primary business activity of your firm at this location? *(circle only one)*

- 01 Agriculture, Mining, Natural Resources
- 02 Architecture, Construction
- 03 Communications
- 04 Consulting, Training
- 05 Consumer Packaged Goods
- 06 Data Processing
- 07 Education
- 08 Engineering
- 09 Financial Services
- 10 Government—Federal, Local, State, Other
- 11 Government—Military
- 12 Health Care
- 13 Manufacturing—Aerospace, Defense
- 14 Manufacturing—Computer Hardware
- 15 Manufacturing—Noncomputer Products
- 16 Real Estate, Insurance
- 17 Research & Development
- 18 Human Resources
- 19 Retailing, Wholesaling, Distribution
- 20 Software Development
- 21 Systems Integration, VAR, VAD, OEM
- 22 Transportation
- 23 Utilities (Electric, Gas, Sanitation)
- 24 Other Business and Services ____________

2 Which of the following best describes your job function? *(circle only one)*

CORPORATE MANAGEMENT/STAFF

- 01 Executive Management (President, Chair, CEO, CFO, Owner, Partner, Principal)
- 02 Finance/Administrative Management (VP/Director/ Manager/Controller, Purchasing, Administration)
- 03 Sales/Marketing Management (VP/Director/Manager)
- 04 Computer Systems/Operations Management (CIO/VP/Director/ Manager MIS, Operations)
- 05 Other Finance/Administration Staff
- 06 Other Sales/Marketing Staff

IS/IT Staff

- 07 Systems Development/ Programming Management
- 08 Systems Development/ Programming Staff
- 09 Consulting
- 10 DBA/Systems Administrator
- 11 Education/Training
- 12 Engineering/R&D/Science Management
- 13 Engineering/R&D/Science Staff
- 14 Technical Support Director/ Manager
- 15 Webmaster/Internet Specialist
- 16 Other Technical Management/ Staff

3 What is your current primary operating platform? *(circle all that apply)*

- 01 DEC UNIX
- 02 DEC VAX VMS
- 03 Java
- 04 HP UNIX
- 05 IBM AIX
- 06 IBM UNIX
- 07 Macintosh
- 08 MPE-ix
- 09 MS-DOS
- 10 MVS
- 11 NetWare
- 12 Network Computing
- 13 OpenVMS
- 14 SCO UNIX
- 15 Sun Solaris/ SunOS
- 16 SVR4
- 17 Ultrix
- 18 UnixWare
- 19 VM
- 20 Windows
- 21 Windows NT
- 22 Other ______
- 23 Other UNIX ______

4 Do you evaluate, specify, recommend, or authorize the purchase of any of the following? *(circle all that apply)*

- 01 Hardware
- 02 Software
- 03 Application Development Tools
- 04 Database Products
- 05 Internet or Intranet Products

5 In your job, do you use or plan to purchase any of the following products or services? *(check all that apply)*

	Use	Plan to buy
SOFTWARE		
01 Business Graphics	☐	☐
02 CAD/CAE/CAM	☐	☐
03 CASE	☐	☐
04 CIM	☐	☐
05 Communications	☐	☐
06 Database Management	☐	☐
07 File Management	☐	☐
08 Finance	☐	☐
09 Java	☐	☐
10 Materials Resource Planning	☐	☐
11 Multimedia Authoring	☐	☐
12 Networking	☐	☐
13 Office Automation	☐	☐
14 Order Entry/ Inventory Control	☐	☐
15 Programming	☐	☐
16 Project Management	☐	☐
17 Scientific and Engineering	☐	☐
18 Spreadsheets	☐	☐
19 Systems Management	☐	☐
20 Workflow	☐	☐
HARDWARE		
21 Macintosh	☐	☐
22 Mainframe	☐	☐
23 Massively Parallel Processing	☐	☐
24 Minicomputer	☐	☐
25 PC	☐	☐
26 Network Computer	☐	☐
27 Supercomputer	☐	☐
28 Symmetric Multiprocessing	☐	☐
29 Workstation	☐	☐
PERIPHERALS		
30 Bridges/Routers/Hubs/ Gateways	☐	☐
31 CD-ROM Drives	☐	☐
32 Disk Drives/Subsystems	☐	☐
33 Modems	☐	☐
34 Tape Drives/Subsystems	☐	☐
35 Video Boards/Multimedia	☐	☐
SERVICES		
36 Computer-Based Training	☐	☐
37 Consulting	☐	☐
38 Education/Training	☐	☐
39 Maintenance	☐	☐
40 Online Database Services	☐	☐
41 Support	☐	☐
42 **None of the above**	☐	☐

6 What Oracle products are in use at your site? *(circle all that apply)*

SERVER/SOFTWARE

- 01 Oracle8
- 02 Oracle7
- 03 Oracle Application Server
- 04 Oracle Data Mart Suites
- 05 Oracle Internet Commerce Server
- 06 Oracle InterOffice
- 07 Oracle Lite
- 08 Oracle Payment Server
- 09 Oracle Rdb
- 10 Oracle Security Server
- 11 Oracle Video Server
- 12 Oracle Workgroup Server

TOOLS

- 13 Designer/2000
- 14 Developer/2000 (Forms, Reports, Graphics)
- 15 Oracle OLAP Tools
- 16 Oracle Power Object

ORACLE APPLICATIONS

- 17 Oracle Automotive
- 18 Oracle Energy
- 19 Oracle Consumer Packaged Goods
- 20 Oracle Financials
- 21 Oracle Human Resources
- 22 Oracle Manufacturing
- 23 Oracle Projects
- 24 Oracle Sales Force Automa
- 25 Oracle Supply Chain Management
- 26 Other ____________
- 27 **None of the above**

7 What other database products are i at your site? *(circle all that apply)*

- 01 Access
- 02 BAAN
- 03 dbase
- 04 Gupta
- 05 IBM DB2
- 06 Informix
- 07 Ingres
- 08 Microsoft Access
- 09 Microso SQL Ser
- 10 Peoples
- 11 Progres
- 12 SAP
- 13 Sybase
- 14 VSAM
- 15 **None of above**

8 During the next 12 months, how mu you anticipate your organization wi spend on computer hardware, softw peripherals, and services for your location? *(circle only one)*

- 01 Less than \$10,000
- 02 \$10,000 to \$49,999
- 03 \$50,000 to \$99,999
- 04 \$100,000 to \$499,999
- 05 \$500,000 to \$999,999
- 06 \$1,000,000 and over